THE MEDIA CONTRACTS HANDBOOK

AUSTRALIA
LBC Information Services
Sydney

CANADA AND USA
Carswell
Toronto

NEW ZEALAND
Brooker's
Auckland

SINGAPORE AND MALAYSIA
Sweet and Maxwell Asia
Singapore and Kuala Lumpur

THE MEDIA CONTRACTS HANDBOOK

by

DEBORAH FOSBROOK B.A. (Hons)

Barrister, of Grays Inn

Co-author of The A-Z of Contract Clauses

ADRIAN C. LAING LLB (Exon)

Barrister, of Inner Temple

Director of Legal Affairs and Company Secretary

HarperCollins Publishers Limited

Co-author of The A-Z of Contract Clauses

SECOND EDITION

LONDON
SWEET &MAXWELL
2001

Published in 2001
by Sweet and Maxwell Limited
of 100 Avenue Road, Swiss Cottage
London NW3 3PF.
Typeset by J&L Composition Ltd, Filey, North Yorkshire.
Printed in England by Bookcraft, Bath Ltd.

No natural forests were destroyed to make this product; only farmed timber was used and replanted.

A CIP catalogue record for this book is available from the British Library.

ISBN 0 421 661305

For our children Katie, David, William, George and Peter.

THE MEDIA CONTRACTS HANDBOOK

CONTENTS

INTRODUCTION

The first edition of the Media Contracts Handbook was originally published in two volumes over ten years ago. The original books have become established as an excellent training tool and precedent guide for drafting and analysing contracts. Copies of the books have been sold all over the world from India and Brazil, to Europe and the United Kingdom. Many concepts which we proposed at the time have now been adopted in the media industry. These books are used by leading television, video and publishing companies as well as lawyers and agents.

The object throughout is to provide working agreements, which are clear and comprehensible to enable you to make the process of negotiating and concluding an agreement quick and efficient. There is no such thing as a standard agreement in any industry. Negotiating a contract should be enjoyable and interesting. The key word is to be prepared and to do your homework so that you understand the issues that matter and, where additional unforeseen costs are likely to occur, who is responsible. These are our own contracts in our own style, some of which are deliberately brief, some longer and others are more innovative, designed to create new contractual concepts.

USING THIS BOOK

1. AS A FRAMEWORK FOR AN AGREEMENT

Each contract is designed to be used as a starting-point for negotiation and consequently as a master reference and precedent to be completed, adapted and amended to suit your own particular circumstances.

2. TO COMPARE AND ANALYSE WITH ANOTHER CONTRACT

These agreements will be helpful where you are issued with a contract which is of a similar nature to one contained in this book. It will not necessarily be obvious at first glance that the issued contract is of a similar nature. Every company has its own style and layout and often uses confusing and sometimes misleading terminology. Only by close inspection, analysis and comparison will you be able to fully appreciate the exact details of the terms proposed or omitted. Few companies would expect an issued contract to be signed without some form of alteration and amendment. Both this book and *The A–Z of Contract Clauses* will allow you to not only request additional clauses but to propose the exact wording you require to meet your needs. It is fully expected that you may add additional clauses to our proposed contracts to fit your particular circumstances.

3. AS A BACKGROUND GUIDE

This book may also be used as a means of comprehending licensing, assignment and other agreements in the media world for either business or academic reasons.

4. OUTLINE OF EACH AGREEMENT

We have supplied a summary of each contract at the end, and highlighted some of the issues which may cause problems.

5. ACCOUNT OF RECENT DEVELOPMENTS IN THE LAW

The contracts take into account all recent legislation, regulations, directives and developments relating to the internet and as well as other relevant areas of the law. We do not believe in quoting legislation in contracts as this often imposes unnecessary restrictions on the parties at a later date, which were not envisaged at the time. Clear, precise language specifying the exact intentions of each of the parties is the main purpose.

6. CHECKLIST OF CLAUSE HEADINGS

The checklist of clause headings and rights is included to help you verify whether you have dealt with issues which are better resolved before the contract is signed than left unanswered. This list relates to our other book, *The A–Z of Contract Clauses* and is very comprehensive.

WEBSITE COMMISSIONING AGREEMENT

AN AGREEMENT dated this [____________] day of [____________]

BETWEEN:

(1) Website Designer ("the Designer")
of [Address of business or registered office]

AND

(2) Commissioning Party ("the Company")
of [Address of business or registered office].

WHEREAS:

(a) The Website Designer has experience in developing and implementing websites for marketing and commercial purposes.

(b) The Company wishes to engage the services of the Designer to assist in the design, development and implementation of a fully functional website dedicated to the Company's requirements.

IT IS AGREED as follows:

1. DEFINITIONS

1.1 "Additional Fees" shall mean such fees in addition to the Initial Fee to be paid by the Company to the Designer in accordance with the terms of this Agreement as specified and detailed in Schedule 1, which is attached to and forms part of this Agreement.

1.2 "Escrow Agreement" shall mean the agreement between the parties and an escrow agent whereby the source code of the computer software generated in furtherance of this Agreement is deposited with a third party which shall be released to the Company in accordance with the terms of this Agreement

1.3 "Initial Fee" shall mean the sum of [figure/currency] to be paid by the Company to the Designer in consideration of the services provided under this Agreement, which shall be payable in accordance with Schedule 2 the Payment Schedule.

1.4 "Material" shall mean any and all materials of any nature whether comprising of text, images, whether visual or subliminal internal or external, whether a graphics interchange format or joint photographics export group or portable network graphics, photographs, drawings, plans, sketches, electronically generated material, sounds, sound effects, music, logos, trademarks, design rights, background, banners, bookmarks, borders, tables, captions, characters, clip art, cartoons, computer generated art, maps, image map links, common gateway interface script, data, domain names, footnotes, headings, hypertext, video, and the combination of any or all such elements, software, and information.

1.5 "Payment Schedule" shall mean Schedule 2, which specifies the date(s) or terms required to be fulfilled prior to payment by the Company to the Designer.

1.6 "Product Specification" shall mean the detailed technical commercial and marketing requirements of the Company in respect of the Website as specified under Schedule 3 of this Agreement.

1.7 "Proposal" shall mean the detailed report in writing of the Designer which gives details of

(a) the exact technical nature of the work to be provided including diary of completion dates;
(b) a full example of the finished Product showing all components and functional image, text, sound and links;
(c) a full breakdown of the cost and personnel involved;
(d) the layout and functioning of the Homepage and other elements of the Website;
(e) the Initial Fee, Additional Fee, and Payment Schedule relating to completion of the Work; and
(f) details of any copyright, and all other rights of any nature which must be cleared and/or paid for relating to the Website which it is proposed to include when it is fully functional.

1.8 "Maximum Fee" shall mean the sum of [figure/currency] which, for avoidance of doubt, will be the combined total costs of the Initial Fee and such Additional Fees as may be paid by the Company to the Designer.

1.9 "Launch Date" shall mean the date by which the Website is intended to be fully functional and ready for access by members of the public.

1.10 "Support Services" shall mean such services as are agreed between the parties and specified under Schedule 4, which detail the nature and cost of any post-Launch Date services to be provided by the Designer to the Company.

1.11 "The Domain Name" of the Website shall be: [____________].

2. ENGAGEMENT OF THE DESIGNER

In consideration of the mutual promises and representations made by one party to the other under this Agreement including the payments agreed to be made by the Company to the Designer, the Company agrees to engage the non-exclusive services of the Designer to design, develop, integrate and support the Company's Website in accordance with the terms of this Agreement.

3. COPYRIGHT

3.1 The source code created in furtherance of this Agreement shall belong to the Designer.

3.2 All copyright and any other intellectual property rights in the Domain Name and all the Material defined in clause 1.4 in respect of the Website shall at all times be vested in and belong to or be under the control of the Company.

3.3 The Designer shall not acquire any rights or interest in the Website of any nature except the source code. Nor shall the Designer will entitled at anytime to review, register, and/or claim any rights, interest or equity in the domain name, or any Material which has been created or developed for the purpose of the Company's Website under the terms of this Agreement.

3.4 The Designer in consideration of the sums paid under the Payment Schedule assigns to the Company the sole and exclusive rights in the media including internet rights whether now known or hereinafter discovered in any rights owned or controlled by the Designer in the Product Specification, Proposal, Material, Domain Name, and Website which may arise in pursuance of this Agreement whether in existence now or created in the future throughout the universe for the full period of copyright and any extensions or renewals.

3.5 The Designer waives all moral rights in respect of Clause 3.4 both to the Company and any licensees and in respect of any successors in title. The Designer agrees that it shall not be entitled to any credit, notice, acknowledgment or otherwise in respect of the Website or any subsequent development thereof.

4. OBLIGATIONS OF THE COMPANY

4.1 The Company shall make such payments as are agreed under this Agreement, in accordance with the Payment Schedule subject to the completion of the required work to a satisfactory standard, to the Designer within [14] days of receipt of a VAT invoice. Further the Company agrees to make such payments to the Designer as may be agreed in accordance with the Support Services under Schedule 4 if agreed between the parties.

4.2 The Company shall provide such resource material and assistance to the Designer as is reasonably required for the proper performance of this Agreement and the fulfilment of the Designer's obligations.

4.3 The Company warrants that it has full power and authority to enter into and perform its obligations under this Agreement and is not bound by any previous agreement which adversely affects this Agreement.

4.4 The Company confirms that any and all rights in any resource material supplied to the Designer under this Agreement shall be owned or controlled by the Company unless expressly stated to belong to a third party.

4.5 The Company shall endeavour to ensure that all such approvals as may be required by the Designer under this Agreement shall be carried out in as timely a manner as possible. The parties shall operate by allowing each other at least seven working days to respond to any request.

4.6 Unless there is an agreement in writing to the contrary, the Company confirms that the Designer shall not be responsible for the acts or omissions of any third party to which the Website is associated, whether by linking or through hyperlinks.

4.7 The Company confirms and warrants that it has or will register the Domain Name with a recognised domain name provider. The Company agrees that it shall be solely responsible for the registration and protection of the Domain Name.

4.8 The Company agrees that it shall be responsible for all copyright and other fees due to third parties arising from the operation of the Website from the Launch Date for the Material. Prior to that date the cost of any copyright and other fees for such Material shall have been included in the report of the Designer and included in the total cost of the Payment Schedule.

4.9 The Company agrees that all agreements to be negotiated with third parties for the Website by the Designer on behalf of the Company shall be subject to the prior approval of the Company and shall be between the Company and the third party without reference to the Designer for any period after the Launch Date.

5. OBLIGATIONS OF THE DESIGNER

5.1 The Designer shall perform its obligations under this Agreement to the best of its skill and ability and shall maintain such high standards as are reasonably expected by the Company to create a fully functional website for the Company's commercial and marketing purposes on or before the Launch Date.

5.2 The Designer confirms and undertakes that it will not directly or indirectly seek to register or exploit the Domain Name or any other domain name which might reasonably be construed as competing with the Domain Name.

5.3 The Designer shall at all times employ suitably qualified and experienced staff (whether full time, temporary or freelance) who are able to contribute to the successful completion of the obligations under this Agreement.

5.4 The Designer agrees not to incur any Additional Fees nor exceed the Maximum Fee without the Company's prior written approval.

5.5 The Designer confirms that it has full power and authority to enter into this Agreement and is not bound by any previous agreement which adversely affects this Agreement.

5.6 The Designer warrants that the entire product of its services shall be original and that the performance of the obligations by the Designer under this Agreement shall not contravene any rights of any third party and that where the Material to be included in the Website is not the original Work of the Designer that it shall be set out in detail in the report specifying the type of material, the name of the Company, the nature of their rights and the expected cost for both pre-launch and post-launch.

5.7 The Designer confirms and warrants that the Website shall be fully compliant and consistent with the Product Specification in Schedule 3.

5.8 The Designer shall use its best endeavours to ensure that the Website is completed to a high standard, and is fully operational by the Company in accordance with the

Proposal costing no more than the Maximum Fee consistent with the time-scale stated in the Payment Schedule.

5.9 The Designer undertakes that it shall enter into an Escrow Agreement with the Company and an escrow agent which will entitle the Company to access the source code of the Website if the Designer goes into liquidation or receivership, or in circumstances where this Agreement is terminated due to a material breach by the Designer.

5.10 The Designer agrees to provide such Support Services as is specified in Schedule 4 to this Agreement for [two] years at the sums stated and thereafter on terms to be agreed between the parties. In the event that the parties cannot agree terms after the first [two] years then the Company may use any third party to provide such services.

5.11 The Designer acknowledges that the Company shall not be obliged to set up and/or exploit and/or use the Website.

5.12 The Designer acknowledges that the Company may decide at any time not to use the service of the Designer subject to payment in full of the sums set out in the Payment Schedule.

5.13 The Designer agrees that the Company may at any time engage any other third party at its sole discretion to carry out work on the Website or any other internet project for the Company. This shall include the right of the Company to use any third party to provide Support Services at any time.

6. TIME OF THE ESSENCE

Both parties agree that all times, dates, and deadlines referred to in this Agreement shall be of the essence of the Agreement unless the parties agree otherwise.

7. MUTUAL INDEMNITY

7.1 The Company and the Designer mutually undertake to indemnify the other against all claims, liabilities, demands, actions, costs, damages or reasonably foreseeable loss arising directly out of any breach by the defaulting party under the terms of this Agreement.

7.2 In the event of any claim, dispute, action, writ, summons, Letter Before Action or formal documentation indicating or threatening legal proceedings of any nature, in connection with Clause 7.1 above, the parties agree to notify the other party as soon as is reasonably practicable and to provide full access to all records or documentation relating thereto. Neither party shall incur any costs of any nature, whether legal or otherwise, which they intend to seek to claim back under the indemnity without first obtaining the prior written approval of the other party and such approval is not to be unreasonably withheld or delayed.

7.3 In the event that for any reason one party refuses to co-operate or disclose information. Then the party threatened shall after [seven] days be entitled to incur reasonable costs which it shall seek to claim under the indemnity. Provided that it shall keep the other party informed by a monthly report of the steps taken.

8. LEGAL PROCEEDINGS

8.1 In the event that any legal proceedings are commenced by any third party against either the Designer and/or the Company in respect of the Proposal or the Website or some other matter relating to this Agreement. Then written notice of such claim shall immediately be given to the other party. Each party agrees to provide such assistance as may reasonably be required in order to settle or defend such proceedings.

8.2 Each party shall bear its own legal costs and both agree to consult with each other before settling any claim.

8.3 Where any action relates to work requested by the Company for the Website then the Company agrees to act on behalf of the Company and the Designer and shall pay all legal costs relating thereto. The Designer agrees to act on the advice of the Company and shall execute all such documents as may be necessary.

9. RIGHTS OF THIRD PARTIES

Any body, corporate or otherwise, which is a not a party to this Agreement, shall have no right to enforce any obligation or right against the Company or the Designer.

10. CONFIDENTIALITY

10.1 The Designer and the Company shall not disclose at any stage to any third party any confidential, business or future plans of the other party, including but not limited to the commercial terms of this Agreement unless a public disclosure, press statement or similar release or any advertising, publicity or promotional document has been specifically agreed to by a duly authorised representative of both parties.

10.2 Where the Designer is approaching third parties for contributions and/or assistance in respect of the Website, then the information to be disclosed shall be kept to a minimum and a representative of the Company shall attend all meetings with the Designer.

10.3 The Designer shall keep a proper record of all discussions with all third parties relating to the Website.

11. ENTIRE AGREEMENT

This Agreement represents the entire agreement between the parties and supersedes all previous agreements, promises and representations made by one party to the other. Any amendment or alteration to this Agreement shall be in writing and signed by a duly authorised representative of both parties.

12. NO PARTNERSHIP OR EMPLOYMENT

This Agreement shall not be deemed to create any partnership or employment relationship between the parties.

13. NOTICES

13.1 The parties agree to serve notices to each other by first class post, facsimile or by e-mail. Irrespective of the manner used to serve notice, for the purposes of this Agreement, once notice is sent, such notice shall be deemed to have been served by the end of the following business day on which the notice was sent.

13.2 Notice to the Company shall be to: [Person] [Fax] [e-mail].
Notice to the Designer shall be by: [Person] [Fax] [e-mail].

14. VALUE ADDED TAX

All sums payable under this Agreement are exclusive of value added tax (VAT) that may be payable by either party. VAT shall not be payable however unless a VAT invoice is sent to the paying party which provides details of a registered VAT number.

15. FORCE MAJEURE

Neither party shall be responsible to the other party in circumstances where the obligations under this Agreement cannot be performed due to circumstances outside the reasonable control of the defaulting party. However, if such circumstances persist for more than five working days, the non-defaulting party may terminate this Agreement in writing having made reasonable compensation to the other party for such work completed to the date of termination.

16. TERMINATION OF THE AGREEMENT

16.1 In addition to any rights or remedies at law, this Agreement may be terminated by giving written notice to the defaulting party who has committed a material breach of this Agreement. The defaulting party shall be given not less than ten working days to remedy the grievance following formal notice and the Agreement shall be terminated if they have not complied.

16.2 Either party shall have the right but not the obligation to terminate this Agreement in the event that the other party becomes insolvent, enters into an arrangement with its creditors, a receiver or receiver and administrator is appointed over the business of the defaulting party or the directors or shareholders of the company pass a resolution to suspend trading, wind up or dissolve the company other than for the purposes of amalgamation or reconstruction.

16.3 The Designer shall upon the expiry or termination of this Agreement deliver to the Company all the property of the Company which is in its possession or under its control, save that the Designer may retain such reference material as the Company may permit for personal use only.

16.4 Upon the expiry or termination of this Agreement all rights granted to the Company in respect of the work done and the services provided and the products thereof to that date that belong solely to the Company.

16.5 The Company shall pay to the Designer the balance of any sums due which have accrued and/or are payable to the expiry or termination date. Subject to any claim which either party may have for any breach or non-performance or out of which such termination shall have arisen shall not be affected or prejudiced.

17. THIRD PARTY TRANSFER

17.1 After the Launch Date the Designer shall be limited to the provision of Support Services if agreed between the parties. The Company shall be entitled, either before or after the Launch Date, to sell, transfer, charge or otherwise dispose of the Domain Name and/or Website as it thinks fit. The consent and/or approval of the Designer is not required and the Designer waives any such rights and/or interest provided that he is paid for the completion of the work set out in the Proposal.

17.2 The benefit and burden of this Agreement shall be binding upon the successors in business and/or title to the Company.

18. LIMITATION OF LIABILITY

Notwithstanding any other provision of this Agreement neither party shall be liable to the other for any indirect or consequential loss or damage and the maximum liability of one party to the other shall be restricted to [figure/currency].

19. GOVERNING LAW

This Agreement shall be construed under and governed by the Laws of England.

Signed by: [____________]
FOR AND ON BEHALF OF THE COMPANY

Date: [____________]

Signed by: [____________]
FOR AND ON BEHALF OF THE DESIGNER

Date: [____________]

The Schedules set out below are attached to and form part of this Agreement.

SCHEDULE 1: **[Additional Fees]**

SCHEDULE 2: **[Pay Schedule]**

SCHEDULE 3: **[Product Specification of the Website]**

SCHEDULE 4: **[Support Services]**

OUTLINE—WEBSITE COMMISSIONING AGREEMENT

The Company is commissioning a specialist Designer to create a Website suitable for their purposes. The Designer is to create a Product Specification, which incorporates the Company's technical, commercial and marketing requirements. This should be analysed in detail to establish that the Website will fulfil all the functions required by the Company. The Company will register and protect the Domain Name.

The Designer will create a Proposal document, which is in fact a full report setting out the actions and steps to be taken, the relevant completion dates, the specification of the Materials involved and the associated costs both before and after the launch date. Third party costs will be set out and all such contracts shall be concluded with the Company directly for any post-launch use. Third party costs incurred prior to the launch date will be part of the payment to the Designer and paid by the Company under the Payment Schedule relating to the Proposal.

The only interest the Designer should retain is the source code and an Escrow Agreement must be set up with an agent in case the Designer goes out of business so that the Company doesn't lose access to the source code.

Payment must be joined to the completion of work by the Designer and it must be made clear that it is only completed when the Website is fully functional. Insurance has not been addressed, but it is recommended that this be considered by the Company, as well as cover for breakdowns and defamation.

The Designer is not entitled to any credit or acknowledgment for his work on the Website, and waives all moral rights and right to any credit. The Designer is transforming any rights that they may hold in the work that they are doing under this contract including the Product Specification, Material, and Website. This is very important as you want to keep the number of parties due any copyright payments to a minimum. The Company is allowed to engage any other third party to work on the project and no approval is required by the Designer.

PRODUCT SUPPLY AGREEMENT FOR ON-LINE PURCHASING

AN AGREEMENT dated this [____________] day of [____________]

BETWEEN:

(1) [____________] registered in [country/address] whose principal place of business is at [address] (to be known as the Supplier)

AND

(2) [____________] registered in [country/address] whose principal place of business is at [address] (to be known as the Seller)

WHEREBY IT IS AGREED THAT:

(a) The Supplier intends to supply products to the Seller to be sold on-line over the Internet.

(b) The Seller has experience and expertise in selling products direct to the public from its website and wishes to sell the Supplier's products on the terms set out below.

IT IS AGREED as follows:

1. DEFINITIONS

1.1 "The Product" shall mean such items, goods or products including any packaging and instructions as are specified in Schedule 1, which is attached to and forms part of this Agreement. Together with such other products which may be added to Schedule 1 by agreement and amendment in writing by both parties. Reference in this Agreement to the Product shall include the plural where the context so determines.

1.2 "Dealer Price" shall mean the price per unit of each Product which the Seller shall pay to the Supplier with respect to each unit of the Product supplied to the Seller.

1.3 "Firm Sale" shall mean that the Seller shall pay the Supplier for all the Product supplied and the Seller shall have no right to return the Product to the Supplier unless the Product is rejected in accordance with the terms of this Agreement.

1.4 "Accounting Period" shall mean [figure/days/weeks] following the receipt by the Seller of an invoice for the Product.

1.5 "Delivery Address" shall be the following address to which the Supplier shall supply the Product: [___________].

1.6 "Seller's Website" shall mean the following website from which the Product will be available to be purchased by the public: [Domain Name] [Location/Internet Address]. A copy of the two dimensional representation of the Sellers Website which is specified in Schedule 2 is attached to and forms part of this Agreement.

1.7 "Territory" shall mean all countries, bases, locations and sites throughout the universe.

1.8 "Duration of this Agreement" shall be deemed to have commenced on [date] and shall continue for a period of [12 months] unless extended or terminated in accordance with the terms of this Agreement.

1.9 "The Suppliers Logo" shall be the following design logo and trademark including any accompanying words which are briefly described as follows: [___________]. A copy of the two dimensional representation of the Suppliers Logo is specified in Schedule 3 and is attached to and forms part of this Agreement.

2. NON-EXCLUSIVE ENGAGEMENT OF THE SELLER BY THE SUPPLIER

2.1 The Supplier agrees to deliver the Product to the Seller for sale on the Sellers Website on a non-exclusive basis for the Duration of this Agreement in consideration for the payments to be made hereunder.

2.2 The Seller agrees to promote and market the Product on the Sellers Website and to make prompt payment to the Supplier of all sums due whether during the Duration of this Agreement or thereafter.

2.3 The Seller and the Supplier agree that the price of any unit of the Product to be paid by the Seller shall be at the Dealer Price and that payment shall be made by the Seller within the Accounting Period.

3. OBLIGATIONS OF THE SUPPLIER

3.1 The Supplier confirms and agrees that it is free to enter into this Agreement and that it is not under any restriction or prohibition which might prevent it from performing any of the obligations under this Agreement.

3.2 The Supplier confirms that it has not entered into and shall not enter into any arrangement which has or might conflict with this Agreement.

3.3 The Supplier warrants to the Seller that it has full power and authority to enter into this Agreement and is not bound by any previous agreement which adversely effects this Agreement.

3.4 The Supplier confirms that it is the sole owner of or controls all copyright, design right, trade marks and service marks and any other rights in the Product and the

Suppliers Logo throughout the Territory, except as otherwise disclosed in writing to the contrary to the Seller.

3.5 The Supplier agrees that the Seller may market, promote and sell the Product at any price it deems fit on the Sellers Website, provided that the Dealer Price shall be paid for each unit of the Product to the Supplier in each case, whether or not any sums have been received by the Seller.

3.6 The Supplier agrees that the Seller shall have the final editorial decision in respect of the position and size of the representation of the Product and the Suppliers Logo on the Seller's Website and any updates and changes that may be necessary. Provided that the Seller shall ensure as far as reasonably possible that the details of the Product and the Suppliers Logo are accurate in terms of the image, text and sound and the purpose for which the Product is intended.

3.7 The Supplier agrees that the Product shall comply and continue to comply with all provisions relating to the design, manufacture, supply and use of any unit of the Product relating to any statute, regulation, order, directive or other governing law in force at the time of delivery to the Seller in the [United Kingdom/Europe/Territory].

3.8 The Seller shall ensure that each Product is supplied with suitable packaging and supporting literature which clearly sets out the purpose for which each unit of the Product is suitable and the steps and precautions that should be taken to ensure that the Product is safe and will not put the public at risk.

3.9 The Supplier agrees that it shall take out adequate insurance for the benefit of itself and the Seller in respect of any death, injury, loss or damage that may arise as a consequence of this Agreement.

3.10 The Supplier confirms that a comprehensive public and product liability insurance policy for the benefit of the Supplier and the Seller is and will be in force covering any claims, actions or damages which may arise as a direct or indirect result of the use by the public of the Product. The Supplier agrees to provide a copy of such policy, or a relevant extract to the Seller upon reasonable request. The cost of the policy shall be split evenly between the parties who shall both be named on the policies. The minimum value per claim cover shall be: [____________].

3.11 The Supplier agrees that it shall be the decision of the Seller as to the nature of the image, display, text and method of marketing and exploiting the Product on the Sellers Website. Provided that the combined effect shall not be offensive or demeaning or derogatory of the Supplier and/or its Products or to any third party.

3.12 The Supplier agrees that it shall not issue any statement to the media regarding either the Products on the Sellers Website and/or the Seller without prior consultation with the press office of the Seller.

3.13 The Supplier shall be responsible for any and all export duties and until the Product is delivered to the Delivery Address all property, rights and risks and liabilities shall remain with the Supplier.

3.14 The Supplier shall deliver the Product in accordance with the delivery dates and quantities specified in accordance with Schedule 2. Thereafter the Supplier shall provide each unit of the Product upon written request in accordance with an agreed format.

3.15 The Supplier will replace free of charge any Product proved to the Supplier's reasonable satisfaction to have been lost or damaged in transit provided that within [ten] days after acceptance of the delivery statement at the Delivery Address the Supplier has received notification in writing of the loss or damage.

3.16 The Supplier agrees that it shall provide the Seller with a full list of the details of :

(a) the Product;
(b) number, dimensions, weight content and description;
(c) method of transport together with shipment and/or carriage cost;
(d) import/export taxes and duties;
(e) value including dealer price and retail price; and
(f) insurance policy cost.

3.17 The packaging of the Product shall be at the sole cost of the Supplier; shipping and carriage shall be at the Sellers cost.

3.18 The Supplier agrees that time is of the essence and where an agreed delivery date cannot be met the Supplier will promptly notify the Seller.

3.19 The Supplier shall provide a delivery statement with each assignment of the Product which shall be agreed by the Seller and returned to the Supplier on each occasion.

3.20 The Supplier agrees that the Seller may engage any person(s) to endorse and/or promote the Product on the Sellers Website. The Supplier agrees that the appointment is entirely at the discretion and cost of the Seller, provided that the person(s) behave in professional manner and do not bring the Supplier and/or its Products into disrepute.

3.21 The Supplier confirms that the Product is safe and satisfactory for its intended purpose if used properly according to the accompanying instructions.

3.22 The Supplier confirms that the Product conforms with the quality and description and other particulars stated and are free from all defects.

3.23 The Supplier confirms that it shall own and/or control the Products at the time of delivery and that it shall be responsible for all sums due to third parties in respect of the production of the Product and that no such sums shall be the responsibility of the Seller.

3.24 The Supplier agrees that it shall not acquire any rights or interest in the Sellers Website except those which relate to the development or variation of the Suppliers existing Product and/or Suppliers Logo.

4. OBLIGATIONS OF THE SELLER

4.1 The Seller agrees and undertakes that the following details are true and accurate and that it is the owner and/or controls all rights and interest in:

(a) the Domain Name: [specify]
(b) the Sellers Website: [specify]
(c) the main business address: [specify]

4.2 The Seller confirms and undertakes that the selling process and dealings with the public will conform in all material respects with all relevant legislation, regulations, directives and codes of conduct (voluntary or otherwise), whether the source of such rules or guidelines are U.K. or E.U. based or otherwise in the Territory.

4.3 The Seller agrees that it has full power and authority to enter into this Agreement and is not bound by any previous agreement which adversely affects this Agreement.

4.4 The Seller agrees that the Product will only be sold from the Seller's Website and not from any other website unless the Supplier's prior approval has been obtained in writing, such approval not to be unreasonably withheld or delayed.

4.5 The Seller undertakes that it has fully disclosed and will continue to fully disclose to the Supplier upon request all other websites which are directly linked to the Seller's Website by whatever means which enables the public to gain direct access to the Seller's Website from another website.

4.6 The Seller agrees and undertakes that the Seller's Website does not and will not contain any sound, music, literature, slogans, straplines, banners or images of any nature which are defamatory, offensive, obscene or which could reasonably be construed as bringing the Supplier or its Product into disrepute or cause loss or damage to their business or reputation.

4.7 The Seller warrants and confirms that it will keep true and accurate records of all orders from the public and shall meet such requests promptly and will pay the Supplier for all the Product delivered.

4.8 The Seller agrees that its maximum order for the Product shall be the quantity and specification stated on the Schedule 4 and that all repeat or additional orders for supply of the Product shall be in writing to the Supplier in an agreed format.

4.9 All payments for the Product shall be in accordance with the agreed stated Dealer Price in the Schedule 4 unless agreed and amended in writing by both parties.

4.10 The Seller shall advertise and promote the Product and the Suppliers Logo on the Sellers Website as specified in Schedule 3, which shall detail the precise relative position, size, colours and accessibility of the advertisement from the public's point of perception.

4.11 The Seller agrees that no other product or advertisement shall be displayed on or featured on the Seller's Website where there is a direct conflict of interest with any product supplied under this Agreement.

4.12 The Seller agrees that in any associated publicity, advertising, promotional material, e-mails, webpages or other marketing material by the Seller of the Seller's website that where appropriate the Suppliers Logo and the Product shall be given reasonable promience, recognition and credit.

4.13 The Seller confirms that it shall be solely responsible for all costs in respect of the exploitation and sale of the Product by the Seller on the Sellers Website and that the Supplier shall not liable for any such sums.

4.14 In the event of delay by the Seller in taking delivery of the Product then the Seller agrees to pay the Supplier storage charges for the Product and any other expenses that the Supplier may sustain in the event that the delay exceeds [fourteen] days in any one delivery consignment. Any such additional payment shall be without prejudice to any other rights and remedies available to the Supplier.

4.15 The Seller agrees that the Supplier shall not be responsible for the delay in delivery of the Product or any other consequence arising from a request for the supply of the Product by the Seller which is late, overdue or due to increased demand.

4.16 Shipments shall be made to the Delivery Address unless notice in writing is received by the Supplier from the Seller.

4.17 The Seller agrees that it shall not issue any statement to the media regarding the Product and/or the Supplier without prior consultation with the press office of the Supplier. The Seller agrees that it shall not bring the Supplier or its Product into disrepute or act in a derogatory or offensive manner or cause loss or damage to their business or reputation.

4.18 The Seller agrees to provide the following copyright notice, credit, service mark, trademark or logo to the Supplier in respect of the Product as is specified in Schedule 4 in the Seller's Website and any advertising, marketing, publicity, promotional and packaging material and shall provide the Supplier with copies and samples at the Seller's cost on a regular basis.

4.19 The Seller agrees that the Supplier shall be entitled to refer to the Seller's Website in its own marketing, publicity and advertising material in the form set out in Schedule 5. Provided that all such use shall be subject to the prior written approval of the Seller.

4.20 The Seller agrees that time is of the essence in this Agreement. The Seller agrees to provide detailed statements for any request for the Product and shall duly sign and retain the delivery statement with each consignment.

4.21 The Seller agrees that the risk in the Product delivered by the Supplier shall be the responsibility of the Seller immediately on receipt by the Seller of the Product but the property and title rights in the Product shall remain with the Supplier until all sums due to the Supplier in respect of that consignment of Product have been paid to the Supplier.

4.22 The Seller agrees to pay the Supplier the Dealer Price in respect of the Product upon demand by the Supplier subject to completion of delivery and any such sum shall be made within the Accounting Period.

4.23 The Seller agrees that it shall not be entitled to adapt and/or alter the Product in any way without the prior written consent of the Supplier.

4.24 The Seller agrees that any modification, variation, adaptation or development of the Product and/or the Supplier's Logo and/or any logo, service mark, trademark or similar image, text or slogan or other identifying sign of the Supplier on the Seller's Website and/or on any associated material of any nature by, created or commissioned by the Seller. That all such material shall be the property of the Supplier and that the Seller shall use its best endeavours to ensure that any necessary documentation is concluded by the Seller to confirm or transfer ownership to the Supplier at the Supplier's cost and expense.

4.25 The Seller agrees that it shall not acquire any copyright, design rights, trademark or service mark or logo associated with the Product and/or the Supplier's Logo and/or the Supplier it shall be the sole and exclusive property of the Supplier together with any goodwill and that the Seller shall not acquire any rights therein including any developments or variations. Further the Seller agrees that the Seller shall provide to the Supplier any necessary documentation to support or transfer any such rights to the Supplier at the Supplier's cost and expense.

4.26 The Seller shall endeavour to promote and market the Product on the Sellers Website in a professional manner throughout the Duration of this Agreement.

4.27 The Seller agrees that the Supplier shall be entitled to deal with, sell, loan or hire or otherwise exploit the Product at anytime to any third parties, whether on the internet or otherwise, provided that where the Supplier intends to provide the Product to a direct competitor of the Seller namely another Website selling the same type of products that the Supplier shall notify the Seller of its intentions.

4.28 The Seller agrees to advise the Supplier in writing with the reason(s) for rejecting any order in writing within [five] working days of delivery in each case.

4.29 The Seller agrees that any order for the Product is on a Firm Sale basis and is not returnable unless faulty or defective or not fit for the intended purpose.

5. LEGAL PROCEEDINGS

In the event of any claim, demand or action by any third party against the Supplier or Seller in respect of the supply and/or sale to the public of the Product on the Sellers Website and/or the Suppliers Logo and/or the Sellers Website that it may become aware of or be served upon it by any third party. Then each party shall notify the other immediately of the nature and detail of any such matter of which they have knowledge. In the event that any party intends to seek to be indemnified from the other for the legal costs or damages then it is under an obligation to allow the other party to have an opportunity to assist in the defence of such case and make no admission or settlement without the consent of such party. Further that it shall allow the party who is to pay the costs and/or damages under any indemnity to control and dispose of the matter as it deems fit provided that it does not impugn on the business of the Seller and/or Supplier.

6. CLAIMS AGAINST THIRD PARTIES

In the event that circumstances arise which give reasonable cause for action to be taken against any third party by virtue of a breach of either party's intellectual property rights or any other rights. Then both parties agree that they shall provide such reasonable assistance to each other and provide such information and other relevant documentation or records as may be within its possession or control. Provided that neither party shall be obliged to take any legal proceedings and shall not be liable to the other party for any failure to do so.

7. RIGHTS OF THIRD PARTIES

Any body, corporate or otherwise, which is a not a party to this Agreement, shall have no right to enforce any obligation or right against the Supplier or the Seller.

8. CONFIDENTIALITY

The Supplier and the Seller shall not disclose at any stage to any third party (except their respective professional legal advisors, accountants and banks) any confidential, business or future plans of the other party including but not limited to the commercial terms of this Agreement which is acquired pursuant to this Agreement. Provided that the reliance on confidentiality does not apply if the information is already in the public domain or the parties propose to agree an advertising publicity or promotional document or event.

9. ENTIRE AGREEMENT

This Agreement represents the entire terms agreed between the parties and supersedes all previous agreements undertakings, promises and representations made by one party to the other, whether oral or in writing. Any amendment or alteration to this Agreement shall be in writing and signed by a duly authorised representative of both parties.

10. NO PARTNERSHIP OR EMPLOYMENT

This Agreement shall not be deemed to create any partnership or employment relationship between the parties.

11. LIMITATION OF LIABILITY

11.1 Neither party shall be liable to the other for any indirect or consequential loss or damages of any kind whether due to a loss of profits and/or interruption of business.

11.2 Any claim relating to the Product by the Seller against the Supplier shall be limited to personal injury or death due to the negligence or fault of the Supplier and shall be settled on the advice of Counsel.

11.3 The Supplier and the Seller mutually undertake to indemnify the other against all claims, liabilities, demands, actions, costs, damages or reasonably foreseeable loss and expenses arising directly out of any breach by the defaulting party under the terms of this Agreement. The total maximum liability of either party in total for the Duration of this Agreement shall be:[____________] excluding any liability for death and / or personal injury.

12. NOTICES

The parties agree to serve notices to each other by recorded first class post, fax or by e-mail to the Managing Director of the relevant company. Where notice is by fax or e-mail then confirmation must also be made by a telephone call to that respective office making them aware of the service of notice. In any event notice is deemed to have been received within [two] working days after the notice was sent.

13. TAXES

13.1 The Dealer Price is exclusive of tax and must be paid without any deduction whatsoever. Where relevant Value Added Tax (VAT) Sales Tax or any other tax shall be paid by the Seller. VAT shall only be paid provided that there is an invoice provided stating the registered VAT number.

13.2 The Seller shall be responsible for complying with all national and international tax and import and export laws applicable under this Agreement and shall bear the cost thereof.

14. FORCE MAJEURE

14.1 Neither party shall be responsible to the other party in circumstances where the obligations under this Agreement cannot be performed due to circumstances outside the reasonable control of the defaulting party. However, if such circumstances persist for more than [25] working days then non-defaulting party may terminate this Agreement by notice in writing.

14.2 Any party which is unable in whole or part to carry out its obligations under this Agreement shall promptly give written notice to that effect to the other party stating in detail the circumstances for such force majeure and the estimated time to remedy such event.

14.3 Both parties agree that in such event they shall reach an amicable settlement to resolve the matter. Each party shall bear its own losses and costs except that the Seller shall pay for all units of the Product which have already been delivered. The Supplier shall not be under any obligation to repurchase product already supplied.

15. TERMINATION OF THE AGREEMENT

15.1 In addition to any rights or remedies at law, this Agreement may be terminated by giving immediate written notice to the defaulting party who has committed a material breach of this Agreement provided the defaulting party has been given not less than [30] working days to remedy the grievance following formal notice.

15.2 Either party shall have the right but not the obligation to terminate this Agreement immediately by notice in writing in the event that the other party becomes insolvent, enters into an arrangement with its creditors, a receiver or receiver/administrator is appointed over the business of the defaulting party or the directors or shareholders of the company pass a resolution to suspend trading, wind up or dissolve the company other than for the purposes of amalgamation or reconstruction.

16. THIRD PARTY TRANSFER

16.1 Both parties shall be entitled to assign the benefit of this Agreement in whole or in part to any third party provided that no such assignment shall relieve the Seller or Supplier of its obligations under this Agreement in the event of a breach by the company receiving the benefit of the assignment. Further the party assigning of this Agreement must:

(a) undertake that the rights of the other party under this Agreement shall not be adversely affected by such assignment; and
(b) agree to indemnify the other party against any loss damage or claim arising in consequence of such assignment.

16.2 This Agreement shall bind and ensure to the benefit of the parties and the respective personal representatives, assigns or other successors in title.

17. GOVERNING LAW

This Agreement shall be construed under and governed by the Laws of England.

Signed by: [______________] [NAME & TITLE IN CAPITALS]
FOR AND BEHALF OF [THE SELLER]

Date: [______________]

Signed by: [______________] [NAME & TITLE IN CAPITALS]
FOR AND ON BEHALF OF [THE SUPPLIER]

Date: [______________]

SCHEDULE 1: **[The Product List]**

SCHEDULE 2: **[Seller's Website]**

SCHEDULE 3: **[Supplier's Logo]**

SCHEDULE 4: **[Quantity and Specification of Product]**

SCHEDULE 5: **[Format of advertising of Seller's Website by Supplier]**

OUTLINE—PRODUCT SUPPLY FOR ON-LINE PURCHASING

This Agreement is a non-exclusive agreement for the supply of goods to an on-line website seller, where goods are being sold directly to the public via a website. Due to the nature of the internet, the territory envisaged is worldwide. The goods are being sold "Firm Sale", as opposed to sale or return. Therefore once the order has been made, the Seller has no right to return the goods unless they are the wrong goods, of the wrong quantity or are faulty. The Agreement is website specific; the Seller is not allowed to sell the Product from another website. The goods are being sold at a "Dealer Price" without reference to a recommended retail price. The Supplier is making a number of representations concerning the goods, the most important of which is that the goods are suitable for their intended purpose.

The Supplier will provide the Product according to the figures and costs set out in the Schedule 1, then according to orders placed. Payment by the Seller is within a specified number of days of delivery and is not linked to the number or volume of sales to the public. The Seller is not bound to sell the Product at an agreed price which may be given away or sold at an inflated price. The Supplier only gets an agreed Dealer Price which is connected to delivery not sales.

The separate Schedules lists are very important as they provide the essence of what the contract is about. These documents should be very detailed. It is important that public liability insurance is taken out and that it is realised that the level of legal responsibility is very much higher in Europe and the United States.

As much information as possible should be established prior to the Agreement about the website and the method of delivery and payment as these are both areas in which problems can occur.

The Agreement makes it clear that the Seller is not acquiring any rights in any copyright trademarks, service marks or logo relating to the Product or the Supplier's business or any development or variations that are created for the Website.

A ceiling has been put on the maximum indemnity liability that may be paid by either party in total for the duration of the Agreement excluding death or personal injury which is not limited.

CONTENT SUPPLY AGREEMENT TO AN INTERNET SERVICE PROVIDER

AGREEMENT DATED: [________________]

BETWEEN:

(1) [Internet Service Provider] whose registered office is at [address]
("the ISP" in this Agreement)

AND

(2) [The Owner] whose registered office is at [address]
("the Licensor" in this Agreement)

WHEREAS:

a) The Licensor owns and controls the rights to the Work as set out below and is able to licence the work for exploitation on the internet.

b) The ISP has experience and expertise in providing an internet based service to the public and wishes to obtain a non-exclusive licence to make the Work available to the public through the ISP's Websites.

IT IS AGREED as follows:

1. DEFINITIONS

1.1 "Consumer" means any individual, body corporate or otherwise which accesses the ISP's Website and the references throughout this Agreement to the singular shall include all references to the plural.

1.2 "Licence Fee" shall mean the sum of [figure/currency].

1.3 "Internet Rights" shall mean the right to display, disseminate, supply, sell, dispose of, or otherwise exploit the work in whole or in part whether for free, or for financial or other consideration electronically throughout the world on any on-line services or networks irrespective of the nature of the method of delivery or reception whether internet, intranet, worldwide web, telephone, television or otherwise whether in existence now or created in the future. This shall include the right to exploit and use the work and/or any part in any media and in any format electronically including but not limited to text, visual images, photos, drawings, plans, sketches, electronically generated material, sounds, sound effects, music, background, banners, bookmarks, border, captions, characters, clip art, cartoon, computer generated art, maps, links, footnotes, headings, hypertext and video.

1.4 "The Work" means the text of the Work specified in the attached Schedule 1 to this Agreement including any other material which may be specifically agreed in writing between the parties as forming part of the Work.

1.5 "The Licence Period" shall mean the period of [12 months] commencing from the [Go Live Date] and shall continue for such other period as may be agreed between the parties by amendment in writing in accordance with the terms of this Agreement.

1.6 "The Territory" means all countries bases and locations throughout the world, outer space and the universe.

1.7 "The ISP's Websites" shall mean the registered domain names owned or controlled at any time by the ISP and set out in Schedule 2 to this Agreement.

1.8 "The Author" is the creator of the Work: [Name].

2. EXCLUSIVE GRANT OF INTERNET RIGHTS

2.1 In consideration of the Licence Fee, the Licensor grants to ISP the non-exclusive Internet Rights in the Work for the duration of the Licence Period throughout the Territory for exploitation on the ISP's Website and make copies for security purposes.

2.2 The Licensor agrees that for the duration of the Licence Period, the Licensor shall not directly or indirectly license, sub-license, promote, distribute or make available the Work or any part(s) in any electronic form within the Territory during the Licence Period to any other party in contravention of the Intranet Rights granted under this Agreement. Nor shall the Licensor license or permit or authorise any third party to copy, produce, manufacture, develop or distribute any development or variation for the World Wide Web.

2.3 The licence is specifically limited to the grant of the Internet Rights on the ISP Websites and all other rights are reserved by the Licensor.

2.4 The ISP acknowledge that they shall not be entitled to license any third party to exploit the Work and/or part(s) in any form except to members of the public accessing one of the ISP's Websites.

2.5 The ISP agrees to pay the Licence Fee on [date] subject to the delivery of the Work by the Licensor in a suitable format in consideration of the rights granted.

3. OBLIGATIONS OF THE LICENSOR

3.1 The Licensor warrants that it has full title, power and authority to enter into this Agreement and is not bound by any previous agreement which adversely effects this Agreement.

3.2 The Licensor confirms that it owns or controls all rights in the Work (in whole or in part) granted to the ISP under this Agreement and that the exercise of such right will not expose the ISP to any civil and/or criminal proceedings.

3.3 The Licensor confirms that it has not granted a licence or other authorisation to any third party to make the Work (in whole or in part) available over the World Wide Web.

3.4 The Licensor undertakes that the Work and any part(s) does not contain anything which is defamatory, libellous, obscene, pornographic or otherwise in breach of the [Law of England]. No such undertaking is being given by the Licensor in respect of any other jurisdiction.

3.5 The Licensor asserts the moral rights of the Author to be reasonably clearly and prominently identified at all times as the creator of the Work as follows: [____________] and in any advertising, publicity, marketing and distribution material.

3.6 The Licensor agrees to provide for use by the ISP in conjunction with the Work one copy of the Author's name, signature, biography, photograph and likeness for promotion and advertising purposes. Any additional material which is required shall be agreed and negotiated directly with the Author as an additional cost to be paid for by ISP. All copyright on any new material which may be created by ISP under this Agreement shall be assigned by the ISP to the Author as a condition of the supply of such original material.

3.7 The supply of any jacket, cover, photographs, logo, artwork or material other than the text in a suitable format for the ISP by the Licensor shall be an additional cost to be agreed between the parties and paid for by ISP.

3.8 The Licensor shall be responsible for the clearance of all contractual copyright and any other rights in respect of the Work and any part(s) and any other associated copyright notices, credits, moral rights, trademarks, service marks and logos. Save that the ISP shall bear the cost of all payments relating to all material for use on its ISP Websites except the text which shall be the responsibility of the Licensor.

4. OBLIGATIONS OF THE ISP

4.1 The ISP shall ensure that the presentation and display of the Work and any part(s) on the ISP Website shall correspond as far as is reasonably practicable in its style, presentation and quality to the version of the Work provided by the Licensor.

4.2 The ISP shall not amend, alter, abridge, expand or modify the content of the Work and/or any part(s) without the prior written approval of the Licensor and the Author.

4.3 The ISP shall ensure that any copyright notices, credits, moral rights, trademarks, service marks and logos included in the publication of the Work [in hardback] shall appear in the same form on the ISP Websites. In particular the ISP recognises that the moral rights of the Author have been asserted in relation to the Work to be identified reasonably prominently and clearly as: [____________] and in all associated promotional, advertising, marketing and distribution material.

4.4 In addition the ISP shall ensure that the Licensor shall be provided with the following copyright notice, credit, trademark and logo in respect of the use of the

Work by ISP and in any advertising, publicity, marketing and distribution material as follows: [____________].

4.5 The ISP agrees to provide copies and samples of any such material referred to in clause [4.4] at the ISP's cost.

4.6 The ISP shall ensure that the ISP Websites include an End-User Licence agreement which purports to prohibit consumers from copying or using the Work except for personal and non-commercial use.

4.7 The ISP agrees to bear the cost of any clearance payments of any nature due or arising from its use of the Work and/or parts under this Agreement except for the text.

5. FIRST REFUSAL

5.1 This Agreement shall commence on the [Go Live Date] as specified and shall continue for the duration of the Licence Period unless continued or terminated in accordance with the terms of this Agreement.

5.2 The ISP shall be entitled to have the first right of refusal to acquire the Work for a further period. First refusal shall mean the obligation of the Licensor to provide an opportunity to the ISP to acquire the same or similar rights as those granted under this Agreement with respect to the Work prior to the Work being offered to any third party. For the avoidance of doubt the ISP shall be under no obligation to acquire the Work nor shall the Licensor be obliged to accept the same Licence Fee. The right of refusal shall continue until such time as the parties agree final terms or [six weeks] from the end of the Licence Period under this Agreement, whichever is the sooner. The right of refusal shall not apply to any subsequent work of the Author.

6. TIME OF THE ESSENCE

Both parties agree that all times and dates referred to in this Agreement shall be of the essence of the Agreement unless both parties agree at a later date in writing to vary all or part of the times and dates.

7. MUTUAL INDEMNITY

7.1 The ISP and the Licensor mutually undertake to indemnify the other against all claims, liabilities, demands, actions, costs, damages or reasonably foreseeable loss arising directly out of any breach by the other defaulting party under the terms of this Agreement.

7.2 In the event of any claim, dispute, action, writ, summons, Letter Before Action, formal documentation indicating or threatening legal proceedings of any nature the parties agree that they shall be obliged to notify the other party as soon as is reasonably practicable. Neither party shall incur any costs of any nature in such circumstances without first obtaining the prior written approval of the other party based on a full disclosure of the facts, such approval not to be unreasonably withheld or delayed.

8. CLAIMS AGAINST THIRD PARTIES

8.1 In the event that circumstances arise which give reasonable cause for action to be taken against any third party by virtue of a breach of either party's proprietary or intellectual property rights of any kind, the parties shall provide such reasonable assistance to each other as is required to protect such rights.

8.2 The parties agree that the general principle with regard to any and all costs which may be incurred taking action against a third party, will be that one party shall agree to take the action on behalf of both parties, and shall ensure that any and all monies recovered from any third party or parties shall be divided equally between the ISP and the Licensor after the party taking the action has recovered all of its costs incurred.

9. RIGHTS OF THIRD PARTIES

Any body, corporate or otherwise, which is a not a party to this Agreement, shall have no right to enforce any obligation or right against the ISP or the Licensor.

10. CONFIDENTIALITY

The Licensor and the ISP shall not disclose to any third party except professional legal advisors, consultants and accountants any confidential information, business, future plans of the other party at any time which is acquired prior to the conclusion of or pursuant to this Agreement. Both parties agree that no reference is to be made to the terms or discussions or information or material made available under this Agreement in any advertising, promotional, publicity or marketing material in any media without the prior written approval of the [Managing Director] of the other party.

11. ENTIRE AGREEMENT

This Agreement represents the entire agreement between the parties and supersedes all previous agreements, promises and representations made by one party to the other. Any amendment or alteration to this Agreement shall be in writing and signed by a duly authorised senior representative of both parties.

12. NO PARTNERSHIP OR EMPLOYMENT

This Agreement shall not be deemed to create any partnership or employment relationship between the parties.

13. NOTICES

Notices pursuant to this Agreement shall be in writing by recorded delivery post as follows:
[Licensor]: [Person] at [address]
[ISP]: [Person] at [address].

14. VAT

All sums payable under this Agreement are exclusive of value added tax (VAT) that may be payable by either party. VAT shall not however be payable unless a VAT invoice is sent which provides details of a registered VAT number.

15. FORCE MAJEURE

Neither party shall be responsible to the other party for any loss or damage in circumstances where the obligations under this Agreement cannot be performed due to circumstances outside the reasonable control of the defaulting party. However, if such circumstances persist for more than [two months] then the non-defaulting party may terminate this Agreement by notice in writing and both parties shall negotiate in good faith to agree to an equitable settlement of this Agreement.

16. TERMINATION OF THE AGREEMENT

16.1 In addition to any rights or remedies at law, this Agreement may be terminated by giving immediate written notice to the defaulting party who has committed a material breach of this Agreement provided the defaulting party has been given not less than [ten] working days to remedy the grievance following formal notice.

16.2 Either party shall have the right but not the obligation to terminate this Agreement in the event that the other party becomes insolvent, enters into an arrangement with its creditors, a receiver or receiver/administrator is appointed over the business of the defaulting party or the directors or shareholders of the company pass a resolution to suspend trading, wind up or dissolve the company other than for the purposes of amalgamation or reconstruction.

16.3 After the expiry or termination of this Agreement the Licensor shall be entitled to instruct the ISP to return or destroy all the master material and any copies in the possession or under the control of the ISP relating to the rights granted under this Agreement subject to the payment by the Licensor of a reasonable sum for such material equivalent to that paid by the ISP for such item.

17. THIRD PARTY TRANSFER

This Agreement is restricted to the contracting parties. Neither party may seek to assign, transfer, charge or otherwise dispose of at any time this Agreement to any third party nor grant any sub-licence of any part nor cause it to be carried out or performed by third parties without the prior written approval of the other party which shall not be unreasonably withheld or delayed. Even where either party consents no assignment, transfer, charge or other disposal shall relieve the Licensor or ISP of their undertakings and obligations under this Agreement.

18. LIMITATION OF LIABILITY

Notwithstanding any other provision of this Agreement neither party shall be liable to the other for any indirect or consequential loss or damage. The maximum liability of the Licensor shall be [figure/currency] in total. The maximum liability of the ISP shall be [figure/currency] in total.

19. GOVERNING LAW

This Agreement shall be construed under and governed by the Laws of England.

Signed: [____________]
FOR AND ON BEHALF OF THE ISP

Date: [____________]

Signed: [____________]
FOR AND ON BEHALF OF THE DESIGNER

Date: [____________]

SCHEDULE 1: **[Full details of the Work: Title, number of pages, ownership of third party material, list of all photographs, maps, drawings, sketches, etc.; description of type of material.] Specify and attach two-dimensional copies of any logos, trademarks, service marks, design rights of Licensor and/or any third party surrounding or contained in the Works].**

SCHEDULE 2: **[Full details of ISP website: Domain Name/Location/Reference].**

OUTLINE—CONTENT SUPPLY AGREEMENT TO AN INTERNET SERVICE PROVIDER

This is a non-exclusive licence to an internet service provider (ISP) authorising the display of a book on the internet, via the ISP's website. The restrictions on the public who have access to the work on the web should be specified in an end-user licence. The payment is a one-off licence fee for an exclusive 12-month period with a right of first refusal after the expiry of the initial period of one year. The Licensor is representing that the rights granted have not been licensed previously and the territory is without restriction.

The Agreement is deliberately short and limited in the undertakings that each party is given.

Any additional services to be provided by the writer are an extra cost and should be negotiated separately.

There is no reference to the then work having been published elsewhere. The work could be a short process or several volumes of more complex material. There are no translation or sub-licensing rights and the license is restricted to the named ISP websites.

The ISP must use the work in its correct form and cannot change the text or associated material although they may create new visual images and break up the text which is suitable for its intended purpose on the Websites. The Licensor will acquire any rights in any new developments or variations. The Licensor cannot use the work elsewhere on the internet while it is under licence to the ISP. The limitation of liability can be different for each party; the figures do not have to be the same.

PERMISSION FORM FOR ELECTRONIC DISTRIBUTION ON THE INTERNET

I, the undersigned, am the sole author and copyright owner of the following Work:

Title: [______________]

Number of pages: [______________]

a copy of which is held at the British Library ISBN reference [______________].

I consent to the following extract of my work being displayed on the internet at the website location and address [______________] under the Domain Name [______________] which is held on behalf of [______________] ("the Company") whose registered address is at [______________] and whose main place of business is at [______________].

The duration of the consent is to be for a minimum of [three] months and is subject to the written withdrawal of my consent at anytime by notice in writing or e-mail to the Company.

The fee for my consent is [______________] which shall be payable for each [three] month period commencing [date].

I understand and accept that:

(a) Once transmitted electronically and displayed on the World Wide Web the extract may be copied onto computer software, onto the hard drive of the consumer's personal computer and may also be downloaded as a hard copy.

(b) The website which is hosting the extract of my work is linked by various electronic means to numerous other website addresses around the world.

(c) The Company has no means of monitoring or controlling the numerous websites on which the extract of my work may appear nor ensuring that my moral rights are observed.

(d) The extract is capable of being copied and transmitted electronically to anywhere in world.

(e) Once the work has been placed on the internet and is subsequently withdrawn for any reason from the Company's website address, the extract might still be accessible via the internet through another website or other means.

I confirm that the Company has agreed to pay me adequate remuneration for the right to use the extract of my Work in this way.

The Company agrees as far as reasonably possible:

(a) that it shall ensure that the extract of the Work is a true and accurate record.

(b) that a copyright notice shall be displayed showing that the copyright on the extract and Work belongs to [name].

(c) that the Company shall observe and respect the moral rights of [____________] to be reasonably, clearly and prominently identified as the Author of the extract.

(d) further that the extract of the Work shall not be treated in a derogatory or demeaning manner which would impugn on the reputation of the Author or the Work.

(e) that the Company shall allow the Author to be consulted on the detail of the display of Authors extract on the Company's Website.

(f) that the Company shall pay additional fees and expenses for any other material or contribution by the Author.

The Company agrees that it shall pay the fee for the display of the extract on a regular basis, and that if it should fail to do so at the start date of any new [three] month period that it shall not be entitled to display the Work.

The Company agrees that it shall not acquire any rights or interest in the Work or any part at anytime, save as set out in the short form permission, and that any developments or variations of the Work, title, text and artwork or of any other material relating to the Work shall be vested in and belong to the Author and that no rights shall vest in the Company who shall transfer all such interests at the end of this Agreement to the Author.

The Company shall not authorise, permit, allow or encourage others to reproduce or display the extract of the Work on other Websites without the prior express permission of the Author.

The Company shall not seek to take legal action against the Author for any reason for the use by the Company of the Work on the Website whether sued by or threatened by another third party.

Both the Company and the Author agree that this Agreement may not be assigned or transferred or otherwise disposed of to any third party at any time without the prior written consent of the other party.

Name of author:	[____________]	Address:	[____________]
Signature:	[____________]	Date:	[____________]

Name of company:	[____________]	Address:	[____________]
Signature:	[____________]	Date:	[____________]

OUTLINE—PERMISSION FORM FOR ELECTRONIC DISTRIBUTION ON THE INTERNET

This is a short-form permission document to cover circumstances where an extract of a work is being displayed on the internet. The terms are deliberately draconian but are intended to reflect the reality of making material available on the world wide web. It is important to make sure that adequate compensation is made to the consenting party.

The consent is given for a short period with a regular fee for each time period. The Author is not waiving his moral rights, and the Publisher is willing to try to observe them. However, once material is released over the web it is fed into innumerable inter-connecting links. The payment is just for the text and artwork, any other contribution by the Author such as photograph, biography, additional material, video, interactive participation would involve negotiating an extra fee and expenses. Otherwise these could be listed in the Agreement.

This type of short form is suitable for a new start-up website or where little author participation is required; it is not appropriate for endorsement of a website by a celebrity.

We have deliberately left out all undertakings by the Author except the statement that he/she is the author and copyright owner. The Company agrees not to take any legal action against the Author for its use of the work on the Website.

There are no references to the practicalities of this Agreement, such as payment for copying, freight, delivery address, etc., which it is assumed can be dealt with by the purchase of a copy by the Publisher or as a negotiable cost.

It is important that the Website Company does not acquire any rights or interest in the work, or authorise third parties to do so.

AGREEMENT BETWEEN AN ELECTRONIC PUBLISHER AND AN AUTHOR FOR ELECTRONIC DISTRIBUTION ON THE INTERNET OF A WORK

AN AGREEMENT made this [____________] day of [____________]

BETWEEN:

(1) [name]
of [address]
(to be known as the Author in this Agreement)

AND

(2) [name]
of [address]
(to be known as the Publisher in this Agreement).

IT IS AGREED as follows:

1. DEFINITIONS

The words below are agreed to mean as follows:

1.1 "The Work" shall be the following book, including the Artwork, based on the Synopsis, provisionally entitled: [____________], which shall consist of approximately: [____________] typed A4 pages.

1.2 "The Synopsis" shall mean the summary of the Work which sets out the chapter outlines, structure and general content of the Work. A copy of the Synopsis is attached to and forms part of this Agreement.

1.3 "The Artwork" shall mean any photographs, plans, visual images, drawings, sketches, pictures, diagrams, map, image map or any other illustrations or electronically generated material, logos, trademarks, design rights, banner, book mark, table, character, clip art, cartoons, computer generated art, links, data, domain name, footnote, headings and hypertext video image which are intended to be included as part of the Work.

1.4 "The Delivery Date" shall be the following date by which the Work is to be delivered to the Electronic Publisher by the Author: [__________].

1.5 "The E-Price" shall mean the price at which the Work will be sold to the public excluding post and packaging charges which shall be [figure/currency].

1.6 "The Licence Period" shall commence on [start date] and continue until [end date].

1.7 "The Territory" shall be all countries, bases and locations throughout the world.

1.8 "The Author Royalties" shall mean [figure/currency] for each unit of the work sold, disposed of, transferred, copied, supplied, or otherwise distributed whether for free or consideration. This figure applies up to [__________] units; thereafter a higher payment per unit is applicable of [figure/currency].

1.9 "The Advance Royalty" Payment shall mean the sum of [__________] [currency].

1.10 "Volume Form" shall mean the publication of the Work in book form, whether packaged as a hardback or paperback.

1.11 "Electronic Publication Rights" shall mean the right to make available, facilitate or disseminate electronically the disposal, sale or otherwise of the Work in whole or in part whether or not for financial gain to members of the public including in combination with associated text, sound, music, music effects, stills and moving images on any and all on-line services and networks irrespective of the method internet, intranet, extranet or otherwise from a website or other platform via the worldwide web which is owned or controlled by the Publishers or by some third party who has acquired such material via a link.

2. GRANT OF RIGHTS

2.1 In consideration of the Author's Royalties and the Advance Royalty Payment the Author grants to the Publisher the sole and exclusive Electronic Publication Rights to the Work throughout the Territory for the duration of the Licence Period.

2.2 The Publisher acknowledges that all copyright in the Work remains vested with the Author and that this Agreement does not effect any transfer of copyright ownership to the Publisher.

2.3 The Author specifically reserves the right to publish the Work in Volume Form and all other rights in all media not specifically granted in clause 2.1.

2.4 For the avoidance of doubt, this Agreement does not purport to grant to the Publishers the right to display the Work to the public in a way which does not involve the purchase and/or right to read and financial benefit to the Publisher and Author for the Work. The Publisher may display no more than [number] pages of the Work in total in a manner that does not require payment by a third party.

3. COPYRIGHT NOTICE AND MORAL RIGHTS

3.1 The Publisher acknowledges that the Author asserts his moral rights generally in respect of the Work and in particular to be reasonably, prominently and clearly identified as: [____________] in connection with all references to the Work and/or any part including the title by the Publisher.

3.2 The Publisher undertakes to respect the moral rights of the Author and to ensure that where part or all of the Work is sold that the following copyright notice will be displayed on the Work or any part on each occasion: [____________].

4. OBLIGATIONS OF THE AUTHOR

4.1 The Author agrees to deliver a software disc containing a complete copy of the Work based on the Synopsis to the Publisher on or before the Delivery Date.

4.2 The Author confirms that he has full authority to enter into and perform this Agreement and that he is not bound by any previous agreement which adversely affects this Agreement.

4.3 The Author confirms that the Synopsis is and that the Work shall be the original work of the Author and does not and will not infringe the copyright or any other rights of any party in respect of the rights granted under this Agreement.

4.4 The Author confirms that the Electronic Publication Rights in the Work have not been previously licensed or otherwise exploited in any form throughout the Territory except as previously disclosed in writing to the Publisher, a copy of which is attached to and forms part of this Agreement.

4.5 The Author confirms that the Work does not and will not contain any obscene, offensive, defamatory or blasphemous or racially prejudiced material and will not expose the Publisher to any civil or criminal proceedings for the duration of the Licence Period in the following specified countries: [____________].

4.6 The Author confirms, to the best of his knowledge and belief, that all statements purporting to be facts are true and that any recipes, instructions, formulae or advice are accurate and are not likely to cause any loss, damage or injury.

4.7 The Author does not agree to indemnify the Publisher against any action, claim, proceedings, demands, loss, damage or injury and/or any costs or reasonable legal expenses incurred whatsoever. It is the responsibility of the Publisher to take out relevant insurance policies to cover any such matters that may arise.

4.8 The Author agrees that the Publisher may use the Author's name as a party to take legal action against any third party for copyright infringement in respect of the Work provided that:

(a) the Author is fully advised of the details of the action; and,
(b) the Publisher gives a full detailed written indemnity to the Author agreeing to pay all costs and expenses in respect of the action incurred by the Publisher and the Author; and
(c) that in the event that any profits, damages, awards or other sums or benefits are recovered in respect of the Work the Publisher shall share such money on terms to be mutually agreed with the Author after the deduction of all reasonable costs and expenses paid by the Publisher to any third party which are not recovered.

4.9 The Author agrees to amend, alter or edit such parts of the Work as the Publisher may request in the event that its legal advisers consider that the Work contains material which is likely to result in legal proceedings against the Publisher. Provided that the Author may refuse to carry out any such changes and shall have the right to terminate this Agreement and refund all the money paid thereunder to date.

4.10 The Author undertakes to obtain and pay for all copyright clearances and consents necessary for the publication of the Work, including the Artwork, throughout the Territory for the duration of the Licensed Period. The Author agrees to obtain all such clearances and consents in writing and to provide the Publisher with such copies as may be requested provided that the Publisher shall reimburse the Author upon receipt of an invoice for all sums due in respect of obtaining by the Author and the grant by third parties of the cost and expense of all such clearances and consents in respect of the grant of the Electronic Publication Rights in the Work.

4.11 The Author undertakes to prepare an index for the Work. If the Author is unable to prepare an index, the Publisher may assume this responsibility but shall not be entitled to recoup the cost from the Author.

4.12 Any new editions of the Work shall be subject to the payment of an additional advance by the Publisher to the Author which shall be agreed between the parties. In the event that the parties fail to agree satisfactory terms then the Author shall not be obliged to produce and deliver any new editions or update or revise the Work.

4.13 The Author agrees that the Publisher shall be entitled to use and permit the use of his name, photograph, biography and fair likeness in respect of the commercial exploitation of the Work in respect of the rights granted under this Agreement. The material which shall be used by the Publisher shall be photographs and biography supplied by the Author which may already be in existence and which the Author is the copyright owner thereof. In the event that the creation of new material is required involving the services of a third party then such additional cost shall be paid for by the Publisher and copyright for such material shall be held by the Publisher.

4.14 The Author agrees that he shall be responsible for all his own national insurance, personal tax and value added tax which may be due in consequence of this Agreement.

4.15 The Author agrees to retain at least one complete copy of the Work in a secure place and to provide further copies should they be required provided that the Publisher bears the cost of reproducing the material insurance and freight.

4.16 The Author acknowledges that the manner and method of marketing the Work, including electronic cover designs, website material, e-price and terms of the sale of the Work, shall be at the Publisher's sole discretion.

4.17 The Author acknowledges that the Advance Royalty Payment shall be off-set against the Author's Royalties.

4.18 The Author agrees that in the event that the Publisher refuses to accept the manuscript of the Work on reasonable grounds and in good faith and has provided written reasons for its rejection. Then the Author shall be obliged to repay to the Publisher the sum of: [figure/currency], which shall be repayable in instalments without interest over a period of [____________] years.

4.19 The Author shall be entitled to sell, transfer or otherwise dispose of the Work to any third party as soon as notice is received from the Publisher that the Work has been rejected for any reason. The repayment of the sum specified must be agreed in writing between the parties prior to the signature of any new agreement with a third party.

4.20 The Author acknowledges that the Publisher shall be entitled to permit Braille and charitable recordings to be made of the Work for the sole use of the blind and handicapped free of charge during the Licence Period.

4.21 The Author agrees that the Publisher shall have the final decision in respect of the exploitation of the Work except the title text and index in respect of the rights granted in this Agreement.

5. OBLIGATIONS OF THE PUBLISHER

5.1 In consideration of the rights granted by the Author to the Publisher under this Agreement the Publisher agrees to the sale to the public of copies of the Electronic Publication Rights in the Work within [four] calendar months following the acceptance of the manuscript of the Work.

5.2 In the event that the Author delivers the Work on or before the Delivery Date the Publisher further agrees to distribute the Work not later than [date].

5.3 The Publisher agrees to pay the Author's Royalty on all copies of the Work or any part sold, disposed of, transferred, copied, supplied or otherwise distributed whether for free or for any other price or consideration. Payment shall be linked to the unit of the Work or any part and not financial consideration. It shall also be applied to all copies supplied to the press, television, radio, magazines, video, or any other form of promotion, marketing, or review or criticism throughout the Territory.

5.4 The Publisher agrees to pay to the Author the Advance Royalty Payment as follows:

(a) [______________] upon signature of this Agreement;
(b) [______________] upon delivery of an acceptable manuscript of the Work;
(c) [______________] on or before [______________]; and
(d) [______________] upon the first display of the Work on the website by the Publisher.

5.5 The Publisher agrees that no part of the Advance Royalty Payment already paid shall be returnable by the Author once the Publisher has accepted the manuscript of the Work.

5.6 The Publisher agrees either to accept or provide written reasons for its rejection of the Work within [21] days of delivery. The Publisher agrees to reject the Work only on reasonable grounds and in good faith. In the event that the Work is rejected on the grounds of the quality of the writing of the Work. Then the parties shall agree that an independent qualified assessor shall provide a detailed report regarding this aspect at the Publisher's cost and expense within [three] months of receipt of the rejection by the Author.

5.7 The Publisher confirms that if the manuscript of the Work is not accepted by the Publisher for any reason. Then the Author shall be entitled to have the Work published by a third party. Provided that the Author undertakes to repay to the Publisher all sums previously paid in respect of the Advance Royalty Payment within an agreed time limit in which case this Agreement shall be terminated and all rights granted shall revert to the Author.

5.8 The Publisher confirms that if within three years of the date of this Agreement the Author's Royalties actually paid are less than [____________] [currency], including the Advance Royalty Payment. Then the Author shall be entitled to terminate this Agreement by giving written notice to the Publisher and upon such notice being received by the Publisher all rights granted under this Agreement shall revert to the Author. Such reversion of rights shall be without prejudice to any claim the Author may have for money due under this Agreement and/or claim for breach of contract and/or damages and/or any other loss, interest or otherwise.

5.9 The Publisher undertakes to instigate and pursue all necessary legal and practical action to protect all copyright and any other rights in the Work granted under this Agreement and shall bear all the legal, administrative or incidental costs of doing so. The Publisher agrees that the prior written approval of the Author shall be required before any action, claim, writ, summons or any other proceedings is settled.

5.10 The Publisher agrees to indemnify the Author against any action, claim, proceedings, demands, loss, damage or injury and any costs or reasonable legal expenses incurred, including any matter settled on the advice of counsel, by the Author as a result of any breach or alleged breach by the Publisher of its obligations under this Agreement.

5.11 The Publisher undertakes that it shall send a statement to the Author every [two] months commencing [date] in each year during the term of this Agreement.

5.12 The Publisher and its sub-agents, sub-licensees and distributors shall keep for a minimum of [three] years all material on which information is held relating to the Work, books of account, records, invoices, discs, microfilm, computer software, letters and contracts showing the development, production, distribution and sale of the Work and all dealings of any nature, disposal or transfer and all sums received by the Publisher in respect of the Work.

5.13 The Publisher undertakes to the Author that a professional, comprehensive and complete history of the Work being exploited by the Publisher will be kept and recorded so that an accurate audit can be carried out by all parties.

5.14 The Publisher agrees to open a bank account with [____________] for the specific purpose of depositing and dealing with all money relating to the exploitation of the Work.

5.15 By 1st March, 1st June, 1st September and 1st December the Publisher shall provide a detailed report to the Author with a full breakdown of the exploitation of the Work, including the number of copies lost through damage, theft or any other reason, which shall be an accurate and complete record. The report shall be accompanied by a [method of payment] payable to [____________] for the full amount in [currency] shown to be due to the Author.

5.16 The Publisher agrees that the Author shall be entitled to arrange for an annual audit to inspect and make copies of the Publisher's books of account, records, contracts and any other relevant material in order to verify the sums due to the Author. The audit maybe carried out by the Author or any professional advisor. The Publisher acknowledges that the Author should upon request be provided with a copy of any record, document or other material in the possession or under the control of the Publisher relating to any payment to the Author for the Work. In the event that in any audit there is an error to the detriment of the Author, then the Publisher shall be responsible for the payment of all reasonable costs incurred in such audit.

5.17 The Publisher confirms that the Copyright Licensing Agency (C.L.A.) has been or will be empowered to grant non-exclusive licences to reproduce electronically the Work and other literary works published by the Publisher by photocopying and other reprographic means. The Work is accordingly deemed to be included with such literary works and the C.L.A. shall divide the proceeds from the reprographic reproduction of the Work authorised by the C.L.A. equally between the Author and the Publisher. The Author shall receive the Author's share of such proceeds through the Authors' Lending and Copyright Society (A.L.C.S.) in accordance with the A.L.C.S. standard terms and conditions.

5.18 The Publisher shall keep the Author reasonably informed in respect of all material developments regarding the exploitation of the Work, including the Publication Date.

5.19 This Agreement is personal to the Publisher and the Publisher may not assign, sub-license or sub-contract in whole or in part the benefits or obligations under this Agreement without the prior written approval of the Author save to those parties who are specified below and are disclosed at the date of this Agreement: [list name and details].

5.20 If the Author consents to any sub-licence or other third party under this Agreement, then it is a condition of such written approval that any such third party shall be subject to the same obligations to the Author as are set out in this Agreement where applicable including confidentiality and that the sub-licence or contract shall terminate upon the expiry or termination of this Agreement. Further that the Publisher shall assume responsibility for the acts or omissions of such third party and the indemnity provisions in this Agreement to the Author shall apply.

5.21 The Publisher agrees that the Author shall be consulted in relation to material in respect of the Work which shall be of a high professional standard: including but not limited to photographs, illustrations, artwork, typography, design and blurb of the jacket, layout of the website material, biography, image, likeness and representations of the Author and any signature, promotional and publicity material, packaging, brochures, advertising.

5.22 The Publisher agrees that it shall be solely responsible for all costs incurred in respect of the exploitation of the rights granted under this Agreement.

5.23 The Publisher shall use its reasonable endeavours to ensure that the Work is accurately described in any marketing and advertising material and the Author's name is clearly displayed. Further the Publisher shall use its reasonable endeavours to ensure that any quotes or use the of statements by third parties shall be subject to the approval of the Author.

5.24 The Publisher agrees that the total cost allocated to the production of the website material, the marketing and advertising shall not be less than [figure/currency].

5.25 The Publisher shall pay to the Author all reasonable travel and accommodation expenses or otherwise that maybe agreed in advance of the attendance of the Author at any marketing and/or promotion of the Work.

5.26 The Publisher agrees to provide the Author not less than [24] sample copies of the Work in each and every form in which it is made available to the public free of charge to the Author. In the event that the Publisher requires the Author to update the Work upon terms to be agreed, then an agreed number of additional copies shall be supplied at the Publisher's expense.

5.27 The Publisher confirms that in the event of the death of the Author after the acceptance of the manuscript of the Work all sums due to the Author under this Agreement will be made payable to the Author's estate.

5.28 In the event that the Author dies prior to the delivery of the manuscript the Publisher agrees to negotiate in good faith with the administrator(s) of the Author's estate concerning the publication or otherwise of the Work.

5.29 The Publisher agrees that in addition to the moral rights of the Author, the Publisher shall ensure that the Author is provided with the following copyright notice, trademark, logo and credit in the Work in respect of any exploitation of the Work by the Publisher and in any publicity promotion advertising or packaging as follows: [____________].

5.30 The Publisher agrees that the Work is the original creation of the Author who is the copyright owner of all rights in the Work and that the Publisher is only acquiring the rights set out in this Agreement. At the expiry or termination of this Agreement the Publisher agrees to execute any document that maybe necessary to transfer or vest any rights on the developments or variations of the Work created by the Publisher for the purpose of this Agreement in the Author.

6. CONFIDENTIALITY

The Author and the Publisher shall not disclose to any third party, except their repective professional legal, audit, insurance and accounting advisors, any confidential, business or future plans of the other party at any time acquired during the existence of this Agreement. No reference is to be made to the terms of this Agreement by either party in any advertising, publicity or promotional material without the prior written consent of the other party. The parties shall agree a press release to announce this Agreement.

7. AMENDMENTS AND ALTERATIONS

This Agreement supersedes all previous agreements, representations or promises and sets out all the terms agreed between the parties. Any amendment or alteration to this Agreement must be in writing and signed by an authorised signatory of each party.

8. NO PARTNERSHIP OR EMPLOYMENT

This Agreement shall not be deemed to create any partnership or employment relationship between the parties.

9. NOTICES

Notices served under this Agreement shall be in writing whether by letter, fax, e-mail or otherwise. Service shall be addressed to the following persons at the addresses set out below by the relevant codes: [name], [address], [fax/e-mail]. In any event all notices served by any method other than the postal service shall require that notice is also sent by recorded delivery.

10. TAXES

The Publisher shall be responsible for complying with all national tax laws applicable to the Work under this Agreement prior to the payment of any sums due to the Author. All sums are exclusive of tax that may be payable by either party and shall be paid without any deduction whatsoever.

11. FORCE MAJEURE

In the event that this Agreement cannot be performed or its obligations fulfilled for any reason beyond the reasonable control of either party including war, industrial action, flood, or Acts of God then such non-performance or failure to fulfil its obligations shall be deemed not to be a breach of this Agreement. In the event that this Agreement cannot be performed or its obligations fulfilled for any reason beyond either party's reasonable control for a continuous period of [three] months. Then either party may, at its discretion, terminate this Agreement by notice in writing at the end of that period provided that both parties agree to negotiate, in good faith, an equitable settlement in respect of the Work already performed to the date of termination.

12. END OF THE AGREEMENT

In addition to any other rights and remedies at law this Agreement may be terminated by giving written notice to the other party who has breached this Agreement or defaulted in the following circumstances:

(a) where the Publisher has failed to account or make payments as required under this Agreement.

(b) where the Publisher or the Author has committed a serious breach of its obligations under this Agreement unless such party rectifies the position, as far as reasonably possible, within [30] days.

(c) where the Publisher goes into voluntary or involuntary liquidation.

(d) where the Publisher is declared insolvent either in bankruptcy proceedings or other legal proceedings.

(e) where an agreement with creditors has been reached by the Publisher due to its failure or inability to pay its debts as they fall due.

(f) where a receiver or administration receiver is appointed over the whole or part of the Publisher's business.

13. THIRD PARTY TRANSFERS

Neither party shall assign, transfer, charge or make over this Agreement or any of its rights or obligations without the prior written consent of the other party. Such consent may not be unreasonably withheld or delayed. Provided that the party who must consent is satisfied that the person or persons or company to whom it is proposed to transfer the licence would be in the same position to comply with all the conditions for the remainder of the duration of the Agreement.

14. RIGHTS OF THIRD PARTIES

Any body corporate or otherwise which is not a party to this Agreement shall have no right to enforce any obligation against the Electronic Publisher or the Author.

15. GOVERNING LAW

This Agreement shall be interpreted and construed in accordance with [____________] Law and the parties agree to submit to the jurisdiction of the [____________] Courts.

Signed: [____________]
FOR AND ON BEHALF OF THE AUTHOR

Date: [____________]

Signed: [____________]
FOR AND ON BEHALF OF THE PUBLISHER

Date: [____________]

Attach copies of the following documents which form part of this Agreement:

1. the Synopsis;
2. the Artwork if applicable;
3. Disclosure letter(s) relating to previous exploitation of electronic publication rights.

OUTLINE—AGREEMENT BETWEEN AN ELECTRONIC PUBLISHER AND AN AUTHOR FOR ELECTRONIC DISTRIBUTION ON THE INTERNET OF A WORK

This is an exclusive electronic distribution agreement between an Author (or copyright owner of such rights) and a purely electronic Publisher. It is very important to ensure that any previous publishing arrangement is not undermined by this Agreement. The electronic Publisher may or may not be selling what is sometimes called an "e-book" to the public but has the right under this Agreement to exercise such rights or license the rights to a third party.

As the book is only in synopsis form, it is important that the working title is as near as possible to the final title of the book, and that the length of the book is realistic and achievable. In the first section of the Agreement there is deliberately no reference to the Publisher being allowed to transfer the business to "executors administrators assigns and successors in business" which is slipped in at this stage in many publishing agreements.

Important documents that should be attached to the Agreement as they form an integral part include the Synopsis, a list of the artwork if possible or the number of pages, and any disclosure letters relating to previous exploitation of the rights.

Do not bind yourself to an unrealistic delivery date so that you will inevitably be in breach of contract. It is essential that the format in which the work is to be delivered is specified, and whether, as is often the case nowadays, both the typewritten manuscript and the associated disc are required. If you believe that there may be a considerable amount of typing to be costed either ask the Publisher to pay for this or factor it into the advance.

Delete from the artwork definition any references which are not relevant. It is likely with an internet publication that the Author will want to create his own additional artwork for the site to surround the text, *i.e.* banner, headings and links. It is advisable that the electronic Publisher gives a real life demonstration of the expected use of the work, so that it becomes clear what new material is to be created to surround the work.

The electronic publication rights definition is very wide to encompass the very fast changing technology and recognises that once on the web little can be done to control third parties.

If the Author won't change the work if the Publisher's lawyers request amendments, then the Agreement can be ended, and all sums repaid.

There is no prejudicial sales clause limiting the Author's ability to sell other works.

For reasons of expediency it is better that the Author clear and pay for any copyright and other consents required and be reimbursed by the Publisher upon receipt of an invoice.

The Author is receiving a fixed price per unit which is not linked directly to the e-price and avoids percentage calculations of fluctuating figures.

There is a brief escalating royalty provision linked to sales of volume of units. A unit must be more than a specified number of pages of the Work. Rights on the work can revert to the Author if the amount received over a fixed period is low. We have not incorporated additional payment linked to "hits" to a website but this is also an additional possibility for payment to the Author.

Although the Author can approve third party sub-licencees and distributors it is better to resolve this at an early stage as to the mechanics of the exploitation.

The Publisher is giving an indemnity to the Author because he is exploiting the work worldwide, there is none from the Author although this could be limited to just the U.K. or Europe. We prefer that the electronic Publisher take out relevant insurance as it is impractical and too expensive to clear a work for legal issues worldwide. There is, however, an undertaking by the Author that the work does not include any obscene, offensive or defamatory material in clause 4.5 but this is limited to the specified countries (we recommend the United Kingdom or members of certain European countries).

A clause has been added providing for a separate bank account. If this is not appropriate then some other method of separating monetary payments is advisable.

FREELANCE CONTRIBUTOR'S AGREEMENT FOR WEBSITE DESIGN

TITLE OF AGREEMENT: [____________]

BETWEEN:

(1) The Website Owner ("the Owner")
of [registered and business address]

AND

(2) The Freelance Contributor ("the Contributor")
of [address].

WHEREAS:

(a) The Owner is creating a website and wishes to engage the freelance services of the Contributor to assist in the process.

(b) The Contributor has expertise and experience in website design and creation and wishes to be engaged on a freelance basis to make a contribution to the Owner's website.

IT IS AGREED as follows:

1. DEFINITIONS

1.1 "The Contributor's Work" shall mean the specific detailed aims and work required of the Contributor under the terms of this Agreement as specified in the attached Schedule [1] to this Agreement.

1.2 "The Territory" shall mean all countries, bases and location throughout the universe.

1.3 "The Contributor's Fee" shall mean the hourly sum of [figure/currency].

2. ENGAGEMENT OF THE CONTRIBUTOR

The Owner agrees to engage the non-exclusive services of the Contributor on an hourly basis and to pay the Contributor the Contributor's Fee in accordance with the terms of this Agreement provided that the Owner may terminate this Agreement at any time by notice in writing.

3. COPYRIGHT

3.1 The Contributor agrees that such present and future copyright as may exist in the product of the Contributor's Work provided to the Owner during the course of this Agreement is hereby assigned solely and exclusively to the Owner for the full period of copyright, including any extensions or renewals throughout the Territory and that the Contributor shall not acquire any rights or interest of any nature whether originated by the Contributor or not.

3.2 The Contributor waives any and all moral rights in the product of the Contributor's Work and in particular waives any right to be identified as the author and creator of the Contributor's Work.

3.3 The Contributor acknowledges that such copyright or any other rights of any nature as may exist now or in the future with respect to any element of the website to which he is contributing shall belong absolutely to the Owner.

3.4 The Contributor accepts and acknowledges that no other sums shall be due to the Contributor except the Contributor's Fee. Any request for out-of-pocket expenses will be dealt with in good faith (but without obligation) by the Owner, subject always to the Contributor informing the Owner in advance of any such expenditure.

4. OBLIGATIONS OF THE OWNER

4.1 The Owner will pay to the Contributor the Contributor's Fee one week in arrears, the first payment to be made one week following the signing of this Agreement by both parties (if applicable). Payment shall be made by cheque to the Contributor unless the Contributor and the Owner mutually agree an alternative method of payment.

4.2 The Owner will at its sole discretion approve and pay any additional sums to the Contributor such as expenses within [seven] days following receipt by the Owner of a fully itemised invoice with such documentation as may reasonably be expected for the Owner to verify the expenses which have been incurred by the Contributor wholly and exclusively as a result of the Contributor's performance of such duties as have been agreed with the Owner in accordance with the terms of this Agreement.

5. OBLIGATIONS OF THE CONTRIBUTOR

5.1 The Contributor warrants that the Contributor has full power and authority to enter into this Agreement and is not bound by any previous agreement which adversely affects this Agreement.

5.2 The Contributor confirms that he is and will be the sole owner and originator of the product of his services performed under this Agreement.

5.3 The Contributor confirms that the product of his services provided under this Agreement will not infringe the rights of any third party.

5.4 The Contributor shall at all times provide his services to the best of his skill and ability and will at no stage make any public statement which might reasonably be construed as bringing the Owner into disrepute.

5.5 The Contributor agrees to be responsible for his own national insurance, personal tax and VAT.

5.6 The Contributor shall keep full and accurate records of all expenses claimed in accordance with this Agreement and provide any relevant original documentation to the Owner upon receipt of a reasonable request to do so.

5.7 The Contributor confirms that he is registered for VAT and shall provide the Owner with his VAT registered number on all invoices sent to the Owner.

5.8 The Contributor confirms that he is a British subject [or holds a passport of a Member State of the E.U.] and shall remain so during the course of this Agreement.

6. MISCELLANEOUS

TIME OF THE ESSENCE

6.1 Both parties agree that all delivery dates, times, and deadlines referred to in this Agreement or agreed subsequently between the Owner and the Contributor shall be of the essence of the Agreement unless the parties agree otherwise.

INDEMNITY

6.2 The Contributor undertakes to indemnify the Owner against all claims, liabilities, demands, actions, costs, damages or reasonably foreseeable loss arising directly out of any breach by the Contributor of the terms of this Agreement.

CLAIMS AGAINST THIRD PARTIES

6.3 In the event that circumstances arise which give reasonable cause for action to be taken against any third party by virtue of a breach of the Owner's proprietary or intellectual property rights of any kind. The Contributor shall provide such reasonable assistance to the Owner, as is required to protect the Owner's rights.

RIGHTS OF THIRD PARTIES

6.4 Any body, corporate or otherwise, which is a not a party to this Agreement, shall have no right to enforce any obligation or right against the Owner or the Contributor.

CONFIDENTIALITY

6.5 The Contributor shall not disclose at any stage to any third party any confidential, business or future plans of the Owner including but not limited to the commercial terms of this Agreement.

ENTIRE AGREEMENT

6.6 This Agreement represents the entire agreement between the parties and supersedes all previous agreements, promises and representations made by one party to the other. Any amendment or alteration to this Agreement shall be in writing and signed by both parties.

NO PARTNERSHIP OR EMPLOYMENT

6.7 This Agreement shall not be deemed to create any partnership or employment relationship between the parties.

NOTICES

6.8 Any notice under this Agreement shall be in writing and sent by first class pre-paid post to the Contributor at [name/address] and to the Owner at [name/address]. Notice shall be deemed to be received within two days of it being sent. Otherwise notice may be served by personal delivery by hand to this recipient.

VALUE ADDED TAX

6.9 All sums payable under this Agreement are exclusive of value added tax (VAT) that may be payable by either party. VAT shall not however be payable unless a VAT invoice is sent to the Owner which provides details of the Contributor's registered VAT number.

FORCE MAJEURE

6.10 Neither party shall be responsible to the other party in circumstances where the obligations under this Agreement cannot be performed due to circumstances outside the reasonable control of the defaulting party.

TERMINATION OF THE AGREEMENT

6.11 In addition to any rights or remedies at law, this Agreement may be terminated by giving immediate written notice to the Contributor if he commits a material breach of this Agreement subject always to the Contributor's right to be fairly remunerated for such work as may have been provided to the Owner prior to the serving of such notice.

6.12 The Owner shall have the right but not the obligation to terminate this Agreement in the event that the Contributor becomes bankrupt, insolvent, enters into an arrangement with his creditors, or a receiver or receiver/administrator is appointed over the business of the Contributor.

6.13 Upon termination of this Agreement for any reason, the Contributor will, upon request, return any and all material, software, items, papers, and any other matter which relates to any work on behalf of the Owner under this Agreement.

THIRD PARTY TRANSFER

6.14 This Agreement shall be binding upon the successors in business and or title to the Owner and may in any event be transferred to any third party by the Owner provided the transferee agrees to be bound by the benefit and burden of this Agreement.

GOVERNING LAW

6.15 This Agreement shall be subject to the Laws of England and any dispute concerning it or its interpretation shall be adjudicated in that jurisdiction.

Full name in print: [____________]
Signed by: [____________]
FOR AND BEHALF OF THE OWNER

Date: [____________]

Full name in print: [____________]
Signed by: [____________]
FOR AND ON BEHALF OF THE CONTRIBUTOR

Date: [____________]

Attached to and forming part of this Agreement:

SCHEDULE 1: [The Contributor's Work]

OUTLINE—FREELANCE CONTRIBUTOR'S AGREEMENT FOR WEBSITE DESIGN

This is a contract between a freelance Contributor and a website designer, sometimes called a "work-for-hire" agreement. The important element is for the freelance Contributor to assign the rights which they may have in such elements of the website which they create. If the relationship between the Contributor and the commissioning party is one of employer and employee, the intellectual property rights would remain with the Contributor unless assigned in writing. The Agreement is also a useful vehicle with which to address issues of confidentiality. The Contributor is being paid an hourly rate and is not entitled to expenses, which is at the discretion of the Owner. The fee could be daily and a maximum ceiling included in the contract.

AGREEMENT BETWEEN WEBSITE OWNER AND CONTRIBUTOR FOR PERSONAL INTERACTIVE WEBSITE

AN AGREEMENT dated: [____________]

BETWEEN:

(1) The Website Owner ("the Owner")
of [registered office/business address]

AND

(2) The Contributor ("the Contributor")
of [address]

WHEREAS:

(a) The Owner owns or controls a website and wishes to engage the on-line interactive services of the Contributor.

(b) The Contributor is an individual with a particular area of expertise who has agreed to provide an interactive on-line service to members of the public hosted by the Owner's website.

IT IS AGREED as follows:

1. DEFINITIONS

1.1 "The Engagement Period" shall mean [twelve months] from the date of this Agreement unless extended or terminated in accordance with the terms of this Agreement.

1.2 "The Territory" shall mean all countries, bases, ships, aeroplanes, oil rigs and other locations throughout the world, universe and outer space.

1.3 "The Basic Fee" shall mean the sum of [figure/currency].

1.4 "Contributor's Expenses" shall mean such sums as are reasonably and properly incurred by the Contributor in performing the obligations under this Agreement.

1.5 "Bonus Fee" shall mean a one-off fee of [figure/currency] which is separate and additional to the Basic Fee and the Contributor's Expenses which shall be payable to the Contributor by the Owner in the event that the number of responses made by the Contributor to the public exceeds [2,000] during the Engagement Period.

1.6 "The Contributor's Services" shall mean the provision of a professional and expert interactive service to such members of the public who indicate by virtue of their response to the Owner's Website that they wish personal advice, recommendations or guidance as might reasonably be expected by the nature of their queries or questions to the Owner's Website.

1.7 "The Owner's Website" shall mean the registered domain name [____________].

2. ENGAGEMENT OF THE CONTRIBUTOR

2.1 In consideration of the mutual promises and undertakings contained in this Agreement, the Owner agrees to engage the services of the Contributor throughout the Engagement Period and to pay the Contributor the Basic Fee, the Contributor's Expenses and the Bonus Fee (if applicable) in accordance with the terms of this Agreement.

2.2 For the duration of the Engagement Period, the Contributor agrees to provide his professional on-line services exclusively to the Owner and not to any other website or on-line service.

2.3 The Owner acknowledges that the Contributor shall be entitled to offer his services in any other media during the Engagement Period to third parties. That where for reasons beyond the control of the Contributor such material should appear on another website or the internet, the Contributor shall not be held to be in breach or liable in any manner under this Agreement.

3. COPYRIGHT

3.1 In consideration of the Basic Fee the Contributor agrees to assign to the Owner all the product of his services under this Agreement whether in existence now or created in the future in all media throughout the Territory for the full period of copyright and any extensions or renewals including but not limited to documents, recordings, photographs, and interactive responses, provided that the Owner shall not acquire any rights or interest in any material in which the copyright already exists which is owned or controlled by the Contributor which is supplied under this Agreement including photographs, documents, biography, and books, slogans, name, business names.

3.2 The Owner agrees that it shall not be entitled to exploit any of the product of the services of the Contributor outside the Engagement Period or in any other media without the negotiation and settlement of additional payments to the Contributor for each different type, method and length of exploitation. Both parties shall use their endeavours to reach agreement in good faith. Failure to do so shall result in the material not being exploited at any time and destroyed by the Owner within [one] year.

4. OBLIGATIONS OF THE OWNER

4.1 The Owner warrants that it has full authority and power to enter into this Agreement and is not bound by any previous agreement which adversely affects this Agreement.

4.2 The Owner will pay to the Contributor the Basic Fee in equal monthly instalments, one month in advance, the first payment to be made immediately following the signing of this Agreement by both parties. Payment shall be made directly into the Contributor's bank account by electronic transfer.

4.3 The Owner will approve (such approval not to be unreasonably withheld or delayed) and pay the Contributor's Expenses within [seven] days following receipt by the Owner of a fully itemised invoice. Together with such documentation as may reasonably be expected for the Owner to verify the sums which have been incurred by the Contributor wholly and exclusively as a result of the Contributor's performance of such duties as are required under this Agreement.

4.4 The Owner will pay to the Contributor the Bonus Fee within [28] days of the expiry of the Engagement Period in a manner to be agreed between the parties. The Owner will provide to the Contributor such information and detail as is reasonably practicable to verify the exact number of responses made by the Contributor to the public during the course of this Agreement.

4.5 The Owner warrants to the Contributor that the Owner will use all reasonable endeavours to ensure that Owner's website will contain no sound, text, music, literature, slogans, strap lines, banners, banner headlines, scream lines or images of any nature or any other reference for any purpose which is defamatory, offensive, obscene or which could reasonably be construed as bringing the Contributor into disrepute.

4.6 The Owner agrees that the Contributor's name, image and endorsement of the Owner's Website shall not be used for any purpose other than the promotion and marketing of the Contributor's interactive response service to the public.

4.7 The Owner agrees and undertakes that it shall not be entitled to use exploit or license any of the material produced or created for the purpose of this Agreement in which the Contributor appears by sound, vision, text or otherwise at any time for the promotion or advertising of the Owner's Website in general or any associated products without the prior approval of the Contributor such approval not to be unreasonably withheld or delayed.

4.8 The Owner agrees that this Agreement only relates to the provision of services by the Contributor for the Engagement Period. The Owner does not acquire any rights, interest, option or other right to exploit any other works of the Contributor.

4.9 The Owner agrees that the Contributor shall be entitled upon request to be provided at the Owner's cost with a copy of any material of any nature in the provision or under the control of the Owner featuring or relating to the Contributor including publicity, advertising, promotional and marketing material.

5. OBLIGATIONS OF THE CONTRIBUTOR

5.1 The Contributor warrants that the Contributor has full power and authority to enter into this Agreement and is not bound by any previous agreement which adversely affects this Agreement.

5.2 The Contributor confirms that he is and will be the sole owner and originator of the product of his services performed under this Agreement.

5.3 The Contributor confirms that the product of his services provided under this Agreement will not infringe the rights of any third party save that the Contributor shall not be liable for any material included at the request of or supplied by the Owner under this Agreement.

5.4 The Contributor shall at all times provide his services to the best of his skill and ability and agrees to respond to the public in a timely and professional manner and will not make any response which is offensive, defamatory or might be construed as bringing the Owner into disrepute.

5.5 The Contributor agrees to be responsible for his own national insurance, personal tax and VAT.

5.6 The Contributor shall keep full and accurate records of all the Contributor's Expenses claimed in accordance with this Agreement and provide such original documentation to the Owner upon reasonable request.

5.7 The Contributor agrees to provide the Owner with such personal bank details as are necessary for the Basic Fee, and other remuneration agreed between the parties, to be paid by the Owner directly into the Contributor's designated bank account by electronic means.

5.8 The Contributor agrees to attend at such times and locations as may reasonably be requested of the Contributor by the Owner in order to promote the Contributor's services on the Owner's Website but on not more than [number] occasions in total.

5.9 The Contributor agrees that the Owner may use the Contributor's name, biography, photograph and fair likeness in the promotion and marketing of the Contributor's services under this Agreement to the Owner's Website.

5.10 The Contributor confirms that he is registered for VAT and shall provide the Owner with his VAT number on all invoices sent to the Owner.

5.11 The Contributor confirms that he is a British subject or a member of a national state of the E.U. and shall remain so during the course of this Agreement.

5.12 At the end of the term of this Agreement the Contributor agrees to return and/or deliver to the Owner all material in his possession or control which belongs to the Owner. The Contributor shall be entitled to retain a copy for his own personal use or references.

5.13 The Contributor asserts all moral rights in the product of his services under this Agreement and requires that the following identification be reasonably and prominently displayed for it to be bought to the attention of the public in relation to all the work created under this Agreement: [______________]. Nor does the Contributor agree that the Owner is entitled to subject any material to derogatory treatment at any time.

5.14 The Contributor acknowledges and agrees that all present and future copyright and any other rights in the Owner's Website shall be and remain the property of the Owner including any developments or variations subject to any interests of third parties. That the Contributor shall not acquire any rights or interest by virtue of this Agreement to any copyright or any other rights in the Owner's Website. At the end of the Engagement Period the Contributor shall execute any document or do anything required by the Owner to confirm or transfer any rights which may be held by the Contributor in the Website.

6. TIME OF THE ESSENCE

Both parties agree that all delivery dates, times, and deadlines referred to in this Agreement shall be of the essence unless the parties agree in writing that they may be varied in any instance.

7. MUTUAL INDEMNITY

7.1 The Contributor undertakes to indemnify the Owner against all liabilities, claim, actions, costs, damages or losses arising out of any breach or alleged breach by the Contributor of any of the terms of this Agreement up to a total maximum liability of [figure/currency].

7.2 The Owner undertakes to indemnity the Contributor against all liabilities, claims, actions, costs, damages or losses arising out of any breach or alleged breach by the Owner of any of the terms of this Agreement.

7.3 The Owner and the Contributor agree that in order to seek indemnity from the other party in any case they must comply with the following conditions:

7.3.1 notify the other party of the full details of the allegations which have been made and supply copies of relevant documentation.

7.3.2 consult with the other party as to the best cause of action in dealing with such matter.

7.3.3 not incur significant legal costs or pay any third party any sum for any reason to restore or settle such matter without the prior written approval of the other party. Such approval not to be unreasonably withheld or delayed.

7.4 The indemnity of the Owner shall continue after the expiry or termination of this Agreement. The indemnity of the Contributor shall end at the expiry or termination of this Agreement.

8. CLAIMS AGAINST THIRD PARTIES

8.1 In the event that circumstances arise which give reasonable cause for action to be taken against any third party by virtue of a breach of either party's proprietary or intellectual property rights of any kind. The parties shall provide such reasonable assistance to each other, as is required to protect such rights.

8.2 The parties agree that the general principle with regard to any and all costs which may be incurred taking action against a third party, will be that one party shall agree to take the action on behalf of both parties, and shall ensure that any and all money recovered from any third party or parties shall divided equally between the Owner and the Contributor after the party taking the action has recovered all of its costs and expenses whether legal fees or otherwise.

9. RIGHTS OF THIRD PARTIES

Any body, corporate or otherwise, which is a not a party to this Agreement, shall have no right to enforce any obligation or right against the Owner or the Contributor.

10. CONFIDENTIALITY

10.1 The Contributor shall not issue any statement in public or to the media including press, radio or television concerning any confidential business or future plans of the Owner or the Owner's Website without the prior consent of an authorised officer of the Owner.

10.2 The Contributor and the Owner shall not disclose to any third party any confidential business plans or profits of the other party at any time acquired during the existence of this Agreement. No reference is to be made to the terms of this Agreement by either party in any advertising, publicity or promotional material without the prior consent of the other party on each occasion.

10.3 After the expiry or termination of this Agreement all parties undertake not to make any disclosure to the press, media or publisher, or otherwise put in the public domain events, conversations, documents, financial details, private family or personal details of the other party without the specific consent of that person except professional legal and financial and other advisors.

11. ENTIRE AGREEMENT

This Agreement represents the entire agreement between the parties and supersedes all previous agreements, promises and representations made by one party to the other. Any amendment or alteration to this Agreement shall be in writing and signed by a duly authorised representative of both parties.

12. NO PARTNERSHIP OR EMPLOYMENT

This Agreement shall not be deemed to create any partnership or employment relationship between the parties.

13. NOTICES

Any notice given under this Agreement must be in writing in the [English Language] in legible form. Notice may be sent by any method but it shall not be deemed to have been received unless there is sufficient evidence that it was properly served on the Owner or Contributor.

14. VALUE ADDED TAX

All sums payable under this Agreement are exclusive of value added tax (VAT) that may be payable by either party. VAT shall not however be payable unless a VAT Invoice is sent to the paying party which provides details of a registered VAT number.

15. FORCE MAJEURE

In the event that this Agreement cannot be performed or its obligations fulfilled for any reason beyond the reasonable control of either party for a continuous period of [one] month. Then either party may at its discretion terminate this Agreement by notice in writing provided that, where notice is given by the Owner, the Owner shall pay a fair and reasonable sum to the Contributor taking into account work completed and any financial loss suffered by the Contributor as a direct result.

16. TERMINATION OF THE AGREEMENT

16.1 Without prejudice to any rights claim or interest of the Contributor the Owner shall have the right by notice to the Contributor to end this Agreement:

16.1.1 if the Contributor fails or neglects to perform or observe any term or condition of this Agreement. In any case which is capable of remedy the Contributor shall be given the opportunity to do so within [ten] days of the Owner notifying the Contributor.

16.1.2 if the Contributor is unable to devote the whole of his attention and ability to performing the services to be provided hereunder for any reason including seriously incapacitating illness or disability.

16.2 Upon the expiry or termination of this Agreement all rights granted to the Owner in respect of the work done and services rendered and the products thereof shall vest absolutely in the Owner. Provided that the Owner shall pay to the Contributor all and any unpaid sums due to the date of expiry or termination.

16.3 The Contributor may without prejudice to any right claim or interest of the Owner have the right to serve notice to the Owner to end this Agreement if the Owner becomes insolvent, enters into an arrangement with its creditors, a receiver or administrator is appointed over the business, or the direction or shareholders of the Owner pass a resolution to suspend trading, wind up or dissolve the Owner other than for the purpose of amalgamation or reconstruction.

17. THIRD PARTY TRANSFER

This Agreement is personal to the contracting parties. Neither party may seek to transfer, charge or make over this Agreement to any third party without the prior written approval of the other party, except to the extent that the benefit and burden of this Agreement shall be binding upon the successors in business and or title to the Owner.

18. LIMITATION OF LIABILITY

Notwithstanding any other provision of this Agreement neither party shall be liable to the other for any indirect or consequential loss or damage and the maximum liability of one party to the other shall be restricted to [figure/currency] in total.

19. GOVERNING LAW

This Agreement shall be construed under and governed by the Laws of England.

Full Name in Print: [______________]
Signature: [______________]
FOR AND BEHALF OF THE OWNER

Date: [______________]

Full Name in Print: [______________]
Signature: [______________]
FOR AND ON BEHALF OF THE CONTRIBUTOR

Date: [______________]

OUTLINE—AGREEMENT BETWEEN WEBSITE OWNER AND CONTRIBUTOR FOR PERSONAL INTERACTIVE WEBSITE

This Agreement is between an individual and the owner of a website. Members of the public would access the Owner's Website and ask questions or make queries to which the Contributor would respond. It is anticipated that the individual has a particular area of expertise which might be anything from astrology to finance. The individual is being paid a basic fee which is paid monthly in advance, agreed expenses subject to receipts and a bonus if the number of responses exceed a specific target. Most commonly this would be e-mail traffic and a suggested target of 2,000 responses within a six-month period is suggested. The Agreement is exclusive to the extent that the Contributor will not enter into a similar on-line relationship with another third party, but is otherwise entitled to pursue other business interests.

The Contributor is expected to be an established professional reputable person. A schedule could be attached as to the specific detail of the type of work required.

The Contributor is agreeing to assign all rights in the product of his services which are created under the Agreement to the Owner whatsoever type of material is created. The Owner is not acquiring any rights in anything already owned by the Contributor. This may include title, slogan, business name. The Owner is not entitled to exploit any material outside the Engagement Period unless additional sums are paid to the Contributor under separate agreements. If no agreement is reached the material must be destroyed.

The Owner must get the Contributor's approval to use the Contributor's name, image or endorsement of the website for any purpose other than the promotion of the Contributor's interactive response service.

The Contributor is not providing an unlimited indemnity to the Owner although he does agree not to use offensive or defamatory material. The Owner's indemnity is not limited, but both parties must be sure to disclose any threat of legal proceedings at any early stage in order to seek to rely on this provision.

SHORT FORM FOR SPONSORSHIP ON WEBSITE

1. **WEBSITE DETAILS**

Domain name:	[__________]
Owner of website:	[__________]
Registered address:	[__________]
Main place of business:	[__________]
Nature of business:	[brief description]
Website reference:	[__________]

2. **SPONSOR'S DETAILS**

Company:	[__________]
Registered address:	[__________]
Main place of business:	[__________]
Nature of business:	[__________]

3. **SPECIFIC NATURE OF SPONSORSHIP**

Website page reference:	[__________]
Exact on-screen position:	[__________]

4. **PAYMENT DETAILS**

Sponsorship fee:	[__________]
Payable as follows:	[__________]

5. **TERM OF AGREEMENT:** [__________]

6. **CONTRACT DETAILS**

Website owner:	[__________]
Sponsor:	[__________]

7. FORMAT DELIVERY

Materials to be supplied by Sponsor to Website Owner in following format: [_____________]

8. DATE OF THE AGREEMENT: [_____________]

9. SIGNED BY

WEBSITE OWNER: [_____________]

SPONSOR: [_____________]

OUTLINE—SHORT FORM FOR SPONSORSHIP ON WEBSITE

This is intended as a basic form for the recording of the bare of essentials of an arrangement to sponsor a website, either in its entirety or as a single page. The Sponsor should be clear as to the notice of the format of the materials (*e.g.* artwork, images, illustrations, logo, etc.) and also be clear as to how the materials will look on screen by reference to other images (*e.g.* of the proportionality of the logo).

A detailed schedule should be attached specifying every image and text of the sponsorship including slogans, trademarks and pictures of goods.

We have left out all undertakings and descriptions of rights intentionally and each party bears its own risk. It is therefore important with this type of paperwork that questions are asked as to ownership of companies and goods and these can be set out in an attached schedule.

SHORT FORM FOR ADVERTISING ON WEBSITE

1. WEBSITE DETAILS

Domain name:	[____________]
Owner of Website:	[____________]
Registered address:	[____________]
Main place of business:	[____________]
Nature of business:	[brief description]
Website reference:	[____________]

2. ADVERTISER'S DETAILS

Company:	[____________]
Registered address:	[____________]
Main place of business:	[____________]
Nature of business:	[____________]

3. PRODUCT/SERVICES TO BE ADVERTISED BY OWNER OF WEBSITE FOR WHICH MATERIALS ARE SUPPLIED BY ADVERTISER:

[____________]

4. ADVERTISING RATE: [____________]

5. PAYMENT DETAILS: [____________]

6. TERM OF AGREEMENT: [____________]

7. CONTRACT DETAILS

Website owner:	[____________]
Advertiser:	[____________]

8. **DATE OF THE AGREEMENT:** [________________]

9. **SIGNED BY**

WEBSITE OWNER: [________________]

ADVERTISER: [________________]

OUTLINE—SHORT FORM FOR ADVERTISING ON WEBSITE

This document is intended to record the basic details of an arrangement for a product or services to be advertised on a website. The advertising rate can be calculated in different ways: by reference to the number of "hits" to the website home page, or the number of "impressions" to a particular page, by a flat fee or by a period of time. There are no undertakings, conditions or clauses which specify who owns any rights or any other details normally associated with a contract. This is a deliberately brief note which sets out only the mechanics.

GENERAL ALL MEDIA BUY-OUT OF A WORK

AGREEMENT dated this [____________] day of [____________]

BETWEEN:

(1) [____________] ["The Assignor"]
of [address]

AND

[____________] [The Assignee]
of [address]

IT IS AGREED as follows:

1. DEFINITIONS

1.1 "All Media Rights" shall mean all intellectual property rights of whatever nature including without limitation all copyright, trademarks, service marks, design rights, trade secrets, moral rights, and confidential information and domain names and sole and exclusive right to adapt, use, copy, licence, authorise, print, transmit, disseminate, store, retrieve, display, process, record, play back, rent, lend, supply or sale, promote or otherwise exploit by any method, medium or process whether created in the future or in existence now of any nature and any developments or variations or adaptations whether text, visual images, photographs, drawings, plans, sketches, electronically generated material, sounds, sound effects, music combination software and information logos, background, banner, bookmark, border table, caption, character, clip art, cartoons computer generated art, map image, map link, common gateway interface script, data, domain name, footnotes, headings, hypertext, video or computer generated graphics including but not limited to:

(a) all forms of television including standard, cable, digital, satellite,
(b) all forms of radio;
(c) all forms of telecommunication systems including telephones and mobile phones, pagers;
(d) all mechanical forms of reproduction including videograms laser discs cassette DVD;
(e) all forms of non-theatric audiences whether for business or commercial use, educational, cultural, religious or social, schools, museums, readings, plays, speeches, addresses or lectures;

(f) all forms of Theatric exploitation including cinemas;
(g) all forms of publishing in printed form, hardback, paperback, digests, serialisation, newspapers, magazines, comics, periodicals, quotation, anthologies or translations;
(h) all forms of publishing and/or dissemination of information by any electronic method and process, internet, worldwide web or intranet;
(i) all forms of computer software and interactive multi-media such as compact discs, CD ROMS, computer games including all circumstances where there is an element of interactivity and/or there is a combination of sound text vision graphics or otherwise;
(j) all forms of merchandising, toys, clothing, mugs, stationery, games and any two or three dimensional representation;
(k) theatre and stage plays;
(l) films;
(m) advertisements;
(n) title rights;
(o) format in any form; and
(p) any character in any form.

1.2 "The Assignment Fee" shall mean the sum of [____________] [currency].

1.3 "The Territory" shall mean all countries, bases and locations throughout the world, the universe or otherwise without limitation of boundary including outer space.

1.4 "The Assignment Period" shall mean the full period of copyright including any extensions or renewals to continue indefinitely in perpetuity.

1.5 "The Work" shall mean the following:

Title: [____________]

Author: [____________]

ISBN no: [____________]

Pages: [____________]

Description: [____________]

1.6 "The Work Material" shall mean all the material of the Work in the possession or under the control of the Assignor including:

(a) all copies of any master material in any form;
(b) a list of locations at which any material is held together with access letters giving irrevocable authority for the Assignee to remove such material; and
(c) all documents, records, data in any form including contracts, licenses, consents, waivers, lists, proofs, scripts, publicity, advertising material, computer software, photographs, negatives, posters, catalogues, drawings, plans, sketches, electronically generated material, sounds, sound effects, music combination, software and information, tables, computer generated art, image map, video, film or otherwise.

2. ASSIGNMENT OF ALL MEDIA RIGHTS

2.1 In consideration of the payment of the Assignment Fee by the Assignee to the Assignor. The Assignor assigns All Media Rights which are in existence now or which may be created in the future in the Work or part(s) to the Assignee for the Assignment Period throughout the Territory.

2.2 The Assignor also grants to the Assignee all property rights and any other rights in the Work Material which are owned or controlled by the Assignor for the Assignment Period throughout the Territory.

2.3 The Assignor agrees that it shall not retain any interest or rights in the Work and/or the Work Material.

2.4 The Assignor also transfers and grants to the Assignee All Media Rights in the Work and the Work Material in respect of the following matters which may be part of the Work or Work Material except those owned or controlled by a third party including any association goodwill:

(a) trade marks;
(b) design rights;
(c) service marks;
(d) logos;
(e) domain name; and
(f) trade secrets.

3. MORAL RIGHTS

3.1 The Assignor waives any and all moral rights under existing or future legislation and the Assignor shall not be entitled to any credit or acknowledgement with respect to the exploitation of the Work and the Work Material by any party in any media at any time. The Assignor unconditionally waives all moral rights in the Work and the Work Material.

3.2 The Assignee recognises and acknowledges that the waiver only applies to the Assignor individually and does not apply to any other third party who may be due a credit or other acknowledgement in respect of the Work Material.

4. OBLIGATIONS OF THE ASSIGNOR

4.1 The Assignor undertakes and agrees that he is the original creator and sole owner of all copyright and any other rights in the Work which are assigned under this Agreement.

4.2 The Assignor agrees that he has full power and authority to enter into this Agreement and that the Assignor has not exploited the Work in any form except those matters listed in Schedule [1].

4.3 The Assignor agrees that it is the sole owner of all property rights and any other rights in the Work Material except for the obligations, credits and moral rights, a complete list of which is set out in Schedule [2] to this Agreement. The Assignor shall be responsible for all sums due to up to the day before this Agreement and the Assignee shall bear all costs and expenses owed to any third party from the date of this Agreement.

4.4 The Assignor makes no warranty or undertaking as to whether any of the Work and/or Work Material is obscene, defamatory, or may expose the Assignee to civil or criminal proceedings. That is the responsibility of the Assignee from the date of this Agreement.

4.5 The Assignor agrees that it has fully disclosed any rights or interests of third parties in the Work Material.

4.6 The Assignor shall arrange for the collection of the Work Material by the Assignee within [seven] days of the date of this Agreement.

4.7 The risk and ownership in respect of the Work Material shall fall to the Assignee on the date of this Agreement.

4.8 From the date of this Agreement the Assignor shall not be responsible or bear any liability in respect of the sale to the pubic of any associated products in respect of the Work.

4.9 The Assignor agrees that from the date of this Agreement it shall not have any rights or interest in the promotion, marketing or exploitation of the Work of any nature provided that the Assignment Fee is paid in full.

4.10 The Assignor agrees that it shall not at anytime seek to undermine or prejudice the goodwill and reputation of the Work by making statements to the media which are intended to criticise the Work.

4.11 The Assignor confirms that he is a British subject or national of a Member State of the European Union.

5. OBLIGATIONS OF THE ASSIGNEE

5.1 In consideration of the rights assigned under this Agreement, the Assignee agrees to pay to the Assignor the Assignment Fee as follows:

(a) [____________] [currency] upon full signature of this Agreement by both parties;
(b) [____________] on or before [date];
(c) [____________] subject to satisfactory collection of the Work Material.

5.2 The Assignee agrees that it shall be entirely responsible for all costs and expenses and/or any other sums due in respect of the exploitation of the Work from the date of this Agreement.

5.3 The Assignee agrees that from the date of this Agreement it shall be liable to bear the cost and expense for clearing and paying for all copyright, consents and any other rights in the Work and the Work Material of any nature and that the Assignor shall not be liable for such sums whether or not such matter was disclosed and/or known by the Assignee at the time of the date of this Agreement.

5.4 The Assignee agrees to provide and observe the copyright notices, credits, moral rights and any applicable other conditions to third parties in respect of the Work and Work Material.

5.5 The Assignee agrees to assume responsibility for and bear the burden of all obligations to third parties in respect of the Work and the Work Material.

5.6 The Assignee agrees that in the event that for any reason, except failure to arrange collection of the Work Material, the Assignment Fee is not paid. Then the Assignee shall pay an additional sum [____________] [currency] for each day the Assignment Fee remains unpaid.

6. TIME OF THE ESSENCE

All dates and times referred to in this Agreement are significant and must be adhered to by both parties.

7. MUTUAL INDEMNITY

7.1 The Assignor agrees to indemnify the Assignee against all claims, liabilities, demands, actions, costs, damages or reasonably foreseeable loss arising directly out of any breach by the Assignor of any terms, warranties or representations made under this Agreement which may arise before [date]. After that time the Assignor shall not be liable to pay the Assignee any sums whatsoever however they may arise. The Assignee agrees that the indemnity shall not continue after [date].

7.2 In the event of any claim, dispute, action, writ, summons, Letter Before Action or formal documentation indicating or threatening legal proceedings of any nature, in connection with clause 6.2 above before the end of the indemnity the parties agree to notify the other party as soon as is reasonably practicable. Neither party shall incur any costs of any nature in such circumstances without first obtaining the prior written approval of the other party, such approval not to be unreasonably withheld or delayed.

7.3 In any event no settlement shall be made to the claim of any third party unless the other party has had an opportunity to review the case and offer its opinion unless there is no intention to rely on the indemnity.

8. CLAIMS AGAINST THIRD PARTIES

8.1 The Assignee shall from the date of this Agreement be entitled entirely at its own discretion to mitigate and proceed with any actions, proceedings, claims and demands against any third party who have or may have infringed any rights held by the Assignee in the Work and/or the Work Material.

8.2 The Assignor agrees that after the date of this Agreement all damages, costs and expenses and any other sums due or arising hereunder shall belong to the Assignee. Where necessary the Assignee agrees to be a party to the action in name, but all co-operation and assistance shall be paid for on terms to be agreed.

9. CONFIDENTIALITY

Neither party to this Agreement shall disclose at any stage to any third party any confidential, business or future plans of the other party including but not limited to the commercial terms of this Agreement unless a public disclosure, press statement or similar release or any advertising, publicity or promotional document has been specifically agreed by a duly authorised representative of both parties.

10. ENTIRE AGREEMENT

This Agreement represents the entire agreement between the parties and supersedes all previous agreements, promises and representations made by one party to the other. Any amendment or alteration to this Agreement shall be in writing and signed by a duly authorised representative of both parties.

11. NO PARTNERSHIP OR EMPLOYMENT

This Agreement shall not be deemed to create any partnership or employment relationship between the parties.

12. NOTICES

The parties agree to serve notices to each other by first class post, facsimile or by e-mail. Irrespective of the manner used to serve notice, for the purposes of this Agreement, once notice is sent, such notice shall be deemed to have been served by the end of the following business day on which the notice was sent.

13. VALUE ADDED TAX

All sums payable under this Agreement are exclusive of value added tax (VAT) that may be payable by either party. VAT shall not however be payable unless a VAT invoice is sent to the Assignee by the Assignor which provides details of the registered VAT number of the Assignor.

14. FORCE MAJEURE

Neither party shall be responsible to the other party in circumstances where the obligations under this Agreement cannot be performed due to circumstances outside the reasonable control of the Assignor or Assignee. In the event that this Agreement is not fulfilled by [date] it will terminate with immediate effect.

15. THIRD PARTY TRANSFER

This Agreement is personal to the contracting parties. Neither party may seek to transfer, charge or make over this Agreement to any third party without the prior written approval of the other party except to the extent that the benefit and burden of this Agreement shall be binding upon the successors in business and/or title of the Assignee.

16. LIMITATION OF LIABILITY

Notwithstanding any other provision of this Agreement neither party shall be liable to the other for any indirect or consequential loss or damage and the maximum liability of the Assignor to the Assignee shall be restricted to [____________] [currency].

17. RIGHTS OF THIRD PARTIES

Any body corporate or otherwise which is not a party to this Agreement shall have no right to enforce any obligation or right against the Assignor or Assignee.

18. GOVERNING LAW

This Agreement shall be governed and construed in accordance with the Laws of England and the European Court of Justice.

Name: [____________]
Title: [____________]
Signed by: [____________]
FOR AND ON BEHALF OF THE ASSIGNOR

Date: [____________]

Name: [____________]
Title: [____________]
Signed by: [____________]
FOR AND ON BEHALF OF THE ASSIGNEE

Date: [____________]

Executed and Delivered as a deed by: [____________]
Signed by: [____________] [Witness]
Signed by: [____________] [Company Secretary]

OUTLINE—GENERAL ALL MEDIA BUY-OUT OF A WORK

This is a short form assignment giving the Assignee all media rights in the Work and the Work material for a fixed sum called the Assignment Fee. The Assignor is providing only limited warranties and undertakings and is not responsible for ensuring that the material is not obscene or defamatory. Although the Assignor may own all rights in the Work he may not own all those in the actual work material. Schedule 2 should provide a full list of all copyright notices, credits, moral rights and other obligations to third parties. The Assignee is to bear all clearance and payment costs to third parties from the date of the Agreement. The Assignor has waived all moral rights regarding credit and derogatory treatment and will have no control over the Work after it becomes the property of the Assignee from the date of the Agreement.

All costs and expenses after the date of the Agreement are the responsibility of the Assignee who will be entitled to exploit the Work and Work material as he sees fit at his total discretion in all formats. The Agreement will require a full list of the description of the Work and the material to be drawn up at an early stage specifying in as much detail as possible what is available. If the background is so complex that it is difficult to set out a list of issues a schedule to the relevant documents referred to could be listed. There are only two important stages: the payment of the Assignment Fee and the handing over of the work material. The risk in the material falls to the Assignee on the date of the Agreement not when it is collected.

It is possible that the Assignor could assign the rights but require a payment not only under the Assignment Fee, but linked to exploitation of the Work and Work Material.

We have included a reference in the signatory section to execution of a deed but this is not absolutely necessary.

SHORT FORM EMPLOYMENT LETTER AGREEMENT

LETTER OF APPOINTMENT dated the [____________] day of [____________].

Name of Employer: [____________] Address: [____________]

Name of Employee: [____________] Address: [____________]

Dear [Employee],
We are delighted to confirm the particulars of your employment with us as follows:

GENERAL

1. The first day of your employment will be [date].
2. The date for the purposes of calculating continuous employment is [date].
3. Your [annual/monthly/weekly/hourly] basic salary will be [figure] [currency].
4. Your basic salary will be paid at regular intervals as follows: [week/month].
5. You will be paid in the following manner: [direct debit / cheque].
6. Your normal working hours will be [start / end].
7. Your holiday entitlement will be [days / months].
8. In the event that this contract of employment comes to an end, and at that time you have an outstanding holiday entitlement, we will pay you in lieu of days not taken off as holidays as follows: [amount per day].
9. In the event that you cannot attend work due to ill-health we will abide by the following ill health policy: [____________]
10. Your pension entitlement is as follows: [____________]
11. You may bring this contract to an end by serving on us the following notice period: [____________]
12. We may bring this contract to an end by serving on you the following notice period: [____________]
13. Your job title will be [____________]
14. Your job description is [____________]
15. We agree that this contract is intended [to be continuous / last for X months].
16. You have agreed to work at the following address(es): [____________].

17. There are other [collective] agreements which are already in force which will effect your terms and conditions of employment. Particulars of the agreements are: [__________].

18. We can confirm at this stage that you will not be expected to work outside the United Kingdom for more than [one month] [per year].

19. In the event that we do require you to work outside the United Kingdom for more than [one month] we will confirm with you before you leave the length of time involved, the currency in which you will be paid, any other benefits to which you will be entitled because you are working abroad and the terms and conditions relating to your return to the United Kingdom.

20. If you have a grievance relating to your employment, in the first instance, please bring the matter to the attention of [person] [title].

21. Our disciplinary rules and procedures are contained in a separate document and you will be provided with all relevant details upon request.

22. In the event there are any material changes to these particulars, we will notify you in writing as soon as reasonably practicable.

DATA PROTECTION POLICY

23. We will respect your right to privacy and shall treat all personal information obtained about you in a strictly professional and confidential manner and shall only pass on personal details to third parties in the following circumstances: [__________].

24. However, we will not under any circumstances pass on details to any third party which are obviously sensitive to you unless we have been specifically requested to do so by you and you have agreed in writing to such disclosure.

TAX NATIONAL INSURANCE

25. The Employee shall be responsible for his own national insurance, personal tax and any other taxes arising under this Agreement in respect of the sums received by the Employee.

Signed for and on behalf of the Employer: [__________]

Signed for and on behalf of the Employee: [__________]

OUTLINE—SHORT FORM EMPLOYMENT LETTER AGREEMENT

This short form letter agreement is intended to cover those issues which need to be confirmed in writing and be provided to the Employee shortly after he starts. It is important to leave all the headings in, and state whether it is appropriate or not. For example, if the business is small and there are no formal disciplinary rules, that should be stated. Also included is a data protection policy.

Since this Agreement will probably only be looked to for the establishment of payment for work, the job title and description and when either party is dissatisfied, it is important that sufficient thought is given to the notice periods, and the process to be followed when either party wishes to resolve a problem. The job description should specify areas of responsibility, the person to whom the Employee reports and those to whom they must provide supervision, if appropriate.

This contract does not apply to a Senior Executive, and it is assumed that the person is normally based in the United Kingdom.

There is no expenses provision, clothing or car allowance, bonus, share option or other benefits listed.

Issues such as ill health medical certificates, pension and other company policy and staff-related matters are often dealt with in an enclosed handbook issued by human resources.

CONTRACT OF EMPLOYMENT FOR EXECUTIVE DIRECTOR

AN AGREEMENT dated this [____________] day of [____________]

BETWEEN:

(1) [Name of Company], the registered address of which is [____________]
(to be known as the Company in this Agreement)

AND

(2) [Name of Executive] of [address] (to be known as the Executive in this Agreement)

IT IS AGREED as follows

1. DEFINITIONS

1.1 "The Services" shall mean the product of the services of the Executive to be provided to the Company under this Agreement which are described in the Executive Job Description attached (Annex A).

1.2 "Executive's Title of Employment" shall be as follows: [____________].

1.3 "Term of the Agreement" shall commence on [date] and shall continue until terminated by either party in accordance with the terms of this Agreement.

1.4 "Executive's Basic Remuneration" shall mean the annual sum of [figure] [currency] which shall be the gross sum payable by the Company to the Executive in accordance with the terms of this Agreement.

1.5 "Additional Remuneration" shall mean such financial or benefit in kind to which the Executive may be entitled, including an annual bonus of [one-third Basic Remuneration] in the event the Company achieves specified turnover, profit and/or cashflow targets as specified in the Executive Bonus Scheme attached as Annex I. Such Additional Remuneration will also include the benefit of any Executive Share Option Scheme details of which are attached as Annex J.

1.6 "The Company" shall mean the Company and all other registered companies owned or controlled by or associated with the Company.

1.7 "The Board" means the Board of Directors for the time being of the Company formally appointed under current Companies Act or any modifying or similar legislation.

1.8 "Bank Holidays" shall mean all recognised Bank and Public Holidays in [England].

1.9 "Continuous Employment" for legal purposes shall mean the period of continuous employment beginning on the commencement of this Agreement under clause 1.3.

1.10 "Executive's Holidays" shall be [25] working week days in any calendar year in addition to Bank Holidays.

1.11 "Normal Working Hours" shall mean from [08.50] to [17.45], Monday to Friday inclusive [with the exception of one hour between the hours of 12.00 and 14.30 for a lunch break].

1.12 "PPP" shall mean [Private Patient's Plan].

1.13 "Work Premises" shall mean all offices, studios and locations owned and controlled by the Company at the date of this Agreement or any time thereafter [in the United Kingdom].

1.14 "Statutory Particulars" shall mean the following:

1.14.1 Continuous Employment: see clause 1.9;
1.14.2 Remuneration: see clause 1.4;
1.14.3 Hours of Work: see clause 1.11;
1.14.4 Sickness: see clauses 4.24, 4.25 and 5.17–5.22;
1.14.5 Pension Scheme: see clause 4.15 and 4.16;
1.14.6 Notice: see clause 6.3;
1.14.7 Job Title: see clause 1.2;
1.14.8 Grievance Procedure: see clause 5.12;
1.14.9 Disciplinary Procedure: see clause 4.1;
1.14.10 Maternity Rights: see clause 4.10; and
1.14.11 Paternity Rights: see clause 4.11.

2. APPOINTMENT OF THE EXECUTIVE

2.1 In consideration of the Services provided under this Agreement the Company agrees to employ the Executive and to pay the Executive's Remuneration in accordance with the terms of this Agreement.

2.2 In consideration of the Executive's Remuneration the Executive agrees to provide the Services in accordance with the terms of this Agreement.

2.3 The Company and the Executive acknowledge that this Agreement is a contract of employment.

2.4 The duties of the Executive as a director of the Company, if appointed, shall be subject to the Memorandum and Articles of Association of the relevant company for the time being and (subject to clause 2.5 below) shall be separate from and additional to his duties pursuant to the Appointment. His salary under this Agreement is inclusive of any Remuneration to which the Executive may be entitled as a director of the Company or any associated body.

2.5 Upon termination of the appointment for whatever reason or at any time during the course of the appointment the Executive shall at the request of the Company forthwith in writing resign his position as a director of the Company without compensation for any loss of office as director.

2.6 The Executive shall participate in any scheme considered by the Board to be appropriate to the Executive for directors' and officers' liability insurance.

2.7 The Executive shall report to [designated title] of the Company.

3. COPYRIGHT AND ANCILLARY RIGHTS

3.1 The Executive acknowledges that all intellectual property rights including copyright, design rights, property rights, rights to data and data bases, trademarks, service marks and any other rights in the Services shall remain the sole and exclusive property of the Company. This Agreement does not purport to grant, assign or transfer any rights in the Services to the Executive. For the avoidance of doubt, all rights, including copyright, in any work or invention created at any time by the Executive in the course of or in connection with his employment will belong by law to the Company.

3.2 The Executive waives all statutory moral rights in respect of the Services provided under this Agreement. Provided that no product of the services attributed to the Executive shall be treated in a manner which will impugn the reputation of the Executive.

3.3 The Executive may not reproduce any work created in the course of his employment or at the Company's request (whether published or not) without the Board's prior consent. Payments for the syndication of works are to be due to the Company.

3.4 Without prejudice to the Executive's statutory rights the Executive shall when so requested by the Company at any time during or after the termination of the Appointment at the expense of the Company execute and make all such documents and do all things as the Company shall deem necessary in order to apply for and obtain letters patent or like monopoly privileges for any such invention or discovery in all such countries as the Company may require. Any such letters patent or other monopoly privileges shall when granted belong absolutely to the Company. the Executive shall at the request and expense of the Company assign them to the Company or as the Company may direct.

4. OBLIGATIONS OF THE COMPANY

DISCIPLINARY RULES

4.1 In the event that the Executive conducts himself in such a way as to justify his possible dismissal the Company agrees to abide by the Disciplinary Procedure as set out in Annex C.

EXPENSES

4.2 In addition to his remuneration hereunder the Executive shall be reimbursed for travelling, telephone, fax, e-mail, hotel and other expenses properly and reasonably incurred by him in the discharge of his duties and in accordance with the relevant rules and practices of the Company for the time being in force. Any credit and charge cards supplied to the Executive by the Company shall be returned to the Company on leaving the Company's employment. Any money paid to the Executive to meet expenses incurred on a Company credit or charge card shall be used for that purpose and no other. The Executive shall be liable for the discharge of any personal expenses incurred by him using the Company credit or charge card.

COMPANY CAR

4.3 The Company shall provide a motor car (of a type determined in accordance with the policy of the Company for the time being) for the use by the Executive in the performance of his duties. The Company shall pay testing, taxation, insurance premiums and the running expenses of the car subject to the terms (if any) which the Company may impose (including terms regarding taking the car outside the United Kingdom as laid down from time to time). The Executive shall be entitled to use the car for his private purposes. The Executive shall take good care of the car and ensure that it is in the state and condition required by law, the Company's car policy and (if applicable) the leasing agents and shall procure that the provisions and conditions of any policy of insurance are observed. The car will be changed at such intervals as may be laid down in the Company's car policy from time to time. The car shall remain the property of the Company or its leasing agents as applicable and shall be returned to the Company upon the determination of the Agreement.

PRIVATE HEALTH CARE

4.4 The Executive shall be entitled to the level of private health care of a senior executive in accordance with the Company's private health policy as amended from time to time. The Company shall provide and pay for cover for the Executive himself and his partner and their unmarried children aged under 21 of any medical insurance scheme in force for the time being and applicable to full-time employees or officers of the Company at the Company's expense. A copy of the policy shall be supplied to the Executive upon request.

4.5 The Company acknowledges its duty to make available to all employees and to keep up-to-date a statement of the Company's general policy with respect to the health and safety at work of its employees and of the arrangements for carrying out that policy.

4.6 The Company acknowledges its duty to consult such representatives as may be appointed by the Secretary of State for Employment with a view to making and maintaining effective arrangements for the health and safety of its employees a copy of which is attached to and forms part of this agreement as Health and Safety Policy as [Annex B].

HOLIDAYS

4.7 The Company acknowledges that the Executive is entitled to the Executive's Holidays in addition to Bank Holidays. The Company agrees that Bank Holidays and the Executive's Holidays shall be subject to the agreed rates of payment in accordance with the Executive Remuneration.

4.8 The Company confirms that in the event that the Executive is requested to work on Bank Holidays or on days which have been agreed as the Executive's Holidays then such work will be paid for on an ad hoc basis on terms to be agreed between the Company and the Executive.

LIFE ASSURANCE

4.9 Subject to Inland Revenue limits, the Company agrees to provide life assurance cover in respect of the Executive at rates acceptable to the Company and to any conditions the Company may from time to time lay down. The Company will make arrangements for the provision by an Insurance Company of life assurance for the Executive of [four times the basic salary], subject to the terms and conditions from time to time of the insurance policy.

MATERNITY RIGHTS

4.10 The Company acknowledges its responsibilities under any legislation or directive in force with respect to leave taken by reason of pregnancy, delivery and post-natal recovery. The detailed guidelines which the Company agrees to abide by are attached to and form part of this Agreement as Maternity Rights Policy as Annex D.

PATERNITY RIGHTS

4.11 The Company acknowledges its responsibility under any legislation or directive in force with respect to the right of the father to take leave in connection with and commencing with the birth of his children. Details of the Company's Paternity Rights Policy is attached as Annex E.

MEDICAL EXAMINATION

4.12 The Executive is eligible for an annual medical screening at the Company's cost by a qualified medical practitioner specified by the Company. The Executive shall agree to a medical examination including an HIV test, at the request and expense of the Company at any time during the continuance of his appointment hereunder whether or not the Executive is absent by reason of sickness, injury or other incapacity. The Executive hereby authorises the [Chief Executive] to have unconditional access to any report or reports (including copies thereof) prepared as a result of any such examination, subject to his statutory rights.

NATIONAL INSURANCE AND TAX PAYMENT

4.13 The Company confirms that he shall be responsible for the Executive's National Insurance payments and personal tax payments whether due under the PAYE scheme or similar arrangement.

PAY REVIEW

4.14 The Company agrees that the Executive's Remuneration shall be subject to regular reviews at yearly intervals. The first review being on the first anniversary of the date of this Agreement: [date].

PENSION SCHEME

4.15 The Executive shall be eligible to be a member of the Company's Pension Scheme upon the terms and conditions from time to time applicable under the Scheme and the Company's pensions policy, Company contributions in respect of the Executive at all times shall be subject to applicable Inland Revenue limits.

4.16 If the Executive chooses not to be a member of the Company's Pension Scheme the basis on which the Company will contribute to a personal pension taken out by the Executive will be agreed with the Company, but in any event the contribution by the Company shall not be less than [15] per cent of the Executive's Basic Remuneration.

PUBLIC AND COMPANY'S LIABILITY INSURANCE

4.17 The Company confirms that there will be in existence during the term of this Agreement adequate public and employer's liability insurance cover for the benefit of the Company and the Employee.

REMUNERATION

4.18 The Company agrees to pay The Executive's Remuneration by credit transfer to The Executive's personal bank or building society account on the [last Thursday] of each month. In the event that a Bank Holiday falls on a Thursday The Company shall be entitled to make payment to The Executive on the next working day unless some other arrangement is made between parties.

4.19 The Company agrees to make all payments required under this Agreement to the Executive personally unless otherwise advised or required by law.

CHANGE OF CONTROL

4.20 The employment of the Executive under this Agreement is deemed to have commenced on the date specified in clause 1.3 and subject to the terms of the

Agreement shall continue unless or until there is a change of control of the Company. Where any person, company or organisations acquires, whether by a series of transactions pursuant to a scheme of arrangement or otherwise, shares in the Company which if taken together with all other shares held by the acquirer, and persons acting in concert with it (as defined in the City Code on Take-Overs and Mergers) resulting in the acquirer obtaining control of the Company as statutorily defined for tax purposes. Then the Executive shall be entitled for up to a period of three months following the date the acquirer obtains control as aforesaid to terminate his employment with immediate effect by notice in writing to the Company subject to the Company paying the sums set out in clause 4.21 to which the Executive shall be entitled forthwith. For the avoidance of doubt this clause shall not apply on a change in control where the acquirer is an associated corporate body of the Company.

4.21 In the event of a change of control in accordance with clause 4.20, the Company and the Executive agree that the Executive shall be entitled to a gross sum equivalent to [two] years Basic Remuneration in addition to financial compensation for all other benefits which the Executive would have been entitled had the contract run its two-year course including compensation for loss of car, pension, private health care, life assurance and any minimum bonus to which the Executive would have been entitled. Further an additional sum shall be paid which shall not be less than [______________] which shall be for loss of office, loss of status, and title, prejudice of future career prospects, stress and derogatory publicity associated therewith.

DATA PROTECTION

4.22 The Company shall abide fully with the spirit and intent of all relevant data protection legislation, directives or governmental guidelines.

4.23 In particular the Company shall abide by its Data Protection Policy in force from time to time and shall not disclose to any third party such information personal and private to the Executive without the Executive's prior approval whether such information is deemed by him to be sensitive or otherwise.

SICKNESS AND INJURY

4.24 The Company agrees to make all payment to the Executive in accordance with the Executive's remuneration in the event of the inability of the Executive to provide his services due to sickness or injury on condition that a medical certificate is produced upon request where the Executive is unavailable to work for a continuous period of five working days or more.

STATUTORY SICK PAY

4.25 The Company reserves the right to set off against payment made to the Executive any statutory sick pay benefits received by it.

5. OBLIGATIONS OF THE EXECUTIVE

THE SERVICE

5.1 The Executive confirms that his services shall be as set out to in accordance with clause 1.1 and shall include the specific duties as described in the Executive's Job Description, as set out in Annex A, which is attached to and forms part of this Agreement.

5.2 The Executive confirms that he has full title and authority to enter into this Agreement and is not bound by any previous agreements which adversely affects this Agreement.

5.3 The Executive is not permitted to undertake any other employment outside working hours, whether paid (financially or otherwise) or unpaid, nor is he permitted to have any interest in any business or undertakings which directly or indirectly competes with the same or similar business interests of the Company (which shall include the interests of an of its subsidiaries or associate companies), without the written permission of the Board. Provided that it is agreed that the Executive may continue to carry on with the following matters already disclosed: [____________].

DUTIES

5.4 During the continuance of the Appointment the Executive shall well and faithfully serve the Company and use his best endeavours to promote the interest of the Company and shall in particular:

5.4.1 provide his services to the best of his skill and ability on a full-time and exclusive basis and shall perform all services diligently to ensure that the obligations under this agreement are satisfactorily performed. The Executive confirms that he shall not during the course of this Agreement supply services of the same or similar nature to the Services provided under the Agreement to any third party without the prior consent of the Company;

5.4.2 carry out the duties described in the Executive's job description as specified from time to time;

5.4.3 undertake such other duties and exercise such other powers in relation to the conduct and management of the Company or its associated bodies and their businesses and affairs as the Board shall from time to time assign or vest in him;

5.4.4 in the discharge of such duties and in the exercise of such powers observe and comply with all resolutions regulations and directions from time to time made or given by the Board;

5.4.5 unless prevented by ill-health from so doing subject to any consent given by the Company devote the whole of his time, attention and abilities to the discharge of his duties hereunder;

5.4.6 conform to such hours of work as may from time to time be reasonably required of him outside Normal Working Hours without further remuneration;

5.4.7 in pursuance of his duties hereunder perform such services for companies with which the Company may now be or subsequently become associated and accept such offices in such associated companies as the Board may from time to time reasonably require.

DISCLOSURE OF INFORMATION AND CONFIDENTIALITY

5.5 The Executive shall not divulge nor communicate to any person (other than those who need to know or with proper authority) any of the business plans or trade secrets or other confidential information of or relating to the Company which he may have received or obtained while in the service of the Company. This restriction shall continue to apply after the termination of his engagement for a period of [three years] but shall cease to apply to information or knowledge which may come into the public domain otherwise than through the default of the Executive or which shall have been received by the Executive from a third party not entitled to disclose the same.

5.6 The Executive is not permitted to publish any letters or articles purporting to represent the views of the Company unless prior permission is obtained from the Board. Failure to comply with the above provisions may, if the circumstances warrant, be regarded as gross misconduct for which the Executive may be liable to summary dismissal.

5.7 The Executive must not contact or communicate with any member of the press or media or anyone so connected, on behalf of the Company unless prior [written] permission has been obtained from the Board.

5.8 The Executive shall not during the period of two years after the determination of his engagement hereunder take any step to solicit or entice away from the Company any individual, partnership, firm or company who at any time during period [twelve months] prior to such determination shall have been a customer or client where any such solicitation or enticement would cause damage to the business of the Company.

5.9 The Executive shall not during the period of [two years] after the termination of his engagement hereunder induce or seek to induce any employee of the Company to leave its service.

ACCEPTANCE OF GIFTS OR LOAN

5.10 The Executive must not accept at any time any gifts or loans of any nature from any individual, partnership, firm, company or other body with whom the Company has or is likely to have business relations, or from any representative of such individual, partnership, firm, company or other body with the exception of small gifts of nominal value (*e.g.* stationery)

CHANGE IN PERSONAL CIRCUMSTANCES

5.11 The Executive shall inform the Company immediately of any alteration to his name, permanent address, telephone or fax number (if any), or any alteration of relevant personal details including next of kin or person to be contacted in case of emergency.

GRIEVANCE PROCEDURE

5.12 The Executive agrees to be bound by the terms of the Grievance Procedure which is attached to and forms part of this Agreement as Annex G.

HOLIDAYS

5.13 The Executive accepts that the precise dates relating to the Executive's Holidays if not already specified shall agreed between the Company and the Executive. The Executive shall be required to give reasonable notice with respect to taking of any holidays other than Bank Holidays. The Company will be entitled to deduct payment for any holidays taken in excess of this entitlement.

LIMITATION OF AUTHORITY

5.14 Subject to the specific authority contained in the Executive's Job Description, the Executive agrees not to pledge, either during the term of this Agreement or any time thereafter, the Company on the Company's behalf without the specific [written] authority of the Board unless such authorisation is within the general parameters of the Executive's Job Description.

MOBILITY

5.15 The Executive shall if called upon to do so and without any further remuneration perform his duties hereunder at the offices of the Company [in London] or elsewhere in [the United Kingdom] as the Company may in its absolute discretion from time to time require. The Executive may be obliged to go outside [the United Kingdom]. If the Executive is required to change his residence in accordance with this clause, the Company will reimburse the Executive with regard to such removal and other expenses incidental to such change of residence as the Company may consider fair and reasonable in the circumstances.

OVER PAYMENT

5.16 The Executive is required to disclose and repay all over-payment of any nature or made by mistake, misrepresentation or otherwise.

SICKNESS, INJURY OR ABSENCE

5.17 In the case of absence from work the Executive must notify the Company as soon as possible, in person wherever possible, or by the best available means at his disposal in the circumstances. In any event, the Executive agrees to provide the Company with as much notice as possible in the event that the Executive is unable whether as a result of sickness or general circumstances beyond the control of the Executive, to perform any of his obligations under this Agreement.

5.18 The Executive must provide a medical certificate for periods of sickness or injury of more than [five working days], and thereafter at weekly intervals and must produce a final certificate before resuming normal duties. The Executive agrees that entitlement to sickness pay is dependent on the above procedure being followed.

5.19 The Executive shall whenever reasonably requested by [the Chief Executive] agree to a medical examination (and requests to submit to such examination at reasonably periodic intervals shall be deemed to be reasonable requests) by such doctor or doctors as the [Chief Executive] may nominate and the Company shall receive a copy of the medical report resulting from such examination. The Executive may arrange for his own qualified medical advisor to be present at such examination who shall be entitled to a copy of such medical report.

5.20 The Executive shall not be entitled to payment by the Company for sickness or injury benefit after the date on which the employment has been terminated either by notice of termination or by expiry of an individual contract.

5.21 Where the Executive is sick or injured whilst on annual holiday he will be entitled to take holiday at a later date within the holiday year provided that the Executive has obtained an acceptable medical certificate for the period of sickness.

5.22 If the Executive is absent from duty without permission and without a reason acceptable to the Company. The Company reserves the right to withhold payment or deduct from the Executive's salary a day's pay for each day of unauthorised absence. Disciplinary action may also be taken in accordance with the Disciplinary Procedure as set out in Annex C.

PERFORMANCE OF PUBLIC DUTIES

5.23 The Executive will be entitled to up to five days additional paid leave of absence with respect to the performance of any recognised public duties including acting as a Justice of the Peace or local authority Councillor but otherwise will be expected to use his own annual leave except to the extent that the number of days permitted as additional paid leave shall be [14] with respect to jury service.

5.24 The Executive will be entitled to up to three days additional paid leave of absence with respect to attendance in his capacity as a member of a recognised education establishment including schools, colleges and universities in the United Kingdom but otherwise will be expected to use his own annual leave.

5.25 The Executive must obtain prior approval for time off in respect of the public duties referred to above from the Board.

PROCEDURE UPON TERMINATION OF THIS AGREEMENT

5.26 The Executive is required to deliver to the Company at the end of his employment (howsoever terminated) all papers, documents, keys, credit cards, cars and all property properly belonging to the Company of any nature. The Executive agrees to sign an undertaking that all such property has been duly returned.

6. MISCELLANEOUS

ALTERATIONS AND AMENDMENTS

6.1 This Agreement supersedes all previous agreements, representations or promises and sets out all the terms agreed between the parties. Any amendment or alteration to this Agreement must be in writing and signed by an authorised signatory of each party. Although the Executive understands and accepts that he will be bound by any reasonable variation or amendments to the Company's policies attached to this Agreement notified in writing to the Executive.

NOTICES

6.2 Notices pursuant to this Agreement shall be in writing by first class recorded delivery to the following parties:

[Name] [Address] in respect of service on the Executive
[Name] [Address] in respect of service on the Company.

Any change or alteration of these details must be notified in writing and confirmed as agreed by the other party. No other method of notification whether by fax, e-mail, telex or otherwise shall be accepted as proper notice.

TERMINATION OF AGREEMENT

6.3 This Agreement may be terminated by the Executive or the Company by giving [12 months] notice to the other party [EXCEPT that the period of notice required to be given by the Company to the Executive shall be three months throughout the first year of service].

6.4 Subject to the Grievance Procedure as set out in Annex G, the Appointment may be terminated forthwith by the Company without prior notice and without pay in lieu if the Executive shall at any time:

6.4.1 be guilty of serious misconduct or any other conduct including criminal convictions likely to affect prejudicially the interests of the Company;
6.4.2 become of unsound mind or incapable of functioning normally due to psychiatric or mental problems;
6.4.3 where the Executive is declared insolvent in bankruptcy or any other legal proceedings;
6.4.4 be guilty of any breach or non-observance of any of the provisions of this Agreement on his part to be performed or observed;

and such termination shall be without prejudice to any other rights of the Company against the Employee.

6.5 In addition to any other rights and remedies at law and notwithstanding clauses 4 and 5, this Agreement may be terminated by the Company by giving written notice to the Executive where the Executive has failed to attend to his duties under this Agreement, for any reason, for a continuous period of [three months] or more. The

Company undertakes not to invoke this procedure in circumstances where it would be manifestly unfair to do so.

6.6 The Company shall be entitled to request the Executive be on paid leave from the Company for a total period not exceeding [one month] for the purpose of investigating any allegations concerning the conduct or well-being of the Executive.

6.7 Upon termination of his employment by the Company for whatever reason the Executive shall (without prejudice to any claim for damages or other remedy which either party may have) immediately upon written request by the Company return or arrange for the collection by the Company of all material of any nature in any medium in the possession or control of the Executive which belongs to the Company. Save that where any material is required by the Executive for the purpose of evidence in proposed future legal proceedings then the Executive shall not be under any obligation to return such material immediately, but shall place it in the possession of his legal advisors.

THIRD PARTY TRANSFER

6.8 Neither party shall assign, transfer, charge or make over this Agreement or any of its rights or obligations without the prior consent of the other party.

THIRD PARTY RIGHTS

6.9 This Agreement is personal to the Company and the Employee. No third party shall be entitled to seek to enforce or rely on the benefits or obligations set out in this Agreement.

GOVERNING LAW

6.10 Both parties agree and acknowledge and confirm that any dispute, litigation, interpretation, damages or losses which arise directly or indirectly as a result of this Agreement shall be subject to the Laws of [______________] and no other jurisdiction shall be applicable.

Name: [____________]
Designation: [____________]
Signed by: [____________]
FOR AND ON BEHALF OF THE COMPANY

Date: [____________]

Name: [____________]
Designation: [____________]
Signed by: [____________]
FOR AND ON BEHALF OF THE EXECUTIVE

Date: [____________]

ATTACHED TO AND FORMING PART OF THIS AGREEMENT

ANNEX A: **EXECUTIVE JOB DESCRIPTION**

ANNEX B: **HEALTH & SAFETY POLICY**

ANNEX C: **DISCIPLINARY PROCEDURE**

ANNEX D: **MATERNITY RIGHTS POLICY**

ANNEX E: **PATERNITY RIGHTS POLICY**

ANNEX F: **EXECUTIVE PENSION SCHEME**

ANNEX G: **GRIEVANCE PROCEDURE**

ANNEX H: **DATA PROTECTION POLICY**

ANNEX I: **EXECUTIVE BONUS SCHEME**

ANNEX J: **EXECUTIVE SHARE OPTION SCHEME**

OUTLINE—CONTRACT OF EMPLOYMENT FOR EXECUTIVE DIRECTOR

This is a contract of employment for a senior Executive who is expected to take a seat on the board of the Company. Numerous annexes will need to be attached as specified. In addition to the basic salary, the Company is providing private health care, life assurance, a car, pensions and participation in the Company's bonus and share option scheme.

The Company is also agreeing to seek the Executive's express approval to the disclosure any private and personal information to any third party, whether such information is deemed by law to be sensitive or otherwise.

The job description should be detailed as should the reporting structure within the organisation. All the benefits under the contract should be examined in some depth and the documentation reviewed prior to signature. Although it is not strictly necessary to attach so many annexes, this has been done to clarify the range of policies and procedures that most people only read once they have joined a company.

There is no indemnity provision by either party. No reference is made to public liability insurance by the Company but it may be relevant to address this issue purely as background.

We have not included a "golden hello" payment which could be on signature or spread over the first few years, but in some industries they are becoming more common.

There is no arbitration clause, but a corporate grievance procedure. The main concern of the Executive will be the salary and benefits. Other benefits not included are clothing allowances, equipment, standard of travel, entertainment or research material allowance.

We have not included a restriction on the type of employment the Executive may be involved in after the end of this contract, nor have we included a non-solicitation clause. These type of restrictions are often unenforceable as they are so widely drafted as to affect the livelihood of the individual which is these days viewed as unacceptable.

STANDARD EMPLOYEE REFERENCE LETTER

A. N. Other
[Job title]
[Address]

[Date]

Dear Sir/Madam,

This letter is to confirm that [Employee name] has been employed by [Company] since [date of first employment]. Since joining [company] in [date], [employee name] has been promoted to the position of [up-graded job title] in [date].

[Employee name] has consistently performed the duties required and expected of her in a competent, diligent and professional manner and has gained the respect of her peer group and manager.

We fully recommend [employee name] to your company and we are confident that [employee name] will prove to be a valuable asset to your company. We have no hesitation in making this recommendation and have no reason to believe that [employee name] will not perform equally well in your organisation.

We are sorry to lose [employee name] but wish her all the best in the new challenges ahead.

Yours sincerely,

[Authorised manager]

OUTLINE—STANDARD EMPLOYEE REFERENCE LETTER

This is a brief reference for an Employee to a prospective new Employer. Although the reference is fairly glowing, the issue to be sure of is that the statements made are true and accurate and are made in good faith.

Where no recommendation can be made then a simple letter setting out the job description and period of employment is sufficient. The Company should be very careful before it makes any derogatory comments concerning a previous employee which could be defamatory or damaging.

SHORT FORM CONFIDENTIALITY LETTER AGREEMENT

I, the undersigned, being a full time senior employee of [____________] ("the Company") in consideration of the sum of [figure/currency] (receipt of which is hereby acknowledged), agree as follows:

(1) I acknowledge receipt of a document entitled [____________] ("the Work") which is [number] pages in length.

(2) I confirm that the Work has been supplied to me by [____________] ("the Grantor").

(3) I confirm that the sole purpose of being granted access to the Work is as follows: [____________]

(4) I confirm that I shall not make nor authorise or permit copies of the Work at any stage for any purpose whilst it is in my control or possession.

(5) I will use my best endeavours to ensure that the Work is at all times kept in a safe and secure manner and all reasonable steps will be taken to ensure that no unauthorised party may gain access to the Work.

(6) I will keep the existence and content of the Work strictly confidential and will only disclose the existence and contents of the Work to those senior executives of the Company on a strictly need-to-know basis.

(7) In the event that the existence and/or the contents of the Work are disclosed to senior personnel of the Company I will ensure that such individuals are made fully aware of this Agreement and the need to maintain strict confidentiality in the Work.

(8) I will immediately return the Work as soon as reasonably practicable following a request from the Grantor and will ensure that the Work is delivered in a safe and secure manner. In any event the Work will be returned by: [date].

(9) I further agree to indemnify and hold harmless the Grantor in the event of any breach of the above promises and undertakings.

Name: [_______________]
Designation: [_______________]
Signature: [_______________]
FOR AND ON BEHALF OF THE GRANTOR

Date: [_______________]

Name: [_______________]
Designation: [_______________]
Signature: [_______________]
FOR AND ON BEHALF OF THE COMPANY

Date: [_______________]

Name: [_______________]
Designation: [_______________]
Signature: [_______________]
WITNESS TO THIS AGREEMENT

Date: [_______________]

OUTLINE—SHORT FORM CONFIDENTIALITY LETTER AGREEMENT

The occasion often arises when a document needs to be disclosed to a third party in confidential circumstances. This short from agreement is intended to cover those circumstances where a specific document (*e.g.* a transcript) is to be disclosed to a third party (*e.g.* a features editor of a newspaper) who needs to read the document to assess its commercial value. Although the enforceability of its terms can sometimes be difficult, the very act of signing the document tends to heighten the recipient's awareness of the need for confidentiality and the consequences which may follow unauthorised disclosure.

The Grantor is providing the document referred to as the Work to a senior employee of the Company.

The clauses are deliberately short and kept to a minimum to avoid delay in allowing access to the material.

LONG FORM CONFIDENTIALITY LETTER AGREEMENT

LETTER OF CONFIDENTIALITY

Strictly private and confidential

From:
[Name of company]
[Address]

To:
[Name of company]
[Address]

[Date]

For the attention of [name of recipient]

Dear Sirs,

We acknowledge that discussions are taking place between your company ("the Buyer") and our company ("the Seller") to enable the Buyer to make a commercial decision as to whether a formal offer should be made to the Seller to acquire in whole or in part the goodwill, assets, liabilities, and contracts ("the Business") of the Seller. In furtherance to these discussions, the Seller has requested information ("Confidential Information") to be supplied by the Seller to the Buyer pursuant these discussions.

The Seller is willing to provide Confidential Information to the Buyer concerning the Business on the following terms and conditions:

PURPOSE OF DISCLOSURE

(1) The Buyer will act in good faith at all times and shall only use the Confidential Information for the purpose for which it is intended and for no other purpose, and will

not under any circumstances seek to take commercial advantage over the Seller by virtue of acquiring the Confidential Information.

NEED TO KNOW POLICY

(2) The Buyer will only disclose the Confidential Information to those employees of the Buyer on a need-to-know basis. The Buyer will also be entitled to disclose the Confidential Information on a need-to-know basis to such professional advisers as are required to assist the Buyer to evaluate the Confidential Information with a view to the acquisition of the Business.

CASCADING UNDERTAKINGS

(3) The Recipient shall use his best endeavours to ensure that all those to whom the Confidential Information is disclosed are made aware of the existence and terms of this Letter of Confidentiality and each individual shall be required to give written acknowledgement that he or she is aware of this document and has agreed to be bound by its terms. A record of the names and signatures of those individuals allowed access will be kept by the Buyer and delivered to the Seller when the material supplied under this Agreement is returned.

COPYING CONFIDENTIAL INFORMATION

(4) Under no circumstances will the Buyer make copies (in any manner or format) of any Confidential Information without the prior approval of the Seller.

SECURITY

(5) The Buyer will use its best endeavours to ensure that all Confidential Information is kept in a safe and secure environment.

RETURN OF CONFIDENTIAL INFORMATION

(6) The Buyer will return, at the Buyer's cost, as soon as is reasonably practicable to the Seller all originals and copies (as may be authorised under this Letter) of all materials relating to the Confidential Information in accordance with the Seller's instruction. The Seller acknowledges that the Buyer will be entitled to keep and retain correspondence relating to these discussion for its own purposes.

SCOPE OF CONFIDENTIAL INFORMATION

(7) The Buyer acknowledges that such Confidential Information as is disclosed under the terms of this document may not be complete and will not constitute a representation of any nature and such representations and warranties as may be formally and contractually made will be contained in the formal transfer document relating to the Business ("the Purchase Agreement").

NON-TRANSFER OF RIGHTS

(8) No rights of any nature are intended to be transferred by virtue of this Letter of Confidentiality by the Seller to the Buyer except as expressly stated.

PUBLIC DOMAIN

(9) The Seller acknowledges that Confidential Information shall not include any information which has or may become public knowledge unless such information has come into the public domain by virtue of a breach of this Letter of Confidentiality by the Buyer.

DISCLOSURE REQUIRED BY LAW

(10) The Buyer shall be deemed not to be in breach of this Letter of Confidentiality if required to make disclosures relating to the Confidential Information by virtue of an order of a court or tribunal of competent jurisdiction or as a result of proceedings which require such disclosure.

NON-SOLICITATION

(11) In addition to any general prohibition under this Letter of Confidentiality against the Buyer using Confidential Information for purposes not intended or agreed, the Buyer expressly undertakes not to use the Confidential Information for the purposes of enticing, poaching or soliciting employees or customers of the Seller to the Buyer.

INDEMNITY

(12) The Buyer will hold harmless and indemnify the Seller for any breach of the terms of this Letter of Confidentiality for any reasonable and direct loss suffered by the Seller as a result of any breach by the Buyer of the terms of this Letter of Confidentiality.

REMEDIES FOR BREACH

(13) The Buyer acknowledges that damages may not be an adequate remedy for a breach or anticipated breach of the terms of this Letter of Confidentiality and in addition to any other remedies available in law or equity to the Seller, the Seller shall be entitled to immediate injunctive relief against the Buyer in such circumstances.

GOVERNING LAW

(14) The Letter of Confidentiality shall be construed under and governed by the Laws of England.

SIGNED FOR AND ON BEHALF OF THE BUYER:

Name: [____________]

Title: [____________]

Witnessed by: [____________]

Date: [____________]

OUTLINE—LONG FORM CONFIDENTIALITY LETTER AGREEMENT

This confidentiality letter agreement is intended to cover circumstances where confidential and commercially sensitive information is being passed to a potential purchaser of a business or part of a business. The clause addressing the issue of cascading the information, can be more specific and actually name those other individuals who have to be aware of the details being disclosed. Whilst the terms of the Agreement may be difficult to enforce in practice, the act of signing is likely to have the effect of increasing the recipients' diligence in maintaining confidence in the disclosed confidential information.

AGREEMENT BETWEEN AN ARTISTE AND AN AGENT

AN AGREEMENT dated: [____________]

BETWEEN:

(1) [Name] whose business address is at: [____________]

(to be known as the Artiste in this Agreement)

AND

(2) [Name of Agent/Company] whose registered office is at: [____________] and who carries on business at: [____________]

(to be known as the Agent in this Agreement).

IT IS AGREED as follows:

1. DEFINITIONS

The words below are agreed to mean as follows:

1.1 "The Agent's Commission" shall be the following percentage of the Gross Receipts: [figure]% [words].

1.2 "The Gross Receipts" shall be the total proceeds from the exploitation of the performances, appearances, recordings, endorsements or the commercial exploitation in any other form of the Artiste throughout the Territory at any time directly or indirectly received by or credited to the Agent or any sub-agent after the deduction of any value added tax whether received during the Term of this Agreement or thereafter.

1.3 "The Nett Receipts" shall be the Gross Receipts less the Agent's Commission.

1.4 "The Term of the Agreement" shall commence on [date] and unless terminated earlier in accordance with the provisions of this Agreement shall continue for [two] years up to and including [date]. This Agreement shall thereafter automatically be renewed for periods of [six months] unless either party shall give the other party [two months] prior written notice that the Agreement is at an end either before the expiry of the initial or any renewed period.

1.5 "The Territory" shall be the United Kingdom of Great Britain, Northern Ireland, Republic of Ireland, The Channel Islands and The Isle of Man, Europe which shall be construed as meaning those countries which are full Member States of the

European Union at the date of this Agreement which are Great Britain, Belgium, Denmark, France, Greece, Italy, Germany, Ireland, Luxembourg, Netherlands, Spain and Portugal.

2. ENGAGEMENT OF THE AGENT

2.1 In consideration of the Agent's Commission, the Agent agrees to provide his non-exclusive services to the Artiste for the Term of the Agreement throughout the Territory.

2.2 In consideration of the Nett Receipts, the Artiste agrees to engage the exclusive services of the Agent for the Term of the Agreement throughout the Territory to engage and commercially exploit the Artiste in all media including but not limited to all forms of films, video, television, theatric and non-theatric, merchandising, publications, advertising, promotional work, electronic dissemination of information including the internet, and interactive multimedia whether as performances, appearances, recordings, photographs, texts, sound, or images.

2.3 The Agent agrees that any form of exploitation of the product of the Artiste's services shall require the prior consent of the Artiste. The Artiste shall be entitled to refuse to carry out any work for any reason whether or not the Agent will not suffer a financial or other loss. The Agent shall not be entitled to seek any compensation, loss or damages from the Artiste which arises from such failure to provide consent.

3. COPYRIGHT

The Agent acknowledges that he is not acquiring any copyright or other rights in any material owned or controlled by the Artiste or in the name of the Artiste and any goodwill and reputation created in respect of any trademark, business name or logo shall remain the sole property of the Artiste. No part of this Agreement is intended to transfer, grant or vest any such rights in the Agent whether in existence prior to this Agreement or created at any time thereafter.

4. OBLIGATIONS OF THE AGENT

4.1 The Agent shall provide his services to the best of his skill and ability and shall perform all services diligently to ensure that the Artiste is regularly engaged by third parties on the best possible terms.

4.2 The Agent shall use his best endeavours to promote and publicise the Artiste in all forms of the media including television, radio, video, film, newspapers and periodicals, books, records and public appearances.

4.3 The Agent shall, as far as possible, keep the Artiste fully informed on a regular basis as regards any negotiations with any third party and agrees that he shall not be entitled to conclude any agreement relating to the Artiste without the prior verbal consent of the Artiste.

4.4 The Agent acknowledges that the Artiste shall be entitled, upon request, to be provided with a copy of any contract, record, document or any other material of any nature in the possession or under the control of the Agent relating to the Artiste.

4.5 The Agent undertakes not to disclose any material nor make any statement, whether true or not, concerning the Artiste's private and sexual life, politics and personal views to the media (including newspapers, television and radio) at any time without the prior written consent of the Artiste.

4.6 The Agent confirms that he had full authority to enter into and perform this Agreement and that he is not bound by any previous Agreement which adversely affects this Agreement.

4.7 The Agent acknowledges that he shall not be entitled to any commission in respect of any work done or for which the Artiste is already committed prior to the date of this Agreement whether that work is performed during the Term of the Agreement or not. A brief summary of the engagements is listed below: [____________].

4.8 The Agent acknowledges that he is not entitled to negotiate or promote in any manner or form the commercial interests of the Artiste outside the Territory unless specifically agreed in advance with the Artiste on each occasion. Any consent given by the Artiste outside the Territory does not mean there is a waiver of consent for any subsequent matter.

4.9 The Agent undertakes that he shall not for the Term of the Agreement assign, transfer or charge any of the rights or obligations in this Agreement to any third party without the prior written consent of the Artiste.

4.10 The Agent shall keep full and accurate separate books of account, records and contracts showing the Gross Receipts, the Agent's Commission and the Nett Receipts under this Agreement. All sums relating to the Artiste shall be kept separate and apart from all other monies received by the Agent. The sums received by the Agent shall be deposited at [name] Bank within one working day of payment. There shall be two signatories to the account and no sums may be withdrawn for any reason except with the required signature of the Artiste and the Agent. Both parties shall be entitled to receive statements and other transaction records, and documents from the [name] Bank.

4.11 The Agent agrees to pay the Nett Receipts to the Artiste on the last day of each calendar month in each year during the Term of this Agreement and thereafter on a quarterly basis.

4.12 On the last day of March, June, September and December in each year the Agent agrees to provide the Artiste with a detailed report containing a full breakdown of the Gross Receipts, the Agent's Commission, and the Nett Receipts.

4.13 The Agent agrees that the Artiste shall be entitled at his own expense to arrange for an annual audit to inspect and make copies of the Agent's books of account, records, contracts and any other relevant material in order to verify the sums due to the Artiste under this Agreement.

4.14 The Agent acknowledges that if within 12 months of the date of this agreement the Nett Receipts paid are less than [figure/currency]. Then the Artiste shall be entitled to terminate this Agreement by notice in writing.

4.15 The Agent agrees to keep all material relating to the Artiste for a period of not less than [two] years after the end of this Agreement.

4.16 Where after inspection and audit it is clear that the Agent has not fulfilled the terms of this Agreement and a serious error of more than [figure/currency] has occurred, then the Agent shall pay the sum due in full together with interest at [figure/per cent] and damages on each occasion of [figure/currency], together with the cost of the accountant or other professional consultant or legal advisor engaged by the Artiste.

4.17 The Agent shall not be responsible for nor bear the cost of arranging insurance cover for the Artiste for the performance of his services under this Agreement. Where appropriate the Agent shall request that a third party take out and bear the cost of additional insurance cover.

4.18 The Agent agrees not to promote, advertise or market the Artiste in any way which may impugn the reputation or embarrass the Artiste. As far as possible the Agent shall provide samples of all material and agrees to adhere to any changes requested by the Artiste. The Agent agrees that it shall be entirely responsible for the cost of all such material and it shall not be deducted from any sums due to the Artiste.

4.19 At the end of this Agreement the Agent agrees to transfer any copyright in the advertising, marketing and promotional material relating to the Artiste under the Agreement provided that the Artiste shall pay the sum of [figure/currency].

4.20 The Agent agrees and undertakes that he shall not seek to be reimbursed by the Artiste in respect of any costs and expenses occurred by the Agent in respect of the performance of his duties under this Agreement unless specifically agreed in detail in advance with the Artiste.

5. OBLIGATIONS OF THE ARTISTE

5.1 The Artiste agrees to provide his/her exclusive services to the best of his/her skill and ability and shall perform his/her duties under this Agreement at such times, dates and locations as may be agreed with the Agent.

5.2 The Artiste confirms that he/she is a British subject or a national of a Member State of the European Union and will remain so during the Term of the Agreement.

5.3 The Artiste confirms that he/she has full authority to enter into and perform this Agreement and that he/she is not bound by any previous Agreement which adversely affects this Agreement except for the following commitments made prior to the date of this Agreement: [____________]

5.4 The Artiste confirms that all the product of his/her services shall be original and will not infringe the copyright or any other right of any third party throughout the Territory.

5.5 The Artiste confirms that all the product of his/her services will not contain any obscene or defamatory material and will not expose the Agent to criminal or civil proceedings.

5.6 The Artiste agrees that the Agent shall be entitled to use and permit the use of the Artiste's name, image, biography, signature, photograph and likeness for the purposes of promoting, advertising and marketing the Artiste. Provided that the Agent shall provide the Artiste with exact samples of all material in any medium which it is intended to refer in any manner to the Artiste prior to production or distribution. In the event that the Artiste requests any changes or alterations the Agent must agree to such amendments.

5.7 The Artiste is not granting the Agent any option to renew or extend this Agreement nor is there any first right of refusal.

5.8 The Artiste agrees not to issue any statement to the media at any time concerning any confidential business or future plans of the Agent or details of any negotiations or terms of any agreements in progress or concluded by the Agent without the prior consent of the Agent.

5.9 The Artiste agrees to keep the Agent informed of his/her telephone number, address and whereabouts at all times during the Term of the Agreement.

5.10 The Artiste confirms that he/she shall be responsible for his/her own expenses, value added tax, personal insurance, national insurance and personal tax arising under this Agreement.

5.11 The Artiste agrees that to the best of his knowledge and belief he is not now nor has at any time been subject to or suffered from any illness or injury which would in any way prevent him from providing his services. That the Artiste will at all times do all that is reasonably necessary to attain and maintain such sound state of health as will enable him to fully perform his services and will not undertake any hazardous pursuits.

6. MISCELLANEOUS

MUTUAL INDEMNITY

6.1 The Artiste and the Agent mutually undertake to indemnify each other against all liabilities, claims, demands, actions, costs, damages and loss arising out of any breach by either party of any of the terms of this Agreement.

6.2 In the event of any claim, dispute, action, writ or summons in connection with clause 6.1, the Artiste and the Agent agree to provide full details to the other party at the earliest opportunity and shall not settle any such matter without first consulting the other party.

CONFIDENTIALITY

6.3 The Artiste and the Agent shall not disclose to any third party any confidential business or future plans of the other party acquired at any time during the existence of this Agreement and no reference is to be made to the terms of this Agreement by either party in any advertising, publicity or promotional material without the prior consent of the other party.

6.4 The Agent and the Artiste mutually agree and undertake that each of them shall not during the Term of this Agreement publish in writing or otherwise make known to the public or act in any way likely to result in publication of any matter concerning the business affairs of the other party without the other party providing their prior written consent.

AMENDMENTS AND ALTERATIONS

6.5 This Agreement supersedes all previous agreements, representations or promises and sets out all the terms agreed between the parties. Any amendment or alteration to this Agreement must be in writing and signed by an authorised signatory of each party.

NO PARTNERSHIP OR EMPLOYMENT

6.6 This Agreement shall not be deemed to create any partnership or employment relationship between the parties.

NOTICES

6.7 Any notice shall be served under this Agreement if it is handed directly in person to the Artiste or Agent or sent by recorded or first class post.

VALUE ADDED TAX

6.8 All sums payable under this Agreement are exclusive of any value added tax that may be payable by either party.

THIRD PARTY TRANSFERS

6.9 Neither party shall assign, transfer, charge or make over this Agreement or any of its rights or obligations without the prior written consent of the other party.

FORCE MAJEURE

6.10 In the event that this Agreement cannot be performed or its obligations fulfilled for any reason beyond the reasonable control of either party including war, industrial action, floods or Acts of God then such non-performance or failure to fulfil its obligations shall be deemed not to be a breach of this Agreement. Any party which is unable in whole or in part to carry out its obligations under this Agreement shall if reasonably possible give written notice to that effect to the other party. The notice should state in detail the circumstances for such force majeure and the estimated time to remedy such event. If this Agreement cannot be performed or its obligations fulfilled for a continuous period of [two months] then either party may terminate this Agreement by notice in writing at the end of that period. Then both parties shall agree a fair and reasonable settlement for all monies due under this Agreement.

TERMINATION

6.11 Either party shall be entitled to terminate this Agreement immediately by serving written notice on the other if that other party shall:

6.11.1 Commit a breach of its obligations under this Agreement which is not capable of remedy or which is capable of remedy but is not rectified within [fourteen days] of receipt of notice.

6.11.2 Make any arrangement for the benefit of or make any composition or arrangement with its creditors or any action or proceeding in bankruptcy or insolvency is taken including but not limited to the appointment of a receiver, administrator, liquidator or other trustee which is not dismissed or discharged within [sixty days] of the start of the action or if the other party shall go into liquidation (whether voluntary or compulsory) other than for the purpose of amalgamation or reconstruction.

6.11.3 Termination shall not prejudice the rights and remedies of the parties. All terms and conditions set out in this Agreement which relate to the period after the expiry or the termination of this Agreement shall continue in full force and effect.

THIRD PARTY RIGHTS

6.12 This Agreement is personal to the Agent and the Artiste. No party who is not a signatory of this Agreement may seek to rely on the obligations and benefits set out herein.

SIGNATURE OF CONTRACTS

6.13 The Agent and the Artiste agree that in the normal course of business all third party contracts shall be directly with the Artiste and signed by the Artiste. The Artiste agrees that in each third party contract the Agent shall be entitled to a clause which remits all sums to the Agent. However both parties shall be permitted to inspect and audit any accounts.

GOVERNING LAW

6.14 Both parties to this Agreement agree and confirm that any dispute, litigation, interpretation, damages or losses which arise directly or indirectly as a result of this Agreement shall be subject to the Laws of [__________] and no other jurisdiction shall be applicable.

LEGAL ADVICE

6.15 The Artiste confirms that he has been advised by the Agent to take legal advice and fully understands the consequences of signing this Agreement.

AGE

6.16 The Artiste confirms that he is aged eighteen years or over at the date of signing this Agreement.

Signed by: [____________]
FOR AND ON BEHALF OF THE ARTISTE

Print name: [____________]
Date: [____________]

Signed by: [____________]
FOR AND ON BEHALF OF THE AGENT

Print name: [____________]
Date: [____________]

OUTLINE—AGREEMENT BETWEEN AN ARTISTE AND AN AGENT

This is a short agreement between an agent which will normally be through a company and an artiste. The Agent is authorised to negotiate contracts for the Artiste in the U.K and Europe only in a wide range of media. In return the Artiste will sign the agreements, but all sums due will be paid direct under such contracts to the Agent. The Agent is to set up a separate account at a bank in the U.K where all sums are to be deposited. It is advisable that an Artiste's income is not mixed with other monies from other artistes as if the Agent gets into financial difficulties it is difficult to separate the Artiste's payments. The new account will have two signatories, the Artiste and the Agent. The Agent will receive an agreed percentage of the money held in the account and is not to claim any additional expenses or costs unless agreed in advance by the Artiste. The term of the Agreement is for a fixed period of two years and then will renew for six-monthly periods unless either party gives prior written notice.

The Artiste may end the Agreement unless he receives an agreed amount within the first year.

The Agent is not acquiring any copyright or other rights in any material owned or controlled by the Artiste including name and photographs. The Artiste must arrange his own insurance and agrees not to pursue any hazardous activities.

The Artiste is not bound to fulfil or agree to any work which he does not wish to do for any reason. The Agent is agreeing to provide copies of all marketing material and to make any alterations that the Artiste may require.

AGREEMENT BETWEEN AN AUTHOR AND A LITERARY AGENT

AN AGREEMENT made this [____________] day of [____________]

BETWEEN:

(1) [____________]
of [____________] (to be known as the Author in this Agreement)

AND

(2) [____________]
of [____________] (to be known as the Agent in this Agreement).

IT IS AGREED as follows:

1. DEFINITIONS

The words below are agreed to mean as follows:

1.1 "The Work" shall be the following book, including the Artwork, based on the Synopsis, entitled [____________] which shall consist of approximately [____________] typed A4 pages.

1.2 "The Synopsis" shall mean the summary of the Work which sets out the chapter outlines, structure and general content of the Work. A copy of the Synopsis is attached to and forms part of this Agreement.

1.3 "The Artwork" shall mean any photographs, drawings, sketches, pictures, diagrams, maps or any other illustrations or visual images which are intended to be included as part of the Work.

1.4 "The Delivery Date" shall be the following date by which the manuscript of the Work is to be completed for publication purposes: [____________].

1.5 "The Term of the Agreement" shall commence on [date] and continue until: [date].

1.6 "The Territory" shall be all countries, bases and locations throughout the world.

1.7 "The Gross Receipts" shall be the total proceeds from the exploitation of the Work in any form throughout the Territory at any time directly or indirectly received by or credited to the Agent or any sub-agent after the deduction of any value added tax.

1.8 "The Nett Receipts" shall be the Gross Receipts less the Agent's Commission.

1.9 "The Agent's Commission" shall mean the following percentage of the Gross Receipts in respect of the following forms of exploitation of the Work:

1.9.1 Hardback and paperback copies of the Work sold in the United Kingdom of Great Britain, Northern Ireland, The Republic of Ireland, the Channel Islands and the Isle of Man: [____________]%

1.9.2 Hardback and paperback copies of the Work sold throughout the Territory excluding the United Kingdom of Great Britain, Northern Ireland, the Republic of Ireland, the Channel Islands, the Isle of Man, the United States of America and Canada: [____________]%

1.9.3 Hardback and paperback copies of the Work sold in the United States of America and Canada: [____________]%

1.9.4 Copies of the Work which are disposed of by a third party throughout the Territory at a discount, reduced price, remainder or overstock: [____________]%

1.9.5 Copies of the Work which are disposed of throughout the Territory as a premium offer, book club or educational editions: [____________]%

1.9.6 Anthologies and quotations: [____________]%

1.9.7 Mechanical reproduction including reproduction of the Work by means of computer disk or in any other electronic or software form including the internet but excluding video exploitation: [____________]%

1.9.8 Translations: [____________]%

1.9.9 Straight non-dramatic radio and television reading: [____________]%

1.9.10 First serialisation of the Work in any newspaper, magazine or periodical: [____________]%

1.9.11 Second and subsequent serialisations of the Work in any newspaper, magazine or periodical: [____________]%

1.9.12 Strip-cartoon or picturisation: [____________]%

1.9.13 Merchandising [____________]%

1.9.14 Theatrical film dramatisation: [____________]%

1.9.15 All forms of television dramatisation: [____________]%

1.9.16 Radio or stage dramatisation: [____________]%

1.9.17 Video exploitation for home use: [____________]%

1.9.18 Any other forms of exploitation: [____________]%

2. ENGAGEMENT OF THE AGENT

2.1 In consideration of the Agent's Commission, the Agent agrees to provide his non-exclusive services to the Author as a literary agent for the Work for the term of the Agreement throughout the Territory.

2.2 In consideration of the Nett Receipts, the Author agrees to engage the exclusive services of the Agent as a literary agent for the Work for the Term of the Agreement throughout the Territory for the purpose of the commercial exploitation of the Work in all media.

3. COPYRIGHT

3.1 The Agent acknowledges that all copyright and any other rights in the Work in all media throughout the Territory and any associated title, artwork and developments or variations are and shall remain the sole property of the Author and that the Agent shall not acquire any rights in the Work.

3.2 The Agent shall ensure that all third parties who are licensed to exploit the Work shall not aquire any rights in the Work other than those set out under the terms of such agreement. The Agent shall at his cost ensure that any necessary documentation is executed to ensure an assignment to the Author by such third parties of any rights that may be created in any development or variation of the Work.

4. ASSERTION OF THE AUTHOR'S MORAL RIGHTS

4.1 The Agent acknowledges that the Author asserts his moral rights generally in respect of the Work under the Copyright, Designs and Patents Act 1988 and in particular to be reasonably, prominently and clearly identified as follows: [____________] on all copies of the Work in all media.

4.2 The Agent agrees to advise and make it a condition of any contract with third parties that the Author must be identified in relation to the Work in all publicity, promotional and marketing material.

4.3 The Author further asserts the right not to have the Work subject to derogatory treatment and/or to have any other work falsely attributed to him. The Agent acknowledges this assertion and agrees to advise and make it a condition of any contract with third parties.

5. OBLIGATIONS OF THE AGENT

5.1 The Agent shall provide his services to the Author to the best of his skill and ability and shall perform his duties diligently to ensure that an agreement is negotiated with a reputable publisher or publishers in respect of the Work as follows:

5.1.1 For publication of the Work in the United Kingdom of Great Britain, Northern Ireland, the Republic of Ireland, the Channel Islands and the Isle of Man in hardback and paperback form on or before [____________].

5.1.2 For publication of the Work in the United States of America and Canada in hardback and paperback form on or before [____________].

5.2 The Agent shall use his best endeavours to exploit commercially and promote the Work in all forms of the media throughout the Territory for the Term of the Agreement including anthologies, quotations, mechanical reproduction, translations, radio, television, serialisations or articles in any newspapers, magazine or periodical, merchandising, theatre performances, film, and video.

5.3 The Agent shall, as far as possible, keep the Author fully informed on a regular basis as regards any negotiations concerning the Work with any third party and agrees that the Agent shall not be entitled to commit the Author or conclude any agreement relating to the Work without the prior written consent of the Author.

5.4 The Agent confirms that the Author shall have the final decisions to conclude and sign any agreement, contract or other document relating to the exploitation of the Work and that no authority is granted under this Agreement for the Agent to sign any contract, record or other document on behalf of the Author.

5.5 The Agent acknowledges that the Author shall be entitled, upon request, to be provided with a copy of any contract, record, document or other material in the possession or under the control of the Agent relating to the Author and the Work.

5.6 The Agent undertakes not to disclose any material nor make any statement, whether true or not, concerning the Author's private and sexual life, politics and personal views to the media (including newspapers, television and radio) at any time without the prior written consent of the Author.

5.7 The Agent confirms that he has full authority to enter into and perform this Agreement and that he is not bound by any previous agreement which adversely affects this Agreement

5.8 The Agent acknowledges that this Agreement relates exclusively to the Work and that the Agent is not entitled to exploit any other material (including any books) created by the Author whether prior to the date of this Agreement, during the term of this Agreement or at any time thereafter without the prior written consent of the Author.

5.9 The Agent agrees that he shall not be entitled to alter, amend, adapt or edit the Synopsis of the Work without prior written consent of the Author.

5.10 The Agent shall keep full and accurate separate books of account, records and contracts showing the Gross Receipts, the Agent's Commission and the Nett Receipts under this Agreement.

5.11 The Agent agrees to pay the Nett Receipts to the Author within 14 days of the last day of March, June, September and December in each year during the Term of the Agreement and thereafter on a half-yearly basis.

5.12 Within 14 days of the last day of March, June, September and December in each year the Agent agrees to provide the Author with a detailed report containing a full breakdown of the Gross Receipts, the Agent's Commission, and the Nett Receipts.

5.13 The Agent agrees that the Author shall be entitled to arrange for an annual audit to inspect and make copies of the Agent's books of account, records, contracts and any other relevant material in order to verify the sums due to the Author under this Agreement. In the event that in any audit there is an error to the detriment of the Author in respect of the amount to be paid by the Agent which is in excess of [10]% then the Agent shall be responsible for the payment of all reasonable costs incurred in such audit.

5.14 The Agent acknowledges that if, within [six months] of the date of the Agreement, the Agent has not negotiated an agreement with a reputable publisher for the Work. Then the Author shall be entitled to terminate this Agreement by notice in writing to end on any date specified by the Author.

5.15 The Agent confirms that in addition to the moral rights of the Author asserted under this Agreement the Agent shall ensure that the Author is provided with the following copyright notice, credit, trademark or logo in the Work in any form and in any publicity, promotional, advertising or packaging material in respect of the marketing and distribution of the Work: [____________].

5.16 The Agent agrees to ensure as far as reasonably possible that the Author shall be entitled to approve all proposed copies, samples and other material of the Work, including book covers, together with any publicity, promotional, advertising or packaging material in respect of the marketing and exploitation of the Work.

5.17 The Agent agrees to keep the Author informed of all proposed release dates in respect of the exploitation of the Work throughout the Territory.

5.18 The Agent confirms that in the event of the death of the Author after the conclusion of a written agreement with a publisher for the publication of the Work. The Agent agrees to ensure that all sums which are due to the Author are made payable to the Author's estate.

5.19 The Agent confirms that the Author shall not be responsible for any costs or expenses incurred by the Agent pursuant to this Agreement and that the Agent shall only be entitled to receive the Agent's Commission.

5.20 The Agent must ensure that any third parties who publish or exploit the Work anywhere in the Territory analyse the Work for any problems relating to obscenity, defamation, or offensive material, and the risk of criminal or civil proceedings.

5.21 The Agent agrees that the artistic and editorial control of the Work shall be at the sole discretion and decision of the Author.

5.22 The Agent shall use all reasonable endeavours to ensure that any third party shall not be entitled to edit, adapt or alter the Work without the prior consent of the Author.

5.23 The Agent agrees that it shall provide full details of any proposed changes to the Author of the Work.

5.24 The Agent acknowledges that it shall not be entitled itself or to authorise any third party to adapt, alter, edit, add to or delete from or in any way change the Work without the prior [written] consent of the Author.

5.25 The Agent agrees to consult with the Author in respect of any proposed translation of the Work in a foreign language. The Agent shall endeavour to ensure that such translations are at the third parties' cost and expense.

6. OBLIGATIONS OF THE AUTHOR

6.1 The Author agrees to write and deliver two copies of the Work to the Agent based on the Synopsis on or before the Delivery Date.

6.2 The Author undertakes that the Work will be of a standard and quality suitable for commercial exploitation and in any event shall consist of not less than

[____________] A4 typed pages, together with a sufficient number of black and white photographs to make [____________] pages of illustration.

6.3 The Author authorises the Agent to collect all sums due to the Author in respect of the Work from any source throughout the Territory during the Term of the Agreement and at any time thereafter relating to any agreement negotiated by the Agent during the Term of the Agreement.

6.4 The Author confirms that he has full authority to enter into and perform this Agreement and that he is not bound by any previous agreement which adversely affects this Agreement.

6.5 The Author confirms that the Synopsis and the Work are and will be the original work of the Author and do not and will not infringe the copyright or any other rights of any third party throughout the Territory.

6.6 The Author undertakes to obtain and pay for all copyright clearances and consents necessary for the publication of the Work, including the Artwork throughout the Territory. The Author agrees to obtain all such clearances and consents in writing and to provide the Agent with such copies as may be requested.

6.7 The Author undertakes that the Synopsis and the Work do not and will not contain any obscene, offensive or defamatory material and will not expose the Agent to civil or criminal proceedings in [the United Kingdom]. No such undertaking shall apply to any other countries in the Territory.

6.8 The Author undertakes to prepare an index for the Work if requested to do so by the Agent.

6.9 The Author confirms that he is a British subject or a national of a Member State of the European Union and will remain so during the Term of the Agreement.

6.10 The Author undertakes that he shall not disclose any confidential information concerning the business or future plans of the Agent to any third party which is acquired during the Term of the Agreement.

6.11 The Author agrees that the Agent shall be entitled to use his name, photograph, biography and fair likeness in respect of the commercial exploitation of the Work, subject to prior approval by the Author.

6.12 The Author agrees that he shall be responsible for all national insurance, personal tax and value added tax which may be due in consequence of this Agreement.

6.13 The Author agrees to attend at such times, dates, places, locations and meetings as may reasonably required by the Agent to assist in the exploitation of the Work. Provided that the cost of any hotel and travel expenses outside of [London] shall be met by the Agent or the third party if applicable.

6.14 The Author agrees that where any alteration in the title or text of the Work is required prior to exploitation in the Territory due to factual errors or the serious threat of legal action then the Author shall not unreasonably withhold or delay his comment to such changes.

7. FIRST REFUSAL

7.1 Nothing stated in this Agreement shall be taken as granting or implying the grant of an option to the Agent over any of the Author's future works.

7.2 In consideration of the sum of [figure/currency] which shall be paid to the Author on: [date]. The Author grants the Agent the right of first refusal with respect to the next literary work of the Author on the following basis:

7.2.1 The Author shall provide the Agent with a copy of the synopsis.
7.2.2 Then the Agent shall have [28 days] to express interest in the work and offer terms of agreement.
7.2.3 The Agent shall be permitted a total of [two months] from the date of delivery of the synopsis to settle terms acceptable to the Author for the work.
7.2.4 The Author is not bound to accept any offer by the Agent nor shall he be obliged to give any reason for rejection. The Author shall be entitled to agree any terms which are in his best interests and is not bound by the terms of this agreement.
7.2.5 This right of first refusal is not applicable to any later work thereafter.

8. MISCELLANEOUS

MUTUAL INDEMNITY

8.1 The Author and the Agent mutually undertake to indemnify each other against all liabilities, claims, demands, actions, costs, damages or loss arising out of any breach by either party of any of the terms of this Agreement.

8.2 In the event of any claim, dispute, action, writ or summons in connection with clause 8.1, the Author and the Agent agree to provide full details to the other party at the earliest opportunity and shall not settle any such matter without first consulting the other party.

CONFIDENTIALITY

8.3 The Author and the Agent shall not disclose to any third party any confidential business or future plans of the other party at any time acquired during the existence of this Agreement and no reference is to be made to the terms of this Agreement by either party in any advertising, publicity or promotional material without the prior consent of the other party. In the event that the Author and the Agent agree to make a joint statement to the press concerning this agreement the following press release shall be issued: [____________].

AMENDMENTS AND ALTERATIONS

8.4 This Agreement supersedes all previous agreements, representations or promises and sets out all the terms agreed between the parties. Any amendment or alteration to this Agreement must be in writing and signed by an authorised signatory of each party.

NO PARTNERSHIP OR EMPLOYMENT

8.5 This Agreement shall not be deemed to create any partnership or employment relationship between the parties.

NOTICES

8.6 Without prejudice to the right to serve notices by any other means, any notice serviced under this Agreement shall be in writing. Any notice which has been sent by first class, pre-paid post shall be deemed to be received 48 hours thereafter (excluding Saturdays, Sundays and public holidays). For the purposes of this Agreement all notices shall be sent to the following addresses:

The Author: [____________];
The Agent: [____________].

VALUE ADDED TAX

8.7 All sums payable under this Agreement are exclusive of any value added tax that may be payable by either party.

FORCE MAJEURE

8.8 In the event that this Agreement cannot be performed or its obligations fulfilled for any reason beyond the reasonable control of the Agent or the Author, including events such as war, industrial action, floods, Acts of God or unforeseen technical failure, then such non-performance or failure to fulfil its obligations shall not be deemed to be a breach of this Agreement. In the event that this Agreement cannot be performed or its obligations fulfilled for any reason beyond the reasonable control of the defaulting party for a continuous period of [three months]. Then the non-defaulting party may, at its discretion, terminate this Agreement by notice in writing at the end of that period. Both parties agree to negotiate, in good faith, an equitable settlement in respect of work already performed to the date of the termination.

TERMINATION AND EXPIRY OF THE AGREEMENT

8.9 In addition to any other rights and remedies at law this Agreement may be terminated by giving written notice to the other party who has breached this Agreement or has defaulted in the following circumstances:

8.9.1 where the Agent has failed to account or make payments as required under this Agreement;

8.9.2 where the Agent or The Author has committed as serious breach of its obligations under this Agreement unless such party rectifies the position, as far as reasonably possible, within [30 days];

8.9.3 where the Agent goes into voluntary or involuntary liquidation;

8.9.4 where the Agent is declared insolvent either in bankruptcy proceedings or other legal proceedings;

8.9.5 where an agreement with creditors has been reached by whe Agent due to his failure or inability to pay his debts as they fall due; or

8.9.6 where a receiver is appointed over the whole or part of the Agent's business.

THIRD PARTY TRANSFERS AND RIGHTS

8.10 Neither party shall assign, charge or make over this Agreement or any of its rights or obligations without the prior written consent of the other party.

8.11 This Agreement is between the Agent and the Author. No third party shall be entitled to seek to rely on the obligations or benefits under this Agreement.

GOVERNING LAW

8.12 This Agreement shall be governed and construed in accordance with the Laws of England in respect of any dispute relating to the performance or interpretation of this Agreement.

A Synopsis is attached to and forms part of this Agreement.

Signed by: [____________]
[Name][Title]
FOR AND ON BEHALF OF THE AUTHOR

Date: [____________]

Signed by: [____________]
[Name][Title]
FOR AND ON BEHALF OF THE AGENT

Date: [____________]

OUTLINE—AGREEMENT BETWEEN AN AUTHOR AND A LITERARY AGENT

This is an Agreement between an Author and a literary Agent for just one Work which is not yet in existence based on a Synopsis. The Agent is providing his non-exclusive services to the Author to exploit and promote a specified book referred to as "the Work". The Author is agreeing to engage the exclusive services of the Agent for a fixed period to commercially exploit the Work, including its publication. The Author is agreeing to write and deliver the Work to the Agent, based on the Synopsis, by a specified delivery date. A copy of the Synopsis which sets out the structure and general content of the Work should be attached to and form part of the Agreement. It is important to note that the Agent is not acquiring any copyright or other rights in the Work, which remain with the Author. Accordingly, it is intended that any agreement negotiated by the Agent should be signed by the Author.

The Agent is receiving a percentage of the Gross Receipts in respect of the exploitation of the Work in all media throughout the world at any time, whether during the term of the Agreement or not. The Agent is only entitled to receive payments relating to contracts he negotiated which were concluded during the term of the Agreement. The Author is entitled to receive all the Nett Receipts, namely the Gross Receipts less the Agent's Commission, on a quarterly basis.

Although the moral rights of the Author do not strictly need to be asserted in this type of agreement, the Agent is effectively being put on notice to ensure that such assertion is incorporated in any subsequent agreement between the Author and a third party.

In the event that the Agent does not secure a publication agreement with a reputable publisher within six months of the date of the Agreement, then the Author is entitled to terminate the Agreement upon notice.

This Agreement is mainly related to an agent based in the U.K, but could be adapted. It is important that the outline details of the Work, the Synopsis and the list of Artwork are comprehensive.

Although the Author is allowing the Agent to exploit the Work throughout the world, the Territory could be adapted to specify each country.

The internet rights come within the broad electronic section, but they could be separated and be subject to separate terms on each occasion.

The rights clause has a variety of different percentages for different media; they could be broken down further for a longer list or all media could be just one percentage.

The contract is limited to just the one work of the Author, but it could be amended to included all work created by the Author and all the product of his services.

The Author is clearing and paying for all copyright and other comments required in the Work. If it is expected to involve a significant amount of third party material then the Author could agree to clear it, and the Agent to pay the cost but be able to deduct it from the Gross Receipts.

The Author is only giving a limited undertaking regarding obscenity, defamation or the threat of criminal or civil proceedings and it is limited to the U.K.

Both parties are, however, giving each other the same indemnity which is unlimited. This could be capped to a maximum limit in total or in each year.

The Work is not to be edited, adapted or changed without the consent of the Author. The Agent has a limited right of first refusal on the next work of the Author which is completely subject to fresh terms being agreed with the Author.

AGREEMENT BETWEEN AN AGENT AND AN ACTOR

AGREEMENT dated: [____________]

THE CONTRACTING PARTIES TO THIS AGREEMENT ARE AS FOLLOWS:

(1) [Name]
of [Address] (referred to as "the Actor")

AND

(2) [Company] registered office at: [____________] and main place of business: [____________] (referred to as "the Agent").

IT IS AGREED as follows:

1. DEFINITIONS

The words below are agreed to mean as follows:

1.1 "The Agent's Commission" shall be the following percentage of The Gross Receipts: [figure]%.

1.2 "The Gross Receipts" shall be the total proceeds from the exploitation of the performances, appearances, recordings, or the commercial exploitation in any other form specified under this Agreement of the Actor throughout the Territory at any time, directly of indirectly received by or credited to the Agent or any sub-agent after the deduction of any value added tax.

1.3 "The Nett Receipts" shall be the Gross Receipts less the Agent's Commission.

1.4 "The Term of the Agreement" shall commence on the date of this Agreement and shall continue until: [date].

1.5 "The Territory" shall be the United Kingdom of Great Britain, Northern Ireland, the Republic of Ireland, the Channel Islands, the Isle of Man and the following countries: [____________].

2. ENGAGEMENT OF THE AGENT

2.1 In consideration of the Agent's Commission, the Agent agrees to provide his non-exclusive services to the Actor for the Term of the Agreement throughout the Territory.

2.2 The Actor agrees to engage the exclusive services of the Agent for the Term of the Agreement throughout the Territory to exploit the services of the Actor in all media whether in existence now or created in the future including but not limited to television, video, film, theatre, radio, commercials, publications, the internet, merchandising.

2.3 It is the intention of both parties that all products of the business services of the Actor should be dealt with by the Agent whether performances, appearances, recordings or otherwise and whether for financial gain or not.

3. COPYRIGHT

3.1 The Agent acknowledges that the name of the Actor and any goodwill and reputation created in respect of any trademark, business name or logo shall remain the sole and exclusive property of the Actor whether in existence now or created during the Term of this Agreement and that no part of this Agreement is intended to transfer any copyright or any other rights vested in the Actor to the Agent.

3.2 The Agent shall use his reasonable endeavours to protect the copyright and any other rights of the Actor which may be created or developed under any contract with a third party. As far as reasonably possible the Agent shall ensure that any photographs, images, text or other material which is created concerning the Actor shall become the property of the Actor and that such third party shall execute any document required to confirm that such copyright and any other rights shall be rested in the Actor.

4. OBLIGATIONS OF THE AGENT

4.1 The Agent shall provide his services to the best of his skill and ability and shall perform all duties diligently to ensure the Actor is regularly engaged by third parties on the best possible terms available in the circumstances.

4.2 The Agent shall use his best endeavours to promote, publicise and advertise The Actor generally and in particular to do the following: [______________].

4.3 The Agent shall, as far as possible, keep the Actor fully informed on a regular basis as regards any negotiations with any third party and agrees that he shall only be entitled to sign and conclude any agreement with the prior consent of the Actor.

4.4 The Agent agrees to arrange and pay for a promotional portfolio of the Actor to be used solely for the purpose of promoting the Actor in accordance with the terms of this Agreement.

4.5 The Agent shall provide the Actor with reasonable notice of all rehearsals, recordings, appearances, performances, auditions, meetings and any other commitments at which the Actor is required to attend under this Agreement.

4.6 The Agent acknowledges that the Actor shall be entitled, upon request, to be provided with a copy of any contract, record, document or any other material in the possession or under the control of the Agent relating to the Actor.

4.7 The Agent undertakes not to disclose any material nor make any statement, whether true or not, concerning the Actor's private and sexual life, politics and personal views to the media (including newspapers, television and radio) at any time without the prior written consent of the Actor.

4.8 The Agent confirms that he has full authority to enter into and perform this Agreement and that he is not bound by any previous agreement which adversely affects this Agreement.

4.9 The Agent acknowledges that he shall not be entitled to any commission in respect of any work done or agreed to be done by the Actor prior the date of this Agreement whether that work is performed during the Term of the Agreement or not.

4.10 The Agent confirms that he shall not enter into negotiations with any third party in respect of the Actor where such Agreement, if fulfilled, would involve the Actor in any degrading, obscene or demeaning activity.

4.11 The Agent shall keep full and accurate separate books of accounts, records and contracts showing the Gross Receipts, the Agent's Commission and the Nett Receipts under this Agreement for a period of [six years] after the expiry or termination of this Agreement.

4.12 The Agent agrees to pay the Nett Receipts to the Actor on the last day of each calendar month in the first year during the Term of the Agreement and thereafter on a quarterly basis.

4.13 On the last day of March, June, September and December in each year the Agent agrees to provide the Actor with a detailed report containing a full breakdown of the Gross Receipts, the Agent's Commission, and the Nett Receipts.

4.14 The Agent agrees that the Actor shall be entitled to arrange for an annual audit to inspect and make copies of the Agent's books of accounts, records, contracts and any other relevant material in order to verify the sums due to the Actor under this Agreement. In the event that in any audit there is an error to the detriment of the Actor in respect of the amount to be paid by the Agent which is in excess of [figure/currency], then the Agent shall be responsible for the payment of all reasonable costs incurred in such audit.

4.15 The Agent acknowledges that if within [six months] of the date of this Agreement the Nett Receipts paid to the Actor are less than [figure/currency]. Then The Actor shall be entitled to terminate this Agreement by notice in writing.

4.16 The Agent agrees to ensure that both he and any third party shall provide the following [credit, copyright notice, trademark and logo] to the Actor in any material relating to the Actor including any advertising, publicity, promotional or packaging material: [______________].

4.17 The Agent agrees to consult with the Actor in respect of any artwork, stills, photographs, biography or other material that may be used to market and exploit the Actor.

4.18 The Agent acknowledges that he shall be solely responsible for all costs incurred by him in respect of his services under this Agreement including the promotion, marketing and advertising of the Actor.

5. OBLIGATIONS OF THE ACTOR

5.1 The Actor confirms that he is a bona fide member of the following unions: [____________].

5.2 The Actor agrees that the Agent shall be his exclusive agent for all business work in any media for the Term of the Agreement throughout the Territory.

5.3 The Actor agrees to provide his services to the best of his skill and ability and shall perform his duties under this Agreement at such times, dates and locations as may reasonably be agreed with the Agent.

5.4 The Actor confirms that he shall be available for all work arranged for him by the Agent under the terms of this Agreement except for the following times and dates: [____________].

5.5 The Actor confirms that he holds a passport for [country] and is resident in [country].

5.6 The Actor confirms that he has full authority to enter into and perform this Agreement and that he is not bound by any previous Agreement which adversely affects this agreement except for the following commitments made prior to the date of this Agreement: [____________].

5.7 The Actor confirms that all the product of his services shall be original and will not infringe the copyright or any other rights of any third party throughout the Territory except where any material is included at the request of the Agent or any third party.

5.8 The Actor confirms that he is in good health and is physically adept and proficient in the following activities: [____________].

5.9 The Actor confirms that all the products of his services will not contain any obscene, offensive or defamatory material and will not expose the Agent to criminal or civil proceedings except where any material is included at the request of the Agent or any third party.

5.10 The Actor agrees not to issue any statement to the media at any time concerning any confidential business or future plans of the Agent or details of any negotiations or the terms of any agreements in progress or concluded by the Agent without the prior consent of the Agent.

5.11 The Actor agrees to keep the Agent informed of his telephone number, address and whereabouts as far as reasonably possible during [all working weekdays] during the Term of the Agreement.

5.12 Subject to prior consultation the Actor agrees that the Agent shall be entitled to use his name, signature, biography, photograph, image and stage name in the promotion, advertising and marketing of the Actor, provided that a copy of any such material shall in due course be provided by the Agent to the Actor upon request.

5.13 The Actor agrees that the Agent is not under any obligation to hold any monies received in a separate account.

5.14 The Actor confirms that the Agent shall be entitled to collect and deposit the Gross Receipts at the following bank account: [____________].

5.15 The Actor confirms that he shall be responsible for his own expense, value added tax, personal, insurance, national insurance and personal tax arising under this Agreement.

6. MISCELLANEOUS

THIRD PARTIES

6.1 This Agreement is purely personal between the Actor and the Agent and may be terminated with immediate effect by notice in writing if either party is not available for a period of not less than [three months] continuously to perform the obligations set out.

6.2 The Agent shall at all times be responsible for the acts, omissions and other matters arising directly or indirectly from any third parties to whom the Agent has arranged for the Actor to provide his services.

6.3 Neither party shall assign, transfer, charge or make over this Agreement or any part of its rights and obligations without the prior written consent of the other party.

CONFIDENTIALITY

6.4 The Actor and the Agent shall not disclose to any third party any confidential business or future plans of the other party at any time acquired during the existence of this Agreement and no reference is to be made to the terms of this Agreement by either party in any advertising, publicity or promotional material without the prior consent of the other party.

AMENDMENTS AND ALTERATIONS

6.5 This Agreement sets out the full and complete terms agreed between the parties. No prior promise written or oral shall be taken into account unless specified in this Agreement. Any amendment or variation must be in writing on a document signed by the Agent and the Actor.

NO PARTNERSHIP OR EMPLOYMENT

6.6 This Agreement shall not be deemed to create any partnership or employment relationship between the parties.

NOTICES

6.7 Without prejudice to the right to serve notices by any other means any notice serviced under this Agreement shall be in writing. Any notice which has been sent by first class, pre-paid post shall be deemed to be received 48 hours thereafter (excluding

Saturdays, Sundays and public holidays). For the purposes of this Agreement all notices shall be sent to the following addresses shall apply:

The Agent: [____________];

The Actor: [____________].

VALUE ADDED TAX

6.8 All sums payable under this Agreement are exclusive of any value added tax that may be payable by either party.

FORCE MAJEURE

6.9 In the event that this Agreement cannot be performed or its obligations fulfilled for any reason beyond the reasonable control of the Agent or the Actor, including the ill-health of the Actor, war, industrial action, floods or Acts of God. Then such non-performance or failure to fulfil its obligations shall be deemed to be a breach of this Agreement. In the event that this Agreement cannot be performed or its obligations fulfilled for any reason beyond the reasonable control of the defaulting party for a continuous period of [one month] then the other party who has not breached this Agreement may, at its discretion, terminate this Agreement by notice in writing at the end of that period.

TERMINATION AND EXPIRY OF THE AGREEMENT

6.10 In addition to any other rights and remedies at law this Agreement may be terminated by giving written notice to the other party who has breached this Agreement or has defaulted in the following circumstances:

6.10.1 where the Agent has failed to account or make payments as required under this Agreement;

6.10.2 where the Agent or the Actor has committed as serious breach of its obligations under this Agreement unless such party rectifies the position, as far as reasonably possible, within [10 days];

6.10.3 where the Agent goes into voluntary or involuntary liquidation;

6.10.4 where the Agent is declared insolvent either in bankruptcy proceedings or other legal proceedings;

6.10.5 where an Agreement with creditors has been reached by the Agent due to his failure or inability to pay his debts as they fall due; or

6.10.6 where a receiver is appointed over the whole or part of the Agent's business.

GOVERNING LAW

6.11 This Agreement shall be subject to the Laws of England.

Signed by: [_______________]
[Name] [Title]
FOR AND ON BEHALF OF THE ACTOR

Date: [_______________]

Signed by: [_______________]
[Name/Title/Company]
FOR AND ON BEHALF OF THE AGENT

Date: [_______________]

Witnessed by: [_______________]

OUTLINE—AGREEMENT BETWEEN AN AGENT AND AN ACTOR

This is an Agreement between an Agent and an Actor. The primary duty of the Agent is to keep the Actor gainfully employed, although the Actor would not be in breach of the Agreement if he turned down work which would involve the Actor in any degrading, obscene or demeaning activity.

The Agent's commission is an agreed percentage of all the Gross Receipts received by him on behalf of the Actor. The Actor is entitled to be paid all the Nett Receipts, which are defined as the Gross Receipts less the Agent's Commission. Both the Agent and the Actor bear their own costs and expenses.

The Actor is agreeing to engage the exclusive services of the Agent for a fixed term in all media in the U.K. and named countries of the Territory. The Agent is not entitled to receive any commission for work done or agreed to be done prior to the signing of the Agreement, even if the money is received during the term of the contract.

The Agent is entitled to mix any monies received with other sums he holds for other clients, and may also sign the contracts provided that the Actor has given his consent. Neither party is giving the other an indemnity. The Agent agrees that he is not to acquire any copyright in the name and rights held by the Actor, and will arrange for any new developments to be transformed to the Actor. The Actor will be consulted about marketing material, part of which will be a promotional portfolio. If no money is received by the Actor or very little, then after six months the contract can be terminated. The Actor is responsible for his own insurance but, where the activity is hazardous, additional cover may be required.

AGREEMENT BETWEEN PROFESSIONAL SPORTSPERSON AND MANAGER

AN AGREEMENT made this [____________] day of [____________]

BETWEEN:

1) [Name]
of [Address] ("the Sportsperson")

AND

2) [Company] whose registered office is at [address] and whose business is mainly based at [address] ("the Manager").

IT IS AGREED as follows:

1. DEFINITIONS

The words below are agreed to mean as follows:

1.1 "The Gross Receipts" shall be the total proceeds from all events, competitions, promotions, sponsorship fees, public appearances and performances, television and radio appearances, recordings, endorsements or any other sums from the commercial exploitation in any other form in any media of the Sportsperson throughout the Territory at any time directly or indirectly received by or credited to the Manager or any sub-agent or sub-licensee after the deduction of any value added tax and any sales tax.

1.2 "The Nett Receipts" shall be the Gross Receipts less the Authorised Expenses.

1.3 "The Authorised Expenses" shall be the following sums reasonably and properly expended by the Manager for and on behalf of the Sportsperson which are not recovered through any third party:

1.3.1 the first class travelling costs of the Sportsperson to all competitions, events and appearances attended by the Sportsperson under the terms of this Agreement or at the specific request of the Manager,

1.3.2 the cost of all accommodation incurred by The Sportsperson through the attendance at all competitions, events and appearances attended by the Sportsperson under the terms of this Agreement or at the request of the Manager;

1.3.3 the following credit and charge card shall be supplied by the Company to the Sportsperson which shall be used by the Sportsperson for the purposes of settling his expenses under this Agreement which shall be the responsibility of the Company to pay: [____________] which shall be returned at the end of this Agreement;

1.3.4 the following equipment or goods shall be supplied for the Sportsperson to retain and own: [____________] and which he is not obliged to return at the end of this Agreement;

1.3.5 a clothing allowance for the Sportsperson up to a monthly limit of: [____________];

1.3.6 the cost of a comprehensive insurance policy in respect of the Sportsperson and his personal property for the benefit of the Sportsperson and his family which should be for not less than: [figure];

1.3.7 specialist medical benefits as specified: [____________];

1.3.8 training facilities as specified: [____________];

1.3.9 any other costs specifically listed: [____________].

1.4 "The Manager's Commission" shall be the following percentage of the Nett Receipts: [____________]%.

1.5 "The Sportsperson's Fees" shall be the Nett Receipts less the Manager's Commission.

1.6 "The Term of the Agreement" shall commence on the date of this agreement and shall continue until [date].

1.7 "The Territory" shall be all countries, bases and locations throughout the world.

1.8 "The Holiday Schedule" shall mean the times and dates during which the Sportsperson shall not be obliged to provide his services under this Agreement. A copy of the Holiday Schedule is attached to and forms part of this Agreement.

1.9 "The Work Schedule" shall mean the times, dates and locations of all competitions, events, promotions, appearances and meetings at which the Sportsperson is obliged to attend under this Agreement. A copy of the Work Schedule is attached to and forms part of this Agreement.

2. ENGAGEMENT OF THE MANAGER

2.1 In consideration of the Manager's Commission, the Manager agrees to provide his non-exclusive services to the Sportsperson to act as agent and manager in all media for the Term of the Agreement throughout the Territory.

2.2 In consideration of the Sportsperson's Fees, the Sportsperson agrees to engage the exclusive services of the Manager for the Term of the Agreement throughout the Territory in all media including television, radio, video, film, newspapers and periodicals, books, records, professional and public appearances, sponsorship arrangements, competitions, events, promotions and any other commercial exploitation of the Sportsperson.

3. COPYRIGHT

3.1 The Manager acknowledges that the name of the Sportsperson and any goodwill and reputation created in respect of any trademark, business name or logo shall remain the sole and exclusive property of the Sportsperson and that no part of this Agreement is intended to transfer any copyright or any other rights vested in the Sportsperson to the Manager.

3.2 The Manager agrees to ensure that the following: [credit/copyright notice/trademark and logo] of the Sportsperson shall appear prominently in any arrangements with a third party and in all publicity, advertising, promotional and packaging material: [details description].

3.3 The Manager acknowledges that he is not acquiring any copyright or any other rights in any name, logo, trademark, image or any other material owned or controlled by the Sportsperson.

3.4 The Manager shall ensure that any developments or variation of any rights owned or controlled by the Sportsperson which may be created by a third party under any agreement shall be assigned to the Sportsperson by such third party before the end of that agreement.

4. OBLIGATIONS OF THE MANAGER

4.1 The Manager shall provide his services to the best of his skill and ability and shall perform all duties diligently to ensure that the Sportsperson is regularly engaged by third parties on the best possible terms throughout the Territory for the Term of the Agreement.

4.2 The Manager shall use his best endeavours to promote and publicise the Sportsperson in all forms of the media but in particular in the following areas: [____________].

4.3 Where the Manager enters into an agreement which concerns the Sportsperson and any other person on whose behalf the Manager acts, then unless such agreement specifically states the sums due to the Sportsperson. The Manager agrees to consult with the Sportsperson in order to agree a fair and equitable allocation of such sums to the Gross Receipts.

4.4 The Manager agrees that the Sportsperson shall be entitled to such holiday and other leave as is set out in the Holiday Schedule together with such other dates as may be agreed between the Manager and the Sportsperson.

4.5 The Manager shall, as far as possible, keep the Sportsperson fully informed on a regular basis as regards any negotiations with any third party and agrees that he shall not be entitled to conclude any agreement or sign any document or other record on behalf of the Sportsperson without the prior consent of the Sportsperson.

4.6 The Manager acknowledges that the Sportsperson shall be entitled, upon request, to be provided with a copy of any contract, record, document, or other material in the possession or under the control of the Manager relating to the Sportsperson.

4.7 The Manager undertakes not to disclose any material nor make any statement, whether true or not, concerning the Sportsperson's private and sexual life, politics and personal views to the media (including newspapers, television and radio) at any time without the prior written consent of the Sportsperson.

4.8 The Manager confirms that he has full authority to enter into and perform this agreement and that he is not bound by any previous Agreement which adversely affects this Agreement.

4.9 The Manager acknowledges that he shall not be entitled to any commission in respect of any work done or agreed to be done by the Sportsperson prior to the date of this Agreement whether that work is performed during the Term of the Agreement or not.

4.10 The Manager undertakes that he shall not for the Term of the Agreement assign, transfer or charge any of the rights or obligations in this Agreement to any third party without the prior written consent of the Sportsperson.

4.11 The Manager shall keep full and accurate separate books of account, records and contracts showing the Gross Receipts, the Manager's Commission, the Authorised Expenses, the Nett Receipts and the Sportsperson's Fees under this Agreement and shall not destroy any such material for [three years] from the date the relevant report is supplied to the Sportsperson.

4.12 The Manager agrees to pay the Sportsperson's Fees to the Sportsperson on the last day of each calendar month in each year during the Term of this Agreement and thereafter on a quarterly basis.

4.13 By [date] and [date] in each year the Manager agrees to provide the Sportsperson with a detailed report containing a full breakdown of the Gross Receipts, the Authorised Expenses, the Manager's Commission, the Nett Receipts and the Sportsperson's Fees.

4.14 The Manager agrees that the Sportsperson shall be entitled to arrange for an annual audit to inspect and make copies of the Manager's books of account, records, contracts and any other relevant material in order to verify the sums due to the Sportsperson under this Agreement. In the event that in any audit there is an error to the detriment of the Sportsperson in respect of the amount to be paid by the Manager. Then the Manager shall be responsible for the payment of all reasonable costs incurred in such audit by the Sportsperson.

4.15 The Manager acknowledges that if within [12 months] of the date of this Agreement the Sportsperson's Fees received by the Sportsperson are less than [figure]. Then the Sportsperson shall be entitled to terminate this Agreement immediately by notice in writing.

4.16 The Manager agrees to be responsible for the Authorised Expenses and where the Sportsperson pays for any such sums the Manager agrees to reimburse the Sportsperson within [7 days] of such expenditure subject to satisfactory receipts or other records being produced upon request.

4.17 The Manager undertakes to arrange comprehensive insurance cover for the Sportsperson and his personal property during the Term of the Agreement and shall provide the Sportsperson with a copy of such insurance policy upon request.

4.18 The Manager agrees to provide the Sportsperson with reasonable notice of all competitions, appearances, promotional and public events and any meetings at which the Sportsperson is obliged to attend under this Agreement.

4.19 The Manager agrees to provide the Sportsperson with all copies and samples of any proposed publicity, promotional, advertising, merchandising and packaging material in respect of the promotion and commercial exploitation of the Sportsperson.

4.20 The Manager agrees to assist the Sportsperson in general with the financial management of all the Sportsperson's Fees and the Sportsperson's financial affairs generally including tax, value added tax, national insurance, pension and health contributions and personal insurance. Provided that the Sportsperson shall seek the benefit of specialist professional advice where appropriate and shall not seek to rely on the Manager to arrange for and pay the cost of such matters.

4.21 The Manager acknowledges that he shall be solely responsible for all his own expenses and costs in providing his services under this Agreement and shall only be entitled to receive the Managers Commission.

4.22 The Manager agrees to open a bank account at [_____ Bank] for the specific purpose of depositing and dealing in all monies received from the commercial exploitation of the product of the services of the Sportsperson. The following person: [Name] shall be the sole signatory for the withdrawal or transfer of any funds. This arrangement shall not be changed without the prior written consent of the Sportsperson.

4.23 The Manager agrees that it shall not be entitled to use that bank account for the purpose of providing a lien or charge to any third party for any purpose.

4.24 The Manager accepts that the Sportsperson shall be entitled to refuse to carry out any work which he deems to be in conflict with his image and reputation as a Sportsperson or which is demeaning, offensive or would be hazardous or which conflicts with his undertakings or code of conduct for any sports organisation of which he is a member. The Manager accepts that the Agreement will only work effectively by mutual co-operation and consultation.

5. OBLIGATIONS OF THE SPORTSPERSON

5.1 The Sportsperson agrees to refer all requests of a commercial nature to the Manager and agrees that the Manager shall have the sole and exclusive right to negotiate with third parties for the commercial services of the Sportsperson during the Term of the Agreement.

5.2 The Sportsperson confirms that his final consent to the conclusion of any commercial agreement negotiated by the Manager under this Agreement shall not be unreasonably delayed or withheld.

5.3 The Sportsperson confirms that he is a bona fide member of the following professional sports organisation: [_____________].

5.4 The Sportsperson agrees to wear the clothing and use the equipment provided by the Manager under this Agreement where an agreement has been concluded with a third party to endorse a product or exclusive clothing equipment or logo as far as reasonably and legally possible and appropriate, at all promotional and television appearances, press calls, and any other competitions, events or exhibitions throughout the Term of the Agreement.

5.5 The Sportsperson agrees to provide his exclusive services to the best of his skill and ability and shall perform his duties under this Agreement at such times, dates and locations as may reasonably be agreed with the Manager including the attendance at and participation in all events, competitions, promotions, appearances and meetings as specified in the Work Schedule.

5.6 The Sportsperson agrees to conduct himself in a fit, proper and professional manner at all times during the Term of the Agreement.

5.7 The Sportsperson confirms that he holds a passport for: [____________] and is mainly resident in: [____________].

5.8 The Sportsperson confirms that he has full authority to enter into and perform this Agreement and that he is not bound by any previous agreement which adversely affects this Agreement except for the following commitments made prior to the date of this Agreement:[____________].

5.9 The Sportsperson confirms that all the products of his services shall be original and will not infringe the copyright or any other right of any third party throughout the Territory except where the work is based on or incorporates material of any third party which is supported by a third party under an agreement concluded by the Manager or is included at the request of the Manager.

5.10 The Sportsperson agrees that the Manager shall be entitled to use and permit the use of the Sportsperson's name, signature, biography, photograph and image for the purposes of the marketing and commercial exploitation of the Sportsperson under this Agreement.

5.11 The Sportsperson agrees not to issue any statement to the media at any time without the prior consultation of the Manager concerning any confidential business or future plans of the Manager or details of any negotiations or the terms of any agreements in progress or concluded by the Manager in respect of the Sportsperson.

5.12 The Sportsperson agrees to keep the Manager informed of his telephone number, address and whereabouts as far as reasonably possible at all times during the Term of the Agreement.

5.13 The Sportsperson authorises the Manager to receive and deposit the Gross Receipts on behalf of the Sportsperson in the following bank account:[____________].

5.14 The Sportsperson acknowledges that although the Manager shall assist in the Sportsperson's financial affairs, The Sportsperson shall be ultimately responsible for seeking expert professional advice, and paying for such costs and expenses together with his own value added tax, national insurance and personal tax arising under this Agreement.

5.15 The Sportsperson acknowledges that the Manager shall be entitled to the Manager's Commission after the expiry of this Agreement in respect of all agreements negotiated by the Manager and concluded during the Term of the Agreement.

5.16 The Sportsperson confirms that at the date of signing this Agreement he is [____________] years old and that he has been advised to seek legal advice before signing this Agreement.

5.17 The Sportsperson agrees to submit to [one] reasonable and professional medical examination required by the Manager in order to arrange suitable insurance cover throughout the Terms of this Agreement. Provided that the following conditions are applied:

5.17.1 the Sportsperson should agree to the choice of Consultant;
5.17.2 the full cost of the medical report and to be paid for by the Manager;
5.17.3 the Manager is to pay the Sportsperson's reasonable expenses;
5.17.4 that the medical report shall only be supplied to and read by the following persons: [____________].

6. MISCELLANEOUS

MUTUAL INDEMNITY

6.1 The Sportsperson and the Manager mutually undertake to indemnify the other against all liabilities, claims, demands, actions, costs, damages or loss arising out of any breach by either party of any of the terms of this Agreement.

6.2 In the event of any claim, dispute, action, writ or summons in connection with clause 6.1, the Sportsperson and the Manager agree to provide full details to the other party at the earliest opportunity and shall not settle any such matter without first consulting the other party.

CONFIDENTIALITY

6.3 The Sportsperson and the Manager shall not disclose to any third party any confidential business or future plans of the other party at any time acquired during the existence of this Agreement and no reference is to be made to the terms of this Agreement by either party in any advertising, publicity or promotional material without the prior consent of the other party.

AMENDMENTS AND ALTERATIONS

6.4 This Agreement supersedes all previous agreements, representations or promises and sets out all the terms agreed between the parties. Any amendment or alteration to this Agreement must be in writing and signed by an authorised signatory of each party.

NO PARTNERSHIP OR EMPLOYMENT

6.5 This Agreement shall not be deemed to create any partnership or employment relationship between the parties.

NOTICES

6.6 Without prejudice to the right to serve notices by any other means, any notice served under this Agreement shall be in writing. Any notice which has been sent by first class, pre-paid post shall be deemed to be received 48 hours thereafter (excluding Saturdays, Sundays and public holidays). For the purposes of this Agreement the following addresses shall apply:

The Sportsperson: [____________]
The Manager: [____________]

VALUE ADDED TAX

6.7 All sums payable under this Agreement are exclusive of any value added tax that may be payable by either party.

THIRD PARTY TRANSFERS AND RIGHTS

6.8 Neither party shall assign, transfer, charge or make over this Agreement or any of its rights or obligations without the prior written consent of the other party. This Agreement is personal to the parties and no third party may seek to benefit or enforce its obligations unless it has been agreed to by both parties.

FORCE MAJEURE

6.9 In the event that this Agreement cannot be performed or its obligations fulfilled for any reason beyond the reasonable control of the Manager or the Sportsperson, including injury to the Sportsperson, war, industrial action, floods or Acts of God, then such non-performance or failure to fulfil its obligations shall be deemed not to be a breach of this Agreement. In the event that this Agreement cannot be performed or its obligations fulfilled for any reason beyond the reasonable control of the defaulting party for a continuous period of [two months]. Then the other party may, at its discretion, terminate this Agreement by notice in writing at the end of that period.

TERMINATION AND EXPIRY OF THE AGREEMENT

6.10 In addition to any other rights and remedies at law this Agreement may be terminated by giving written notice to the other party who has breached this Agreement or defaulted in the following circumstances:

6.10.1 where the Manager has failed to account or make payments as required under this Agreement;

6.10.2 where the Manager or the Sportsperson has committed a serious breach of its obligations under this Agreement unless such party rectifies the position, as far as reasonably possible, within [one month];

6.10.3 where the Manager goes into voluntary or involuntary liquidation;
6.10.4 where the Manager is declared insolvent either in bankruptcy proceedings or other legal proceedings;
6.10.5 where an agreement with creditors has been reached by the Manager due to his failure or inability to pay his debts as they fall due;
6.10.6 where a receiver is appointed over the whole or part of the Manager's business; or
6.10.7 where the Sportsperson is convicted of a serious criminal offence or a serious breach of the rules of the professional sports association specified in clause 5.3.

MEDIATION

6.11 The Manager and the Sportsperson agree that prior to the commencement of any legal proceedings in the event of any dispute, difference or other problems which arise pursuant to this Agreement which cannot be resolved by negotiation between the parties. That without prejudice to any legal rights of any party they shall endeavour to agree the appointment of a third party to assist in the resolution of the matter. The cost of such mediator shall be shared equally between the parties.

GOVERNING LAW

6.12 This Agreement shall be subject to the Laws of England.

Attached to and forming part of this Agreement is the Holiday Schedule and the Work Schedule.

Signed by: [____________]
FOR AND ON BEHALF OF THE SPORTSPERSON

Date: [____________]

Signed by: [____________]
FOR AND ON BEHALF OF THE MANAGER

Date: [____________]

Witnessed by: [____________]

OUTLINE—AGREEMENT BETWEEN PROFESSIONAL SPORTSPERSON AND MANAGER

The Manager under this Agreement has a duty to promote and exploit the Sportsperson in all media including competitions, events, exhibitions, television, radio, film, publishing and sponsorship deals. The Manager collects all the money due to the Sportsperson which is referred to as the Gross Receipts and deposited in a named bank account. The Nett Receipts are calculated by making the deductions in respect of the authorised expenses which have been incurred by the Sportsperson. The Manager takes his commission, which should include his expenses, from the Nett Receipts. The Sportsperson's Fee is defined as the Nett Receipts less the Manager's commission. The Sportsperson would be entitled to terminate the Agreement in the event that he does not receive a specified sum within an agreed period from the date of the Agreement. The Manager has the right to terminate the Agreement if the Sportsperson is convicted of a serious criminal offence or the Sportsperson commits a serious breach of the rules of the professional sports association to which he belongs.

In addition to his general responsibilities, the Manager is also agreeing to take out a comprehensive insurance policy for the Sportsperson and his personal property for the term of the Agreement. The Sportsperson is agreeing to a medical by a consultant for insurance purposes but only on a number of conditions.

The Sportsperson has agreed to conduct himself in a professional manner, therefore we have deliberately left out a clause referring to obscene or offensive material.

The Sportsperson is not to unreasonably withhold or delay his consent to any of the projects which are proposed by the Manager, but we have not set out a number of grounds on which it is clear that refusal can be justified.

We have included a mediation route as a feasible choice for both parties prior to taking legal proceedings. There is no statement that it will be binding and should be without prejudice to any legal rights of either party.

The additional items being provided under this Agreement should be specified in detail to avoid disputes at a later stage.

A schedule may also be attached of any copyright, logos, trademarks, or other rights which the Sportsperson owns or controls at the date of this Agreement.

As with most types of agency agreements, the contract is exclusive in respect of the sportsperson and non-exclusive on the manager's side. The territory is for all countries in the world but could, of course, be for a limited territory, such as the United States, or for a number of specified countries. The term of the Agreement, especially for a sportsperson, is likely to be for a small number of years. As with other agreements of this type, we have avoided an option or renewal clause.

To be attached to and forming part of this Agreement are a Schedule of Holiday Leave and a Work Schedule.

GENERAL CONTRACT FOR SERVICES

AN AGREEMENT made this [____________] day of [____________]

BETWEEN:

(1) [____________]
of [____________] (to be known as the Originator in this Agreement)

AND

(2) [____________]
of [____________] (to be known as the Company in this Agreement).

IT IS AGREED as follows:

1. DEFINITIONS

The words below are agreed to mean as follows:

1.1 "The Work Plan" shall mean the detail of the nature of the services of the Originator to be provided to the Company under this Agreement, which are described as follows: [____________].

1.2 "The Term of the Agreement" shall commence on: [date] and shall continue until: [date].

1.3 "The Territory" shall mean the following specific countries: [____________].

1.4 "The Originator's Fee" shall mean the sum of: [figure/currency].

1.5 "The Originator's Expenses" shall mean all expenses reasonably and properly incurred by the Originator in providing his services under this Agreement, including the cost of raw materials, travel and accommodation.

1.6 "The Work Schedule" shall mean such times, dates and locations at which the Originator has agreed to provide his services. A copy of the Work Schedule is attached to and forms part of this agreement.

2. ENGAGEMENT OF THE ORIGINATOR

2.1 The Company agrees to engage the Originator for the purpose of providing his non-exclusive services to the Company throughout the Territory for the Term of the Agreement as set out in the Work Plan and in accordance with the Work Schedule.

2.2 In consideration of the Originator's Fee and the Originator's Expenses, the Originator agrees to provide his non-exclusive services to the Company throughout the Territory for the Term of the Agreement as set out in the Work Plan and in accordance with the Work Schedule.

3. COPYRIGHT

3.1 The Company acknowledges that all copyright, design rights and any other rights in the product of the services provided by the Originator excluding any material provided by the Company shall remain the sole and exclusive property of the Originator and this Agreement does not purport to grant, assign, or transfer any rights to the Company.

3.2 The Company and the Originator agree that any material arising from the services of the Originator as set out in the Work Plan shall only be used by the Company for the following specific purposes: [____________]

3.3 In the event that the Company wishes to use any material arising from the services of the Originator as set out in the Work Plan for any purpose other than those specified in clause 3.2 then the prior written consent of the Originator shall be required, together with an additional payment to be agreed between the parties.

3.4 The Company acknowledges that the Originator shall be entitled to exploit any material created by the Originator under this Agreement provided that all references to and any confidential information and material provided by the Company are deleted.

4. MORAL RIGHTS

4.1 The Company acknowledges that the Originator asserts his moral rights generally in respect of the product of his services under this Agreement as set out in the Work Plan including any documents, artwork, and other material and in particular to be reasonably, prominently and clearly identified as follows: [____________] on all copies in all media.

4.2 The Originator asserts the right to object to derogatory treatment of his work under this Agreement whether addition to, deletion from, or alteration or adaptation which is a distortion or mutilation or is otherwise prejudicial to the honour or reputation of the Originator.

5. OBLIGATIONS OF THE COMPANY

5.1 The Company agrees to pay the Originator's Fee as follows:

5.1.1 [__________] upon signature of this Agreement;
5.1.2 [__________] on or before [__________] subject to supply of: [__________];
5.1.3 [__________] on or before [__________] subject to delivery of: [__________].

5.2 The Company agrees to pay to the Originator the Originator's Expenses as follows: [____________].

5.3 The Company undertakes that the products of the Originator's services provided under this Agreement shall be entitled to the following on-screen credit: [____________].

5.4 The Company agrees to provide the following copyright notice, credit, trademark and logo to the Originator in all publicity, advertising, promotional and packaging material in respect of the marketing, distribution and exploitation of the product of the Originator's services provided under this Agreement: [____________].

5.5 The Company undertakes that the products of the services provided to the Company by the Originator under this Agreement shall not be used in an obscene, offensive or derogatory manner and will not expose the Originator to any civil or criminal proceedings.

5.6 The Company agrees to make all payments required under this Agreement to the Originator personally unless otherwise advised. The Company shall only be obliged to pay value added tax upon receipt of a formal invoice.

5.7 The Company acknowledges that the Originator is already committed and entitled to carry out the following work for third parties during the Term of the Agreement: [____________].

5.8 The Company agrees that no alteration shall be made to the Work Plan or the Work Schedule without the prior approval of the Originator.

5.9 The Company agrees that the use of the name, photograph, image, or other material relating to the Originator in respect of this Agreement shall require his specific consent on each occasion for its use in any commercial exploitation or marketing material under this Agreement.

6. OBLIGATIONS OF THE ORIGINATOR

6.1 The Originator confirms that he is the original creator and sole owner of or controls all copyright, design rights and any other rights in the product of his services to the Company under this Agreement excluding any information or material supplied by or included at the request of the Company.

6.2 Subject to clause 5.7, the Originator confirms that he has full title and authority to enter into this Agreement and is not bound by any previous agreement which adversely affects this Agreement.

6.3 The Originator confirms that the products of his services under this Agreement will not involve the use of any material which infringes the copyright or any other rights of any third party in the Territory except for any information or material supplied by or included at the request of the Company.

6.4 The Originator confirms that the Services will not contain any obscene, offensive or defamatory material and will not expose the Company to any civil or criminal proceedings except for any information or material supplied by or included at the request of the Company.

6.5 The Originator agrees to attend at all such times, dates (excluding bank holidays and weekends), and locations including press calls and promotional events and recordings as the Company and the Originator have agreed in the Work Schedule.

6.6 The Originator confirms that he is a bona fide member of the following trade/professional organisation: [______________].

6.7 The Originator agrees not to issue any statement to the media at any time concerning any confidential business or future plans of the Company or the Company's business acquired during the Term of the Agreement.

6.8 The Originator shall provide his services to the best of his skill and ability and shall perform all services diligently to ensure that the obligations under this Agreement are satisfactorily performed in accordance with the Work Plan.

6.9 The Originator agrees that his consent as may be required for the purposes of this Agreement is provided.

6.10 The Originator agrees to be responsible for his own national insurance, personal tax and Value Added Tax.

6.11 The Originator undertakes that all information, advice, material and statements provided to the Company by the Originator shall, to the best of his knowledge and belief, be true and accurate except for information and material provided by or included at the request of the Company.

6.12 In respect of the Originator's Expenses, the Originator agrees to provide the Company with all receipts or other sufficient evidence of expenditure upon request by the Company.

6.13 The Originator confirms that he is a British subject or a member of a national state of the European Union.

7. MISCELLANEOUS

MUTUAL INDEMNITY

7.1 The Originator and the Company mutually undertake to indemnify the other against all liabilities, claims, demands, actions, costs, damages or loss arising out of any breach by either party of any of the terms of this Agreement.

7.2 In the event of any claim, dispute, action, writ or summons in connection with clause 7.1, the Originator and the Company agree to provide full details to the other party at the earliest opportunity and shall not settle any such matter without first consulting the other party.

CONFIDENTIALITY

7.3 The Originator and the Company shall not disclose to any third party (except professional legal advisors and accountants) any confidential information, business finance or future plans of the other party which is acquired as a direct result of this

Agreement. The Originator and the Company agree to make a joint statement to the press concerning this Agreement, the following press release shall be issued: [____________].

7.4 All records and other materials received by either party which belong to the other shall be returned upon termination or expiry of this Agreement.

7.5 After the expiry or termination of this Agreement all parties undertake not to disclose to the press or any other media company, publisher or otherwise information relating to events, conversations, finance, documents, or general behaviour of the other party without their prior consent.

AMENDMENTS AND ALTERATIONS

7.6 This Agreement supersedes all previous agreements, representations or promises and sets out all the terms agreed between the parties. Any amendment or alteration to this Agreement must be in writing and signed by an authorised signatory of each party.

NOTICES

7.7 Any notice shall be served personally on the [Managing Director] of the Company or the Originator by hand or shall be by first class recorded delivery to the following addresses:

Company [address] to [Managing Director];
Originator [address] to [Originator];
No other method is accepted a proper notice.

VALUE ADDED TAX

7.8 All sums payable under this Agreement are exclusive of any Value Added Tax that may be payable by either party.

FORCE MAJEURE

7.9 In the event that this Agreement cannot be performed or its obligations fulfilled for any reason beyond the reasonable control of the Originator or the Company, including such events as war, industrial action, floods or Acts of God, then such non-performance or failure to fulfil its obligations shall be deemed not to be a breach of this Agreement. In the event that this Agreement cannot be performed or its obligations fulfilled for any reason beyond the reasonable control of the defaulting party for a continuous period of [____________]. Then the other party may, at its discretion, terminate this Agreement by notice in writing at the end of that period provided that both parties agree to negotiate, in good faith, an equitable settlement in respect of work already performed to the date of termination.

TERMINATION AND EXPIRY OF THE AGREEMENT

7.10 In addition to any other rights and remedies at law, this Agreement may be terminated by giving written notice to the other party who has breached this Agreement or defaulted in the following circumstances:

7.10.1 where the Company has failed to account or make payments as required under this Agreement;

7.10.2 where the Company or the Originator has committed a serious breach of its obligations under this Agreement unless such party rectifies the position, as far as reasonably possible, within [____________];

7.10.3 where the Company goes into voluntary or involuntary liquidation;

7.10.4 where the Company is declared insolvent either in bankruptcy proceedings or other legal proceedings;

7.10.5 where an agreement with creditors has been reached by the Company due to its failure or inability to pay its debts as they fall due; or

7.10.6 where a receiver is appointed over the whole or part of the Company's business.

THIRD PARTY TRANSFERS AND RIGHTS

7.11 Neither party shall assign, transfer, charge or make over this Agreement or any of its rights or obligations without the prior written consent of the other party.

NO PARTNERSHIP OR EMPLOYMENT

7.12 This Agreement shall not be deemed to create any partnership or employment relationship between the parties.

GOVERNING LAW

7.13 This Agreement shall be subject to the Laws of England.

Attached to and forming part of this Agreement are the Work Plan and the Work Schedule.

Signed by: [____________]
THE ORIGINATOR

Date: [____________]

Signed by: [____________]
THE COMPANY

Date: [____________]

OUTLINE—GENERAL CONTRACT FOR SERVICES

This is a general contract for the services. The parties are referred to as the Company and the Originator. This Agreement should be used where the parties wish to minimise the possibility of the relationship between them being construed as an employment contract or partnership. In the event that a contract is a contract of employment, the employee is the first owner of copyright in respect of an original literary, dramatic, musical or artistic work made by an employee in the course of his employment, unless there exists an agreement to the contrary.

The Originator is to supply his non-exclusive services for a short period in a named country. In return the Company will pay the Originator's fee and expenses.

A Work Schedule should be attached to and form part of the Agreement setting out in as much detail as possible the exact times, dates and locations to which the Originator is committing himself.

The Company is acknowledging that the parties do not intend to create an employment relationship between them and that the copyright and design rights in all original material remain the property of the Originator. There is no provision for insurance by the Company. There is no license by the Originator of the product of his services except agreement that the Company may use it for the purpose set out. Any additional use by the Company will require the payment of additional fees.

There are mutual indemnity provisions but this could either be deleted or limited in value.

TELEVISION PRESENTER'S CONTRACT

AN AGREEMENT made this [____________] day of [____________]

BETWEEN:

(1) [____________]
of [____________] (to be known as the Presenter in this Agreement)

AND

(2) [____________]
of [____________] (to be known as the Company in this Agreement).

IT IS AGREED as follows:

1. DEFINITIONS

The words below are agreed to mean as follows:

1.1 "The Term of the Agreement" shall commence on the date of this Agreement and shall continue until [____________].

1.2 "The Presenter's Fee" shall be the following sums:

[____________] for the first 12 calendar months;
[____________] for the following 12 calendar months;
[____________] thereafter.

1.3 "The Programme" shall be the following film and any associated sound recording entitled [____________] which shall be [____________] minutes in duration.

1.4 "The Territory" shall be the following specified countries: [____________].

2. EXCLUSIVE ENGAGEMENT OF PRESENTER

2.1 The Company and the Presenter agree that in consideration of the Presenter's Fee the Presenter shall provide his/her exclusive services to the Company as presenter of the Programme and provide such other contributions as may reasonably be required by the Company in respect of recordings, appearances, meetings and other work directly related to presenting and promoting the programme for the Term of the Agreement in the Territory.

2.2 The Presenter agrees not to provide his/her services for any other television company other than for a charitable nature and purpose throughout the Term of the Agreement without the prior written consent of the Company.

2.3 The Company confirms that the Presenter is entitled to make contributions of a charitable nature and purpose to any third party provided the Presenter gives to the Company reasonable notice of the event and undertakes that no such engagement shall take precedence over any obligations of the Presenter under this Agreement.

3. ASSIGNMENT OF COPYRIGHT

3.1 In consideration of the Presenter's Fee the Presenter assigns to the Company all present and future copyright and any other rights in all media throughout the world and universe in the product of his/her services and any other material created hereunder for the purpose of this Agreement for the full period of copyright and any extensions and renewals including but not limited to photographs, films, sound or other recordings, advertisements, or scripts.

3.2 The Presenter acknowledges that any intellectual property of any kind including but not limited to copyright, design rights, service marks, trademarks, logos, inventions, titles, slogans, property rights and any other rights held by the Company or which are created or developed in conjunction with the services by the Presenter under this Agreement shall be the sole and exclusive property of the Company. The Presenter shall not acquire any rights or interest nor does this Agreement purport to grant, assign or transfer any such rights on the product of the services to the Presenter.

4. ASSERTION OF PRESENTER'S MORAL RIGHTS

4.1 The Company acknowledges that the Presenter asserts his/her moral rights generally in respect of the Programme and any other contributions in sound, text or vision that may be created by the Presenter under this Agreement and in particular to be identified in a reasonably prominent and clear manner as follows: [____________].

4.2 The Presenter asserts the moral right not to have any work which he/she has contributed to or created, treated in a derogatory manner at any time.

5. OBLIGATIONS OF THE COMPANY

5.1 The Company agrees to engage the exclusive services of the Presenter in respect of the Programme for the Term of the Agreement.

5.2 In consideration of the Presenter's services the Company agrees to pay the Presenter's Fee in equal installments throughout the Term of the Agreement on the last day of each calendar month. The first installment shall be due on: [date].

5.3 The Company agrees to pay the Presenter throughout the Term of the Agreement a monthly clothing and hairdressing allowance of: [figure/currency].

5.4 In addition to the Presenter's Fee and the hairdressing and clothing allowance,the Company agrees to reimburse the Presenter in respect of all expenses reasonably and properly incurred for the purpose of fulfilling his/her obligations under this Agreement including taxis, petrol, telephone charges and business lunches subject to satisfactory receipts or other records being produced on request up to a maximum limit of: [figure/currency] per calendar month.

5.5 The Company agrees that it shall provide the Presenter with a new executive car for his/her own personal use for the Term of the Agreement which shall be comprehensively insured, taxed and serviced entirely at the Company's expense and shall remain the property of the Company.

5.6 The Company shall ensure that suitable insurance cover is arranged for the Presenter and his/her personal property for the benefit of the Presenter and his/her family and shall provide him/her with a copy of the insurance policy upon request. The Company confirms that the Presenter's personal life insurance for the benefit of his/her estate shall not be less than: [figure/currency].

5.7 The Company agrees to provide the following items and benefits to the Presenter at the Company's sole cost and expense for the duration of the Agreement: [____________].

5.8 If after one year of the continuation of this Agreement the Company is sold in a takeover, or floated on the Stock Exchange. Then the Presenter shall be entitled to receive the equivalent value of [figure/currency] in shares or money within [one month] of such event occurring.

5.9 The Company agrees to arrange and pay for any travel and accommodation required of the Presenter by the Company under this Agreement and undertakes, as far as possible, that all accommodation will be a minimum of a four star hotel and all forms of travel will be business or first class.

5.10 The Company agrees to provide the Presenter with reasonable notice of all rehearsals, recordings and any other meetings and promotional events which the Presenter is required to attend under this Agreement.

5.11 The Company acknowledges that there is no option or first right of refusal in respect of the Presenter's services after the expiry or termination of this Agreement.

5.12 The Company agrees that in the event that it is intended to exploit the Programme or any other contributions by the Presenter for any other medium except television or that it requires additional work by the Presenter for the purpose of merchandising material. Then it is agreed that the Company shall negotiate in good faith with the Presenter to agree an additional payment to the Presenter in each case.

5.13 The Company agrees that the Presenter's name, image, signature and endorsement shall not be used for any other purpose than the marketing of the Programme, and Company unless agreed in advance with the Presenter. The Company agrees to provide the Presenter with exact samples of all materials in any medium in which it is intended to use the name, image or endorsement of the Presenter. Such material whether for promotional, advertising, publicity or packaging shall not be at the Company's cost prior to the production or distribution of such material. In the event that the Presenter requests alterations or changes in any form then the Company agrees to carry out their request provided that it is reasonable in the circumstances.

5.14 The Company agrees that the Presenter shall only be responsible for any loss or damage directly arising from a breach of this Agreement. The Presenter shall not be liable for any matter relating to the presentation of the content of the programme which shall be entirely at the Company's cost and risk. The Company shall arrange publicity, liability, defamation, breach of copyright and other comprehensive insurance policy for the benefit of the Company and the Presenter.

6. AVAILABILITY OF THE PRESENTER

6.1 The Presenter agrees to attend at all such times, dates (including bank holidays and weekends), and locations including press calls and promotional events as the Company may require except in respect of such times, dates and locations which are specified and set out in the attached Schedule A.

6.2 The Company confirms that in any event the Presenter shall be entitled to not less than: [____________] holiday leave per annum, excluding public holidays and weekends.

6.3 Irrespective of any holiday leave the Company agrees that the Presenter's Fee shall not be affected by any leave due to illness, provided that such leave does not exceed more than [ten days] per annum and is supported by a medical certificate.

6.4 The Presenter shall inform the Company, at the earliest opportunity, of all leave which he/she intends to take under the terms of this Agreement which are not in the attached Schedule A and in any event to give the Company not less than [14 days] advance notification.

7. OBLIGATIONS OF THE PRESENTER

7.1 The Presenter agrees to provide his/her exclusive services to the Company as presenter of the Programme for the Term of the Agreement, including acting as interviewer, commentator and reporter, whether live or pre-recorded. Together with such other contributions as may reasonably be required by the Company in respect of recordings, appearances, meetings and other work directly related to presenting or promoting the Programme.

7.2 The Presenter shall comply with all the rules in force at such places and locations at which he/she is required to attend and shall observe all reasonable directions as may be given to him/her on behalf of the Company.

7.3 The Presenter agrees that in the event that the Company decides for any reason to discontinue the production of the Programme. Then the Company shall only be liable for the Presenter's Fee and [the hairdressing and clothing allowance] due for the rest of the Term of the Agreement.

7.4 The Presenter shall provide his/her services to the best of his/her skill and ability to ensure the fulfillment of his/her obligations under this Agreement.

7.5 The Presenter confirms that he/she is a [British] subject or national of a Member State of the [European Union] and will remain so during the Term of the Agreement.

7.6 The Presenter confirms that he/she has full authority to enter into and perform this Agreement and that he/she is not bound by any previous agreement which adversely affects this Agreement.

7.7 The Presenter undertakes that all the products of his/her services under this Agreement shall be original and will not infringe the copyright or any other right of any third party throughout the Territory except where the work is based on or incorporates material of any third party which is included at the Company's request.

7.8 The Presenter undertakes that all the products of his/her services under this Agreement will not contain any obscene or defamatory material or anything of an advertising nature and will not expose the Company to civil or criminal proceedings except where the work is based on or incorporates material of any third party which is included at the Company's request.

7.9 The Presenter agrees that his/her consent as may be required is provided for the purposes of this Agreement in respect of the product of the services or the performances or other contributions of the Presenter.

7.10 Subject to prior consultation, the Presenter agrees that the Company shall be entitled to use his/her name, biography, photograph and fair likeness in respect of the promotion and advertising of the Company and the Programme provided that any commercial exploitation of the Presenter's name, biography, photograph and image shall be subject to prior agreement between the parties.

7.11 The Presenter undertakes that he/she shall not during the Term of the Agreement issue any statement to the media in respect of the Programme without the prior consent of the Company nor at any time disclose any confidential information concerning the business or future plans of the Company to any third party which is acquired during the Term of the Agreement.

7.12 The Presenter shall, on the expiry or termination of this Agreement, deliver to the Company, upon request, all property of the Company which is in his/her possession save that the Presenter may retain such material as may be agreed with the Company for his/her own personal reference.

7.14 The Presenter undertakes to keep the Company informed of his/her telephone number, address and whereabouts during the Term of the Agreement.

7.15 The Presenter confirms that he/she shall be responsible for his own value added tax, national insurance and personal tax arising under this Agreement.

7.16 The Presenter agrees to submit to any medical examination by a reputable consultant required by the Company's insurers at the Company's cost in order to insure the Presenter throughout the Term of the Agreement. Provided that any medical report is disclosed only to the Managing Director of the Company, the Insurers and the Presenter.

7.17 The Presenter acknowledges that he/she is not entitled to order any goods or services, or to pledge or commit the credit of the Company nor make any payment or agree to pay any person whosoever without the prior consent of the Company except in relation to his/her own personal expenses.

8. MISCELLANEOUS

8.1 In the event of any claim, dispute, action, writ or summons in connection with this Agreement, the Presenter and the Company agree to provide full details to the other party at the earliest opportunity and shall not settle any such matter without first consulting the other party.

8.2 No reference is to be made to the terms of this Agreement by either party in public without the prior consent of the other party.

8.3 This Agreement supersedes all previous agreements, representations or promises and sets out all the terms agreed between the parties. Any amendment or alteration to this Agreement must be in writing and signed by an authorised signatory of each party.

8.4 Without prejudice to the right to serve notices by any other means any notice served under this Agreement which has been sent by first class, pre-paid post shall be deemed to be received 48 hours thereafter (excluding Saturdays Sundays and public holidays).

8.5 All sums payable under this Agreement are exclusive of any value added tax that may be payable by either party.

8.6 Neither party shall assign, transfer, charge or make over this Agreement or any of its rights or obligations without the prior written consent of the other party.

8.7 In the event that this Agreement cannot be performed or its obligations fulfilled for any reason beyond its reasonable control including war, industrial action, floods or Acts of God then such non-performance or failure to fulfil its obligations shall be deemed not to be a breach of this Agreement. In the event that this Agreement cannot be performed or its obligations fulfilled for any reason beyond either party's reasonable control for a continuous period of [two] months then either party may, at its discretion, terminate this Agreement by notice in writing at the end of that period.

8.8 In addition to any other rights and remedies at law the non-defaulting party may, by giving written notice to the other party who is in breach, terminate this Agreement on the following grounds:

8.8.1 where the Company has failed to make payments as required under this Agreement;

8.8.2 where either party has committed a serious breach of its obligations under this Agreement unless such party rectifies the position, as far as reasonably possible, within [30 days]; or

8.8.3 where the Company goes into voluntary or involuntary liquidation or is declared insolvent either in bankruptcy proceedings or other legal proceedings or has reached an agreement with creditors due to its failure or inability to pay its debts as they fall due, or where a receiver is appointed over the whole or part of the Company's business.

8.9 This Agreement shall be subject to the Laws of England.

Signature: [_______________]
Name: [_______________]
Title: [_______________]
Date: [_______________]
ON BEHALF OF THE PRESENTER

Signature: [_______________]
Name: [_______________]
Title: [_______________]
Date: [_______________]
ON BEHALF OF THE COMPANY

OUTLINE—TELEVISION PRESENTER'S CONTACT

This is an agreement between an on-screen presenter and a television company. The Presenter is agreeing to provide his exclusive services to the Company for a specified period of time in specified countries, not the world. The Presenter is not allowed to work for any third party during the term of the Agreement without the prior consent of the Company but would be entitled to make contributions of a charitable nature subject to certain conditions.

The Presenter is entitled to an annual fee, payable monthly, a hairdressing and clothing allowance, reasonable expenses and the use of an appropriate car and such other benefits as may be set out.

The Presenter is asserting his moral rights to be identified and also not to be subject to derogatory treatment.

The Presenter is assigning all copyright in the product of his services to the Company which is a complete transfer of all rights in all media without any right to any additional money should the material be exploited at any time. The Presenter is not giving an indemnity to the Company regarding his performance or the content of the Programme. This is best dealt with by the Company taking out insurance cover.

If the Company discontinues the Programme for which the Presenter has specifically agreed to provide his services. Then the Company will still be liable to pay the Presenter's fee and the hairdressing and clothing allowance for the outstanding period of the Agreement. The Company shall not be bound to pay any compensation or damages.

The Company is agreeing to provide personal insurance cover for the Presenter and life insurance cover.

The Presenter is entitled to a specified amount of holiday leave and sick leave per annum. A schedule should be attached to and form part of the Agreement, which specifies exactly which days of the year, times of the day and locations are specifically not included.

The Presenter is agreeing not to issue any statement to the media or disclose any confidential information concerning the company. No clause has been included relating to public statements or involvement by the Presenter in activities of a political nature.

It should be noted that there is no renewal option in this Agreement.

AGREEMENT BETWEEN CELEBRITY AND COMPANY FOR ADVERTISING CAMPAIGN

AN AGREEMENT made this [____________] day of [____________]

BETWEEN:

(1) [____________]
of [____________] (to be known as the Celebrity in this Agreement)

AND

2) [____________]
of [____________] (to be known as the Company in this Agreement)

IT IS AGREED as follows:

1. DEFINITIONS

The words below are agreed to mean as follows:

1.1 "The Company's Product" shall be the following product and/or services: [____________].
A two-dimensional copy of the Company's Product is attached to and forms part of this Agreement.

1.2 "The Company's Logo" shall mean the following artwork, design, logo and trade-mark and any associated words or slogan: [____________].
A two-dimensional copy of the Company's Logo is attached to and forms part of this Agreement.

1.3 "The Term of the Agreement" shall commence on: [date] and shall continue until: [date].

1.4 "The Celebrity's Fee" shall be the following sum: [figure/currency].

1.5 "The Repeat Fees" shall be the following sums to be paid by the Company to the Celebrity in addition to the Celebrity's Fee when any of the advertisements or any sections or parts which include the performance, recordings, films, photographs, image, voice-over, personal appearances, or otherwise of the Celebrity of material produced under this Agreement which shall be due to the Celebrity on each occasion such material is exploited in that medium at any time throughout the Territory:

Standard Television Commercial:	[____________];
Cable Television Commercial:	[____________];
Satellite Television Commercial:	[____________];
Radio Commercial:	[____________];
Telephone Commercial:	[____________];
Internet Computer Software Commercial:	[____________];
Cinema Commercial:	[____________];
Theatre Commercial:	[____________];
Video [in any form] Commercial:	[____________];
Non-Theatric Audiences:	[____________];
Publishing:	[____________];
Merchandising:	[____________];
All other forms of any nature:	[____________].

1.6 "The Territory" shall be all countries, bases and locations throughout the world and universe.

1.7 "The Agent" shall mean the following [company] who is authorised to act on behalf of the Celebrity: [____________] whose registered address is at [____________].

1.8 "The Work Schedule" shall mean such times, dates and locations at which the Celebrity has agreed to provide his services to the Company during the Term of the Agreement. A copy of the Work Schedule is attached to and forms part of this Agreement.

2. ENGAGEMENT OF CELEBRITY

2.1 The Company agrees that the Celebrity shall be the sole and exclusive personality to be engaged by the Company for the Term of this Agreement in the Territory to endorse, provide and advertise the Company's Product.

2.2 In consideration of the Celebrity's Fee and the Repeat Fees, the Celebrity agrees to provide his exclusive services to the Company to endorse, promote and advertise the Company's Product by personal appearances, performances and recordings, films, images, photographs or otherwise of material of the Celebrity for advertisements for use in all media in accordance with the Work Schedule and on such other occasions as may be agreed for the Term of the Agreement throughout the Territory in accordance with the terms of this Agreement.

2.3 The Celebrity undertakes not to provide his services to any third party for the endorsement, advertisement or promotion of any other product or service of any type whether it directly competes with the Company's Product or not other than services of a charitable nature throughout the Term of the Agreement without the prior written consent of the Company except in respect of the following services which the Celebrity shall carry out in the normal course of his career: [specify].

2.4 The Company confirms that the Celebrity is entitled to make contributions of a charitable nature and purpose to any third party provided that the Celebrity gives to the

Company reasonable notice of the event and undertakes that no such engagement shall take precedence over any obligations of the Celebrity under this Agreement.

2.5 The Company acknowledges that the Celebrity is already committed and entitled to carry out the following work during the Term of the Agreement: [____________].

2.6 The Company specifically acknowledges that the Celebrity shall be entitled during the Term of the Agreement to provide his services to any third party for work in addition to that set out in clauses 2.3 and 2.5, provided that it is not for the endorsement, advertisement or promotion of a product or service of a third party.

3. COPYRIGHT

3.1 In consideration of the Celebrity's Fee and the Repeat Fees, the Celebrity assigns to the Company all present and future copyright and any other rights in all media throughout the Territory in the products of his services and any other material created for the purpose of this Agreement for the full period of copyright and any extensions and renewals.

3.2 The Company agrees that it shall not be entitled to use, exploit or license any of the material produced or created for the purposes of this Agreement in which the Celebrity appears in sound or vision or by any other reference for any purpose at any time other than the endorsement, promotion or advertising of the Company's Product during the Term of the Agreement. Where the Company wishes to use any such material at any time for any purpose or to license a third party. Then it is clear that the prior written consent of the Celebrity is required and the negotiation and settlement of a new agreement to the satisfaction of both parties.

3.3 The Company confirms that it is the sole owner of or controls all copyright and any other rights on the Company's logo and the Company's Product in all media throughout the Territory and any developments or variations.

3.4 The Company agrees that all copyright design right and any other right in the Celebrity's name, image, slogan, trademark, logo or any other rights supplied by the Celebrity under this Agreement shall be the sole and exclusive property of the Celebrity and the Company shall not acquire any rights or interests or in any development or variations pursuant to this Agreement.

4. ASSERTION OF CELEBRITY'S MORAL RIGHTS

4.1 The Company acknowledges and the Celebrity asserts his moral rights in general in respect of the services to be provided under this Agreement. The Celebrity shall be reasonably, prominently and clearly identified at all times in the following: [style/manner/format] and in particular by the following: [name] whether in any original material created and exploited under this Agreement, supplied by the Celebrity, or issued in supporting press releases, or otherwise.

4.2 The Company acknowledges and the Celebrity asserts his right not to be subject at any time in any material to derogatory treatment, obscene, racist, offensive, demeaning, defamatory, or any distortion, or other development which may impugn the character of the Celebrity or his work.

5. OBLIGATIONS OF THE COMPANY

5.1 The Company agrees to engage the exclusive services of the Celebrity to endorse, promote and advertise the Company's Product throughout the Territory for the Term of the Agreement.

5.2 The Company agrees that the Celebrity shall be the sole and exclusive personality to endorse, present, promote and advertise the Company's Product throughout the Territory during the Term of the Agreement.

5.3 In consideration of the Celebrity's Services, the Company agrees to pay the Celebrity's Fee as follows:

5.3.1 [____________] upon signature of this Agreement;
5.3.2 [____________] on or before [____________];
5.3.3 [____________] on or before [____________];
5.3.4 [____________] on or before [____________].

5.4 In addition to the Celebrity's Fee, the Company agrees to pay to the Celebrity the Repeat Fees within [28 days] of each of the dates upon which the event takes place at any time.

5.5 In addition to the Celebrity's Fees and the Repeat Fees the Company agrees to pay the Celebrity throughout the Term of the Agreement a monthly expense allowance which includes provision for hairdressing, clothing, taxis, petrol, telephone charges and business lunches. Such monthly allowance shall be [____________] and shall be paid one month in advance during the Term of this Agreement. No supporting documentation shall be required.

5.6 The Company shall ensure that comprehensive insurance cover is arranged for the Celebrity and his personal property in respect of the provision of his services for the Term of the Agreement for the benefit of the Celebrity and shall provide the Celebrity with a copy of the insurance policy upon request. The Company confirms that the Celebrity's personal life insurance for the benefit of his estate shall not be less than: [figure/currency].

5.7 In addition to the expense allowance under clause 5.5, the Company agrees to arrange and pay for any travel and accommodation required of the Celebrity by the Company under this Agreement and undertakes, as far as possible, that all accommodation will be a minimum of [4-star hotel] and all forms of travel will be first class.

5.8 The Company acknowledges that the Celebrity shall be entitled, upon request, to be provided at the Company's sole cost with a copy of any material produced under this Agreement which it is intended to release to the public including any publicity, advertising, promotional and marketing material in the possession or under the control of the Company featuring or relating to the Celebrity.

5.9 The Company undertakes not to disclose any material nor make any statement, whether true or not, concerning the Celebrity's private and sexual life, politics and personal views to the media (including newspapers, television and radio) at any time without the prior written consent of the Celebrity or his Agent.

5.10 The Company agrees that the Celebrity shall not be requested to be involved in any derogatory, obscene, offensive, racist or demeaning activity or any other work which would impugn the character of the Celebrity in respect of the provision of his services under this Agreement.

5.11 The Company agrees to consult with the Celebrity and the Agent in respect of all proposed scripts, photographs, films, videos, sound recordings, posters, computer software, packaging, advertising, promotional, publicity and marketing material in all media prior to the production, manufacture and distribution of such material.

5.12 The Company confirms that it has full authority to enter into and perform this agreement and that it is not bound by any previous Agreement which adversely affects this Agreement.

5.13 The Company undertakes that no material of any nature concerning the Celebrity shall be used by the Company or any third party in an offensive, obscene, derogatory, defamatory or demeaning manner.

5.14 The Company undertakes that it shall ensure that no material produced under this Agreement will infringe the copyright or any other rights of any third party throughout the Territory and will not expose the Celebrity to any civil or criminal proceedings.

5.15 The Company agrees to provide the Celebrity or the Agent with reasonable notice of all rehearsals, film and sound recordings and any other meetings and promotional events at which the Celebrity is required to attend under this Agreement which shall not be less than: [____________].

5.16 The Company agrees that all costs and expenses incurred in respect of the development, production, distribution and exploitation of the Company's Product and any advertisements, promotional events and any other material shall be at the Company's sole cost and that the Celebrity shall not be liable to pay any such sums.

5.17 The Company confirms that there exists a comprehensive product and public liability insurance policy which shall remain in force at all material times covering any claims, actions or damages which may arise as a direct or indirect result of the use by the public of the Company's Product, together with all other products or services owned or controlled by the Company which the public would reasonably associate with the Company. The Company agrees to provide the Celebrity with a copy upon request. Further the Company agrees to take out and bear the cost of an insurance policy for the benefit of the Celebrity which provides full protection to the Celebrity arising from a civil or criminal action against the Celebrity in respect of the Company's Product or any other material exploited by them under this Agreement for not less than: [____________].

5.18 The Company confirms that the Company's Product and all other products owned or controlled by the Company are safe and fit for their intended use and comply with all statutes, regulations, directives and codes in force.

5.19 The Company agrees that the Celebrity is not obliged to provide personal medical details or to agree to a medical examination for the purpose of this Agreement.

5.20 The Company shall be fully liable to the Celebrity for all acts and omissions with respect to any of the Company's sub-licenses, sub-agents or any third party it uses for the purposes of its business whether there is a contractual relationship or not.

5.21 The Company shall at the end of each calendar month for the duration of the Term of this Agreement and thereafter send to the Celebrity a statement showing any sums due and a detailed breakdown of the date, method, and medium of which use has been made under this Agreement. Disclosure shall be as specific and full as known to the Company itself and no information shall be withheld for any reason.

5.22 The Company agrees that upon request it shall provide a copy of any record, document, accounts, or other material which assist the Celebrity in establishing the validity and accuracy of the information provided in the accounts and the sums due.

5.23 The Company agrees that the professional advisors of the Celebrity namely legal, accountant and agent shall each be entitled to inspect the accounts once in each six-month period during normal business hours with [_____days'] notice. In the event that an error is found to the detriment of the Celebrity. Then the Company shall pay twice that sum in compensation together with the payment due within [_____days'] notice of the error by the Celebrity.

6. OBLIGATIONS OF THE CELEBRITY

6.1 The Celebrity agrees to provide his services to the best of his skill and ability and to attend at all such times, dates (including bank holidays and weekends), and locations, including press calls and promotional events and recordings, during the Term of the Agreement as the Company and the Celebrity have agreed in the Work Schedule and on the following additional number of days: [_____________].

6.2 In accordance with the Work Schedule the Celebrity agrees to provide the following specific services:

6.2.1 the presentation of and performance in not less than [_____________] advertisements for the purpose of [_____________];
6.2.2 the presentation of a corporate video which shall be of [_____________] minutes in duration;
6.2.3 the attendance at not less than [_____________] official functions and promotional events organised by the Company;
6.2.4 photographic sessions: [_____________]
for: [_____________];
6.2.5 sound recordings: [_____________]
for: [_____________]; and
6.2.6 other: [_____________].

6.3 The Celebrity confirms that he is a bona fide member of [union].

6.4 The Celebrity confirms that he holds a valid passport for: [_____________] and is resident in: [_____________] and will remain so during the Term of the Agreement.

6.5 The Celebrity confirms that he has full authority to enter into and perform this Agreement and that he is not bound by any previous agreement which adversely affects this Agreement.

6.6 The Celebrity confirms that all the product of his services shall be original and will not infringe the copyright or any other right of any third party throughout the Territory, except where any material is included at the request of the Company or other third party engaged by the Company.

6.7 The Celebrity confirms that all the products of his services will not contain any obscene or defamatory material and will not expose the Company to criminal or civil proceedings, except where any material is included at the request of the Company or any other third party engaged by the Company.

6.8 The Celebrity agrees that the Company shall be entitled to use and permit the use of the Celebrity's name, biography, photograph and fair likeness for the purposes of promoting and advertising the Company's Product but not for any other purpose during the Term of the Agreement. Provided that the Agent is notified on each occasion of the proposed use, and is fully consulted as regards the exact form and medium in which it is intended to be exploited.

6.9 The Celebrity agrees not to issue any statement to the media at any time concerning any confidential business or future plans of the Company or the Company's Product acquired during the Term of the Agreement.

6.10 The Celebrity agrees not to participate in any dangerous sport, drugs except for medicinal purposes, political controversies or other activities which would prejudice the goodwill and reputation of the Company and the Company's Product during the Term of the Agreement.

6.11 The Celebrity confirms that all sums due to the Celebrity shall be paid directly to the Agent.

6.12 The Celebrity confirms that he shall be responsible for his own value added tax, national insurance and personal tax due as a consequence under this Agreement.

6.13 The Celebrity agrees to comply with all the rules in force at such places and locations at which he is required to attend and shall observe all directions as may reasonably be given to him by or on behalf of the Company.

6.14 The Celebrity acknowledges that subject to the final editorial decision in respect of all advertisement publicity, promotional and any other material created under this agreement shall be at the sole discretion of the Company subject to the undertakings given in this Agreement.

7. MISCELLANEOUS

MUTUAL INDEMNITY

7.1 The Celebrity and the Company undertake to indemnify the other against all liabilities, claims, demands, actions, costs, damages or loss arising out of any breach by either party of any of the terms of this Agreement.

7.2 In the event of any claim, dispute, action, writ or summons in connection with clause 7.1, the Celebrity and the Company agree to provide full details to the other party at the earliest opportunity and shall not settle any such matter without first consulting the other party.

7.3 In the event of any legal proceedings being commenced by any third party against either the Company or the Celebrity or both in respect of any material under this Agreement. Then written notice shall immediately be given to the other on such occasion. Both parties shall assist each other as may reasonably be required to settle or defend such action and will execute any documents which their own lawyers shall deem appropriate to supply or provide. Each party shall bear its own legal costs.

CONFIDENTIALITY

7.4 No reference is to be made to the terms of this Agreement by either party in any media at any time without the prior written consent of the other party in each case.

AMENDMENTS AND ALTERATIONS

7.5 This Agreement supersedes all previous agreements, representations, undertakings and assurances given prior to this Agreement and sets out all the terms agreed between the parties. Any amendment or alteration to this Agreement must be in writing and signed by the Company and the Celebrity.

NOTICES

7.6 Any notice or direction to be given by the Company to the Celebrity shall be made by only the following person: Managing Director/Company Secretary/Film Director/Art Director or other person of comparable position who is in charge of the project. Any formal notice shall be in writing and sent by e-mail or fax but will not be deemed served until a copy has been received by recorded post or by hand to:

[Celebrity/Agent] at [address] [fax/e-mail]
[Name] at [address] [fax/e-mail].

VALUE ADDED TAX

7.7 All sums payable under this Agreement are exclusive of any value added tax that may be payable by either party.

FORCE MAJEURE

7.8 In the event that this Agreement cannot be performed or its obligations fulfilled for any reason beyond the reasonable control of the Company or the Celebrity, including such events as ill-health of the Celebrity, war, industrial action, floods, Acts of God or unforeseen technical failure. Then such non-performance or failure to fulfil its obligations shall be deemed not to be a breach of this Agreement. In the event that this Agreement cannot be performed or its obligations fulfilled for any reason beyond the reasonable control of the defaulting party for a continuous period of [six months]. Then the non-defaulting party may, at its discretion, terminate this Agreement by notice in writing at the end of that period. Provided that both parties agree to negotiate, in good faith, an equitable settlement in respect of work already performed to the date of termination and the proposed use of such material.

TERMINATION AND EXPIRY OF THE AGREEMENT

7.9 In addition to any other rights and remedies at law this Agreement may be terminated by giving written notice to the other party who has breached this Agreement or defaulted in the following circumstances:

7.9.1 where the Company has failed to account or make payments as required under this Agreement;
7.9.2 where the Company or the Celebrity has committed a serious breach of its obligations under this Agreement unless such party rectifies the position, as far as reasonably possible, within [30 days];
7.9.3 where the Company goes into voluntary or involuntary liquidation;
7.9.4 where the Company is declared insolvent either in bankruptcy proceedings or other legal proceedings;
7.9.5 where an agreement with creditors has been reached by the Company due to its failure or inability to pay its debts as they fall due;
7.9.6 where a receiver is appointed over the whole or part of the Company's business;
7.9.7 where the Celebrity is convicted of a serious criminal offence, including all drink-driving related offences and any criminal offence concerned with illegal drugs.

7.10 In the event of termination of the Agreement the following events shall occur:

7.10.1 All sub-licenses and sub-agents rights shall be revoked.
7.10.2 All master material shall be retained for [_____ years].
7.10.3 All property of the Celebrity shall be returned.

NO PARTNERSHIP OR EMPLOYMENT

7.11 This Agreement shall not be deemed to create any partnership or employment relationship between the parties.

THIRD PARTIES

7.12 Neither party shall assign, transfer, charge or make over this Agreement or any of its rights or obligations without the prior written consent of the other party.

7.13 This Agreement is personal to the Company and the Celebrity and no third party may seek to rely on its obligations and benefits except the Agent.

GOVERNING LAW

7.14 This Agreement shall be subject to the Laws of [England]. A copy of:

(a) the Company's product
(b) the Company's logo
(c) Work Schedule shall be attached to and form part of this Agreement.

SIGNED BY [THE CELEBRITY]
SIGNATURE [____________] DATE [____________]

SIGNED BY [THE COMPANY]
SIGNATURE [____________] DATE [____________]

WITNESSED BY AGENT: [____________]

OUTLINE—AGREEMENT BETWEEN CELEBRITY AND COMPANY FOR ADVERTISING CAMPAIGN

The Company is engaging the sole and exclusive services of the Celebrity to front a campaign and is not to use any other personality. The campaign would involve television commercials, advertisements in the press, promotional appearances and a corporate video but could encompass the wide range of media including radio, telephone, internet, videos. The services provided by the Celebrity are exclusive, and an undertaking is given not to advertise or promote the product or services of any third party during the term of the Agreement with the exception of charity work. This restriction should not interfere with the normal career and work commitments of the Celebrity which should be set out.

The Company is agreeing to pay to the Celebrity a fixed sum referred to as "the Celebrity's fee". In addition, repeat fees are to be paid by the Company when each of the advertisements are used in different media.

A work schedule should be attached setting out the times, dates and locations at which the Celebrity has agreed to provide his services to the Company. The Company is also agreeing to pay the Celebrity a monthly expense allowance which covers personal requirements such as clothes and hairdressing. The Company is responsible for arranging and paying for the Celebrity's first-class travel and accommodation together with insurance cover.

No option or renewal clause has been included.

The Agent is to receive payment and may audit the accounts but is not a party to the Agreement except as a witness.

If it is too difficult for the Company to account for each use in each media a blanket fee could be paid per day/month or for a fixed period.

The use of the material produced under this Agreement by the Company is limited to the purpose of advertising or promoting the Company's Products and the Term of the Agreement.

SPONSORSHIP AGREEMENT BETWEEN SPONSOR AND PROFESSIONAL SPORTSPERSON

BETWEEN:

(1) [____________]
of [____________] (to be known as the Sponsor in this Agreement)

AND

(2) [____________]
of [____________] (to be known as the Sportsperson in this Agreement)

IT IS AGREED as follows:

1. DEFINITIONS

The words below are agreed to mean as follows:

1.1 "The Sponsor's Logo" shall be the following design, logo and trademark, including any accompanying words, which are briefly described as follows: [____________]. A copy of the two-dimensional representation of the Sponsor's Logo is attached to and forms part of this Agreement.

1.2 "The Sponsor's Product" shall be the following item(s): [____________].

1.3 "The Sponsorship Fee" shall be the sum of: [figure/currency].

1.4 "The Performance Related Fee" shall be the sums to be paid by the Sponsor to the Sportsperson in the event that the Sportsperson wins or achieves any of the events, records or other matters which are set out in the Performance Related Schedule which is attached to and forms part of this Agreement.

1.5 "The Events Schedule" shall mean all the competitions, sporting and promotional events and meetings which the Sportsperson agrees to attend and participate in during the Sponsorship Period. A copy of the Events Schedule setting out the names, times, dates and locations of all such events is attached to and forms part of this Agreement.

1.6 "The Territory" shall be all countries, bases and locations throughout the [world, universe and outer space].

1.7 "The Sponsorship Period" shall commence on the date of this agreement and shall continue until: [____________].

2. SPONSORSHIP

2.1 In consideration of the Sponsorship Fee and the Performance Related Fee, the Sportsperson agrees to provide his non-exclusive services to the Sponsor to promote and endorse the Sponsor's Product for the duration of the Sponsorship Period throughout the Territory in accordance with the terms of this Agreement.

2.2 The Sponsor agrees to engage the non-exclusive services of the Sportsperson to promote and endorse the Sponsor's Product throughout the Territory for the duration of The Sponsorship Period.

2.3 The Sportsperson undertakes that he will not enter into any other sponsorship agreement with any third party concerning the same or similar items in respect of the Sponsor's Product, namely: [____________] for the duration of the Sponsorship Period without the prior written consent of the Sponsor.

2.4 The Sportsperson undertakes not to enter into an agreement to promote or endorse the products of the following companies for the duration of the Sponsorship Period: [____________].

3. COPYRIGHT

3.1 The Sponsor confirms that it is the sole owner of or controls all copyright and any other rights in the Sponsor's Logo and the Sponsor's Product and that any use by the Sportsperson under this Agreement of the Sponsor's Logo and the Sponsor's Product will not expose him to any criminal or civil proceedings.

3.2 The Sportsperson acknowledges that all copyright and any other rights in the Sponsor's Logo and the Sponsor's Product together with any goodwill shall belong to and remain the sole property of the Sponsor and that the Sportsperson shall not acquire any rights or interests in the Sponsor's Logo or the Sponsor's Product, including any trademark, design, title and artwork and any developments or variations.

4. OBLIGATIONS OF THE SPONSOR

4.1 In consideration of the services provided under this Agreement, the Sponsor shall pay to the Sportsperson the Sponsorship Fee as follows:

4.1.1 [____________] upon signature of this Agreement;
4.1.2 [____________] on or before;
4.1.3 [____________] on or before.

4.2 The Sponsor acknowledges that the Sponsorship Fee shall be paid notwithstanding that the Sportsperson may be unable to provide his services under this Agreement due to illness or injury which is supported by a medical certificate from a qualified doctor.

4.3 In addition to the Sponsorship Fee, the Sponsor agrees to pay to the Sportsperson any of the sums set out in the Performance Related Schedule within:[__________] of the event or occasion on which the Sportsperson becomes entitled to such payment and notice in writing by the Sportsperson.

4.4 The Sponsor agrees to provide the following items and benefits to the Sportsperson at the Sponsor's sole cost and expense for the duration of the Sponsorship Period:

The Sponsor's Product: [______________];
Clothing: [______________];
Equipment: [______________];
Facilities: [______________];
Medical benefits: [______________];
Other specific benefits: [______________].

4.5 The Sponsor agrees that it shall provide the Sportsperson with a new car, bearing the Sponsor's Logo, described below, for his personal and professional use throughout the Sponsorship Period, which shall be comprehensively insured, taxed and serviced entirely at The Sponsor's expense and shall remain the property of The Sponsor.

The car shall be: [description/colour].

4.6 The Sponsor agrees to arrange and pay for any travel and accommodation for the Sportsperson in respect of the promotion and endorsement of the Sponsor's Product and any other events or meetings agreed with the Sponsor under this Agreement. The Sponsor undertakes that all accommodation and all forms of travel shall be: [______________].

4.7 The Sponsor shall ensure that suitable comprehensive insurance cover is arranged for the Sportsperson and all items and materials provided under this Agreement for the duration of the Sponsorship Period at the Sponsor's sole cost. The Sponsor confirms that the Sportsperson's personal life insurance for the benefit of his estate shall not be less than: [figure/currency]. A copy of all relevant insurance policies shall be provided to the Sportsperson as soon as it is available.

4.8 The Sponsor agrees to provide the Sportsperson with reasonable notice of all promotional events and any other meetings at which the Sportsperson is required to attend under this Agreement.

4.9 The Sponsor agrees to provide the Sportsperson with samples of all proposed promotional, advertising, publicity, packaging and other material in which it is intended to use the name, image, endorsement or any other contribution in any form of the Sportsperson under this Agreement.

4.10 The Sponsor agrees that the name, image and endorsement of the Sportsperson shall not be used for any purpose other than the promotion and endorsement of the Sponsor's Product for the duration of the Sponsorship Period.

4.11 The Sponsor undertakes that it will not do anything or permit any third party to do anything which is likely to be derogatory, detrimental or damaging to the reputation of the Sportsperson. In the event that the Sportsperson advises the Company of any such material it will be withdrawn from the public and destroyed. The Company shall then negotiate in good faith with the Sportsperson to agree compensation for loss or damages together with any costs incurred.

4.12 The Sponsor acknowledges that this Agreement does not oblige the Sportsperson to make any personal appearances in any film, video or sound recording for the Sponsor in respect of the Sponsor's Product, including personal appearances on radio or television. Any such additional work shall be the subject of separate negotiation on each occasion.

4.13 The Sponsor confirms that it has full title and authority to enter into this Agreement and is not bound by any previous Agreement which adversely affects this Agreement.

4.14 The Sponsor undertakes that all material produced by the Sponsor under this Agreement will not be offensive or obscene in nature or derogatory or defamatory to any third party.

4.15 The Sponsor agrees to ensure that the size, shape, nature and use of the Sponsor's Logo and the Sponsor's Product will not infringe any statutes, rules, directives or guidelines currently in existence with regard to the following sports organisations: [____________] and [____________].

4.16 The Sponsor confirms that it shall be solely responsible for all costs incurred in respect of the production, distribution, promotion and exploitation of the Sponsor's Logo and the Sponsor's Product and that the Sportsperson shall not be liable for any such sums.

4.17 The Sponsor undertakes that the Sponsor's Product shall be safe for its intended use and shall comply with all statutes, regulations, directives and codes in force and that the Sportsperson shall not be responsible at any time in respect of any civil or criminal proceedings that may arise concerning the Sponsor's Product.

5. OBLIGATIONS OF THE SPORTSPERSON

5.1 The Sportsperson agrees to attend and participate to the best of his skill and ability at all events and occasions specified in the Events Schedule.

5.2 The Sportsperson confirms that he is a bona fide member of the following sports organisation: [____________].

5.3 The Sportsperson confirms that he has full title and authority to enter into this Agreement and is not bound by any previous agreement or professional rules and codes of conduct which adversely affects this Agreement.

5.4 The Sportsperson agrees to wear the clothing and use the equipment and car with the Sponsor's Logo provided by the Sponsor under this Agreement, as far as reasonably possible and appropriate at all competitions, promotional and televised events, appearances, press-calls, and any other organised sporting events held throughout the Sponsorship Period attended by the Sportsperson throughout the Territory.

5.5 The Sportsperson acknowledges that the Sponsor's Logo shall be on each item provided by the Sponsor to the Sportsperson under this Agreement.

5.6 The Sportsperson agrees that the Sponsor shall be entitled to use the Sportsperson's name, biography, photograph and fair likeness in respect of the packaging, promotion, publicity and advertising of the Sponsor's Product for the duration of the

Sponsorship Period throughout the Territory, provided that any other commercial exploitation of the Sportsperson's name, biography and fair likeness shall be subject to prior written agreement between the parties.

5.7 The Sportsperson acknowledges that the car shall remain the property of the Sponsor and shall be returnable to the Sponsor upon the termination or expiry of this Agreement.

5.8 The Sportsperson agrees that he shall be responsible for all his own national insurance, personal tax and value added tax which shall be due in consequence of this agreement.

5.9 The Sportsperson agrees to provide his services to the best of his skill and ability to ensure the fulfilment of his obligations under this Agreement. The Sportsperson further agrees to conduct himself in a fit and proper manner and agrees not to engage in any public activities which are detrimental, derogatory or offensive to the Sponsor or the Sponsor's Product.

5.10 The Sportsperson confirms that he is primarily resident in: [____________].

6. MISCELLANEOUS

INDEMNITY

6.1 The Sponsor undertakes to indemnify the Sportsperson against all liabilities, claims, demands, actions, costs, damages or loss arising out of any breach by the Sponsor of any of the terms of this Agreement.

CONFIDENTIALITY

6.2 The Sponsor and the Sportsperson shall not disclose to any third party any confidential business or future plans of the other party at any time acquired during the existence of this Agreement and no reference is to be made to the terms of this Agreement by either party in any advertising, publicity or promotional material without the prior written consent of the other party.

AMENDMENTS AND ALTERATIONS

6.3 This Agreement supersedes all previous agreements, representations or promises and sets out all the terms agreed between the parties. Any amendment or alteration to this Agreement must be in writing and signed by an authorised signatory of each party.

NO PARTNERSHIP OR EMPLOYMENT

6.4 This Agreement shall not be deemed to create any partnership or employment relationship between the parties.

NOTICES

6.5 Notices pursuant to this Agreement shall be in writing and must be served personally by courier or by registered post. Any notice shall be effective on the day it is received.

VALUE ADDED TAX

6.6 All sums payable under this Agreement are exclusive of any value added tax that may be payable by either party.

THIRD PARTY TRANSFERS

6.7 Neither party shall assign, transfer, charge or make over this Agreement or any of its rights or obligations without the prior written consent of the other party.

FORCE MAJEURE

6.8 No party shall be liable for its inability or delay in performing any of its obligations if caused by any reason beyond the reasonable control of the Sponsor or the Sportsperson, including ill-health of the Sportsperson, war, industrial action, floods or Acts of God. Either party shall, due to reasons beyond its control, be entitled to serve notice to suspend performance of its obligations for [10 days]. After such time the non-defaulting party may terminate the Agreement by notice in writing which shall be without prejudice to the rights and remedies of either party.

TERMINATION AND EXPIRY OF THE AGREEMENT

6.9 In addition to any other rights and remedies at law, this Agreement may be terminated by giving written notice to the other party who has breached this Agreement or defaulted in the following circumstances:

6.9.1 where the Sponsor has failed to account or make payments as required under this Agreement;

6.9.2 where the Sponsor or the Sportsperson has committed a serious breach of its obligations under this Agreement, unless the defaulting party rectifies the position, as far as reasonably possible, within: [____________];

6.9.3 where the Sponsor goes into voluntary or involuntary liquidation;

6.9.4 where the Sponsor is declared insolvent either in bankruptcy proceedings or other legal proceedings;

6.9.5 where an agreement with creditors has been reached by the Sponsor due to its failure or inability to pay its debts as they fall due;

6.9.6 where a receiver is appointed over the whole or part of the Sponsor's business;

6.9.7 where the Sportsperson is convicted of a serious criminal offence anywhere throughout the Territory, including a drink-driving offence which results in the Sportsperson being banned from driving or where the Sportsperson is convicted of a drug related offence; or

6.9.8 where the Sportsperson is found to be in serious breach of the rules of the sports organisation of which he is a member.

GOVERNING LAW

6.10 Any dispute, litigation or issues of construction should be subject to the exclusive jurisdiction of: [____________].

Attached to and forming part of this Agreement are:

Schedule 1. Sponsor's Logo
Schedule 2. Performance Related Payments
Schedule 3. Events List

[____________] Title/Name
[Sponsor]

[____________] Title/Name
[Sportsperson]

This Agreement is dated: [____________]

OUTLINE—SPONSORSHIP AGREEMENT BETWEEN SPONSOR AND PROFESSIONAL SPORTSPERSON

This is a sponsorship agreement between a Company and an individual professional Sportsperson. Special care should be taken not to jeopardise the amateur status of an individual which should be checked with the appropriate governing sports body at the time.

The Sponsor is providing a "Sponsorship Fee" for the non-exclusive services of the individual. The Sportsperson is agreeing not to enter into a sponsorship agreement with respect to the same or similar items as the Sponsor's product for the duration of the sponsorship period so the type of item should be stipulated, *i.e.* shoe. The parties should also list those specific companies with which the Sportsperson has agreed not to enter into a sponsorship agreement. There are two conflicts here, one with a similar product and another with a rival company. We have not provided consent for a medical, nor covered ill health by the Sportsperson except under force majeure. The indemnity is from the Sponsor and is not limited in size.

The Sponsor is also agreeing to pay a series of sums referred to as the "Performance Related Fee" which is linked to the individual's success in certain events. Schedule 2 should specify the amount, the event and the requirements for such payments to be made. For example, a payment may be due as a result of the individual winning a competition and/or achieving a record-breaking time or distance. The events list sets out all promotional events, competitions and meetings at which the Sportsperson is required to attend and participate including the times, dates and locations.

Under this Agreement the Sponsor is providing a branded product, whether clothing or equipment, which the individual, where appropriate, is agreeing to wear or use to the exclusion of all items of a similar nature for a specified period of time. The Sponsor would be entitled to use the Sportsperson's name, image and fair likeness for the promotion and advertising of the Sponsor's product. Personal television, film, video and radio appearances by the Sportsperson are the subject of separate negotiations. This should not be confused with the obligation of the Sportsperson to wear the sponsored equipment and clothing at televised events. A copy of the Sponsor's logo should be attached as Schedule 1.

The Sponsor is agreeing to arrange and pay for all travel and accommodation expenses of the individual for such work but it should be noted that there is no general expense clause. Other benefits provided include sports facilities, a car, personal insurance and medical cover.

AGREEMENT BETWEEN ON-SCREEN CONTRIBUTOR AND COMPANY

BETWEEN:

(1) [______________]
of [______________] (to be known as the Contributor in this Agreement)

AND

(2) [______________]
of [______________] (to be known as the Company in this Agreement).

IT IS AGREED as follows:

1. ENGAGEMENT OF CONTRIBUTOR

The Company and the Contributor agree that the Contributor shall provide his/her non-exclusive services to the Company for the Films as specified below.

2. DETAILS OF THE FILMS

The Company confirms that the Contributor is engaged to provide his/her services for the Films described as follows:

Title: [______________];
Number of episodes: [______________];
Duration of each episode: [______________];
Approximate broadcast/release date: [______________].

3. NATURE OF SERVICES

3.1 The Contributor agrees to provide the following services to the Company under this Agreement:

3.1.1 all necessary background and research work;
3.1.2 preparation of the Contributor's scripts;
3.1.3 presentation to camera as required; and
3.1.4 special requirements: [______________].

4. DETAILS OF REHEARSALS

Dates: [____________]

Times: [____________]

Locations: [____________]

5. DETAILS OF RECORDINGS/FILMING

Dates: [____________]

Times: [____________]

Locations: [____________]

6. CONTRIBUTOR'S FEES

In consideration of the services provided by the Contributor and the rights assigned to the Company under this Agreement the Company shall pay to the Contributor the fee of: [figure/currency].

7. EXPENSES

The Company agrees to pay all the Contributor's expenses reasonably and properly incurred in providing his/her services under this Agreement, subject to satisfactory receipts or records being produced subject to a total maximum of: [__________] and provided that any claim is made during the existence of this Agreement or written [one month] of the expiry or termination of this Agreement.

8. TRAVEL AND ACCOMMODATION

The Company agrees to arrange and pay for any travel and accommodation requested of the Contributor under this Agreement. The Company undertakes that, as far as possible, all accommodation shall be in a minimum of [a three-star hotel] and all forms of travel will be [business class].

9. INSURANCE

In respect of the Contributor's services the Company agrees to arrange and pay full and comprehensive insurance cover for the Contributor, including his/her personal belongings and shall provide the Contributor with a copy of such insurance policy upon request. The loss of life cover shall not be less than: [__________].

10. ADDITIONAL FEES

In the event that the Contributor is requested by the Company to provide services over and above those set out in clauses 3, 4 and 5. Then the Company undertakes to agree with the Contributor payment of an additional fee for such work.

11. PAYMENT OF FEES

11.1 The Company agrees to pay the Contributor's Fees as follows:

11.1.1 [____________] upon signature of this Agreement;
11.1.2 [____________] on or before [____________];
11.1.3 [____________] on or before [____________].

12. VALUE ADDED TAX, NATIONAL INSURANCE AND PERSONAL TAX

12.1 All fees are exclusive of value added tax. The Contributor agrees to be responsible for his/her own national insurance and personal tax. The Company agrees to make all payments required under this Agreement to the Contributor personally unless otherwise advised. The Company shall only be obliged to pay value added tax upon receipt of a formal invoice.

13. THE CONTRIBUTOR'S UNDERTAKINGS

13.1 The Contributor undertakes that he/she shall not disclose any confidential information concerning the business or future plans of the Company or relating to the Films to any third party acquired in the course of his/her engagement under this Agreement.

13.2 The Contributor undertakes that all his/her contributions to the Series will be original unless based upon or incorporating material specifically included at the request of the Company.

13.3 The Contributor undertakes that his/her contributions shall not contain anything which is an infringement of copyright or any other right of any third party or is defamatory or obscene or will expose the Company to criminal or civil proceedings or anything of an advertising nature unless specifically included in the Films at the request of the Company.

13.4 The Contributor undertakes that he/she shall observe all rules and regulations in force at any locations where he/she may be required to provide his/her services and shall carry out and observe all directions as may reasonably be given to him/her on behalf of the Company.

13.5 The Contributor agrees that the Company shall have the final editorial decision in aspect of the Films and shall be entitled to alter, amend, adapt, edit and delete the Films as it fits. The Company shall not be obliged to include the product of the services of the Contributor in the Films.

13.6 The Contributor agrees that the Company shall have the sole discretion as to the manner and method to be used in the production and exploitation of the Films and that no further sums shall be due to the Contributor except those set out in this Agreement.

13.7 The Contributor agrees that the Company shall be entitled to assign transfer sub-license or otherwise exploit any of the product of the services of the Contributor created under this Agreement.

14. THE COMPANY'S UNDERTAKINGS

14.1 The Company undertakes that the Contributor shall be entitled to the following on-screen credit at the end of the Films: [____________] and where applicable in any associated advertising, publicity and promotional material.

14.2 The Company undertakes that any material produced under this Agreement shall not be used in an offensive, defamatory or derogatory manner in respect of the Contributor.

14.3 The Company agrees to provide the Contributor with samples of all proposed promotional, advertising, publicity and packaging for which it is intended to use more than just the name of the Contributor.

14.4 The Company confirms and undertakes that it shall be the sole owner of and/or control all copyright and any other rights in the Films and that any exploitation of the Films shall not expose the Contributor to any criminal or civil proceedings.

14.5 The Company agrees that it will be solely responsible for the clearance and payment for all contractual, copyright, consent payment and other for obligations owed to third parties arising out of the production and exploitation of the Films.

15. COPYRIGHT

15.1 In consideration of the payments under this Agreement the Contributor assigns to the Company the sole and exclusive rights in all media whether now known or hereinafter invented in the Film(s) and part(s) including the soundtrack and in any other product of the services of the Contributor under this Agreement throughout the Territory for the full period of copyright and any extensions or renewals including but not limited to:

15.1.1 all forms of television, digital, cable, satellite;
15.1.2 all forms of video;
15.1.3 merchandising, publishing;
15.1.4 interactive, multi-media, electronic information, storage and dissemination.

15.2 The Contributor agrees on request to execute and sign any other documents which may be required at a later date to effect the assignment to the Company.

16. MORAL RIGHTS

In consideration of the payments under this Agreement the Contributor waives all moral rights except to the extent that the Contributor shall be given the credit set out in Clause 14.

17. ALTERATIONS AND AMENDMENTS

The parties agree that any representation, promise or undertaking, whether provided by either party in writing or verbally, shall not be binding unless specifically set out as a term of this Agreement. This Agreement sets out the entire terms agreed and any amendment or variation must be in writing and signed by both parties in one document.

18. GOVERNING LAW

This Agreement shall be subject to the Laws of England.

Signed by: [____________]
FOR AND ON BEHALF OF THE CONTRIBUTOR

Signed by: [____________]
FOR AND ON BEHALF OF THE COMPANY

Agreement dated: [____________]

OUTLINE—AGREEMENT BETWEEN ON-SCREEN CONTRIBUTOR AND COMPANY

The on-screen contributor is to make a small and non-dramatic presentation for a documentary, educational or game show programme. The details of the type of work, the recording dates and as such details as is known of the Films should be included in the contract.

The Contributor is only providing his non-exclusive services, and may work for any third party.

The Company will pay the fees and expenses and no further sums shall be due for any exploitation of the Films in any media. The final editorial decision is at the sole discretion of the Company.

All moral rights are waived except the right to a credit which must be specified. The Contributor is giving the Company all rights in all media and shall hold no copyright in the Films.

This Agreement is deliberately short to ensure that it is completed prior to the start of production.

AGREEMENT BETWEEN CONSULTANT AND COMPANY

AN AGREEMENT made this [____________] day of [____________]

BETWEEN:

(1) [____________]
of [____________] (to be known as the Consultant in this Agreement)

AND

(2) [____________]
of [____________] (to be known as the Company in this Agreement).

IT IS AGREED as follows:

1. ENGAGEMENT OF CONSULTANT

The Company and the Consultant agree that the Consultant shall provide his/her non-exclusive services to the Company for the Series as specified below.

2. PERIOD OF ENGAGEMENT

The period of the engagement of the Consultant by the Company shall commence on: [date] and continue until the completion of the Series but in any event not later than: [____________].

3. DETAILS OF THE SERIES

The Company confirms that the Consultant is engaged to provide his/her services for the Series described as follows:

Title of Series: [____________];
[____________] number of episodes of [____________] minutes each;
Proposed broadcast/release date: [____________];
Brief description of content: [____________].

4. NATURE OF SERVICES

4.1 The Consultant agrees to provide his/her specialist advice and knowledge as may be required under this Agreement in respect of the Series, including the following:

4.1.1 to prepare detailed background information and such other material that may from time to time be requested by: [name];
4.1.2 to review and report on the synopsis, scripts, stills and other content of the Series;
4.1.3 to co-operate with the writer and director as required;
4.1.4 to attend such meetings and filming as may be requested and agreed; and
4.1.5 other particular requirements: [____________].

5. THE CONSULTANT'S FEE

In consideration of the services provided by the Consultant under this Agreement and the rights assigned, the Company shall pay to the Consultant a fee of [____________].

The Company agrees to pay the Consultant's Fee as follows:

5.1.1 [____________] upon signature of this Agreement;
5.1.2 [____________] on or before: [____________];
5.1.3 [____________] on or before: [____________].

6. ADDITIONAL FEES

In addition to the Consultant's Fee in clause 5, the Company agrees to pay to the Consultant in respect of his/her attendance at any viewings, meetings and filming locations which may be agreed between the parties an additional daily fee of: [____________] which shall be paid for any work on any day. The Company agrees to pay the Consultant any additional daily fees within [14 days] of receipt of a suitable invoice for that work.

7. THE CONSULTANT'S UNDERTAKINGS

7.1 All information, advice and material provided to the Company by the Consultant shall, to the best of his knowledge and belief, be true and accurate.

7.2 Where requested by the Company and/or its legal advisors, the Consultant should assist in providing supporting documentation to support the matters upon which the Consultant has advised.

7.3 The Consultant is a professional: [____________] and a member of the following bodies: [____________].
The Consultant's professional qualifications are: [____________] and he is an expert in the field of: [____________].

7.4 The Consultant assigns all copyright and any other rights in the Series to the Company, whether in existence now or created in the future, in the product of his services under this Agreement in all media throughout the world, universe and outer space for the full period of copyright and any extensions or renewals.

7.5 The Consultant acknowledges that the final editorial decision in respect of the content and exploitation of the Series shall be at the sole discretion of the Company.

7.6 The Consultant agrees that his main role shall be to assist the Company in: [____________] but that he may be interviewed, filmed, or otherwise appear in sound or vision.

7.7 The Consultant acknowledges that the Company shall not be liable for any expenses, material charges, telephone, meals, insurance, travel, accommodation or otherwise unless specifically agreed in advance on each occasion or booked by the Company.

7.8 The Consultant shall not be entitled to any credit or acknowledgment unless he appears in sound or vision. Then the following credit shall appear in the Series: [____________].

7.9 The Consultant agrees that, notwithstanding any publicity or promotional material which may or will be issued, the Company shall be under no obligation to transmit or otherwise exploit the Series nor shall any further payments be due to the Consultant.

7.10 The Consultant agrees to provide a biography to allow photographs to be taken for a portrait, and to allow the Company to use his name in any publicity or promotional material relating to the Series.

7.11 The Consultant shall not order or pledge any goods or products on behalf of the Company.

7.12 The Consultant agrees that, during the continuance of this engagement under this Agreement, the Consultant shall carry out his obligations to the best of his skill and ability. The Consultant agrees to observe all directions and restrictions as may be reasonably given to him by the Company.

8. COMPANY'S UNDERTAKINGS

8.1 The Company confirms that it shall be solely responsible for any sums due in respect of the production and exploitation of the Series and that the Consultant shall not be liable for any such sums.

8.2 The Company shall ensure that the Series shall not include any reference to the Consultant in sound or vision which is likely to bring the Consultant into disrepute, is derogatory or is defamatory.

8.3 The Company shall only be liable for the Consultant fee in the event that it decides for any reason to end the production of the Series or not use the services of the Consultant.

8.4 The Company shall not seek any indemnity from the Consultant in respect of this Agreement and fully accepts that any risk or threat of legal proceedings arising from the Series or any exploitation is entirely at the Company's cost and expense.

9. VALUE ADDED TAX, NATIONAL INSURANCE AND PERSONAL TAX

All fees are exclusive of value added tax. The Consultant agrees to be responsible for his/her own personal insurance, national insurance and personal tax. The Company agrees to make all payments required under this Agreement to the Consultant personally unless otherwise advised. The Company shall only be obliged to pay value added tax upon receipt of a formal invoice.

10. NO RENEWAL

Any failure to renew or extend the terms of this Agreement following its expiry shall not constitute grounds for any claim or payments whatsoever to the Consultant.

11. NOTICES

Notices shall be in writing and may be by fax, e-mail, or any other method to the last notified address of the party.

12. TERMINATION

Upon expiry or termination of this Agreement the Consultant shall immediately arrange for the return of all Company property.

13. TIME OF THE ESSENCE

Both parties agree that all dates referred to in this Agreement shall be important.

14. AMENDMENTS

Any amendment or alteration to this Agreement must be in writing and signed by both parties.

15. GOVERNING LAW

This Agreement shall be subject to the laws of [____________].

SIGNED BY THE CONSULTANT: [____________] DATE: [____________]
Name/Title

SIGNED BY THE COMPANY: [____________] DATE: [____________]
Name/Title

OUTLINE—AGREEMENT BETWEEN CONSULTANT AND COMPANY

The consultant is providing his services to the production company in an advisory capacity in a specialist field. The consultant may be appearing on-screen in sound or vision, but it is uncertain. The consultant is expected to be an authority in his field and will be providing the production company with important background information and detail. The consultant is undertaking that, to the best of his knowledge and belief, all such material is true and accurate.

Although in most cases the distinction between a contract of service between an employee and an employer and a contract for services is easily recognisable, there is a large grey area, especially in respect of contracts concerning freelance or consultancy work.

There is an assignment of any rights that the Consultant may acquire during the course of this Agreement to the Company. Normally it is assumed under a contract of employment that the employer owns the rights, but this type of arrangement may cause confusion later so a full, all-media assignment avoids any claims for royalties when the Series is exploited elsewhere.

There are no indemnity or insurance provisions except that the Consultant is responsible for his own personal insurance. It is assumed but could be stated that the Company will have public liability insurance.

The threat of litigation is entirely at the Company's risk and cost, and the Company has agreed not to seek any indemnity from the Consultant.

If the Company decides not to use the services of the Consultant or to discontinue the series it shall only pay the Consultant fee, and not the additional daily fees.

There is no mention of moral rights, but the Consultant will get a credit if he appears in sound or vision, and the Company is agreeing not to be derogatory to or to defame the Consultant.

AGREEMENT BETWEEN RESEARCHER AND COMPANY

AGREEMENT DATED: [____________]

BETWEEN:

(1) [____________]
of [____________] (to be known as the Researcher in this Agreement)

AND

(2) [____________]
of [____________] (to be known as the Company in this Agreement).

IT IS AGREED as follows:

1. ENGAGEMENT OF RESEARCHER

The Company and the Researcher agree that the Researcher shall provide his/her exclusive services to the Company for the Series as specified below.

2. PERIOD OF ENGAGEMENT

The period of the engagement of the Researcher by the Company shall commence on the date of this Agreement and continue until: [date].

3. DETAILS OF THE SERIES

The Company confirms that the Researcher is engaged to provide his/her services for the Series entitled: [____________].

4. NATURE OF SERVICES

4.1 The Researcher agrees to carry out such work diligently and expeditiously to the best of his/her skill and ability as may be requested by the Company in respect of the Series, including the following responsibilities:

4.1.1 to provide detailed facts and research material and background information and to state the source of any such material;

4.1.2 to report on the existence of any stills, photographs, newspapers cuttings, film and video material and sound recordings and to include in the report ownership of copyright, any contractual consent, moral rights and credit requirements, the estimated cost of reproduction and copyright clearance payments, and the format and quality of any such material;

4.1.3 to trace and contact any individual or company as may be required and to arrange interviews and recordings if specifically requested to do so;

4.1.4 to co-operate with the producer and any assistant;

4.1.5 to attend such meetings, filming and recordings as may be requested and agreed;

4.1.6 to provide all reports on typed A4 paper; and

4.1.7 other particular requirements: [____________].

5. THE RESEARCHER'S FEE

5.1 In consideration of the services provided by the Researcher and the rights assigned under this agreement the Company shall pay to the Researcher a daily fee of [____________].

5.2 The Researcher acknowledges that the above daily fee shall be for an eight-hour day and pro-rata payments may be made where appropriate.

5.3 No overtime or additional fees shall be due unless specifically agreed between the parties in advance.

6. PAYMENT OF FEES

The Company agrees to pay the Researcher's Fee within seven days of the end of each working week following receipt of a suitable invoice setting out the hours and days worked by the Researcher and the details of all such work.

7. EXPENSES

The Researcher agrees to obtain the prior consent of the Company in respect of all expenses to be incurred in excess of: [____________] in any one week. The Company agrees to pay the Researcher's expenses reasonably and properly incurred for the purpose of this Agreement, subject to satisfactory receipts or records being produced upon request.

8. VALUE ADDED TAX, NATIONAL INSURANCE AND PERSONAL TAX

All fees are exclusive of value added tax. The Researcher agrees to be responsible for his/her own personal insurance, national insurance and personal tax. The Company agrees to make all payments required under this Agreement to the Researcher personally unless otherwise advised. The Company shall only be obliged to pay value added tax upon receipt of a formal invoice.

9. THE RESEARCHER'S UNDERTAKINGS

9.1 The Researcher undertakes that he/she shall not disclose any confidential information concerning the business or future plans of the Company to any third party acquired in the course of his/her engagement under this Agreement.

9.2 The Researcher undertakes that he/she shall observe all rules and regulations in force at any locations where he/she may be required to provide his/her services and shall carry out and observe all directions as may reasonably be given to him/her on behalf of the Company.

9.3 The Researcher undertakes that he/she shall not order any goods or services or commit or make payment on behalf of the Company without the prior consent of the Company.

10. THE COMPANY'S UNDERTAKINGS

10.1 The Company undertakes that the Researcher shall be entitled to the following on-screen credit in the Series: [____________].

10.2 The Company undertakes that the Researcher shall be required to provide a minimum of [____________] days work for the Series.

11. COPYRIGHT

The Researcher agrees to assign to the Company all present and future copyright and any other rights in the product of his/her services under this Agreement in all media throughout the world for the full period of the copyright and any extensions or renewals.

12. EDITORIAL CONTROL

The final editorial decision in respect of all matters relating to the Series shall be at the sole discretion of the Company.

13. ALTERATIONS AND AMENDMENTS

Any amendment or alteration to this Agreement must be in writing and signed by an authorised signatory of both parties.

14. GOVERNING LAW

This Agreement shall be subject to the Laws of England.

Signed by Researcher: [_______________] [Date]

Signed by Company: [_______________] [Date]

OUTLINE—AGREEMENT BETWEEN RESEARCHER AND COMPANY

The Researcher is being paid at a daily eight-hour rate by the Production Company. The Researcher is not verifying the truth of any material or information, he is only providing the source details. The Researcher is not giving any undertakings regarding any research material or its content but merely providing reference lists. This therefore follows that there should be no indemnity, moral rights, legal proceedings clauses. This type of arrangement is merely to establish that it is short term and temporary.

AGREEMENT BETWEEN FILM DIRECTOR AND COMPANY

AN AGREEMENT made this [____________] day of [____________]

BETWEEN:

(1) [____________]
of [____________] (to be known as the Director in this Agreement)

AND

(2) [____________]
of [____________] (to be known as the Company in this Agreement).

IT IS AGREED as follows:

1. DEFINITIONS

The words below are agreed to mean as follows:

1.1 "The Programme" shall be the film and any associated sound recording to be produced by the Company provisionally entitled: [____________] which shall be [____________] minutes in duration.

1.2 "The Director's Fee" shall be the sum of: [figure/currency].

1.3 "The Assignment Fee" shall be the sum of: [____________].

1.4 "The Production Period" shall commence on: [date] and shall continue throughout and in accordance with the Production Schedule but shall end in any event no later than: [date].

1.5 "The Production Schedule" shall be the agreed dates, times and locations of the Programme, including development, casting, pre-production, production, post-production (including post-shooting, rostrum camera work, shooting of titles and credits and dubbing) and delivery to the Company of a first class quality master tape of the Programme of broadcast quality in the following format: [____________]. A copy of the Production Schedule is attached to and forms part of this Agreement.

2. ENGAGEMENT OF DIRECTOR

The Company and the Director agree that in consideration of the Director's Fee, the Director shall provide his/her exclusive services as director and such other contributions as specified under this Agreement in respect of the Programme for the Production Period.

3. ASSIGNMENT OF COPYRIGHT

In consideration of the Assignment Fee, the Director assigns all present and future copyright and any other rights in all media throughout the world and universe in the product of his/her services and in the Programme and any other material created for the purpose of this Agreement to the Company for the full period of copyright and any extensions and renewals.

For the avoidance of doubt all media shall include but not be limited to television, internet, telephone, radio, video, computer software, publishing, merchandising.

4. MORAL RIGHTS

4.1 The Director asserts all moral rights in respect of the product of his services with respect to the Programme.

4.2 The Director asserts his right to be reasonably prominently and clearly identified as the Director of the Programme as follows: [____________].

4.3 The Director asserts his right to object to derogatory treatment of his work in the Programme.

4.4 The Company agrees that it shall be obliged to notify all third parties who may exploit the Programme of the assertion of moral rights by the Director.

4.5 In the event that the Programme is completed using the services of the Director, the Director shall be accorded a credit in the following manner: [____________] in all publicity, advertising and promotional material and in the end credits of the Programme.

4.6 The Director acknowledges that he shall not be entitled to a credit in the following circumstances:

4.6.1 Short extracts of the Programme to promote, advertise and/or exploit the Programme in any media including television and radio.

4.6.2 Where the advertising relates to work on which the Programme is based or the script or any members of the cast or other persons associated with the Programme.

4.6.3 Where due to lack of time or space in any media no other artist or person involved in the production of the Programme is credited.

4.6.4 Associated merchandising in any form.

4.7 The Director accepts that the Company shall not be responsible for the failure by third parties to provide a credit to the Director which was unintentional. Provided that when the Company becomes aware of any such failure or default it shall use its endeavours to remedy the position.

5. OBLIGATIONS OF THE DIRECTOR

5.1 The Director agrees to provide his/her exclusive services to the Company as the Director of the Programme for the Production Period and in accordance with the Production Schedule and to assist in such other matters including script revisions, meetings and other arrangements as may be required for the completion of the Programme.

5.2 The Director agrees to attend at such times, dates and locations as the Company may require and shall comply with all the rules in force at such locations and shall observe all directions as may reasonably be given to him/her on behalf of the Company.

5.3 The Director shall not alter, amend or deviate from the Production Schedule, the budget, or the final script provided by the Company without the prior consent of the Company in each case and any such consent may only be given by the following person: [Name].

5.4 The Director acknowledges that he/she is not entitled to order any goods or services, or to pledge or commit the credit of the Company nor make any payment or agree to pay any person whosoever without the prior consent of the Company.

5.5 In the event of disagreement between the Director and the Company, the Director acknowledges that the Company's decision shall be final.

5.6 The Director shall provide his/her services to the best of his/her technical and artistic skill and ability and shall perform his/her services diligently and expeditiously to ensure the completion of the Programme.

5.7 The Director confirms that he/she is a [British] subject or national of a Member State of the E.U.

5.8 The Director confirms that he/she has full authority to enter into and perform this Agreement and that he/she is not bound by any previous agreement which adversely effects this Agreement.

5.9 The Director undertakes that all the product of his/her services under this Agreement shall be original and will not infringe the copyright or any other rights of any third party, except where the work is based on or incorporates material of any third party which is included at the Company's request or with their knowledge.

5.10 The Director undertakes that all the product of his/her services under this Agreement will not contain any obscene, defamatory, derogatory or offensive material and will not expose the Company to any civil or criminal proceedings, except where the work is based on or incorporates material of any third party which is included at the Company's request or with their knowledge.

5.11 Subject to prior consultation, the Director agrees that the Company shall be entitled to use his/her name, biography, photograph and image in any commercial exploitation of the Programme.

5.12 The Director undertakes that he/she shall not at any time issue any statement to the media in respect of the Programme without the prior consent of the Company until: [date]. Nor shall the Director at any time disclose any confidential information concerning the business or future plans of the Company to any third party which is acquired during the Production Period.

5.13 The Director shall at the end of the Production Period deliver to the Company all material whatsoever prepared by him/her or in his/her possession in connection with the Programme. The Director may retain a copy of the script and Programme and such other material as may be agreed with the Company for his/her own personal reference.

5.14 The Director undertakes to keep the Company informed of his/her telephone number, address and whereabouts as far as possible during the Production Period.

5.15 The Director confirms that he/she shall be responsible for his/her own value added tax, national insurance and personal tax arising under this Agreement.

5.16 The Director agrees to submit to any medical examination required by the Company's insurers in order to provide suitable insurance for the Director throughout the Production Period. The medical shall be with a competent and professional doctor at the Company's sole cost. The medical report shall only be made available to the insurer, the Company and the Director.

5.17 The Director agrees that the artistic and editorial control of the Programme shall be at the sole discretion and decision of the Company. Provided that the Company shall in good faith consider the requests and proposals of the Director in respect of the production and exploitation of the Programme.

5.18 The Director acknowledges that the Company shall have the sole discretion as to the manner and method to be used in the production, manufacture, distributing and marketing of the Programme.

5.19 The Director agrees that during the course of this Agreement he shall act in a professional manner and shall do no act, or omit to do, or otherwise do anything which would bring the Company into disrepute.

5.20 The Company shall not be under any liability to the Director in respect of any claim for loss of publicity or opportunity to enhance the Director's reputation whether or not the Company stops production or exploitation of the Programme and/or the use of the Director's services.

6. OBLIGATIONS OF THE COMPANY

6.1 The Company agrees to engage the exclusive services of the Director for the Programme for the duration of the Production Period.

6.2 In consideration of the services of the Director, the Company agrees to pay the Director's Fee as follows:

6.2.1 [______________] upon signature of this Agreement;

6.2.2 [______________] upon the commencement of filming; and

6.2.3 [______________] at the end of the Production Period.

6.3 In consideration of the rights assigned under this agreement, the Company agrees to pay the Assignment Fee to the Director upon signature by both parties of this Agreement.

6.4 The Company agrees to reimburse the Director in respect of all expenses reasonably and properly incurred by the Director for the purpose of fulfilling his/her obligations under this Agreement, subject to satisfactory receipts or other records being produced on request which shall be no more than: [____________] per calendar month.

6.5 The Company shall arrange suitable insurance cover for the Director and his/her personal property for the benefit of the Director for the Production Period at the Company's cost and shall provide him/her with a copy of the insurance policy.

6.6 The Company agrees to arrange and pay for any travel and accommodation required by the Director under this Agreement and undertakes, as far as possible, that all accommodation will be in a minimum of [a three-star hotel] and all forms of travel will be: [____________].

6.7 The Company confirms that it shall be solely responsible for any sums due in respect of the production and exploitation of the Programme and the Director shall not be liable for any such payments.

6.8 The Company confirms that the script for the Programme shall be original and that the Company shall own or control the copyright and all other rights of any nature in the Programme whether in existence now or created in the future in [the world] for [the full period of copyright and any extensions or renewals].

7. MISCELLANEOUS

MUTUAL INDEMNITY

7.1 The Director and the Company mutually undertake to indemnify the other against all liabilities, claims, demands, actions, costs, damages and loss arising out of any breach by either party of any of the terms of this Agreement.

7.2 In the event of any claim, dispute, action, writ or summons in connection with clause 7.1, the Director and the Company agree to provide full details to the other party at the earliest opportunity and shall not settle any such matter without first consulting the other party.

CONFIDENTIALITY

7.3 The Director and the Company shall not disclose to any third party any confidential business or future plans of the other party at any time acquired during the existence of this Agreement and no reference is to be made to the terms of this Agreement by either party in any advertising, publicity or promotional material without the prior consent of the other party.

AMENDMENTS AND ALTERATIONS

7.4 This Agreement supersedes all previous agreements, representations or promises and sets out all the terms agreed between the parties. Any amendment or alteration to this Agreement must he in writing and signed by an authorised signatory of each party.

NO PARTNERSHIP OR EMPLOYMENT

7.5 This Agreement shall not be deemed to create any partnership or employment relationship between the parties.

NOTICES

7.6 Without prejudice to the right to serve notices by any other means any notice served under this Agreement shall be in writing. Any notice which has been sent by first class, pre-paid post shall be deemed to be received 48 hours thereafter (excluding Saturdays, Sundays and public holidays).

VALUE ADDED TAX

7.7 All sums payable under this Agreement are exclusive of any value added tax that may be payable by either party.

THIRD PARTY TRANSFERS

7.8 Neither party shall assign, transfer, charge or make over this Agreement or any of its rights or obligations without the prior written consent of the other party.

FORCE MAJEURE

7.9 Any party which is unable in whole or part to carry out its obligations under this Agreement shall promptly notify the other party. The reasons for such force majeure should be stated and the estimated time before the Agreement can be performed. In the event that the Agreement cannot be fulfilled or its obligations fulfilled for any reason beyond the reasonable control of either party including acts of war, industrial action, technical failure, floods and Acts of God. Then such failure shall be deemed not to be a breach of this Agreement. Where the situation is not and cannot be remedied within [three] months then either party may terminate this Agreement without prejudice to any legal rights and remedies.

ILL HEALTH OF DIRECTOR

7.10 In the event that the Director is unable to perform his/her obligations under this Agreement for any reason, including ill health, the Company shall be entitled to terminate this Agreement subject to making fair and reasonable payment to the Director in respect of services already provided under this Agreement.

TERMINATION

7.11 Each party may at its own discretion and without being required to pay compensation, terminate this Agreement by serving formal notice [two months] in advance. Where notice is given by the Company, the Director shall be entitled to payment of all the fees due under this Agreement to the end of the Production period.

GOVERNING LAW

7.12 This Agreement shall be governed by and construed in accordance with the Laws of England.

A PRODUCTION SCHEDULE IS ATTACHED TO AND FORMS PART OF THIS AGREEMENT.

Signed by the Director: [______________]
[Print name in full]

Signed by the Company: [______________]
[Print name in full]

Agreement Dated : [______________]

OUTLINE—AGREEMENT BETWEEN FILM DIRECTOR AND COMPANY

This Agreement is between a Director and a Production Company for a single Programme for television or video, although it could easily be adapted for a television series or a low-budget feature film.

The Director is to provide his exclusive services for the production period for a one-off director's fee which is paid in stages or it could be adjusted to be monthly. There is no restraint of work clause either during the production period or thereafter.

The Production Schedule should be as detailed as possible and form part of the Agreement with the Director.

The Director is assigning all copyright in all media in the product of his services to the Company, so he will retain no rights in the Programme.

The Director is asserting his moral rights, but accepts that there are some circumstances in which a credit may not be applicable.

Any deviation by the Director from the production schedule, budget or script requires the consent of a particular named person from the Company.

The Director accepts that the decision of the Company shall be final if there is any conflict of opinion. The Company agreeing to consult with the Director and consider his views.

No additional sum of compensation shall be due if the Company stops production or no longer wishes to use the Director.

The Company will pay the Director's expenses subject to a monthly limit and will also arrange insurance cover. The Director accepts that he will attend a medical examination for this purpose. The Director will not be entitled to any other sums or royalties from the exploitation of the Programme in any media.

In the event that the Director is unable through ill health or other reason to carry out his duties, the Company may end the contract provided they agree a reasonable payment for work that he has completed.

GENERAL RELEASE FORM

1. PRODUCTION COMPANY: [Name]
   Address: [____________]
   Fax/e-mail: [____________] Tel.: [____________]
   Contact Person: [____________]

2. CONTRIBUTOR: [Name]
   Address: [____________]
   Fax/e-mail: [____________] Tel.: [____________]
   Contact Person: [____________]

3. The Production Company has [filmed/recorded/photographed/interviewed] the Contributor who has carried out the following work on the [subject]: [List full details].

4. In consideration of the work by the Contributor the Production Company is to pay a fee of: [figure/currency] by: [date] in: [cash/cheque/other] to the Contributor which shall be in full and final settlement. No further sums of any nature for any reason shall be due to the Contributor for the provision of his/her services or the exploitation of the material in any media at any time.

5. The Contributor understands that the Production Company shall not be obliged to use, keep, or exploit the material created under this Agreement, nor shall it be obliged to provide a credit or acknowledgment to the Contributor.

6. The Contributor agrees that the Production Company may alter, adapt or edit the material created under this Agreement, and market and exploit it entirely at the Production Company's sole discretion.

7. The Production Company agrees that it shall not use the material [or permit others to do so] in any way which is derogatory of or is likely to impugn the reputation of the Contributor.

8. The Contributor assigns to the Production Company all present and future copyright and any other rights in all media in the product of his services and any material created under this Agreement throughout the world, outer space and the universe for the full period of copyright and any extensions or renewals. All media shall include but not be limited to television, video, radio, publishing, internet, merchandising, computer software.

9. The Contributor agrees that he shall be responsible for his own insurance, personal tax, and expenses which may arise under this Agreement.

Signed by Contributor: [____________] Date: [____________]

Signed by Production Company: [____________] Date: [____________]

If Contributor is under 18 signed by Parent/Guardian: [____________]

OUTLINE—GENERAL RELEASE FORM

This is a general release form, mainly used for members of the public who appear in a programme in more than just the background. This is a contract like any other and to be enforceable there must be some quid pro quo or consideration. The consideration need not be adequate but should be more than token. It should also be borne in mind that a minor under the age of 18 cannot provide his legally binding consent and the signature of a parent or guardian would be required. The individual signing the Agreement should be provided with a copy of the signed document.

There is no indemnity, moral rights, or force majeure. You may wish to delete the reference to not impugning the character of the Contributor. However, if the person is actively misled as to the use of the material, then this document may be invalid.

The Contributor is responsible for his own insurance, tax, and no further sums are to be paid for exploitation of the material created.

There is a full assignment clause giving all rights in all media to the Production Company.

AGREEMENT BETWEEN COMPANY AND PRESENTER FOR SERIES WITH PROFIT SHARE

AN AGREEMENT made this [____________] day of [____________]

BETWEEN:

(1) [____________]
of [____________] (to be known as the Presenter in this Agreement)

AND

(2) [____________]
of [____________] (to be known as the Company in this Agreement).

IT IS AGREED as follows:

1. DEFINITIONS

The words below are agreed to mean as follows:

1.1 "The Series" shall be the series of films and any associated sound recordings based on the Treatment and the Scripts entitled [____________] comprising of [____________] episodes, each of which shall be [____________] minutes in duration.

1.2 "The Treatment" shall be the summary of each of the episodes of the Series based on [____________].
A copy of the Treatment is attached to and forms part of this Agreement.

1.3 "The Scripts" shall be the draft and final scripts based on The Treatment to be prepared by The Presenter.

1.4 "The Presenter's Fee" shall be the sum of [____________].

1.5 "The Presenter's Royalties" shall be [____________] percentage of The Nett Receipts.

1.6 "The Key Personnel" shall be as follows:

1.6.1 the Producer: [____________];
1.6.2 the Director: [____________];
1.6.3 the Narrator: [____________];

1.6.4 Senior Cameraman: [____________];
1.6.5 Editor: [____________];
1.6.6 Any other: [____________].

1.7 "The Term of the Engagement" shall commence on: [date] and shall continue until: [date].

1.8 "The Production Schedule" shall be the agreed dates, times and locations of making the Series, including pre-production, production and post-production. A copy of the Production Schedule is attached to and forms part of this Agreement.

1.9 "The Gross Receipts" shall be the total proceeds from the exploitation of the Series and any part(s) throughout the Territory at any time received by or credited to the Company or its sub-agents or its sub-licensees after the deduction of the Sales Tax and any value added tax paid by the Company.

1.10 "The Production Costs" shall be the total costs, whether direct or indirect, of making the Series, including all items necessary for the development, pre-production, production, post-production and delivery of the Series (including the Presenter's Fee) which are not recovered from any third party.

1.11 "The Distribution Expenses" shall be the following costs reasonably and properly expended in respect of the exploitation of the Series by the Company which are not recouped from any third party:

1.11.1 duplication such as prints, duplicate negatives, cassettes (including repairs and replacements);
1.11.2 delivery, storage, shipping, customs duties, freight, handling charges and insurance;
1.11.3 making trailers of the Series;
1.11.4 publicity and advertising material;
1.11.5 copyright and music clearance;
1.11.6 distributor's commission;
1.11.7 dubbing, editing and subtitling for exploitation to a foreign country;
1.11.8 any other costs: [____________].

1.12 "The Nett Receipts" shall be the Gross Receipts less the Production Costs and the Distribution Expenses.

1.13 "The Sales Tax" shall be any sales or other taxes levied by any Member State of the E.U. government or foreign authority on the sale or supply of the Series which form a distinct element in the sale or rental price and which is recovered as part of the price, directly or indirectly, by the Company.

1.14 "The Territory" shall be all countries, bases and locations throughout the world, universe and outer space.

1.15 "The Television Rights" shall mean the right to broadcast, transmit, deliver, provide the Series on all forms of television in existence now or created in the future whatever the method of supply of the sound and vision including but not limited to cable, satellite, digital and over the air and/or whatever the method of payment is required or not as the case may be such as rental, subscription, free, pay per view or otherwise.

1.16 "The Videogram Rights" shall mean the right to transfer, manufacture and duplicate the Series by means of electronic reproduction in the form of any disc or magnetic tape (including but not limited to cassettes, cartridges or reel to reel) which consists of a sequence of visual images, with or without sound and/or subtitles, capable of being shown as a moving picture and to sell, rent, supply, distribute and have distributed the Series in any such form for private home use only by the public.

1.17 "The Non-Theatric Rights" shall mean the right to permit or license, sale or hire the exhibition of the Series to non-paying audiences in all formats in business and commercial industries and organisations of an educational, cultural, religious, charitable and social nature, including but not limited to schools, churches, evening institutions, museums, hospitals, prisons, summer camps, drama groups, film societies, professional associations, public libraries, colleges, universities, hotels, private clubs.

1.18 "The Theatric Rights" shall mean the right to exhibit the Series to audiences where a charge for admission is made, including but not limited to public and private cinemas, concert and lecture halls and arenas.

2. ENGAGEMENT OF PRESENTER

The Company and the Presenter agree that in consideration of the Presenter's Fee and the Presenter's Royalties, the Presenter shall provide his/her exclusive services as principal presenter for the Series and provide such other contributions as may be set out in this Agreement for the Term of The Engagement.

3. ASSIGNMENT OF RIGHTS

3.1 In consideration of the Presenter's Fee and the Presenter's Royalties, the Presenter assigns to the Company the Television Rights, the Videogram Rights, the Theatric Rights and the Non-Theatric Rights in the product of his/her services in the Series (including the scripts and sound recordings) under this Agreement throughout the Territory for the full period of copyright and any extensions and renewals thereto.

3.2 The Company agrees that all rights not specifically assigned to the Company in Clause 3.1 are reserved by the Presenter.

4. ASSERTION OF THE PRESENTER'S MORAL RIGHTS

The Presenter asserts all his/her moral rights in respect of the Series, the Company and any third parties or successors in title. The Presenter asserts that he/she must be identified in the form and style: [____________] in respect of the Series, and all copies and any adaptations whether during the Term of the Engagement or not. The identification must be clear and sufficiently prominent for him/her to be brought to the attention of the public.

5. OBLIGATIONS OF THE PRESENTER

5.1 The Presenter agrees to provide his/her exclusive services to the Company for the Term of The Engagement at such times, dates, and locations as the Company may reasonably require, subject to sufficient prior notice and shall comply with all the rules in force at such locations and shall observe all reasonable directions as may be given to him/her on behalf of the Company in respect of the Series by: [____________].

5.2 In addition to presenting the Series, the Presenter agrees to assist in background research work and to prepare and write the Scripts for the Series.

5.3 The Presenter agrees to be available for the post-production of the Series for any work which may be necessary for a period of up to [two working days] and thereafter on terms to be agreed.

5.4 The Presenter confirms that be/she is a British subject or national of a Member State of the E.U. and will remain so during the Term of the Engagement.

5.5 The Presenter confirms that he/she has full authority to enter into and perform this Agreement and that he/she is not bound by any previous agreement which adversely affects this Agreement.

5.6 The Presenter undertakes that all the products of his/her services under this Agreement shall be original and will not infringe the copyright or any other right of any third party, except where the work is based on or incorporates material of any third party which is included at the Company's request or is in the public domain.

5.7 The Presenter undertakes that all the products of his/her services under this Agreement will not contain any obscene or defamatory material and will not expose the Company to civil or criminal proceedings, except where the work is based on or incorporates material of any third party which is included at the Company's request or is in the public domain.

5.8 Subject to prior consultation the Presenter agrees that the Company shall be entitled to use his/her name, biography, photograph, image, signature and recordings in any commercial exploitation of the Series under this Agreement.

5.9 The Presenter agrees to keep the Company, as far as reasonably possible, informed of his/her address, whereabouts and telephone number during the Term of the Engagement.

5.10 The Presenter agrees that his/her consent as may be required under [the Copyright, Designs and Patents Act 1988] is provided for the purpose of the exercise of the rights assigned under this Agreement.

5.11 The Presenter agrees that he/she shall be responsible for all his/her own national insurance, personal tax and value added tax which may become due as a consequence of this Agreement.

5.12 The Presenter agrees that the Company shall have the sole discretion as to the manner and method to be used in producing, marketing and exploiting the Series.

6. OBLIGATIONS OF THE COMPANY

6.1 The Company agrees to engage the exclusive services of the Presenter for the Term of the Engagement and confirms that the Presenter shall be the principal presenter of the Series.

6.2 The Company agrees to produce the Series using the Key Personnel in accordance with the Treatment and the Production Schedule and confirms that the Series will be in colour, in the English language and primarily in the following format: [____________].

6.3 In consideration of the rights assigned under this Agreement, the Company undertakes that it shall pay the Presenter's Fee to the Presenter as follows: [____________].

6.4 The Company undertakes that it shall pay the Presenter's Royalties to the Presenter within [14 days] of the last day of June and December in each year.

6.5 The Company agrees to arrange and pay for any travel and accommodation for the Presenter required by the Company under this Agreement which shall be of a standard acceptable to the Presenter.

6.6 The Company agrees to pay or reimburse the Presenter in respect of all expenses reasonably and properly incurred in the provision of the services under this Agreement, including taxis, clothes and hairdressing, subject to satisfactory receipts or records being produced upon request.

6.7 The Company undertakes that it shall arrange suitable insurance cover for the Presenter and his/her personal property for the benefit of the Presenter during the Term of the Engagement and shall provide the Presenter with a copy of the policy upon request.

6.8 The Company agrees to provide the Presenter with reasonable notice of all alterations to the Production Schedule and any meetings and events which the Presenter is required to attend under this Agreement.

6.9 The Company and its sub-agents and sub-licensees shall keep full and accurate books of account, records and contracts showing the Gross Receipts, the Production Costs, the Distribution Expenses, the Nett Receipts, the Sales Tax and the Presenter's Royalties in respect of the commercial exploitation of the Series.

6.10 Within [14 days] of the last day of June and December in each year the Company shall provide a detailed report to the Presenter with a full breakdown of the exploitation of the Series setting out the Gross Receipts, the Production Costs, the Nett Receipts, the Distribution Expenses, the Presenter's Royalties and the Sales Tax.

6.11 The Company agrees that the Presenter shall be entitled to arrange for an annual audit to inspect and make copies of the Company's books of account, records, contracts and any other relevant material in order to verify the sums due to the Presenter.

6.12 The Company confirms that it shall be solely responsible for any sums due in respect of the production and exploitation of the Series and that the Presenter shall not be liable for any such payments.

6.13 The Company agrees to provide the following on-screen credit to the Presenter in the Series and in any publicity, promotional or packaging material in respect of the marketing and distribution of the Series: [____________] and the following copyright notice in respect of the Scripts: [____________].

6.14 The Company agrees to provide at its sole cost copies and samples of any proposed publicity, promotional, advertising and packaging material in respect of the exploitation of the Series upon request by the Presenter.

6.15 The Company agrees that in the Series and in all publicity, advertising and exploitation no other party than the Company shall have a more dominant, frequent or greater allocation of image or name than the Presenter.

6.16 The Company agrees that the Presenter shall only be liable for any breach of the undertakings by the Presenter given in this Agreement. In the event that the Company is to seek any indemnity from the Presenter, it agrees that it must promptly notify the Presenter of any claim or legal proceeding and make no admission or settlement proposal unless the Presenter has had reasonable opportunity to comment on and assist in any such matter.

6.17 The Company accepts and agrees that it shall be solely responsible for the legal consequences and liabilities that may arise in respect of the content and exploitation of the Series, and that where any claim, action, loss or damage results in the Presenter incurring legal costs that the Company shall pay all reasonable legal costs and expenses.

7. MISCELLANEOUS

CONFIDENTIALITY

7.1 The Presenter and the Company shall not disclose to any third party any confidential business or future plans of the other party at any time acquired during the existence of this Agreement and no reference is to be made to the terms of this Agreement by either party in any advertising, publicity or promotional material without the prior consent of the other party.

AMENDMENTS AND ALTERATIONS

7.2 This Agreement supersedes all previous agreements, representations or promises and sets out all the terms agreed between the parties. Any amendment or alteration to this Agreement must be in writing and signed by an authorised signatory of each party.

NO PARTNERSHIP OR EMPLOYMENT

7.3 This Agreement shall not be deemed to create any partnership or employment relationship between the parties.

NOTICES

7.4 Notices pursuant to the Agreement shall be by hand or first class registered or recorded post addressed as follows:

The Company: [Address] to [Name]
The Presenter: [Address] to [Name].

VALUE ADDED TAX

7.5 All sums payable under this Agreement are exclusive of any value added tax that may be payable by either party.

THIRD PARTY TRANSFERS

7.6 Neither party shall assign, transfer, charge or make over this Agreement or any of its rights or obligations without the prior written consent of the other party.

FORCE MAJEURE

7.7 In the event that this Agreement cannot be performed or its obligations fulfilled for any reason beyond the reasonable control of either party including war, industrial action, floods or Acts of God then such non-performance or failure to fulfil its obligations shall be deemed not to be a breach of this Agreement. In the event that this Agreement cannot be performed or its obligations fulfilled for any reason beyond either party's reasonable control for a continuous period of [three] months, then either party may, at its discretion, terminate this Agreement by notice in writing at the end of that period.

MEDIATION

7.8 If any dispute or difference of any nature shall occur which cannot be resolved by negotiation between the parties then, prior to the start of any legal proceedings, the parties agree to appoint a mediator at the cost of both parties to resolve the matter. The decision of the mediator is not binding, but the parties must agree in advance in writing as to the allocation and liability of the cost.

GOVERNING LAW

7.9 This Agreement shall be construed and interpreted in accordance with [European Law] and subject to the jurisdiction of: [____________].

NO RENEWAL

7.10 Any failure to renew or extend the terms of this Agreement shall not constitute grounds for any claim or payment whatsoever.

8. TERMINATION

8.1 The Presenter shall on expiry or termination of this Agreement arrange for the collection by the Company of any property which is in his possession or control belonging to the Company. The Presenter may keep some material for personal reference only.

8.2 The Company shall have the right by notice in writing to end this Agreement if the Presenter is unavailable through ill health or any other reason for more than [14 days] to provide his services as agreed.

8.3 The Presenter shall have the right by notice in writing to end this Agreement if the Production Schedule is delayed by more than [one month] or the Company is about to be wound up, or a receiver appointed, or is taken over, or has been publicly discredited.

ATTACHED TO AND FORMING PART OF THIS AGREEMENT:

SCHEDULE A: TREATMENT
SCHEDULE B: PRODUCTION SCHEDULE

Signed by the Presenter: [____________]

Signed by the Company: [____________]

OUTLINE—AGREEMENT BETWEEN COMPANY AND PRESENTER FOR SERIES WITH PROFIT SHARE

This Agreement is between a presenter and a production company for a series of programmes drafted mainly in favour of the Company. The Presenter is providing his exclusive services to the Production Company for the duration of the term of his engagement and would be available, as required, during the post-production.

The Presenter is expected to be the author of the draft and final scripts and involved in the choice of locations and key personnel.

The Production Company is agreeing to pay the Presenter's fee and a percentage of the nett receipts of any income received from the exploitation of the Series throughout the world. The nett receipts are calculated by deducting the production costs and the distribution expenses from the gross receipts. The Presenter is not assigning all rights in the Series to the Company, only the television rights, together with the videogram, theatric and non-theatric rights. All other rights are reserved. The non-theatric definition could be expanded to cover closed circuit TV on shops, aeroplanes and oil rigs, otherwise it falls within the video rights.

The Presenter asserts his moral rights but there is no specific reference to derogatory treatment.

The persons who can give directions to the Presenter should be named (or their level of position).

If the Presenter is writing scripts then a credit and copyright notice should be agreed with the Company.

There is no limit on the Presenter's expense account which the Company is paying.

It is not a requirement that there be a medical for insurance purposes.

The Presenter has no right of approval in respect of the exploitation of the Series, but copies of marketing material will be provided on request.

The production schedule should be sufficiently detailed so that the workload required is clear.

APPOINTMENT OF MERCHANDISING AGENT

BETWEEN:

(1) [____________]
of [____________] (to be known as the Licensor in this Agreement)

AND

(2) [____________]
of [____________] (to be known as the Agent in this Agreement).

IT IS AGREED as follows:

1. DEFINITIONS

The words below are agreed to mean as follows:

1.1 "The Character" shall be the original concept and novel idea for a character which is briefly described as follows:

Name of Character: [____________];
Trademark/Logo: [____________].

Full details of the Character are attached to and form part of this Agreement.

1.2 "The Licensed Articles" shall be any licensed product based on or derived from the Character to be produced and distributed under agreements to be negotiated and concluded by the Agent or any sub-agent or sub-licensee.

1.3 "The Licence Fee" shall be the sum of: [figure/currency].

1.4 "The Territory" shall be the United Kingdom of Great Britain, Northern Ireland, the Republic of Ireland, the Channel Islands and the Isle of Man.

1.5 "The Licence Period" commences on the [date of this Agreement] and shall continue until: [date].

1.6 "The Agent's Commission" shall be the following percentage of the Gross Receipts: [figure] per cent [__________%].

1.7 "The Gross Receipts" shall be the total proceeds from the exploitation of the Licensed Articles throughout the Territory at any time directly or indirectly received by or credited to the Agent or any sub-agent or sub-licensee after the deduction of any value added tax.

1.8 "The Nett Receipts" shall be the Gross Receipts less the Agent's Commission.

2. ENGAGEMENT OF THE AGENT

2.1 In consideration of the Agent's Commission,the Agent agrees to provide his/her non-exclusive services to the Licensor for the Licence Period throughout the Territory.

2.2 In consideration of the Nett Receipts, the Licensor agrees to engage the exclusive services of the Agent for the Licence Period throughout the Territory and grants to the Agent the sole and exclusive right to negotiate and conclude agreements for the manufacture, distribution and sale of the Licensed Articles and the associated trade mark or logo for the Licence Period throughout the Territory.

2.3 The Agent acknowledges that he/she shall not he entitled to commit the Licensor to any agreement, whether in writing or not, without the prior consent of the Licensor and that all licence agreements must be in writing and may only be signed and authorised by the Licensor.

3. OBLIGATIONS OF THE AGENT

3.1 The Agent shall provide his/her services to the best of his/her skill and ability and shall perform all services diligently to ensure that the Character is commercially exploited on the best possible terms.

3.2 The Agent shall, as far as possible, keep the Licensor fully informed on a regular basis as regards any negotiations with any third party in respect of the Licensed Articles.

3.3 In consideration of the rights granted under this Agreement, the Agent shall pay to the Licensor the Licence Fee as follows:

3.3.1 [____________] upon signature of this Agreement;
3.3.2 [____________] on or before [____________].

3.4 The Agent acknowledges that the Licence Fee is not returnable and is not to be off-set against the Gross Receipts.

3.5 The Agent undertakes that he/she shall pay the Nett Receipts to the Licensor within [14 days] of the last day of March, June September and December in each year.

3.6 The Agent and his/her sub-agents and sub-licensees shall keep full and accurate books of account, records and contracts and prices showing all dealings of the Licensed Articles, including the total number of units of the Licensed Articles manufactured, distributed and sold, whether by wholesale or retail, distributed without charge for promotional purposes and all units lost, damaged or stolen and the calculation of the Gross Receipts, the Agent's Commission and the Nett Receipts.

3.7 Within [14 days] of the last day of March, June, September and December in each year, the Agent shall provide a detailed report to the Licensor showing all dealings of the Licensed Articles including the total number of units of the Licensed Articles manufactured, distributed and sold whether by wholesale or retail, all prices and details of units distributed without charge for promotional purposes and all units lost, damaged or stolen and the calculation of the Gross Receipts, the Agent's Commission and the Nett Receipts.

3.8 The Agent agrees that the Licensor shall be entitled to arrange for an annual audit to inspect and make copies of the Agent's books of account, records, contracts and any other relevant material in order to verify the sums due to the Licensor.

3.9 The Agent agrees to ensure that any third party shall agree to provide the following credit, copyright notice, trademark or logo to the Licensor in respect of the Licensed Articles and in all publicity, advertising, promotional and packaging material in respect of the marketing and distribution of the Licensed Articles: [____________].

3.10 The Agent agrees to ensure that all third parties to be licensed by the Licensor under this Agreement shall agree that the prior written approval of the Licensor shall be required to approve The Licensed Articles prior to manufacture and distribution.

3.11 The Agent agrees to ensure that all third parties to be licensed by the Licensor under this Agreement shall agree that the prior written approval of the Licensor shall be required to approve such samples of the Licensed Articles in the exact form and material in which such third party proposes to manufacture, distribute and sell any of the Licensed Articles.

3.12 The Agent agrees to ensure that all third parties to be licensed by the Licensor under this Agreement shall agree that the prior written approval of the Licensor shall be required to approve all publicity, promotional, advertising and packaging material in respect of the Licensed Articles.

3.14 The Agent acknowledges and agrees to ensure that all third parties to be licensed by the Licensor under this Agreement shall agree that all copyright and any other rights in the Character and any trademark or logo, together with any goodwill, shall remain the sole property of the Licensor and that the Agent and all such third parties shall not acquire any rights in the Character or in any associated trademark, logo, title, artwork and any developments or variations thereto.

3.15 The Agent acknowledges that he/she is solely responsible for all costs he/she may incur in respect of his/her services under this Agreement.

3.16 The Agent agrees to ensure that all third parties to be licensed by the Licensor under this Agreement shall agree to undertake that all the Licensed Articles shall be safe for their intended use and shall comply with all applicable statutes, regulations, directives and codes in force and that prior to distribution to the public liability comprehensive insurance cover shall be arranged for not less than: [____________] per claim in each case.

3.17 The Agent acknowledges that the Licensor shall be entitled, upon request, to be provided with a copy of any contract, record, document or other material in any form in the possession or under the control of the Agent relating to the Licensor or the Licensed Articles.

3.18 The Agent confirms that he/she has full authority to enter into and perform this Agreement and that he/she is not bound by any previous agreement which adversely affects this Agreement.

3.19 The Agent acknowledges that he/she is not entitled to negotiate or promote in any manner or form the commercial interests of the Character outside the Territory, unless specifically agreed in advance with the Licensor.

3.20 The Agent agrees that all sums received in respect of the exploitation of the Character under this Agreement shall be deposited in a separate account at a bank to be agreed with the Licensor. Further that the Licensor shall be permitted access at all times to statements of the account directly with the bank. The Agent shall not be entitled to create any charge or lien over the monies.

3.21 The Agent acknowledges that he is not acquiring any copyright or any other rights in the Character and/or any Licensed Articles and/or any logo, trademark, or otherwise which shall remain with and belong solely to the Licensor.

4. OBLIGATIONS OF THE LICENSOR

4.1 The Licensor confirms that he/she is the original creator and sole owner of or controls all copyright and any other rights in the Character, which are granted under this Agreement.

4.2 The Licensor confirms that he/she has full title and authority to enter into this Agreement and is not bound by any previous Agreement which adversely affects this Agreement.

4.3 The Licensor confirms that the Character does not contain any obscene or defamatory material and will not expose the Agent to any civil or criminal proceedings.

4.4 The Licensor confirms that the Character does not contain any material which infringes the copyright or any other rights of any third party in the Territory.

4.5 Subject to prior approval, the Licensor agrees that the Agent shall be entitled to use the Licensor's name, biography, photograph and image in the promotion and advertising of the Character.

4.6 The Licensor agrees that he/she shall be responsible for all national insurance, personal tax and value added tax which shall be due in consequence of this Agreement.

4.7 The Licensor agrees to supply on loan such copies of artwork of the Character and any trademark, logo or other credit which may be required by the Agent for the purposes of this Agreement.

4.8 The Licensor agrees that all sums due under any licence agreements shall be paid direct to the Agent.

5. MISCELLANEOUS

MUTUAL INDEMNITY

5.1 The Licensor and the Agent mutually undertake to indemnify the other against all liabilities, claims, demands, actions, costs, damages or loss arising out of any breach by either party of any of the terms of this Agreement.

5.2 In the event of any claim, dispute, action, writ or summons in connection with clause 5.1, the Licensor and the Agent agree to provide full details to the other party at the earliest opportunity and shall not settle any such matter without first consulting the other party.

CONFIDENTIALITY

5.3 The Licensor and the Agent shall not disclose to any third party any confidential business or future plans of the other party at any time acquired during the existence of this Agreement and no reference is to be made to the terms of this Agreement by either party in any advertising, publicity or promotional material without the prior consent of the other party.

AMENDMENTS AND ALTERATIONS

5.4 This Agreement supersedes all previous agreements, representations or promises and sets out all the terms agreed between the parties. Any amendment or alteration to this Agreement must be in writing and signed by an authorised signatory of each party.

NO PARTNERSHIP OR EMPLOYMENT

5.5 This Agreement shall not be deemed to create any partnership or employment relationship between the parties.

NOTICES

5.6 Any notice served under this Agreement shall be in writing and the sender must be able to provide proof that it was received.

VALUE ADDED TAX

5.7 All sums payable under this Agreement are exclusive of any value added tax that may be payable by either party.

THIRD PARTY TRANSFERS

5.8 Neither party shall assign, transfer, charge or make over this Agreement or any of his/her rights or obligations without the prior written consent of the other party.

FORCE MAJEURE

5.9 In the event that this Agreement cannot be performed or its obligations fulfilled for any reason beyond the reasonable control of either party including war, industrial action, floods or Acts of God then such non-performance or failure to fulfil its obligations shall be deemed not to be a breach of this Agreement. In the event that this Agreement cannot be performed or its obligations fulfilled for any reason beyond either party's reasonable control for a continuous period of [six] months, then either party may, at its discretion, terminate this Agreement by notice in writing at the end of that period.

TERMINATION AND EXPIRY OF THE AGREEMENT

5.10 In addition to any other rights and remedies at law either party specified below may, by giving written notice to the other party, terminate this agreement on the following grounds:

- 5.10.1 where the Agent has failed to account or make payments as required under this Agreement;
- 5.10.2 where either party has committed a serious breach of his/her obligations under this Agreement, unless such party rectifies the position, as far as reasonably possible, within: [____________];
- 5.10.3 where the Agent goes into voluntary or involuntary liquidation;
- 5.10.4 where the Agent is declared insolvent, either in bankruptcy proceedings or other legal proceedings;
- 5.10.5 where an agreement with creditors has been reached by the Agent due to his/her failure or inability to pay his/her debts as they fall due; or
- 5.10.6 where a receiver is appointed over the whole or part of the Agent's business.

GOVERNING LAW

5.11 This Agreement shall be subject to the Laws of England.

ATTACHED TO AND FORMING PART OF THIS AGREEMENT ARE DETAILS OF THE CHARACTER.

Signed by: [____________]
FOR AND ON BEHALF OF THE LICENSOR

Signed by: [____________]
FOR AND ON BEHALF OF THE AGENT

This Agreement is dated: [____________]

OUTLINE—APPOINTMENT OF MERCHANDISING AGENT

This is an agreement to engage the services of an agent for the general merchandising of a character. The copyright owner of the Character is referred to as the Licensor. The Licensor is granting the Agent an exclusive licence to negotiate and conclude licensing agreements for the manufacture and distribution of Licenced Articles derived from the Character in the U.K. and the Republic of Ireland, but this could be extended to Europe or wider.

The Agent is not authorised to commit the Licensor to any agreement, whether in writing or not, without the prior consent of the Licensor who should sign the agreements.

The Agent is paying the Licensor a Licence Fee, which is not returnable or to be off-set. The Agent is entitled to deduct from the Gross Receipts his agreed percentage commission only, and the remainder, referred to as the Nett Receipts, are to be paid to the Licensor on a quarterly basis for the term of the Agreement. It is a condition that a separate account be opened at a bank which allows the Licensor access to the statements at all times. It maybe that the Licensor could also be a joint signatory.

The Agent is not acquiring any copyright or other rights in the Character or Licensed Articles.

The Agent is to ensure that any third party who is to be granted a licence has agreed to provide an agreed credit and copyright notice to the Licensor (including any trademark or logo) and that the written approval of the Licensor is required to approve an exact sample of the product to be manufactured.

PUBLISHING AGREEMENT BETWEEN PUBLISHER AND AUTHOR

AN AGREEMENT made this [____________] day of [____________]

BETWEEN:

(1) [____________]
of [____________] (to be known as the Author in this Agreement)

AND

(2) [____________]
of [____________] (to be known as the Publisher in this Agreement).

IT IS AGREED as follows:

1. DEFINITIONS

The words below are agreed to mean as follows:

1.1 "The Work" shall be the following book, including the Artwork, based on the Synopsis, provisionally entitled [____________] which shall consist of: [_______] typed A4 pages.

1.2 "The Synopsis" shall mean the summary of the Work which sets out the chapter outlines, structure and general content of the Work. A copy of the Synopsis is attached to and forms part of this Agreement.

1.3 "The Artwork" shall mean any photographs, tapes, drawings, sketches, pictures, diagrams, maps, charts or plans or any other illustrations which are intended to be included as part of the Work.

1.4 "The Delivery Date" shall be the following date by which the Work is to be delivered to the Publisher by the Author: [date].

1.5 "The Licence Period" shall commence on the [date of this Agreement] and continue until [____________].

1.6 "The Territory" shall be all countries, bases, ships, aeroplanes, oil rigs and any other locations throughout the world.

1.7 "The Author's Royalties" shall mean the following percentages in respect of all sums received by or credited to the Publisher in respect of the Work:

THE HOME MARKET

1.7.1 Hardback copies of The Work sold in the United Kingdom of Great Britain, Northern Ireland, the Republic of Ireland, the Channel Islands and the Isle of Man:

in respect of the first 2,000 copies:	[figure] per cent	[________%]
in respect of the next 3,000 copies:	[figure] per cent	[________%]
in respect of the next 10,000 copies:	[figure] per cent	[________%]
thereafter:	[figure] per cent	[________%]

Such percentages are to be calculated on the United Kingdom recommended retail price except where copies of the Work are sold for export including sales to the Publisher's branches and subsidiaries overseas, in which case the percentages shall be based on the nett amounts received by or credited to the Publisher.

1.7.2 Paperback copies of the Work sold in the United Kingdom of Great Britain, Northern Ireland, the Republic of Ireland, the Channel Islands and the Isle of Man:

in respect of the first 5,000 copies:	[figure] per cent	[________%]
in the respect of the next 10,000 copies:	[figure] per cent	[________%]
in respect of the next 15,000 copies:	[figure] per cent	[________%]
thereafter:	[figure] per cent	[________%]

Such percentages are to be calculated on the United Kingdom recommended retail price except where copies of the Work are sold for export including sales to the Publisher's branches and subsidiaries overseas in which case the percentages shall be based on the nett amounts received by or credited to the Publisher.

UNITED STATES OF AMERICA AND CANADA

1.7.3 Hardback copies of the Work sold throughout the United States of America and Canada and their respective territories and dependants, and the Philippine Islands:

in respect of the first 2,000 copies:	[figure] per cent	[________%]
in respect of the next 3,000 copies:	[figure] per cent	[________%]
in respect of the next 10,000 copies:	[figure] per cent	[________%]
thereafter:	[figure] per cent	[________%]

Such percentages are to be calculated on the nett amount received by or credited to the Publisher.

1.7.4 Paperback copies of the Work sold throughout the United States of America and Canada and their respective territories and dependants, and the Philippine Islands:

in respect of the first 5,000 copies:	[figure] per cent	[________%]
in the respect of the next 10,000 copies:	[figure] per cent	[________%]
in respect of the next 15,000 copies:	[figure] per cent	[________%]
thereafter:	[figure] per cent	[________%]

Such percentages are to be calculated on the nett amount received by or credited to the Publisher.

THE OVERSEAS MARKET, EXCLUDING THE UNITED STATES AND CANADA

1.7.5 Hardback copies of the Work sold throughout the Territory excluding the United Kingdom of Great Britain, Northern Ireland, the Republic of Ireland, the Channel Islands, the Isle of Man, the United States of America and Canada and their territories and dependants, and the Philippine Islands:

in respect of the first 2,000 copies:	[figure] per cent	[________%]
in respect of the next 3,000 copies:	[figure] per cent	[________%]
in respect of the next 10,000 copies:	[figure] per cent	[________%]
thereafter:	[figure] per cent	[________%]

Such percentages are to be calculated on the nett amount received by or credited to the Publisher.

1.7.6 Paperback copies of the Work sold throughout the Territory excluding the United Kingdom of Great Britain, Northern Ireland, the Republic of Ireland, the Channel Islands, the Isle of Man, the United States of America and Canada and their territories and dependants, and the Philippine Islands:

in respect of the first 5,000 copies:	[figure] per cent	[________%]
in the respect of the next 10,000 copies:	[figure] per cent	[________%]
in respect of the next 15,000 copies:	[figure] per cent	[________%]
thereafter:	[figure] per cent	[________%]

Such percentages are to be calculated on the nett amount received by or credited to the Publisher.

REMAINDER, DISCOUNTED AND REDUCED HARDBACK AND PAPERBACK COPIES

1.7.7 Where the Publisher disposes of copies of the Work throughout the United Kingdom of Great Britain, Northern Ireland, the Republic of Ireland, the Channel Islands and the Isle of Man at a discount, reduced price, remainder or overstock. The Author agrees that he shall only be entitled to receive [figure] per cent in respect of all the sums actually received by or credited to the Publisher where the Work is sold at less than [figure] per cent of the recommended retail price.

1.7.8 Where the Publisher disposes of copies of the Work throughout the Territory, excluding the United Kingdom of Great Britain, Northern Ireland, the Republic of Ireland, the Channel Islands and the Isle of Man at a discount reduced price, remainder or overstock. The Author agrees that he shall only be entitled to receive [figure] per cent in respect of all the sums actually received by the Publisher where the Work is sold at less than [figure] per cent of the recommended retail price.

PREMIUM OFFERS, BOOK CLUB, EDUCATIONAL EDITIONS AND SUBSCRIPTIONS

1.7.9 Where the Publisher disposes of copies of the Work throughout the United Kingdom of Great Britain, Northern Ireland, the Republic of Ireland, the Channel Islands and the Isle of Man as a premium offer, book club, as educational editions or subscriptions. Then the Author agrees that he shall only be entitled to receive [figure] per cent in respect of all the sums received by or credited to the Publisher where the Work is sold at less than [figure] per cent of the recommended retail price.

1.7.10 Where the Publisher disposes of copies of the Work throughout the Territory excluding the United Kingdom of Great Britain, Northern Ireland, the Republic of Ireland, the Channel Islands and the Isle of Man as a premium offer, book club, as educational editions or subscriptions. Then the Author agrees that he shall only be entitled to receive [figure] per cent in respect of all the sums actually received by or credited to the Publisher where the Work is sold at less than [figure] per cent of the recommended retail price.

MAIL ORDER

1.7.11 Where the Publisher sells copies of the Work throughout the United Kingdom of Great Britain, Northern Ireland, the Republic of Ireland, the Channel Islands and the Isle of Man through mail order or other direct selling method. The Author agrees that he shall only be entitled to receive [figure] per cent of the price of the Work by mail order or other direct selling method.

1.7.12 Where the Publisher sells copies of the Work throughout the Territory excluding the United Kingdom of Great Britain, Northern Ireland, the Republic of Ireland, the Channel Islands and the Isle of Man through mail order or other direct selling method. The Author agrees that he shall only be entitled to receive [figure] per cent of the sums actually received by or credited to the Publisher.

SMALL REPRINTS

1.7.13 Where the Work is reprinted in hardback for sale in the United Kingdom of Great Britain, Northern Ireland, the Republic of Ireland, the Channel Islands and the Isle of Man in the quantity of [____________] copies or less. Then, in respect of those small reprint hardback copies, the Author shall only be entitled to [figure] per cent of the recommended retail price of the Work.

1.7.14 Where the Work is reprinted in paperback for sale in the United Kingdom of Great Britain, Northern Ireland, the Republic of Ireland, the Channel Islands and the Isle of Man in the quantity of [____________] copies or less. Then, in respect of those small reprint paperback copies, the Author shall only be entitled to the [figure] per cent of the recommended retail price of the Work.

SUBSIDIARY RIGHTS

1.8 The Author shall be entitled to receive the following percentages of the nett sums received by the Publisher in respect of the exploitation of the following rights in the Work throughout the Territory:

		PER CENT	%
1.8.1	anthologies and quotations:	[______]	[______]
1.8.2	translations:	[______]	[______]
1.8.3	cassette or talking book:	[______]	[______]
1.8.4	straight non-dramatic radio and television readings:	[______]	[______]
1.8.5	dramatic adaptations for all forms of television, radio, film and theatre excluding the home video market:	[______]	[______]
1.8.6	dramatic or non-dramatic adaptations for the home video market:	[______]	[______]
1.8.7	first serialisation published prior to publication in hardback form:	[______]	[______]
1.8.8	first serialisation published after the publication in hardback form:	[______]	[______]
1.8.9	second and subsequent serialisation after publication, in hardback form:	[______]	[______]
1.8.10	hardback reprint rights licensed to another publisher, including large prints and educational editions:	[______]	[______]
1.8.11	paperback reprint rights licensed to another publisher:	[______]	[______]
1.8.12	digest book condensation in volume form:	[______]	[______]
1.8.13	one-shot digest to publish an abridgement of the Work in a periodical or newspaper:	[______]	[______]
1.8.14	book club editions sold to another publisher on a royalty inclusive basis:	[______]	[______]
1.8.15	book club editions licensed to another publisher on a separate royalty basis:	[______]	[______]
1.8.16	merchandising:	[______]	[______]
1.8.17	strip-cartoons or picture form:	[______]	[______]
1.8.18	any electronic or mechanical reproduction in information, storage and retrieval systems excluding the Internet:	[______]	[______]
1.8.19	the Internet:	[______]	[______].

ADVANCE

1.9 "The Advance Royalty Payment" shall be the sum of: [______] [______].

2. EXCLUSIVE LICENCE

2.1 In consideration of the Author's Royalties and the Advance Royalty Payment, the Author grants to the Publisher the sole and exclusive right to publish, exploit and license the Work and any parts thereof in all media including but not limited to all methods of publication and reproduction including hardback, paperback, serialisation, translations, anthologies, quotations, mechanical reproduction, radio, theatre, film, television merchandising and the Internet throughout the Territory for the duration of the Licence Period.

2.2 The Publisher agrees that the Author shall remain the copyright owner of the Work and that the Author has not granted any rights to the Publisher in respect of outer space and the rest of the universe except that set out in the Territory.

2.3 Where the Publisher decides to allow the Work to go out of print throughout the Territory or where the Work is not available to the public through retail outlets or if no new editions are issued. Then the Author shall be entitled to terminate this agreement by giving the Publisher [six] months' written notice. In such circumstances all rights granted under this Agreement shall revert to and be vested in the Author without prejudice to any claim that the Author may have for money due under this Agreement and/or any claim for breach of contract and/or damages.

3. COPYRIGHT NOTICE AND MORAL RIGHTS

3.1 The Publisher acknowledges that the Author asserts his moral right to be identified as the Author of the Work and in particular to be reasonably, prominently and clearly identified as follows: [____________] on all copies of the Work in all media and on all publicity, promotional, marketing and packaging material. This assertion shall bind both the Publisher and any other third party who acquires any interest or rights in the Work at any time. The Publisher shall be obliged to notify in writing all third parties of this assertion by the Author.

3.2 The Author asserts his right to object to derogatory treatment of his Work.

3.3 The Publisher undertakes that the following copyright notice will be incorporated on every copy of the Work: [____________] [year of first publication] and any associated material in all media.

The Publisher shall not at any time delete or authorise the removal or omission of such copyright notice. The copyright notice shall be placed on such manner and position as to give reasonable notice to the public of the claim of copyright.

3.4 The Publisher agrees to identify the Author as the Author of the Work in a suitable and prominent position of the cover, binding and inside front pages of the Work on all copies and in all marketing, advertising and publicity material.

4. OBLIGATIONS OF THE AUTHOR

4.1 The Author agrees to deliver [two] legible copies of the typescript and in disk form using the software: [____________] based on the Synopsis to the Publisher on or before the Delivery Date.

4.2 The Author confirms that he has full authority to enter into and perform this Agreement and that he is not bound by any previous agreement which adversely affects this Agreement.

4.3 The Author confirms that the Synopsis is and that the Work shall be the original work of the Author and does not and will not infringe the copyright, design right, moral right, trade or service mark or other intellectual property right of any third party in respect of the rights given by the Author under this Agreement.

4.4 The Author confirms that the Work has not been previously published or otherwise exploited in any form throughout the Territory.

4.5 The Author confirms that the Work does not and will not contain any obscene, offensive, defamatory, blasphemous material, commit any breach of privacy, contract, duty of confidence, Official Secrets Act, or contempt of court, and will not expose the Publisher to any civil or criminal proceedings throughout the Territory [during the Licence Period].

4.6 The Author confirms that as far as reasonably possible he has sought to verify and check all statements in the Work which he purports to be true and accurate and is able to provide documentary evidence in support. Further that, insofar as there may be instructions, directions, recipes, formulae or advice to be acted upon or copied by the public, the Author has personally verified such material and is certain that it does not pose any risk to the health and safety of the public and especially children. The Author undertakes that it is not likely to and shall not cause or result in any loss, damage or injury of any nature.

4.7 The Author agrees to indemnify the Publisher against any action, claim, proceedings, demands, loss, damage or injury and any costs or reasonable legal expenses incurred, including any matter settled on the advice of counsel, by the Publisher as a result of any breach or alleged breach by the Author of his obligations under this Agreement subject to a maximum liability of: [____________]. If the Publisher wishes to assert its right to be indemnified it must:

4.7.1 promptly notify the Author of any claim or legal proceedings which have arisen and make no admission or offer of settlement at that stage; and

4.7.2 provide the Author with the opportunity to be fully consulted as regards any proposed steps to be taken and any settlement of the matter.

4.7.3 The Publisher shall not be entitled to deduct any sums owed under the indemnity from the payments due in respect of the Work without the prior written consent of the Author.

4.8 The Author agrees that the Publisher may use the Author's name as a party to take legal action against any third party for copyright infringement in respect of the Work provided that:

4.8.1 the Author is fully advised of the details of the action;

4.8.2 the Publisher gives a written indemnity to the Author agreeing to pay all costs and expenses in respect of the action incurred by the Publisher and the Author; and

4.8.3 that in the event that any profits, damages, awards or other sums or benefits are recovered in respect of the Work, the Publisher shall share such money on terms to be mutually agreed with the Author after the deduction of all reasonable costs and expenses paid by the Publisher to any third party which are not recovered.

4.9 The Author agrees to amend, alter or edit such parts of the Work as the Publisher may request in the event that the Publisher's legal advisers consider that the Work contains material which is likely to result in legal proceedings being brought against the Publisher.

4.10 The Author undertakes to obtain and pay for all copyright clearances and consents necessary for the publication of the Work, including the Artwork, throughout the Territory. The Author agrees to obtain all such clearances and consents in writing and to provide the Publisher with such copies as may be requested.

4.11 The Author shall not, without the prior written consent of the Publisher (which consent shall not be unreasonably withheld or delayed), enter into any agreement for the publication of any other work which is reasonably likely to affect prejudicially the sale of the Work throughout the Territory for the duration of the Licence Period.

4.12 The Author agrees to read and correct the proof-sheets of the Work and to return them to the Publisher within [40 days] of their receipt or within such other period as may be agreed between the Author and the Publisher. The Publisher shall pay for delivery of the proofs and the Author shall bear the cost of arranging their return.

4.13 The Author undertakes to make such additions and alterations in respect of any new editions of the Work as may be reasonably required by the Publisher. In the event that the Author is unable or unwilling to make such additions and alterations. Then the Publisher shall negotiate in good faith to resolve the matter. In the event that no arrangement can be reached the Publisher shall [not] be entitled to use a third party [at the Publisher's cost].

4.14 The Author undertakes to prepare an index for the Work. If the Publisher prepares an index as a result of the Author's inability or unwillingness to do so, then the cost shall be paid for by the Publisher.

4.15 The Author agrees that the Publisher shall be entitled to use and permit the use of an agreed style and material for his name, photograph, biography and image but not his signature in respect of the publication and any other commercial exploitation of the Work.

4.16 The Author agrees that he shall be responsible for all his own national insurance, personal tax and value added tax which may be due in consequence of this Agreement.

4.17 The Author agrees to retain at least one complete copy of the Work for future reference purposes.

4.18 The Author acknowledges that the manner and method of producing, distributing and marketing the Work, including cover designs, selling price and terms of the sale of the Work, shall be at the Publisher's sole discretion subject to clause 3.

4.19 The Author acknowledges that the Advance Royalty Payment shall be off-set against the Author's Royalties.

4.20 The Author agrees that in the event that the Publisher refuses to accept the manuscript of the Work on reasonable grounds and in good faith and has provided written reasons for its rejection. Then the Author shall be obliged to repay to the Publisher the following sum: [____________].

4.21 The Author acknowledges that the Publisher shall be entitled to permit braille and charitable recordings to be made of the Work for the sole use of the blind and handicapped free of charge during the Licence Period.

4.22 The Author confirms that all payments under this Agreement shall be made payable to: [Name] c/o [Account] [Bank] [Address].

4.23 The Author shall make himself available as reasonably required by the Publisher for the promotion of the Work for the following periods provided that the Publisher pay all the costs and expenses:

4.23.1 [____________] appearances and interviews up to [____________] months after the date of publication of the hardback.

4.23.2 [____________] appearances and interviews up to [____________] months after the date of publication of the paperback.

5. OBLIGATIONS OF THE PUBLISHER

5.1 In consideration of the rights granted by the Author to the Publisher under this Agreement, the Publisher agrees to produce and publish the Work within a reasonable period of time following the acceptance of the manuscript of the Work but in any event no later than: [date]. Provided that the Author delivers the Work on or before the Delivery Date, the Publisher agrees to publish the Work no later than: [date].

5.2 The Publisher confirms that the published selling price of the Work shall not be less than:
[figure] in hardback form where the Work is sold in the United Kingdom of Great Britain, Northern Ireland, the Republic of Ireland, the Channel Islands and the Isle of Man and;
[figure] in paperback form where the Work is sold in the United Kingdom of Great Britain, Northern Ireland, the Republic of Ireland, the Channel Islands and the Isle of Man.

5.3 The Publisher agrees to pay to the Author the Advance Royalty Payment as follows:
[____________] upon signature of this Agreement;
[____________] upon delivery of an acceptable manuscript of the Work;
[____________] on or before [____________]; and
[____________] upon first publication of the Work.

5.4 The Publisher agrees that no part of the Advance Royalty Payment already paid shall be returnable by the Author once the Publisher has accepted the manuscript of the Work.

5.5 The Publisher agrees either to accept or provide written reasons for its rejection of the Work within [28 days] of delivery of the manuscript. The Publisher agrees to reject the Work only on reasonable grounds and in good faith.

5.6 The Publisher confirms that if the manuscript of the Work is not accepted by the Publisher for any reason. Then the Author shall be entitled to have the Work published by a third party, provided that the Author repays to the Publisher all sums previously paid in respect of the Advance Royalty Payment. In which case this Agreement shall be terminated and all rights granted shall revert to the Author.

5.7 The Publisher confirms that if within three years of the date of this Agreement the Author's Royalties actually paid are less than: [_____________] including the Advance Royalty Payment. Then the Author shall be entitled to terminate this Agreement by giving written notice to the Publisher and upon such notice being received by the Publisher all rights granted under this Agreement shall revert to the Author without prejudice to any claim the Author may have for money due under this Agreement and/or any claim for breach of contract and/or damages.

5.8 The Publisher undertakes to instigate and pursue all necessary legal and practical action to protect all copyright and any other rights in the Work granted under this Agreement and shall bear all the legal, administrative or incidental costs of so doing. The Publisher agrees that the prior written approval of the Author shall be required before any action, claim, writ, summons or any other proceedings are settled.

5.9 The Publisher agrees to indemnify the Author against any action, claim, proceeding, demand, loss, damage or injury and any costs or reasonable legal expenses incurred by the Author, including any matter settled on the advice of counsel, as a result of any breach or alleged breach by the Publisher of its obligations under this Agreement.

5.10 The Publisher undertakes that it shall make accounts twice yearly as at June 30 and December 31 and shall pay the Author's Royalties within [10 days] of the last day of June and December in each year. The Publisher shall not be obliged to make any royalty payments to the Author if the amount due in any accounting period is less than: [_____________] in which case such sums shall be carried forward to the next accounting period.

5.11 The Publisher and its sub-agents, sub-licensees and distributors shall keep full and accurate books of account, records and contracts showing all sums received by or credited to the Publisher in respect of the Work. This material shall be preserved and kept secure by the Publisher for a minimum of [three years] after the expiry or termination of the Agreement or, in the event that there is a dispute between the parties, for such longer period as may be necessary. In any event they shall not be destroyed without prior written notice to the Author of the Publisher's intention to do so.

5.12 Within [28 days] of the last day of June and December in each year the Publisher shall provide a detailed report to the Author with a full breakdown of the exploitation of the Work setting out the total sales, including the number of copies of the Work used for publicity or review purposes and the number of copies lost through damage or theft, destroyed, pulped or remaindered or for any other reason for which no royalty has been paid to the Author.

5.13 The Publisher agrees that the Author shall be entitled to arrange for an annual audit to inspect and make copies of the Publisher's books of account, records, contracts and any other relevant material in order to verify the sums due to the Author. In the event that in any audit there is found an error to the detriment of the Author in respect of the amount to be paid by the Publisher which is in excess of: [figure/currency]. Then the Publisher shall be responsible for the payment of all reasonable costs incurred in such audit by the Author including personal expenses, accountants' fees, and legal costs.

5.14 The Publisher shall keep professional, comprehensive and complete records of all dealings of any nature, disposal or transfer in respect of the Work. The Publisher shall co-operate fully with the Author in any audit and assist in providing such information as the Author may request to establish whether there are any errors or omissions and to fully audit the accounts.

5.15 In the event that any sums are deducted or withheld from the Author's royalties due under this Agreement. Then the Publisher agrees to provide satisfactory evidence of the reason to the Author and to make this clear in the statement of accounts.

5.16 The Publisher confirms that the Copyright Licensing Agency (C.L.A.) have been or will be empowered to grant non-exclusive licences to reproduce the Work and other literary works published by the Publisher by photocopying and other reprographic means. The Work is accordingly deemed to be included with such literary works and the C.L.A. shall divide the proceeds from the reprographic reproduction of the Work authorised by the C.L.A. equally between the Author and the Publisher. The Author shall receive the Author's share of such proceeds through the Authors' Lending and Copyright Society (A.L.C.S.) in accordance with the A.L.C.S. standard terms and conditions.

5.17 The Publisher will have the entire control of the format, paper, binding, typography, layout and design of the jacket and the position of any images, names, titles, or otherwise of the Work. All decisions in respect of the production, publication, distribution, advertising, price, marketing and exploitation of the Work shall be at the Publisher's sole discretion.

5.18 The Publisher agrees to supply a copy of the proposed jacket, marketing notes and biographical material to the Author to provide him with an opportunity to be consulted.

5.19 The Publisher shall consult with the Author in respect of the appointment of any third party to exploit the Work.

5.20 The Publisher shall provide the Author with details of all proposed release dates in respect of the exploitation of the Work.

5.21 The Publisher agrees to provide to the Author not less than [24] sample copies of the Work [in each and every form] in which it is made available to the public free of charge to the Author.

5.22 The Publisher confirms that in the event of the death of the Author after the acceptance of the manuscript of the Work all sums due to the Author under this Agreement will be made payable to the Author's estate.

5.23 In the event that the Author dies prior to the delivery of the manuscript the Publisher agrees to negotiate in good faith with the administrator(s) of the Author's estate concerning the publication or otherwise of the Work.

5.24 The Publisher agrees that it shall be solely responsible for all costs incurred in publishing, distributing, marketing and exploiting the Work throughout the Territory and that no such sums shall be deducted from the payments due to the Author under this Agreement.

5.25 The Publisher shall endeavour to ensure:

5.25.1 that the Work is accurately and adequately described in its catalogues, brochures and marketing material;

5.25.2 that sufficient copies of the Work are printed for distribution and sale to the public by the publication date and shall not be less than: [number];

5.25.3 that the cover of the Work, text and artwork shall be of a high, professional standard;

5.25.4 that all quotes and use of statements from third parties by the Publisher of the Work shall be subject to approval by the Author;

5.25.5 that the total marketing budget for the Work is not less than: [figure/currency];

5.25.6 that review copies will be sent to [____________] persons recommended by the Author;

5.25.7 that the marketing of the Work will cover the following media: [____________];

5.25.8 that the Publisher, unless prevented by force majeure or the delay of the Author, shall publish or exploit the Work in the following formats by the following date(s):
Hardback: [date]
Paperback: [date]
Film: [date]
Video: [date]
Merchandising: [date].

6. MISCELLANEOUS

CONFIDENTIALITY

6.1 The Author and the Publisher shall not disclose to any third party any confidential business or future plans of the other party at any time acquired during the existence of this Agreement and no reference is to be made to the terms of this Agreement by either party in any advertising, publicity or promotional material without the prior consent of the other party. In the event that the Author and the Publisher agree to make a joint statement to the press concerning this Agreement the following press release shall be issued: [____________].

AMENDMENTS AND ALTERATIONS

6.2 This Agreement supersedes all previous agreements, representations or promises and sets out all the terms agreed between the parties. Any amendment or alteration to this Agreement must be in writing and signed by an authorised signatory of each party.

NO PARTNERSHIP OR EMPLOYMENT

6.3 This Agreement shall not be deemed to create any partnership or employment relationship between the parties.

NOTICES

6.4 Without prejudice to the right to serve notices by any other means any notice served under this agreement shall be in writing. Any notice which has been sent by first class prepaid post shall be deemed to be received 48 hours thereafter (excluding Saturdays, Sundays and public holidays). For the purposes of this agreement all notices shall be sent to the following addresses:

The Author: [____________];
The Publisher: [____________].

VALUE ADDED TAX

6.5 All sums payable under this Agreement are exclusive of any value added tax that may be payable by either party.

FORCE MAJEURE

6.6 In the event that this Agreement cannot be performed or its obligations fulfilled for any reason beyond the reasonable control of the Author or the Publisher, including ill-health of the Author, war, industrial action, floods or Acts of God, then such non-performance or failure to fulfil its obligations shall be deemed not to be a breach of this Agreement. In the event that this Agreement cannot be performed or its obligations fulfilled for any reason beyond the reasonable control of the defaulting party for a continuous period of [six] months. Then the other party may, at its discretion, terminate this Agreement by notice in writing at the end of that period, provided that both parties agree to negotiate, in good faith, an equitable settlement in respect of the work already performed to the date of termination.

TERMINATION AND EXPIRY OF THE AGREEMENT

6.7 In addition to any other rights and remedies at law this Agreement may be terminated by giving written notice to the other party who has breached this Agreement or defaulted in the following circumstances:

6.7.1 where the Publisher has failed to account or make payments as required under this Agreement;
6.7.2 where the Publisher or the Author has committed a serious breach of its obligations under this Agreement, unless such party rectifies the position, as far as reasonably possible, within [30 days];
6.7.3 where the Publisher goes into voluntary or involuntary liquidation;

6.7.4 where the Publisher is declared insolvent either in bankruptcy proceedings or other legal proceedings;

6.7.5 where an agreement with creditors has been reached by the Publisher due to its failure or inability to pay its debts as they fall due; or

6.7.6 where a receiver is appointed over the whole or part of the Publisher's business.

6.8 The delivery date of the Work shall be of the essence of this Agreement. If the Author shall fail to deliver the Work by the delivery date. Then the Publisher shall give the Author [two months] written notice to deliver the Work and may at its discretion extend this period. If the Author fails to deliver the Work by the new notified delivery date then the Publisher may terminate the Agreement by notice in writing and the Advance Royalty Payment shall be due to be repaid by the Author.

THIRD PARTY TRANSFERS

6.9 Neither party shall assign, transfer, charge or make over this Agreement or any of its rights or obligations without the prior written consent of the other party.

ARBITRATION

6.10 Both the Author and the Publisher agree to resolve any disputes concerning this Agreement either through referral to arbitration under the Arbitration Rules of the Chartered Institute of Arbitrators or to the Informal Disputes Settlement Procedure of the Publishers Association.

GOVERNING LAW

6.11 This Agreement shall be construed, interpreted and subject to the Laws of England.

A COPY OF THE SYNOPSIS IS ATTACHED TO AND FORMS PART OF THIS AGREEMENT.

FOR AND ON BEHALF OF THE AUTHOR: [____________]
[Name/Title]

FOR AND ON BEHALF OF THE PUBLISHER: [____________]
[Name/Title/Company]

OUTLINE—PUBLISHING AGREEMENT BETWEEN PUBLISHER AND AUTHOR

This is an exclusive publishing agreement between an Author and a Publisher which is not intended in any way to reflect industry practice. If an Agent is acting on behalf of the Author and is to receive any payments under this Agreement, then the Publisher would normally require written authorisation to that effect from the Author.

There are provisions for escalating royalties for both hardback and paperback editions of the Work for the home and overseas market. The units relating to the royalties are for guidance only. The Author's royalties are based on the recommended price of the Work or the nett sums received by the Publisher, depending on the circumstances.

The Publisher is paying an advance against royalties, which is payable by instalments. This advance is not returnable in the event that the sales do not cover the advance.

The Publisher is being granted an exclusive licence to publish and exploit the Work in all media throughout the world for a fixed licence period. An Author may, of course, wish to reserve and retain some of the subsidiary rights.

The Author remains the copyright owner of the Work. The Author asserts his moral right to be identified as the Author and is also to receive a copyright notice on all copies.

The Publisher is to pay for all the Author's corrections of the proofs. It is important to allow sufficient time for the Author to read and amend them.

There is a total limit of liability of the indemnity by the Author to the Publisher. The Publisher will not be able to claim any sums from the Author under the indemnity if the Author is not advised of any problems that may arise.

The Publisher is not entitled to use a third party to edit the Work. The Publisher is to keep professional accounting records and must not destroy them without notifying the Author. All copies whether given away, or destroyed must be accounted for. Normally Publishers only account in the royalty statements for books on which sums are received. It is better to link payment by the Publisher of the cost of the audit to a fixed financial error rather than a percentage.

Normally no undertakings are given by the Publisher in the production, marketing and selling of the Work, which we have included. This element is most important to Authors particularly as regards the jacket, biographical material and the marketing content of any catalogues.

No option or access to other works of the Author is being given.

The Author should retain those rights, which he cannot reasonably expect the Publisher to exploit. Often overseas sales are inhibited in the smaller markets overseas if the Publisher has to account on the recommended retail price, so a net receipts provision may actually increase revenue to the Author.

GHOST-WRITER'S AGREEMENT

BETWEEN:

(1) [____________]
of [____________] (to be known as the Originator in this Agreement)

AND

(2) [____________]
of [____________] (to be known as the Ghost-Writer in this Agreement)

IT IS AGREED as follows:

1. DEFINITIONS

The words below are agreed to mean as follows:

1.1 "The Work" shall be the following book, including the Artwork, based on the Synopsis and entitled [____________] which consist of approximately [____________] typed A4 pages.
1.2 "The Synopsis" shall mean the summary of the Work, which sets out the structure and general content of the Work, including a chapter breakdown. A copy of the Synopsis is attached to and forms part of this Agreement.
1.3 "The Artwork" shall mean any photographs, drawings, sketches, pictures, diagrams, maps or any other illustrations which are intended to be included as part of the Work.
1.4 "The Target Date" shall be the following date by which the Work is intended to be completed and delivered to a publisher: [____________].
1.5 "The Territory" shall mean all countries, bases and locations throughout the world, outer space and the universe.
1.6 "The Term of the Agreement" shall commence on the [date of this Agreement] and shall continue until: [date].
1.7 "The Ghost-Writer's Fee" shall be the following sum: [figure/currency].

2. ENGAGEMENT OF THE SERVICES OF THE GHOST-WRITER

2.1 In consideration of the Ghost-Writer's Fee, the Ghost-Writer agrees to provide his non-exclusive services to the Originator for the Term of the Agreement to write, research and produce the Work.

2.2 The Originator agrees to engage the non-exclusive services of the Ghost-Writer to write, research and produce the Work for the Term of the Agreement.

2.3 The Ghost-Writer agrees that the Originator shall be entitled to engage or enter into any agreement with any third party to write, research or produce the Work or any other book or publication based on the Synopsis or any development or variation thereof at any time during the Term of the Agreement throughout the Territory.

3. COPYRIGHT AND MORAL RIGHTS

3.1 In consideration of the Ghost-Writer's Fee, the Ghost-Writer assigns to the Originator all present and future copyright and all other rights in the product of his services under this Agreement, including all drafts, scripts, notes, photographs or other material which is created by him under this Agreement and in the Work in all media whether in existence now or created in the future, including but not limited to the title, publication, anthology, quotations, mechanical reproductions, serialisations, translations, dramatic and non-dramatic adaptations for radio, television, film, theatre or video and any merchandising throughout the Territory for the full period of copyright and any extensions or renewals thereof.

3.2 The Ghost-Writer agrees that he/she shall not be entitled to any copyright notice, credit or acknowledgment in respect of the exploitation of the Work by the Originator or any third party in any media at any time. The Ghost-Writer agrees that the Originator shall be entitled to receive the sole credit for producing and writing the Work.

3.3 The Ghost-Writer unconditionally waives all moral rights in any of the material created under this Agreement and in the Work. The waiver shall apply to the right to be identified as the Author and the right to object to any derogatory treatment of the Work. The waiver shall apply to the Originator and any publisher, licensees, assignees or other third party who may require any rights or interest. The Ghost-Writer accepts that the waiver cannot be revoked or otherwise altered at any time even after the death of the Originator.

3.4 The Originator agrees that the Ghost-Writer shall be entitled for biographical purposes only to state that the Work was written by the Originator with the research assistance of the Ghost-Writer.

4. EDITORIAL CONTROL

4.1 The Ghost-Writer acknowledges and agrees that the Originator shall have the sole and exclusive discretion as to the research, interviews and content of the Work and the Artwork.

4.2 The Ghost-Writer agrees to adapt, alter, edit and amend the Work as requested by the Originator during the Term of the Agreement and prior to acceptance of the Work by the Originator.

5. OBLIGATIONS OF THE GHOST-WRITER

5.1 The Ghost-Writer agrees to provide his non-exclusive services to the Originator for the Term of the Agreement to research, write and produce the Work at such times, dates, and locations as the Originator may reasonably require subject to sufficient prior notice and shall observe all reasonable directions and requests by The Originator.

5.2 The Ghost-Writer shall provide his services to the best of his skill and ability to ensure the successful completion of the Work.

5.3 The Ghost-Writer agrees that he shall carry out the following specific duties as the Originator may direct:

- 5.3.1 to trace and contact any individual or company as may be required and to arrange interviews and recordings if specifically requested to do so;
- 5.3.2 to interview such persons for the purpose of dealing with such issues, subjects, details, history, documents or any other material;
- 5.3.3 to keep full and accurate tape-recordings of all interviews;
- 5.3.4 to keep full and accurate records of all sources of information, documents, records and any other material relied upon in the Work;
- 5.3.5 to report on the existence of any stills, photographs, newspaper cuttings, film and video material and sound recordings and to include in the report ownership of copyright, any contractual and credit requirements, the estimated cost of reproduction and copyright clearance payments, and the format and quality of any such material;
- 5.3.6 to obtain such copyright clearances and other consents as may be required;
- 5.3.7 to proof-read the Publisher's copy of the Work; and
- 5.3.8 to prepare an index for the Work.

5.4 The Ghost-Writer undertakes to prepare and write not less than: [____________] typed A4 pages in relation to the Work which shall consist of approximately [____________] words.

5.5 In addition to clause 5.4, the Ghost-Writer agrees to provide sufficient material for the Artwork in order to ensure no less than [____________] A4 pages of illustrations.

5.6 The Ghost-Writer agrees to deliver two copies of the Work and the Artwork to the Originator on or before the Target Date. The Ghost-Writer agrees that such typed material will be of a standard and quality suitable for publication by a reputable publisher.

5.7 The Ghost-Writer agrees to provide regular reports to the Originator and to make available all material which he has obtained or recorded in furtherance of this Agreement.

5.8 The Ghost-Writer agrees that to the best of his knowledge and belief the facts and information contained in the Work shall be true and accurate, except where any material is supplied by and specifically included at the request of the Originator.

5.9 The Ghost-Writer confirms that he has full authority to enter into and perform this Agreement and that he is not bound by any previous Agreement which adversely affects this Agreement.

5.10 The Ghost-Writer undertakes that all the products of his services under this Agreement shall be original and will not infringe the copyright or any other rights of any third party, except where the work incorporates material of any third party or is supplied by the Originator and which is specifically included at the Originator's request.

5.11 The Ghost-Writer agrees to keep the Originator, as far as reasonably possible, informed of his whereabouts and telephone number during the Term of the Agreement.

5.12 The Ghost-Writer undertakes not to disclose any material nor make any statement, whether true or not, concerning the private or sexual life, political or personal views of the Originator or any third party interviewed for the purposes of the preparation and writing of the Work to any third party at any time without the prior written consent of the Originator.

5.13 The Ghost-Writer confirms that the Originator shall be solely entitled to retain all sums received from the exploitation of the material created, collected and obtained during the course of this Agreement and in the Work and the Artwork in any media throughout the Territory at any time and that the Ghost-Writer shall not be entitled to any such sums.

5.14 The Ghost-Writer agrees that he shall be responsible for all his own national insurance, personal tax and value added tax which may become due as a consequence of this Agreement.

5.15 The Ghost-Writer confirms that he holds a [____________] passport.

5.16 The Ghost-Writer agrees to deliver to the Originator (at the Originator's sole cost) all documents, writings, recordings, photographs, artwork and all other material created, collected or obtained relating to the Work in the possession of or under the control of the Ghost-Writer after the expiry or completion of this Agreement.

5.17 The Ghost-Writer agrees that the Originator shall be entitled to assign, transfer, change or make over the benefit and obligations of this Agreement to any third party at any time.

6. OBLIGATIONS OF THE ORIGINATOR

6.1 In consideration of the services provided by the Ghost-Writer under this Agreement and the rights assigned, the Originator shall pay to the Ghost-Writer the Ghost-Writer's Fee as follows:

[____________] upon signature of this Agreement;

[____________] on or before [____________] subject to delivery and approval of written evidence of sufficient progress such as outlines of chapters and draft chapters;

[____________] subject to delivery and acceptance of the Work and the Artwork by the Originator;

[____________] on or before: [____________].

6.2 The Originator agrees to pay or reimburse the Ghost-Writer in respect of all expenses reasonably and properly incurred in providing his services during the Term of the Agreement, including telephone, fax, stationery, travel and accommodation, subject to satisfactory receipts or records being produced upon request.

6.3 The Originator agrees either to accept or provide written reasons for the rejection of the Work, the Artwork or any parts within 21 days of delivery. The Originator agrees to reject the Work only on reasonable grounds and in good faith.

6.4 The Originator confirms that he shall bear the cost of any copyright clearance, consent, or other acquisition of rights or permission for the use of any material for the Work, including the Artwork, which is owned or controlled by a third party.

6.5 The Originator confirms that the exploitation of the Work in any form will be at the sole cost and expense of the Originator and that the Ghost-Writer shall not be liable for any such payments.

6.6 The Originator agrees to provide such assistance, background detail, access to all relevant documents and other records, information which may be available concerning persons to be interviewed and any other matters to the Ghost-Writer as may be necessary for the completion of the Work by the Target Date.

6.7 The Originator agrees to provide the Ghost-Writer, free of charge, with not less than [2 copies] of the Work in hardback and [2 copies] of the Work in paperback.

6.8 The Originator agrees to arrange and bear the cost of a comprehensive insurance policy for the Work, the Artwork and all other relevant material in the possession or under the control of the Originator and the Ghost-Writer during the Term of the Agreement.

7. MISCELLANEOUS

INDEMNITY AND LEGAL LIABILITY

7.1 The Ghost-Writer is not providing any general indemnity to the Originator under this Agreement arising out of the provision of his services.

7.2 The Originator accepts that it shall not be entitled to seek any sums from the Ghost-Writer in respect of this Agreement provided that he fulfils the obligation to deliver the Work by the Target Date. All responsibility for any legal liability or proceedings, which may arise from the use of any material collected, obtained, or provided under this Agreement and in the Work shall be at the sole risk and expense of the Originator. No liability shall be attributed to the Ghost-Writer in the event that there are errors or omissions in respect of the permissions, consents or clearances in the Work. Nor shall the Ghost-Writer be liable in the event that any third party shall sue for infringement of copyright, trademark, service mark, design right or any other intellectual property rights or alleges that any material is obscence, offensive, defamatory, derogatory or otherwise at any time.

7.3 The Originator shall be entitled to deal with legal proceedings at its own discretion without consultation with the Ghost-Writer and to retain any damages or other sums received.

CONFIDENTIALITY

7.4 The Originator and the Ghost-Writer shall not disclose to any third party any confidential business or future plans of the other party at any time acquired during the existence of this Agreement and no reference is to be made to the terms of this Agreement by either party in any advertising, publicity or promotional material without the prior consent of the other party.

AMENDMENTS AND ALTERATIONS

7.5 This Agreement supersedes all previous agreements, representations or promises and sets out all the terms agreed between the parties. Any amendment or alteration to this Agreement must be in writing and signed by an authorised signatory of each party.

NO PARTNERSHIP OR EMPLOYMENT

7.6 This Agreement shall not be deemed to create any partnership or employment relationship between the parties.

NOTICES

7.7 Without prejudice to the right to serve notices by any other means any notice served under this Agreement shall be in writing. Any notice which has been sent by first class, pre-paid post shall be deemed to be received 48 hours thereafter (excluding Saturdays, Sundays and public holidays). For the purposes of this Agreement, all notices shall be sent to the following addresses:

The Originator: [____________]
The Ghost-Writer: [____________]

VALUE ADDED TAX

7.8 All sums payable under this Agreement are exclusive of any value added tax that may be payable by either party.

FORCE MAJEURE

7.9 In the event that this Agreement cannot be performed or its obligations fulfilled for any reason beyond the reasonable control of the Originator or the Ghost-Writer, including such events as war, industrial action, floods, Acts of God or the ill-health of the Ghost-writer, then such non-performance or failure to fulfil its obligations shall be deemed not to be a breach of this Agreement. In the event that this Agreement cannot be performed or its obligations fulfilled for any reason beyond the reasonable control of the defaulting party for a continuous period of [____________], then the other party may, at its discretion, terminate this Agreement by notice in writing at the end of that period, provided that both parties agree to negotiate, in good faith, an equitable settlement in respect of work already performed to the date of termination.

TERMINATION OF THE AGREEMENT

7.10 In addition to any other rights and remedies at law this Agreement may be terminated by giving written notice to the other party who has breached this Agreement in the following circumstances:

7.10.1 where the Originator has failed to account or make payments as required under this Agreement;

7.10.2 where the Ghost-Writer or the Originator has committed a serious breach of his obligations under this Agreement, unless such party rectifies the position, as far as reasonably possible, within [____________].

GOVERNING LAW

7.11 This Agreement shall be subject to the laws of England.

A COPY OF THE SYNOPSIS IS ATTACHED TO AND FORMS PART OF THIS AGREEMENT.

THE ORIGINATOR: [____________] [Date]

THE GHOST-WRITER: [____________] [Date]

OUTLINE—GHOST-WRITER'S AGREEMENT

An example of the application of this type of agreement would be where a person engages a writer to work at their direction to research, prepare and write an autobiography for which the actual writer receives no public credit or acknowledgment.

The Ghost-Writer is providing his non-exclusive services, so he could do work elsewhere and is being paid an agreed sum, the Ghost-Writer's Fee, and is not entitled to receive any money from the exploitation of the Work. The Ghost-Writer is also entitled to an expense allowance, to travel and accommodation costs incurred in the course of fulfilling his obligations under the Agreement for which there is no maximum limit. The Originator could also use someone else to work on the project if they choose. The Ghost-Writer is giving all rights in all media everywhere to the Originator and will retain no interest. All moral rights are waived and there is no right to a copyright notice. Effectively the Ghost-Writer is a shadow. The Originator does not have to let the Ghost-Writer know when the Work is published, but is to provide some free copies. There are no undertakings by the Ghost-Writer regarding the nature of the material for legal purposes, although he will provide a list of copyright clearances and consents. All legal liability and risk for the exploitation of the Work is at the Originator's cost and risk, who is also giving only limited undertakings.

A copy of the Synopsis should be attached to the Agreement, and it should be realised that the Artwork definition could be varied.

COLLABORATION AGREEMENT BETWEEN TWO AUTHORS

BETWEEN:

[Author A]
of [____________]

AND

[Author B]
of [____________]

IT IS AGREED between Author A and Author B as follows:

1. DEFINITIONS

The words below are agreed to mean as follows:

1.1 "The Authors" shall mean Author A and Author B.

1.2 "The Work" shall be the following book, including the Artwork, based on the Synopsis entitled: [____________] which shall consist of approximately [____________] typed A4 pages.

1.3 "The Synopsis" shall mean the summary of the Work which sets out the structure and general content of the Work including a chapter breakdown. A copy of the Synopsis is attached to and forms part of this Agreement.

1.4 "The Artwork" shall mean any graphic work, photograph, drawing, sketch, picture, diagram, map, chart, or any other illustration which is intended to be included as part of the Work.

1.5 "The Delivery Date" shall be the following date by which the Work is to be ready for delivery to a publisher by the Authors: [____________].

1.6 "The Territory" shall mean all countries, bases and locations throughout the world, outer space and the universe.

2. COLLABORATION

2.1 The Authors agree that the Work and the Artwork are to be produced for the purpose of publication in hardback and paperback form primarily in [the United Kingdom of Great Britain, Northern Ireland, the Republic of Ireland, the Channel Islands and the Isle of Man] and in as many countries throughout the Territory as reasonably possible.

2.2 The Authors agree that the Work shall be in a fit and proper form to be delivered to a reputable publisher by the Delivery Date.

2.3 The Authors agree that their individual contributions to the Work and the Artwork may fairly be described as follows:

Author A: [____________];
Author B: [____________].

3. ORIGINALITY

The Authors undertake to each other that their contributions to the Work and the Artwork shall be original and shall not infringe the copyright or any other rights of any third party throughout the Territory without informing the other Author of any material which is not original.

4. CAPACITY AND PREVIOUS AGREEMENTS

The Authors confirm that they have full power and authority to enter into this Agreement and that neither is bound by any previous agreement which adversely affects this Agreement.

5. AGENTS

5.1 The Authors confirm that neither party has entered into or is bound by an agreement with an agent in respect of the Work.

5.2 The Authors agree that an agent shall not be appointed for the purpose of negotiating a publishing agreement or any other form of exploiting the Work without the knowledge and consent of both parties to this Agreement.

6. JOINT COPYRIGHT

6.1 The Authors agree that notwithstanding the nature of their individual contributions to the Work, the copyright and any other rights in all media in the Work, and the Artwork shall belong to the Authors jointly and equally during the existence of this Agreement.

6.2 The Authors confirm that if this Agreement is terminated for any reason then Author A and Author B shall only hold the copyright in their individual contributions to the

Work and shall be entitled to exploit their own individual contributions without the consent of or payment to the other party.

6.3 In the event of any dispute concerning the copyright ownership of any parts of the Work after termination of this Agreement then Author A and Author B agree that the starting point for the division of copyright in the Work shall be as set out in clause 2.3 of this Agreement.

7. PUBLICATION OF THE WORK

7.1 The Authors agree that no formal approach to a publisher in respect of the Work shall be made without the written consent of both parties to this Agreement.

7.2 No publication agreement shall be entered into without the written consent of both parties to this Agreement.

8. THE PUBLICATION AGREEMENT

8.1 In respect of any publishing agreement which is to be made between the Authors and a publisher, the Authors confirm the following arrangements:

8.1.1 All proceeds from the exploitation of the Work and the Artwork shall be divided equally between the Authors including all royalty payments which become due and any advance made by a publisher against such royalties.

8.1.2 Payment by the publisher shall be made in the following manner:

Author A: [____________]
Address: [____________]
Author B: [____________]
Address: [____________]

8.2 The Authors shall not enter into an agreement with a publisher or with any third party which has the effect of assigning any copyright in the Work or the Artwork to the publisher unless agreed between the parties.

8.3 The Authors shall not enter into an agreement with a publisher unless the total advance against royalties to be made by a publisher to the Authors is equal to or more than: [____________]

8.4 The Authors shall not enter into an agreement with a publisher unless the royalties are of the following minimum percentages:

8.4.1 first hardback edition of the Work published in the United Kingdom of Great Britain, Republic of Ireland, Northern Ireland, the Channel Islands and the Isle of Man: [____________]%

8.4.2 first paperback edition of the Work published in the United Kingdom of Great Britain, Republic of Ireland, Northern Ireland, the Channel Islands and the Isle of Man: [____________]%

9. ACCURACY

The Authors mutually undertake that all material provided for the purpose of inclusion in the Work shall be, to the best of each author's knowledge and belief, true and accurate.

10. OBSCENE OR DEFAMATORY MATERIAL

The Authors undertake to each other that their contributions to the Work and the Artwork shall not contain any material which is obscene, offensive or defamatory of any third party and will not expose the Authors to any criminal or civil proceedings.

11. EXPENSES

The Authors agree to be personally responsible for their own expenses incurred in respect of the preparation, research and writing required for the satisfactory completion of the Work and the Artwork.

12. VAT, NATIONAL INSURANCE AND PERSONAL TAX

The Authors agree to be individually responsible for their own national insurance and personal tax and any value added tax which may become due as result of this Agreement or any publication Agreement.

13. CONFIDENTIALITY

The Authors confirm that neither shall disclose to any third party any confidential information concerning the Work or the Artwork or the business or future plans of the other author acquired during the course of this Agreement without the prior consent of the other party.

14. MUTUAL INDEMNITY

The Authors mutually undertake to indemnify the other against all liabilities, claims, demands, actions, costs, damages or loss arising out of any breach by either party of any of the terms of this Agreement, save that both parties agree to provide full details to the other party at the earliest opportunity and shall not settle any such matter without first consulting the other party.

15. EDITORIAL CONTROL

The Authors agree that no material is to be included in the Work or the Artwork unless both parties agree that the material is to be included.

16. ALTERATIONS AND AMENDMENTS

The Authors agree that this Agreement supersedes all previous agreements, representations or promises and sets out all the terms agreed between the Authors. Any amendment or alteration to this Agreement must be in writing and signed by each of the Authors.

17. THIRD PARTY TRANSFER

The Authors agree that neither party shall be entitled to assign, transfer, charge or make over this Agreement or any of the rights or obligations to any third party without the prior written consent of the other party.

18. NO PARTNERSHIP OR EMPLOYMENT

This Agreement shall not be deemed to create a partnership or employment relationship between the Authors.

19. NON-PERFORMANCE

In the event that either one of the Authors is unable to perform his duties under this Agreement due to circumstances beyond his reasonable control, including ill-health. Then such non-performance shall not be deemed to be a breach of any term of this Agreement. If such non-performance continues for a period of [________] or more then the other party shall be entitled to terminate this Agreement by notice in writing.

20. DEATH OF THE AUTHORS

The Authors agree that in the event of the death of one of the Authors after the delivery of the Work for publication, then the joint copyright ownership in the Work of the deceased author shall be vested in his estate, which shall be entitled to any sums which would have been due to the author under the terms of the Agreement.

21. TERMINATION

Either party shall have the right by summary notice in writing to the other Author to terminate this Agreement if the other Author fails or neglects to perform or observe any condition of this Agreement.

22. GOVERNING LAW

This Agreement shall be subject to the Laws of England.

A COPY OF THE SYNOPSIS IS ATTACHED TO AND FORMS PART OF THIS AGREEMENT.

Signed by: [____________]
FOR AND ON BEHALF OF AUTHOR A

Date: [____________]

Signed by: [____________]
FOR AND ON BEHALF OF AUTHOR B

Date: [____________]

Witnessed by: [____________]

OUTLINE—COLLABORATION AGREEMENT BETWEEN TWO AUTHORS

This is a collaboration agreement between two authors. The stage at which this agreement applies is where the authors have agreed an outline to the work but no approach has been made to a publisher.

The nature of the individual contributions of each author must be clarified. They may be responsible for specific chapters, or they may work closely on the whole work but agree to be responsible for different areas of research.

The authors are agreeing to be joint and equal copyright owners of the work as a whole, notwithstanding their individual contributions, and that they must both agree on the contents of the material to be included in the work. In the event of the agreement being terminated, then the division of copyright in the work will be based on their individual contribution.

No third party will publish the work or act as an agent to exploit the work unless they both consent. Preliminary business points are raised such as the proposed delivery date by which the work should be finished; the basic terms which they will seek from a publisher such as advances against royalties and percentages. All proceeds from the exploitation of the work are to be split equally between the authors.

Upon the death of one of the authors prior to publication, the surviving author would become the sole copyright owner in the work. The proceeds which would have been due to the deceased author had he not died, would go to his estate. This Agreement is unlikely to be a formal document between two authors but a letter agreement highlighting agreed issues which should be resolved before a publisher is approached.

BUY-OUT OF ALL RIGHTS IN AN AUTHOR'S WORK

BETWEEN:

(1) [____________]
of [____________] (to be known as the Author in this Agreement)

AND

(2) [____________]
of [____________] (to be known as the Assignee in this Agreement)

IT IS AGREED as follows:

1. DEFINITIONS

The words below are agreed to mean as follows:

1.1 "The Work" shall mean the original work by the Author entitled [____________], which is [____________] typed A4 pages and which includes: [____________] pages of the Artwork.

1.2 "The Artwork" shall mean any photograph, drawing, sketch, picture, diagram, map, chart, plan or any other illustration or any engraving, lithograph, woodcut or similar work and any other material listed: [____________] which forms part of or is attached to the Work.

1.3 "The Assignment Fee" shall be the sum of: [figure/currency].

1.4 "The Territory" shall be all countries, ships, aeroplanes, oilrigs, bases and locations throughout the world, outer space and the universe.

1.5 "All Media Rights" shall mean the sole and exclusive right to produce, manufacture, supply, sell, rent, distribute, license, market, and exploit the Work and any part(s) in all forms of the media whether in existence now or created in the future including but not limited to all forms of publication; hardback, paperback; all forms of radio, television and video; cable; satellite; digital; cassette; laser; disk; any technical method of delivery; any method of payment, charging, subscription, rental, lease, and for free; all forms of telecommunication systems; sound; vision; graphics; text; icons; images; all forms of theatric and non-theatric exploitation; all forms of mechanical and electronic reproduction, dissemination, or otherwise, internet, intranet and multimedia exploitation; CD-ROMs; all methods of merchandising; any other developments, variations or adaptation of any nature.

2. FULL ASSIGNMENT OF RIGHTS

2.1 In consideration of the Assignment Fee the Author assigns to the Assignee all present and future copyright and All Media Rights and any other rights of any nature whether in existence now or created in the future in the Work and any parts including the Artwork and the material in Schedule A throughout the Territory for the full period of any copyright and any extensions and renewals thereof and in perpetuity.

2.2 The Author agrees that on request by the Assignee at the Assignee's sole cost and expense he shall execute and sign such other documents as may reasonably be required by the Assignee to vest the copyright and other rights assigned under this Agreement in the Assignee.

3. WAIVER OF AUTHOR'S RIGHTS

3.1 In consideration of the Assignment Fee, the Author agrees that he shall waive all moral rights in the Work and any parts including the Artwork and the material in Schedule A. Therefore the Author shall not object to any failure to identify him as the author of the Work and/or Artwork and/or the material. The Author waives all rights to object to derogatory treatment of the Work and/or Artwork and/or material. Both these waivers are unconditional and shall extend to all third parties and successors in title.

3.2 The Author agrees that he waives all right to a copyright notice in respect of the Work and any parts and the Artwork and material in Schedule A in all media at any time in the Territory.

4. OBLIGATIONS OF THE AUTHOR

4.1 The Author confirms that the Work and the Artwork are the sole and original creation of the Author and confirms that he is the sole owner of all copyright and any other rights in the Work and the Artwork which are assigned under this Agreement.

4.2 The Author shall deliver all the material of the Work and the Artwork set out in the attached Schedule A [_____________] to the Assignee on or before: [date]. The risk in the material shall pass on delivery, which shall be at the Author's cost.

4.3 The Author confirms that he has and will retain good title and authority to enter into this Agreement and is not bound by any previous agreement which adversely affects this Agreement except: [_____________].

4.4 The Author confirms that the Work and the Artwork do not contain any material which he believes infringes the copyright or any other rights of any third party in the Territory.

4.5 The Author acknowledges that the Assignee shall be entitled to edit, adapt, alter or amend the Work and the Artwork entirely at its own sole cost and discretion.

4.6 The Author confirms that the Work has not been previously licensed to any third party and has not been previously exploited in any form at any time throughout the Territory except: [____________].

4.7 The Author confirms that he has taken specialist legal advice and fully comprehends the consequences of signing this Agreement.

5. OBLIGATIONS OF THE ASSIGNEE

5.1 In consideration of the rights assigned by the Author, the Assignee shall pay to the Author the Assignment Fee as follows:

[figure/currency] upon signature of this Agreement;
[figure/currency] upon acceptance of the material under clause 4.2;
[figure/currency] on or before [date].

5.2 The Assignee confirms that it has and will retain good title and authority to enter into this Agreement and is not bound by any previous agreement which adversely affects this Agreement.

5.3 The Assignee confirms that it shall be solely responsible for all costs incurred in respect of the distribution, marketing and exploitation of the Work and the Artwork and the material in Schedule A in any media at any time throughout the Territory and that the Author shall not be liable for any such sums.

5.4 The Assignee undertakes that the Work and the Artwork and the material in Schedule A will not be used in any manner or form which is obscene, offensive or defamatory or derogatory and will not expose the Author to any civil or criminal proceedings.

6. MISCELLANEOUS

MUTUAL INDEMNITY

6.1 The Author and the Assignee mutually undertake to indemnify the other against all liabilities, claims, demands, actions, costs, damages or loss arising out of any breach by either party of any of the terms of this Agreement.

6.2 In the event of any claim, dispute, action, writ or summons in connection with clause 6.1, the Author and the Assignee agree to provide full details to the other party at the earliest opportunity and shall not settle any such matter without first consulting the other party.

CONFIDENTIALITY

6.3 The Author and the Assignee shall not disclose to any third party any confidential business or future plans of the other party at any time acquired during the existence of this Agreement and no reference is to be made to the terms of this Agreement by either party in any advertising, publicity or promotional material without the prior consent of the other party.

AMENDMENTS AND ALTERATIONS

6.4 This Agreement supersedes all previous undertakings, representations or promises and sets out all the terms agreed between the parties. Any amendment or alteration to this Agreement must be in writing and signed by the Assignee and the Assignor.

NO PARTNERSHIP OR EMPLOYMENT

6.5 This Agreement shall not be deemed to create any partnership or employment relationship between the parties.

VALUE ADDED TAX

6.6 All sums payable under this Agreement are exclusive of any value added tax that may be payable by either party.

FORCE MAJEURE

6.7 In the event that this Agreement cannot be performed or its obligations fulfilled for any reason beyond the reasonable control of the Author or the Assignee, including such events as war, industrial action, floods or Acts of God, then such nonperformance or failure to fulfil its obligations shall be deemed not to be a breach of this Agreement. In the event that this Agreement cannot be performed or its obligations fulfilled for any reason beyond the reasonable control of the defaulting party for a continuous period of [three months] then the other party may, at its discretion, terminate this Agreement by notice in writing at the end of that period.

TERMINATION OF THE AGREEMENT

6.8 In addition to any other rights and remedies at law, this Agreement may be terminated by giving written notice to the other party who has breached this Agreement or defaulted on the grounds that the Assignee has failed to account or make payments as required under this Agreement or where the Author or the Assignee has committed a serious breach of its obligations under this Agreement and has not rectified the position within [30 days].

GOVERNING LAW

6.9 This Agreement shall be subject to the Laws of [____________].

ATTACHED TO AND FORMING PART OF THIS AGREEMENT IS SCHEDULE A, A LIST OF THE MATERIAL OF THE WORK AND ARTWORK.

FOR AND ON BEHALF OF THE AUTHOR: [____________]

FOR AND ON BEHALF OF THE ASSIGNEE: [____________]

DATE OF THIS AGREEMENT: [____________]

OUTLINE—BUY-OUT OF ALL RIGHTS IN AN AUTHOR'S WORK

This is a short-form, full assignment of the copyright and all other rights in an author's work, which is also known as a complete buy-out. The Author is confirming that he is the sole and original creator of the Work and that no copyright of any third party exists in the Work. There is also an undertaking by the Author that the Work has not been previously exploited in any form. If there are agreements in existence which relate to the Work, then they should be comprehensively declared.

Upon signing this Agreement and receiving the Assignment Fee, the Author would have no property rights left in the Work. The Author is being paid an Assignment Fee (which should be adequate consideration and not a nominal sum). This Agreement is to be used where the copyright in a Work is being bought and sold in the same manner as tangible property. In addition to selling the property rights in the Work, the Author is waiving his moral rights, including the right to be identified as the author or to object to derogatory treament. It should be remembered, however, that moral rights may be waived but the right to moral rights cannot be transferred to a third party. The Author has waived his right to a copyright notice in the Work, Artwork and material. The Assignee may exploit the Work without giving any credit in any form to the fact that the Work was created by the Author.

We have deliberately left out any reference to the nationality of the Author and left the issue of governing law to be decided between the parties.

The Assignee is to agree not to use the Work, Artwork or material in any way which is obscene, defamatory or derogatory to the Author. The Author is not giving any such undertaking. The buyer is taking the material as it exists and must check it for legal problems.

However both parties are giving an indemnity, the Author may wish to limit his responsibilities to a fixed sum. The Author is still undertaking that there are no copyright problems with the Work, Artwork or material.

SERIALISATION OF A BOOK

AN AGREEMENT DATED: [____________]

BETWEEN:

(1) [____________]
of [____________] (to be known as the Licensor in this Agreement)

AND

(2) [____________]
of [____________] (to be known as the Licensee in this Agreement)

IT IS AGREED as follows:

1. DEFINITIONS

The words below are agreed to mean as follows:

1.1 "The Work" is the following book entitled: [____________].

1.2 "The Periodical" is the following publication owned or controlled by the Licensee in which the Work is to be serialised: [____________]

1.3 "The Publisher" shall mean the following company with which the Licensor has entered into an agreement for the publication of the Work in hardback and paperback form: [____________].

1.4 "The Publication Agreement" shall mean the written agreement between the Publisher and the Licensor entitling the Publisher to publish the Work in hardback and paperback form.

1.5 "The Licence Period" shall commence on the [date of this Agreement] and continue until: [date/event].

1.6 "The Serialisation Rights" shall mean the right to publish the Extracts in the Periodical.

1.7 "The Extracts" shall mean the following parts of the Work:

1.7.1 From the written text of the original hardback edition of the Work:

pages: [____________];
pages: [____________];
pages: [____________];
pages: [____________].

1.7.2 The following illustrated parts of the Work:

pages: [____________];
pages: [____________];
pages: [____________];
pages: [____________].

1.8 "The Territory" shall be all countries, locations and bases throughout the world.

1.9 "The Serialisation Fee" shall be the sum of: [figure/currency].

2. LICENCE OF EXCLUSIVE SERIALISATION RIGHTS

2.1 In consideration of the Serialisation Fee, the Licensor grants to the Licensee the sole and exclusive Serialisation Rights throughout the Territory for the duration of the Licence Period.

2.2 The Licensee undertakes not to edit, adapt, alter or amend or in any way change the Extracts without the prior written consent of the Licensor.

2.3 The Licensee undertakes not to permit, license or transfer any of the Serialisation Rights to any third party without the prior written consent of the Licensor.

2.4 The Licensor undertakes not to permit, license or transfer the right to publish the Extracts or any other part(s) of the Work in any other newspaper, periodical or magazine owned or controlled by any third party throughout the Territory for the duration of the License Period except for the purposes of review, criticism or other fair dealing.

3. MORAL RIGHTS

3.1 The Licensee acknowledges that the Licensor asserts his moral rights generally in respect of the Work and the Extracts and in particular to be identified on each and every occasion that the Extracts appear in the Periodical as follows: [__________].

3.2 The Licensee acknowledges that the Licensor asserts his moral right to object to derogatory treatment of the Work and the Extracts.

3.3 The Licensor agrees that he has reviewed the Extracts and their proposed layout in the Periodical and does not object to any such treatment.

4. COPYRIGHT NOTICE

4.1 The following copyright notice and words shall be displayed in the precise manner and order set out: [____________] and printed at the end of the Extract in each copy of the Periodical together with the name of the Publisher and the title of the Work. The Licensee agrees that it shall not at any time delete or authorise the removal or omission of such copyright notice which shall be placed in such a manner and location as to give reasonable notice of the copyright owner's rights.

4.2 The Licensee agrees to acknowledge by suitable words, credit or copyright notice the ownership of any copyright in any material in the Extract. Provided that the Licensor shall advise the Licensee in writing of the conditions required to be fulfilled.

4.3 The Licensee agrees to provide the following copyright notice, trademark, logo and credit to the Licensor in the Periodical in respect of the Extracts and in any publicity, promotional, advertising and packaging material associated with the Extracts as follows: [____________].

5. OBLIGATIONS OF THE LICENSEE

5.1 The Licensee agrees to pay to the Licensor the Serialisation Fee as follows:

[____________] upon signature of this Agreement;
[____________] on or before [date/event].

5.2 The Licensee undertakes to publish the Extracts in the Periodical in the following manner:

approximately [____________] words on each of the following dates: [____________].

5.3 The Licensee confirms that it has and will retain good title and authority to enter into this Agreement and is not bound by any previous agreement which adversely affects this Agreement.

5.4 The Licensee undertakes to instigate and pursue all necessary legal and practical action to protect all copyright and any other rights in the Extracts granted under this Agreement and shall bear all the legal, administrative or incidental costs of so doing. The Licensee agrees that the prior written approval of the Licensor shall be required before any action, claim, writ, summons or any other proceedings are settled.

5.5 The Licensee agrees that the Licensor shall be entitled to be consulted in relation to any artwork and designs to be created by the Licensee in respect of the Extracts.

5.6 The Licensee agrees to provide the Licensor with not less than [24 sample copies] of every edition of the Periodical in which the Extracts appear, free of charge.

5.7 The Licensee agrees to provide the Licensor with copies and samples of any proposed publicity, promotional, advertising and packaging material in respect of the marketing and commercial exploitation of the Serialisation Rights.

5.8 The Licensee agrees that it shall be solely responsible for the cost including the Extracts and the Periodicals and the distribution, marketing and publicity.

5.9 The Licensee agrees to be responsible for the cost of any additional material or photographs that may be required for the article and in the event of the creation of any such new material shall provide a copy to the Licensor.

6. OBLIGATIONS OF THE LICENSOR

6.1 The Licensor confirms that he has full title and authority to enter into and perform this agreement and that he is not bound by any previous Agreement which adversely affects this Agreement.

6.2 The Licensor confirms that the Publication Agreement entitles the Licensor to grant to the Licensee the Serialisation Rights under this Agreement.

6.3 The Licensor confirms that the Work is the original work of the Licensor and that he is the sole owner of or controls all copyright and any other rights in the Work granted under this Agreement.

6.4 The Licensor confirms that all copyright clearances and consents necessary for the publication of the Extracts have been obtained and have or will be paid for by the Licensor.

6.5 The Licensor confirms that the Extracts have been reviewed by their legal advisors for legal problems prior to the proposed publication of the Work in hardback. The Licensor does not accept any responsibility for any legal action which may arise form the publication of the Extracts by the Licensee and the Licensee must seek its own specialist legal advice in respect of the threat of potential claims or actions by the public or any third party.

6.6 The Licensor confirms that the Work does not contain any material which infringes the copyright or any other rights of any third party in the Territory in respect of the rights granted under this Agreement.

6.7 The Licensor agrees that the Licensee shall be entitled to use the name, photograph, biography and image of the Licensor in respect of the exercise of the Serialisation Rights granted under this Agreement.

6.8 The Licensor agrees to arrange one photographic session of [____________] length with the Licensee at the Licensee's sole cost for the purpose of photographs to be used in the Periodical in association with the Extracts and one interview of [____________] duration. Provided that the Licensee agrees to assign copyright and all other rights in the photographs and the interview and any material related there to the Licensor.

6.9 The Licensor agrees that he shall be responsible for all his own national insurance, personal tax and value added tax which may be due in consequence of this Agreement.

7. MISCELLANEOUS

CONFIDENTIALITY

7.1 The Licensor and the Licensee shall not disclose to any third party any confidential business or future plans of the other party at any time acquired during the existence of this Agreement and no reference is to be made to the terms of this Agreement by either party in any advertising, publicity or promotional material without the prior consent of the other party.

AMENDMENTS AND ALTERATIONS

7.2 This Agreement supersedes all previous agreements, representations or promises and sets out all the terms agreed between the parties. Any amendment or alteration to this Agreement must be in writing and signed by an authorised signatory of each party.

NO PARTNERSHIP OR EMPLOYMENT

7.3 This Agreement shall not be deemed to create any partnership or employment relationship between the parties.

VALUE ADDED TAX

7.4 All sums payable under this Agreement are exclusive of any value added tax that may be payable by either party.

THIRD PARTY TRANSFERS

7.5 Neither party shall assign, transfer, charge or make over this Agreement or any of its rights or obligations.

FORCE MAJEURE

7.6 In the event that this Agreement cannot be performed or its obligations fulfilled for any reason beyond the reasonable control of the Licensor or the Licensee, including such events as war, industrial action, floods or Acts of God, then such non-performance or failure to fulfil its obligations shall be deemed not to be a breach of this Agreement. In the event that this Agreement cannot be performed or its obligations fulfilled for any reason beyond the reasonable control of the defaulting party for a continuous period of [one month]. Then the other party may, at its discretion, terminate this Agreement by notice in writing at the end of that period.

TERMINATION AND EXPIRY OF THE AGREEMENT

7.7 If either party fails to perform or observe any of the terms of this Agreement and if the defaulting party fails to remedy such failure or breach with [three days] of receipt of a notice in writing which sets out the alleged default and the remedy required. Then if the failure or breach is not rectified the party may serve a further notice, which will terminate the Agreement with immediate effect upon receipt. Any such termination shall be without prejudice to the legal rights and remedies available to either party.

GOVERNING LAW

7.8 This Agreement shall be governed by and construed in accordance with the Laws of [____________] and no other jurisdiction shall be applicable.

Signed by: [____________]
FOR AND ON BEHALF OF THE LICENSOR

Signed by: [____________]
FOR AND ON BEHALF OF THE LICENSEE

AGREEMENT DATED: [____________]

OUTLINE—SERIALISATION OF A BOOK

This is a deliberately short serialisation agreement between an author and a newspaper/magazine. The parties are referred to as the Licensor and the Licensee. The Agreement presumes that the Author has reserved the serialisation rights in any publishing agreement which he may have entered into concerning the Work.

The Licensee is to publish an agreed number of pages and artwork in the Periodical.

There is to be an additional photographic session for some new photographs to surround the text, and there may also be an interview. The Licensor has requested that all copyright in the material be assigned to the Licensor. Normally it would be kept by the party that pays for the Work—in this case the Licensee.

There are no indemnity or notice provisions. The termination is short, so that the Agreement can be terminated if one party is in breach and fails to remedy the matter.

Although the Licensor is stating that their legal advisors have looked at the Work for legal problems, it is the responsibility of the Licensee to do the same before publishing the Extracts. The Licensor is not giving an undertaking that the Extracts are not obscene or defamatory.

The Licensor is, however, obtaining and paying for all copyright clearances and consents.

PRE-PRODUCTION OPTION TO ACQUIRE AN EXCLUSIVE LICENCE IN AN AUTHOR'S WORK

BETWEEN:

(1) [______________]
of [______________] (to be known as the Author in this Agreement)

AND

(2) [______________]
of [______________] (to be known as the Production Company in this Agreement).

IT IS AGREED as follows:

1. DEFINITIONS

1.1 "The Author's Work" shall be the original work by the Author entitled [______________] and published by [______________].

1.2 "The Series" shall be the series of films and any associated sound recordings based on the Author's Work entitled [______________] comprising of [______________] episodes, each of which shall be [______________] minutes in duration.

1.3 "The Option Fee" shall be the sum of: [figure/currency].

1.4 "The Option Period" commence on the [date of this Agreement] and shall continue until: [date].

2. GRANT OF EXCLUSIVE OPTION

2.1 In consideration of the Option Fee, the Author grants to the Production Company the sole and exclusive right to exercise an option to produce the Series based on the Author's Work. The right to exercise the option shall be for the duration of the Option Period.

2.2 In the event that the Production Company exercises the option. Then the Author and the Production Company both agree to sign the exclusive licence agreement, which is attached to and forms part of this Agreement.

2.3 The Production Company acknowledges that after the expiry of the Option Period the Production Company shall have no further rights in the Author's Work and shall not be entitled to produce the Series.

2.4 The Author undertakes that he/she will not grant an option nor authorise, licence or permit any third party to produce a film based on the Author's Work or any adaptation, variation or development during the Option Period without the prior written consent of the Production Company.

2.5 In the event that the option is not exercised then all copyright, property and all other rights shall remain vested in and belong only to the Author.

2.6 Any failure to renew or extend the Option Period following the expiry shall not be grounds for any claim or payments for any reason and the Author and the Production Company agree that they shall not be entitled to any claim or sums for any failure to renew, extend or negotiate a further period.

3. OBLIGATIONS OF THE AUTHOR

3.1 The Author confirms that he/she has full authority to enter into and perform this Agreement and that he/she is not bound by any previous agreement which adversely affects this Agreement.

3.2 The Author confirms that the Author's Work is the original work of the Author and does not infringe the copyright or any other right of any third party in the following countries: [____________]. Except for the following material which is owned or controlled by a third party which has been included in the Author's Work: [____________].

3.3 The Author agrees that he/she shall be responsible for all national insurance, personal tax and value added tax which may be due in consequence of this Agreement.

4. OBLIGATIONS OF THE PRODUCTION COMPANY

4.1 In consideration of the Author granting to the Production Company the option rights under this Agreement. The Production Company agrees that it shall pay to the Author the Option Fee within [14 days] of both parties signing this Agreement.

4.2 The Production Company agrees that it will not assign, transfer or charge any of the rights or obligation under this Agreement to any third party without the prior written consent of the Author.

4.3 The Production Company undertakes that it shall be responsible for any sums due in respect of the production and the exploitation of the rights in the Series including any sums due in respect of any third party from the clearance, consent or otherwise of any material which is in the Work which is not owned or controlled by the Author.

4.4 The Production Company acknowledges that it shall not be entitled to arrange or permit the development and writing of any treatment, scripts or other material relating to the Author's Work unless it has exercised the option granted under this Agreement and signed the exclusive licence agreement attached to this Agreement.

4.5 The Production Company acknowledges that it shall not be entitled to off-set the option fee paid under this Agreement against any sums due to the Author under the exclusive licence agreement attached to this Agreement.

5. MORAL RIGHTS AND COPYRIGHT NOTICE

5.1 The Author asserts his moral right to be reasonably, prominently and clearly identified as the original creator of and author of the Work in the following form and style: [____________] on all copies of any material based on the Author's Work in any form.

5.2 The Author requests the following copyright notice in the following form and style: [____________] on all copies of any material based on the Author's Work.

5.3 The Publisher is entitled to the following credit in the following form and style: [____________] on all copies of any material based on the Author's Work.

5.4 The Author asserts his moral right not to have the Author's Work subject to derogatory treatment. However, the Author accepts that adaptation, development, editing and variation of the Author's Work is necessary to create a treatment or script for the Series.

6. MISCELLANEOUS

6.1 The Author and the Production Company undertake to indemnify the other against all liabilities, claims, demands, actions, costs, damages and loss arising out of any breach by either party of any of the terms of this Agreement.

6.2 In the event of any claim, dispute, action, writ or summons in connection with clause 6.1, the Author and the Production Company agree to provide full details to the other party at the earliest opportunity and shall not settle any such matter without first consulting the other party.

6.3 No reference is to be made to the terms of this Agreement by either party in public without the prior consent of the other party.

6.4 Any amendment or alteration to this Agreement must be in writing and signed by an authorised signatory of each party.

6.5 Without prejudice to the right to serve notices by any other means any notice served under this Agreement which has been sent by first class, pre-paid post shall be deemed to be received [48 hours] thereafter (excluding Saturdays, Sundays and public holidays).

6.6 All sums payable under this Agreement are exclusive of any value added tax that may be payable by either party.

6.7 No party shall be liable to any other for any loss or damage arising from any failure to perform any of its obligations in this Agreement or for any cause whatsoever beyond its control.

6.8 This Agreement shall not be deemed to create any partnership or employment relationship between the parties.

6.9 In addition to any other rights and remedies at law either party may, by giving written notice to the other party, terminate this Agreement on the grounds that:

6.9.1 the Production Company has failed to make payments as required under this Agreement;

6.9.2 where either party has committed a serious breach of its obligations under this Agreement and has not rectified the position within [30 days]; or

6.9.3 where the Production Company goes into voluntary or involuntary liquidation or is declared insolvent, either in bankruptcy proceedings, or other legal proceedings or has reached an agreement with creditors due to its failure or inability to pay its debts as they fall due, or where a receiver is appointed over the whole or part of the Production Company's business.

6.10 This Agreement shall be subject to the Laws of England.

ATTACHED TO AND FORMING PART OF THIS AGREEMENT IS AN EXCLUSIVE LICENCE AGREEMENT.

THE AUTHOR: [____________]

NAME/TITLE: [____________]

THE PRODUCTION COMPANY: [____________]

NAME/TITLE: [____________]

DATE OF THIS AGREEMENT: [____________]

OUTLINE—PRE-PRODUCTION OPTION TO ACQUIRE AN EXCLUSIVE LICENCE IN AN AUTHOR'S WORK

This is a short option agreement between an author and a production company. The Production Company is agreeing to pay the Author an Option Fee and in return the Author is granting the exclusive right to exercise an option to produce a Series based on the Author's Work. The option lasts for a limited period, referred to as the Option Period. If the option is exercised then both parties are agreeing to sign an exclusive licence agreement which should be attached to this Option Agreement.

This Option Agreement may be adapted to suit a wide variety of circumstances. As far as possible, the agreement which is to be concluded if the Option is exercised should be attached to the Agreement.

The Author asserts his moral rights to be identified, and the right to have a copyright notice.

If the parties do not wish to attach an exclusive licence then a list of main agreed issues could be attached.

Although the Author is giving an undertaking that the copyright is clear, he may only wish to do this for named countries. There are no undertakings regarding the content of the Work such as obscenity, defamation as it is not envisaged that the Work will be distributed to the public in general by the Production Company at this stage. An undertaking by the Production Company to this effect could be provided.

Either Contract 37 or 38 could be adopted to be attached to this Option.

EXCLUSIVE LICENCE BETWEEN AN AUTHOR AND PRODUCTION COMPANY FOR FILM BASED ON BOOK

AN AGREEMENT made this [____________] day of [____________] 2[____]

BETWEEN:

(1) [____________]
of [____________] (to be known as the Author in this Agreement)

AND

(2) [____________]
of [____________] (to be known as the Production Company in this Agreement)

IT IS AGREED as follows:

1. DEFINITIONS

The words below are agreed to mean as follows:

1.1 "The Author's Work" shall be the [original] work by the Author, including the Artwork, entitled [____________].

1.2 "The Publishers" shall mean the following publishers of the Author's Work with whom the Author has entered into a written agreement for the publication of the Author's Work in respect of the hardback and paperback as follows: [____________].

1.3 "The Artwork" shall mean any photographs, drawings, sketches, pictures, diagrams, maps, charts, plans, graphic work or any other illustrations which are included as part of the Author's Work.

1.4 "The Film" shall be the feature-length, cinematic film and any associated sound recordings to be produced by the Production Company based on and adapted from the Author's Work entitled [____________] which shall be [____________] minutes in duration in the [____________] language.

1.5 "The Scripts" shall be all draft and final scripts to be prepared by the screen-play writer based on the Author's Work.

1.6 "The Key Personnel" shall be as follows:

1.6.1 the producer: [______________];
1.6.2 the director: [______________];
1.6.3 the screen-play writer: [______________];
1.6.4 senior cameraman: [______________];
1.6.5 senior film editor: [______________];
1.6.6 leading actor: [______________];
1.6.7 leading actress: [______________];
1.6.8 any other: [______________].

1.7 "The Production Schedule" shall be the provisional dates, times and locations of making the Film, including pre-production, production, post-production and completion of the Film. A copy of the Production Schedule is attached to and forms part of this Agreement.

1.8 "The Licence Fee" shall be the sum of: [figure/currency].

1.9 "The Author's Royalties" shall mean the following percentage of the Gross Receipts: [______________].

1.10 "The Licence Period" shall commence on the [date of this Agreement] and shall continue until: [date/event].

1.11 "The Territory" shall be all countries, bases and locations throughout the world.

1.12 "All Media Rights" shall mean the sole and exclusive right to produce, manufacture, supply, sell, rent, distribute, license, market and export the Film and any part(s) in all forms of the media whether in existence now or created in the future including but not limited to all forms of publication; hardback, paperback; all forms of radio, television and video; cable; satellite; digital; cassette; laser; disk, and any technical method of delivery; any method of payment, charging, subscription, rental, lease, and for free; all forms of telecommunication systems; sound; vision; graphics text; icons; images; all forms of theatric and non-theatric exploitation; all forms of electronic, internet, intranet and multi-media exploitation; CD-ROMs; all methods of merchandising; any other developments, variations or adaptations of any nature.

1.13 "The Gross Receipts" shall be all sums and the total proceeds actually received by or credited to the Production Company or any of its sub-agents, sub-licencees or any other third party arising from the exploitation of the Film and any part(s) and all the media rights under this Agreement after the deduction of such commission; agency and distributor charges and expenses which shall be specified in the account in detail and the deduction of Sales Tax.

1.14 "Sales Tax" shall be any sales or other taxes levied by the E.U., British or foreign authorities on the sale or supply of the Film which form a distinct element in the sale or rental price and which are not recovered as part of the price directly or indirectly by the Production Company.

2. EXCLUSIVE LICENCE OF RIGHTS

2.1 In consideration of the Licence Fee and the Author's Royalties, the Author grants to the Production Company the sole and exclusive right to produce and exploit all the

Media Rights in the Film based on the Author's Work for the duration of the Licence Period throughout the Territory.

2.2 The Author agrees that he will not from the date of this Agreement until the expiry of the Licence Period and/or the termination of this Agreement exercise and/or license, and/or authorise and/or suffer the exercise in the Territory the exploitation in any media of a film of any type based on the Author's Work.

2.3 The Author agrees that he shall not be entitled to license or otherwise exploit any other media of any nature based on the Author's Work until the expiry or termination of this Agreement.

2.4 The Author reserves the right in respect of all other areas outside the Territory.

3. ASSERTION OF THE AUTHOR'S MORAL RIGHTS

3.1 The Production Company acknowledges that the Author asserts his moral rights generally in respect of the Film and in particular to be reasonably, clearly and prominently identified as follows: [____________] on all copies based on the Author's Work in all media.

3.2 The Author conditionally waives his moral right to object to derogatory treatment of the Film and its exploitation in any media under this Agreement. Provided that the Production Company use its reasonable endeavours to comply with the following conditions:

3.2.1 that the Author shall be provided with a reasonable opportunity to review and comment on the draft script, the key personnel, and the Production Schedule together with any later major or significant changes that may occur.

3.2.2 that the Author shall be entitled to approve the final script prior to production of the Film and shall be consulted on all changes except minor editing.

3.2.3 that the Author shall be provided with and approve a sample of each type of proposed form of exploitation in each form of the media.

3.3 The Author shall be entitled to revoke the waiver if these conditions are not fulfilled at any time by notice in writing to the Production Company.

4. OBLIGATIONS OF THE PRODUCTION COMPANY

4.1 In consideration of the rights granted under this Agreement, the Production Company agrees that it shall pay to the Author the Licence Fee as follows:

[____________] upon signature of this Agreement;
[____________] on or before: [date];
[____________] upon first video release of the Film to the public anywhere throughout the Territory but in any event no later than: [date];
[____________] upon first broadcast or transmission of the Film on television in any form but in any event no later than: [date].

4.2 The Production Company agrees that the Licence Fee shall not be returnable by the Author and shall be due in its entirety to the Author on or before the specified dates, irrespective of whether the production of the Film is delayed or stopped for any reason.

4.3 The Production Company undertakes that it shall produce the Film using the Key Personnel and in accordance with the Production Schedule at its sole cost and expense.

4.4 The Production Company confirms that the proposed budget for the Film is not less than: [figure/currency].

4.5 The Production Company agrees that the Author shall be entitled to approve the Scripts and shall deliver the Scripts to the Author for approval on or before the following dates:

the draft script: [date]
the final script: [date].

4.6 The Production Company agrees that the Author shall be entitled to view the rushes of the Film subject to adequate prior notice being given to the Production Company.

4.7 The Production Company confirms that it will be the sole owner of or control all copyright and any other rights in the Film except for the Author's Work.

4.8 The Production Company confirms that it has and will retain good title and authority to enter into this Agreement and is not bound by any previous agreement which adversely affects this Agreement.

4.9 The Production Company undertakes that it shall be solely responsible for all costs incurred and sums due in respect of the development, production, distribution, marketing and exploitation of the Film and part(s) in any form and that the Author is not and will not be liable for any such payments and that the Production Company will not be entitled to deduct any such sums from the Gross Receipts.

4.10 The Production Company agrees that it shall be solely responsible for obtaining and paying for all copyright clearances, consents, waivers, licences, contractual obligations and any other rights which are due or owed to any third parties arising directly or indirectly in respect of any material in the Film or part(s). Together with the cost of any exploitation of any of the media rights granted under this Agreement and including but not limited to artistic, musical, literary works, sound recordings, films, performing rights in any music and mechanical reproduction of any recordings, and actors. None of these costs shall be the responsibility of the Author and they shall not be deducted from the Gross Receipts.

4.11 The Production Company undertakes that the Film will not contain any obscene, offensive, blasphemous or defamatory material and will not expose the Author to any civil or criminal proceedings throughout the Territory at any time.

4.12 The Production Company undertakes that the Film will not contain any material which infringes the copyright or any other rights of any third party throughout the Territory at any time.

4.13 In addition to the Licence Fee, the Production Company undertakes that it shall pay the Author's Royalties to the Author within [seven days] of the last day of June and December in each year.

4.14 The Production Company and its sub-agents, sub-licensees, distributors and any other third parties involved in the exploitation of the Film shall keep professional, complete and accurate books of account, records, contracts, computer data, and other material showing the Gross Receipts and the Sales Tax and the Author's Royalties in respect of the commercial exploitation of the Film throughout the Territory at any time.

4.15 Within [seven days] of the last day of June and December in each year, the Production Company shall provide a detailed report to the Author with a full breakdown of the exploitation of the Film setting out the Gross Receipts, the Author's Royalties and the Sales Tax. Any deductions shall be set out and supported by documentation.

4.16 The Production Company agrees that the Author shall be entitled to arrange for an annual audit to inspect and make copies of the Production Company's books of account, records, contracts, computer data and any other material in order to verify the sums due to the Author. In the event that any audit shows a deficit to the Author of [____________] or more then the Production Company shall pay [double] the sum owed to the Author and all costs of such audit.

4.17 The Production Company agrees to provide the following on-screen credit, copyright notice, trademark or logo to the Author in the Film and in any publicity, promotional, advertising and packaging material in respect of the marketing distribution and exploitation of the Film: [____________].

4.18 The Production Company agrees to provide copies and samples at its own cost of any publicity, promotional, advertising and packaging material in respect of the marketing and commercial exploitation of the Film when requested to do so by the Author.

4.19 Upon request the Production Company agrees to keep the Author informed of the progress of the production of the Film and any exploitation in any media.

4.20 The Production Company shall provide the Author with details of all proposed release dates in respect of the exploitation of the Film.

4.21 The Production Company agrees that it shall not be entitled to exploit the Film in any form after the expiry of the Licence Period without the prior written consent of the Author. The Author shall still receive annual reports and continue to receive the Author's Royalties at any time until no further sums are due.

4.22 The Production Company acknowledges that the Author has asserted his moral rights to be identified as the author and the right to object to derogatory treatment. The Production Company agrees to observe these moral rights and to notify all third parties that may be engaged in the exploitation of the Film in any manner.

4.23 The Production Company agrees that all sums received in respect of the exploitation of the Film shall be kept in a separate account over which no lien or charge may be given without the prior written consent of the Author.

4.24 The Production Company shall not permit the Author any editorial control in respect of the Film, but shall agree that the Author may approve the draft and final script.

4.25 The artistic and editorial control of the exploitation of all media rights in the Film shall be at the discretion of the Production Company. The Production Company shall in good faith consider the requests and suggestions of the Author in respect of content, interpretation and presentation.

4.26 The Production Company agrees that it shall be responsible for and bear the cost of all legal proceedings which may arise in respect of the production and exploitation of the Film.

4.27 The Production Company agrees that the Author shall be entitled to approve the final edit of the Film.

5. OBLIGATIONS OF THE AUTHOR

5.1 The Author confirms that he has full authority to enter into and perform this Agreement and that he is not bound by any previous agreement which adversely affects this Agreement.

5.2 The Author confirms that no agreement which has been signed by or on behalf of the Author concerning the publication of the Author's Work throughout the Territory prohibits the Author from granting the rights in the Author's Work to the Production Company provided under this Agreement.

5.3 The Author confirms that the Author's Work is the original work of the Author and does not infringe the copyright or any other rights of any third party throughout the Territory in respect of the rights granted to the Production Company under this Agreement.

5.4 The Author undertakes that he shall not disclose any confidential information concerning the business or future plans of the Production Company to any third party which is acquired during the Licence Period. Provided that any such information is not released by the Production Company to the public or in the public domain.

5.5 The Author shall not make any statement in public or to the press concerning the Film or any business of the Production Company prior to the completion of the Film without the prior consent of the Production Company which shall not be unreasonably withheld or delayed. The Author is entitled to make a statement which is a review, criticism or assessment or the Film once it is released.

5.6 Subject to prior consultation, the Author agrees that the Production Company shall be entitled to use his name, photograph, biography and fair likeness in respect of the commercial exploitation of the Film.

5.7 The Author agrees either to accept or provide written reasons for his rejection of the Scripts for the Film within [21 days] of delivery in each case and undertakes that such rejection shall not be unreasonably withheld or delayed.

5.8 The Author acknowledges that the Production Company shall be entitled to make alterations to the Scripts during the course of production of the Film, provided that such amendments are not substantial and do not amount to unjustified modifications or derogatory treatment of the Author's Work.

5.9 The Author acknowledges that the Production Company shall have the final editorial decision in respect of the production and exploitation of the Film.

5.10 The Author acknowledges that the copyright in the Scripts and the Film shall belong to the Production Company and/or the Screen-play Writer, as the case may be.

5.11 The Author confirms that he is a British subject or national of a Member State of the E.U. and is resident in: [____________].

5.12 The Author acknowledges that the Production Company shall have the sole discretion as to the manner and method to be used in the distribution, marketing and promotion of the Film.

5.13 The Author acknowledges that the Licence Fee shall be off-set against the Author's Royalties.

5.14 The Author agrees that he shall be responsible for the cost of all his own national insurance, personal tax and value added tax, which may be due in consequence of this Agreement.

5.15 The Author has had the Author's Work reviewed by legal advisers for the purpose of the publication of the Work in hardback and paperback. The Author's Work in its present state does not contain any material of any nature which is obscene or defamatory or will expose the Production Company to civil or criminal proceedings under the Laws of England. The Author's Work has not been reviewed for legal purposes in any other countries of the Territory.

5.16 The Author asserts his moral rights to be clearly, prominently and reasonably identified to the public on each copy of the Film and on all other copies in any form which are exploited in any media under this Agreement as follows: [____________] as the author of the Author's Work on which the Film is based.

5.17 The Author has the right to object to derogatory treatment of the Author's Work on which the Film is based and does not waive any right to do so by approving the scripts. The Author accepts that the Film will not be an exact reproduction of the Author's Work.

5.18 The Author agrees that if the Production Company shall stop and not continue production of the Film. Then it is agreed that the total limit of the liability to the Author shall be the Licence Fee. No compensation shall be due or payable for any alleged loss of income, publicity, enhancement of reputation or injury or damage.

6. MISCELLANEOUS

MUTUAL INDEMNITY

6.1 In the event of any claim, dispute, action, writ or summons arising out of this Agreement, each party agrees to provide full details to the other party at the earliest opportunity and shall not settle any matter without first consulting with the other party if they intend such to be indemnified.

6.2 No settlement shall be made to the claim of any third party unless such claim is settled on reasonable grounds and in good faith taking into account the opinion of a legal advisor who is an expert in that field.

6.3 Either party shall be entitled to institute legal proceedings against a third party who has infringed their rights. Where the consent of both parties is required, they agree to co-operate subject to an agreement as to costs and the allocation of damages.

6.4 The Author indemnifies the Production Company up to a maximum of: [____________] in respect of any loss, damage, or costs arising out of any undertakings by the Author in this Agreement.

6.5 The Production Company indemnifies the Author in respect of any loss, damage, or costs arising out of any breach of the undertakings by the Production Company in this Agreement including any liability, claim, action, demand, writ or summons.

CONFIDENTIALITY

6.6 The Author and the Production Company shall not disclose to any third party any confidential business or future plans of the other party at any time acquired during the existence of this Agreement and no reference is to be made to the terms of this Agreement by either party in any advertising, publicity or promotional material without the prior consent of the other party.

AMENDMENTS AND ALTERATIONS

6.7 This Agreement supersedes all previous agreements, representations or promises and sets out all the terms agreed between the parties. Any amendment or alteration to this Agreement must be in writing and signed by an authorised signatory of each party.

THIRD PARTY TRANSFERS

6.8 Neither party shall assign, transfer, charge or make over this Agreement or any of its rights or obligations without the prior written consent of the other party.

NO PARTNERSHIP OR EMPLOYMENT

6.9 This Agreement shall not be deemed to create any partnership or employment relationship between the parties.

NOTICES

6.10 Without prejudice to the right to serve notices by any other means any notice served under this Agreement shall be in writing and by recorded delivery post.

VALUE ADDED TAX

6.11 All sums payable under this Agreement are exclusive of any value added tax that may be payable by either party.

FORCE MAJEURE

6.12 In the event that this Agreement cannot be performed or its obligations fulfilled for any reason beyond the reasonable control of the Author or the Production Company, including such events as war, industrial action, floods, Acts of God or unforeseen technical failure, then such non-performance or failure to fulfil its obligations shall be deemed not to be a breach of this Agreement. In the event that this Agreement cannot be performed or its obligations fulfilled for any reason beyond the reasonable control of the defaulting party for a continuous period of [six months]. Then the other party may, at its discretion, terminate this Agreement by notice in writing at the end of that period. Provided that both parties agree to negotiate, in good faith, an equitable settlement.

TERMINATION AND EXPIRY OF THE AGREEMENT

6.13 In addition to any other rights and remedies at law, this Agreement may be terminated by giving written notice to the other party who has breached this Agreement or has defaulted in the following circumstances:

6.13.1 where the Production Company has failed to account or make payments as required under this Agreement;

6.13.2 where the Production Company or the Author has committed a serious breach of its obligations under this Agreement, unless such party rectifies the position, as far as reasonably possible, within: [____________];

6.13.3 where the Production Company goes into voluntary or involuntary liquidation;

6.13.4 where the Production Company is declared insolvent either in bankruptcy proceedings or other legal proceedings;

6.13.5 where an agreement with creditors has been reached by the Production Company due to its failure or inability to pay its debts as they fall due; or

6.13.6 where a receiver is appointed over the whole or part of the Production Company's business.

GOVERNING LAW

6.14 This Agreement shall be subject to the Laws of England.

A COPY OF THE PRODUCTION SCHEDULE IS ATTACHED TO AND FORMS PART OF THIS AGREEMENT.

Signed by: [____________] [Title/Name]
THE AUTHOR

Signed by: [____________] [Title/Name]
THE PRODUCTION COMPANY

AGREEMENT DATED: [____________]

OUTLINE—EXCLUSIVE LICENCE BETWEEN AN AUTHOR AND PRODUCTION COMPANY FOR FILM BASED ON BOOK

This is an exclusive licence between an Author and a Production Company for a Film based on the Author's Work. The Agreement therefore presumes that the Author has reserved such rights in the publication agreement between himself (or an agent) and the Publisher(s) of the Work. The Production Company is paying the Author a Licence Fee, which is non-returnable but is to be off-set against the Author's Royalties.

The Author is to receive an agreed percentage of all money received by the Production Company from the exploitation of the Film. This percentage is referred to as the Author's Royalties. These royalties are derived from the Gross Receipts. The Production Company is not entitled to deduct any sums, such as the production costs or distribution expenses or other sums, prior to payment to the Author. It is therefore likely that the percentage due to the Author would, in these circumstances, be relatively small but far easier to determine and verify. The Author, under this Agreement, would be entitled to receive his percentage even where the Film makes a loss as long as his Licence Fee has been recouped.

The Author is granting the Production Company an exclusive licence to produce and exploit the Film based on the Author's Work in all media for a fixed Licence Period. All rights revert to the Author after expiry or termination. The Author may well receive reports and royalties after the expiry of the Licence Period.

The Author asserts his moral rights to be identified.

The Author does not waive his moral right not to be subject to derogatory treatment by approving the scripts. The Production Company should take its own legal advice as regards the content of the Film. There is only a limited undertaking by the Author regarding obscurity or defamation in the Work.

EXCLUSIVE LICENCE BETWEEN AUTHOR AND PRODUCTION COMPANY FOR A SERIES BASED ON THE AUTHOR'S WORK

AN AGREEMENT made this [____________] day of [____________]

BETWEEN:

(1) [____________]
of [____________] (to be known as the Author in this Agreement)

AND

(2) [____________]
of [____________] (to be known as the Company in this Agreement).

IT IS AGREED as follows:

1. DEFINITIONS

1.1 "The Author's Work" shall be the original work by the Author entitled [____________] and published by [____________].

1.2 "The Series" shall be the series of films and any associated sound recordings based on the Author's Work entitled [____________] comprising of [____________] episodes, each of which shall be [____________] minutes in duration.

1.3 "The Treatment" shall be the summary of the storylines to be prepared by the scriptwriter based on the Author's Work.

1.4 "The Scripts" shall be all draft and final scripts to be prepared by the scriptwriter from the Treatment and based on the Author's Work.

1.5 "The Licence Fee" shall be the non-returnable and recoupable advance against the Author's Royalties which is the sum of: [figure/currency].

1.6 "The Licence Period" commence on the date of this Agreement and shall continue until: [date].

1.7 "The Territory" shall be all countries throughout the world, universe and outer space.

1.8 "The Television Rights" shall mean the right to broadcast, transmit or otherwise exploit the Series by all forms of television including digital, satellite, cable and terrestrial whatever the method of charge, whether it is free, and whatever the method of delivery whether in existence now or developed in the future.

1.9 "The Videogram Rights" shall mean the right to exploit the Series by all forms of videograms whether capable of being recorded, played or stored or replayed by any format of cassette, disk, laser and irrespective of the method of distribution or the persons including sales, retail, closed circuit user, to the general public or to businesses, commercial industries or other educational institutions.

1.10 "The Theatric Rights" shall mean the right to exhibit the Series to audiences where a charge for admission is made, including but not limited to public and private cinemas, concert and lecture halls and arenas.

1.11 "The Author's Royalties" shall be [figure per cent] [______%] of the Nett Receipts.

1.12 "The Gross Receipts" shall mean one hundred per cent of all sums, received or credited to the Company [in sterling] in the [United Kingdom] arising directly, indirectly or otherwise from the use and exploitation of the Series in the Territory at any time after the deduction of any taxes and currency conversion charges.

1.13 "The Production Costs" shall be the total costs, whether direct or indirect including the Licence Fee, of making the Series, including all items necessary for the development, pre-production, production, post-production and completion of the Series which are not recovered from any third party.

1.14 "The Distribution Expenses" shall be the following costs reasonably and properly expended in respect of the exploitation of the Series by the Company, which are not recouped from any third party:

1.14.1 duplication such as prints, duplicate negatives, cassettes, repairs and replacements;
1.14.2 delivery, storage, shipping, customs duties, freight, handling charges and insurance;
1.14.3 trailers and promotional material;
1.14.4 publicity and advertising material;
1.14.5 copyright, permissions, consents, clearances and performing rights payments and other fees and expenses to individuals, companies or collecting societies for any material;
1.14.6 any distributor's, sub-distributor's, sub-agent's and sub-licensee's commission;
1.14.7 dubbing, editing, subtitling and translating for the purpose of exploitation to a foreign country;
1.14.8 accounting and legal fees whether for debt collection and/or protection of legal rights and/or auditing; and
1.14.9 any other: [____________].

1.15 "The Nett Receipts" shall be the Gross Receipts less the Distribution Expenses.

1.16 "The Taxes" shall be any sales or other taxes levied by the E.U., British or foreign authorities on the sale, supply or exploitation of the Series which form a distinct element in the price or charge and which are not recovered.

2. EXCLUSIVE LICENCE OF RIGHTS

2.1 In consideration of the Licence Fee and the Author's Royalties. The Author grants to the Company the sole and exclusive right to produce the Series based on the Author's Work and to exploit all the Television Rights and all the Videogram Rights in the Series based on the Author's Work throughout the Territory for the duration of the Licence Period.

2.2 The Company acknowledges that after the expiry of the Licence Period. The Company shall have no rights in the Author's Work and shall only not be entitled to exploit the Series.

2.3 The Company undertakes that at the end of the Licence Period it shall execute any document or do anything required by the Author to vest all copyright in any variations or developments of the Author's Work in the Author except the Series.

2.4 The Author agrees that he/she will not licence or authorise any third party to produce any other film based on the Author's Work during the Licence Period.

2.5 The Company agrees that all rights not specifically granted under the Agreement are reserved by the Author.

3. MORAL RIGHTS

3.1 The Author declares his moral right to be recognised and acknowledged as the original writer of the Author's Work and to be identifiably, clearly and sufficiently prominently brought to the attention of the public to be known as: [____________] on all copies of any material distributed or exploited by the Company.

3.2 The Author declares his right to object to derogatory treatment of the Author's Work unless the Author has given his prior written approval to the Company in which case there shall be a conditional waiver. A waiver in any other case shall be applicable to any other act by the Company.

3.3 The Company acknowledges both the moral rights of the Author and agrees that it shall be bound to honour such rights and shall ensure that all third parties and successors in title of the business agree to accept such conditions.

4. COPYRIGHT NOTICE AND CREDIT

4.1 The Company agrees to provide the following copyright notice, credit, trademark and logo to the Author [____________] in the Series and in any advertising, publicity, packaging material, and any associated material in any media in respect of the exploitation of the Series.

4.2 The Company agrees to provide the Author with copies and samples of any advertising, publicity and packaging material together with one copy of each version in which the Series is exploited.

4.3 The Company agrees to ensure that any third party or successor in title shall agree to provide the conditions set out in Clause 4.1 to the Author.

5. OBLIGATIONS OF THE AUTHOR

5.1 The Author confirms that he/she has full authority to enter into and perform this Agreement and that he/she is not bound by any previous agreement which adversely affects this Agreement.

5.2 The Author confirms that the Author's Work is the original work of the Author and does not infringe the copyright or any other right of any third party in respect of the rights granted under this Agreement.

5.3 The Author confirms that the Author's Work does not contain any obscene or defamatory material and will not expose the Company to civil or criminal proceedings in [the United Kingdom].

5.4 The Author undertakes that he/she shall not disclose any confidential information concerning the business or future plans of the Company to any third party, which is acquired during the Licence Period.

5.5 The Author agrees to either accept or provide written reasons for his/her rejection of the Treatment and the Scripts for the Series within [30 days] of delivery in each case and undertakes that such rejection shall only be made on reasonable grounds and in good faith.

5.6 The Author agrees that he/she shall be responsible for all national insurance, personal tax and value added tax which may be due in consequence of this Agreement.

5.7 The Author agrees to provide to the Company on loan such artwork, stills, photographs and biographies of the principal persons or other material which he owns or controls that may assist the Company to exploit the rights granted under this Agreement. The Author agrees that the Company shall be entitled to arrange for copies to be made at the Company's cost so that the original material may be returned by an agreed date.

5.8 The Author acknowledges that the Company shall have the sole discretion as to the production, distribution, marketing and exploitation of the Series which shall be entirely at the Company's cost and expense.

5.9 Subject to prior consultation the Author agrees that the Company shall be entitled to use his name, biography, image and signature in the marketing and exploitation of the Series provided that it shall not be used for any product endorsement.

The Author shall be provided at the Company's cost with a sample of each and every item of material which features the name, biography or image of the Author created pursuant to this Agreement. Where it is intended to use it on the packaging of videos, then the Author shall be given the opportunity to view the final proof of any proposed cover.

Provided that the Author provides a response within [three days]. Then the Company agrees to incorporate all reasonable changes requested by the Author.

5.10 The Author agrees that the Licence Fee is non-returnable but can be off-set against the Author's Royalties.

6. OBLIGATIONS OF THE COMPANY

6.1 In consideration of the rights granted under this Agreement, the Company shall pay the Author the Licence Fee as follows:

[______] upon signature by both parties to this Agreement;
[______] on or before: [date];
[______] upon acceptance by the Author of the final Script;
[______] upon first television release in [the United Kingdom] but no later than: [date];
[______] upon first video release in [the United Kingdom] but no later than: [date].

6.2 The Company agrees that the Author shall be entitled to approve the Treatment and the Scripts which shall be delivered on or before:

Treatment: [date]
Draft Script: [date]
Final Script: [date].

6.3 The Company undertakes that it shall pay the Author's Royalties to the Author by the following dates for the preceding [three-month] period:

January, February, March	by: [date]
April, May, June	by: [date]
July, August, September	by: [date]
October, November, December	by: [date]

and at the same time provide a comprehensive and detailed report on each occasion which sets out a complete list of the exploitation of the Series with the Gross Receipts, the Distribution Expenses, the Nett Receipts and the Author's Royalties.

6.4 The Company agrees and undertakes that it shall be responsible for all the production costs and that it shall not be entitled to deduct or off-set them under this Agreement.

6.5 The Company agrees that, except for minor alterations, the final Script shall be used for the Series unless there is a material alteration in the circumstances which demand changes in which case the Author shall be consulted for his approval.

6.6 The Company shall arrange for the Author and his representatives to view the final version of the Series before it is made available to a third party.

6.7 The Company agrees not to use permit or license the Series to endorse any product without the prior written consent of the Author.

6.8 The Company agrees that it shall remain liable to the Author for all acts, omissions and errors of any third parties engaged by the Company including sub-licensees, agents and distributors.

6.9 The Company agrees that it shall be solely responsible for any damage, loss or copying of any material provided by the Author under this Agreement.

6.10 The Author shall at all times be allowed to inspect the accounts, software, records, documents, contracts or other material owned, controlled or in the possession of the

Company or to appoint a suitably qualified person to do so in order to verify the payments due to the Author. If such inspection reveals an error of [figure/currency] due to the Author. Then the Company shall pay the sum due immediately plus all costs of the audit and compensation of [____________].

6.11 The Company agrees that all accounting records and other material shall be kept until [date] and shall not be erased or destroyed without written notification to the Author.

6.12 The Company agrees that the Author's Work has only been reviewed for copyright, defamation and other legal problems in [the United Kingdom] and that it is the sole responsibility of the Company to arrange for and ensure that there is no threat of legal action from the Scripts or the Series. Such costs shall not be part of the Distribution Costs and shall be at the Company's sole expense.

6.13 The Company agrees to keep the Author advised on a regular basis as regards the production and exploitation of the Series.

7. MISCELLANEOUS

INDEMNITY AND LEGAL PROCEEDINGS

7.1 The Author and the Company mutually undertake to indemnify the other against all liabilities, claims, demands, actions, costs, damages and loss arising out of any breach by either party of any of the terms of this Agreement.

7.2 In the event of any claim, dispute, action, writ or summons in connection with clause 7.1, the Author and the Company agree to provide full details to the other party at the earliest opportunity and shall not settle any such matter without first consulting the other party.

7.3 In the event that the parties cannot agree the terms upon which to settle a matter. Then it is agreed that the advice or the opinion of Counsel shall be sought at the Company's cost but shall not be considered binding.

7.4 In the event that there is an allegation that the Author's Work and/or the Series infringes any third party rights. Then the party against whom the claim is made shall be entitled to defend it without prejudice to the right of that party to take third party proceedings or any other action against the Company whether for a contribution to indemnity or claim for damages.

CONFIDENTIALITY

7.5 The Author and the Company shall not disclose to any third party any confidential business or future plans of the other party at any time acquired during the existence of this Agreement and no reference is to be made to the terms of this Agreement by either party in any advertising, publicity or promotional material without the prior consent of the other party.

AMENDMENTS AND ALTERATIONS

7.6 This Agreement supersedes all previous agreements representations or promises and sets out all the terms agreed between the parties. Any amendment or alteration to this Agreement must be in writing and signed by an authorised signatory of each party.

NO PARTNERSHIP OR EMPLOYMENT

7.7 This Agreement shall not be deemed to create any partnership or employment relationship between the parties.

NOTICES

7.8 All notices under this Agreement must be in writing and delivered by courier, hand delivered, or first class or recorded post, not fax, e-mail or text messages.

VALUE ADDED TAX

7.9 All sums payable under this Agreement are exclusive of any value added tax that may be payable by either party.

THIRD PARTY TRANSFERS

7.10 Neither party shall assign, transfer, charge or make over this Agreement or any of its rights or obligations without the prior written consent of the other party.

FORCE MAJEURE

7.11 In the event that this Agreement cannot be performed or its obligations fulfilled for any reason beyond the reasonable control of either party including war, industrial action, floods or Acts of God. Then such non-performance or failure to fulfil its obligations shall be deemed not to be a breach of this Agreement. In the event that this Agreement cannot be performed or its obligations fulfilled for any reason beyond either party's reasonable control for a continuous period of [three months] then either party may, at its discretion, terminate this Agreement by notice in writing at the end of that period.

TERMINATION

7.12 In addition to any other rights and remedies at law, either party may, by giving written notice to the other party, terminate this Agreement on the grounds that:

7.12.1 the Company has failed to account or make payments as required under this Agreement;

7.12.2 where either party has committed a serious breach of its obligations under this Agreement and has not rectified the position within [30 days]; or

7.12.3 where the Company goes into voluntary or involuntary liquidation or is declared insolvent either in bankruptcy proceedings or other legal proceedings or has reached an agreement with creditors due to its failure or inability to pay its debts as they fall due, or where a receiver is appointed over the whole or part of the Company's business.

GOVERNING LAW

7.13 This Agreement shall be subject to the Laws of England.

Signed by: [____________]
FOR AND ON BEHALF OF THE AUTHOR

Signed by: [____________]
FOR AND ON BEHALF OF THE COMPANY

OUTLINE—EXCLUSIVE LICENCE BETWEEN AUTHOR AND PRODUCTION COMPANY FOR A SERIES BASED ON THE AUTHOR'S WORK

This is an exclusive licence between an Author and a Production Company for a Series of Films based on the Author's Work. The Agreement therefore presumes that the Author has reserved such rights in the publication agreement between himself (or an agent) and the Publisher(s) of the Work. The Production Company is paying the Author a Licence Fee, which is non-returnable but is to be off-set against the Author's Royalties. The Production Company is also paying to the Author an agreed percentage of all money received by the Production Company from the exploitation of the Film. The Author's Royalties are a percentage of the Nett Receipts. The Nett Receipts are the Gross Receipts less the Distribution Expenses. All the production costs are to be met by the Company and cannot be deducted from the Gross Receipts. Similarly the Company is to pay all legal costs for the Series.

The definition of television and videogram rights are wider than normal, but do not cover telecommunication use on small screens and the internet.

The Author is entitled to a copyright notice and credit as writer of the original Work. There is also an assertion of moral rights.

There are no restrictions placed on the Author making statements about the Film, although there is one of confidentiality regarding the Company's business.

The Author is granting the Production Company the right to produce the Film based on the Author's Work. The Production Company is entitled to exploit all forms of television and video for a specified period referred to as the Licence Period throughout the Territory.

It is not envisaged under this Agreement that the Author is writing or assisting in the preparation of the screen-play. The screen-play writer is named in the Agreement, as are all other key personnel. The Author has, nevertheless, a right of approval over the Scripts. In any event, the Production Company is entitled to make alterations to the Scripts during the course of production, provided that such amendments are not substantial and do not amount to an unjustified modification or derogatory treatment of the Work.

As the Author is not the writer of the Scripts, the copyright position in relation to the Scripts as opposed to the original Work should be made clear. In this Agreement, the Author accepts that the copyright in the Scripts and the Film do not belong to him. The Author is entitled to view the rushes but final editorial control rests with the Production Company.

EXCLUSIVE LICENCE FOR A FILM TO BE SHOWN ON STANDARD TELEVISION

AN AGREEMENT made this [____________] day of [____________]

BETWEEN:

(1) [____________]
of [____________] (to be known as the Licensor in this Agreement)

AND

(2) [____________]
of [____________] (to be known as the Licensee in this Agreement).

IT IS AGREED as follows:

1. DEFINITIONS

The words below are agreed to mean as follows:

1.1 "The Film" shall be the following film and any associated sound recording entitled [____________] which is [____________] minutes in duration.

1.2 "The Licence Fee" shall be the sum of: [figure/currency].

1.3 "The Film Package" shall be the following material of the Film:

1.3.1 technical material of first class quality comprising of [____________];
1.3.2 laboratory access letter;
1.3.3 typed transcript of final script;
1.3.4 typed copy of action continuity/shot list;
1.3.5 music cue sheet listing each musical work with the name of the composer, author and publisher including the duration of each musical work and the description of use in each case;
1.3.6 statement of on-screen, publicity, advertising, and promotional credit obligations and moral rights;
1.3.7 such publicity material including photographs and stills as may be available; and
1.3.8 such promotional material including trailers, promos and posters as may be available.

1.4 "The Territory" shall be the United Kingdom of Great Britain, Northern Ireland, the Channel Islands, the Isle of Man.

1.5 "The Standard Television Rights" shall mean the right to broadcast the Film on conventional VHF or UHF broadcast television in digital or analogue form transmitted by means of over the air standard television signals (including free, pay per view, subscription, licence and rental) for general reception excluding cable television and satellite television.

1.6 "The Cable Television Rights" shall mean the right to broadcast or transmit the Film by means of basic cable or pay cable, (including free, pay per view, subscription, license and rental) or by way of any other cable medium whether in existence now or developed in the future.

1.7 "The Satellite Television Rights" shall mean the right to broadcast or transmit the Film by means of a satellite, (including free, pay per view, subscription, license and rental), whether encrypted or not.

1.8 "The License Period" shall commence of the date of this Agreement and shall continue until [date].

2. EXCLUSIVE LICENSE OF RIGHTS

2.1 In consideration of the License Fee, the Licensor grants to the Licensee the sole and exclusive Terrestrial Television Rights throughout the Territory for the Licence Period.

2.2 The Licensee shall be entitled to [number] broadcasts of the Film.

2.3 The Licensee shall be entitled to broadcast not more than [__________] minutes of the Film for the purpose of programme announcement, trailing and post-broadcast comment or review in each case, without further payment.

2.4 The Licensee shall be entitled to authorise the use of not more than [___________] minutes for the purpose of programme comment or review on radio.

3. EDITORIAL CONTROL

The Licensee shall not be entitled to edit, adapt or alter the Film, except for minor editing and deletions for the purpose of complying with the Licensee's programme policy and scheduling.

4. OBLIGATIONS OF THE LICENSOR

4.1 The Licensor confirms that it is the sole owner of or controls all copyright and any other rights in the Film which are granted to the Licensee under this Agreement.

4.2 The Licensor confirms that it has and will retain good title and authority to enter into this Agreement and is not bound by any previous agreement which adversely affects this Agreement.

4.3 The Licensor confirms and undertakes that all copyright and any other rights consents, releases, or licenses including consents under the Copyright Designs and Patents Act 1988 in respect of all material of any nature in the Film has been or shall be cleared and paid for. This undertaking includes but is not limited to stills, music, footage, performers, artists, products, text, recordings, images, crew, editing and that the Licensee shall not be liable for any such payments.

The Licensee shall only be liable to pay any sums due from the recording and transmission of music in the Film namely the mechanical reproduction and performing rights payments.

4.4 The Company undertakes that it was the maker of the Film and the person by whom the arrangements necessary for the making of the Film were made and the first owner of copyright in the Film and acquired all rights in all material on which the Film is based and is incorporated in it as are necessary for the exercise of the rights printed in this Agreement.

4.5 The Licensor confirms that the Film does not and will not contain any material of any nature which is obscene or defamatory or will expose the Licensee to civil and/or criminal proceedings. The Licensor confirms and undertakes that the version of the Film supplied under the Agreement will be that which has been reviewed by the Licensee and rated by the censorship authority [____________].

4.6 The Licensor agrees that the Licensee shall be entitled to make such changes, cuts or alterations as may be required to comply with its own programming requirements and policy provided that the copyright notices and credits are not deleted and the moral rights of the following parties are observed: [____________].

4.7 The Licensor agrees that the Film Package shall be delivered by: [date]. The risk on the Film Package shall pass on delivery to the Licensee. The material shall be supplied at the Licensee's cost and returned at the end of the Licence Period at the Licensee's cost.

4.8 The Licensor agrees and undertakes that it shall not exercise and release to the public the following other rights on the Film in the Territory before the dates set out below:

Satellite Television Rights: [date]
Videogram Rights: [date]
Cable Television Rights: [date]

5. OBLIGATIONS OF THE LICENSEE

5.1 In consideration of the rights granted, the Licensee shall pay to the Licensor the Licence Fee as follows:

5.1.1 [____________] upon signature of this Agreement;
5.1.2 [____________] upon acceptance by the Licensee of the Film Package;
5.1.3 [____________] on or before [____________].

5.2 The Licensee agrees to reimburse the Licensor in respect of all the reproduction, insurance, and delivery costs incurred in providing an acceptable Film Package, subject to satisfactory receipts being provided on request.

5.3 The Licensee agrees that the Film Package shall remain the property of the Licensor and that at the end of the Licence Period the Film Package shall be returned to the Licensor at the Licensee's expense.

5.4 The Licensee agrees either to accept or provide written reasons for its rejection of the Film Package within [____________] of its delivery.

5.5 In the event that the Film is not of suitable technical quality and the Licensor cannot deliver an acceptable replacement within [21 days]. Then the Licensee shall be entitled to terminate this Agreement and the Licensor shall repay all sums paid to it in respect of the Licence Fee immediately.

5.6 The Licensee agrees to use all reasonable endeavours to ensure that the Film is shown on channel [____________] after [time] by [date].

5.7 The Licensee shall be responsible for all payments due in respect of the performing rights in any music and the mechanical reproduction of the Film.

5.8 The Licensee agrees and acknowledges that it shall use and shall not delete the credits, copyright notices, moral rights, trademarks, service marks, logos, titles or otherwise set out in Schedule A which is attached to and forms part of this Agreement. Except that the failure to broadcast any item listed on Schedule A due to unexpected lack of broadcast time, failure of facilities or other unforeseen circumstance shall not be a breach of this Agreement provided that reasonable endeavours had been made to comply with this Agreement.

5.9 The Licensee agrees that no third party shall be entitled to sponsor the Film or have its logo, trademark, service mark, design, product or image associated with or incorporated in the introduction trailer, or end credits whether for the purpose of corporate promotion, advertising or other publicity during the Licence Period in the Territory.

5.10 The Licensee agrees that it must provide the following credits in any advertising, publicity, promotional release in respect ot the Film: [____________].

5.11 The Licensee shall be entitled not to broadcast the Film for any reason and its maximum liability to the Licensor shall be: [____________]. No sum shall be due in compensation for any other claim.

6. MISCELLANEOUS

MUTUAL INDEMNITY

6.1 The Licensor and the Licensee mutually undertake to indemnify the other against all liabilities, claims, demands, actions, costs, damages and loss arising out of any breach by either party of any of the terms of this Agreement. In the event of any claim, dispute, action, writ or summons in connection with clause 6.1, the Licensor and the Licensee agree to provide full details to the other party at the earliest opportunity.

6.2 If either party wishes to assert its right to be indemnified then it must promptly:

6.2.1 notify the other party of any threat or claim which may arise and make no admission or settlement; and

6.2.2 provide the other party with the opportunity to be fully consulted in respect of the proposed course of action.

6.3 In the event that there is an allegation of infringement of copyright. Then the party against whom the claim is made may defend it and shall be entitled at its own discretion to join the other party or take third party proceedings for a contributory indemnity, damages or otherwise.

CONFIDENTIALITY

6.4 The Licensor and the Licensee shall not disclose to any third party any confidential business or future plans of the other party acquired at any time during the existence of this Agreement and no reference is to be made to the terms of this Agreement by either party in any advertising, publicity or promotional material without the prior written consent of the other party.

AMENDMENTS AND ALTERATIONS

6.5 This Agreement supersedes all previous agreements, representations or promises and sets out all the terms agreed between the parties. Any amendment or alteration to this Agreement must be in writing and signed by an authorised signatory of each party.

NOTICES

6.6 Without prejudice to the right to serve notices by any other means any notice served under this Agreement shall be in writing. Any notice which has been sent by first class, pre-paid post shall be deemed to be received 48 hours thereafter (excluding Saturdays, Sundays and public holidays).

VALUE ADDED TAX

6.7 All sums payable under this Agreement are exclusive of any value added tax that may be payable by either party.

THIRD PARTY TRANSFERS

6.8 Neither party shall assign, transfer, charge or make over this Agreement or any of its rights or obligations without the prior written consent of the other party.

FORCE MAJEURE

6.9 In the event that this Agreement cannot be performed or its obligations fulfilled for any reason beyond the reasonable control of either party including war, industrial action, floods or Acts of God then such non-performance or failure to fulfil its obligations shall be deemed not to be a breach of this Agreement. In the event that this Agreement cannot be performed or its obligations fulfilled for any reason beyond either party's reasonable control for a continuous period of [three months]. Then either party may, at its discretion, terminate this Agreement by notice in writing at the end of that period.

RIGHTS OF THIRD PARTIES

6.10 Any body, corporate or otherwise, which is not a party to this Agreement, shall have no right to enforce any obligation or right against the Licensor or the Licensee.

TERMINATION PROVISIONS

6.11 In addition to any other rights and remedies at law either party may, by giving written notice to the other party, terminate this agreement on the following grounds:

6.11.1 where either party has failed to account or make payments as required under this Agreement;

6.11.2 where either party has committed a serious breach of its obligations under this Agreement, unless such party rectifies the position, as far as reasonably possible, within [_______] days;

6.11.3 where either party goes into voluntary or involuntary liquidation;

6.11.4 where either party is declared insolvent either in bankruptcy proceedings or other legal proceedings;

6.11.5 where an agreement with creditors has been reached by either party due to its failure or inability to pay its debts as they fall due; or

6.11.6 where a receiver is appointed over the whole or part of either party's business.

EXPIRY OR TERMINATION OF THE AGREEMENT

6.12 After the expiry or the termination of this Agreement, the Licensor shall be entitled to instruct the Licensee to return or destroy all master material and any copies thereof in the possession of or under the control of the Licensee relating to the rights granted under this Agreement.

GOVERNING LAW

6.13 This Agreement shall be subject to the Laws of England.

ON BEHALF OF THE LICENSOR: [____________] [NAME/TITLE]

ON BEHALF OF THE LICENSEE: [____________] [NAME/TITLE]

THIS AGREEMENT IS DATED: [____________]

A COPY OF THE SCHEDULE A [Credit List] IS ATTACHED TO AND FORMS PART OF THIS AGREEMENT.

OUTLINE—EXCLUSIVE LICENCE FOR A FILM TO BE SHOWN ON STANDARD TELEVISION

This is an exclusive licence for a completed Film to be shown on standard terrestrial television in the U.K. The parties in this Agreement are referred to as the Licensor and the Licensee. The Licensor is the copyright owner of the Film and the Licensee is the company to whom the licence is being granted. The Licensee is paying the Licensor a Licence Fee. In return, the Licensor is granting to the Licensee an exclusive licence to broadcast the Film on a specific number of occasions within an agreed time period. The payment of the Licence Fee is subject to specific conditions and linked to the delivery of the Film Package.

The Licensee is not acquiring the cable or satellite television rights in the Film. The Licensor is agreeing, however, that the Film will not be shown on cable or satellite television before an agreed date.

The Licensor is confirming that all payments in respect of the Film, including any appropriate copyright clearances in respect of the licence, have been dealt with. The Licensee is agreeing to pay any sums due for the performing rights and the mechanical reproduction of the Film.

The Licensee is agreeing to abide by Schedule A which sets out credits, copyright notices, moral rights and other conditions of title.

Where the Licensee also transmits by satellite or cable to other countries in Europe, the licence should be adapted accordingly, but these additional uses could be non-exclusive.

EXCLUSIVE LICENCE FOR A FILM TO BE SHOWN ON SATELLITE TELEVISION

AN AGREEMENT made this [____________] day of [____________]

BETWEEN:

(1) [____________]
of [____________] (to be known as the Licensor in this Agreement)

AND

(2) [____________]
of [____________] (to be known as the Licensee in this Agreement).

IT IS AGREED as follows:

1. DEFINITIONS

The words are agreed to mean as follows:

1.1 "The Film" shall be the following film and any associated sound recording entitled [____________], which is [____________] minutes in duration.

1.2 "The Licence Fee" shall be the sum of: [figure/currency].

1.3 "The Film Package" shall be the following material of the Film:

1.3.1 technical material of first class quality of: [____________];
1.3.2 music cue sheet listing each musical work with the name of the composer, author and publisher, including the duration of each musical work and the description of use in each case;
1.3.3 statement of on-screen, publicity, advertising, and promotional credit and moral right obligations;
1.3.4 such publicity material including photographs and stills as may be available; and
1.3.5 such promotional material including trailers, promos and posters as may be available.

1.4 "The Territory" shall be the footprint of the satellite which is called [____________], which is capable of being received or is directed at the following countries: [____________].

1.5 "The Satellite Television Rights" shall mean the right to transmit the Film and/or part(s) by means of a satellite and the signals transmitted by a satellite which creates a footprint or similar technology whether in existence now or created in the future regardless of the method of charging, payment or whether the service is free and whether or not the service is encrypted, scrambled or otherwise distorted to avoid illegal reception or not.

1.6 "The Cable Television Rights" shall mean the right to transmit the Film and/or part(s) by means of a cable system or similar technology whether in existence now or created in the future regardless of the method of charging, payment or whether the service is free and whether or not the service is encoded, or otherwise distorted to avoid illegal reception.

1.7 "The Licence Period" shall commence on the [date of this Agreement] and shall continue until: [date] or the completion of all the transmissions, whichever is the earlier.

2. EXCLUSIVE LICENCE OF RIGHTS

2.1 In consideration of the Licence Fee, the Licensor grants to the Licensee the sole and exclusive Satellite Television Rights throughout the Territory for the Licence Period.

2.2 The Licensee shall only be entitled to: [number] total transmissions of the full length of the Film.

2.3 The Licensee shall be entitled to transmit excerpt of any part of the Film for the purpose of programme announcement and trailing without any further payment. Provided that the total duration of each excerpt shall not exceed [____________] minutes in duration and the total length of all aggregate excerpts shall not exceed [____________] minutes in relation to each proposed transmission of the Film.

2.4 In addition the Licensor agrees that where in the Territory the service provided by the Licensee is supplied by cable operators for that purpose only. Then the Licensee shall be entitled and authorise the exercise by such cable operators of the cable television rights in the Film and/or part(s) in the Territory for [two] transmissions only.

3. OBLIGATIONS OF THE LICENSOR

3.1 The Licensor shall deliver the Film Package to the Licensee on or before: [date] at the Licensee's cost and expense.

The risk in respect of the Film Package shall pass to the Licensee on delivery.

3.2 The Licensor confirms and undertakes that it is the sole owner of or controls all copyright and any other rights in respect of the Film and/or part(s) and the Film Package which are granted under this Agreement. That such rights are vested in the Licensor free from encumbrances and that the Licensor is not bound by any prior agreement which adversely effects or restricts his authority to enter into this Agreement.

3.3 The Licensor shall be exploited in all other rights in the Film and/or part(s) in the

Territory including but not limited to the standard television, cable and digital television and videogram rights at any time.

3.4 The Licensor confirms that the Licensee shall not be entitled to edit, adapt, alter, translate or subtitle or distort the Film and/or part(s) in any form or to use it for the purposes of product endorsement or sponsorship at any time without the prior written consent of the Licensor which the Licensor shall not be obliged to provide. The Licensor agrees that the Licensee may at its discretion undertake minor editing of and deletions from the Film in pursuance of its programme policy governing the suitability of material and/or the requirement of accurate timing of its schedules. The Licensee shall not exercise this right unreasonably or unnecessarily and any editing or deletions shall be of a minor nature and not impair continuity.

3.5 The Licensor acknowledges that it shall have no editorial control in respect of the times, dates, duration and marketing of the Film and/or part(s) by the Licensee.

3.6 The Licensor notifies the Licensee of the moral rights of the parties specified in the Film Package who are entitled to be identified as the authors of original works on the Film, namely: [____________].

3.7 The Licensor agrees and undertakes that the Film is not obscene, defamatory, and/or does not contravene any codes of practice in any of the following countries: [____________] and shall not expose the Licensee to civil or criminal proceedings in those countries.

3.8 The Licensor confirms that all trademarks, service marks, logos, titles, slogans, designs and other works, images, and marks in the Film and Film Package are specifically authorised for use by the relevant parties for the purpose of this Agreement and that proof of ownership will be provided if required upon request by the Licensee.

3.9 At the end of the Licence Period the Licensor agrees to instruct the Licensee to destroy all copies of the Film and Film Package or to return the material.

4. OBLIGATIONS OF THE LICENSEE

4.1 In consideration of the rights granted by the Licensor, the Licensee shall pay to the Licensor the Licence Fee as follows:

4.1.1 [____________] upon signature of this Agreement;
4.1.2 [____________] on acceptance by the Licensee of the Film Package;
4.1.3 [____________] on or before [____________].

4.2 The Licensee agrees to reimburse the Licensor in respect of all the reproduction, insurance, and delivery costs incurred in providing an acceptable Film Package, subject to satisfactory receipts being provided on request.

4.3 The Licensee agrees that the Film Package shall remain the property of the Licensor and that at the end of the Licence Period all copies of the Film and the Film Package shall be destroyed or shall be returned to the Licensor at the Licensee's expense.

4.4 The Licensee agrees either to accept or provide written reasons for its rejection of the Film Package within [______ days] of delivery. The Licensee accepts that risk in the Film Package shall pass to the Licensee upon delivery.

4.5 In the event that the Film is not of suitable technical quality and the Licensor cannot deliver an acceptable replacement within [______ days]. Then the Licensee shall be entitled to terminate this Agreement and the Licensor shall repay all sums paid to it in respect of the Licensee Fee.

4.6 The Licensee agrees to provide the Licensor with written details of the cable operators with which it has concluded agreements for the supply of its satellite transmissions on the dates on which the Film is transmitted.

4.7 The Licensee agrees to use all reasonable endeavours to ensure that the Film is transmitted within [six months of the date of this Agreement].

4.8 The Licensee shall be responsible for all payments due in respect of the performing rights in any music as are controlled by the Performing Right Society (or any society affiliated to it) in respect of the exercise of the rights granted under this Agreement.

4.9 The Licensee agrees to transmit the on-screen credits and to observe all moral rights notified in respect of the Film.

4.10 The Licensee shall, as far as is reasonably possible, provide the Licensor with the details of all transmission dates of the Film.

4.11 The Licensee agrees not to arrange any sponsorship or endorsement of any product in respect of the Film or any part(s) without the prior notification to and consent of the Licensee.

4.12 The Licensee agrees that it shall be entitled to alter, amend, adapt or change the Film or any parts except for minor editing because of programme schedules, or due to removal of material which is unacceptable due to legal reasons or a code of practice. In any event it shall not impair continuity or affect the moral rights of any party.

4.13 The Licensee shall not authorise or permit any use by any third party of the Film and/or part(s) except for those cable operators specified under this Agreement in the Territory.

5. MISCELLANEOUS

MUTUAL INDEMNITY

5.1 The Licensor and the Licensee mutually undertake to indemnify the other against all liabilities, claims, demands, actions, costs, damages and loss arising out of any breach by either party of any of the terms of this Agreement. In the event of any claim, dispute, action, writ or summons in connection with clause 6.1, the Licensor and the Licensee agree to provide full details to the other party at the earliest opportunity. The maximum liability of either party under this Agreement shall be limited to: [figure/currency] in total including legal costs for each party. The indemnity shall only apply if the party seeking to rely on the indemnity has notified the other of the full nature of the claim.

CONFIDENTIALITY

5.2 The Licensor and the Licensee shall not disclose to any third party any confidential business or future plans of the other party at any time acquired during the existence of this Agreement and no reference is to be made to the terms of this Agreement by either party in any advertising publicity or promotional material without the prior written consent of the other party.

AMENDMENTS AND ALTERATIONS

5.3 This Agreement supersedes all previous agreements, representations or promises and sets out all the terms agreed between the parties. Any amendment or alteration to this Agreement must be in writing and signed by an authorised signatory of each party.

NOTICES

5.4 Without prejudice to the right to serve notices by any other means any notice served under this Agreement shall be in writing whether by post, fax, e-mail or otherwise but must also be confirmed by telephone.

VALUE ADDED TAX

5.5 All sums payable under this Agreement are exclusive of any value added tax that may be payable by either party.

THIRD PARTY TRANSFERS

5.6 Either party shall be entitled to transfer, assign or charge the benefit or obligations under this Agreement provided that the rights granted under this Agreement are not adversely affected and that the indemnity by the Licensor and Licensee shall continue in existence.

FORCE MAJEURE

5.7 In the event that this Agreement cannot be performed or its obligations fulfilled for any reason beyond the reasonable control of either party including failure of facilities, war, industrial action, floods or Acts of God. Then such non-performance or failure to fulfil this Agreement by either party shall be deemed not to be a breach of this Agreement. In the event that this Agreement cannot be performed or its obligations fulfilled for any reason beyond either party's reasonable control for a continuous period of [three months]. Then either party may, at its discretion, terminate this Agreement by notice in writing at the end of that period.

TERMINATION PROVISIONS

5.8 In addition to any other rights and remedies at law either party may, by giving written notice to the other party, terminate this Agreement where either party has failed to make payments or has committed a serious breach of its obligations, unless such party rectifies the position, as far as reasonably possible, within [_____ days]; where either party goes into voluntary or involuntary liquidation, is declared insolvent, reached an agreement with creditors due to its failure or inability to pay its debts as they fall due, or a receiver is appointed.

GOVERNING LAW

5.9 This Agreement shall be subject to the Laws of [____________].

THE LICENSOR: [____________] [TITLE/NAME]

THE LICENSEE: [____________] [TITLE/NAME]

OUTLINE—EXCLUSIVE LICENCE FOR A FILM TO BE SHOWN ON SATELLITE TELEVISION

This contract is an exclusive licence for a completed Film to be shown on satellite television. The Licensor is the copyright owner of the Film and the Licensee is the company to whom the licence is being granted. The Licensee is paying the Licensor a Licence Fee and in return, the Licensor is granting the Licensee an exclusive licence to transmit the Film on a specific number of occasions, for the Licence Period on satellite television. The countries which are capable of receiving the satellite transmission should be named. The Licensor accepts that the satellite transmission of the Film may be received by cable companies who then deliver the Film to the public for which a non-exclusive licence has been given. The Licensee is agreeing to provide the Licensor with details of the cable operators with which it has concluded agreements on the dates on which the Film is transmitted.

The Licensor is confirming that all payments in respect of the production of the Film, including the appropriate copyright clearances, have been dealt with. The Licensee is agreeing to pay any sums due in respect of the performing rights in any music.

The Licensee is notified of the moral right obligations in the Film which it has agreed to abide by. The content of the Film has only been looked at for obscenity, defamation and other legal problems in named countries and not in the total number of countries which the Territory of the licence covers.

Both parties have agreed a maximum liability under the contract which is the same level, but it could be different.

This Agreement can be assigned or transferred provided that the licence is not adversely affected and the indemnity continues.

There is no restriction on any other rights not granted under this Agreement, and this licence does not entitle the Film to be shown on the internet or telephones.

NON-EXCLUSIVE LICENCE FOR A FILM TO BE SHOWN ON CABLE TELEVISION

BETWEEN:

(1) [____________]
of [____________] (to be known as the Licensor in this Agreement).

AND

(2) [____________]
of [____________] (to be known as the Licensee in this Agreement).

IT IS AGREED as follows:

1. DEFINITIONS

The words below are agreed to mean as follows:

1.1 "The Film" shall mean the film entitled: [____________] with a running time of not less than: [____________] which shall include the sound recordings and/or music associated with the Film.

1.2 "The Licence Fee" shall be the sum of: [figure/currency].

1.3 "The Film Package" shall be the following material of the Film:

1.3.1 Technical material of first class quality comprising of: [____________];
1.3.2 laboratory access letter;
1.3.3 typed transcript of final script;
1.3.4 typed copy of action continuity/shot list;
1.3.5 music cue sheet listing each musical work with the name of the composer, author and publisher, including the duration of each musical work and the description of use in each case;
1.3.6 statement of on-screen, publicity, advertising, and promotional credit obligations;
1.3.7 such publicity material including photographs and stills as may be available; and
1.3.8 such promotional material including trailers, promos and posters as may be available.

1.4 "The Territory" shall be the following [Licensed Areas/Countries]: [____________] and all ships, oil rigs, aircraft and military installations in that location.

1.5 "The Cable Television Rights" shall mean the right to transmit and/or deliver the Film by all forms of cable whether in existence now or developed in the future for reception by television regardless of whether to the public, commercial use, closed circuit television, and by all methods of payment, free or otherwise. Provided that it shall not include telephones, the internet or other merchandise, or other devices except televisions.

1.6 "The Licence Period" shall commence on [date] and shall continue for a period of [____________] or until such time as all the transmissions licensed under this Agreement have been completed whichever is the earlier.

2. NON-EXCLUSIVE LICENCE OF RIGHTS

2.1 In consideration of the Licence Fee, the Licensor grants to the Licensee the non-exclusive Cable Television Rights throughout the Territory for the Licence Period.

2.2 The Licensee shall be entitled to: [____________] transmissions of the Film during the Licence Period in the Territory.

2.3 The Licensee shall be entitled to transmit not more than [____________] in duration of the Film for the purpose of programme announcement, trailing and post-transmission comment or review in respect of each transmission, without any further payment.

3. OBLIGATIONS OF THE LICENSOR

3.1 The Licensor shall deliver the Film Package on or before: [date] at the Licensor's cost. The Licensee shall receive the material on loan for the duration of the Licence Period at the Licensee's risk.

3.2 The Licensor agrees and undertakes that it controls and is an exclusive distributor of the rights in the Film which are granted to the Licensee under this Agreement, and that there is no third party except the copyright owner: [____________] who has a claim to own or control the rights which have been granted.

3.3 The Licensor confirms that it has good title and authority to enter into this Agreement and that it is not bound by a conflicting or previous agreement which adversely affects or would jeopardise this Agreement.

3.4 In respect of the rights granted in this Agreement the Licensor confirms that all copy-right, consorts, moral rights, contracts, artistic, musical, literary works, sound recordings, dramatic works, trademarks, service marks, design rights, logos, credits, titles, slogans, text, images and sounds and any other rights have been cleared and paid for in respect of the Film and the Film Package.

Further that the Licensor shall hold the Licensee liable for any such sums except the mechanical reproduction of any music and the performing rights in any music which may arise from the exercise of the rights by the Licensee.

3.5 The Licensor shall include in the Film Package a full list of credit obligations and moral rights.

3.6 The Licensor has not licensed nor does it permit the Licensee to edit, adapt, alter or change the Film or to use it to endorse a product or third party or for the purposes of sponsorship or advertisement.

3.7 The Licensor agrees and undertakes that to the best of its knowledge and belief the Film does not contain any material which is obscene, defamatory, libellous, offensive, or likely to incite violence or [____________] in the jurisdiction of [country]. The Film has not been cleared for each country in the world.

4. OBLIGATIONS OF THE LICENSEE

4.1 In consideration of the rights granted by the Licensor the Licensee shall pay to the Licensor the Licence Fee as follows:

4.1.1 [____________] upon signature of this Agreement;
4.1.2 [____________] on acceptance by the Licensee of the Film Package;
4.1.3 [____________] on or before [____________].

4.2 The Licensee agrees to reimburse the Licensor in respect of all the reproduction, insurance, and delivery costs incurred in providing an acceptable Film Package, subject to satisfactory receipts being provided on request.

4.3 The Licensee agrees that the Film Package shall remain the property of the Licensor and that at the end of the Licence Period, the Film Package will be returned to the Licensor at the Licensee's cost.

4.4 The Licensee agrees either to accept or provide written reasons for its rejection of the Film Package within [____________] of delivery.

4.5 In the event that the Film is not of a suitable technical quality and an acceptable replacement is not agreed. Then the Licensee shall be entitled to terminate this Agreement and the Licensor shall repay all sums paid.

4.6 The Licensee agrees to use all reasonable endeavours to ensure that the Film is first transmitted by: [date].

4.7 The Licensee shall be responsible for all payments due in respect of the performing rights in any music and the mechanical reproduction of any recordings.

4.8 The Licensee agrees to keep the Licensor informed of proposed transmission dates, and to provide the Licensor with copies of any associated publicity and advertising material that may be available at the Licensee's cost.

4.9 The Licensee agrees and undertakes that it shall not use the Film for the purposes of endorsement of a product, advertising or sponsorship of a third party or otherwise except with the prior written approval of the Licensor in each case, which the Licensor shall not be obliged to provide.

4.10 The Licensee agrees to carry out the credit, copyright notice, moral right, contractual and trademark obligations or otherwise which are included in the Film Package and shall ensure that as far as possible that they are fulfilled in respect of the promotion of the transmission of the Film if required.

4.11 The Licensee shall not alter, amend, adapt, subtitle or otherwise vary or change the Film in any way. It shall be transmitted in the form that it is delivered unless deletions are requested on the advice of legal advisors or in order to conform with the programme policy requirements of: [____________]. In that event the Licensee shall notify the Licensor of the proposed alterations and request written consent.

4.12 The Licensee accepts that there is no first right of refusal or option to extend the Licence Period. In the event for any reason that the Licensee fails to exercise any of the transmissions under this Agreement. Then the Licensor shall not be obliged to extend the Licence Period.

5. INDEMNITY

5.1 The Licensor agrees to indemnify the Licensee in respect of any third party claim, loss, damage, settlement, legal costs and expenses which may be paid to such third party as a result of any matter in the Film in respect of the exercise of the rights granted under this Agreement. Provided that in all cases the Licensee shall:

5.1.1 Notify the Licensor as soon as possible of the details of any claim, loss or damage.

5.1.2 Consult with the Licensor as to the best course of action in dealing with such matter.

5.1.3 Not agree to pay any third party any sum without the prior approval of the Licensor.

5.2 The Licensee shall only indemnify the Licensor in respect of any breach of this Agreement where the Licensee has suffered a quantifiable loss or damage.

6. CONFIDENTIALITY

Both parties agree not to use any commercially sensitive and confidential information provided under this Agreement without the prior written consent of the other party.

7. AMENDMENTS

This Agreement sets out all matters agreed between the parties relating to the Film and no other earlier documents, records or conversations shall be relied upon at a later date to supersede these terms. All future amendments to this Agreement must be in writing and signed by both parties.

8. NOTICES

All notices must be legible and in writing, and evidence must be provided that it was received by the recipient.

9. VALUE ADDED TAX

All sums payable under this Agreement are exclusive of any value added tax that may be payable by either party.

10. THIRD PARTY TRANSFERS

Neither party shall assign, transfer, charge or make over this Agreement or any of its rights or obligations without the prior written consent of the other party.

11. FORCE MAJEURE

No party shall be liable for its inability or delay in performing any of its obligations if such delay is caused by circumstances beyond the reasonable control of the party including but not limited to industrial action, fire, Act of God, earthquake, facilities failure due to weather or explosion.

12. TERMINATION

12.1 In addition to any other rights and remedies at law either party may, by giving written notice to the other party, terminate this Agreement on the following grounds:

12.1.1 where the Licensee has failed to make payments as required;

12.1.2 where either party has committed a serious breach of its obligations under this Agreement unless such party rectifies the position;

6.9.3 where either party goes into voluntary or involuntary liquidation or is declared insolvent, either in bankruptcy proceedings or other legal proceedings, or where an agreement with creditors has been reached and a receiver is appointed.

13. GOVERNING LAW

This Agreement shall be subject to the Laws of [____________].

FOR AND ON BEHALF OF THE LICENSOR: [____________] [NAME/TITLE/ COMPANY]

FOR AND ON BEHALF OF THE LICENSEE: [____________] [NAME/TITLE/ COMPANY]

DATE OF THIS AGREEMENT: [____________]

OUTLINE—NON-EXCLUSIVE LICENCE FOR A FILM TO BE SHOWN ON CABLE TELEVISION

The Licensor is a distributor of a film and is not the copyright owner who made the Film. The Licensee is a cable company who may want the Film for a small licensed area, or a whole country.

If the Agreement was for a package of films you would make the film reference a list in a schedule to be attached. The Licensee is acquiring the non-exclusive cable rights. The rights clause has, however, been drafted broadly to cover non-theatric uses as whole commercial companies and closed circuit television but it is limited to reception by television whatever the method of payment. A narrower definition could be included. The licence period will end by a fixed date or when all transmissions are completed, which could be much earlier.

Moral rights, copyright notices, credits and all that type of detailed obligations should be set out clearly at the time of the contract or when the film package is delivered as in this case.

The Licensor has agreed that all copyright and other rights have been cleared and paid for and that the Licensee shall only pay sums due for performing rights in any music and the mechanical reproduction of any recordings. The latter could be amended and be met by the Licensor.

The Licensee is not entitled to any editing of the Film, and any changes for legal or policy reasons must be agreed in advance in writing.

The undertaking by the Licensor in respect of obscenity and defamation is limited to a named country, but could be wider. No mention is made of other rights not provided except in the cable rights clause.

EXCLUSIVE LICENCE FOR A FILM TO BE SHOWN ON ALL FORMS OF TELEVISION (INCLUDING CABLE, SATELLITE, STANDARD AND DIGITAL)

AN AGREEMENT made this [____________] day of [____________]

BETWEEN:

(1) [____________]
of [____________] (to be known as the Licensor in this Agreement)

AND

(2) [____________]
of [____________] (to be known as the Licensee in this Agreement).

IT IS AGREED as follows:

1. DEFINITIONS

The words below are agreed to mean as follows:

1.1 "The Film" shall be the following film and any associated sound recording entitled [____________] which is [____________] minutes in duration.

1.2 "The Licence Fee" shall be the sum of: [figure/currency].

1.3 "The Film Package" shall be the following material of the Film:

1.3.1 technical material of first class quality comprising of: [____________]
1.3.2 laboratory access letter;
1.3.3 typed transcript of final script;
1.3.4 typed copy of action continuity/shot list;
1.3.5 music cue sheet listing each musical work with the name of the composer, author and publisher including the duration of each musical work and the description of use in each case;
1.3.6 statement of on-screen, moral rights, publicity, advertising, and promotional credit obligations;
1.3.7 such publicity material including photographs and stills as may be available; and

1.3.8 such promotional material including trailers, promos and posters as may be available.

1.4 "The Territory" shall be all countries, locations and bases throughout the world and universe.

1.5 "The Standard Television Rights" shall mean the right to broadcast the Film on conventional VHF or UHF broadcast television transmitted by means of over the air standard television signals (including free, pay per view, subscription, licence and rental) for general reception, excluding cable television and satellite television

1.6 "The Cable Television Rights" shall mean the right to broadcast or transmit the Film by means of basic cable or pay cable (including free, pay per view, subscription, license and rental) or by way of any other cable medium, whether in existence now or developed in the future.

1.7 "The Satellite Television Rights" shall mean the right to broadcast or transmit the Film by means of a satellite (including free, pay per view, subscription, license and rental), whether encrypted or not.

1.8 "The Digital Television Rights" shall mean the right to convert the Film into a digitised format and to transmit the Film using digital means and the further right for viewers to interact with the on-screen display of the Film in a manner consistent with the enabling technology now known or invented in the future.

1.9 "The DVD Rights" shall mean the right to convert the Film into a digitised format enabling the Film to be stored onto a disc referred to as a 'digital visual display device' or otherwise and the right for such disc to be played on an enabling device, including but not limited to a personal computer, television apparatus, or a device specifically designed or enabled to use the disc for the purpose for which it is intended.

1.10 "The License Period" shall commence of the date of this Agreement and shall continue until [date].

2. EXCLUSIVE LICENSE OF RIGHTS

2.1 In consideration of the License Fee, the Licensor grants to the Licensee the sole and exclusive right to broadcast and transmit the Film on all forms of television, whether in existence now or created in the future, including without limitation the Standard Television Rights, Cable Television Rights, Satellite Rights and Digital Television Rights throughout the Territory for the Licence Period.

2.2 The Licensee shall be entitled to unlimited transmissions and broadcasts of the Film and/or part(s).

2.3 For the avoidance of doubt, any rights not specifically granted under this Agreement are expressly reserved to the Licensor, including but not limited to the DVD Rights.

3. EDITORIAL CONTROL

The licensee shall not be entitled to edit, adapt or alter the Film or authorise others to do so except for minor editing and deletions for the purpose of complying with legal advice, programme policy and scheduling.

4. OBLIGATIONS OF THE LICENSOR

4.1 The Licensor shall deliver the Film Package to the Licensee on or before: [date].

4.2 The Licensor confirms that it is the sole owner of or controls all copyright and any other rights in the Film which are granted to the Licensee under this Agreement.

4.3 The Licensor confirms that it has and will retain good title and authority to enter into this Agreement and is not bound by any previous agreement which adversely affects this Agreement.

4.4 The Licensor confirms that all sums due in respect of the production of the Film have been paid, including the acquisition of all consents, copyright and any other rights in the Film granted to the Licensee and that the Licensee is and will not be liable for any such payments.

4.5 The Licensor confirms that the Film does not contain any obscene or defamatory material and will not expose the Licensee to any civil or criminal proceedings.

4.6 The Licensor confirms that the Film does not contain any material which infringes the copyright or any other rights of any third party in the Territory.

4.7 The Licensor acknowledges and agrees that the Licensee shall be entitled to authorise and permit third parties to exercise the rights granted in this Agreement provided that they abide by the obligations set out. Further that the Licensee shall remain liable for the acts, omissions and errors of all such third parties and shall be entitled to retain all sums received from such exploitation.

5. OBLIGATIONS OF THE LICENSEE

5.1 In consideration of the rights granted, the Licensee shall pay to the Licensor the Licence Fee as follows:

5.1.1 [______________] upon signature of this Agreement;
5.1.2 [______________] upon acceptance by the Licensee of the Film Package;
5.1.3 [______________] on or before [______________].

5.2 The Licensee agrees to reimburse the Licensor in respect of all the reproduction, insurance, and delivery costs incurred in providing an acceptable Film Package, subject to satisfactory receipts being provided on request.

5.3 The Licensee agrees that the Film Package shall be the property of the Licensee upon payment of all sums due under this Agreement. That at the end of the Licence Period the Film Package shall be returned to the Licensor if so requested and the Licensor shall pay a reasonable sum for it or it shall be destroyed or stored as the Licensee thinks fit.

5.4 The Licensee agrees either to accept or provide written reasons for its rejection of the Film Package. In the event that the Film is not of first-class technical quality and the Licensor cannot deliver an acceptable replacement. Then the Licensee shall be entitled to terminate this Agreement and the Licensor shall repay all sums previously paid under this Agreement.

5.5 The Licensee shall be responsible for all payments due in respect of the performing rights in any music as are controlled by the Performing Right Society (or any society affiliated to it) in respect of the exercise of the rights granted under this Agreement and any sums due for the mechanical reproduction of the Film whether by the Licensee directly or any third party.

5.6 The Licensee shall be responsible for such costs as are incurred in the conversion of the Film into a digitised format.

5.7 The Licensee agrees to broadcast the on-screen credits in the Film and to fulfil any moral right obligations notified by the Licensor.

6. MISCELLANOUS

MUTUAL INDEMNITY

6.1 The Licensor and the Licensee mutually undertake to indemnify the other against all liabilities, claims, demands, actions, costs, damages and loss arising out of any breach by the defaulting party of any of the terms of this Agreement.

6.2 In the event of any claim, dispute, action, writ or summons in connection with clause 6.1, the Licensor and the Licensee agree to provide full details to the other party at the earliest opportunity and shall not settle any such matter without first obtaining the prior written consent of the other party, such consent not to be unreasonably withheld or delayed.

CONFIDENTIALITY

6.3 The Licensor and the Licensee shall not disclose to any third party any confidential business or future plans of the other party acquired at any time during the existence of this Agreement and no reference is to be made to the terms of this Agreement by either party in any advertising, publicity or promotional material without the prior written consent of the other party.

AMENDMENTS AND ALTERATIONS

6.4 This Agreement supersedes all previous agreements, representations or promises and sets out all the terms agreed between the parties. Any amendment or alteration to this Agreement must be in writing and signed by an authorised signatory of each party.

NOTICES

6.5 Without prejudice to the right to serve notices by any other means any notice served under this Agreement shall be in writing. Any notice which has been sent by first class, pre-paid post shall be deemed to be received 48 hours thereafter (excluding Saturdays, Sundays and public holidays). Notice may not be served by e-mail.

VALUE ADDED TAXES

6.6 All sums payable under this Agreement are exclusive of any value added tax that may be payable by either party.

THIRD PARTY TRANSFERS

6.7 Neither party shall assign, transfer, charge or make over this Agreement or any of its rights or obligations without the prior written consent of the other party.

FORCE MAJEURE

6.8 In the event that this Agreement cannot be performed or its obligations fulfilled for any reason beyond the reasonable control of either party including war, industrial action, floods or Acts of God then such non-performance or failure to fulfil its obligations shall be deemed not to be a breach of this Agreement. In the event that this Agreement cannot be performed or its obligations fulfilled for any reason beyond either party's reasonable control for a continuous period of [six months] then either party may, at its discretion, terminate this Agreement by notice in writing at the end of that period.

TERMINATION PROVISIONS

6.9 In addition to any other rights and remedies at law either party may, by giving written notice to the other party, terminate this Agreement on the following grounds:

6.9.1 where either party has failed to account or make payments as required under this Agreement;

6.9.2 where either party has committed a serious breach of its obligations under this Agreement, unless such party rectifies the position, as far as reasonably possible, within 30 days;

6.9.3 where either party goes into voluntary or involuntary liquidation;

6.9.4 where either party is declared insolvent, either in bankruptcy proceedings or other legal proceedings;

6.9.5 where an agreement with creditors has been reached by either party due to its failure or inability to pay its debts as they fall due; or

6.9.6 where a receiver or administrative receiver is appointed over the whole or part of either party's business.

EXPIRY OR TERMINATION OF THE AGREEMENT

6.10 After the expiry or the termination of the Agreement the Licensor shall be entitled to instruct the Licensee to return or destroy all master material and any copies thereof in the possession of or under the control of the Licensee relating to the rights granted under this Agreement.

THIRD PARTY RIGHTS

6.11 This Agreement is not intended to confer any right upon any third party to enforce the terms of this Agreement against either contracting party.

GOVERNING LAW

6.12 This Agreement shall be subject to the Laws of England.

Signed by:
FOR AND ON BEHALF OF THE LICENSOR

Date:

Signed by:
FOR AND ON BEHALF OF THE LICENSEE

Date:

Witnessed by:

OUTLINE—EXCLUSIVE LICENCE FOR A FILM TO BE SHOWN ON ALL FORMS OF TELEVISION (INCLUDING CABLE, SATELLITE, STANDARD AND DIGITAL)

This contract is an exclusive licence for the broadcast and transmission of a completed film on all forms of television, including standard television, cable, satellite and digital. The relevance of the digital transmission can arise in different ways. First, the right is being expressly granted for the Film to be converted into a digitised format (at the Licensee's cost) and secondly for the Film to be transmitted digitally. Thirdly, an express right is granted to enable viewers to interact with the on-screen display of the Film (*e.g.* the broadcaster may encourage viewers to watch from different angles, replay at will, store and play-back or link to other broadcast material). In other words, the nature of the behaviour of the viewer is fundamentally different due to the interactivity element and the contract is designed to make sure no issue is taken against a possible expectation that the transmission of the Film would be restricted to passive viewing of a film broadcast using the old analogue method. A definition of DVD rights is included so that such rights can be expressly reserved. The concern is that without directly addressing the issue, the Licensor may have an expectation that digital rights includes the right for the Film to be converted into a DVD and played on a personal computer, a specifically designed DVD player or even an adapted television set, which is not the intention of this licence.

The undertakings are intentionally short and brief, and the Licensor is not concerned about the use of the Film which is unlimited in whole or part. The Film can also be licensed to third parties, but the Licensee remains liable for the acts, errors or omissions of such sub-licensees.

COMMISSIONING OF A PILOT FOR A TELEVISION SERIES

AN AGREEMENT made this [____________] day of [____________]

BETWEEN:

(1) [____________]
of [____________] (to be known as the Assignor in this Agreement)

AND

(2) [____________]
of [____________] (to be known as the Company in this Agreement).

IT IS AGREED as follows:

1. DEFINITIONS

The words below are agreed to mean as follows:

1.1 "The Format" shall be the novel idea for and structure of a series of films created by the Assignor, details of which are set out in Appendix A which is attached to and forms part of this Agreement.

1.2 "The Treatment" shall be the summary of the Pilot which is based on the Format, details of which are set out in Appendix B which is attached to and forms part of this Agreement.

1.3 "The Pilot" shall be the film and any associated sound recording based on the Treatment and provisionally entitled [____________], which shall be [____________] minutes in duration.

1.4 "The Key Personnel" shall be as follows:

1.4.1 the producer: [____________];
1.4.2 the director: [____________];
1.4.3 the presenter: [____________]; and
1.4.4 any other: [____________].

1.5 "The Approved Budget" shall be the agreed cost of making the Pilot, whether direct or indirect, necessary for the development, pre-production, production, post-production completion and delivery of the Pilot, including but not limited to facilities, location costs, insurance, personnel, copyright clearance, consents, music, artistes, equipment, technical material, contingency allowance, any completion guarantee and the producer's fee. A copy of the Approved Budget is set out in Appendix C which is attached to and forms part of this Agreement.

1.6 "The Production Schedule" shall be the agreed dates, times and locations of making the Pilot, including pre-production, production, post-production completion and delivery of the Pilot. A copy of the Production Schedule is set out in Appendix D which is attached to and forms part of this Agreement.

1.7 "The Payment Schedule" shall be the details of the cashflow from the Approved Budget. A copy of the Payment Schedule is set out in Appendix E which is attached to and forms part of this Agreement.

1.8 "The Series" shall be the series of films and any associated sound recordings based on the Pilot, which both parties may agree to produce following satisfactory completion of the Pilot.

1.9 "The Pilot Package" shall be the following material of the Pilot:

1.9.1 Technical material of first class quality: [____________];
1.9.2 laboratory access letter;
1.9.3 typed transcript of final script/dialogue/commentary;
1.9.4 typed copy of running order/action continuity;
1.9.5 music cue sheet listing each musical work with the name of the composer, author and publisher including the duration of each musical work and the description of use in each case; and
1.9.6 statement of on-screen credit and moral right obligations.

1.10 "Media Rights" shall mean the right to produce, manufacture, supply, sell, rent, distribute license, market, and exploit the Pilot and/or any part(s) and the Series and/or any part(s) in all forms of the media whether in existence now or created in the future including but not limited to all forms of publication; hardback, paperback; all forms of radio, television and video; cable; satellite; digital; cassette; laser; disk; any technical method of delivery; any method of payment, charging, subscription, rental, lease, and for free; all forms of telecommunication systems; sound; vision; graphics; text; icons; images; all forms of theatric and non-threatric exploitation; all forms of electronic, internet, intranet and multi-media exploitation; CD-Roms; DVD; all methods of merchandising; any other developments, variations or adaptations of any nature.

2. RIGHTS

2.1 The Company acknowledges and agrees that all copyright and any rights in the format shall remain vested in the Assignor.

2.2 The Assignor and the Company agree that, in consideration of the Company funding the full cost of the Pilot, the Company shall become joint copyright owner of the Pilot with the Assignor. The Assignor therefore assigns to the Company joint copyright ownership with the Assignor in the Pilot whether in existence now or created in the future in all the Media Rights throughout [the world] for the full period of copyright and any extensions or renewals [except for any rights in the Format].

2.3 In addition the Assignor agrees that the Company shall have the sole and exclusive right to exercise, and conclude an agreement with the Assignor to produce the Series.

2.4 The option shall lapse in the event that no agreement has been concluded between the Assignor and the Company by: [date].

2.5 In the event that the option lapses or the Company advises the Assignor in writing that it does not wish to produce the Series. Then the Company agrees that it shall not be entitled to develop, arrange, or permit any other material to be produced based on the Format, the Pilot or the Series unless an agreement has been concluded with the Assignor.

2.6 The Company agrees and undertakes that, in the event of the lapse of the option or the failure to conclude an agreement for the Series, all rights in the Pilot shall be assigned by the Company to the Assignor provided that, in the event that the Assignor concludes an agreement with a third party to produce the Series, the Company shall be repaid the sum of [figure/currency] only on terms to be agreed.

2.7 The Company undertakes to execute all such documents as may be required by the Assignor at the Assignor's cost to effect such reversion of copyright subject to the conditions as regards recoupment by the Company of part of the cost of the Pilot.

3. OBLIGATIONS OF THE ASSIGNOR

3.1 The Assignor undertakes that it shall produce the Pilot using the Key Personnel, in accordance with the Treatment, the Approved Budget and the Production Schedule and that the Pilot shall be produced in colour and in the English language.

3.2 The Assignor shall deliver the Pilot Package to the Licensee on or before [____________]. The risk in the Pilot Package shall pass on delivery.

3.3 The Assignor confirms that the Format is an original idea created solely by the Assignor and has not been previously exploited in its present form and is not in the public domain.

3.4 The Assignor confirms that it is the sole owner of all copyright and any other rights in the Format.

3.5 The Assignor confirms that it has and will retain good title and authority to enter into this Agreement and is not bound by any agreement which adversely affects this Agreement.

3.6 The Assignor undertakes that all sums due in respect of the production of the Pilot will be paid and that the Company is not and will not be liable for any such payments.

3.7 In respect of the Pilot the Assignor undertakes that all copyright and any other rights, consents, clearances, music or otherwise shall be cleared for private viewing only and for such clearance payments as are set out in the Approved Budget.

3.8 The Assignor undertakes that the Pilot will not contain any obscene or defamatory material and will not expose the Company to any civil or criminal proceedings in respect of the proposed use under this Agreement.

3.9 The Assignor undertakes to open a production account specifically for the purpose of using the Approved Budget and shall keep accurate books of account and records of the costs of production of the Pilot, which shall be made available for inspection by the Company upon request.

3.10 In the event of the Approved Budget being exceeded the Assignor agrees to inform the Company in advance and provide a statement of costs incurred to date and details of the proposed additional costs. The Assignor agrees that the prior written approval of the Company shall be required in order to authorise any further expenditure.

3.11 The Assignor agrees that in the event that the parties conclude an agreement for the exploitation of the Series, the Assignor shall assign the same rights in the Series to the Company as the Pilot and that both parties shall share equally in all sums received from the exploitation of the Series.

4. OBLIGATIONS OF THE COMPANY

4.1 In consideration of the rights assigned and the production of the Pilot the Company shall pay to the Assignor the Approved Budget as set out in the Payment Schedule.

4.2 The Company agrees to reimburse the Assignor in respect of all the reproduction, insurance and delivery costs incurred in providing an acceptable Pilot Package, subject to satisfactory receipts being provided upon request.

4.3 The Company agrees either to accept or provide written reasons for its rejection of the Pilot Package within [____________] of delivery.

4.4 The Company agrees that the Pilot Package shall be the joint property of both parties. Provided that in the event that the option lapses or there is no agreement concluded for the production of the Series. Then the Pilot Package and any copies shall be returned to the Assignor.

4.5 When the option lapses or there is no agreement concluded between the parties of the Series. Then the Company shall at the Assignor's cost execute any document necessary for the reversion of copyright and all other rights in the Pilot to the Assignor.

4.6 The Company agrees that it is not acquiring any rights in the Format and all rights to be acquired shall be limited to the Pilot and the Series. All sums received from the exploitation of the Series shall be shared equally between the parties in the event that an agreement is concluded.

5. INDEMNITY

The Assignor and the Company both agree that insurance cover be taken out in respect of the production of the Pilot to indemnify each party against any liabilities, claims, demands, actions, costs, losses, damages, legal costs or otherwise arising out of the performance, non-performance, alleged breach or actual breach or any legal proceedings under or relating to this Agreement.

6. CONFIDENTIALITY

The Assignor and the Company shall not disclose to any third party except professional legal advisors, accountants, or companies or persons involved in the Pilot any confidential information, business or future plans of the other party.

7. AMENDMENTS

This Agreement supersedes all previous agreements, representations or promises and sets out all the terms agreed between the parties. Any amendment or alteration to this Agreement must be in writing and signed by an authorised signatory of each party.

8. NO PARTNERSHIP

This Agreement shall not be deemed to create any partnership or employment relationship between the parties.

9. VALUE ADDED TAX

All sums payable under this Agreement are exclusive of any value added tax that may be payable by either party.

10. THIRD PARTY TRANSFERS

Neither party shall assign, transfer, charge or make over this Agreement or any of its rights or obligations without the prior written consent of the other party.

11. FORCE MAJEURE

In the event that this Agreement cannot be performed or its obligations fulfilled for any reason beyond the reasonable control of either party including war, industrial action, floods or Acts of God. Then such non-performance or failure to fulfil its obligations shall be deemed not to be a breach of this Agreement. In the event that this Agreement cannot be performed or its obligations fulfilled for any reason beyond either party's reasonable control for a continuous period of [three months]. Then either party may, at its discretion, terminate this Agreement by notice in writing at the end of that period.

12. TERMINATION

In addition to any other rights and remedies at law either party may, by giving written notice to the other party, terminate this Agreement on the following grounds.

Where either party has failed to take account or make payments, or has committed a serious breach of its obligations unless such party rectifies the position within [____________]. Where either party goes into voluntary or involuntary liquidation, is declared insolvent in bankruptcy or other legal proceedings, an agreement with creditors has been reached due to failure or inability to pay debts as they fall due, or a receiver is appointed.

13. GOVERNING LAW

This Agreement shall be subject to the [Laws of England].

ATTACHED TO AND FORMING PART OF THIS AGREEMENT:

APPENDIX A	FORMAT
APPENDIX B	TREATMENT
APPENDIX C	APPROVED BUDGET
APPENDIX D	PRODUCTION SCHEDULE
APPENDIX E	PAYMENT SCHEDULE

[____________] [NAME/TITLE]
SIGNED BY THE ASSIGNOR

[____________] [NAME/TITLE]
SIGNED BY THE COMPANY

OUTLINE—COMMISIONING OF A PILOT FOR A TELEVISION SERIES

This contract is between a commissioning company, "the Company", and a production company, "the Assignor", to produce a pilot programme for a Series. The idea for the pilot (*e.g.* game show, format for a factual series, studio based programme, etc.) belongs to the Assignor and is referred to as the Format.

This Agreement mainly refers to the Pilot which is based on the Format. The Pilot is to be produced by the Assignor using the Approved Budget provided by the Company. The money is to be kept in a separate account which the Company is entitled to inspect. The Assignor is giving the Company joint copyright ownership of the Pilot and an option for a Series.

All rights revert to the Assignor if the option lapses or the Company do not want to produce the Series. The Pilot is budgeted to be cleared for private viewing only to assess it for the Series and not to be exploited.

If the Assignor goes over budget, then the consent of the Company is required to approve any further expenditure.

There is no mutual indemnity, but an agreement to take out insurance cover to protect the parties against all claims. Although initially more expensive, this could turn out to be a cheaper option if legal problems arise.

The Assignor is giving ownership of all media rights jointly to the Company and this could be limited to separate types of rights and a short licence period if required.

COMMISSIONING OF A FILM FOR TELEVISION WITH PARTIAL ASSIGNMENT

AN AGREEMENT made this [____________] day of [____________]

BETWEEN:

(1) [____________]
of [____________] (to be known as the Assignor in this Agreement)

AND

(2) [____________]
of [____________] (to be known as the Assignee in this Agreement).

IT IS AGREED as follows:

1. DEFINITIONS

The words below are agreed to mean as follows:

1.1 "The Film" shall be the film and any associated sound recordings based on the Treatment and the Scripts entitled [____________], which shall be [____________] minutes in duration.

1.2 "The Treatment" shall be the summary of the Film based on [____________]. A copy of the Treatment is attached to and forms part of this Agreement as Schedule 1.

1.3 "The Scripts" shall be the draft and final scripts based on the Treatment to be prepared by the Writer.

1.4 "The Key Personnel" shall be as follows:

1.4.1 the producer: [____________];
1.4.2 the director: [____________];
1.4.3 the writer: [____________];
1.4.4 the Presenter: [____________];
1.4.5 the narrator: [____________];
1.4.6 senior cameraman: [____________];
1.4.7 editor: [____________];
1.4.8 any other(s): [____________].

1.5 "The Budget" shall mean the fixed sum of [figure/currency] exclusive of VAT which shall be the entire cost of the development, pre-production, production, post-production and delivery of the Film in accordance with the terms of this Agreement. A copy of the Budget is attached to and forms part of this Agreement as Schedule 2. For the avoidance of doubt the Budget shall include:

1.5.1 the fees and exploitation fees to be paid to all performers, artists, contributors, or other persons who appear in sound and/or vision;
1.5.2 the cost of film and/or studio hire, laboratory processing, editing, reproduction and storage costs;
1.5.3 the cost of ancillary personnel, crew, creative, technical, and legal support, and graphic, photographic and music facilities for the production and delivery of the Film;
1.5.4 the cost of telephone, stationery, travel, accommodation, meals, clothing;
1.5.5 the provision of all necessary consents, clearances, releases, moral rights, contract, the requisition of any necessary copyright in the relevant media, in any material and any insurance or completion guarantees.

1.6 "The Production Schedule" shall be the agreed dates, times and locations of developing, producing and completing the Film. A copy of the Production Schedule is attached to and forms part of this Agreement as Schedule 3.

1.7 "The Payment Schedule" shall be the dates and terms upon which sums are to be made payable from the Budget. A copy of this Payment Schedule is attached to and forms part of this Agreement.

1.8 "The Film Package" shall be the following material of the Film:

1.8.1 Technical material of first class quality comprising of: [____________];
1.8.2 laboratory access letter;
1.8.3 typed transcript of final script;
1.8.4 typed copy of action continuity/shot list;
1.8.5 music cue sheet listing each musical work with the name of the composer, author and publisher including the duration of each musical work and the description of use in each case;
1.8.6 statement of on-screen, moral right, publicity, advertising and promotional credit obligations and copyright notices;
1.8.7 such publicity material including photographs and stills as may be available; and
1.8.8 such promotional material including trailers, promos and posters as may be available.

1.9 "The Territory" shall be all countries, bases and locations throughout the universe.

1.10 "The Television Rights" shall mean the right to broadcast, transmit, supply or to authorise others to do so the Film and/or any parts by all forms of television including but not limited to terrestrial, cable, satellite, digital or otherwise by any method whether known now or created in the future, whether encrypted or not and whether provided for free or some method of payment such as subscription, pay per view, or licence.

1.11 "The Videogram Rights" shall mean the right to transfer and duplicate the Film and/or any parts in the form of video cassettes, video disks, and any other similar devices or other means known now or created in the future and to sell, supply, hire, exploit and to authorise others to do so. The method of electronic reproduction can be in any form, provided that it creates a recording of a sequence of visual images, and integral sound which can be reproduction and copies supplied to the public to watch on television by means of a machine or device which playback this Film.

1.12 "The Non-Theatric Rights" shall mean the right to exhibit the Film to audiences who are not making any specific payment to view or hear the Film and the right to permit, licence, sale, hire or supply this Film to be exhibited in all formats in business and commercial industries, and organisations of a cultural, educational, religious, charitable and social nature.

1.13 "The Theatric Rights" shall mean the right to exhibit the Film to audiences where a charge for admission is made, including but not limited to public and private cinemas, concert and lecture halls and arenas.

1.14 "The Gross Receipts" shall be the total proceeds of any nature from the exploitation of the Film, including any parts, throughout the Territory at any time received by or credited to the Assignee or its sub-agents or its sub-licensees after the deduction of the Sales Tax and any value added tax.

1.15 "The Distribution Expenses" shall be the following costs reasonably and properly expended in respect of the exploitation of the Film and any parts by the Assignee which are not recouped from any third party:

1.15.1 duplication processing and reproduction costs of all technical and master material including but not limited to negatives, prints, rushes, out-takes, videotapes, recordings, music and effects tracks, title and subtitle tracks, viewing copies.

1.15.2 delivery, storage, shipping, customs duties, freight, handling charges and insurance;

1.15.3 trailers and promotional extracts;

1.15.4 publicity, advertising and promotional material including posters and catalogues;

1.15.5 the clearance of and payment for exploitation of any copyright, consents, moral rights, music, contracts, releases, artists, graphics, stills, credits, trade mark, service marks, design rights and any other rights;

1.15.6 any commission of any sub-licensee, sub-agent or distributor;

1.15.7 dubbing, editing and sub-titling for the purpose of exploitation to a foreign country; and

1.15.8 any other costs listed below specifically agreed between the parties: [_____________].

1.16 "The Nett Receipts" shall be the Gross Receipts less the Distribution Expenses.

1.17 "The Sales Tax" shall be any sales or other taxes levied by any authorities on the sale or supply of the Film, which form a distinct element in the sale or rental price and which are recovered as part of the price directly or indirectly by the Assignee.

1.18 "The Assignor's Royalties" shall be [_____ per cent] of the Nett Receipts [_____%].

1.19 "The Assignment Period" shall commence on the [date of this Agreement] and shall continue until" [date].

2. RIGHTS

2.1 In consideration of the provision of the Budget by the Assignee to the Assignor to make the Film. The Assignor assigns to the Assignee all present and future copyright in respect of the Television Rights, the Videogram Rights, the Non-Theatric Rights and the Theatric Rights in the Film and parts throughout the Territory for the duration of the Assignment Period.

2.2 The Assignee acknowledges that all other rights in the Film not specifically assigned under this Agreement shall remain vested in the Assignor, including but not limited to any merchandising and publication rights.

2.3 The Assignee acknowledges that after the expiry of the Assignment Period, the Assignee shall have no rights in the Film or any parts and that all rights assigned under this Agreement shall revert to the Assignor.

2.4 The Assignee undertakes that at the end of the Assignment Period it shall execute any document or do anything required by the Assignor to confirm the reversion of all copyright and any other rights in the Film to the Assignor.

2.5 In consideration of the assignment of rights, the Assignee agrees to pay the Assignor's Royalties to the Assignor in respect of the exploitation of the Film or any parts.

2.6 The Assignee agrees that it shall not be entitled to offset this Budget from the Gross Receipts, only the Distribution Expenses.

2.7 The Assignor agrees that the royalties shall be due from promotional, review, free or other exploitation of the film and/or parts for which no sums are received by or credited to the Assignee.

2.8 No royalties shall be paid to the Assignor in respect of copies of the Film and/or part(s) which are destroyed in transit, by fire, water, remaindered, sold at cost or on stock transfer provided that no income, benefit or credit is received of any nature from such disposal, loss or damage.

3. OBLIGATIONS OF THE ASSIGNOR

3.1 The Assignor undertakes that it shall produce the Film using the Key Personnel, in accordance with the Treatment, the Budget, the Scripts, the Production Schedule and the Payment Schedule.

3.2 The Assignor confirms that the Film shall be produced in colour, in the English language and in the following format: [____________].

3.3 The Assignor shall deliver the Scripts to the Assignee for approval on or before the following dates:

The draft script: [____________];
The final script: [____________].

3.4 The Assignor shall deliver the rough edited version of the Film to the Assignee for approval on or before: [date] in the following format: [____________] at the Assignor's cost and expense from the Budget.

3.5 The Assignor shall deliver the Film Package at the Assignor's cost to the Assignee on or before: [date].

3.6 The Assignor confirms that it has and will retain good title and authority to enter into this Agreement and is not bound by any previous agreement which adversely affects this Agreement.

3.7 The Assignor agrees that final editorial decisions in respect of the scripts and the Film shall rest solely with the Assignee. The Assignee's representative shall be entitled to attend the production and post-production of the Film at any time and to view and examine the recordings for the Film. Provided that such attendance shall be in such a manner as not to interfere with the completion of the Film.

3.8 The Assignor agrees that, after the delivery of the Film to the Assignee, the Assignee shall be entitled at the Assignee's cost to authorise and permit any alterations, changes, deletions, and/or interruptions to the Film that it may in its sole discretion think fit. Provided that prior to making any material alterations the Assignee shall consult with the Assignor and take into account any requests as far as reasonably possible.

3.9 The Assignor shall give a separate bank account specifically for the Budget and the administration of the Film.

3.10 In the event that it is anticipated that the Budget is to be exceeded or is exceeded. Then the prior written authorisation of the Assignee shall be required before the Assignor incurs any additional costs or expenses or continues production.

3.11 The Assignor agrees that the Budget is a statement of the total cost for the Film and is not for guidance, but the maximum agreed price between the parties. Any additional costs and expenses not agreed and authorised in writing by the Assignee in advance shall be the sole responsibility of the Assignor.

3.12 The Assignor agrees and undertakes that all copyright, consents, releases, moral rights, contractual obligations, music, and any other rights of any nature shall be cleared in respect of all rights granted under this Agreement but shall only be paid for to the extent that such payment is provided for in the Budget. The Assignee shall bear any additional costs of clearance payments which shall be included in the Distribution Expenses. Payments due in respect of the performing rights in any music or the mechanical reproduction of the recordings shall as far as possible be at the cost of any third party who is authorised to exploit the Film.

3.13 The Assignor acknowledges that the Assignee shall have the sole discretion as to the manner and method to be used in the marketing, promoting and advertising the Film.

3.14 The Assignor shall not without the prior written approval of the Assignee inform any person except those absolutely necessary for the production of the Film of any content of the Scripts and/or Film except to agents, advisors, and production personnel. Nor shall the Assignor issue any press releases or statements regarding the development, production or marketing of the Film without the prior consent of the Assignee.

3.15 The Assignor confirms to the Assignee the moral rights of the parties set out in the Film package.

3.16 The Assignor undertakes that it is the sole owner of or will control all copyright and any other rights in the Film and/or parts which are assigned to the Assignee for the purposes of this Agreement.

3.17 That the Assignor has not and will not at any time assign, licence, change, transfer or otherwise deal in the rights in the Film and/or parts to any person or company except the Assignee.

4. OBLIGATIONS OF THE ASSIGNEE

4.1 In consideration of the rights assigned and the production of the Film, the Assignee shall pay to the Assignor the Budget as set out in the Payment Schedule.

4.2 The Assignor agrees to bear the cost of any sums due which exceed the Budget provided that prior written approval has been given to the Assignee.

4.3 The Assignee agrees to reimburse the Assignor in respect of all the reproduction, insurance and delivery costs incurred in providing an acceptable Film Package, subject to satisfactory receipts being produced upon request.

4.4 The Assignee agrees either to accept or provide written reasons for its rejection of the Scripts and the Film Package within [______ days] of delivery in each case.

4.5 The Assignee undertakes that it and its sub-agents and sub-licensees shall keep full and accurate books of account, records and contracts showing the Gross Receipts, the Distribution Expenses, the Sales Tax, the Nett Receipts and the Assignor's Royalties in respect of the exploitation of the Film.

4.6 The Assignee undertakes that it shall pay the Assignor's Royalties to the Assignor by: [date] and [date] in each year.

4.7 The Assignee shall provide a detailed report to the Assignor with a full breakdown of the exploitation of the Film showing the Gross Receipts, the Distribution Expenses, the Sales Tax, the Nett Receipts and the Assignor's Royalties by [date] and [date] in each year. The report shall include details of all units, lost, stolen, or damaged, or given away, currency conversion costs, documentation to support any deduction of Distribution Expenses.

4.8 The Assignee agrees that the Assignor shall be entitled to arrange for an annual audit to inspect and make copies of the Assignee's books of account, records, contracts and any other relevant material of any nature in order to verify the sums due to the Assignor. Where there is discovered to be an error or omission of any type then compensation shall be paid of: [______________] on each audit.

4.9 The Assignee confirms that it shall be solely responsible for any sums due in respect of the exploitation of the Film which are not set out in the Budget and that the Assignor shall not be liable for any such payments.

4.10 The Assignee agrees that the Assignor shall be entitled to the following on-screen credit and copyright notice in the Film and in any publicity, promotional, advertising and packaging material in respect of the exploitation of the Film: [______________].

4.11 The Assignee agrees that it shall use its reasonable endeavours to ensure that all moral rights, credit and other obligations of any nature notified in the Film Package are adhered to by the Assignee in the exploitation of the Film and/or part(s).

4.12 The Assignee agrees that any editing or changes to the Film and/or parts for the purposes of exploitation shall be at the Assignee's sole cost after the acceptance of delivery of the Film.

4.13 The Assignee agrees to consult with the Assignor in respect of any substantial alterations, additions to, changes, deletions, or translations of the Film. The Assignee agrees that it shall not edit the Film in any way which is likely to impair its quality, meaning or integrity or amounts to a breach of any of the notified moral rights.

4.14 The Assignee agrees that it shall consult with the Assignor where it is proposed to use the Film and/or part(s) for the purpose of sponsorship, product endorsement, advertising or otherwise which is not a direct exploitation of the Film.

4.15 The Assignee agrees to provide the Assignor with copies of any marketing material which may be available in respect of the Film upon request by the Assignor.

5. MISCELLANEOUS

INDEMNITY

5.1 The Assignee shall indemnify the Assignor against any liability, loss, damage, expense or cost arising directly or indirectly from the exploitation of the Film and/or parts by the Assignee and the failure to perform any of the obligations set out in this Agreement.

5.2 The Assignor shall indemnify the Assignee against any liability, loss, damage, expense arising directly or indirectly from the breach or non-performance of any of the obligations set out in this Agreement up to a total of: [figure/currency].

CONFIDENTIALITY

5.3 The Assignor and the Assignee shall not disclose to any third party any confidential business or future plans of the other party at any time acquired during the existence of this Agreement and no reference is to be made to the terms of this Agreement by either party in any advertising, publicity or promotional material without the prior written consent of the other party.

AMENDMENTS AND ALTERATIONS

5.4 This Agreement supersedes all previous agreements, representations or promises and sets out all the terms agreed between the parties. Any amendment or alteration to this Agreement must be in writing and signed by an authorised signatory of each party.

NO PARTNERSHIP OR EMPLOYMENT

5.5 This Agreement shall not be deemed to create any partnership or employment relationship between the parties.

VALUE ADDED TAX

5.6 All sums payable under this Agreement are exclusive of any value added tax that may be payable by either party.

THIRD PARTY TRANSFERS

5.7 Neither party shall assign, transfer, charge or make over this Agreement or any of its rights or obligations without the prior written consent of the other party.

FORCE MAJEURE

5.8 In the event that this Agreement cannot be performed or its obligations fulfilled for any reason beyond the reasonable control of either party including war, industrial action, floods or Acts of God. Then such non-performance or failure to fulfil its obligations shall be deemed not to be a breach of this Agreement. In the event that this Agreement cannot be performed or its obligations fulfilled for any reason beyond either party's reasonable control for a continuous period of [12 months]. Then either party may, at its discretion, terminate this Agreement by notice in writing at the end of that period.

TERMINATION

5.9 Each party shall be entitled to terminate this Agreement immediately by serving written notice on the other party if that other party shall:

5.9.1 commit a breach of any of its major obligations under this Agreement which is not capable of being remedied or is not remedied within [____________] of receipt of notice; or

5.9.2 make an arrangement for the benefit of, or make a composition or arrangement with its creditors, or any action or proceedings in bankruptcy or insolvency is taken including the appointment of a receiver, administrator, liquidator or other trustee other than for the purpose of amalgamation or reconstruction of the business.

NOTICES

5.10 Notices pursuant to this Agreement shall be by first class post as follows:

Assignor: [Name] [Address]
Assignee: [Name] [Address].

SELL-OFF PERIOD

5.11 The Assignee shall be entitled to sell off, on a non-exclusive basis, licensed material and stocks previously manufactured under this Agreement for the purpose of commercial sale for a period of [12 months] from the date of expiry or termination of this Agreement, provided that the Assignee adheres to the terms of this Agreement.

EXPIRY OR TERMINATION OF THE AGREEMENT

5.12 After the expiry or the termination or the completion of the sell-off period. Then the Assignor shall be entitled to instruct the Assignee to return or destroy all master material, licensed material, any copies of the master or licensed material and stocks previously manufactured under this Agreement in the possession of or under the control of the Assignee relating to the rights assigned under this Agreement.

GOVERNING LAW

5.13 This Agreement shall be subject to the [Laws of England].

Signed by: [____________]
FOR AND ON BEHALF OF THE ASSIGNOR

Date: [____________]

Signed by: [____________]
FOR AND ON BEHALF OF THE ASSIGNEE

Date: [____________]

THE FOLLOWING DOCUMENTS ARE ATTACHED TO AND FORM PART OF THIS AGREEMENT.

SCHEDULE 1	TREATMENT
SCHEDULE 2	BUDGET
SCHEDULE 3	PRODUCTION SCHEDULE
SCHEDULE 4	PAYMENT SCHEDULE

OUTLINE—COMMISIONING OF A FILM FOR TELEVISION WITH PARTIAL ASSIGNMENT

This contract is between a commissioning company and a production company to produce a Film for worldwide distribution. The production company, the Assignor, is assigning all television rights, the video and theatric rights for a specific period of time throughout the universe. The Assignor is retaining all other rights in the Film, including the merchandising and publication rights. The video rights are drafted broadly to include non-theatric use.

This contract allows for the Assignor to receive a percentage of the nett receipts received by the Assignee from the exploitation of the Film. The nett receipts are defined as the Gross Receipts, less the Distribution Expenses but not the Budget.

The Assignor who is producing this Film will provide copies of the draft and final script for approval, allow the Assignee to view a rough edited version of the Film and deliver all the final material of the Film Package. All these costs should be provided for in the Budget.

The Assignee has final editorial control, and can send a representative at any time to attend filming. The Assignee can edit, alter or change the Film once it is delivered but agrees to consult in advance with the Production Company if there are any material alterations.

The Budget is not an estimate and must be kept in a separate account. Any additional costs must be authorised by the Assignee in advance. The Assignor is to clear all material in the Film, but will only pay for those sums set out in the Budget.

The Assignee must keep proper records of its exploitation of the Film and pay compensation for any errors or omissions which are discovered at a later date by the Production Company. The Assignee will bear the costs of the distribution of the Film but these can be deducted from the Gross Receipts before the Assignee is paid any royalties. The Assignee is to provide the Production Company with an agreed credit, and copyright notice, and to observe all moral rights notified as part of this Film Package.

COMMISSIONING OF SERIES FOR TELEVISION AND WORLDWIDE EXPLOITATION WITH FULL ASSIGNMENT

AN AGREEMENT made this [____________] day of [____________]

BETWEEN:

(1) [____________]
of [____________] (to be known as the Producer in this Agreement)

AND

(2) [____________]
of [____________] (to be known as the Distributor in this Agreement).

IT IS AGREED as follows:

1. DEFINITIONS

The words below are agreed to mean as follows:

1.1 "The Series" shall be the series of films and any associated sound recordings based on the Treatment and the Scripts entitled [____________] and comprising of [____________] episodes, each of which shall be [____________] minutes in duration.

1.2 "The Treatment" shall be the summary of the Series. A copy of the Treatment is attached to and forms part of this Agreement in Appendix A.

1.3 "The Scripts" shall be the draft and final scripts based on The Treatment to be prepared by the Writer.

1.4 "The Key Personnel" shall be as follows:

1.4.1 the producer: [____________];
1.4.2 the director: [____________];
1.4.3 the presenter: [____________];
1.4.4 the narrator: [____________];
1.4.5 senior cameraman: [____________];
1.4.6 editor: [____________];
1.4.7 any other(s): [____________].

1.5 "The Approved Budget" shall be the agreed cost of making the Series, whether direct or indirect, inclusive of all locations, facilities and any other items necessary for the development, pre-production, production, post-production and delivery of the Series, including any contingency allowance and the cost of any completion guarantee and the producer's fee. A copy of the Approved Budget is attached to and forms part of this Agreement set out in Appendix B.

1.6 "The Production Schedule" shall be the agreed dates, times and locations of making the Series, including pre-production, production, post-production and delivery of the Series. A copy of the Production Schedule is attached to and forms part of this Agreement set out in Appendix C.

1.7 "The Series Package" shall be the following material of the Series:

1.7.1 Technical material of first class quality comprising of: [____________];
1.7.2 laboratory access letter;
1.7.3 typed transcript of final script;
1.7.4 typed copy of action continuity/shot list;
1.7.5 music cue sheet listing each musical work with the name of the composer, author and publisher, including the duration of each musical work and the description of use in each case;
1.7.6 statement of credit, copyright notice, trademark, moral right and any other contractual obligations whether in on-screen publicity, advertising, promotional or material;
1.7.7 publicity, advertising and promotional material: [____________].

1.8 "The Territory" shall be all countries, bases, locations throughout the world and the universe.

1.9 "The Gross Receipts" shall be the total proceeds from the distribution and exploitation of the Series, including any parts throughout the Territory at any time received by or created to the Distributor or its sub-agents or its sub-licensees or any other person or body after the deduction of any sales tax and any value added tax.

1.10 "The Distribution Expenses" shall be the following costs, reasonably and properly expended in respect in of the exploitation of the Series by the Distributor which are not recouped from any third party:

1.10.1 reproduction, repair and supply of material;
1.10.2 delivery, storage, shipping customs duties, freight, handling charges and insurance;
1.10.3 publicity, advertising and promotional material;
1.10.4 copyright, music rights, contract, mechanical reproduction and performing rights, moral rights, any clearance of material, and the payment of any fees, royalties or other sums that may arise directly;
1.10.5 any sub-licencee's commission, charges, or fees;
1.10.6 dubbing, editing and subtitling for the purpose of exploitation to a foreign country.

1.11 "The Nett Receipts" shall be the Gross Receipts less the Approved Budget and the Distribution Expenses.

1.12 "The Sales Tax" shall be any sales or other taxes levied by the E.U., British or foreign authorities on the sale or supply of the Series, which form a distinct element in the sale or rental price and which are recovered as part of the price directly or indirectly by the Distributor.

1.13 "The Producer's Royalties" shall be [figure] per cent [____%] of the Nett Receipts.

1.14 "All Media Rights" shall mean the right to produce, manufacture, supply, sell, rent, distribute, license, market, and exploit, the Series and any part(s) in all forms of the media whether in existence now or created in the future including but not limited to all forms of publication; hardback, paperback; all forms of radio, television and video; cable; satellite; digital; cassette; laser; disk any technical method of delivery; any method of payment, charging, subscription, rental, leasing and for free; all forms of telecommunication systems; sound; vision; graphics; text; icons; images; all forms of theatric and non-theatric exploitation; CD-Roms; all methods of merchandising; any other developments, variations or adaptations of any nature.

2. ASSIGNMENT OF RIGHTS

In consideration of the provision of the Approved Budget by the Distributor and the payment of the Producers Royalties, the Producer assigns to the Distributor the sole and exclusive All Media Rights in the Series and/or parts for the full period of copyright and any extensions, renewals or variations continuing in perpetuity indefinitely and without limitation.

3. OBLIGATIONS OF THE PRODUCER

3.1 The Producer undertakes that it shall produce the Series using the Key Personnel in accordance with the Treatment, the Approved Budget, the Scripts and the Production Schedule. The Series shall be produced in colour in the English Language and be of sufficient quality in vision and sound for the purposes of exploiting the distribution rights.

3.2 The Series shall be completed on or by: [date] and the Producer shall deliver the Series Package to the Distributor on or by: [date]. In the event that there is any expected delay, then the producer shall notify the Distributor stating the reasons and keep the Distributor informed of progress.

3.3 The Producer shall permit the Distributor upon request to attend a viewing of the rough cut of the Series.

3.4 The Producer confirms that it has and will retain good title to enter into this Agreement and is not bound by any previous agreement, commitment or undertaking which conflicts with or adversely affects this Agreement.

3.5 The Producer undertakes that neither it nor its predecessors in title have at any time prior to this Agreement assigned, licensed, changed or in any way dealt with the Treatment, the Scripts or the Series which is inconsistent with the terms of this Agreement.

3.6 The Producer agrees and undertakes that has acquired and/or will control All Media Rights in the Treatment, the Scripts and the Series which are assigned to the Distributor under this Agreement.

3.7 The Producer agrees and undertakes that it shall only use and pay for items for the Series out of the Approved Budget and that no such sums shall be used to fund other projects. That the Producer shall pay all costs of the production of the Series out of the Approved Budget and that the Distributor shall not be liable for any such payments once the Approved Budget has been paid to the Producer.

3.8 The Producer agrees that it shall ensure that all artists, stills, music, footage, moral rights, and any other material of any nature in the Series shall be cleared for exploitation by the Distributor. The Producer shall only be liable to pay the costs set out in the Approved Budget; any additional sums that may fall due shall be paid by the Distribution Expenses from the Gross Receipts.

3.9 The Producer agrees that once the Series is delivered to the Distributor that any editorial decisions in respect of the exploitation, marketing and advertisement of the Series shall be at the sole discretion of the Distributor. Provided that the Series is not exploited in any way which would demean the reputation of the Producer and the Distributor observes all notified contractual, moral rights and other binding obligations to all parties involved in the Series.

3.10 The Producer agrees that the Series shall not contain any act, vision or sound which is obscene or defamatory or would expose the Producer or the Distributor to civil or criminal proceedings.

4. OBLIGATIONS OF THE DISTRIBUTOR

4.1 In consideration of the assignment of rights by the Producer to the Distributor under this Agreement, the Distributor agrees to pay the Approved Budget to the approval of the Treatment and the Scripts.

4.2 The delivery of the Series Package to the Distributor shall be at the Producer's cost as part of the Approved Budget.

4.3 In the event that the Distributor cannot accept the delivery of the Scripts or the Series Package. The Distributor shall provide written reasons for the rejection.

4.4 The Distributor agrees that the Producer shall only pay such clearance payments as may be set out in the Approved Budget. Any sums due from the exploitation of the Series by the Distributor shall be paid by the Distributor and recouped under the Distribution Expenses.

4.5 The Distributor agrees that it shall keep all records, contracts, documents, software, and master material relating to the exploitation of the Series in good condition and for a minimum of twenty years from the date of this Agreement.

4.6 The Distributor agrees that it and any third parties engaged to assist in the exploitation of the Series shall be run on a professional and efficient basis and shall follow standard accounting practices in the proper collection and recording of the income and expenses relating to any exploitation of the Series in any form. No sum shall be paid or distributed without sufficient documentary evidence to support the figures in the accounts which shall be provided to this Producer.

4.7 The Distributor shall pay the Producer's Royalties to the Producer on the following dates in each year: [______________] in [currency] by [method].

At the same time the Distributor shall provide a full set of accounts for each such period as appropriate, together with full supporting documentation providing evidence of all contracts, invoices, payments or otherwise of any nature in excess of [figure/currency].

4.8 The Distributor agrees that the Producer or any advisor may provide notice to audit the accounts once in each year at the Producer's cost. The Distributor shall co-operate fully and allow the Producer full access to all information in any format relating to the Series. Provided that in some circumstances a confidentiality access agreement may be concluded to protect commercially sensitive information.

4.9 The Distributor shall endeavour to update the Producer in respect of the marketing and exploitation of the Series and to allow the Producer to assist in the publicity and promotional events.

5. INDEMNITY

The Producer and the Distributor agree that they shall not provide indemnity provisions to each other, but shall arrange insurance cover to cover such eventuality of the breach of this Agreement by either party or the threat of legal action in the sum of: [______________].

6. CONFIDENTIALITY

Both parties recognise that in the course of this Agreement they may become aware of secret, confidential, or private material which is commercially sensitive to their business, and agree not to knowingly disclose it to any third parties.

7. AMENDMENTS

This Agreement sets out the full intent of the parties and all previous representatives shall not apply. Any alteration to these terms must be in writing and signed by both parties.

8. NO PARTNERSHIP

There is no partnership or employment relationship between the parties.

9. NOTICES

All notices must be in writing and by letter by recorded or registered delivery whether by post or courier. Copies may be sent by fax, e-mail or text but shall not constitute sufficient notice.

All notices shall be as follows:

1. Producer: [None] [Address]
2. Distributor: [None] [Address].

A minimum of [____________] days shall be given in each case to remedy the position prior to termination.

10. FORCE MAJEURE

In the event that the services cannot be produced for any reason or the exploitation is delayed due to any reason beyond the reasonable control of either party which is not foreseen at the time of this Agreement. Then both parties agree that the performance or fulfilment of the terms may be suspended for [one year] only. Thereafter the parties may bring the Agreement to an end by negotiating a settlement.

11. TERMINATION

This Agreement may be terminated by notice in writing by the Producer or the Distributor if the other party shall fail to account or make payments as required; be in breach of the negotiations and not remedy the position; go into voluntary or involuntary liquidation; be declared insolvent or be unable to pay its debts or have a receiver appointed.

12. GOVERNING LAW

This Agreement shall be subject to the Laws of England.

[____________] [NAME] [Company Secretary]
[____________] [NAME] [Director]
FOR AND ON BEHALF OF THE PRODUCER

[____________] [NAME] [Title]
[____________] [NAME] [Director]
FOR AND ON BEHALF OF THE DISTRIBUTOR

ATTACH TO THIS AGREEMENT:

APPENDIX A:	TREATMENT
APPENDIX B:	APPROVED BUDGET

OUTLINE—COMMISSIONING OF SERIES FOR TELEVISION AND WORLDWIDE EXPLOITATION WITH FULL ASSIGNMENT

This contract is a commissioning agreement between a Distributor and a Producer. The Distributor will pay for the cost of making the Series in accordance with the Approved Budget. The Producer will deliver the Series and receive a percentage royalty of the net receipts referred to as the Producer's Royalty. The Distributor shall deduct the Distribution Expenses from the Gross Receipts and the Approved Budget before any sums are paid out to the Producer. All rights in the Series are assigned in all media by the Producer and the Distributor. There is no assertion of moral rights by the Producer but nor is there a waiver. More detailed reference may need to be made as to the major artistes in the Series or the Presenter. The Distributor may exploit the Series as it thinks fit once it is delivered. More detailed marketing conditions maybe appropriate in some circumstances to set targets.

COMMISSIONING OF SERIES FOR WORLDWIDE VIDEO DISTRIBUTION

AGREEMENT DATED: [____________]

PARTIES TO THIS AGREEMENT:

(1) [COMPANY] TRADING AS: [____________]
of [ADDRESS] (to be known as the Assignor in this Agreement)

AND

(2) [COMPANY] TRADING AS: [____________]
of [ADDRESS] (to be known as the Assignee in this Agreement).

1. DEFINITIONS

It is agreed that the words below shall be defined as follows:

1.1 "The Series" shall be the following series of films and any associated sound recordings based on the Treatment and the Scripts entitled [____________] and comprising of [____________] episodes, each of which shall be [____________] minutes in duration.

1.2 "The Treatment" shall be the summary of each of the episodes of the Series based on the original idea of [the Assignor] and a copy of the Treatment is attached to and forms part of this Agreement as Schedule [1].

1.3 "The Scripts" shall be the draft and final scripts based on the Treatment.

1.4 "The Key Personnel" shall be as follows: [____________].

1.5 "The Budget" shall be all the expenses, costs and payments made to make the Series, whether arising directly or indirectly which are necessary for the development, pre-production, production, post-production and delivery of the Series, including any contingency allowance, completion guarantee, the producer's fee and the reproduction, insurance and freight charges. A copy of the Budget is attached to and forms part of this Agreement as Schedule [2].

1.6 "The Production Schedule" shall be the proposed dates, times, locations and scheduling of the Series at all stages until completion and delivery. A copy of the Production Schedule is attached to and forms part of this Agreement as Schedule [3].

1.7 "The Series Package" shall be the following material of the Series:

1.7.1 technical material of first class quality comprising of: [____________];
1.7.2 laboratory access letter;
1.7.3 typed transcript of final script;
1.7.4 music cue sheet listing each musical work with the name of the composer, author and publisher, including the duration of each musical work and the description of use in each case; and
1.7.5 statement of on-screen, publicity, advertising, promotional credit obligations and copyright notices, trademarks, service marks, logos and moral right obligations, waivers, or assertions which shall be set out in words, description and image if appropriate.

1.8 "The Territory" shall be all countries, bases and locations throughout the planet Earth.

1.9 "The Videogram Rights" shall mean the right to transfer, manufacture and duplicate the Series by means of electronic reproduction in the form of any disc or magnetic tape (including but not limited to cassettes, cartridges or reel to reel), which consists of a sequence of visual images, with or without sound, capable of being shown as a moving picture by means of a playback device which is separate from or an integral part of the television but the Series is displayed on the television screen. It shall include the right to sell, rent, supply, distribute and have distributed the Series in any such form for private home use only by the public.

1.10 "The Non-Theatric Rights" shall mean the right to exhibit the Series to non-paying audiences in all businesses and commercial industries and organisations of an educational, cultural, religious, charitable and social nature, including but not limited to schools, churches, evening institutions, museums, hospitals, prisons, summer camps, drama groups, film societies, professional associations, public libraries, colleges and universities, hotels and private clubs.

1.11 "The Gross Receipts" shall be all the monies of any nature whether lending or rental income, sales whether rental or wholesale, or otherwise any other sums or benefits which are credited to, paid to and/or received in respect of the Series by the Assignee and/or any sub-licensee and/or distributor and/or any other third party engaged by the Assignee in respect of the exploitation of the Series at any time from the Videogram Rights and the Non-Theatric Rights.

1.12 "The Assignor's Royalties" shall be the following percentage of the Gross Receipts: [figure] per cent [____________]%.

2. COPYRIGHT AND ASSIGNMENT

2.1 Subject to clause 2.2, the Assignor and the Assignee both acknowledge that they shall hold joint present and future copyright and all other rights in the Series and parts in all media, whether in existence now or created in the future throughout the Territory for the full period of copyright and any extensions and renewals. Further that the consent of both parties shall be required to exploit such rights which shall be the subject of separate agreements in each case.

2.2 In consideration of the Budget for the production of the Series by the Assignor based on a project created by the Assignor. The Assignor agrees to assign to the Assignee the sole and exclusive Videogram Rights and Non-Theatric Rights in the Series and parts throughout the Territory for [____________] years. Upon expiry of that period then the rights shall revert back to joint copyright ownership between the parties.

2.3 The Assignee agrees that it shall pay and the Assignor shall be entitled to the Assignor's Royalties in respect of the exploitation of the Videogram Rights and the Non-Theatric Rights.

2.4 The Assignee shall be entitled to use and permit the use of The Series for the purpose of trade and in-store demonstrations to promote and advertise the Series.

2.5 The Assignee shall be entitled to incorporate any part of the Series on videograms reproducing other films for the purpose of promoting and advertising the Series, provided that the other films will not be derogatory or offensive in manner.

3. EDITORIAL CONTROL

3.1 The Assignee shall be entitled at its sole discretion and cost to make minor changes, deletions, alterations, interruptions or additions to the Series as may reasonably be required of less than [____________] in duration. In the event that significant or major changes are envisaged, the prior approval of the Assignor shall be required in advance.

3.2 The Assignor and Assignee are both responsible for the content of the Series and therefore agree that it shall not contain any offensive, obscene or defamatory material which would expose either party to criminal or civil proceedings.

4. OBLIGATIONS OF THE ASSIGNOR

4.1 The Assignor undertakes that it shall produce the Series using the Key Personnel, in accordance with the Treatment, the Budget, the Scripts and the Production Schedule.

4.2 The Assignor confirms that the Series shall be produced in colour, in the English language and in the following format: [description].

4.3 The Assignor shall deliver the final script to the Assignee for approval on or before: [date].

4.4 The Assignor shall deliver the Series Package to the Assignee on or before: [date].

4.5 The Assignor confirms that the Series is based on an idea by [name] which is original and not copied from any third party. That the copyright in this project has been assigned by [name] to the Assignor.

4.6 The Assignor confirms that it has and will retain good title and authority to enter into this Agreement and is not bound by any previous agreement which adversely affects this Agreement.

4.7 The Assignor undertakes that all sums due in respect of the production of the Series will be paid as set out in the Budget. That in the event that it is expected that the

Budget will be exceeded, the Assignee shall be notified immediately in writing. That no additional costs or expenses of any nature shall be incurred without the prior written consent of the Assignee. That the Budget only sets out the cost of clearance and payments for the Videogram Rights and the Non-Theatric Rights and not all other media.

4.8 Upon request, the Assignor shall advise the Assignee about the progress of the production of the Series and to arrange viewings.

4.9 The Assignor undertakes to open a production account specifically for the purpose of depositing and paying out the Budget and shall keep accurate books of account and records of the costs of production of the Series with supporting documentation, contracts and other material which shall be made available for inspection by the Assignee upon request.

4.10 The Assignor acknowledges that the Assignee shall have the sole discretion as to the manner and method to be used in marketing, promoting and advertising the Series in respect of the Videogram Rights and the Non-Theatric Rights assigned under this Agreement.

4.11 The Assignor shall ensure that the each obligation to third parties in clause 1.7.6 is true and accurate and all have been agreed in writing so that any such material can be inspected by the Assignor if required.

4.12 The Assignor agrees that it shall assist with the marketing and promotion of the Series when requested by the Assignee if convenient at the Assignee's cost.

4.13 The Assignor agrees not to use the Budget to fund or offer as collateral for any other project at any time. That all monies shall only be used in accordance with the terms of this Agreement proposed for the Series.

5. OBLIGATIONS OF THE ASSIGNEE

5.1 In consideration of the rights assigned and the production of the Series, the Assignee shall pay to the Assignor the Budget as follows:

[____________] which shall be paid directly into the bank account opened by the Assignee for that purpose.

5.2 In the event of the Budget being exceeded, the Assignee agrees to pay such additional costs, provided that it has given its prior written approval of the expenditure to the Assignor on each occasion and shall pay such additional costs on dates to be agreed.

5.3 The Assignee agrees either to accept or provide written reasons for its rejection of the final script and the Series Package within [____________] of delivery in each case.

5.4 The Assignee confirms that it shall be responsible for any sums which arise through the exploitation of the Videogram Rights and the Non-Theatric Rights which are not set out in the Budget, including those due in respect of the performing rights in any music or the mechanical reproduction of the Series.

5.5 The Assignee undertakes that it and any third party including sub-agents, sub-licensees and sub-distributors shall keep full and accurate books of account, records and contracts showing the Gross Receipts and the Assignor's Royalties in respect of the exploitation of the Series under this Agreement and shall keep such material for not less than [____________] years in good condition and stored in a professional manner.

5.6 On the first day of March, June, September and December in each year, the Assignee undertakes that it shall pay the Assignor's Royalties due from the Gross Receipts to the Assignor by [method] in [currency].

5.7 On the first day of March, June, September and December in each year, the Assignee shall provide a detailed report to the Assignor with a full breakdown of the exploitation of the Series setting out the Gross Receipts and the Assignor's Royalties together with copies of all significant documentation to support the accounts. Where any sum is withheld, or converted or otherwise not received when due, then a side letter should set out the background information for the reduction, deduction, or delay.

5.8 The Assignee agrees that the Assignor shall be entitled to arrange for an audit at any time to inspect and make copies of the Assignee's books of account, records, contracts and any other relevant material in order to verify the sums due to the Assignor at the Assignor's cost and expense.

5.9 The Assignee confirms that it shall use its endeavours to exploit the Videogram Rights and Non-Theatric Rights assigned under this Agreement and to achieve, as far as possible, the maximum revenues.

5.10 The Assignee agrees to deliver videograms of the Series to retail or rental outlets on or by [____________] subject to satisfactory delivery of the Series Package by the Assignor.

5.11 The Assignee agrees to provide the following copyright notice, trademark, logo and credits to the Assignor in any publicity, promotional, advertising and packaging material in respect of the marketing and distribution of the Series: [____________].

5.12 The Assignee agrees to provide copies and samples of any publicity, promotional, advertising and packaging material in respect of the marketing and distribution of the Series upon request by the Assignor at the Assignee's cost.

5.13 The Assignee acknowledges that it shall be solely responsible for any sums due in respect of the manufacture, distribution, marketing and exploitation of the Videogram Rights and Non-Theatric Rights in the completed Series and that the Assignor shall not be liable for any such payments nor shall the Assignee deduct any such costs or payments from the Gross Receipts prior to the payment of the Assignor's Royalties.

5.14 The Assignee undertakes to provide the Assignor, free of charge, with not less than 12 copies of the Series in such form as will be made available to the general public.

5.15 The Assignee shall ensure as far as possible that all contractual, moral rights and other royalties regarding credits, copyright notices, logos, trademarks and service marks notified in the Series Package are adhered to by the Assignee under this Agreement.

6. LEGAL PROCEEDINGS

6.1 In the event of an action, claim, dispute, writ or proceedings arising out of this performance of this Agreement, the Assignor and the Assignee agree to provide full details to the other party at the earliest opportunity and shall not make an offer, or settle any such matter without full disclosure to the other party and agreement by both parties as to the best course of action. Each party shall bear its own costs unless the problem is directly attributable to one party, in which case the defaulting party shall bear all costs.

6.2 Insurance cover shall be arranged in respect of the Series both for production, distribution and product liability for the benefit of the Assignor and Assignee in the sum of: [figure] per year. The cost shall be part of the Budget for the first five years and thereafter shared equally between the parties.

7. CONFIDENTIALITY

The Assignor and the Assignee shall not disclose to any third party any confidential business or future plans of the other party at any time acquired during the existence of this Agreement. No reference is to be made to the terms of this Agreement by either party in any advertising, publicity or promotional material without the prior written consent of the other party.

8. AMENDMENTS

This Agreement supersedes all previous agreements, representations or promises and sets out all the terms agreed between the parties. Any amendment or alteration to this Agreement must be in writing and signed by an authorised signatory of each party.

9. NO PARTNERSHIP

This Agreement shall not be deemed to create any partnership or employment relationship between the parties.

10. NOTICES

Notices may be sent by fax, e-mail, text messages, letter, or otherwise provided that the sender can provide evidence that it has been received. [____________] must be given on each occasion to remedy a breach of this Agreement. Where notice is to terminate this Agreement it must be sent by recorded delivery or courier at the sender's expense.

11. TAXES

All charges and payments are not inclusive of tax and must be paid as far as legally possible without any deduction including Value Added Tax, Sales Tax or any other tax, levy or assessment. Each party shall be responsible for any national insurance, income tax or otherwise levied on their receipt of the income.

12. THIRD PARTY TRANSFERS

Neither party shall assign, transfer, charge or make over this Agreement or any of its rights or obligations without the prior written consent of the other party.

13. FORCE MAJEURE

In the event that this Agreement cannot be performed or its obligations fulfilled for any reason beyond the reasonable control of either party including war, industrial action, floods or Acts of God. Then such non-performance or failure to fulfil its obligations shall be deemed not to be a breach of this Agreement.

14. GOVERNING LAW

This Agreement shall be subject to the Laws of [____________].

15. TERMINATION

In the event that the Assignor does not deliver the Series Package or the Assignee does not market and distribute the Series in the form of videos as set out in this Agreement. Then as it is agreed that the parties shall be joint copyright owners of the Series unless the parties can resolve the matter within [____________] between themselves. It is agreed that they shall appoint [title] at [address] as arbitrator, the cost of which shall be met by both parties equally, and the parties agree that his/her decision shall be binding and that neither shall institute legal proceedings and that both agree to honour the decision.

SIGNED: [____________] [NAME] [TITLE] [DATE]
THE ASSIGNOR

SIGNED: [____________] [NAME] [TITLE] [DATE]
THE ASSIGNEE

SIGNED: [____________] [NAME] [TITLE] [DATE]
ARBITRATOR

I AGREE TO ACT AS ARBITRATOR TO THIS AGREEMENT IF REQUESTED TO DO SO BY BOTH THE ABOVE PARTIES SUBJECT TO AGREEMENT AS TO MY COSTS.

ATTACH TO AND FORMING PART OF THIS AGREEMENT IS:

SCHEDULE 1: THE TREATMENT
SCHEDULE 2: THE BUDGET
SCHEDULE 3: THE PRODUCTION SCHEDULE

OUTLINE—COMMISSIONING OF SERIES FOR WORLDWIDE VIDEO DISTRIBUTION

This contract is between a commissioning company and a production company to produce a Series of programmes for video distribution worldwide. In all likelihood, the commissioning company is a video distributor. For the purpose of the Agreement the commissioning company is called the Assignee and the production company the Assignor.

The Agreement is on the basis that the original idea behind the Series was created and proposed by the Assignor and is factual in nature.

This contract provides for the joint copyright ownership of the Series, except for the video and non-theatric rights which are being transferred to the Assignee for a fixed term and then will revert back to be held by both parties. Both parties remain joint copyright owners of all other rights, including all forms of television. For these rights to be exploited, the consent of both parties would be required and would need to be agreed as and when the circumstances arise.

The Assignor is entitled to receive a percentage of the Gross Receipts received from the exploitation of the worldwide video and non-theatric rights. This percentage is referred to as the Assignor's Royalties. The Assignee is paying for all the production costs set out in "the Budget", which should be attached to and form part of the Agreement. The Video distributor is not entitled to deduct the Budget or any marketing costs from the Gross Receipts before the payment of the Assignor's Royalties. In many cases a small percentage of gross is better than a large one of net where the production costs and distribution costs are not capped. The production company is agreeing to open a specific bank account for the project through which all money would be directed. No additional sums may be spent without the prior written consent of the video distributor.

The payment schedule of the Budget to the Assignor should be set out and could be one payment or in stages.

As the parties become copyright owners of the Series, there are some clauses which have not been included, such as a no obscenity and defamation undertaking, and no mutual indemnity. In the event of the threat of legal proceedings or some other claim, the parties agree to share information and agree on the best course of action. Insurance cover for the production of the Series and product liability should be arranged for a minimum amount each year which can be part of the Budget for the first five years. In the event that the parties have a major problem which cannot be resolved between them, then an arbitrator named in the contract can be appointed after a certain period whose decision is binding. It is better that it is agreed now; otherwise it will only be an additional point of dispute at a later date. Unusually we have included them as a signatory whereby that person agrees to act subject to costs being determined.

COMMISSIONING AND COMPLETE BUY-OUT OF ALL RIGHTS IN POP VIDEO

DATE OF THIS AGREEMENT: [____________]

THIS AGREEMENT IS BETWEEN THE FOLLOWING PARTIES:

1. [NAME] trading as [____________] at [ADDRESS OF HEAD OFFICE] and [MAIN BUSINESS PREMISES]. "THE ASSIGNOR"
2. [NAME] trading as [____________] at [ADDRESS OF HEAD OFFICE] and [MAIN BUSINESS PREMISES]. "THE ASSIGNEE"

1. DEFINITIONS

The words set out below shall be defined as follows:

1.1 "The Video" shall be the promotional video and any associated sound recording for the Musical Work to be performed by the Artiste.

1.2 "The Artiste" shall be: [Name] performing as: [____________].

1.3 "The Musical Work" shall be the musical composition and recording entitled: A copy of the Musical Work is attached to and forms part of this Agreement as Schedule A.

1.4 "The Artistic Concept" shall be the brief narrative description of the content of the Video, which includes images, location and the technical format. A copy of the Artistic Concept is attached to and forms part of this Agreement as Schedule B.

1.5 "The Assignment Fee" shall be the sum of: [figure/currency].

1.6 "The Key Personnel" shall be as follows: [____________].

1.7 "The Budget" shall be the total cost of making the Video, whether direct or indirect, inclusive of all locations, facilities and other items necessary for the development, pre-production, production, post-production, comprehensive personal injury insurance and product liability, delivery and exploitation of the Video. A copy of the Budget is attached to and forms part of this Agreement as Schedule C.

1.8 "The Production Schedule" shall be the agreed dates, times and locations of making the Video, including pre-production, production, post-production and delivery of the Video. A copy of the Production Schedule is attached to and forms part of this Agreement as Schedule D.

1.9 "The Video Package" shall be the following material of the Video:

1.9.1 technical material of first class quality comprising: [____________];

1.9.2 [____________] copies of the Video in format: [____________];

1.9.3 a complete list of the laboratories and any other locations at which any material relating to the Video is held, together with access letters giving the Assignee irrevocable authority to obtain the material and copies for use at its sole discretion; and

1.9.4 the original copies of the insurance policies arranged for the benefit of the Assignee.

1.10 "The Territory" shall be all countries, bases and locations throughout the universe.

1.11 "All Media Rights" shall mean the sole and exclusive right to produce, manufacture, supply, sell, rent, distribute, license, market, and exploit the Video and any part(s) in all forms of the media whether in existence now or created in the future including but not limited to all forms of publication; hardback, paperback; all forms of radio, television and video; cable; satellite; digital; cassette; laser disc; any technical method of delivery; any method of payment, charging, subscription, rental, lease, and for free; all forms of communication systems; sound; vision; graphics; text; icons; images; all forms of theatric and non-theatric exploitation; all forms of electronic, internet, intranet and multi-media exploitation; CD-Roms; DVD; all methods of merchandising; any other developments, variations or of any nature.

2. ASSIGNMENT

In consideration of the payment of the Budget and the Assignment Fee, the Assignor assigns to the Assignee All Media Rights in the Video and parts throughout the Territory for the full period of copyright and any extensions and renewals which shall continue in perpetuity without limitation of time indefinitely.

3. OBLIGATIONS OF THE ASSIGNOR

3.1 The Assignor undertakes that it shall produce the Video using the Key Personnel, in accordance with the Artistic Concept, the Budget and the Production Schedule subject to the payment of the Budget and the Assignment Fee.

3.2 The Assignor confirms that the Video shall not contain any other music, text or sound effects other than the Musical Work, unless there is prior written consent in advance by the Assignee.

3.3 The Assignor shall deliver the Video Package to the Assignee on or before: [date] at [____________].

3.4 The Assignor confirms that it is the sole owner of or controls all copyright and any other rights in the Video, which are assigned under this Agreement except in respect of the Artiste and the Musical Work.

3.5 The Assignor confirms that it has and will retain good title and authority to enter into this Agreement and is not bound by any previous agreement which adversely affects this Agreement.

3.6 The Assignor undertakes that all sums due in respect of the production and exploitation of the Video will be paid as set out in the Budget and that the Assignee is not and will not be liable for any such payments, except in respect of the Artiste and the Musical Work which are not included in the Budget.

3.7 In respect of the Video, the Assignor undertakes that all copyright and any other rights (except for the Artiste and the Musical Work), including consents required under the Copyright Designs and Patents Act 1988 shall be cleared and paid for in respect of the rights assigned under this Agreement for use by the Assignee of the Video for promotional purposes, provided that the Assignor shall only be responsible for such clearance payments as are set out in the Budget.

3.8 The Assignor undertakes that the Video will not contain any obscene, offensive, defamatory or derogatory material and will not expose the Assignee to any civil or criminal proceedings unless it is agreed in advance in writing between the parties or set out as part of the Artistic Concept or part of the performance by the Artiste or the Musical Work.

3.9 In the event of the Approved Budget being exceeded by up to [____________], the Assignor agrees to inform The Assignee in advance and provide the Assignee with a statement of costs incurred to date and details of the additional costs.

3.10 In the event of the Approved Budget being exceeded by more than 10%, the Assignor agrees that the prior written approval of the Assignee shall be required in order to authorise any further expenditure and that any further payment shall be at the Assignee's sole discretion.

3.11 The Assignor agrees to provide original copies or, where not, appropriate copies of all parties engaged in the production of the Video or who provided material or locations for retention by the Assignee for future reference and, in particular, those documents which relate to moral rights. As far as possible, the Assignor shall ensure that all moral rights of any nature are waived and that all parties sign written letters of agreement or contracts for their work or services.

4. OBLIGATIONS OF THE ASSIGNEE

4.1 In consideration of the production of the Video, the Assignee shall pay to the Assignor the Budget as follows:

4.1.1 [____________] upon signature of this Agreement; and
4.1.2 [____________].

4.2 In consideration of rights assigned under this Agreement, the Assignee shall pay to the Assignor the Assignment Fee as follows:

4.2.1 [____________] upon signature to this Agreement; and
4.2.2 [____________] on or before [____________].

4.3 In the event of the Budget being exceeded by up to 10%, the Assignee agrees to pay such additional costs, provided that the Assignor informs the Assignee in advance and provides upon request to the Assignee a statement of costs incurred to date and details of the additional costs.

4.4 In the event of the Budget being exceeded by more than 10%, the Assignee agrees to pay such additional costs, provided that it has provided prior written approval of the expenditure to the Assignor.

4.5 The Assignee agrees either to accept or provide written reasons for their rejection of the Video Package within seven days of delivery.

4.6 The Assignee confirms that it shall be responsible for providing the services and attendance of the Artiste as required by the Assignor for the purpose of producing the Video.

4.7 The Assignee confirms that it shall provide to the Assignor such recordings of the Musical Work at its sole discretion and cost for the purpose of the production of the Video.

4.8 The Assignee agrees that it shall be responsible for any payments in respect of the Artiste and the Musical Work and any sums due in respect of the distribution and exploitation of the Video in any media throughout the Territory not set out in the Budget.

4.9 The Assignee confirms that it shall be responsible for any payments due in respect of the performing rights in any music and the mechanical reproduction of the Video.

5. TIME OF THE ESSENCE

Both parties agree that all times and dates referred to in this Agreement shall be of the essence.

6. CONFIDENTIALITY

The Assignor and the Assignee shall not disclose to any third party any confidential business or future plans of the other party at any time acquired during the existence of this Agreement and no reference is to be made to the terms of this Agreement by either party in any advertising, publicity or promotional material without the prior written consent of the other party. The production of the Video shall not be disclosed by the Assignor to the media; nor shall any statement or reference be made regarding the behaviour or performance of the Artiste without the prior consent of the Assignee.

7. AMENDMENTS

This Agreement supersedes all previous agreements, representations or promises and sets out all the terms agreed between the parties. Any amendment or alteration to this Agreement must be in writing and signed by an authorised signatory of each party.

8. NO PARTNERSHIP

This Agreement shall not be deemed to create any partnership or employment relationship between the parties.

9. NOTICES

Without prejudice to the right to serve notices by any other means any notice served under this Agreement shall be in writing.

10. VALUE ADDED TAX

All sums payable under this Agreement are exclusive of any value added tax that may be payable by either party.

11. FORCE MAJEURE

In the event that this Agreement cannot be performed or its obligations fulfilled for any reason beyond the reasonable control of either party including war, industrial action, floods or Acts of God then such non-performance or failure to fulfil its obligations shall be deemed not to be a breach of this Agreement. In the event that this Agreement cannot be performed or its obligations fulfilled for any reason beyond either party's reasonable control for a continuous period of [two weeks]. Then either party may, at its discretion, terminate this Agreement by notice in writing at the end of that period.

12. TERMINATION

In addition to any other rights and remedies at law, the Assignor or the Assignee may, by giving written notice to the other defaulting party, terminate this Agreement on the grounds that this defaulting party has failed to account or make payments as required under this Agreement or has committed a serious breach of its obligations and has not rectified the position within seven days.

13. GOVERNING LAW

This Agreement shall be subject to the Laws of England.

ATTACHED TO AND FORMING PART OF THIS AGREEMENT:

SCHEDULE A: THE MUSICAL WORK
SCHEDULE B: THE ARTISTIC CONCEPT
SCHEDULE C: THE BUDGET
SCHEDULE D: THE PRODUCTION SCHEDULE

Signed by: [____________]
FOR AND ON BEHALF OF THE ASSIGNOR

Date: [____________]

Signed by: [____________]
FOR AND ON BEHALF OF THE ASSIGNEE

Date: [____________]

OUTLINE—COMMISSIONING AND COMPLETE BUY-OUT OF ALL RIGHTS IN POP VIDEO

This contract is between a record company which wants to commission a pop video and a production company. For the purpose of this Agreement, the record company is called the Assignee and the production company the Assignor. The production company is assigning all copyright in the Video, without limitation of time, to the record company. The record company is paying for all the production costs set out in the Budget.

The Agreement constitutes a complete buy-out of all copyright and all other rights in all media by the Assignee. The consideration for the assignment is the Assignment Fee which is over and above the Budget and the Producer's Fee.

The Agreement is on the basis that the Assignor would be responsible for the clearance and payment of copyright fees as set out in the Budget. These payments are in respect of the Video being used by the Assignee for promotional purposes throughout the world.

The record company is responsible for the attendance and payment of the Artiste at the film location. The record company is entirely responsible for the clearance payments of all music and sound recordings. No moral rights are being asserted.

COMMISSIONING AND COMPLETE BUY-OUT OF ALL RIGHTS IN CORPORATE VIDEO

AN AGREEMENT made this [____________] day of [____________]

BETWEEN:

(1) [____________]
of [____________] (to be known as the Assignor in this Agreement)

AND

(2) [____________]
of [____________] (to be known as the Assignee in this Agreement).

IT IS AGREED as follows:

1. DEFINITIONS

The words below are agreed to mean as follows:

1.1 "The Video" shall be the following film and any associated sound recording based on the Treatment entitled: [____________], duration: [____________].

1.2 "The Treatment" shall be the synopsis of the Video. A copy of the Treatment is attached to and forms part of this Agreement as Appendix 1.

1.3 "The Key Personnel" shall be as follows: [Producer/Director/Presenter].

1.4 "The Budget" shall be the agreed costs of making the Video, whether direct or indirect, inclusive of all locations, facilities and other items necessary for the development, pre-production, production, post-production and delivery of the Video; including insurance and an additional cost for the services of the Assignor. A copy of the Budget is attached to and forms part of this Agreement as Appendix 2.

1.5 "The Production Schedule" shall be the agreed dates, times and locations of making and delivery of the Video. A copy of the Production Schedule is attached to and forms part of this Agreement as Appendix 3.

1.6 "The Payment Schedule" shall be the details of the payment of the Budget by the Assignee to the Assignor. A copy of the Payment Schedule is attached to and forms part of this Agreement as Appendix 4.

1.7 "The Video Package" shall be the following material of the Video:

1.7.1 technical material of first class quality: [____________];

1.7.2 not less than [____________] [format] copies of the Video;

1.7.3 a complete list of the technical and master material and any copies in any format and in any gauge, including but not limited to rushes, out-takes, video tapes, sound recordings, music and effects tracks, title and sub-title tracks and viewing copies in the possession or under the control of the Assignor;

1.7.4 a complete list of the laboratories and any other locations at which any material relating to the Video is held together with access letters giving the Assignee irrevocable authority to obtain the material and copies for use at its sole discretion;

1.7.5 typed manuscript of final script;

1.7.6 Music cue sheet listing each musical work with the name of the composer, author and publisher, including the duration of each musical work and the description of use in each case; and

1.7.7 a detailed statement and copies of all records of the copyright and other clearances obtained and the sums due or paid and all contractual obligations and undertakings and all moral rights waived or asserted in relation to the Video.

1.8 "The Territory" shall be all countries, areas, ships, aeroplanes, oil-rigs and any other location throughout the world.

1.9 "All Media Rights" shall mean the sole and exclusive right to produce, manufacture, supply, sell, rent, distribute, license, market, and exploit the Video and any part(s) in all forms of the media whether in existence now or created in the future including but not limited to all forms of publication; hardback, paperback; all forms of radio, television and video; cable; satellite; digital; cassette; laser disc; any technical method of delivery; any method of payment, charging, subscription, rental, lease, and for free; all forms of telecommunication systems, telephone, mobile phones, pagers, text; icons; images; all forms of theatric and non-theatric exploitation; all forms of electronic; CD-Roms; all methods of merchandising; any other developments, variations or adaptations of any nature.

2. ASSIGNMENT

In consideration of the receipt of all the Budget, the Assignor assigns to the Assignee All Media Rights in the Video and parts throughout the Territory for the full period of copyright and any extensions and renewals.

3. OBLIGATIONS OF THE ASSIGNOR

3.1 The Assignor undertakes that it shall produce the Video using the Key Personnel, in accordance with the Treatment, the Budget and the Production Schedule.

3.2 The Assignor confirms that the Video shall be produced in colour, in the English language and in the following format: [____________].

3.3 The Assignor shall deliver the Video Package to the Assignee on or before: [date].

3.4 The Assignor confirms that it is the sole owner of or controls all copyright and any other rights in the Video, which are assigned under this Agreement.

3.5 The Assignor confirms that it has and will retain good title and authority to enter into this Agreement and is not bound by any previous agreement which adversely affects this Agreement.

3.6 The Assignor undertakes that all sums due in respect of the production of the Video will be paid and that the Assignee is not and will not be liable for any such payments.

3.7 In respect of the Video, the Assignor undertakes that all copyright and any other rights (musical or otherwise), including consents required under the Copyright Designs and Patents Act 1988 shall be cleared in respect of All Media Rights assigned under this Agreement provided that the Assignor shall only be responsible for such clearance payments as are set out in the Budget.

3.8 The Assignor undertakes that the Video will not contain any obscene or defamatory material and will not expose the Assignee to any civil or criminal proceedings.

3.9 In the event of the Budget being exceeded by up to [______] per cent, the Assignor agrees to inform the Assignee in advance and to provide the Assignee with a statement of costs incurred to date and details of the additional costs.

3.10 In the event of the Budget being exceeded by more than [______] per cent, the Assignor agrees that the prior written approval of the Assignee shall be required in order to authorise any further expenditure and that any further payment shall be at the Assignee's sole discretion.

3.11 The Assignor accepts that all editorial decisions in respect of the Video are at the Assignee's sole discretion, and agrees to carry out all such requests as may be made provided that the Assignee shall bear the cost whether included in the Budget or not.

3.12 The Assignor agrees to incorporate all such trademarks, service marks, copyright notices and logos and credits in the Video as the Assignee may request in writing by: [date] provided that, where it is not part of the Budget, the Assignee shall bear all the costs and supply copies of such materials and artwork on loan as may be required.

3.13 The Assignor agrees to incorporate all material in clause 3.12 in the manner, style, size, form and position requested by the Assignee. The Assignor agrees that it shall not assign any rights, interest or goodwill in any such material or any development or variation which shall remain the sole property of the Assignee or the relevant third party.

3.14 The Assignor agrees that the Assignee shall be entitled to retain all income and other sums due from the exploitation of the Film and/or parts and that the Assignee shall not be entitled to receive any royalties, monies or other payment whatsoever except the Assignment Fee under this Agreement.

3.15 The ownership and risk of the Film Package shall pass on delivery to the Assignor.

4. OBLIGATIONS OF THE ASSIGNEE

4.1 In consideration of the production of the Video, the Assignee shall pay to the Assignor the Budget as set out in the Payment Schedule.

4.2 In the event of the Budget being exceeded by up to [______] per cent the Assignee agrees to pay such additional costs, provided that the Assignor informs the Assignee in advance and provides upon request, to the Assignee a statement of costs incurred to date and details of the additional costs.

4.3 In the event of the Budget being exceeded by more than [______] per cent the Assignee agrees to pay such additional costs, provided that it has given prior written approval of the expenditure to the Assignor.

4.4 The Assignee agrees either to accept or provide written reasons for its rejection of the Video Package within [__________] of delivery.

4.5 The Assignee confirms that it shall be responsible for any clearance payments not set out in the Budget including any sums due in respect of the distribution and exploitation of the Video in any media throughout the Territory, including any sums in respect of the performing rights in any music and the mechanical reproduction of the Video.

4.6 The Assignee agrees that it shall not exploit the Video in any manner which would result in a breach of the credits, moral rights, copyright notices, or contractual obligations concluded with third parties in respect of the Video.

4.7 Once the Video is accepted by the Assignee, all further costs and expenses in respect of the exploitation and marketing of the Video are at the Assignee's sole cost and expense.

4.8 The Assignee agrees that where editorial changes are requested by the Assignee that affect the Budget and will result in additional costs, the Assignee shall be responsible for the cost of such additional work.

4.9 The Assignee agrees to provide a list of trademarks, service marks, copyright notice and logos to the Assignor by: [date] and shall supply on loan all such material and artwork as may be required. Where any such costs were not part of the Budget, then the Assignee agrees to pay all such costs.

4.10 The Assignee confirms that it owns or controls or has the consent of the relevant third party in respect of any trademark, service mark, copyright notice, or logos or credits that it shall be requested to include in the Video and that the Assignor shall not be liable where it is acting on the instructions of the Assignee and that it shall be the sole responsibility of the Assignee.

5. CONFIDENTIALITY

The Assignor and the Assignee shall not disclose to any third party any confidential business or future plans of the other party at any time acquired during the existence of this Agreement. No reference is to be made to the terms of this Agreement by either party in any advertising, publicity or promotional material without the prior written consent of the other party.

6. AMENDMENTS

This Agreement supersedes all previous agreements, representations or promises and sets out all the terms agreed between the parties. Any amendment to this Agreement must be in writing and signed by both parties.

7. NO PARTNERSHIP

This Agreement shall not be deemed to create any partnership or employment relationship between the parties.

8. NOTICES

Without prejudice to the right to serve notices by any other means any notice served under this Agreement shall be in writing.

9. VALUE ADDED TAX

All sums payable under this Agreement are exclusive of any value added tax that may be payable by either party.

10. FORCE MAJEURE

In the event that this Agreement cannot be performed or its obligations fulfilled for any reason beyond the reasonable control of either party including war, industrial action, floods or Acts of God. Then such non-performance or failure to fulfil its obligations shall be deemed not to be a breach of this Agreement. In the event that this Agreement cannot be performed or its obligations fulfilled for any reason beyond either party's reasonable control for a continuous period of [three months]. Then the party who is not in default may, at its discretion, terminate this Agreement by notice in writing at the end of that period.

11. TERMINATION

In addition to any other rights and remedies at law, either party may, by giving written notice to the other party, terminate this Agreement on the grounds that the other party has failed to account or make payments as required under this Agreement or has committed a serious breach of its obligations under this Agreement and has not rectified the position within [____________].

12. GOVERNING LAW

This Agreement shall be subject to the Laws of England.

13. THIRD PARTY TRANSFER

13.1 The Assignee shall be entitled to transfer, charge or make over this Agreement to any third party provided that they agree to fulfil the terms of this Agreement.

13.2 The Assignor shall not be entitled to appoint another production company to fulfil any part of the work on the Video unless it is set out in the Budget or agreed with the Assignee in advance. Nor shall the Assignor transfer, charge or make over any of the benefits or obligations under this Agreement without the prior written consent of the Assignee.

Attached to and forming part of this Agreement:

APPENDIX 1: TREATMENT
APPENDIX 2: BUDGET
APPENDIX 3: PRODUCTION SCHEDULE
APPENDIX 4: PAYMENT SCHEDULE

SIGNED: [____________] [NAME]

DATE: [____________] [TITLE]
THE ASSIGNOR

SIGNED: [____________] [NAME]

DATE: [____________] [TITLE]
THE ASSIGNEE

OUTLINE—COMMISSIONING AND COMPLETE BUY-OUT OF ALL RIGHTS IN CORPORATE VIDEO

This contract is between a company which wants to commission a corporate video and a production company. The Video could be for in-house training, promotional purposes, media image projection, etc. For the purpose of the Agreement, the commissioning company is called the Assignee and the production company the Assignor.

The production company is assigning all copyright in the Video to the commissioning company. The commissioning company is paying for all the production costs set out in the Budget. There are provisions for the Budget being exceeded. Details of the payments by the commissioning company should be agreed and set out in a payment schedule.

The Agreement constitutes a complete buy-out of all copyright and all other rights in all media by the Assignee. The consideration for the assignment is the fee which is in the Budget.

The Agreement is made on the basis that the Assignor would be responsible for the clearance of rights in all media but would only make payment provision in the Budget for corporate use only.

The Assignee is to provide details of the trademark, service mark, copyright notices, and logos and credits which may be applicable whether owned by the Assignee or a third party. The Assignor is to follow instructions, and the Assignee is responsible for any errors and the cost.

No moral rights are being asserted, and there are no indemnity provisions.

BUY-OUT OF ALL RIGHTS IN A COMPLETED FILM

AN AGREEMENT made this [____________] day of [____________]

BETWEEN:

(1) [Company Name] trading as: [____________]
of [List of addresses] (to be known as the Licensor in this Agreement)

AND

(2) [Company Name] trading as: [____________]
of [List of addresses] (to be known as the Licensee in this Agreement).

IT IS AGREED as follows:

1. DEFINITIONS

The words below are agreed to mean as follows:

1.1 "The Film" shall be the following film and any associated sound recording entitled [____________] which is [____________], minutes in duration. Full details of the Film are set out in Schedule [1] and are attached to and form part of this Agreement.

1.2 "The Assignment Fee" shall be the sum of: [figure/currency].

1.3 "The Film Package' shall be all the material of the Film and/or part(s) in the possession or under the control of the Assignor including:

1.3.1 all technical and master material and any copies in any format and in any gauge including but not limited to negatives, rushes, out-takes, video tapes, prints, sound recordings, music and effects tracks, title and sub-title tracks, trailers, promos and viewing copies;

1.3.2 a complete list of the laboratories, warehouses and other locations at which any material relating to the Film and/or part(s) are held, together with access letters giving the Assignee irrevocable authority to obtain the material and/or copies for use at its sole discretion;

1.3.3 a complete list of all material relating to the Film and/or part(s) held by any third party;

1.3.4 all originals and all copies of all documents, records and other data in any form including but not limited to dialogue lists, scripts, music cue sheets, publicity, promotional and advertising material including material stored in computerised form;

1.3.5 a detailed statement of all on-screen, publicity, advertising and promotional credit obligations, moral rights and contractual obligations;

1.3.6 all publicity material including photographs and stills negatives, posters and catalogues;

1.3.7 a detailed statement of the copyright and other clearances or permissions obtained; and

1.3.8 music cue sheet listing each musical work with the name of the composer, author and publisher, including the duration of each musical work and the description of use in each case.

1.4 "The Territory" shall be all countries, areas, ships, aeroplanes, oil-rigs, bases and any other locations throughout the universe.

2. ASSIGNMENT

2.1 In consideration of the payment of the Assignment Fee in full by the agreed date. The Assignor assigns to the Assignee all present and future copyright and all other rights in all media, whether in existence now or created in the future, in the Film, including any parts and the Film Package throughout the Territory for the full period of copyright and any extensions and renewals including but not limited to:

2.1.1 all forms of exploitation through the medium of television and radio whether transmission is by cable, digital satellite, microwave, over the air or otherwise whether free or payment-encrypted or not;

2.1.2 all forms of exploitation through telecommunication systems, computers, DVD, CD-Rom software, telephones, mobile phones, pagers, electronic merchandise, the internet;

2.1.3 all forms of exploitation through videos, cassettes, lasers, discs, merchandising, cinemas, non-paying audiences in educational, cultural, religious and social establishments, clubs and universities, commercial use by businesses;

2.1.4 all forms of publishing whether in printed or electronic form;

2.1.5 all other forms not covered above in any medium.

2.2 The Assignor and the Assignee acknowledge that the assignment in clause 2.1 is subject to the following existing agreements: [list documents].

Copies of the existing agreements are attached to and form part of this Agreement as Schedule [2].

2.3 The Assignor acknowledges that the Film Package shall be the sole property of the Assignee and that the Assignor shall not retain any rights or interest in the Film Package.

3. OBLIGATIONS OF THE ASSIGNOR

3.1 The Assignor shall, as far as reasonably possible, deliver the Film Package to the Assignee on or before: [date].

3.2 The Assignor confirms that it is the sole owner of or controls all copyright and any other rights in the Film, which are assigned under this Agreement.

3.3 The Assignor confirms that it has and will retain good title and authority to enter into this Agreement and is not bound by any previous agreement which adversely affects this Agreement, except for those agreements specifically referred to in clause 2 above.

3.4 The Assignor confirms that all sums due in respect of the production of the Film have been paid and that the Assignee is not and will not be liable for any such payments.

3.5 In respect of the Film, the Assignor confirms that all copyright and any other rights (musical or otherwise), including consents required under the Copyright, Designs and Patents Act 1988 have been obtained in respect of the following right only: [____________] and have been paid for in respect of the following rights: [____________].

3.6 The Assignor acknowledges that the Assignee shall be entitled to edit, adapt, alter or amend the Film, including any soundtrack, entirely at its sole cost and discretion.

4. OBLIGATIONS OF THE ASSIGNEE

4.1 In consideration of the rights assigned by the Assignor, the Assignee shall pay to the Assignor the Assignment Fee as follows:

4.1.1 [____________] upon signature of this Agreement;
4.1.2 [____________] on or before [____________];
4.1.3 [____________] on or before [____________].

4.2 The Assignee confirms that it shall be responsible for the clearance of and payment of any sums due in respect of the distribution, marketing and exploitation of the Film in any media throughout the Territory at any time and shall not seek to recover any such sum from the Assignor.

4.3 The Assignee agrees to abide by any contractual, moral and credit obligations specified by the Assignor in clause 1 in the Film Package.

4.4 The Assignee agrees that it has viewed the Film and does not rely on any undertaking by the Assignor as to its content in respect of obscenity, or defamation, and shall seek its own legal advice.

4.5 Where the Assignee changes the Film and breaches any of the previous contractual, moral, or other credit obligations to any third party it shall indemnify the Assignor in respect of any claim provided that the Assignee deals with all matters relating to the claim.

5. CONFIDENTIALITY

The Assignor and the Assignee shall not disclose to any third party any confidential business or future plans of the other party at any time acquired during the existence of this Agreement.

6. INDEMNITY

6.1 The Assignor agrees to indemnify the Assignee in respect of any claim, action, damages, loss or costs which may arise for any reason from the exploitation of the Film and/or part(s) which relates to the failure by the Assignor to have cleared and/or paid for the use of any material or artist or personnel in the Film which the Assignor had undertaken to be cleared. The maximum total liability shall be limited to: [figure/currency] under this Agreement to the Assignee.

6.2 The Assignee shall indemnify the Assignor against any liability, loss, damages, claim or costs which arise directly as a result of the breach by the Assignee of this Agreement.

7. AMENDMENT

This Agreement sets out the entire and complete understanding of the terms agreed between the parties and may not be changed or superseded except in a written document signed by both parties.

8. TAXES

8.1 All sums payable under this Agreement are exclusive of any value added tax that may be payable by either party.

8.2 Each party shall bear the cost of any national insurance, taxes, or otherwise that may arise from the assignment of the Film and Film Package under this Agreement.

9. FORCE MAJEURE

If the ability of the Assignee to accept delivery of the Film Package and/or the provision or performance of the terms of this Agreement is delayed, hindered, or prevented by circumstances beyond the reasonable control of the Assignor or Assignee. Then such delivery and/or performance shall be suspended and if it cannot be effected within a reasonable time after the due date then it shall be cancelled by notice in writing and equitable settlement of the position.

10. GOVERNING LAW

This Agreement shall be construed in accordance with [________ Law] and subject to the exclusive jurisdiction of [_____________].

Attached to this Agreement:

Schedule 1: Film Description
Schedule 2: Pre-existing Agreements.

[_____________] [NAME/TITLE/COMPANY]

[_____________] [NAME/TITLE/COMPANY]

OUTLINE—BUY-OUT OF ALL RIGHTS IN A COMPLETED FILM

This contract is a complete buy-out of all rights in a completed Film for a one-off payment. The Film could be a feature film, documentary, television series, library material, etc. For this Agreement, the copyright owner is the Assignor and the purchasing company is the Assignee.

This Agreement is a full assignment of all copyright and any other rights in all media throughout the universe. The Assignor will no longer have any rights in the Film, in whole or in part, and will not be able to exploit it in any form or receive any more money.

The Assignor is undertaking that all payments in respect of the production of the Film have been paid. The Assignor is confirming that only certain copyright clearances have been obtained. The Assignee will be responsible for all clearance payments and performing rights which become due from the exploitation of the Film.

The rights in the Film and the Film Package are assigned. Property, ownership and risk of the Film Package will pass on delivery. The indemnity by the Assignor is limited to a fixed sum related to not clearing or paying for the rights properly. The indemnity by the Assignee is wider and relates to its non-fulfilment of notified contractual, copyright and moral right obligations.

This Agreement is given as to obscenity or defamation as it is accepted the Assignee has viewed the Film.

BUY-OUT OF ALL VIDEO RIGHTS IN A COMPLETED FILM

AGREEMENT DATED: [____________]

PARTIES TO THIS AGREEMENT:

(1) [____________] a company incorporated in [____________] number [____________] registered office at: [address] main place of business at: [address] of [____________]

[THE ASSIGNOR]

(2) [____________] a company incorporated in [____________] number [____________] registered office at: [address] main place of business at: [address] of [____________]

[THE ASSIGNEE]

IT IS AGREED as follows:

1. DEFINITIONS

The words below are agreed to mean as follows:

1.1 "The Film" shall be the following film and any associated sound recording entitled [____________], which is [____________] minutes in duration

1.2 "The Assignment Fee" shall be the sum of: [figure/currency].

1.3 "The Master Material" shall be the following material of the Film:

1.3.1 technical material of first class quality comprising of: [____________];
1.3.2 laboratory access letter;
1.3.3 typed transcript of final script;
1.3.4 music cue sheet listing each musical work with the name of the composer, author and publisher, including the duration of each musical work and the description of use in each case;
1.3.5 such publicity and marketing material including photographs, posters, stills, packaging and labels as may be available;

1.3.6 A full written and comprehensive statement together where appropriate with copies of all supporting documents, contracts and records relating to the exploitation of the Videogram Rights in the Film including consents, clearances, contractual obligations, moral right assertions or waivers, copyright, trademarks, service marks, logos, credits, or copyright notices.

1.4 "The Territory" shall be all countries, bases and locations throughout the world.

1.5 "The Videogram Rights" shall mean the right to transfer, manufacture, duplicate, sell, rent, supply, distribute and have distributed the Film for home use by the public and to non-paying audiences in educational, cultural, religious, social and other institutions of any kind, and to commercial companies and businesses such as hotels, clubs, airlines, ships, by means of electronic and mechanical reproduction whether the existence now or created in the future in the form of any disc, magnetic tape, or other method so that the film shown as a moving image intended for reproduction on copies which are inserted in a machine or device to be played back on a television, computer or other visual screen by a video recorder, DVD player or some other machine whether the two are distinct or one item. These rights shall include videocassette, disc, laser, reel to reel, DVD, CD-ROM, the internet, delivery by telephone and mobile phones by a screen.

2. ASSIGNMENT

In consideration of the payment of the Assignment Fee, the Assignor assigns to the Assignee the sole and exclusive Videogram Rights in the Film, including any parts which are in existence now or created in the future throughout the Territory for the full period of copyright and any extensions and renewals.

3. OBLIGATIONS OF THE ASSIGNOR

3.1 The Assignor shall deliver the Master Material to the Assignee on or before [date] at the Assignor's cost and risk.

3.2 The Assignor confirms that it is the sole owner of or controls all copyright and any other rights in the Film which are assigned under this Agreement except: [____________].

3.3 The Assignor confirms that it has and will retain good title and authority to enter into this Agreement and is not bound by any previous agreement which adversely affects this Agreement.

3.4 The Assignor confirms that all sums due in respect of the production of the Film have been paid and that the Assignee is not and will not be liable for any such payments.

3.5 The Assignor reserves all other rights in the Film and/or parts not assigned to the Assignee.

3.6 The Assignor confirms that all necessary copyright clearances, consents, contracts, waivers, licenses, releases or otherwise have been obtained from all performers, musicians, actors, writers, personnel and any other persons involved and in respect of all master material in the Film and/or part(s). That the details have been fully disclosed and are accurate as set out in the Master Package.

The Assignor confirms that it has fully disclosed the position in respect of the payments made in respect of such third parties. The Assignee shall only be liable to pay such sums for the exploitation of the rights assigned under this Agreement as they fall due which the Assignor have made clear are the responsibility of the Assignee. The Assignee shall in any event bear the cost of all sums due in respect of performing rights, mechanical reproduction, any union members, and any music.

3.7 The Assignor undertakes that the Film and/or parts, its title and content, any sound, text or music and the exploitation of the Videogram Rights will not expose the Assignee to civil or criminal proceedings or infringe or breach the copyright, contract, trademark, service mark, logo, design, literary, dramatic, musical, artistic or other rights of any third party. This undertaking shall not apply to any edited or altered version of the Film and/or parts which is not the same as the original Master Material.

3.8 The packaging, shipping, carriage and insurance of the Master Material shall be at the Assignor's cost and risk. In the event that the delivery date cannot be met, the Assignor shall notify the Assignee at the earliest opportunity. The risk in the Master Material shall pass immediately upon delivery to the Assignee but the property shall remain with the Assignor until all the Assignment Fee has been paid for.

3.9 The Assignor shall only be entitled to receive the Assignment Fee and shall not be entitled to receive any income, royalties or otherwise from the exploitation of the Video Rights.

3.10 The Assignor agrees that the Assignee shall be entitled to edit, revise, change, alter, add to, delete from or amend the Film and/or parts in respect of the exploitation of the Videogram Rights at the Assignee's sole cost and discretion.

4. OBLIGATIONS OF THE ASSIGNEE

4.1 In consideration of the rights assigned by the Assignor the Assignee shall pay to the Assignor the Assignment Fee as follows:

4.1.1 [______________] upon signature of this Agreement;
4.1.2 [______________] on or before;
4.1.3 [______________] subject to the acceptance of the Master Package.

4.2 The Assignee accepts that it is only acquiring the Videogram Rights in the Film and that all other rights are reserved by the Assignor and that the Assignee has no rights or interest in them including, CD-ROMs, transmission by television, radio, publishing, merchandising, music. Nor shall the Assignee be entitled to exploit these other rights in the Film.

4.3 The Assignee agrees to bear the cost of all sums due for the exploitation of the Video Rights in the Film including the performing rights in any music; the mechanical reproduction of the Film; any union members and any music.

4.4 The Assignee accepts that, in the event that it edits or alters the Film, it shall be at the sole discretion, cost, and liability of the Assignee and the Assignor shall not be liable or bear any such cost.

4.5 The Assignee accepts that the risk in the Master Material shall pass on delivery and that property shall pass to the Assignee on full payment of the Assignment Fee.

4.6 The Assignee shall abide by the statement in clause 1.3.6. In the event that there is any failure or breach by the Assignee, the Assignee shall pay all costs, damages and expenses which may be claimed and/or arise in consequence from any third party.

4.7 The Assignee agrees that it shall not be entitled to license any music, characters, images or any other rights or parts except those set out in this Agreement.

5. INDEMNITY

The Assignor and the Assignee mutually undertake to indemnify the other against all liabilities, claims, demands, actions, costs, damages and loss arising out of any breach by either party of any of the terms of this Agreement. In the event of any claim, dispute, action, writ or summons the Assignor and the Assignee agree to provide full details to the other party at the earliest opportunity and shall not settle any such matter without first consulting the other party.

6. PUBLICITY

No reference is to be made to the terms of this Agreement by either party in any advertising, publicity or promotional material without the prior written consent of the other party.

7. AMENDMENTS

This Agreement supersedes all previous agreements, representations or promises and sets out all the terms agreed between the parties. Any amendment or alteration to this Agreement must be in writing and signed by an authorised signatory of each party.

8. VALUE ADDED TAX

All sums payable under this Agreement are exclusive of any value added tax that may be payable by either party.

9. FORCE MAJEURE

In the event that this Agreement cannot be performed or its obligations fulfilled for any reason beyond the reasonable control of either party including war, industrial action, floods or Acts of God for a continuous period of [six months] then either party may, at its discretion, terminate this Agreement by notice in writing at the end of that period provided that no payments have been made and no master material delivered.

10. GOVERNING LAW

This Agreement shall be subject to the Laws of England.

Signed by: [______________]
FOR AND ON BEHALF OF THE ASSIGNOR

Date: [______________]

Signed by: [______________]
FOR AND ON BEHALF OF THE ASSIGNEE

Date: [______________]

OUTLINE—BUY-OUT OF ALL VIDEO RIGHTS IN A COMPLETED FILM

This Agreement is deliberately brief and involves the assignment of all video, DVD, CD-ROM, and non-theatric rights in a film to a new company.

The Video Rights definition is not standard and covers all electronic and mechanical reproduction and dissemination including the internet, images via mobile phone screen or a watch on your wrist. The most important aspect is that it is for private use and not to a paying audience; however, even this could be deleted from the definition.

The Assignor has already paid for all the costs of producing the Film or bought in from a third party. The Assignor will deliver the Master Material by an agreed date and will be paid a fixed Assignment Fee—there is no future income or royalty.

The Assignor is supplying a list of credits, copyright notices, and other moral right contractual obligations which the Assignee is agreeing to abide by.

The Assignee will pay the cost of all sums due for the exploitation of the Video Rights.

It is important that the Assignor has provided an accurate statement regarding sums due and disclosed relevant documentation.

APPOINTMENT OF A FILM DISTRIBUTOR

AN AGREEMENT made this [____________] day of [____________]

BETWEEN:

(1) [____________]
of [____________] (to be known as the Licensor in this Agreement)

AND

(2) [____________]
of [____________] (to be known as the Licensee in this Agreement).

IT IS AGREED as follows:

1. DEFINITIONS

The words below are agreed to mean as follows:

1.1 "The Film" shall be the film entitled: [____________], full details of which are set out in the attached Appendix A.

1.2 "The Non-Returnable Advance" shall be the sum of: [figure/currency].

1.3 "The Film Package" shall be the following material of the Film:

- 1.3.1 technical material of first class quality comprising of: [____________];
- 1.3.2 laboratory access letter;
- 1.3.3 transcript of final script;
- 1.3.4 action continuity/shot list;
- 1.3.5 music cue sheet listing each musical work, the composer, author, publisher, duration and description of use;
- 1.3.6 publicity, advertising, and promotional material;
- 1.3.7 full statement of all copyright, moral and contractual obligations including credits, copyright notices, trademarks, logos, service marks, designs, together with any relevant documents, images, or text.

1.4 "The Territory" shall be all countries, bases and locations throughout the planet Earth including ships, aeroplanes, and other moving objects.

1.5 "The Television Rights" shall mean the right to broadcast, transmit, delivery, distribute or manufacture, duplicate, sell, rent, license, or supply the Film by cable, satellite, terrestrial, digital, or other forms of reception by television whether in existence now or created in the future including free pay per view, subscription, license and rental. The reception device for television shall not include computer screens, merchandising goods, telephones, or other telecommunication methods of reception.

1.6 "The Video Rights" shall mean the right to manufacture, duplicate, sell, rent, license or supply, distribute and have distributed the Film for home use only by the public and to non-paying audiences in educational, cultural, religious, social and other institutions of any kind and to commercial companies and businesses such as hotels, clubs, airlines, ships by means of electronic and mechanical reproduction whether in existence now or created in the future via any disc, magnetic tape or other method so that the Film is shown as a moving image intended for reproduction on copies which are inserted in a machine or device to be played back on a television, computer or other visual screen by a video recorder, DVD player or CD-ROM or some other machine whether the two are distinct or one item.

1.7 "The Gross Receipts" shall mean all sums, benefits or credits received by the Licensee or any third party engaged by or appointed by the Licensee at any time from the distribution and exploitation of the Film and/or parts.

1.8 "The Distribution Expenses" mean the costs and expenses incurred by the Licensee in respect of the distribution and exploitation of the Film but not the administration and business costs of the Licensee.

1.8.1 The cost of reproducing and supplying all Master Material that may be required and viewing copies.

1.8.2 The cost of all alterations that may be required, dubbing, subtitling, editing, adaptations, promotional excerpts.

1.8.3 The cost of all delivery, storage, freight, publicity and marketing material, customs duties, packaging, labels, taxes and fees.

1.8.4 The cost of all clearance, consent, waiver releases, copyright, trademarks, designs, logos, music, performing rights and mechanical reproduction payments.

1.8.5 The cost of all professional advisors and bodies, accountants, legal fees, insurance, professional agencies, trade bodies incurred to exploit the Film, clear material, or collect payment, or provide insurance cover.

The Distribution Expenses shall not exceed: [figure/currency] in any accounting period. Any excess over this sum shall be the responsibility and the cost of the Licensee.

1.9 "The Nett Receipts" shall be the Gross Receipts, less the Distribution Expenses.

1.10 "The Licensee's Commission" shall be the following percentage of the Nett Receipts: [figure] per cent [______ %].

1.11 "The Licensor's Royalties" shall be the Nett Receipts less the Licensee's Commission.

1.12 "The Licence Period" shall commence on: [date] and shall continue until: [date].

2. EXCLUSIVE LICENCE

2.1 In consideration of the payment of the Non-Returnable Advance and the Licensor's Royalties, the Licensor grants to the Licensee the sole and exclusive Television Rights and Video Rights throughout the Territory for the duration of the Licence Period and the right to authorise third parties to exercise such rights.

2.2 The Licensee acknowledges that all other rights are specifically excluded from this Agreement including the merchandising and publication rights.

2.3 The Licensee agrees that, after the end of the Licence Period, the Licensee shall not have any rights in the Film and/or parts or any material developed or created pursuant to this Agreement. All rights shall revert in full to the Licensor.

2.4 The Licensor shall not assign, grant or otherwise exploit the rights granted to the Licensee; nor shall either of them execute any document or do anything in derogation from the grant.

2.5 The Licensee and its sub-licensees may make dubbed and/or subtitled versions in such languages as may be necessary to exploit the Film in [non-English] speaking countries.

3. OBLIGATIONS OF THE LICENSOR

3.1 The Licensor shall deliver the Film Package to the Licensee on or before: [date].

3.2 The Licensor confirms that it is the sole owner of or controls all copyright and any other rights in the Film and/or part(s) which are granted under this Agreement.

3.3 The Licensor confirms that it has and will retain good title and authority to enter into this Agreement and is not bound by any previous agreement which adversely affects this Agreement.

3.4 The Licensor confirms that all sums due to produce the Film have been or will be paid by the Licensor and that no such costs are the responsibility of the Licensee.

3.5 The Licensor has arranged for clearances, consents, waivers, releases and all necessary copyright, moral right and contractual matters for the exploitation of the Television Rights and the Video Rights in the Film. The cost of payment shall be the responsibility of the Licensee under this Agreement not the Licensor including payments for performing rights in any music or the mechanical reproduction of any music.

3.6 The Licensor confirms that its own legal advisors do not believe the Film to be obscene, defamatory or offensive but no such undertaking is given to the Licensee who have viewed the Film and must take their own independent advice. The Licensee must arrange suitable insurance cover for the benefit of the Licensor and Licensee in respect of the threat of any legal action arising from the exploitation of the Film.

3.7 The Licensor shall ensure that the consent and agreement is obtained from all parties involved in the creation or supply of the publicity and promotional material including the artists and where appropriate for the use of their names, image, photograph and likeness in the exploitation of the Television Rights and the Video Rights. The Licensee shall bear the cost of all payments that may fall due arising from their consent or agreement.

3.8 The Licensor confirms that the Film and its title and content including any sound or music will not infringe, breach or otherwise interfere with any copyright, literary, dramatic, musical, artistic, personal, private, trademark, trade name, service mark, logo, design or other right of any third party in the Territory during the Licence Period.

3.9 The Licensor acknowledges that the Non-Returnable Advance shall be offset against The Licensor's Royalties.

3.10 The Licensor acknowledges that the Licensee shall have the sole discretion as to the manner and method to be used in editing, marketing, promoting and advertising the Film and may incorporate the words: [Distributed by Licensee together with logo] in the main and end credits and title.

4. OBLIGATIONS OF THE LICENSEE

4.1 In consideration of the rights granted by the Licensor, the Licensee shall pay to the Licensor Non-Returnable Advance as follows: [figure/currency] upon signature of this Agreement [____________]; upon acceptance by the Licensee of the Film Package.

4.2 The Licensee agrees to reimburse the Licensor in respect of all the reproduction, insurance, and delivery costs incurred in providing an acceptable Film Package subject to satisfactory receipts being provided.

4.3 The Licensee agrees that the Film Package shall remain the property of the Licensor and that at the end of the Licence Period, the Film Package will be returned to the Licensor at the Licensee's cost.

4.4 The Licensee agrees either to accept or provide written reasons for its rejection of the Film Package within [____________] of delivery.

4.5 In the event that the Film is not of suitable technical quality and the Licensor cannot deliver an acceptable replacement. Then the Licensee shall be entitled to terminate this Agreement and the Licensor shall repay all sums received.

4.6 The Licensee confirms that it shall be responsible for all payments which may be due in respect of the exploitation of the Television Rights and Video Rights in the Film, and any advertising, marketing or promotion, including any sums due in respect of the performing rights in any music and the mechanical reproduction of the Film.

4.7 The Licensee undertakes that it and its sub-agents, sub-licensees and any third party engaged by the Licensee shall keep full and accurate books of account, records and contracts showing the Gross Receipts, the Distribution Expenses, the Nett Receipts and the calculation of the Licensee's Commission and the Licensor's Royalties which shall be retained for the Licence Period and for [____________] years thereafter. No documentation or other material shall be destroyed without first offering to make it available to the Licensor.

4.8 The Licensee undertakes that it shall pay the Licensor's Royalties to the Licensor on [date] and [date] in each year.

4.9 The Licensee shall provide a detailed report in writing to the Licensor with a full breakdown of the exploitation of the Film setting out the Gross Receipts, the Distribution Expenses, the Nett Receipts, the Licensee's Commission and the Licensor's Royalties and showing all dealings with the Film on [date] and [date] in each year.

4.10 The Licensee agrees that the Licensor shall be entitled to arrange for an annual audit to inspect and make copies of the Licensee's books of account, records, contracts and any other relevant material in order to verify the sums due to the Licensor. The Licensee shall ensure that such an audit provision is included in any contract or agreement with third parties and that the Licensor shall be entitled to inspect all such third party records and material relating to the exploration of the Film.

4.11 The Licensee confirms that it shall use its best endeavours to exploit the rights granted under this Agreement.

4.12 The Licensee agrees to provide to the Licensor copies and samples of any advertising, publicity, promotional and packaging material in respect of the marketing, distribution and exploitation of the Film.

4.13 The Licensee agrees that it shall not be entitled to recover more than: [____________] costs under Distribution Expenses in any one accounting period. Any excess shall not be carried forward to the next period but shall be at the cost and expense of the Licensee.

4.14 The Licensee agrees that no sums shall be withheld for any reason which are not disclosed to the Licensor.

4.15 The Licensee agrees that the accounting report shall provide copies of supporting documents and records to substantiate the figures for any payment or expense in excess of: [figure/currency].

4.16 The cost and expense of all currency conversions shall be stated in full and any charges itemised and then exchange rates stipulated.

4.17 Where an error is found or later disclosed, whether by the Licensor or Licensee, the Licensee shall not be entitled to a refund of any overpayment to the Licensor. Nor shall the Licensor be entitled to any interest, compensation, or damages for an error, provided the error was not deliberate or fraudulent and payment is made immediately. An error arising from an audit by the Licensor shall result in the Licensee paying all costs of the accountants and legal advisors for each such audit.

4.18 The Licensee shall pay all sums due to the Licensor to a notified account at: [____________] Bank.

4.19 The Licensee agrees that it shall not distort or mutilate the Film in the event that any editing, dubbing or other alterations are required to exploit the Film and shall not add any additional material except to the credits which shall not be changed. The

Licensee may, however, change material which its legal advisors believe is likely to result in legal proceedings against the Licensee.

4.20 The Licensee agrees to provide all copyright notices, credit, trademarks, service marks, designs, logos, moral rights in the Film and in any advertising, publicity or promotional material required and notified by the Licensor with the Film Package and that they shall not be deleted or changed in the exploitation of the Television Rights or the Video Rights in the Film.

4.21 The Licensee agrees that prior to the sale and distribution of the Video Rights in the Film it shall arrange comprehensive Product Liability Insurance for the benefit of the Licensor and Licensee of not less than: [figure] per claim, a copy of which shall be supplied to and provided to the Licensor together with evidence of payment of the premium. Such policy shall be maintained by the Licensee for the term of the Licence Period at the Licensee's sole cost.

4.22 The Licensee undertakes that it shall ensure that all licensed articles under this Agreement shall comply with all legislation codes in respect of the product and that in particular any licensed article shall be safe by use by the public and suitable children.

5. CONFIDENTIALITY

The Licensor and the Licensee shall not disclose to any third party any confidential business or future plans of the other party at any time acquired during the existence of this Agreement and no reference is to be made to the terms of this Agreement by either party in any advertising, publicity or promotional material without the prior consent of the other party.

6. ALTERATIONS

This Agreement supersedes all previous agreements, representations or promises and sets out all the terms agreed between the parties. Any amendment or alteration to this Agreement must be in writing and signed by an authorised signatory of each party.

7. NO PARTNERSHIP OR THIRD PARTY INTEREST

This Agreement shall not be deemed to create any partnership or employment, relationship between the parties and is personal between the parties. No third party shall be entitled to enforce or receive the benefit of this Agreement without the consent of both parties.

8. THIRD PARTY TRANSFERS

Neither party shall assign, transfer, charge or make over this Agreement or any of its rights or obligations without the prior written consent of the other party.

9. FORCE MAJEURE

In the event that this Agreement cannot be performed or its obligations fulfilled for any reason beyond the reasonable control of either party including war, industrial action, floods or Acts of God. Then such non-performance or failure to fulfil its obligations shall be deemed not to be a breach of this Agreement. In the event that this Agreement cannot be performed or its obligations fulfilled for any reason for a continuous period of [six months]. Then either party may, at its discretion, terminate this Agreement by notice in writing at the end of that period subject to an equitable settlement being agreed.

10. TERMINATION

10.1 In addition to any other rights and remedies at law, the Licensor and the Licensee may, by giving written notice to the other party, terminate this Agreement on the following grounds:

- 10.1.1 where the Licensee has failed to account or make payments as required under this Agreement;
- 10.1.2 where the Licensor or the Licensee has committed a serious breach of its obligations under this Agreement; unless such party rectifies the position, as far as reasonably possible, within [____________];
- 10.1.3 where the Licensee goes into voluntary or involuntary liquidation, is declared insolvent either in bankruptcy proceedings or other legal proceedings, or where an agreement with creditors has been reached due to its failure or inability to pay its debts as they fall due, and where a receiver is appointed over the whole or part of the Licensee's business.

10.2 After the expiry or the termination of this Agreement the Licensor shall be entitled to instruct the Licensee to return or destroy all master material, copies and all records and other material in the possession of or under the control of the Licensee relating to the rights granted under this Agreement.

11. TAXES

All sums are exclusive of tax. Sales Tax, Value Added Tax and any other taxes or levies which are due or paid to any government or authority which are not included or withheld must be required by law and justified by original documentation.

12. NOTICES

Notices under this Agreement shall be in writing by recorded delivery addressed as follows:

[NAME] [TITLE] [ADDRESS] The Licensor
[NAME] [TITLE] [ADDRESS] The Licensee.

Information may be sent by other means such as fax, e-mail and telephone but will not constitute service of notice.

13. GOVERNING LAW

This Agreement shall be construed and governed by the jurisdiction of [COUNTRY].

[The Licensor] [NAME] [TITLE] [SIGNATURE]
[The Licensee] [NAME] [TITLE] [SIGNATURE]

Attached to and forming part of this Agreement: Appendix A.

OUTLINE—APPOINTMENT OF A FILM DISTRIBUTOR

This contract is an exclusive licence to appoint a distributor to exploit the worldwide television and video rights in a completed Film. The parties in this Agreement are referred to as the Licensor and the Licensee. The Licensor is the copyright owner of the Film and the Licensee is the company to whom the licence is being granted. The Licensor is grantinig to the Licensee an exclusive worldwide licence to market and distribute the completed Film throughout the world for a limited period. The Television and Video Right definitions are widely drafted to include digital television, and DVD.

The Licensee, being the distributor, will receive all money from the exploitation of the rights in the Film which have been granted. This total figure is called the Gross Receipts. The Licensee is entitled to deduct the expenses incurred in distributing the Film. These costs are referred to as the Distribution Expenses. Once the Distribution Expenses have been deducted from the Gross Receipts, the balance is the Nett Receipts. At this stage the Licensee is entitled to take his commission which is an agreed percentage of the Nett Receipts. The Licensor receives the Gross Receipts, less the Distribution Expenses and the Licensee's commission. This money is defined as the Licensor's Royalties. The Licensor is receiving an advance against his royalties which is called the Non-Returnable Advance. The distributor must report and account twice yearly in addition to allowing the Licensor an annual audit.

The Licensor is undertaking that all payments in respect of the production of the Film and all relevant copyright clearances have been dealt with. The Licensee shall be responsible for such copyright payments which arise in respect of the exploitation of the rights granted, including any payments due for the performing rights in any music and the mechanical reproduction of the Film, which includes the soundtrack.

No moral rights are being asserted under this Agreement. If the Licensor is the director then his moral rights should be asserted. We have limited the Distribution Expenses to a maximum amount in each accounting period for which the Licensee must pay the additional cost and cannot carry it forward.

The Licensee can edit and change the Film for the purposes of exploitation but must not distort or mutilate it. The main and end credits must remain unchanged except the details of the Licensee may be added. There are two lists which it is important are accurate: first the copyright and clearance list and the payments due which were not paid at the production stage, and secondly the list of credits, copyright notices, moral rights and contractual obligations.

APPOINTMENT OF A VIDEO DISTRIBUTOR

AN AGREEMENT made this [____________] day of [____________]

BETWEEN:

(1) [____________]
of [____________] (to be known as the Licensor in this Agreement)

AND

(2) [____________]
of [____________] (to be known as the Licensee in this Agreement).

IT IS AGREED as follows:

1. DEFINITIONS

The words below are agreed to mean as follows:

1.1 "The Film" shall be the following film and any associated sound recording entitled [____________] which is [____________] minutes in duration.

1.2 "The Advance" shall be the sum of: [figure/currency].

1.3 "The Master Material" shall be the following material of the Film:

1.3.1 Technical material of first class quality comprising of: [____________];
1.3.2 Transcript of final script;
1.3.3 Action continuity/shot list;
1.3.4 Music cue sheet listing each musical work with the name of the composer, author and publisher, the duration of each musical work and the description of use;
1.3.5 A written statement together with supporting documents of all credit, contractual, moral right, clearances, contracts, releases, copyright notices, trademarks, logos, designs, service marks or otherwise that the Licensee must ensure are incorporated and all copies of film or undertakings which apply to all publicity, promotional, packaging or advertising material.

1.4 "The Territory" shall be construed as Europe which shall be all full Member States at the date of this Agreement namely Great Britain, Belgium, Denmark, France, Greece, Italy, Germany, Ireland, Luxembourg, Netherlands, Spain, Portugal.

1.5 "The Video Rights" shall mean the right to reproduce, transfer, duplicate, distribute and have distributed the Film and part(s) in the form of video cassettes, video discs, (or other similar devices or means whether in existence now or created in the future) and to sell, hire, export or otherwise deal in videograms and to authorise others to do so. "Videogram" shall mean magnetic tape whether reel to reel or endless loop in cassette or disc form bearing or used for reproducing a sequence of normal images capable of being shown as a moving picture including any soundtrack which is intended for reproduction on copies for supply to the public for home use only or for use by means of a playback device connected to or forming part of a television.

1.6 "The Gross Receipts" shall be the total proceeds from the distribution and exploitation of the Film throughout the Territory at any time (whether derived from the wholesale selling price or not) received by or credited to the Licensee or its sub-agents or its sub-licensees or any third party after the deduction of any value added tax and any sales tax which may from time to time be in force paid by the Licensee.

1.7 "The Sales Tax" shall be any sales or other taxes levied by the government or other authorities on the sale or supply of videograms, which form a distinct element in the wholesale selling price and which are recovered as part of the wholesale selling price directly or indirectly by the Licensee.

1.8 "The Licensor's Royalties" shall be: [figure] per cent [_____]% of the Gross Receipts.

1.9 "The Licence Period" shall commence on the date of this Agreement and shall continue until: [date].

2. EXCLUSIVE LICENCE OF RIGHTS

2.1 In consideration of the Advance and the Licensor's Royalties, the Licensor grants to the Licensee the sole and exclusive Videogram Rights in the Film and part(s) throughout the Territory for the duration of the Licence Period.

2.2 The Licensee shall be entitled to use and permit the use of extracts of the Film to be shown on television for the purpose of trade and in-store demonstrations to promote and advertise the Film.

2.3 The Licensee shall be entitled to incorporate parts of the Film on videograms reproducing other films for the purpose of promoting and advertising the Film, provided that the other films will not be derogatory or offensive in manner.

2.4 The Licensee acknowledges that all other rights, including all television rights (whether standard, cable, digital or satellite) and the theatric and the non-theatric rights are specifically excluded from this Agreement and are retained by the Licensor. Nor does this Agreement include any use in connection with computers such as DVD or CD-ROM.

3. EDITORIAL CONTROL

3.1 The Licensee shall not be entitled itself or to authorise any third party to edit, adapt or alter the Film without the prior written consent of the Licensor.

3.2 The Licensor agrees that subject to consent the Licensee may carry out minor edits of up to [____________] duration of the Film provided that it does not interfere with the integrity of the Film or impair continuity.

4. OBLIGATIONS OF THE LICENSOR

4.1 The Licensor shall deliver the Master Material to the Licensee on or before: [date] and property and risk shall pass on delivery.

4.2 The Licensor confirms that it is the sole owner of or controls all copyright and any other rights in the Film which are granted under this Agreement.

4.3 The Licensor confirms that it has and will retain good title and authority to enter into this Agreement and is not bound by any previous agreement which adversely affects this Agreement.

4.4 The Licensor confirms that all sums due in respect of the production of the Film have been paid and that the Licensee is not and will not be liable for any such payments.

4.5 In respect of the Film, the Licensor confirms that all copyright consents and any other rights musical or otherwise, have been obtained in respect of the rights granted under this Agreement. That the Licensee shall not be responsible for any such payments, except for any sums which arise through the exploitation of the Videogram Rights under this Agreement due in respect of the mechanical reproduction of the Film or the performing rights in any music.

4.6 The Licensor confirms that the Film does not contain any obscene or defamatory material and will not expose the Licensee to any civil or criminal proceedings. Provided that the Licensor shall not be liable for any sum in excess of: [figure/ currency] which shall be the maximum limit of any claim the Licensee may make under this clause in this Agreement.

4.7 The Licensor confirms that the Film does not contain any material of any nature, title, artist, music, text, sounds or otherwise which breaches the contract or infringes the copyright, moral right, trademark, logo, service mark or any other rights of any third party in the Territory.

4.8 The Licensor agrees that the Advance may be returned if the terms of this Agreement are not fulfilled. The Licensor agrees that the Advance may be offset against the Licensor's Royalties.

4.9 The Licensor shall provide at the Licencee's cost copies of any promotional or publicity material and photographs relating to the Film that may be available which the Licensee may be permitted to use, together with biographical details of the principal artists and personnel.

4.10 The Licensor agrees that the Licensee shall have the sole right and discretion to decide upon the production schedule, the release dates, the sale, rental and supply prices and the marketing and promotional strategy.

4.11 The Licensor agrees that, in the event that the Master Material is not delivered by the agreed date, there shall be an agreed extension of the Licence Period.

5. OBLIGATIONS OF THE LICENSEE

5.1 In consideration of the rights granted by the Licensor the Licensee shall pay to the Licensor the Advance as follows:

5.1.1 [____________] upon signature of this Agreement;
5.1.2 [____________] upon acceptance by the Licensee of the Master Material;
5.1.3 [____________] on or before [____________].

5.2 The Licensee agrees to reimburse the Licensor in respect of all the reproduction, insurance, and delivery costs incurred in providing the Master Material, subject to satisfactory receipts being provided on request.

5.3 The Licensee agrees either to accept or provide written reasons for its rejection of the Master Material within [____________] of delivery.

5.4 In the event that the Film is not of suitable technical quality and the Licensor is unable to deliver an acceptable replacement within [____________]. Then the Licensee shall be entitled to terminate this Agreement and the Licensor shall repay all sums paid immediately upon notice.

5.5 The Licensee confirms that it shall be responsible for payment of any sums which arise through the exploitation of the Videogram Rights under this Agreement due to the Performing Right Society or the Mechanical Copyright Protection Society.

5.6 The Licensee undertakes that it and its sub-agents and sub-licensees shall keep full and accurate books of account, records and contracts showing the Gross Receipts, the Sales Tax and the Licensor's Royalties in respect of the exploitation of the Film under this Agreement.

5.7 The Licensee undertakes that it shall pay the Licensor's Royalties within 28 days of the last day of March, June, September and December in each year.

5.8 The Licensee shall provide a detailed report to the Licensor within 28 days of the last day of March, June, September and December in each year with a full breakdown of the exploitation of the Film, setting out the Gross Receipts, the Sales Tax and the Licensor's Royalties.

5.9 The Licensee agrees that the Licensor shall be entitled to arrange for an annual audit to inspect and make copies of the Licensee's books of account, records, contracts and any other relevant material in order to verify the sums due to the Licensor.

5.10 The Licensee confirms that it shall use its endeavours to exploit the rights granted under this Agreement and to achieve, as far as possible, the maximum Gross Receipts.

5.11 The Licensee agrees to deliver videograms of the Film to retail or rental outlets on or by: [date].

5.12 The Licensee agrees to provide the following copyright notice, trademark or logo and credits to the Licensor in any publicity, promotional, advertising and packaging material in respect of the marketing, distribution and exploitation of the Film: [______________].

5.13 The Licensee agrees to provide copies and samples of any publicity, promotional, advertising and packaging and other material in respect of the marketing, distribution and exploitation of the Film.

5.14 The Licensee acknowledges that it shall be solely responsible for any sums due in respect of the manufacture, distribution, marketing and exploitation of the Videogram Rights in the Film and that the Licensor shall not be liable for any such payments.

5.15 The Licensee agrees that neither it nor any third party shall be entitled to edit, adapt or alter the Film without the prior written consent of the Licensor. Provided that minor edits of up to [______________] duration shall be permitted if it does not impair continuity or the integrity of the Film.

The Licensee agrees to notify the Licensor of all proposed edits, changes or alterations including extracts to be used for trade and exhibition purposes. All such work once agreed shall be at the Licensee's sole cost.

5.16 The Licensee agrees that in all publicity, promotional and advertising material for the Film no other artists shall appear more prominently or frequently than [name].

5.17 The Licensee undertakes that the minimum retail/wholesale sale price of each copy shall be not less than: [______________] and that not less than: [______________] shall be manufactured by: [date].

5.18 The Licensee shall ensure that the Film and any credits, copyright, or other contractual obligations and rights are accurately and adequately described and set out in the packaging, catalogues, brochures and other marketing material. That the packaging and all text and artwork shall be of a high professional standard.

5.19 The Licensee agrees that all quotes and use of statements from third parties to be used in any packaging or marketing material shall be subject to the prior approval of the Licensor.

5.20 The Licensee agrees that a total marketing and promotion budget of not less than: [______________] shall be allocated and spent by the Licensee. That the Licensee shall pay the expenses of any persons who contributed to the Film who are asked to appear at any marketing event.

5.21 The Licensee agrees that it shall not be entitled to use the Film or the Video Rights to endorse or promote any other product or person at any time nor license the use of the Film in another film.

5.22 The Licensee shall use the efforts to ensure that videograms of the Film are available in all markets of the Territory.

5.23 The Licensee agrees to fulfil the terms of the statement delivered in clause 1.3.5.

6. MUTUAL INDEMNITY

The Licensor and the Licensee mutually undertake to indemnify each other against all liabilities, claims, demands, actions, costs, damages or loss arising out of any breach by them of the terms of this Agreement. The Licensor and the Licensee agree to provide full details to the other party at the earliest opportunity and shall not settle any such matter without first disclosing all the facts, notifying their intention to such an indemnity and providing them with an opportunity to resolve the matter. Each party shall be subject to a maximum indemnity of: [____________] for the duration of this Agreement. Over that amount each party shall bear its own loss and costs.

7. CONFIDENTIALITY

The Licensor and the Licensee shall not disclose to any third party any confidential business or future plans of the other party at any time acquired during the existence of this Agreement. No reference is to be made to the terms of this Agreement by either party in any advertising, publicity or promotional material without the prior consent of the other party.

8. AMENDMENTS AND ALTERATIONS

This Agreement supersedes all previous agreements, representations or promises and sets out all the terms agreed between the parties. Any amendment or alteration to this Agreement must be in writing and signed by an authorised signatory of each party.

9. CONTRACTING PARTIES

This Agreement shall not be deemed to create any partnership or employment relationship between the parties. Nor shall it permit or allow any third party to enforce or rely on the terms agreed between the parties.

10. NOTICES

Without prejudice to the right to serve notices by any other means any notice served under this Agreement shall be in writing.

11. VALUE ADDED TAX

All sums payable under this Agreement are exclusive of any value added tax that may be payable by either party.

12. THIRD PARTY TRANSFERS

Neither party shall assign, transfer, charge or make over this Agreement or any of its rights or obligations without the prior written consent of the other party.

13. FORCE MAJEURE

Neither party shall be liable to the other for any loss or damage arising from its failure to perform any of its obligations under this Agreement for any reason whatsoever beyond its reasonable control.

14. TERMINATION

14.1 The Licensee agrees that in the event that the Licensor's Royalties received by the Licensee are less than: [figure/currency] by: [date]. Then the Licensor may terminate this Agreement by notice in writing to that effect.

14.2 In the event that this Agreement is revoked, terminated or withdrawn, the Licensee shall immediately revoke termination or withdraw all third party sub-licences or sub-distributors which it may have granted in respect of the Film.

14.3 This Agreement may be terminated without prejudice to the rights of the parties on the following grounds:

14.3.1 the Licensor or the Licensee has committed a material breach which is incapable of remedy or has not been remedied within [____________];

14.3.2 the Licensee has been declared bankrupt, or is insolvent, or a receiver, administrator, liquidator or other trustee has been appointed, or the Licensee has gone into voluntary or compulsory liquidation;

14.3.3 the conduct of the Licensee's business is prejudicial to or damaging to the Licensor's business.

14.4 Upon the expiry or termination of this Agreement all rights in the Film and any other Master Material or other property shall revert in total to the Licensor.

15. GOVERNING LAW

This Agreement shall be governed by and construed in accordance with [_____ law] in [country].

[THE LICENSOR]: [____________] NAME/TITLE

[THE LICENSEE]: [____________] NAME/TITLE

OUTLINE—APPOINTMENT OF A VIDEO DISTIBUTOR

This contract is an exclusive licence between a company which owns or controls the copyright in a completed film and a video distributor. For this Agreement, the copyright owner is the Licensor and the distribution company is the Licensee. This is not a typical video deal which usually relies on the Licensor receiving a small cut of the wholesale price after deduction of packaging and marketing costs which are not specified.

The Licensor is granting to the distribution company an exclusive licence to market the completed Film on video including cassette and disc in Europe for a fixed Licensed Period. All other rights, including the television rights, non-theatric and computer use are specifically excluded and retained by the Licensor. The distribution company is paying the Licensor a fixed percentage of the Gross Receipts, referred to as the Licensor's Royalties. The Licensor is receiving an advance to be off-set against any future royalties. The Licensee is solely responsible for all costs and expenses arising from the distribution, marketing and exploitation of the Film under the Agreement. The Licensor is undertaking that all payments in respect of the production of the Film have been dealt with.

There is a limit set on the liability for the obscurity and defamation undertaking by the Licensor. In addition there is a ceiling for the indemnity provisions.

The Licensee is not to edit the Film without the written consent of the Licensor, but minor changes are permitted. The marketing budget, sale price and other factors are specified, which most video distributors refuse to do.

The accounting provisions could be expanded and could specify the type of records which the distributor keeps as well as many compensation to be paid for errors.

APPOINTMENT OF A NON-THEATRIC DISTRIBUTOR

AN AGREEMENT made this [____________] day of [____________]

BETWEEN:

(1) [____________]
of [____________] (to be known as the Licensor in this Agreement)

AND

(2) [____________]
of [____________] (to be known as the Licensee in this Agreement).

IT IS AGREED as follows:

1. DEFINITIONS

The words below are agreed to mean as follows:

1.1 "The Series" shall be the series of films and any associated sound recordings entitled [____________] and comprising of [____________] episodes; each of which is [____________] minutes in duration.

1.2 "The Non-Returnable Advance" shall be the sum of: [figure/currency].

1.3 "The Series Package" shall be the following first class quality material of the Series comprising of: [____________] together with the music cue sheet and synopsis.

1.4 "The Territory" shall be the following countries: [____________].

1.5 "The Non-Theatric Rights" shall mean the right to exhibit the Series to non-paying audiences in all businesses and commercial industries and organisations of an educational, cultural, religious, charitable and social nature including but not limited to schools, churches, evening institutions, museums, hospitals, prisons, summer camps, drama groups, film societies, professional associations, public libraries, colleges and universities, hotels and private clubs.

1.6 "The Gross Receipts" shall be the total proceeds from the exploitation of the Series throughout the Territory at any time received by or credited to the Licensee or its sub-agents or its sub-licensees after the deduction of any taxes which may from time to time be in force and paid by the Licensee.

1.7 "The Distribution Expenses" shall be the following costs reasonably and properly expended in respect of the exploitation of the Series by the Licensee which are not recouped from any third party including but not limited to advertising and promotion costs, all clearance, consent and copyright fees, legal and accounting costs, all reproduction costs of material, foreign language versions, insurance, freight, packaging, commissions, distribution fees.

1.8 "The Nett Receipts" shall be the Gross Receipts less the Distribution Expenses.

1.9 "The Licensee's Commission" shall be: [figure] per cent [_____]% of the Nett Receipts.

1.10 "The Licensor's Royalties" shall be the Nett Receipts after the deduction of the Licensee's Commission.

1.11 "The Licence Period" shall commence on: [date] and shall continue until: [date].

2. EXCLUSIVE LICENCE

In consideration of the payment of the Non-Returnable Advance and the Licensor's Royalties, the Licensor grants to the Licensee the sole and exclusive Non-Theatric Rights in the Series and the right to authorise any third party to exercise such rights throughout the Territory for the duration of the Licence Period.

3. EDITORIAL CONTROL

The Licensee shall not be entitled itself or to authorise any third party to edit, adapt or alter the Series without the prior written consent of the Licensor.

4. OBLIGATIONS OF THE LICENSOR

4.1 The Licensor shall arrange for the delivery of the Series Package to the Licensee on or before: [date] by: [name].

4.2 The Licensor confirms that it is the sole owner of or controls all copyright and any other rights in the Series which are granted under this Agreement.

4.3 The Licensor confirms that it has and will retain good title and authority to enter into this Agreement and that there is no previous agreement in respect of the Non-Theatric Rights in the Series.

4.4 The Licensor confirms that all sums due in respect of the production of the Series have been paid and that the Licensee is not and will not be liable for any such payments.

4.5 The Licensor confirms that the Series does not contain any obscene or defamatory material and will not expose the Licensee to any civil or criminal proceedings.

4.6 The Licensor acknowledges that the Non-Returnable Advance shall be off-set against the Licensor's Royalties.

4.7 The Licensor undertakes that all copyright and any other rights in respect of all material in the services of any nature have been cleared and paid for including music, stills, footage, artistes, products or otherwise in respect of the exploitation of the Non-Theatric Rights throughout the Territory. That the Licensee shall not be liable for any such payments and shall only pay for sums due for the mechanical reproduction of the Series and the performing rights in any music.

5. OBLIGATIONS OF THE LICENSEE

5.1 In consideration of the rights granted by the Licensor the Licensee shall pay to the Licensor the Non-Returnable Advance as follows: [____________] upon signature of this Agreement; [____________] upon acceptance by the Licensee of the Series Package.

5.2 The Licensee agrees that the Series Package shall remain the property of the Licensor and that at the end of the Licence Period the Series Package will be returned to the Licensor at the Licensee's risk and cost.

5.3 The Licensee agrees either to accept or provide written reasons for its rejection of the Series Package within [____________] of delivery.

5.4 The Licensee confirms that it shall be responsible for any payments due in respect of the exploitation of the Series under this Agreement, including any sums due in respect of the performing rights in any music and the mechanical reproduction of the Series.

5.5 The Licensee undertakes that it and its sub-agents and sub-licensees shall keep full and accurate books of account, records and contracts showing the Gross Receipts, the Distribution Expenses, the Nett Receipts, any taxes, and the calculation of the Licensee's Commission and the Licensor's Royalties in respect of the exploitation of the Series under this Agreement.

5.6 The Licensee undertakes that it shall pay the Licensor's Royalties on: [dates] every year.

5.7 The Licensee shall provide a detailed report to the Licensor by [date] and [date] in each year with a full breakdown of the exploitation of the Series together with copies of all relevant documents and records.

5.8 The Licensee agrees that the Licensor shall be entitled to arrange for an audit at any time to inspect and make copies of the Licensee's, any sub-agents' and sub-licensees' books of account, records, contracts and any other relevant material in order to verify the sums due to the Licensor.

5.9 The Licensee confirms that it shall use its best endeavours to exploit the rights granted under this Agreement and to achieve, as far as possible, the maximum Gross Receipts.

5.10 The Licensee agrees to ensure, as far as possible, that all third parties shall exhibit the on-screen credits for the Series.

5.11 The Licensee agrees to provide the following copyright notice, trademark, logo and credits to the Licensor in any publicity, promotional, advertising and packaging material in respect of the marketing and distribution of the Series: [______________].

5.12 The Licensee agrees to provide copies and samples of any publicity, promotional, advertising and packaging material in respect of the marketing and distribution of the Series upon request at the Licensee's cost.

6. CONFIDENTIALITY

The Licensor and the Licensee shall not disclose to any third party any confidential business or future plans of the other party at any time acquired during the existence of this Agreement. No reference is to be made to the terms of this Agreement by either party in any advertising, publicity or promotional material without the prior consent of the other party.

7. AMENDMENTS

This Agreement supersedes all previous agreements, representations or promises and sets out all the terms agreed between the parties. Any amendment or alteration to this Agreement must be in writing and signed by an authorised signatory of each party.

8. NO PARTNERSHIP OR EMPLOYMENT

This Agreement shall not be deemed to create any partnership or employment relationship between the parties.

9. THIRD PARTY TRANSFERS

Neither party shall assign, transfer, charge or make over this Agreement or any of its rights or obligations without the prior written consent of the other party.

10. FORCE MAJEURE

In the event that this Agreement cannot be performed or its obligations fulfilled for any reason beyond the reasonable control of either party including war, industrial action, floods or Acts of God. Then such non-performance or failure to fulfil its obligations shall be deemed not to be a breach of this Agreement. In the event that this Agreement cannot be performed or its obligations fulfilled for any reason beyond either party's reasonable control for a continuous period of [three months]. Then either party may, at its discretion, terminate this Agreement by notice in writing at the end of that period.

11. TERMINATION

11.1 In addition to any other rights and remedies at law either party may, by giving written notice to the other party, terminate this Agreement: where the other party has failed to account or make payments as required or has committed a serious breach of its obligations under this Agreement, unless such party rectifies the position, as far as reasonably possible, within 30 days; where the other party goes into voluntary or involuntary liquidation, is declared insolvent either in bankruptcy or other legal proceedings; where an agreement with creditors has been reached due to failure or inability to pay its debts as they fall due; or where a receiver is appointed over the whole or part of the business.

11.2 After the expiry or termination or completion of this Agreement, the Licensor shall be entitled to instruct the Licensee to return or destroy all master material and any copies thereof in the possession of or under the control of the Licensee or any third party relating to the rights granted under this Agreement.

12. GOVERNING LAW

This Agreement shall be subject to the Laws of England.

13. TAXES

All sums are exclusive of tax where value added tax, sales tax or other tax is levied on the goods or service and it is deducted by the Licensee. This must be justified in the accounts. Each party shall be responsible for its own tax, value added tax, national and personal insurance.

14. NOTICES

All notices may be given by any reasonable material available provided that it is supported by evidence to justify that it was properly given to a senior person of the Licensor or Licensee.

15. LEGAL PROCEEDINGS

In the event that legal proceedings are threatened or some other claim, action or breach is made by any third party in respect of the Series against the Licensor or the Licensee. Then the other party shall be notified that there is a case. The Licensor shall assume all responsibility for all such matters and shall bear the costs of both parties where the matter relates to the Series.

Signed by: [______________] Date: [______________]
FOR AND ON BEHALF OF THE LICENSOR

[NAME, TITLE]

Signed by: [______________] Date: [______________]
FOR AND ON BEHALF OF THE LICENSEE

[NAME, TITLE]

OUTLINE—APPOINTMENT OF A NON-THEATRIC DISTRIBUTOR

This contract is an exclusive licence between a company which owns or controls the copyright in a completed Series and a distribution company in the non-theatric market. For this Agreement the copyright owner is the Licensor and the distribution company is the Licensee. The Licensor is granting to the distribution company an exclusive licence to market the Non-Theatric Rights in the Series in specified countries.

The Licensee will receive all money from the exploitation of the Non-Theatric Rights in the Series, referred to as the Gross Receipts. The Licensee is entitled to deduct his expenses incurred in distributing the Series. The Nett Receipts are calculated by deducting the Distribution Expenses from the Gross Receipts. The Licensee is then entitled to a fixed percentage commission from those Nett Receipts. The Licensor receives everything thereafter once the Non-Returnable Advance has been recouped.

The Licensor is undertaking that all payments in respect of the production of the Series and all relevant copyright clearances and payments have been paid.

There is no indemnity provision, but a legal proceedings clause which provides that the Licensor will take over the case and bear the legal costs.

PRE-SALE OF A FILM FOR VIDEO AND NON-THEATRIC DISTRIBUTION

THIS AGREEMENT is dated: [____________] and made

BETWEEN the following parties:

(1) [Company] of [Address] ["The Licensor"]

AND

(2) [Company] of [Address] ["The Licensee"].

IT IS AGREED as follows:

1. DEFINITIONS

The words below are agreed to mean as follows:

1.1 "The Film" shall be the following film and any associated sound recording based on the Treatment entitled [____________], which is summarised and described in the attached Schedule 1.

1.2 "The Treatment" shall be the summary of the Film. A copy of the Treatment is attached in Schedule 2.

1.3 "The Licence Fee" shall be the sum of: [figure/currency].

1.4 "The Film Package" shall be the following material of the Film:

1.4.1 Technical material of first class quality comprising: [____________];
1.4.2 Laboratory access letter;
1.4.3 Typed transcript of final script;
1.4.4 Music cue sheet; and
1.4.5 Comprehensive written report and images of all credits, copyright notices, moral rights, trademarks service marks, logos, designs, copyrights, consent and clearance acknowledgments and any other contractual obligations which relate to the Film any other material supplied as part of the Film Package and any publicity, advertising, promotion and exploitation of the rights granted under this Agreement. The detail must include a description, and image, the duration, position, colour and context and background.

1.5 "The Gross Receipts" shall mean one hundred per cent of all sums actually received by or credited to the Licensee arising directly and indirectly from the use or exploitation of the rights granted under this Agreement in the Film and/or part(s) by the Licensee or any other third party appointed or engaged by the Licensee in respect thereof.

1.6 "The Licensor's Royalties" shall be [figure] per cent/[_____]% of the Gross Receipts.

1.7 "The Territory" shall be the following countries: [____________].

1.8 "The Sales Tax" shall be any sales or other taxes levied by the E.E.C., British or foreign authorities on the sale or supply of the Film, which form a distinct element in the sale or rental price and which are recovered as part of the price directly or indirectly by the Licensee.

1.9 "The Video and Non-Theatric Rights" shall mean the right to transfer, manufacture, duplicate, sell, rent, supply, distribute and have distributed the Film and/or part(s) for home use by the public and to non-paying audiences in educational, cultural, religious, social and other institutions of any kind, and to commercial companies and businesses such as hotels, clubs, airlines and ships by means of electronic and mechanical reproduction whether in existence now or created in the future in the form of any disc, magnetic tape, or other method so that the Film is shown as a moving image intended for reproduction on copies which are inserted in a machine or device to be played back on a television, computer or other visual screen by a video recorder, DVD player or some other machine whether the two are distinct or one item. These rights shall include video cassette, disc, laser, reel to reel, DVD.

1.10 "The Licence Period" shall commence on: [date] and expire on: [date].

2. EXCLUSIVE LICENCE

2.1 In consideration of the payment of the Licence Fee and the Licensor's Royalties, the Licensor grants to the Licensee the sole and exclusive Video and Non-Theatric Rights in the Film and/or part(s) and to the right to authorise any third party to exercise such rights throughout the Territory for the duration of the Licence Period.

2.2 The Licensee shall only be entitled to use or license parts of the Film for the promotion, advertising and marketing of the Videogram and Non-Theatric Rights in the Film granted to the Licensee.

2.3 The Licensee is not being granted the CD-ROM rights in the Film, nor any right to transmit the Film via any telecommunication system whether mobile phones, terrestrial telephonic lines, cable or otherwise. All rights not specifically granted to the Licensee are reserved by and belong to the Licensor.

2.4 The Licensee shall not be entitled to edit, adapt, alter or change the Film without the prior written consent of the Licensor which shall not be unreasonably withheld or delayed. No changes shall be permitted which would affect the contractual, moral rights, copyright or credit obligations of the Licensor. All changes that may be agreed shall be at the Licensee's sole cost and shall not be offset or deducted from any sums due to the Licensor.

3. OBLIGATIONS OF THE LICENSOR

3.1 The Licensor confirms that it intends to produce the Film in colour, in the English language and in the following format: [____________].

3.2 The Licensor shall deliver the Film Package to the Licensee on or before: [date].

3.3 The Licensor confirms that it is the sole owner of or will control all copyright and any other rights in the Film which are granted under this Agreement.

3.4 The Licensor confirms that it has and will retain good title and authority to enter into this Agreement and is not bound by any previous agreement which adversely affects this Agreement.

3.5 The Licensor confirms that it shall be solely responsible for all sums which are or may be due in respect of the production of the Film and that the Licensee is not and will not be liable for any such payments.

3.6 In respect of the Film, the Licensor confirms that all copyright and any other rights have been obtained in respect of the rights granted under this Agreement and that the Licensee shall not be responsible for any such payments, except for any sums which arise through the exploitation of the Video and the Non-Theatric Rights under this Agreement due for the performing rights in any music and/or the mechanical reproduction of the Film.

3.7 The Licensor confirms that the Film will not contain any obscene or defamatory material and will not expose the Licensee to any civil or criminal proceedings.

3.8 The Licensor confirms that the Film will not contain any material which infringes the copyright or any other rights of any third party in the Territory in respect of the rights granted under this Agreement.

3.9 The Licensor acknowledges that the Licence Fee shall be offset against the Licensor's Royalties.

3.10 The Licensor acknowledges that the Licensee shall have the sole discretion as to the manner and method to be used in marketing, promoting and advertising the Film in respect of the rights granted under this Agreement.

4. OBLIGATIONS OF THE LICENSEE

4.1 In consideration of the rights granted by the Licensor, the Licensee shall pay to the Licensor the Licence Fee within [____________] of both parties signing this Agreement.

4.2 The Licensee agrees to reimburse the Licensor in respect of all the reproduction, insurance, and delivery costs incurred in providing an acceptable Film Package, subject to satisfactory receipts being provided on request.

4.3 The Licensee agrees either to accept or provide written reasons for its rejection of the Film Package within [____________] of delivery.

4.4 In the event that the Film is not of a suitable technical quality and the Licensor cannot deliver an acceptable replacement. Then the Licensee shall be entitled to terminate this Agreement and the Licensor shall repay all sums paid to it immediately.

4.5 The Licensee confirms that it shall be responsible for any sums which arise through the exploitation of the Video and the Non-Theatric Rights under this Agreement due for the performing rights in any music and/or the mechanical reproduction of the Film.

4.6 The Licensee undertakes that it and its sub-agents and sub-licensees shall keep full and accurate books of account, records and contracts showing the Gross Receipts and the calculation of the Licensor's Royalties.

4.7 The Licensee undertakes that it shall pay the Licensor's Royalties to the Licensor on: [dates] in each year.

4.8 On [dates] in each year, the Licensee shall provide a detailed report to the Licensor with a full breakdown of the exploitation of the Film showing the Gross Receipts and the Licensor's Royalties together with copies of all relevant contracts and documents for any sum in excess of: [figure/currency]. The Licensee agrees that the Licensor shall be entitled to arrange for an audit at any time to inspect and make copies of the Licensee's books of account, records, contracts and any other relevant material in order to verify the sums due to the Licensor at the Licensor's cost.

4.9 The Licensee confirms that it shall be solely responsible for any sums due in respect of the exploitation of the Film and that the Licensor shall not be liable for any such payments nor shall any such sums be deducted from the Gross Receipts or the sums due to the Licensor.

4.10 Provided that the Film Package is delivered on schedule, the Licensee agrees to deliver video of the Film to retail or rental outlets on or by: [date].

4.11 The Licensee agrees to provide one copy and one sample of each and every publicity, promotional, advertising and packaging material in respect of the marketing, distribution and exploitation of the Film, including any video cassettes or discs or other products to the Licensor upon request at the Licensee's cost and expense.

4.12 The Licensee agrees to adhere to all credit, copyright notice, moral right, contractual obligation, trademark, logo, service mark or other rights notified by the Licensor in the written statement of the Film Package. The Licensee shall add its own distribution name as: Distributed by: [____________] with the following logo/mark: [____________]. In both the exploitation of the Video and Non-Theatric Rights and any associated packaging, publicity, advertising or otherwise by the Licensee or any other third party.

4.13 The Licensee agrees that prior to the sale of the Videos to the public it shall arrange public liability insurance for any products to be used by the public of not less than: [____________] for any one claim in favour of the Licensor and Licensee and shall maintain the policy for the term of this Agreement at the Licensee's expense.

5. MUTUAL INDEMNITY

The Licensor and the Licensee mutually undertake to indemnify the other against all liabilities, claims, demands, actions, costs, damages and loss arising out of any breach by either party of any of the terms of this Agreement. The Licensor and the Licensee agree to provide full details to the other party at the earliest opportunity and shall not settle any such matter without first consulting the other party.

6. CONFIDENTIALITY

The Licensor and the Licensee shall not disclose to any third party any confidential business or future plans of the other party at any time acquired during the existence of this Agreement. No reference is to be made to the terms of this Agreement by either party in any advertising, publicity or promotional material without the prior consent of the other party.

7. AMENDMENTS

This Agreement supersedes all previous agreements, representations or promises and sets out all the terms agreed between the parties. Any amendment or alteration to this Agreement must be in writing and signed by an authorised signatory of each party.

8. RELATIONSHIP

This Agreement shall not be deemed to create any partnership or employment relationship between the parties. Nor shall it create any relationship which permits a third party to enforce the terms of this Agreement without the consent of both parties.

9. NOTICES

Without prejudice to the right to serve notices by any other means any notice served under this Agreement shall be in writing and sent by recorded or registered courier or postal service.

10. TAXES

All sums payable under this Agreement are exclusive of any tax that may be payable by either party.

11. THIRD PARTY TRANSFERS

Neither party shall assign, transfer, charge or make over this Agreement or any of its rights or obligations without the prior written consent of the other party.

12. FORCE MAJEURE

In the event that this Agreement cannot be performed or its obligations fulfilled for any reason beyond the reasonable control of either party including war, industrial action, floods or Acts of God for any reason beyond either party's reasonable control for a continuous period of [____________]. Then either party may, at its discretion, terminate this Agreement by notice in writing at the end of that period provided that an equitable settlement is made in respect of payments made and work done.

13. TERMINATION

13.1 In addition to any other rights and remedies at law, either party may, by giving written notice to the other party, terminate this Agreement on the following grounds:

13.1.1 where the Licensee has failed to account or make payments as required under this Agreement;

13.1.2 where either party has committed a serious breach of its obligations under this Agreement, unless such party rectifies the position, as far as reasonably possible, within [____________];

13.1.3 where the other party goes into voluntary or involuntary liquidation or is declared insolvent, either in bankruptcy proceedings or other legal proceedings, or where an agreement with creditors has been reached by either party due to its failure or inability to pay its debts as they fall due, or where a receiver is appointed over the whole or part of either party's business.

13.2 After the expiry or the termination or the completion of the sell off period. Then the Licensor shall be entitled to instruct the Licensee to return or destroy all master material, licensed material, any copies of the master or licensed material and stocks previously manufactured under this Agreement in the possession of or under the control of the Licensee relating to the rights granted under this Agreement.

14. SELL-OFF PERIOD

The Licensee shall be entitled to sell off, on a non-exclusive basis, licensed material and stocks previously manufactured under this Agreement for the purpose of commercial sale for a period of six months from the date of expiry or termination, provided that the Licensee adheres to the terms of this Agreement.

15. GOVERNING LAW

This Agreement shall be subject to the Laws of England.

Attached to this Agreement:

Schedule 1—Film
Schedule 2—Treatment

Signed by: [____________]
FOR AND ON BEHALF OF THE LICENSOR

Signed by: [____________]
FOR AND ON BEHALF OF THE LICENSEE

OUTLINE—PRESALE OF A FILM FOR VIDEO AND NON-THEATRIC DISTRIBUTION

This Agreement is between a production company and video distribution company. The production company is called the Licensor and the distribution company the Licensee.

The Licensor is producing a Film and is entirely responsible for the production costs, which may have come from various sources. This contract is a pre-sale to the Licensee. The Licensor is agreeing to grant the Licensee an exclusive worldwide home video and non-theatric licence in return for an advance against future royalties which, for the purpose of this Agreement, is called a Licence Fee. It is accepted between the parties that the advance is to be put towards the production costs. As this is not a commissioning deal, the video company is not entitled to any editorial control or approval of the scripts or key personnel. In the event that the project falls through for any reason the video company is entitled to recover its investment in its entirety.

In addition to the Licence Fee the Licensor receives an agreed percentage, known as the Licensor's Royalties, from the Gross Receipts. The grant of rights is limited to the video and non-theatric market. Video therefore includes DVD players but not CD-ROM nor the licensing of the use of the Film for mobile phones or watches. The Licensee is not entitled to edit or change the Film without the consent of the Licensor. The Licensor must not withhold consent to any changes unreasonably. Any excerpts of the Film can only be used to promote the Film. This Agreement has very short undertaking, and the mutual indemnity is unlimited. A product liability insurance clause has been added for the Licensee.

EXCLUSIVE LICENCE FOR THE USE OF ORIGINAL FORMAT FOR TELEVISION SERIES

AN AGREEMENT made this [____________] day of [____________]

BETWEEN:

(1) [Writer] care of [Agent's Name]
of [Address] (to be known as the Licensor in this Agreement)

AND

(2) [Company] trading as: [____________]
of [Address] (to be known as the Licensee in this Agreement).

IT IS AGREED as follows:

1. DEFINITIONS

The words below are agreed to mean as follows:

1.1 "The Format" shall be the original concept and novel idea for and structure of a series of films which is briefly described as follows: [____________];
full details of which are attached to and form part of this Agreement in Appendix 1 [title, script, characters, plot, storyline, location, intellectual property rights, running order and sequence, design and layout of set, presentation of questions/answers, score system, prizes, slogans, graphics, costumes].

1.2 "The Series" shall be the series of films and any associated sound recordings based on the Format entitled [____________] and comprising of [____________] episodes, each of which shall be [____________] minutes in duration. Full details of the Series are set out in Appendix 2 which is attached to and forms part of this Agreement.

1.3 "The Licence Fee" shall be the sum of: [figure/currency].

1.4 "The Licence Period" shall commence on [the date of this Agreement] and shall continue until [date].

1.5 "The Territory" shall be all countries throughout the world.

1.6 "The Television Rights" shall mean the right to broadcast, transmit, deliver or supply this Series based on the Format by means of all forms of reception by television whether terrestrial, cable, digital, satellite, whether in existence now or created in the future for domestic home viewing by the public. Regardless of the form of method of payment or not including free, subscription, rental, pay per view, licence or otherwise whether encrypted or not and shall include the right to authorise others to do any such things.

1.7 "The Video and Non-Theatric Rights" shall mean the right to transfer, manufacture, duplicate, sell, rent, supply, distribute and have distributed this Series for domestic home viewing by the public and to non-paying audiences. In educational, cultural, religious, social and other institution of any kind and to commercial companies and businesses such as hotels, clubs, airlines and ships by means of electronic and mechanical reproduction whether in existence now or created in the future in the form of any disc, magnetic tape or other method so that the Film is shown as a moving image intended for reproduction on copies which are inserted in a machine or device to be played back on a television computer or other visual screen by a video recorder DVD player or some other machine whether the two are distinct or one item. These rights shall include video cassette, disc, laser, reel to reel and DVD.

1.8 "The Licensor's Royalties" shall be: [figure] per cent [_____]% of the Nett Receipts.

1.9 "The Gross Receipts" shall be the total proceeds from the exploitation of the Series and/or part(s) throughout the Territory at any time received by or credited to the Licensee or its sub-agents or its sub-licensees or any other third party engaged by the Licensee.

1.10 "The Production Budget Costs" shall be the total costs and expenses of making and delivering the Series. For the avoidance of doubt this shall include but not be limited to; fees to be paid to performers, cost of film, studio hire, processing, storage, editing, and artistic, photographic, graphic, technical, legal, accounting and production personnel, transport, accommodation, entertainment, stationery, acquisition of rights, clearance of all third-party material including music.

1.11 "The Distribution Expenses" shall mean all the costs and expenses incurred in respect of the distribution and marketing of the Series which shall include but not be limited to:

1.11.1 the cost of reproducing, making, repairing and supplying all material that may be required cassettes, videos, films, prints, tapes, brochures, photographs, posters; scripts, music one sheets;

1.11.2 the cost of all translations, dubbing, subtitling, editing, adaptations and excerpts;

1.11.3 the cost of delivery, storage, publicity, marketing, labels, packaging, freight, shipment, customs duties, fees, or payments for export and import purposes;

1.11.4 the cost of all accountant, legal, professional agencies, collection agencies or other bodies or persons;

1.11.5 the cost of obtaining clearance of and payment for consent, waiver, authority to export any material in the Series whether copyright, moral rights, trademark, service mark, design right, logo, product, music, stills, footages or any other rights, all costs and payments for the use and performance of any music to any collecting society;

1.11.6 all costs of any personal or public liability and other insurance including indemnity provisions that may be required;

1.11.7 all fees, charges, commissioning and costs by third-party distributors, or agents who assist in the exploitation of the Series.

1.12 "The Nett Receipts" shall be the Gross Receipts less the Distribution Expenses.

2. EXCLUSIVE LICENCE

2.1 In consideration of the payment of the Licence Fee, the Licensor grants to the Licensee the sole and exclusive right to produce the Series based on the Format for the duration of the Licence Period throughout the Territory.

2.2 In consideration of the Production Budget Costs being borne entirely by the Licensee and not being off-set against the Gross Receipts. The Licensee shall be entitled to transmit the Series on Channel [____________] [number] times without payment to the Licensee or the Gross Receipts.

2.3 In consideration of the payment of the Licensor's Royalties the Licensor grants to the Licensee the sole and exclusive right to the Television Rights and the Video and Non-Theatric Rights in the Series and/or part(s) in the Territory for the duration of the Licence Period and to authorise third parties to exercise such rights.

2.4 The Licensee agrees that all other rights not specifically granted are reserved by the Licensor in the Format including but not limited to computer CD-ROM, internet, publishing, and merchandising. That the Licensee shall not be entitled to exploit such rights nor receive any payment from their exploitation.

2.5 At the end of the Licence Period the Licensee agrees it shall not be entitled to exploit the Series without further agreement with the Licensor. The Licensee agrees to transfer or vest any developments or variations of the Format in the Licensor at such time and shall at the Licensor's cost execute any document or do anything that may be required to do so.

3. MORAL RIGHTS

The Licensee acknowledges that the Licensor asserts his/her moral rights generally in respects of the Series and in particular to be identified as follows: [__________] in the Series and in respect of all copies of the Series and any packaging, marketing and publicity material.

4. OBLIGATIONS OF THE LICENSEE

4.1 In consideration of the rights granted under this Agreement, the Licensee shall pay to the Licensor the Licence Fee as follows: [figure/currency] upon signature of this Agreement; [figure/currency] on or before: [date].

4.2 The Licensee undertakes that it shall pay the Licensor's Royalties to the Licensor on: [dates] in each year.

4.3 The Licensee and its sub-agents and sub-licensees and any other third party engaged by the Licensee shall keep full and accurate books of account, records and contracts and any other material showing the Gross Receipts, the Distribution Expenses, the Nett Receipts and the Licensor's Royalties in respect of the exploitation of the Series for a minimum of [____________] years.

4.4 The Licensee shall provide a detailed report to the Licensor with a full breakdown of the exploitation of the Series setting out the Gross Receipts, the Distribution Expenses, the Nett Receipts and the Licensor's Royalties on: [dates] in each year.

4.5 The Licensee agrees that the Licensor shall be entitled to arrange for an audit to inspect and make copies of the Licensee's books of account, records, contracts and any other relevant material in order to verify the sums due to the Licensor at any time within [____________] months of receipt of each report. Such audit to be at the Licensors cost and by such reputable professional advisor as the Licensor may so choose. The Licensor and the Licensor's advisor may be required to provide a written confidentiality undertaking to the Licensee prior to such audit.

4.6 The Licensee agrees to provide the following on-screen credit, copyright notice, trademark or logo to the Licensor in the Series and in any publicity, promotional, advertising or packaging material in respect of the marketing and distribution of the Series: [____________]. Position/Background: [____________].

4.7 The Licensee agrees to provide a copy of the Series and samples of any publicity, promotional, advertising and packaging material in respect of the marketing and commercial exploitation of the Series to the Licensor for information purposes at the Licensee's cost.

4.8 The Licensee agrees that all sums relating to the Gross Receipts for the Series shall be kept in a separate bank account and not mixed with the other monies of the Licensee. Nor shall a charge, lieu, or other security be given in respect of the Agreement or the Gross Receipts or the bank account by the Licensee.

4.9 The Licensee agrees to provide the Licensor with a copy of the bank statement relating to the account upon request at any time.

4.10 The Licensee agrees that it shall pay all the Production Budget Costs and shall not seek to reclaim any such sum from the Licensor or to offset it against the License Fee or the Gross Receipts whether the original proposed costs are excluded or not.

4.11 The Licensee shall ensure that all rights not required from the Licensor which need to be required for the exploitation of this Series shall be cleared and paid for under the Distribution Expenses.

4.12 The Licensee agrees that all sums due and paid for in respect of the marketing and exploitation of the Series shall be at the Licensee's sole cost and may be deducted as Distribution Expenses from the Gross Receipts prior to the payment of the Licensors Royalties of the Nett Receipts.

4.13 The Licensee agrees that the Licensee shall not be entitled to deduct any sums for the provision of the Licensee's services under this Agreement.

4.14 The Licensee agrees that no sponsorship, logo or product shall be used to endorse the Series without the prior written consent of the Licensor which shall not be unreasonably withheld or delayed.

4.15 The Licensee agrees that all goodwill generated as a result of the use by the Licensee of any trademark, logo design or other material provided by the Licensor shall belong to the Licensor.

4.16 The Licensee shall be fully liable for all acts and omissions with respect to any sub-distributor, agent or sub-licence.

5. OBLIGATIONS OF THE LICENSOR

5.1 The Licensor confirms that he/she is the original creator and sole owner of or controls all copyright and any other rights in the Format which are granted under this Agreement.

5.2 The Licensor confirms that he/she has full title and authority to enter into this Agreement and is not bound by any previous agreement which adversely effects this Agreement.

5.3 The Licensor confirms that the Format does not contain any obscene or defamatory material and will not expose the Licensee to any civil or criminal proceedings in [country].

5.4 The Licensor confirms that the Format does not contain any material which infringes the copyright or any other rights of any third party in the Territory in respect of the rights granted under this Agreement.

5.5 Subject to prior consultation the Licensor agrees that the Licensee shall be entitled to use the Licensor's name, biography, photograph, image, fair likeness and signature in the exploitation of the Series.

5.6 The Licensor agrees that it shall be responsible for all insurance, taxes or other personal or corporate liabilities that may be due in consequence of this Agreement.

5.7 The Licensor confirms that it is the sole owner of all rights in the credit, trademark, logo as follows: [______________] that the Licensee is to include in the Series and in all marketing material and that the use will not expose the Licensee to any civil or criminal proceedings.

5.8 That the Licensor will not exploit any of the other rights in the Series which are retained by the Licensor without first giving the Licensee the opportunity to make a better offer than that by a third party.

5.9 The Licensor agrees that it shall not exploit the other rights in the Series which have been retained for release to the public prior to: [date].

5.10 The Licensor agrees that where, in the opinion of the legal advisors of the Licensee, charges, alterations or variations must be made to the Format for the Series due to programme policy, the possibility of legal action or risk of the breach of legislation. Then the Licensor agrees that the Licensee may make such necessary variations provided that the Licensor is consulted in advance and provided with good reason.

6. MUTUAL INDEMNITY

6.1 The Licensor and the Licensee mutually undertake to indemnify the other against all liabilities, claims, demands, actions, costs, damages and loss arising out of any breach of any of the terms of this Agreement. In the event of any claim, dispute, action, writ or summons in connection with this the Licensor and the Licensee agree to provide full details to the other party at the earliest opportunity and shall not settle any such matter without first consulting the other party.

6.2 Neither party shall be liable to the other for indirect or consequential changes including without limitation those arising from delay, interruption or loss of profits.

6.3 The Licensee shall ensure that all due care and attention is made where there is a hazard or higher risk of injury in the Series.

6.4 The Licensee shall ensure that there is sufficient insurance cover in place to protect the Licensor and Licensee in respect of the Series. The cost of such insurance policies shall be part of the Distribution Expenses.

6.5 Each party agrees that in the event of any legal proceedings they shall each bear their own legal costs and shall not be indemnified except under any insurance policy.

7. CONFIDENTIALITY

The Licensor and the Licensee shall not disclose to any third party any confidential business or future plans of the other party at any time acquired during the existence of this Agreement. Where access is required to confidential material a separate confidentiality agreement for that purpose may be requested to be signed.

8. AMENDMENTS

This Agreement supersedes all previous agreements, representations or undertakings and sets out all the terms agreed between the parties. Any amendment must be in writing and signed by both parties.

9. RELATIONSHIP

This Agreement shall not be deemed to create any partnership or employment relationship between the parties nor to affect an acquisition or transfer of rights except those specified. No third party may endorse this Agreement without the written consent of both parties.

10. THIRD PARTY TRANSFERS

Neither party shall assign, transfer, charge or make over this Agreement or any of its rights or obligations without the prior written consent of the other party, which may be withheld

11. FORCE MAJEURE

No party shall be held in any way responsible for any failure to fulfil the obligations if such failure has been caused directly by circumstances beyond the reasonable control of the defaulting party. This shall include accident, equipment failures, war, riot, industrial action, terrorism. The defaulting party shall notify the other as soon as possible, and propose a cause of action and delay which the other party must accept if the situation is to be remedied within [____________] or may reject if a longer period is envisaged.

12. TAXES

All payments and charges are exclusive of tax. Any sums deducted for exchange rate or tax purposes must be specified in the accounts.

13. NOTICES

All notices must be in writing and may be sent by any method provided that delivery of notice is to be acknowledged on receipt and there is evidence of service.

14. TERMINATION

14.1 In addition to any other rights and remedies at law, either party may, by giving written notice to the other party, terminate this Agreement on the grounds that:

14.1.1 the Licensee has failed to account or make payments as required under this Agreement;

14.1.2 where either party has committed a serious breach of its obligations under this Agreement and has not rectified the position within [____________];

14.1.3 where the Licensee goes into voluntary or involuntary liquidation or is declared insolvent, either in bankruptcy proceedings or other legal proceedings, or has reached an agreement with creditors due to its failure or inability to pay its debts as they fall due, or where a receiver is appointed over the whole or part of the Licensee's business.

15. GOVERNING LAW

This Agreement shall be subject to the Laws of [____________].

Attach: Appendix 1—the Format
Appendix 2—the Series.

THE LICENSOR: [____________]
[NAME/TITLE/DATE]

THE LICENSEE: [____________]
[NAME/TITLE/DATE]

OUTLINE—EXCLUSIVE LICENCE FOR THE USE OF ORIGINAL FORMAT FOR TELEVISION SERIES

This Agreement is between the copyright owner of an original format for a game or quiz show and a production company. The production company is likely to be either a television company or an independent production company.

The copyright owner is granting to the Licensee an exclusive licence permitting the production of a television programme based on the format for a specific period of time. The full details of the format should be set out in writing and be attached to and form part of the Agreement in Appendix 1.

The production company would be entitled to exploit the Series throughout the world in the television, video and non-theatric markets. The copyright owner receives a Licence Fee and a percentage of the Nett Receipts from the commercial exploitation of the Series.

After the expiry of the Licence Period, all copyright and any developments or variations of the format would be vested in the Licensor and the Licensee has agreed to confirm this in writing if required. The Licensor is asserting his moral rights in this Agreement.

The Licensee is to pay all the Production Budget Costs in return for the Series being shown on a specified channel a number of times. Only the Distribution Expenses may be deducted from the Gross Receipts prior to the payment of the payment of the Licensor's Royalties of the Nett Receipts. There is no limit to the Distribution Expenses nor how they are to be allocated to each accounting period so that it is left to the discretion of the Licensee. That is why it is often better to have a smaller percentage of the Gross Receipts. The money is to be placed in a separate account, statements provided to the Licensor, and an audit may take place after every report. At the end of the Licence Period the Licensee cannot exploit the Series without further consent from the Licensor. There is some limitation on the licensing of the rights in the Format not granted by the Licensor such as release dates to the public.

BUY-OUT OF ALL RIGHTS IN ORIGINAL FORMAT

AN AGREEMENT made this [____________] day of [____________]

BETWEEN:

(1) [____________]
of [____________] (to be known as the Assignor in this Agreement)

AND

(2) [____________]
of [____________] (to be known as the Assignee in this Agreement).

IT IS AGREED as follows:

1. DEFINITIONS

The words below are agreed to mean as follows:

1.1 "The Format" shall mean but not be limited to all the goodwill and reputation, the title, the basic idea, and concept, the original script, character, plot, storyline, location, running order, design, layout, colour signs, scoreboards and studio equipment, the rules, procedures, catchphrases, questions and answers, slogans, costumes and outfits, all written material and artworks computer generated graphics, all intellectual property rights, design rights, trademarks, service marks, logo, musical, literary, dramatic, artistic and other works, which are described in detail in Appendix 1 and shall form part of this Agreement.

1.2 "The Assignment Fee" shall be the sum of: [figure/currency].

1.3 "The Format Package" shall be all the material of the Format in the possession or under the control of the Assignor including copies of all documents, records and other data and material in any form and a complete list of all material relating to the Format held by any third party.

1.4 "The Territory" shall be all countries, areas, ships, aeroplanes, oil-rigs and bases throughout the world.

2. ASSIGNMENT

2.1 In consideration of the payment of the Assignment Fee, the Assignor assigns to the Assignee all present and future copyright and all other rights in all media in the

Format and/or part(s), whether in existence now or created in the future, throughout the Territory for the full period of copyright and any extensions and renewals as far as possible in perpetuity, including but not limited to:

2.1.1 all forms of exploitation through the medium of television and radio including reception and transmission by standard terrestrial television, cable, satellite, digital regardless of the method of payment or not or the technical method whether encrypted or otherwise;

2.1.2 all forms of exploitation through the medium of videograms whether capable of being recorded stored or played by cassette, disc laser, or DVD whether by any method of payment, sales, rental, lease to the general public;

2.1.3 all forms of television video and non-theatric audiences including but not limited to business and commercial use, educational, cultural, religious and social establishments, schools, churches, prisons, hospitals, camps, workshops, film societies, professional and trade bodies, private and public libraries, colleges, universities, hotels, clubs, shops, airlines;

2.1.4 all forms of theatric exploitation including cinemas;

2.1.5 all forms of publishing whether in printed or electronic form;

2.1.6 all forms of electronic, internet, intranet and multi-media exploitation including CD-ROMS and all other methods of interactivity, sound, noise, text or graphic;

2.1.7 all forms of merchandising whether based on character, logo, images, rules, or otherwise, including commercial exploitation of any item of any nature, toys, clothing, accessories, cutlery, badges, sweets, stickers, stationery or otherwise;

2.1.8 all other forms of adaptation, variation or development of any other rights.

2.2 The Assignor agrees that he/she shall not be entitled to any credit or acknowledgement in respect of the exploitation of the Format in any media by the Assignee or any third party.

2.3 The Assignor waives all moral rights of any nature in respect of the Format.

3. OBLIGATIONS OF THE ASSIGNOR

3.1 The Assignor shall deliver the Format Package to the Assignee on or before: [date].

3.2 The Assignor confirms that he/she is the original creator and sole owner of or controls all copyright and any other rights in the Format which are assigned under this Agreement.

3.3 The Assignor confirms that he/she has and will retain good title and authority to enter into this Agreement and is not bound by any previous agreement which adversely affects this Agreement.

3.4 The Assignor confirms that he/she holds a [____________] passport and lives in [____________].

3.5 The Assignor confirms that the Format does not contain any material which infringes the copyright or any other rights of any third party in [country].

3.6 The Assignor agrees that it shall not be entitled to receive any sums which may arise from the exploitation of the Format by the Assignee.

3.7 The Assignor agrees that all development, variation, charges, production, marketing and exploitation of the Format shall be at the Assignee's sole discretion and cost.

4. OBLIGATIONS OF THE ASSIGNEE

4.1 In consideration of the rights assigned by the Assignor the Assignee shall pay to the Assignor the Assignment Fee as follows:

4.1.1 [____________] upon signature of this Agreement;
4.1.2 [____________] on or before [____________].

4.2 The Assignee confirms that it shall be responsible for any sums due in respect of the development, distribution, marketing and exploitation of the Format in any media at any time and that the Assignor shall not be liable for any such sums.

5. MISCELLANEOUS

5.1 The Assignor and the Assignee undertake to indemnify the other against all liabilities, claims, demands, actions, costs, damages or loss arising out of any breach by either party of any of the terms of this Agreement.

5.2 In the event of any claim, dispute, action, writ or summons in connection with clause 5.1, the Assignor and the Assignee agree to provide full details to the other party at the earliest opportunity and shall not settle any such matter without first consulting the other party.

5.3 The maximum indemnity liability in total of each party under this Agreement shall be: [____________].

5.4 No reference is to be made to the terms of this Agreement by either party in public without the prior written consent of the other party.

5.5 Any amendment or alteration to this Agreement must be in writing and signed by an authorised signatory of each party.

5.6 The Assignment Fee under this Agreement is exclusive of any value added tax.

5.7 No party shall be liable to any other for any loss or damage arising from any failure to perform any of its obligations in this Agreement or for any cause whatsoever beyond its control.

5.8 This Agreement shall be subject to the Laws of England.

Attached to and forming part of this Agreement is Appendix 1.

Signed by: [____________]
FOR AND BEHALF OF THE ASSIGNOR

Date: [____________]

Signed by: [____________]
FOR AND ON BEHALF OF THE ASSIGNEE

Date: [____________]

OUTLINE—BUY-OUT OF ALL RIGHTS IN ORIGINAL FORMAT

This is a deliberately short agreement for the assignment of all rights in an original format for a one-off assignment fee. It is a complete buy-out and the Assignor would not be entitled to any credit or acknowledgment in any future use of the Format. It should be appreciated that no copyright of any kind would remain vested with the Assignor as a result of this Agreement. The Assignor is waiving his moral rights and would therefore not be entitled to any credit or acknowledgment in respect of any exploitation of the Format.

It is important that full details of the Format are attached to the Agreement. It may also be worthwhile for the material of the Format to be noted under the Format Package. The undertakings are brief and minimal. The Assignor receives only the one Assignment Fee and no more from any exploitation by the Assignee. It is the responsibility of the Assignee to check for contact problems and to pay all further costs. The Assignee may do whatever it wants to develop, alter and exploit the Format.

EXCLUSIVE LICENCE FOR SERIES BASED ON A GROUP OF CHARACTERS

AN AGREEMENT made this [____________] day of [____________]

BETWEEN:

(1) [____________]
of [____________] (to be known as the Licensor in this Agreement)

AND

(2) [____________]
of [____________] (to be known as the Licensee in this Agreement).

IT IS AGREED as follows:

1. DEFINITIONS

The words below are agreed to mean as follows:

1.1 "The Characters" shall be the original concept and novel idea for a group of characters which are briefly described as follows: [____________].
Full descriptions, names and details of the Characters and any associated trade mark or logo are attached to and form part of this Agreement in Schedule 1.

1.2 "The Series" shall be the series of films and any associated sound recordings based on the Characters entitled [____________]. Full details of the Series are described in Schedule 2 which is attached to and forms part of this Agreement.

1.3 "The Treatment" shall be the summary of each of the episodes of the Series prepared by the Licensor and a copy of the Treatment is attached to and forms part of this Agreement in Schedule 3.

1.4 "The Scripts" shall be the draft and final scripts based on the Treatment to be prepared by the Licensor.

1.5 "The Licence Fee" shall be the sum of [figure/currency].

1.6 "The Licensor's Royalties" shall be [figure] per cent [_____]% of the Nett Receipts.

1.7 "The Gross Receipts" shall be the total proceeds from the exploitation of the Series throughout the Territory at any time received by or credited to the Licensee or its sub-agents or its sub-licensees or any other third party appointed by the Licensee.

1.8 "The Production Costs" shall be the total costs, whether direct or indirect (excluding the Licence Fee) of making the Series, including all items necessary for the development, pre-production, production, post-production and delivery of the Series which are not recovered from any third party.

1.9 "The Distribution Expenses" shall be the following costs, reasonably and properly expended, in respect of the exploitation of the Series by the Licensee which are not recouped from any third party including but not limited to:

1.9.1 reproduction and supply of technical material and artwork;
1.9.2 delivery, storage, shipping, customs duties, freight, handling charges and insurance;
1.9.3 publicity, advertising and promotional material;
1.9.4 copyright, music and rights clearances and payment of any nature;
1.9.5 dubbing, editing and subtitling for the purpose of exploitation to a foreign country; and
1.9.6 charges, commissions and fees of distributors, or sub-agents, collecting societies, or agents, legal and accounting fees.

1.10 "The Nett Receipts" shall be the Gross Receipts less the Production Costs and the Distribution Expenses.

1.11 "The Key Personnel" shall be as follows:

the producer: [______________];
the director: [______________];
the narrator: [______________];
any other(s): [______________].

1.12 "The Production Schedule" shall be the agreed dates, times and locations of making the Series, including development, production, pre-production, post-production and delivery of the Series. A copy of the Production Schedule is attached to and forms part of this Agreement in Schedule 4.

1.13 "The Licence Period" shall commence on [date] and shall continue until [date].

1.15 "The Territory" shall be all countries throughout the world.

2. EXCLUSIVE LICENCE

2.1 In consideration of the payment of the Licence Fee and the Licensor's Royalties. The Licensor agrees that the Licensor shall grant the Licensee the sole and exclusive right to exercise and exploit all film, video, electronic and mechanical rights in the Characters in the Series and in all other media whether in existence now or created in the future but not the publication and merchandising rights which shall be retained by the Licensor. Therefore for the avoidance of doubt the Licensee shall be granted the following rights:

2.1.1 all forms of television, video, radio, advertisements, theatre, institutions and businesses;

2.1.2 all forms of mechanical and electronic reproduction and distribution videos, discs, CD-ROMS, cassettes, logos, discs, internet, telecommunication systems.

2.2 The Licensor shall retain:

2.2.1 all publications, hardbacks, paperbacks, digests, serialisation and newspapers;

2.2.2 all merchandising such as toys, clothes, mugs, stationery, but not computer games.

2.3 The grant of rights by the Licensor and for the Licence Period and all rights shall revert to the Licensor upon expiry or termination of this Agreement.

2.4 The Licensee agrees that at the end of the Licence Period it shall execute any document or do anything required by the Licensor to vest all copyright in any variations or developments of the Characters in the Licensor.

2.5 The Licensor undertakes that he/she will not licence any third party to produce a television or video programme based on the Characters or any development or variation during the Licence Period.

3. EDITORIAL CONTROL

The final editorial decisions in respect of the Series shall be at the Licensee's sole discretion. The Licensee agrees to consult fully with the Licensor and to take due consideration of any editorial views expressed by the Licensor.

4. OBLIGATIONS OF THE LICENSEE

4.1 In consideration of the rights granted under this Agreement, the Licensee shall pay to the Licensor the Licence Fee as follows:

4.1.1 [____________] upon signature of this Agreement;

4.1.2 [____________] on or before [____________].

4.2 The Licensee agrees to produce the Series using the Key Personnel in accordance with the Treatment, the Scripts and the Production Schedule and confirms that the Series will be in colour and in the English language and primarily in the following format: [____________].

4.3 The Licensee undertakes that it shall pay the Licensor's Royalties to the Licensor within [____________] of the last day of June and December in each year.

4.4 The Licensee agrees to arrange and pay for any travel and accommodation for the Licensor required by the Licensee under this Agreement and undertakes, as far as possible, that all accommodation will be in a minimum of [____________] and all forms of travel will be business or first class.

4.5 The Licensee agrees to pay or reimburse the Licensor in respect of all expenses reasonably and properly incurred in respect of attendance at any meetings, filming and locations requested by the Licensee under this Agreement, subject to satisfactory receipts or records being produced upon request.

4.6 The Licensee undertakes that it will arrange suitable insurance cover for the Licensor and his/her personal property in the event that the Licensor is requested to attend any filming or locations and shall provide the Licensor with a copy of the policy when it is available.

4.7 The Licensee agrees to provide the Licensor with reasonable notice of all alterations to the Production Schedule and any meetings and events which the Licensor is required to attend under this Agreement.

4.8 The Licensee and its sub-agents and sub-licensees and any other third parties appointed by the Licensee shall keep full and accurate books of account, records and contracts and other material showing the Gross Receipts, the Production Costs, the Distribution Expenses, the Nett Receipts and the Licensor's Royalties in respect of the exploitation of the Series.

4.9 Within [____________] of the last day of June and December in each year, the Licensee shall provide a detailed report to the Licensor with a full breakdown of the exploitation of the Series setting out the Gross Receipts, the Production Costs, the Distribution Expenses, the Nett Receipts and the Licensor's Royalties.

4.10 The Licensee agrees that the Licensor shall be entitled to arrange for an annual audit to inspect and make copies of the Licensee's books of account, records, contracts and any other relevant material in order to verify the sums due to the Licensor at the Licensor's cost.

4.11 The Licensee agrees to provide the following on-screen credit, copyright notice, trademark or logo to the Licensor in the Series and in any publicity, advertising, promotional or packaging material in respect of the marketing and distribution of the Series: [____________].

4.12 The Licensee agrees to provide copies and samples of any publicity, promotional, advertising and packaging material in respect of the marketing and commercial exploitation of the Series upon request at the Licensee's cost.

4.13 The Licensee acknowledges that it shall be solely responsible for all costs incurred in respect of the production and exploitation of the Series and that the Licensor shall not be liable for any such payments.

4.14 The Licensee acknowledges that the Licence Fee shall not be off-set against the Gross Receipts or the Licensor's Royalties.

5. OBLIGATIONS OF THE LICENSOR

5.1 The Licensor confirms that he/she is the original creator and sole owner of or controls all copyright and any other rights in the Characters, which are granted under this Agreement.

5.2 The Licensor confirms that he/she has full title and authority to enter into this Agreement and is not bound by any previous agreement which adversely effects this Agreement.

5.3 The Licensor confirms that he/she holds a [____________] passport and is resident in [____________].

5.4 The Licensor confirms that the Characters do not contain any obscene or defamatory material and will not expose the Licensee to any civil or criminal proceedings.

5.5 The Licensor confirms that the Characters do not contain any material which infringes the copyright or any other rights of any third party in the Territory in respect of the rights granted under this Agreement.

5.6 Subject to prior consultation, the Licensor agrees that the Licensee shall be entitled to use the Licensor's name, biography, photograph and fair likeness in any commercial exploitation of the Series.

5.7 The Licensor agrees to write and deliver the Scripts for the Series to the Licensee in accordance with the Production Schedule but in any event no later than: [date].

5.8 The Licensor agrees that he shall be responsible for all national insurance, personal tax and value added tax which shall be due in consequence of this Agreement.

5.9 The Licensor agrees to supply copies of such artwork of the Characters and any trade mark or logo or other credit which may be required by the Licensee under this Agreement at the Licensee's cost.

5.10 The Licensor agrees, subject to sufficient prior notice, to attend at such times, dates, places and locations as the Licensee may reasonably require in order to assist in the production of the Series.

6. MISCELLANEOUS

MUTUAL INDEMNITY

6.1 The Licensor and The Licensee mutually undertake to indemnify the other against all liabilities, claims, demands, actions, costs, damages and loss arising out of any breach by either party of any of the terms of this Agreement.

6.2 In the event of any claim, dispute, action, writ or summons in connection with clause 6.1, the Licensor and the Licensee agree to provide full details to the other party at the earliest opportunity and shall not settle any such matter without first consulting the other party.

CONFIDENTIALITY

6.3 The Licensor and the Licensee shall not disclose to any third party any confidential business or future plans of the other party at any time acquired during the existence of this Agreement and no reference is to be made to the terms of this Agreement by either party in any advertising, publicity or promotional material without the prior written consent of the other party.

AMENDMENTS AND ALTERATIONS

6.4 This Agreement supersedes all previous agreements, representations or promises and sets out all the terms agreed between the parties. Any amendment or alteration to this Agreement must be in writing and signed by an authorised signatory of each party.

NO PARTNERSHIP OR EMPLOYMENT

6.5 This Agreement shall not be deemed to create any partnership or employment relationship between the parties.

NOTICES

6.6 Without prejudice to the right to serve notices by any other means any notice served under this Agreement shall be in writing. Any notice which has been sent by first class, pre-paid post shall be deemed to be received 48 hours thereafter (excluding Saturdays, Sundays and public holidays).

TAXES

6.7 All sums payable under this Agreement are exclusive of any value added tax or sales tax that may be due or paid by either party. Each party shall bear the cost of their own tax liability.

THIRD PARTIES

6.8 Neither party shall assign, transfer, charge or make over this Agreement or any of its rights or obligations without the prior written consent of the other party.

6.9 No third party may take the responsibilities or liabilities of either party.

FORCE MAJEURE

6.10 In the event that this Agreement cannot be performed or its obligations fulfilled for any reason beyond the reasonable control of either party, including war, industrial action, floods or Acts of God. Then such non-performance or failure to fulfil its obligations shall be deemed not to be a breach of this Agreement. In the event that this Agreement cannot be performed or its obligations fulfilled for any reason beyond either party's reasonable control for a continuous period of [three months]. Then either party may, at its discretion, terminate this Agreement by notice in writing at the end of that period.

TERMINATION

6.11 In addition to any other rights and remedies at law, either party may, by giving written notice to the other party, terminate this Agreement on the grounds that:

6.11.1 the Licensee has failed to account or make payments as required under this Agreement;

6.11.2 where either party has committed a serious breach of its obligations under this Agreement and has not rectified the position within [____________]; or

6.11.3 where the Licensee goes into voluntary or involuntary liquidation or is declared insolvent, either in bankruptcy proceedings or other legal proceedings, or has reached an agreement with creditors due to its failure or inability to pay its debts as they fall due, or where a receiver is appointed over the whole or part of the Licensee's business.

GOVERNING LAW

6.12 This Agreement shall be construed, governed and fall within the jurisdiction of [____________].

Attached to and forming part of this Agreement are the following Schedules:

1. The Characters;
2. The Series;
3. The Treatment;
4. The Production Schedule.

Signed by: [____________]
FOR AND ON BEHALF OF THE LICENSOR

Signed by: [____________]
FOR AND ON BEHALF OF THE LICENSEE

OUTLINE—EXCLUSIVE LICENCE FOR SERIES BASED ON A GROUP OF CHARACTERS

This Agreement is between the copyright owner of a group of characters and a production company, referred to as the Licensor and the Licensee respectively. The Characters are to be used for a series for mainly the worldwide television and video markets. The programmes could be real life, animation or puppetry.

The Licensor is granting an exclusive licence to the production company to produce the Series using the Characters. The Licensor is providing the Treatment and Scripts. The production company is paying a Licence Fee and a percentage of the profits earned from the exploitation of the Series worldwide.

The Licensee is not acquiring the merchandising or publication rights for the Characters but all other forms of media for the exploitation of the Series in all forms of television, video, non-theatric, theatric markets and internet.

Under this Agreement, the Licensee has the final editorial control for the Series.

The Licence Fee is not to be off-set against the Licensor's future royalties. The production costs for the Series will be recouped from the Gross Receipts. Although the Licensor is not specifically asserting his moral rights, under clause 4.11 he is entitled to an agreed credit, copyright notice, trademark and logo in respect of the Series and in all associated promotional and packaging material.

The accounting provisions could be expanded to allow for compensation for errors, and provisions could be included to allow greater involvement by the Licensor in the appointment of third parties and the approval of samples. Further, the sums involved in the project could be kept in a separate account.

LICENCE AGREEMENT WITH DISTRIBUTOR FOR CHARACTER FOR SPECIFIC PRODUCT

AN AGREEMENT made this [____________] day of [____________]

BETWEEN:

(1) [____________]
of [____________] (to be known as the Licensor in this Agreement)

AND

(2) [____________]
of [____________] (to be known as the Licensee in this Agreement).

IT IS AGREED as follows:

1. DEFINITIONS

The words below are agreed to mean as follows:

1.1 "The Character" shall be the original concept and novel idea for a character which is briefly described as follows: name of Character: [____________].
Full details of the Character are attached to and form part of this Agreement in Schedule A. [Copyright, and other intellectual property rights, design, trademark, logo, plot, storyline, artwork, colour, sign, scoreboard, equipment, catchphrase, slogan, costumes, outfit, script, 2-D and 3-D drawings.]

1.2 "The Licensed Article" shall be the licensed product to be developed, produced and distributed by the Licensee, which shall be based on or derived from the Character and which is described as follows: [____________].
Full details of the Licensed Article are attached to and form part of this Agreement in Schedule B.

1.3 "The Licence Fee" shall be the sum of [figure/currency].

1.4 "The Territory" shall be the following countries marked on the attached map in Schedule C listed as follows: [____________], and all surrounding territorial waters, and any ships, airlines, vessels or other locations in that Territory.

1.5 "The Licence Period" shall commence on [date] and shall continue until [date].

1.6 "The Licensor's Royalties" shall be [figure] per cent [____]% of the recommended retail selling price for each Licensed Article together with copies of supporting documentation to verify these figures.

2. LICENCE OF RIGHTS

2.1 In consideration of the Licence Fee the Licensor grants to the Licensee the sole and exclusive right to produce, manufacture, distribute, sell and exploit the Licensed Article, based on the Character throughout the Territory for the duration of the Licence Period.

2.2 The Licensee undertakes that at the end of the Licence Period it shall execute any document or do anything required by the Licensor to vest all copyright and any other rights in any variations or developments of the Character in the Licensor at the Licensor's cost.

2.3 The Licensor undertakes that he/she will not licence any third party to produce the Licensed Article based on the Character or any development or variation in the Territory during the Licence Period.

2.4 The Licensor shall not authorise, permit or license any other products in the [______________] field which are to be derived from or incorporate the Character or any part before: [date].

2.5 The Licensee agrees that it is only being licensed to produce the specified product and that it may not sub-license, sub-distribute or otherwise produce any other item based on the Character or engage any third party to exploit the Licensed Article.

2.6 The Licensee agrees that it shall not acquire any interest, goodwill or right in the name of the Character or any associated slogan or words, image or test or any trade-mark or logo of the Licensor under this Agreement except to manufacture and distribute the Licensed Article, and shall not register any such rights or interest.

3. OBLIGATIONS OF THE LICENSEE

3.1 In consideration of the rights granted under this Agreement; the Licensee shall pay to the Licensor the Licence Fee as follows: [______________] upon signature of this Agreement; [______________] on or before [______________].

3.2 The Licensee acknowledges that the Licence Fee is not returnable and is not to be off-set against the Licensor's Royalties and is not contingent on sales of the Licensed Articles.

3.3 The Licensee undertakes that the minimum recommended retail selling price per unit of each Licensed Article shall be: [______________].

3.4 The Licensee undertakes to use and apply the Character and any trade mark and logo for the sole purpose of manufacturing, distributing, selling and marketing the Licensed Article and not for any other purpose.

3.5 The Licensee undertakes that it shall pay the Licensor's Royalties within [______________] of the last day of March, June, September and December in each year.

3.6 The Licensee shall keep professional, accurate and complete books of account, records and contracts and prices showing all dealings of the Licensed Article, including the total number of units of the Licensed Article manufactured, distributed and sold, whether by wholesale or retail, distributed without charge for promotional purposes and all units lost, damaged or stolen and the calculation of the Licensor's Royalties in respect of the Licensed Articles.

3.7 Within [____________] of the last day of March, June, September and December in each year. The Licensee shall provide a detailed written report to the Licensor showing all dealings of the Licensed Article including the total number of units of the Licensed Article manufactured, distributed and sold whether by wholesale or retail prices and details of units distributed without charge for promotional purposes and all units lost, damaged or stolen or any other reason why no royalty is paid to the Licensor and the calculation of the Licensor's Royalties in respect of the Licensed Articles. Together with copies of supporting documentation to verify these figures.

3.8 The Licensee agrees that the Licensor at the Licensor's cost shall be entitled to arrange for its senior executives and/or its legal and/or accountancy advisors to audit, inspect and make copies of all the Licensee's bank statements, accounts, records, contracts, software equipment, or other material relating to Character and the Licensed Articles in order to verify and establish the accuracy of the payment and reports to the Licensor under this Agreement.

3.9 In the event that it is established by the Licensor that there are errors in excess of: [figure/currency] on any accounting period. Then for each such period the Licensee shall pay the sum due in full plus twice the error sum in compensation. The establishment of an overpayment shall not result in a refund, but a correction on the next accounting period that falls due.

3.10 The Licensee agrees to provide the following credit, copyright notice, trademark and logo to the Licensor in respect of the Licensed Article and in all publicity, advertising, promotional and packaging material in respect of the marketing and distribution of the Licensed Article: [____________].

3.11 The Licensee agrees that the Licensor shall be entitled to approve the Licensed Article and any associated leaflets and packaging prior to manufacture and distribution and the Licensee undertakes to supply such samples of the Licensed Article and any leaflets and packaging in the exact form and material in which the Licensee proposes to manufacture, distribute and sell the Licensed Article. The Licensee acknowledges that approval by the Licensor must be in writing.

3.12 The Licensee agrees that the Licensor shall be entitled to approve all publicity, promotional, advertising and packaging material in respect of the Licensed Article. The Licensee acknowledges that such approval must be obtained in writing prior to manufacture, production and distribution of any such material.

3.13 The Licensee acknowledges that all copyright and any other rights in the Character and any trade mark or logo, together with any goodwill, shall remain the sole property of the Licensor and that the Licensee shall not acquire any rights in the Character or in any trademark, logo, title, artwork and any developments or variations thereof.

3.14 The Licensee undertakes that copies of the Licensed Article shall be distributed to the public by: [date] subject to satisfactory approval of the samples by the Licensor.

3.15 The Licensee acknowledges that it is solely responsible for all costs incurred in the commercial exploitation of the Licensed Article including the manufacturing, distribution, selling, advertising and promotion.

3.16 The Licensee agrees that in the event that the Licensor's Royalties received by the Licensor within 12 months of the date of this Agreement are less than [figure/currency]. Then the Licensor shall be entitled to terminate this Agreement immediately by notice in writing to that effect.

3.17 The Licensee undertakes that all the Licensed Articles are and shall be safe for their intended use by the public and particularly children. The Licensee shall ensure that the Licensed Articles shall comply with all statutes, regulations, directives and codes in force and that prior to distribution to the public, comprehensive product liability insurance cover shall be arranged of not less than [____________] per claim.

3.18 The Licensee agrees to provide the Licensor with not less than [____________] Licensed Articles in the form in which they are released to the general public without charge.

3.19 The Licensee acknowledges that any approval of the samples or the Licensed Article by the Licensor shall not detract from or waive any duty by the Licensee to ensure that the product is safe for its intended use and does not contain any material, chemical, or parts which are toxic, dangerous or are likely to result in an accident when played with by a small child.

3.20 The Licensee agrees that a disclaimer shall appear on the packaging relating to the Licensor and that the Licensed Product shall be tested by a trial of: [___________]. The Licensee shall notify the Licensor of any alleged accidents, faults or consumer criticisms of the Product and forward copies of all letters received.

3.21 The Licensee shall be solely responsible for paying any costs or damages arising from any claim action or liability arising from the production, manufacture, sale and distribution of the Licensed Articles.

3.22 The Licensee agrees that it shall not be entitled to appoint or engage any third party to manufacture, distribute or market the Licensed Articles without the prior written approval of the Licensor.

3.23 The Licensee agrees that it has acquired no merchandising rights on the Character except the right to exploit the Licensed Article.

3.24 The Licensee agrees that no film or commercial featuring the Licensed Article shall be made without the prior written consent of the Licensor which owns such rights.

3.25 The Licensee shall ensure that each Licensed Article shall conform in all respects to the quality, design, packaging and materials of the sample submitted to and approved by the Licensor. That the workmanship or materials shall not be defective.

3.26 The Licensee shall indemnify the Licensor from any claim by the public or any third party in respect of any defect or flaw in the Licensed Articles or any injury, damage or loss which is raised directly or indirectly from their use.

4. OBLIGATIONS OF THE LICENSOR

4.1 The Licensor confirms that he/she is the original creator and sole owner of or controls all copyright and any other rights in the Character which are granted under this Agreement.

4.2 The Licensor confirms that he/she has full title and authority to enter into this Agreement and is not bound by any previous agreement which adversely affects this Agreement.

4.3 The Licensor confirms that the Character does not contain any material which infringes the copyright or any other rights of any third party in the Territory in respect of the rights granted under this Agreement and will not expose the Licensee to civil or criminal proceedings.

4.4 Subject to prior written approval, the Licensor agrees that the Licensee shall be entitled to use the Licensor's name, biography, photograph and fair likeness in the exploitation of the Licensed Articles.

4.5 The Licensor agrees that he/she shall be responsible for all national insurance, personal tax and value added tax which shall be due in consequence of this Agreement.

4.6 The Licensor agrees to provide written approval of or reject any of the material provided by the Licensee as soon as reasonably possible after delivery by the Licensee.

4.7 The Licensor agrees to supply at the Licensee's cost copies of such artwork of the Character and any trademark, logo or other credit which may be required by the Licensee to assist in the manufacture and distribution of the Licensed Articles.

4.8 The Licensor agrees that the Licensee may at the Licensee's sole cost make minor changes, developments or variations of the Character in the Licensed Articles for the purposes of safety, marketing or manufacture, but no such alterations shall be unreasonable, unnecessary or offensive or demeaning.

4.9 The Licensor agrees that the Licensee shall have the sole discretion as to the manufacture, production, distribution and marketing of the Licensed Articles subject to the written approval of the samples set out in this Agreement.

4.10 The Licensor asserts his moral right to be identified as: [____________] on all copies of the Licensed Article and on all packaging and marketing material.

5. WAIVER

No waiver of any breach shall be decreed a waiver of any preceding or succeeding breach whether the same or not. No delay or omission in exercising any right or remedy shall operate as a waiver. No waiver shall be binding for any purpose unless put in writing and signed by the party. Any such written waiver shall only be effective for the purpose stated and no other.

6. LEGAL PROCEEDINGS

6.1 In the event that any legal proceedings are commenced by any third party against either the Licensor and/or the Licensee in respect of the Character and/or the Licensed Articles, the written notice of such claim shall immediately be given to the other party who shall provide all assistance as may reasonably be required in order to settle or defend each such case. Each party shall bear its own legal costs and expenses.

6.2 In the event that there is any allegation or claim made that the Character and/or the Licensed Articles infringe any third party rights. Then the party against whom the claim or allegation is made shall notify the other party. Each party shall be entitled to defend itself without prejudice to the right of that party to take third party proceedings or any other steps or actions against the other parties to this Agreement whether under the indemnity or as a claim for damages.

7. INDEMNITY

7.1 The Licensor undertakes to keep the Licensee indemnified for the duration of the Licence Period against all actions, costs, proceedings, claims, demands and expenses that may be brought against, suffered or incurred by the Licensee in consequence of any breach or alleged breach of any undertaking by the Licensor in this Agreement.

7.2 The Licensee undertakes to keep the Licensor indemnified for the duration of the Licence Period against all actions, costs, proceedings, claims, demands and expenses that may be brought against, suffered or incurred by the Licensor in consequence of any breach or alleged breach of any undertaking by the Licensor in this Agreement.

8. THIRD PARTY TRANSFER

The Licensee shall not be entitled to assign, transfer, charge, make over, sub-licence, sub-contract or otherwise attribute any part of this Agreement to any third party except professional legal and accounting advisors who provide for advice and report purposes only. No third party shall be entitled to rely on or enforce the terms of this Agreement which is personal to the parties.

9. TAXES

All charges, payments and sums are exclusive of sales tax, value added tax and any other sum charged on the sale or supply of Products. Each party shall be responsible for its personal and corporate taxes, and insurance.

10. AMENDMENTS

This Agreement sets out the entire and complete agreement between the parties and supersedes all prior arrangements written or oral relating to the subject matter of this

Agreement. This Agreement must be varied only by an exchange of written documents signed by both parties whether separate or one entity.

11. NO AGENT OR PARTNERSHIP

This Agreement shall not constitute or imply a partnership or employment relationship between the parties. Neither party shall be deemed to be an agent of the other for any purpose whatsoever. Neither party shall have any authority or power to bind the other in any way.

12. NOTICES

Any notice shall be in writing and served under this Agreement if it is delivered by hand to the Managing Director of the Licensor or Licensee or sent by recorded delivery. Advance notice may be sent by fax or e-mail but shall not constitute service.

13. FORCE MAJEURE

In the event that this Agreement cannot be performed or its obligations fulfilled for any reason beyond reasonable control including war, hostilities, strikes, acts of God, natural disasters, fire, or breakdown of equipment not caused by negligence or neglect. Then this Agreement shall be suspended for that period up to a period of [____________]. Thereafter either party may terminate this Agreement by notice in writing subject to the conclusion of an equitable settlement giving due regard to the circumstances.

14. TERMINATION

The Licensor may terminate this Agreement by notice in writing in the event that:

14.1 the Licensee shall have failed to manufacture and distribute [____________] units of the Licensed Article before: [date];

14.2 the Licensee shall fail to pay the License Fee in full by date: [____________];

14.3 the Licensee shall fail to make payment of the Licensor's Royalties or report for any accounting period;

14.4 the Licensee shall commit a breach of this Agreement;

14.5 the Licensee is unable to pay its debts or is trading insolvently or is wound up, put into receivership or liquidation or otherwise no longer a viable business. The Licensee may terminate this Agreement if the Licensor is in breach of any of the terms of this Agreement.

15. EXPIRY AND SELL-OFF

15.1 Upon the expiry or termination of this Agreement the Licensee shall be permitted on a non-exclusive basis to sell the Licensed Articles already manufactured in the

Licence Period until: [date] provided that this Licensee adheres to the terms of this Agreement.

15.2 Thereafter the Licensor shall be entitled to instruct the Licensee to return all Master Material, Licensed Articles, artwork, stock, publicity and any other material of any nature in the possession of or under the control of the Licensee.

16. JURISDICTION

Both parties acknowledge and confirm that any dispute litigation, interpretation, damages or loss which arise as a result of this Agreement shall be subject to the Laws of [____________] and no other jurisdiction shall be applicable.

17. CONFIDENTIALITY

The parties agree to not disclose to any third parties any business information or plans which may be disclosed during the course of this Agreement of the other party.

ATTACH: SCHEDULE A—THE CHARACTER
SCHEDULE B—THE LICENSED ARTICLE

[____________] [NAME/TITLE/DATE]
THE LICENSOR

[____________] [NAME/TITLE/DATE]
THE LICENSEE

OUTLINE— LICENCE AGREEMENT WITH DISTRIBUTOR FOR CHARACTER FOR SPECIFIC PRODUCT

This is an Agreement between the copyright owner of a character and a distributor.

The copyright owner is referred to as the Licensor and the distributor as the Licensee. The Licensor is granting to the Licensee an exclusive licence to produce a particular product based on the Character and referred to as "the Licensed Article". This might be anything from a soft toy to a badge. The Licensor has the right to reject the samples of the proposed product and any associated packaging and publicity material which require the written approval of the Licensor prior to manufacture and distribution.

The Licensor is receiving a Licence Fee. This is not an advance against royalties and is not returnable. In addition, the Licensor receives a percentage royalty based on the recommended retail selling price, the Licensor's Royalty. If the Licensor receives less than a stated amount of royalties within, for example, twelve months, then the Licensor may terminate the Agreement.

The Licensor is specifically asserting his moral rights and is also entitled to an agreed credit, copyright notice, trademark and logo in respect of the Licensed Article and in all associated promotional and packaging material.

There are various provisions relating to the safety of the Licensed Product and the requirement to take out product liability insurance.

The Licensee will account regularly and permit frequent audits. Where an error occurs then compensation is fixed at twice the error sum in addition to the payment of the underpayment.

At the end of the Licence Period all rights revert to the Licensor and there is only a brief non-exclusive sell-off period. It is far better with this type of agreement to keep the Licence Period relatively short, and to only licence those countries in the Territory that it is effectively capable of marketing.

Any sub-licenses, agents or otherwise are not to be appointed as a matter of right and must be approved. The attachments relating to the Character and the Licensed Product are important to argument later as to the true nature of the Licence. There is an undertaking not to license other products in a similar field. This is not essential, and the Licence could also be non-exclusive.

EXCLUSIVE LICENCE FOR EXPLOITATION OF BOARD GAME

AN AGREEMENT made this [____________] day of [____________]

BETWEEN:

(1) [____________]
of [____________] (to be known as the Licensor in this Agreement)

AND

(2) [____________]
of [____________] (to be known as the Company in this Agreement).

IT IS AGREED as follows:

1. DEFINITIONS

The words below are agreed to mean as follows:

1.1 "The Board Game" shall be the original concept and novel idea for a board game created by the Licensor which is briefly described as follows:

title: [____________];
brief description: [____________].

A copy of the full two-dimensional illustrative and written details of the Board Game, including the colour, dimensions and materials of each of the components, and a complete list of rules and instructions are attached to and form part of this Agreement as Schedule 1.

1.2 "The Prototype" shall be the three-dimensional reproduction of the Board Game created and produced by the Licensor.

1.3 "The Licensed Articles" shall be the three-dimensional reproductions based on the Prototype to be manufactured and distributed by the Company.

1.4 "The Non-Returnable Advance" shall be the sum of [figure/currency].

1.5 "The Licensor's Royalties" shall be the following percentage of the recommended retail selling price or any other sums at any time received by or credited to the Company in respect of the exploitation of the Licensed Articles:

in respect of units sold within the United Kingdom of Great Britain, Northern Ireland, the Republic of Ireland, the Channel Islands and the Isle of Man:

(i) [____________] % for the first [____________] units of the Licensed Articles;
(ii) [____________] % for the following [____________] units of the Licensed Articles; and
(iii) [____________] % for the following [____________] units of the Licensed Articles.

In respect of units sold throughout the Territory excluding the United Kingdom of Great Britain, Northern Ireland, the Republic of Ireland, the Channel Islands and the Isle of Man:

(i) [____________] % for the first [____________] units of the Licensed Articles;
(ii) [____________] % for the following [____________] units of the Licensed Articles; and
(iii) [____________] % for the following [____________] units of the Licensed Articles.

1.6 "The Territory" shall be all countries, bases and locations throughout the world.

1.7 "The Licence Period" shall commence on the date of this Agreement and shall continue for a period of [date].

2. EXCLUSIVE LICENCE OF RIGHTS

2.1 In consideration of the payment of the Non-Returnable Advance and the Licensor's Royalties, the Licensor grants to the Company the sole and exclusive right to produce, manufacture, distribute, sell and exploit the Licensed Articles based on the Prototype throughout the Territory for the duration of the Licence Period.

2.2 The Company undertakes that at the end of the Licence Period it shall execute any document or do anything required by the Licensor to confirm that all copyright, design rights and any other rights in the Board Game Licensed Article and in any variations or developments of the Licensed Articles are the sole property of the Licensor.

2.3 The Licensor undertakes that he will not license or permit any third party to produce, manufacture or distribute the Board Game or the Prototype, including any developments or variations, throughout the Territory for the duration of the Licence Period.

3. COPYRIGHT AND ANCILLARY RIGHTS

The Company acknowledges and agrees that all present and future copyright and design rights and other rights in the Board Game (including the title) and the Prototype are and will remain the sole property of the Licensor and that this Agreement does not in any way purport to transfer any copyright or design rights or other rights to the Company except a limited licence to produce the Licence Article.

4. MORAL RIGHTS

The Company acknowledges that the Licensor asserts his moral rights generally in respect of the Board Game, the Prototype and the Licensed Articles and in particular to be reasonably, clearly and prominently identified as follows: [____________].

5. OBLIGATIONS OF THE COMPANY

5.1 In consideration of the rights granted under this Agreement, the Company shall pay to the Licensor the Non-Returnable Advance as follows:

5.1.1 [____________] upon signature of this Agreement;
5.1.2 [____________] on or before: [____________];
5.1.3 [____________] upon first release of the Licensed Articles for sale to the public anywhere throughout the Territory but in any event not later than: [____________]

5.2 The Company acknowledges that the Non-Returnable Advance is to be off-set against the Licensor's Royalties but is not returnable nor contingent upon any sales figures in relation to the Licensed Articles.

5.3 The Company confirms that it has full title and authority to enter into this Agreement and is not bound by any previous agreement which adversely affects this Agreement.

5.4 The Company undertakes that the minimum retail selling price for each unit of the Licensed Articles throughout the Territory shall not be less than: [____________].

5.5 The Company undertakes that it shall pay the Licensor's Royalties to the Licensor on [dates] in each year.

5.6 The Company and its sub-agents, sub-licensees and distributors shall keep full and accurate books of account, records and contracts and prices showing all dealings of the Licensed Articles, including the total number of units of the Licensed Article manufactured, distributed and sold, whether by wholesale or retail, or distributed without charge for promotional purposes and all units lost, damaged or stolen and the calculation of the Licensor's Royalties in respect of the Licensed Articles.

5.7 On [dates] in each year the Company shall provide a detailed report to the Licensor showing all dealings of the Licensed Articles, including the total number of units of the Licensed Articles manufactured, distributed and sold, whether by wholesale or retail, all prices and details of units distributed without charge for promotional purposes and all units lost, damaged or stolen and the calculation of the Licensor's Royalties in respect of the Licensed Articles.

5.8 The Company agrees that the Licensor shall be entitled to arrange for an [annual] audit to inspect and make copies of the Company's books of account, records, contracts and any other relevant material in order to verify the sums due to the Licensor.

In the event that in any audit an error is found to the detriment of the Licensor in respect of the amount to be paid by the Company which is in excess of [_____] per cent, then the Company shall be responsible for the payment of all reasonable costs incurred in such audit.

5.9 The Company agrees to provide the following copyright notice, credit, trademark and logo to the Licensor in respect of the Licensed Articles and in all publicity, advertising, promotional and packaging material in respect of the marketing, distribution and exploitation of the Licensed Articles: [_____________].

5.10 The Company agrees that the Licensor shall be entitled to approve the Licensed Articles prior to their production, manufacture and distribution and the Company undertakes to supply at its sole cost such samples of the Licensed Articles in the exact form and material in which the Company proposes to manufacture, distribute and sell the Licensed Articles. The Company acknowledges that such approval by the Licensor must be in writing.

5.11 The Company confirms that it shall be solely responsible for all costs incurred in the development, production, manufacture, distribution, marketing, promotion, advertising and exploitation of the Licensed Articles and that such sums will not be offset against the Licensor's Royalties.

5.12 The Company agrees that the Licensor shall be entitled to approve the appointment of any sub-agent, sub-licensee, distributor and any other third party in respect of the production, manufacture, distribution and exploitation of the Licensed Articles under this Agreement.

5.13 The Company undertakes that not less than: [_____________] units of the Licensed Articles shall be manufactured within [_____________] of the delivery of the Prototype by the Licensor to the Company.

5.14 The Company undertakes that all the Licensed Articles shall be safe for their intended use and shall comply with all statutes, regulations, directives and codes in force and that prior to distribution and sale to the public comprehensive insurance cover for the Company and the Licensor shall be arranged of not less than [_____________] per claim.

5.15 The Company agrees to provide the Licensor at the Company's cost with not less than [_____________] units of the Licensed Articles in the form in which they are distributed to the general public.

5.16 The Company agrees to provide the Licensor with copies of all artwork, packaging, promotional and advertising work in relation to the sale, distribution and marketing of the Licensed Articles.

5.17 The Company agrees that in the event that the Licensor's Royalties (including the Non-Returnable Advance) received by the Licensor within[_____________] of the date of this Agreement are less than: [_____________]. Then the Licensor shall be entitled to terminate this Agreement forthwith by giving notice in writing to that effect.

6. OBLIGATIONS OF THE LICENSOR

6.1 The Licensor confirms that he is the original creator and sole owner of or controls all copyright, design rights and any other rights in the Board Game and the Prototype which are granted to the Company under this Agreement.

6.2 The Licensor confirms that he has full title and authority to enter into this Agreement and is not bound by any previous agreement which adversely affects this Agreement.

6.3 The Licensor confirms that the Board Game and the Prototype do not involve the use of any material which infringes the copyright or any other rights of any third party in the Territory in respect of the rights granted under this Agreement.

6.4 The Licensor confirms that the Board Game and the Prototype do not contain any obscene, offensive or defamatory material and will not expose the Company to any civil or criminal proceedings in [country].

6.5 The Licensor agrees to attend such meetings, exhibitions and promotional events as may reasonably be required by the Company, subject to sufficient prior notice at the Company's cost and expense.

6.7 The Licensor agrees that the Company shall be entitled to use the Licensor's name, biography, photograph and fair likeness in any commercial exploitation of the Licensed Articles subject to prior written approval in each case.

6.8 The Licensor agrees that he shall be responsible for his own national insurance, personal tax and value added tax which shall be due in consequence of this Agreement.

6.9 The Licensor agrees to provide written approval or reject the Licensed Articles or any samples created by the Company as soon as reasonably possible. The Licensor agrees to reject the Licensed Articles only on reasonable grounds and in good faith.

6.10 The Licensor agrees to provide the Company, upon request, with access to all such materials of the Board Game and the Prototype as may be available to assist in the production and manufacture of the Licensed Articles.

6.11 The Licensor confirms that he holds a [______________] passport and is resident in [country].

7. MISCELLANEOUS

MUTUAL INDEMNITY

7.1 The Licensor and the Company mutually undertake to indemnify the other against all liabilities, claims, demands, actions, costs, damages or loss arising out of any breach by either party of any of the terms of this Agreement.

7.2 In the event of any claim, dispute, action, writ or summons in connection with clause 7.1, the Licensor and the Company agree to provide full details to the other party at the earliest opportunity and shall not settle any such matter without first consulting the other party.

7.3 The total liability under this Agreement of the Licensor shall be limited to [figure/currency] to the Licensee. The total liability of the Licensee to the Licensor shall not be limited at all and shall be for any matter within or after the Licence Period.

CONFIDENTIALITY

7.4 The Licensor and the Company shall not disclose to any third party any confidential business or future plans of the other party at any time acquired during the existence of this Agreement and no reference is to be made to the terms of this Agreement by either party in any advertising, publicity or promotional material without the prior written consent of the other party.

AMENDMENTS AND ALTERATIONS

7.5 This Agreement supersedes all previous agreements, representations or promises and sets out all the terms agreed between the parties. Any amendment or alteration to this Agreement must be in writing and signed by an authorised signatory of each party.

NO PARTNERSHIP

7.6 This Agreement shall not be deemed to create any partnership, employment or agency relationship between the parties. Nor shall it entitle either party to commit or enter into any agreement with any third party on their behalf.

NOTICES

7.7 Without prejudice to the right to serve notices by any other means any notice served under this Agreement shall be in writing. Any notice which has been sent by first class, pre-paid post shall be deemed to be received 48 hours thereafter (excluding Saturdays, Sundays and public holidays). For the purposes of this Agreement the following details shall apply in respect of:

The Licensor: [Address] [Name] [Fax/e-mail];
The Company: [Address] [Name] [Fax/e-mail].

TAXES

7.8 All sums payable under this Agreement are exclusive of any taxes or sales or value added tax that may be due as a result of the supply or sale of goods by either party. Each party shall bear its own personal and corporate taxes and national insurance.

THIRD PARTY TRANSFERS

7.9 Neither party shall assign, transfer, charge or make over this Agreement or any of its rights or obligations without the prior written consent of the other party.

FORCE MAJEURE

7.10 In the event that this Agreement cannot be performed or its obligations fulfilled for any reason beyond the reasonable control of the Licensor or the Company, including such events as war, industrial action, floods or Acts of God. Then such non-performance or failure to fulfil its obligations shall be deemed not to be a breach of this Agreement. In the event that this Agreement cannot be performed or its obligations fulfilled for any reason beyond the reasonable control of the defaulting party for a continuous period of [three months] then the other party may, at its discretion, terminate this Agreement by notice in writing at the end of that period.

TERMINATION AND EXPIRY OF THE AGREEMENT

7.11 In addition to any other rights and remedies at law, this Agreement may be terminated by giving written notice to the other party who has breached this Agreement or defaulted in the following circumstances:

7.11.1 where the Company has failed to account or make payments as required under this Agreement;
7.11.2 where the Company or the Licensor has committed a serious breach of its obligations under this Agreement, unless such party rectifies the position, as far as reasonably possible, within [____________];
7.11.3 where the Company goes into voluntary or involuntary liquidation;
7.11.4 where the Company is declared insolvent, either in bankruptcy proceedings or other legal proceedings;
7.11.5 where an agreement with creditors has been reached by the Company due to its failure or inability to pay its debts as they fall due; or
7.11.6 where a receiver is appointed over the whole or part of the Company's business.

7.12 After the expiry or the termination or the completion of the sell-off period, the Licensor shall be entitled to instruct the Company to deliver or destroy all master material, licensed material, any copies of the master or licensed material and stocks previously manufactured under this Agreement in the possession of or under the control of the Company relating to the rights granted under this Agreement.

SELL-OFF PERIOD

7.13 The Company shall be entitled to sell off, on a non-exclusive basis, licensed material and stocks previously manufactured under this Agreement for the purpose of commercial sale for a period of six months from the date of expiry or termination, provided that the Company adheres to the terms of this Agreement.

GOVERNING LAW

7.14 This Agreement shall be subject to the Laws of England.

Attached to and forming part of this Agreement is Schedule 1—The Board Game.

Signed by: [____________]
FOR AND ON BEHALF OF THE LICENSOR

Date: [____________]

Signed by: [____________]
FOR AND ON BEHALF OF THE COMPANY

Date: [____________]

Witnessed by: [____________]

The Licensor confirms that he has received independent legal advice and is over the age of 18 years.

OUTLINE—EXCLUSIVE LICENCE FOR EXPLOITATION OF BOARD GAME

This Agreement is an exclusive licence for the manufacture and exploitation of a Board Game. It is assumed that the drawings and components and rules of the Game have been developed to the extent that a prototype has been produced by the original creator. The actual Licensed Article is a reproduction of the prototype. The original creator is referred to throughout the Agreement as "the Licensor" and the manufacturer and distribution party as "the Company".

The Company is paying to the Licensor a non-returnable advance which is to be off-set against royalties. The royalties are an agreed escalating percentage of the recommended retail selling price of the Licensed Article. The Licence is exclusive to the Company for a specified Licence Period within a specified territory. The copyright and design rights in the Board Game, including the title, remain the property of the Licensor. The moral rights of the Creator are being asserted in addition to the Company agreeing to provide a copyright notice and credit to the Licensor in all packaging and marketing material. The Company is agreeing that there will be a minimum retail selling price in respect of the Licensed Article.

The Licensor has the right to approve the Licensed Articles prior to their manufacture in the exact form in which they are to be sold.

The Company is responsible for all costs of development, production, manufacture and distribution. These costs are not off-set against the Licensor's Royalties.

The Licensor has the right to approve any third party who may become involved in the manufacture or distribution of the Licensed Articles.

A copy of the full two-dimensional illustrative and written details of the Board Game, including the colour, dimensions and materials of each of the components and a complete list of rules and instructions should be attached to and form part of this Agreement.

The indemnity liability of the Licensor to the Licensee has been fixed, but the liability of the Company is unlimited.

The Licensor could be paid fixed sums each year which are an advance against royalties as an alternative, and the type and nature of the accounting records to be examined could be expanded if the Company explains the basis on which it maintains its records. A provision could be added to keep all accounts documents and material for a fixed period, to provide supporting documentation with the report. It would be important that the Licensor saw how other goods had been marketed. The Licensor will only be notified of a claim under the indemnity if the Company intends to seek repayment. Under this type of agreement not all legal proceedings and threats would be notified.

The most likely type of problem is that the Licensed Article is discounted or sold at a lower price and the Company tries to account on the sums received which would inevitably be much lower.

Here there is no clause to allow the Company to deduct the production costs from any sums due to the Licensor.

SPONSORSHIP OF TELEVISION SERIES

BETWEEN:

(1) [______________]
of [______________] (to be known as the Sponsor in this Agreement)

AND

(2) [______________]
of [______________] (to be known as the Television Company in this Agreement).

IT IS AGREED as follows:

1. DEFINITIONS

The words below are agreed to mean as follows:

1.1 "The Programme" shall be the film and any associated sound recording entitled [______________] which shall be [______________] minutes in duration.

1.2 "The Programme Schedule" shall mean the following broadcast, transmission or supply details of the Programme:

Television channel: [______________];
Transmission dates: [______________];
Programme commences: [______________];
Programme ends: [______________].

1.3 "The Outline" means the brief description of the Programme. A copy of the Outline is attached to and forms part of this Agreement in Appendix A.

1.4 "The Sponsor's Logo" shall be the following material, together with any associated words.

A two-dimensional copy of the Sponsor's Logo is attached to and forms part of this Agreement in Appendix B specifying trademarks, designs, logo, slogan, texts, artwork, title, recordings, scripts, music, photographs, business name, graphics, computer generated material.

1.5 "The Sponsorship Fee" shall be the sum of [figure/currency].

1.6 "The Sponsorship Period" shall commence on [date] and shall continue until: [date].

1.7 "The Territory" shall be Europe, namely the following countries: the United Kingdom, Northern Ireland, Belgium, Denmark, France, Greece, Italy, Germany, Luxembourg, Netherlands, Spain, Portugal, Malta and [____________].

2. EXCLUSIVE SPONSORSHIP RIGHTS

2.1 In consideration of the payment of the Sponsorship Fee the Television Company grants to the Sponsor the exclusive right to sponsor and endorse the Programme and have the Sponsor's Logo incorporated in or with the Programme for the duration of the Sponsorship Period throughout the Territory.

2.2 The Television Company undertakes that no other third party will be entitled to sponsor, endorse, advertise on or promote its goods or products in conjunction with the Programme or have its logo, trademark, service mark or design, title, business name, slogan or otherwise incorporated into the Programme for the purpose of product or corporate promotion or advertising for the duration of the Sponsorship Period.

2.3 The Television Company undertakes to broadcast, transmit or supply the Programme in accordance with the Programme Schedule throughout the Territory during the Sponsorship Period.

2.4 The Sponsor acknowledges that all intellectual property rights including copyright, trademarks, designs, logos, slogans, text, artwork, title, recordings, scripts, photographs, business name, graphics, computer generated material and any other rights in the Programme shall remain the sole property of the Television Company and that the Sponsor shall not acquire any rights in the Programme, including any developments or variations.

2.5 The Television Company acknowledges that all intellectual property rights including copyright, trademarks, designs, logos, slogans, text, artwork, title, recordings, scripts, music, photographs, business name, graphics, computer generated material and any other rights in the Sponsor's Logo shall remain the sole and exclusive property of the Sponsor together with any goodwill and that the Television Company shall not acquire any rights in the Sponsor's Logo, including any developments or variation.

2.6 The Sponsor acknowledges that the sponsorship of the Programme does not give the Sponsor the right to use the Television Company's name, logo, programme title or any other material owned or entitled by the Television Company in any promotion, advertising, marketing or product owned or controlled by the Sponsor.

3. EDITORIAL CONTROL

3.1 The Sponsor acknowledges that all editorial decisions concerning the content of the Programme and any material before and after the opening and closing credits are entirely at the sole discretion of the Television Company.

3.2 The Television Company shall be entitled at its sole discretion and cost to make such changes, deletions, alterations, interruptions or additions to the Programme as may be required as a result of programme and editorial decisions. The Television Company agrees to ensure that as far as reasonably possible the Sponsor shall be informed in advance of any significant alterations.

3.3 The Television Company agrees that it shall not alter, change, add to or delete the final version of the Sponsor's logo, which is approved by the Sponsor, before, after or in the Programme unless it is caused by failure of faculties, national emergency, or some other cause beyond the reasonable control of the Television Company.

4. OBLIGATIONS OF THE SPONSOR

4.1 The Sponsor agrees to pay to the Television Company the Sponsorship Fee as follows:

4.1.1 [____________] upon signature of this Agreement;
4.1.2 [____________] within [____________] of the first transmission of the Programme on Channel [____________] and [____________]; and
4.1.3 [____________] on or before: [____________].

4.2 The Sponsor confirms that it is the sole owner of or controls and will have paid for and cleared for all copyright consents, releases, trademarks, logos, service marks, designs, slogans, title, artwork, music, graphics, computer generated material throughout the Territory in the Sponsor's Logo. The Sponsor confirms that the Sponsor's Logo does not infringe the copyright, trademarks or any other rights of any third party throughout the Territory.

4.3 The Sponsor confirms that the Sponsor's Logo does not and will not contain any obscene, defamatory, derogatory or offensive material and will not expose the Television Company to any civil or criminal proceedings.

4.4 The Sponsor undertakes that the specific product or services being promoted under this Agreement are: [____________] and that, together with all other products or services owned or controlled by the Sponsor which the public would reasonably associate with the Sponsor's Logo. The Sponsor shall ensure that they shall be safe and fit for their intended use and comply with all statutes, regulations, directives and codes in force in the Territory.

4.5 The Sponsor confirms that a comprehensive public liability insurance policy will be in force during the Sponsorship Period covering any writs, claims, actions or damages which may arise as a direct or indirect result of the use by the public of the specific product or services being promoted under this Agreement, together with all other products or services owned or controlled by the Sponsor which the public would reasonably associate with the Sponsor's Logo. The Sponsor undertakes to provide the Television Company with a copy of all relevant insurance policies upon request and evidence of payment of the premiums.

4.6 The Sponsor confirms that it has and will retain good title and authority to enter into this Agreement and is not bound by any previous agreement which adversely affects this Agreement.

4.7 The Sponsor acknowledges that the Television Company shall have the sole discretion as to the manner and method to be used in the scheduling, marketing, promoting and advertising of the Programme irrespective of any rights granted under this agreement and that the Television Company shall be entitled to retain all proceeds from the commercial exploitation of the Programme that no sums due from any exploitation of the Programme of any nature shall be due to the Sponsor provided that there is no reference to the Sponsor or the Sponsor's Logo in the Programme or any method of exploitation except television in any form.

4.8 The Sponsor agrees to bear all costs and expenses of developing, creating and producing the Sponsor's Logo and of supplying the Sponsor's Logo in a form acceptable to the Television Company for its incorporation before, after or in the Programme. It is accepted that the Television Company shall not bear any such costs. In the event that the material is developed and produced at the Television Company's studios, the Television Company shall agree a budget and invoice the Sponsor for payment in advance. The Television Company shall assign in full all rights, including copyright, trademarks in all media worldwide to the Sponsor in such material.

4.9 The Sponsor agrees to be bound by the requirements of the Television Company in respect of any sponsorship or advertising rules, directives or statutes which apply to the Television Company concerning the broadcast or transmission of the Sponsor's Logo, including its size, shape, colour, wording, on-screen position and general nature and to agree to be bound by any recommendation of the legal advisors or compliance officers as the case may be.

4.10 In the event that the Television Company does not wish to incorporate the Sponsors Logo due to unfavourable media reports regarding the Sponsor which might damage the Programme or the Television Company. Then the Sponsor agrees that the Television Company may terminate the Agreement subject to repayment of all the Sponsorship Fee paid to that date.

5. OBLIGATIONS OF THE TELEVISION COMPANY

5.1 The Television Company agrees to broadcast or transmit the Programme based on the Outline incorporating the Sponsor's Logo in the following on-screen position: [____________].

5.2 The Television Company confirms that the Sponsor's Logo will be reasonably, prominently and clearly identifiable in the Programme as follows:

Position: [____________]
Duration: [____________]
Background: [____________]
Links: [____________].

5.3 The Television Company undertakes that the Programme will not contain any obscene, offensive, derogatory or defamatory material and will not expose the Sponsor to any civil or criminal proceedings.

5.4 The Television Company undertakes that the Programme will not contain any material which infringes the intellectual property rights, copyright or any other rights of any third party throughout the Territory during the Sponsorship Period.

5.5 The Television Company agrees to ensure that the Sponsor's Logo will not infringe any sponsorship, advertising or promotional rules, directives or statutes which apply to the Television Company or the television industry concerning the Sponsor's Logo, including its size, shape, colour, wording, on-screen position and general nature.

5.6 The Television Company confirms that it is the sole owner of or controls all intellectual property rights, copyright and any other rights in the Programme.

5.7 The Television Company confirms that it shall be solely responsible for all costs incurred in the production, broadcast, transmission, distribution and exploitation of the Programme and that the Sponsor shall not be liable for any such sums.

5.8 The Television Company confirms that the Sponsor shall be entitled to the following text, slogan, trademark, credit in all publicity, promotion and marketing material appearing in any written form: [____________] distributed by the Sponsor in respect of the Programme. There shall be no such mention in any programme schedules issued by the Television Company.

5.9 The Television Company agrees that no part of the Sponsor's Logo shall be incorporated in any part of the Programme for any exploitation except on television.

5.10 In the event that there are changes in the Programme Schedule then the Television Company shall endeavour to notify the Sponsor in advance.

6. CONFIDENTIALITY

The Sponsor and the Television Company shall not disclose to any third party any confidential business or future plans of the other party at any time acquired during the existence of this Agreement. No reference is to be made to the terms of this Agreement by either party in any advertising, publicity or promotional material without the prior written consent of the other party.

7. AMENDMENTS

This Agreement supersedes all previous agreements, representations or promises and sets out all the terms agreed between the parties. Any amendment or alteration to this Agreement must be in writing and signed by an authorised signatory of each party.

8. NO PARTNERSHIP

This Agreement shall not be deemed to create any partnership or employment or agency between the parties, nor may it be relied upon by a third party.

9. NOTICES

Without prejudice to the right to serve notices by any other means any notice served under this Agreement shall be in writing. Any notice which has been sent by first class, pre-paid post shall be deemed to be received 48 hours thereafter (excluding Saturdays, Sundays and public holidays). For the purposes of this Agreement all notices shall be sent to the following addresses:

The Television Company: [____________];
The Sponsor: [____________].

10. TAXES

All sums payable under this Agreement are exclusive of any value added tax, sales tax or otherwise that may be payable by either party.

11. THIRD PARTY TRANSFERS

Neither party shall assign, transfer, charge or make over this Agreement or any of its rights or obligations.

12. FORCE MAJEURE

In the event that this Agreement cannot be performed or its obligations fulfilled for any reason beyond the reasonable control of the Sponsor or the Television Company, including war, industrial action, floods or Acts of God, unforeseen technical failure. Then such non-performance or failure to fulfil its obligations shall be deemed not to be a breach of this Agreement. In the event that this Agreement cannot be performed or its obligations fulfilled for any reason beyond the reasonable control of the defaulting party for a continuous period of [____________]. Then the other party may, at its discretion, terminate this Agreement by notice in writing at the end of that period, provided that both parties agree to negotiate, in good faith, an equitable settlement in respect of work already performed to the date of termination.

13. TERMINATION AND EXPIRY OF THE AGREEMENT

In addition to any other rights and remedies at law, this Agreement may be terminated by a party giving written notice to the other party which has breached this Agreement or has defaulted on any of the following grounds:

13.1.1 where the Sponsor or the Television Company has committed a serious breach of its obligations under this Agreement, unless such party rectifies the position, as far as reasonably possible, within: [____________];

13.1.2 where the Sponsor or the Television Company goes into voluntary or involuntary liquidation, is declared insolvent, either in bankruptcy proceedings or other legal proceedings, or where an agreement with creditors has been reached due to its failure or inability to pay its debts as they fall due, or where a receiver is appointed over the whole or part of the business.

14. LEGAL PROCEEDINGS

In the event that any legal proceedings are commenced or threatened by any third party against the Sponsor or the Television Company in respect of the Sponsors Logo and/or the Programme. The written notice of such claim or action shall be immediately given to the other party. Each party shall be responsible for dealing with its own legal problems and bear its own legal costs. Each party shall be afforded the opportunity to provide its opinion on the best course of action in the circumstances.

15. INDEMNITY

15.1 The Sponsor indemnifies the Television Company against all liabilities, claims, costs, damages, expenses including legal fees, expert witnesses and reports or otherwise reasonably and properly incurred by the Television Company arising out of any breach or alleged breach of this Agreement by the Sponsor up to a maximum total of [figure/currency] per year during the Sponsorship Period.

15.2 The Television Company indemnifies the Sponsor against all liabilities, claims, costs, damages, expenses including legal fees, expert witnesses and reports or otherwise reasonably and properly incurred by the Television Company arising out of any breach or alleged breach of this Agreement by the Sponsor up to a maximum total of: [figure/currency] whether during the existence of the Sponsorship Period or not.

15.3 In order to claim under the indemnity provisions the Sponsor and the Television Company must promptly notify the other party of any claim or legal proceedings and make no settlement or admission at that stage, and provide the other party with the opportunity to participate in or fully control any settlement or compromise or proceedings if appropriate.

16. GOVERNING LAW

This Agreement is subject to the jurisdiction of the [____________].

Attached to this Agreement are the following documents:

Appendix A—Outline
Appendix B—Sponsors Logo

[____________] [NAME/TITLE/DATE]
THE SPONSOR

[____________] [NAME/TITLE/DATE]
THE TELEVISION COMPANY

DATE OF THIS AGREMENT SHALL BE: [____________]

OUTLINE—SPONSORSHIP OF TELEVISION SERIES

This Agreement is between a Sponsor and a Television Company for the broadcast, transmission or supply of a Programme incorporating the Sponsor's Logo. The Sponsor's Logo could be a trademark, brand-name, logo or any words, phrases or images. The Television Company is specifically responsible for ensuring that the details of the Sponsor's Logo (such as relative size, shape, colour, on-screen position and general nature) do not infringe any laws, rules or directives by which the Television Company is bound.

The Sponsor is paying the Television Company a Sponsorship Fee, in return for which the Television Company is agreeing to incorporate the Sponsor's Logo before, after or in the Programme.

The Sponsor is responsible for ensuring that there exists a comprehensive public liability policy in respect of the products or services which are the subject matter of the Logo, together with all other products or services owned or controlled by the Sponsor with which the public would reasonably associate with the Sponsor's Logo.

A copy of the outline of the Programme and a copy of the Sponsor's Logo should be attached to the Agreement which should set out as much detail as possible.

The development and production of the material of the Sponsor's Logo may be supplied in finished form by the Sponsor or made in the Television Company's studios. In any event it is the Sponsor's responsibility to bear the cost of supplying all original material of trademarks, slogans, artwork, etc. that may be needed and the final production costs in the Programme of the Sponsor's Logo. In return the Television Company will transfer and assign all media rights in the Sponsor's Logo material which is produced. External decisions as regard schedules, marketing and exploitation are the Television Company's choice. An agreed credit and publicity statement regarding the sponsorship of the Programme should be set out to be included in all publicity and marketing of the Programme by the Television Company. The Sponsor's Logo is only to be used on television where the Television Company intends to license or exploit the Programme; elsewhere it will be removed.

SPONSORSHIP AGREEMENT FOR RADIO PROGRAMME

AN AGREEMENT made this [____________] day of [____________]

BETWEEN:

(1) [____________]
of [____________] (to be known as the Sponsor in this Agreement)

AND

(2) [____________]
of [____________] (to be known as the Radio Station in this Agreement).

IT IS AGREED as follows:

1. DEFINITIONS

The words below are agreed to mean as follows:

1.1 "The Programme" shall be the sound recording, whether live or prerecorded, broadcast or transmitted by the Radio Station entitled [____________] which shall be [____________] minutes in duration. Brief description: [____________].

1.2 "The Presenter" shall mean the following person who hosts the Programme: [____________].

1.3 "The Programme Schedule" shall mean the following broadcast or transmission details of the Programme:

radio frequencies: [____________];
broadcast/transmission dates: [____________];
time programme commences: [____________];
time programme ends: [____________].

1.4 "The Sponsor's Copy" shall be the following words, slogan, noises, music and lyrics relating to the Sponsor's Product which are to be incorporated into the Programme: [____________], together with a music cue sheet listing each musical work which is included, the name of the composer, author and publisher, the duration, work and the description of use in each case.

1.5 "The Sponsor's Product" shall mean the following materials, goods or services: [____________].

1.6 "The Sponsorship Fee" shall be the sum of: [figure/currency].

1.7 "The Sponsorship Period" shall commence on: [date] and shall continue until: [date].

1.8 "The Territory" shall be the following [countries/licensed area]: [____________].

2. NON-EXCLUSIVE SPONSORSHIP

2.1 In consideration of the Sponsorship Fee, the Radio Station grants to the Sponsor the non-exclusive right to sponsor the Programme and to promote the Sponsor's Product and to have the Sponsor's Copy incorporated into the Programme throughout the Territory for the duration of the Sponsorship Period.

2.2 The Sponsor agrees that the Radio Company shall be entitled to advertise, promote and endorse any third party products in the Programme or in conjunction with it whether or not it directly competes with the Sponsor's business or products.

2.3 The Sponsor acknowledges that all copyright and any other rights in the Programme shall remain the sole property of the Radio Station and that the Sponsor shall not acquire any rights in the Programme and that the Radio Station shall be entitled to retain all sums received from the exploitation of the Programme.

2.4 The Radio Station acknowledges that all copyright and any other rights in the Sponsor's Copy shall remain the sole and exclusive property of the Sponsor, together with any goodwill and that the Radio Station shall not acquire any rights in the Sponsor's Copy, including any developments or variations.

3. EDITORIAL CONTROL

3.1 The Sponsor acknowledges and confirms that all editorial decisions concerning the content of the advertising and sponsorship before, after or in the Programme shall be entirely at the sole discretion of the Radio Station.

3.2 The Radio Station shall be entitled at its sole discretion and cost to make such changes, deletions, alterations, interruptions or additions to the Programme as may be required without any notification to the Sponsor provided that it is an editorial or programme policy decision and overall the balance of the Sponsor's interest is not affected.

4. OBLIGATIONS OF THE SPONSOR

4.1 The Sponsor agrees to pay to the Radio Station, the Sponsorship Fee in full in advance on: [date].

4.2 The Sponsor confirms that it is the sole owner of or controls all copyright and any other rights throughout the Territory in the Sponsor's Copy and the Sponsor's Product. The Sponsor confirms that the Sponsor's Copy and the Sponsor's Product do not infringe the copyright or any other rights of any third party throughout the Territory.

4.3 The Sponsor confirms that the Sponsor's Copy does not contain any obscene, offensive or defamatory material and will not expose the Radio Station to any civil or criminal proceedings.

4.4 The Sponsor undertakes that the Sponsor's Product being promoted under this Agreement, together with all other products or services owned or controlled by the Sponsor which the public would reasonably associate with the Sponsor's Product, shall be safe and fit for their intended use and comply with all statutes, regulations, directives and codes in force.

4.5 The Sponsor confirms that a comprehensive public and product liability insurance policy will be in force for the duration of the Sponsorship Period covering any claims, actions or damages which may arise as a direct or indirect result of the use by the public of the specific product or services being promoted under this Agreement, together with all other products or services owned or controlled by the Sponsor which the public would reasonably associate with the Sponsor's Copy or the Sponsor's Product. The Sponsor undertakes to provide the Radio Station with a copy of all relevant insurance policies upon request.

4.6 The Sponsor confirms that it has and will retain good title and authority to enter into this Agreement and is not bound by any previous agreement which adversely affects this Agreement.

4.7 The Sponsor acknowledges that the Radio Station shall have the sole discretion as to the manner and method to be used in the marketing, promoting and advertising of the Programme.

4.8 The Sponsor agrees to bear all costs of creating the Sponsor's Copy and of supplying the Sponsor's Copy in a technical medium acceptable to the Radio Station for its incorporation in the Programme on or before: [date].

4.9 The Sponsor agrees to be bound by the requirements of the Radio Station in respect of any sponsorship or advertising rules, directives or statutes which apply to the Radio Station concerning the broadcast or transmission of the Sponsor's Copy, including its length, content, time of broadcast or transmission and general nature.

4.10 The Sponsor shall be responsible for the clearance and payment of all consents, clearance, waiver, and licences in respect of all copyright, contract and other rights in the Sponsor's Copy, and the supply of the Sponsors Copy in a technical medium acceptable to the Radio Station under this Agreement. In particular the Sponsor shall clear and pay for any music in respect of the performing rights in any music and the mechanical reproduction of any recordings by the Sponsor. The Radio Station shall be responsible for any sums due through its use of any music in respect of the performing rights.

4.11 The Sponsor agrees that the Radio Station shall be entitled at its sole discretion to replace the Presenter with a person of similar quality.

5. OBLIGATIONS OF THE RADIO STATION

5.1 The Radio Station undertakes to incorporate the Sponsor's Copy before, after or into the Programme and to broadcast or transmit the Programme and hosted by the

Presenter in accordance with the Programme Schedule throughout the Territory for the duration of the Sponsorship Period.

5.2 The Radio Station confirms that the Presenter is contractually bound to the Radio Station to be the on-air host of the Programme for the duration of the Sponsorship Period.

5.3 The Radio Station agrees to broadcast or transmit the Sponsor's Copy on the following number of occasions during the course of the Programme: [____________] of the following duration: [____________] seconds on each occasion in the following circumstances: [____________].

5.4 The Radio Station confirms that the Programme will be lawfully broadcast or transmitted in accordance with a statutory franchise which was granted on [____________] and is operative until [____________] and entitles the Radio Station to broadcast or transmit in the following frequencies throughout the Territory: [____________].

5.5 The Radio Station undertakes that the Programme will not contain any obscene, offensive or defamatory material and will not expose the Sponsor to any civil or criminal proceedings excluding any matters which may arise as a result of the broadcast or transmission of the Sponsor's Copy.

5.6 The Radio Station shall endeavour to ensure that the broadcast or transmission of the Sponsor's Copy will not infringe any sponsorship or advertising rules, directives or statutes which apply to the Radio Station.

5.7 The Radio Station undertakes to include in any programme schedule, promotional, advertising or publicity literature published or issued by the Radio Station in respect of the Programme, the following credit, trademark, logo, slogan and statement to the Sponsor: [____________].

5.8 The Radio Station confirms that it shall be solely responsible for all costs incurred in respect of the production, broadcast or transmission, promotion and marketing of the Programme and that the Sponsor shall not be liable for any such sums.

5.9 The Radio Station agrees that it shall be responsible for any such due in respect of the broadcast and transmission of the Sponsor's Copy in the Programme in respect of any performing rights.

6. INDEMNITY

The Sponsor and the Radio Station mutually undertake to indemnify the other against all liabilities, claims, demands, actions, costs, damages or loss arising out of any breach by either party of any of the terms of this Agreement. The Sponsor and the Radio Station agree to provide full details to the other party at the earliest opportunity.

7. CONFIDENTIALITY

The Sponsor and the Radio Station shall not disclose to any third party any confidential business or future plans of the other party at any time acquired during the existence of this Agreement. No reference is to be made to the terms of this Agreement by either party in any advertising, publicity or promotional material without the prior written consent of the other party. In the event that the Sponsor and the Radio Station agree to make a press statement, the following words shall be used: [____________].

8. AMENDMENTS

This Agreement supersedes all previous agreements, representations or promises and sets out all the terms agreed between the parties. Any amendment or alteration to this Agreement must be in writing and signed by an authorised signatory of each party.

9. NO AGENCY

This Agreement shall not be deemed to create any agency partnership or employment relationship between the parties.

10. NOTICES

Any notice served under this Agreement shall be in writing. For the purposes of this Agreement, all notices shall be sent to the following addresses:

The Radio Station: [Address] [Name/Title];
The Sponsor: [Address] [Name/Title].

11. TAXES

All sums payable under this Agreement are exclusive of any value added tax, sales tax or otherwise that may be payable by either party.

12. THIRD PARTY TRANSFERS

Neither party shall assign, transfer, charge or makeover this Agreement or any of its rights or obligations without the prior written consent of the other party.

13. FORCE MAJEURE

In the event that this Agreement cannot be performed or its obligations fulfilled for any reason beyond the reasonable control of the Sponsor or the Radio Station, including such events as war, industrial action, floods, Acts of God or unforeseen technical failure. Then such non-performance or failure to fulfil its obligations shall result in the temporary suspension of this Agreement. In the event that this Agreement cannot be performed or its obligations fulfilled for any reason beyond the reasonable control of the defaulting party for a continuous period of

[____________]. Then the other, non-defaulting party may, at its discretion, terminate this Agreement by notice in writing at the end of that period.

14. TERMINATION

This Agreement may be terminated by either party by written notice to the other defaulting party in the event that the other party shall have committed any material breach of this Agreement. There shall be no opportunity to remedy the breach.

15. GOVERNING LAW

This Agreement shall be construed, interpreted and fall within the jurisdiction of: [____________].

Signed by: [____________]
FOR AND ON BEHALF OF THE SPONSOR

Signed by: [____________]
FOR AND ON BEHALF OF THE RADIO STATION

OUTLINE—SPONSORSHIP AGREEMENT FOR RADIO PROGRAMME

This is a short, non-exclusive sponsorship agreement between a Sponsor and a Radio Station. The basis of this Agreement is that a Sponsor is providing a Sponsorship Fee to the Radio Company. In return, the Radio Company is agreeing to incorporate the Sponsor's Copy into the Radio Programme. It is important to remember the consequences of music being part of the Sponsor's Copy.

The non-exclusive nature of the Agreement allows any other party to sponsor the Programme.

The Sponsor must clear and pay for the Sponsor's Copy and material in a suitable technical form for the Radio Station. The undertakings are limited and could be reduced further; there is no ceiling on the indemnity provisions. There is no assertion of moral rights but this may be applicable in some cases.

The most important part is to specify the way in which the Sponsor's Copy is to be scheduled after, before or in the Programme.

PRODUCT PLACEMENT IN A TELEVISION PROGRAMME

AN AGREEMENT made this [____________] day of [____________]

BETWEEN:

(1) [____________]
of [____________] (to be known as the Company in this Agreement)

AND

(2) [____________]
of [____________] (to be known as the Television Company in this Agreement).

IT IS AGREED as follows:

1. DEFINITIONS

The words below are agreed to mean as follows:

1.1 "The Programme" shall be the film and any associated sound recording entitled: [____________] which shall be [____________] minutes in duration, briefly described: [____________].

1.2 "The Programme Schedule" shall mean the following broadcast or transmission details of the Programme:

Television channel: [____________];
Broadcast/transmission dates: [____________];
Time programme commences: [____________];
Time programme ends: [____________].

1.3 "The Scripts" shall mean the draft and final scripts of the Programme.

1.4 "The Company's Product" shall be the following product: [____________].
A two-dimensional copy of the Company's Product is attached to and forms part of this Agreement in Schedule A.

1.5 "The Company's Logo" shall mean the following artwork, designs, logos and trade-marks, slogan, computer generated material, text, title and graphics.
A copy of the Company's Product is attached to and forms part of this Agreement in Schedule B.

1.6 "The Placement Fee" shall be the sum of: [figure/currency].

1.7 "The term of the Agreement" shall commence on [the date of this Agreement] and shall continue until: [date].

1.8 "The Territory" shall be all countries, bases and locations throughout the world.

2. EXCLUSIVE RIGHTS

2.1 In consideration of the payment of the Placement Fee the Television Company grants to the Company the exclusive right to have a product in the field of: [____________] in the Programme and that the Company's Product and the Company's Logo shall be incorporated into the Programme for the Term of the Agreement throughout the Territory.

2.2 The Company acknowledges that the Television Company is entitled to arrange for other companies to sponsor, advertise or promote their products or services in the Programme, provided that no third party will be entitled to have its product, logo, trademark or design incorporated into the Programme which directly competes with the sales of the Company's Product in the field of: [____________].

2.3 The Company acknowledges that all copyright, trademarks, logo and title and any other rights in the Programme and any parts excluding the Company's Product and the Company's Logo are and shall remain the sole and exclusive property of the Television Company. That the Television Company shall be entitled to exploit the Programme in all media throughout the Territory and to retain all sums received from the exploitation of the Programme of whatever nature.

2.4 The Company shall not acquire any interest or rights in the Programme or parts, nor shall they be entitled to exploit it in any form except for the Company's Product and Company's Logo.

2.5 The Television Company acknowledges that all copyright, trademarks, logo and title and any other rights in the Company's Product and the Company's Logo are and shall remain the sole and exclusive property of the Company. That the Television Company shall not acquire any goodwill or rights in the Company's Product or the Company's Logo, including any developments or variations, nor shall they be entitled to exploit them.

3. EDITORIAL CONTROL

3.1 The Company acknowledges that all editorial decisions concerning the content of the Programme are entirely at the sole discretion of the Television Company.

3.2 The Company acknowledges that the Television Company shall be entitled, at its sole discretion and cost, to make such changes, deletions, alterations, interruptions or additions to the Programme as may be required by editorial or programming decisions or otherwise.

4. OBLIGATIONS OF THE COMPANY

4.1 The Company agrees to pay to the Television Company; the Placement Fee as follows: [____________].

4.2 The Company confirms that it is the sole owner of or controls all rights in the Company's Product and the Company's Logo and they do not infringe the copyright or any other rights of any third party throughout the Territory.

4.3 The Company confirms that the Company's Product and the Company's Logo do not contain any obscene, offensive or defamatory material and will not expose the Television Company to any civil or criminal proceedings.

4.4 The Company undertakes that the Company's Product being promoted under this Agreement shall be safe and fit for its intended use and comply with all statutes, regulations, directives and codes in force.

4.5 The Company confirms that a comprehensive public and product liability insurance policy is in force covering any claims, actions or damages which may arise as a direct or indirect result of the use by the public of the Company's Product being promoted under this Agreement.

4.6 The Company confirms that it has and will retain good title and authority to enter into this Agreement and is not bound by any previous agreement which adversely affects this Agreement.

4.7 The Company acknowledges that the Television Company shall have the sole discretion as to the manner and method to be used in the production, distribution, marketing, promotion, advertising and exploitation of the Programme.

4.8 The Company agrees to be bound by any sponsorship, advertising or other rules, directives or statutes which apply to the Television Company in respect of the incorporation of the Company's Product and the Company's Logo in the Programme.

4.9 The Company acknowledges that it shall suitable technical material of the Company's Product and the Company's Logo as follows at the Company's cost: [____________] on loan to the Television Company for the purpose of incorporating the Company's Product and Company's Logo in the Programme and such other material as may be required upon request.

4.10 The Company agrees that it shall not be entitled to use, exploit or promote the title of the Programme or any script, artist, music, slogan or any other parts of any nature in conjunction with the Company's products or any other products or services of the Company under any circumstances. This Agreement is solely related to the placement of the Company's Product on the Programme and not a sub-licence or other authority to the Company.

4.11 The Company shall not acquire nor have any interest or rights in any part of the Programme at any time of any nature. The only rights of the Company are limited to the Company's Product and the Company's Logo.

4.12 The Company accepts that the script, Programme Schedule and other aspects of the Programme may be changed for programme policy, editorial and legal reasons at the Television Company's own discretion. In the event that this results in less exposure of the Company's Product and Company's Logo the Company agrees that this is acceptable provided that the Company's Product is visible on screen for at [____________].

4.13 The Company accepts that any reference to the Company's Product and Company's Logo in the Programme in the publicity, advertising and promotional material may differ depending on the circumstances, and on occasions may not be mentioned at all.

5. OBLIGATIONS OF THE TELEVISION COMPANY

5.1 The Television Company agrees to produce the Programme in accordance with the Scripts in colour and in the English language.

5.2 The Television Company undertakes to broadcast, transmit or supply the Programme incorporating the Company's Product and the Company's Logo in accordance with the Programme Schedule in: [country/territory].

5.3 In consideration of the payment of the Placement Fee, the Television Company agrees to incorporate The Company's Product in the Programme in the following manner and scenes with reference to the Scripts: [____________].

5.4 The Television Company confirms that the Company's Product will be reasonably and clearly identifiable in the Programme and in any event will be seen on-screen on not less than [____________] separate occasions and on each occasion will be on-screen for not less than [____________] seconds.

5.5 The Television Company agrees to incorporate the Company's Logo in the Programme in the following manner and scenes with reference to the Scripts: [____________].

5.6 The Television Company confirms that the Company's Logo will be reasonably and clearly identifiable in the Programme and in any event will be seen on-screen on not less than [____________] separate occasions and on each occasion will be on-screen for not less than [____________] seconds.

5.7 The Television Company undertakes that the Programme, except for the Company's Product and the Company's Logo, will not contain any obscene, offensive or defamatory material and will not expose the Company to any civil or criminal proceedings.

5.8 The Television Company undertakes that the Programme, except for the Company's Product and the Company's Logo, will not contain any material which infringes the copyright or any other rights of any third party throughout the Territory.

5.9 The Television Company agrees to ensure that the Programme will not infringe any sponsorship or advertising rules, directives or statutes which apply to the Television Company.

5.10 The Television Company agrees that it will be solely responsible for all costs incurred in respect of the production, distribution, marketing, advertising and exploitation of the Programme.

5.11 The Television Company agrees that it shall pay all the cost of producing and incorporating the Company's Product and Company's Logo in the Programme subject to the supply of the original material from the Company.

5.12 The Television Company confirms that it has and will retain good title and authority to enter into this Agreement and is not bound by any previous agreement which adversely affects this Agreement.

5.13 In all publicity, promotional and advertising material for the Programme it is agreed that no other party shall have their product or logo more frequently or prominently displayed then the Company.

5.14 The Television Company shall include the following mention, credit, photograph and statement relating to the Company's Product and the Company's Logo in the Programme in appropriate publicity, advertising and publicity material.

6. LOSS

It is agreed that neither the Company nor the Television Company shall be held liable to the other party for any damages, loss of production, loss of profit or loss of any kind which arises as an indirect result of this Agreement or as a result of interruptions, delays, inaccuracies, errors, omissions, failure to transmit and [____________].

7. RISK

Risk and responsibility for any material supplied under this Agreement shall not pass until they are delivered and accepted.

8. INDEMNITY

8.1 The Company shall keep the Television Company indemnified from and against all liabilities, actions, claims, proceedings, damages and losses suffered or incurred directly [but not indirectly] by the Television Company or awarded against the Television Company or any corporation or settlement agreed in consequence of any breach or alleged breach of this Agreement by the Company for any other third party appointed by them.

8.2 The Television Company agrees to indemnify the Company in respect of all liabilities, actions, claims, proceedings, damages and losses suffered or incurred directly [but not indirectly] by the Company or awarded against the Company or any compensation or settlement agreed in consequence of any breach or alleged breach of this Agreement by the Company or any other third party appointed by them.

9. CONFIDENTIALITY

9.1 The Company agrees not to disclose any script, text, title, content, artiste details, programme schedule or any other matter which relates to the Programme, or the

Company's Product or Company's Logo in the Programme prior to the transmission of the Programme without the prior written consent of the Television Company. Failure to adhere to this clause will result in the removal of the Company's Product and Company's Logo from the Programme and the right of the Television Company to return all sums paid to the Television Company to that time.

9.2 Both parties shall maintain the following issues in the utmost secrecy and confidence:

9.2.1 the terms of this Agreement;

9.2.2 all representations, documents, e-mails, and recordings viewed or made or exchanged prior to or after this Agreement relating to the Company's Product the Company's Logo and the Programme. Disclosure shall only be on the agreed basis of this Agreement or with the prior approval of the other party.

10. AMENDMENTS

This Agreement must not be changed, modified, amended or supplemented except in one written document signed by both parties.

11. NO PARTNERSHIP

This Agreement does not deem or imply a partnership or agency and neither party shall have the authority or power to bind the other in any way.

12. NOTICES

All notices shall be in writing and sent to the principal office of the parties and addressed to the Managing Director.

13. VALUE ADDED TAX

All sums payable under this Agreement are exclusive of any value added tax that may be payable by either party.

14. THIRD PARTY TRANSFERS

Neither party shall assign, charge or make over this Agreement or any of its rights or obligations without the prior written consent of the other party. Such consent may not be unreasonably withheld or delayed in the case of a parent, subsidiary or associated company seeking consent. Any assignee shall expressly provide a written undertaking that will fulfil the rights and obligations of the Agreement. No such assignment shall relieve the party of its obligations under this Agreement.

15. FORCE MAJEURE

In the event that this Agreement cannot be performed or its obligations fulfilled for any reason beyond the reasonable control of the Company or the Television Company, including such events as war, industrial action, floods or Acts of God, unforeseen technical failure. Then such non-performance or failure to fulfil its obligations shall be deemed not to be a breach of this Agreement. In the event that this Agreement cannot be performed or its obligations fulfilled for any reason beyond the reasonable control of the defaulting party for a continuous period of [____________]. Then the other party may, at its discretion, terminate this Agreement by notice in writing at the end of that period, provided that both parties agree to negotiate, in good faith, an equitable settlement in respect of work already performed to the date of termination.

16. TERMINATION

16.1 In addition to any other rights and remedies at law, this Agreement may be terminated by giving written notice to the other party who has breached this Agreement or defaulted in the following circumstances:

16.1.1 where the Company has failed to account or make payments as required under this Agreement;
16.1.2 where the Company or the Television Company has committed a serious breach of its obligations under this Agreement, unless such party rectifies the position, as far as reasonably possible, within [____________];
16.1.3 where the Company or the Television Company goes into voluntary or involuntary liquidation;
16.1.4 where the Company or the Television Company is declared insolvent either in bankruptcy proceedings or other legal proceedings;
16.1.5 where an agreement with creditors has been reached by the Company or the Television Company due to its failure or inability to pay its debts as they fall due; or
16.1.6 where a receiver is appointed over the whole or part of the Company's or the Television Company's business.

17. JURISDICTION

This Agreement shall be subject to the Laws of [____________] and any dispute concerning it or its interpretation shall be decided in that jurisdiction.

18. WAIVER

No waiver whether express or implied by this Company or the Television Company shall be deemed as waiver or consent to any subsequent or continuing breach of this Agreement. Nor shall any failure to exercise and/or delay in exercising any right or remedy under this Agreement operate as a waiver of such right.

19. MEDIATION

The Company and the Television Company agree that in the event of any dispute difference or other problem that may arise under this Agreement which cannot be resolved by negotiation between the parties. Then without prejudice to any legal rights of either party they shall endeavour to agree the appointment of a third person to mediate between the parties. The cost of such person is to be shared equally between the parties.

WE AGREE TO THE TERMS OF THIS AGREEMENT:

[____________]

THE COMPANY

[NAME/TITLE]

[____________]

THE TELEVISION AGREEMENT

[NAME/TITLE]

Attached to this Agreement are Schedule A [the description of the Company's Product] and Schedule B [the Company's Logo].

OUTLINE—PRODUCT PLACEMENT IN A TELEVISION PROGRAMME

This is an exclusive product placement agreement for a particular type of product, *i.e.* toy, cosmetic, drink or car. It does not exclude other product placement deals for the same Programme. It is only exclusive to a particular area of goods or services. This is just another form of advertising but is not openly recognised by the authorities or the public, although it is clearly present these days. The Company is paying a Placement Fee for its specified Company Product and Company Logo to be in the Programme. The Agreement will be based on the Company having viewed all or part of the Script and it being agreed that the Product will be sited in particular scenes and for a specific period. It is important that the Company is not seen to interfere with the editorial decisions of the Programme, which should be at the Television Company's sole discretion. Both the Script and Programme Schedule may be changed by the Television Company. The Company is not to use the programme or any part to promote the Company's Product, any other product or to use any title, content or music from the Programme without consent.

The Company is to supply suitable technical material of its product and logo, but it will be incorporated at the Television Company's cost into the Programme. A mediation provision has been included if there is a dispute. It may be helpful to nominate a person or company in advance.

SPONSORSHIP AND PRODUCT PLACEMENT IN VIDEO

AGREEMENT BETWEEN THE FOLLOWING PARTIES:

(1) [______________]
of [______________] (to be known as the Sponsor in this Agreement)

AND

(2) [______________]
of [______________] (to be known as the Production Company in this Agreement).

IT IS AGREED by the parties as follows:

1. DEFINITIONS

The words below are to mean as follows:

1.1 "The Programme" shall be the film and any associated sound recording based on the Treatment and the Scripts entitled [______________] which shall be [______________] minutes in duration.

1.2 "The Treatment" shall be the summary of the contents and structure of the Programme. A copy of the Treatment is attached to and forms part of this Agreement in Schedule A.

1.3 "The Scripts" shall be the draft and final scripts based on the Treatment prepared by the Writer.

1.4 "The Production Schedule" shall be the dates, times and locations of making the Programme including pre-production, production, post-production and delivery of the Programme. A copy of the Production Schedule is attached to and forms part of this Agreement in Schedule B.

1.5 "The Sponsorship Fee" shall be the sum of [figure/currency].

1.6 "The Sponsorship Period" shall commence on: [date] and shall continue until: [date].

1.7 "The Key Personnel" shall be as follows:

1.7.1 The Producer [______________];
1.7.2 The Director [______________];

1.7.3 The Writer [____________];
1.7.5 The Presenter [____________]; and
1.7.6 Any other(s) [____________].

1.8 "The Territory" shall mean the following countries and their territorial waters and any ships, aeroplanes, oil rigs and other bases: [____________].

1.9 "The Sponsor's Logo" shall be the following material, together with any allocated words. A two-dimensional copy of the Sponsor's Logo is attached to and forms part of this Agreement in Schedule C, specifying trademarks, designs, logos, slogan, text, artwork, title, recordings, scripts, music, photographs, business name, graphics, computer generated material.

1.10 "The Sponsor's Product" shall be the following item: [____________]. A two dimensional representation of the Sponsors Product is attached to and forms part of this Agreement in Schedule D.

1.11 "The Videogram Rights" shall mean the right to transfer, manufacture, duplicate, distribute, sale, rent, license, supply or otherwise exploit the Programme in the form of videograms, video discs, video cassettes or some other similar device such as DVDs whether invented now or created in the future which is used to play the Programme on a television whether the playback device is a separate machine or an integral part of the television which is intended for home use only by the public.

1.12 "The Non-Theatric Rights" exercise the Video Rights to audiences outside the home and domestic reception for exhibition to businesses, industries, educational, cultural, religious, charitable and social institutions and bodies including but not limited to schools, churches, museums, hospitals, prisons, camps, drama groups, colleges, universities, hotels and private clubs, where no fee is charged for the public to view the Programme in the audience even though payment may be made to the Licensor for the supply of the Master Material for the exhibition.

2. NON-EXCLUSIVE SPONSORSHIP RIGHTS

2.1 In consideration of the Sponsorship Fee the Production Company grants to the Sponsor the non-exclusive right to have the Sponsor's Logo and the Sponsor's Product incorporated in the Programme for the duration of the Sponsorship Period.

2.2 The Sponsor acknowledges that the Production Company is entitled to arrange sponsorship with other third parties for the Programme whether or not it directly competes with the Sponsor's Product.

2.3 The Sponsor acknowledges that all intellectual property rights, including copyright, trademarks, designs, logos, slogan, text, artwork, title, recordings, scripts, photographs, business name, graphics, computer generated material and all other material and any other rights in the Programme and part(s) shall be the sole property of the Production Company and that the Production Company shall be entitled to exploit the Programme in all media throughout the Territory and to retain all sums received from the exploitation of the Programme. That the Sponsor shall not be entitled to any such sums.

2.4 The Production Company acknowledges that the Sponsor's Logo and the Sponsor's Product shall remain the sole and exclusive property of the Sponsor and that the Production Company will not acquire any rights in the Sponsor's Logo or the Sponsor's Product, including any developments or variations.

2.5 The Sponsor agrees that parts of the Programme including the Sponsor's Product and Sponsor's Logo may be included on other third party material for the purpose of advertising and promotion of the Programme.

3. EDITORIAL CONTROL

The Sponsor acknowledges that all editorial decisions concerning the Programme are entirely at the sole discretion of the Production Company.

4. OBLIGATIONS OF THE SPONSOR

4.1 The Sponsor agrees to pay to the Production Company the Sponsorship Fee as follows: [____________].

4.2 The Sponsor confirms that it is the sole owner of or controls all intellectual property rights including copyright and any other rights throughout the Territory in the Sponsor's Logo and the Sponsor's Product. The Sponsor confirms that the Sponsor's Logo and the Sponsor's Product do not and will not infringe the copyright or any other rights of any third party throughout the Territory.

4.3 The Sponsor confirms that the Sponsor's Logo and the Sponsor's Product do not contain any obscene, offensive or defamatory material and will not expose the Production Company to any civil or criminal proceedings.

4.4 The Sponsor undertakes that the Sponsor's Product being promoted under this Agreement, together with all other products or services owned or controlled by the Sponsor which the public would reasonably associate with the Sponsor's Logo, shall be safe and fit for their intended use and comply with all statutes, regulations, directives and codes in force.

4.5 The Sponsor confirms that a product public liability insurance policy is or will be in force covering any claims, actions or damages which may arise as a direct or indirect result of the use by the public of the Sponsor's Product being promoted under this Agreement. The Sponsor undertakes to provide the Production Company with a copy of the policy upon request and proof of its validity.

4.6 The Sponsor confirms that it has and will retain good title and authority to enter into this Agreement and is not bound by any previous agreement which adversely affects this Agreement.

4.7 The Sponsor acknowledges that the Production Company shall decide as to the manner and method to be used in the marketing, promoting and advertising the Programme and not the Sponsor.

4.8 The Sponsor agrees to bear all costs of creating the Sponsor's Logo and of supplying the Sponsor's Logo in a form acceptable to the Production Company for its incorporation in the Programme. The Sponsor agrees to provide at its sole cost [____________]number of the Sponsor's Product.

4.9 The Sponsor agrees to be bound by the requirements of the Production Company in respect of any sponsorship or advertising rules, directives or statutes which apply to the Programme concerning the exploitation of the Videogram Rights and the Non-Theatric Rights within the Territory.

5. OBLIGATIONS OF THE PRODUCTION COMPANY

5.1 The Production Company agrees to produce the Programme using the Key Personnel, in accordance with the Treatment, the Scripts and the Production Schedule.

5.2 The Production Company undertakes to use its endeavours to exploit the Videogram Rights and the Non-Theatric Rights in the Programme throughout the Territory for the duration of The Sponsorship Period.

5.3 The Production Company confirms that the Sponsor's Logo will be reasonably, prominently and clearly identifiable when shown in the Programme and in the following size: [____________].

5.4 During the course of the Programme the Production Company undertakes that the Sponsor's Logo will appear on-screen as follows: [____________].

5.5 The Production Company confirms that the Programme shall be produced in colour, in the English language and in the following format: [____________].

5.6 The Production Company shall deliver the final script to the Sponsor as soon as reasonably possible but in any event on or before: [date].

5.7 The Production Company undertakes that all sums due in respect of the production and exploitation of the Programme will be paid by the Production Company and that the Sponsor is not and will not be liable for any such payments.

5.8 The Production Company undertakes that all rights, copyright, consents, releases, waivers, music of any nature (except the Sponsor's Product and Sponsor's Logo) in respect of the Programme shall be cleared and paid for by the Production Company.

5.9 The Production Company agrees to provide the following credit, trademark, logo, design, copyright notice, statement or otherwise to the Sponsor in the following circumstances:

5.9.1 [____________] on all packaging, labels, jackets, or sleeves;
5.9.2 [____________] on all posters, brochures, catalogues, advertisements;
5.9.3 [____________] on the first press release;
5.9.4 [____________] on display stands at exhibitions.

5.10 The Production Company agrees to provide the Sponsor one copy and one sample of each of the publicity, promotional, advertising and packaging material in respect of the marketing and distribution of the Programme upon request by the Sponsor.

5.11 The Production Company acknowledges that it shall be solely responsible for any sums due in respect of the manufacture, distribution, marketing and exploitation of the Videogram Rights and the Non-Theatric Rights in the Programme and that the Sponsor shall not be liable for any such payments.

5.12 The Production Company undertakes to provide the Sponsor with [____________] number of free copies of the Programme in such form as will be made available to the general public.

5.13 The Production Company undertakes that the Programme will not contain any obscene, offensive or defamatory material and will not expose the Sponsor to any civil or criminal proceedings; excluding the Sponsor's Logo and the Sponsor's Product.

5.14 The Production Company undertakes that the Programme will not contain any material which infringes the copyright or any other rights of any third party in the Territory, excluding the Sponsor's Logo and the Sponsor's Product.

5.15 The Production Company agrees to ensure that the inclusion of the Sponsor's Logo and the Sponsor's Product in the Programme will not infringe any sponsorship or advertising rules, directives or statutes which apply to commercial exploitation of the Videogram Rights and the Non-Theatric Rights in the Programme throughout the Territory during the Sponsorship Period.

6. MISCELLANEOUS

MUTUAL INDEMNITY

6.1 The Sponsor and the Production Company mutually undertake to indemnify the other against all liabilities, claims, demands, actions, costs, damages or loss arising out of any breach by either party of any of the terms of this Agreement.

6.2 In the event of any claim, dispute, action, writ or summons in connection with clause 6.1, the Sponsor and the Production Company agree to provide full details to the other party at the earliest opportunity and shall not settle any such matter without first consulting the other party.

CONFIDENTIALITY

6.3 The Sponsor and the Production Company shall not disclose to any third party any confidential business or future plans of the other party at any time acquired during the existence of this Agreement and no reference is to be made to the terms of this Agreement by either party in any advertising, publicity or promotional material without the prior written consent of the other party.

AMENDMENTS AND ALTERATIONS

6.4 This Agreement supersedes all previous agreements, representations or promises and sets out all the terms agreed between the parties. Any amendment or alteration to this Agreement must be in writing and signed by an authorised signatory of each party.

NO PARTNERSHIP

6.5 This Agreement shall not be deemed to create any partnership or employment or agency relationship between the parties. No party has the authority to commit or pledge the other under any circumstances.

NOTICES

6.6 Any notice served under this Agreement shall be in writing. For the purposes of this Agreement, all notices shall be sent to the following addresses:

The Production Company: [Address] [Name] [Title];
The Sponsor: [Address] [Name] [Title].

VALUE ADDED TAX

6.7 All sums payable under this Agreement are exclusive of any value added tax that may be payable by either party.

THIRD PARTY TRANSFERS

6.8 Neither party shall assign, transfer, charge or make over this Agreement or any of its rights or obligations without the prior written consent of the other party except a parent, associated or subsidiary company which provides a written undertaking and evidence of the intention to fulfil the obligations due under this Agreement.

FORCE MAJEURE

6.9 In the event that this Agreement cannot be performed or its obligations fulfilled for any reason beyond the reasonable control of the Sponsor or the Production Company, including such events as war, industrial action, floods, Acts of God or unforeseen technical failure, then this Agreement shall be suspended from the date of the force majeure. In the event that this Agreement cannot be performed or its obligations fulfilled for any reason beyond the reasonable control of the defaulting party for a continuous period of [____________]. Then the other, non-defaulting party may, at its discretion, terminate this Agreement by notice in writing at the end of that period.

TERMINATION

6.10 This Agreement may be terminated at any time by written notice by either party to the other party that has defaulted and committed a material breach of this Agreement, or is unable to fulfil its obligations due to its inability to pay its debts as they fall due.

STOCK

6.11 After the expiry, termination or end of this Agreement the Production Company shall no longer be entitled to exploit copies of the Programme incorporating the Sponsor's Logo or Product without the consent of the Sponsor. In the event that no consent is provided, all such references should be reserved. This shall only apply to copies of the Programme in the possession or under the control of the Production Company.

GOVERNING LAW

6.12 This Agreement shall be interpreted by and fall within the jurisdiction of any country in the Territory that may be appropriate in the circumstances.

AGREEMENT DATED: [____________]

SIGNED: [____________] **THE SPONSOR**

SIGNED: [____________] **THE PRODUCTION COMPANY**

ATTACHMENTS:

SCHEDULE A—THE TREATMENT
SCHEDULE B—THE PRODUCTION SCHEDULE
SCHEDULE C—THE SPONSOR'S LOGO
SCHEDULE D—THE SPONSOR'S PRODUCT

OUTLINE—SPONSORSHIP AND PRODUCT PLACEMENT IN VIDEO

This is a simple Product placement agreement between a Sponsor and a Production Company. The Programme is aimed primarily at the home video market. The Sponsor is paying the Production Company a Sponsorship Fee, which can be in stages. The Production Company is agreeing that the Sponsor's Product and Logo are to be incorporated into the Programme on a non-exclusive basis. The rules relating to sponsorship of videos for home use are less stringent than those which apply to television programmes. Accordingly, the extent of the exposure of the Sponsor's Logo and Product during the course of the video is governed more by commercial considerations than by statutes and rules.

There are limited undertakings by either party. The document of reassurance relating to the safety of the product is important. An important aspect of this Agreement is the details of the sponsorship in the Programme itself, and elsewhere on labels, catalogues and adverts. None of the production costs are attributed to the Sponsor, but there could be a fixed sum agreed. There is no assertion of moral rights. The Sponsor is not to be allowed direct involvement in the editorial decisions, but this is achieved by looking at the Treatment, Scripts, Production Schedule other elements of the Programme. The Production Company has agreed that it will adhere to these documents, so it is important that they are attached to the Agreement.

PROMOTIONAL USE OF COMPANY'S LOGO

AN AGREEMENT made this [____________] day of [____________]

BETWEEN:

(1) [____________]
of [____________] (to be known as the Licensor in this Agreement)

AND

(2) [____________]
of [____________] (to be known as the Licensee in this Agreement).

IT IS AGREED as follows:

1. DEFINITIONS

The words below are agreed to mean as follows:

1.1 "The Licensor's Logo" shall be the following trademark, service mark, design or logo, slogan, text, graphics or other material.
A two-dimensional copy of the Licensor's Logo is attached to and forms part of this Agreement in Schedule 1.

1.2 "The Licensee's Product" shall be the following product which is produced, manufactured and distributed by or on behalf of the Licensee: [____________].
A two-dimensional copy of the Licensee's Product is attached to and forms part of this Agreement in Schedule 2.

1.3 "The Product Package" shall mean all material associated with the Licensee's Product including any packaging, labels, advertising, promotion and publicity material, films, videos, television and radio commercials and any other visual or sound recordings, photographs, computer generated graphics, scripts, artwork, music, DVD, CD-ROM, internet, mobile phones.

1.4 "The Licence Fee" shall be the sum of [figure/currency].

1.5 "The Territory" shall be the following countries of the world: [____________].

1.6 "The Licence Period" shall commence on: [date] and shall continue until: [date].

2. NON-EXCLUSIVE LICENCE

2.1 In consideration of the payment of the Licence Fee, the Licensor grants to the Licensee the non-exclusive right to reproduce the Licensor's Logo in each and every form of the Product Package throughout the Territory for the duration of the Licence Period in accordance with the terms of this Agreement.

2.2 The Licensee confirms that it owns or controls all intellectual property rights including copyright and any other rights in the Licensee's Product and the Product Package throughout the Territory.

2.3 The Licensor confirms that it is the sole owner of or controls all intellectual property rights including copyright and any other rights in the Licensor's Logo throughout the Territory.

2.4 The Licensee acknowledges that all intellectual property rights including copyright and any other rights in the Licensor's Logo, together with any goodwill shall belong to and remain the sole property of the Licensor. That the Licensee shall not acquire any rights or interests in the Licensor's Logo or in any trademark, design, title or artwork, including any developments or variations. Nor shall the Licensee attempt to register such interest at any time.

2.5 The Licensee shall ensure that the following words are set out on each and every item of the Product Package: [The trademark is manufactured and reproduced under licence from the Licensor and the trademark is the registered trademark of the Licensor.].

3. OBLIGATIONS OF THE LICENSEE

3.1 In consideration of the rights granted under this Agreement, the Licensee shall pay to the Licensor the Licence Fee as follows:

3.1.1 [____________] upon signature of this Agreement;
3.1.2 [____________] on or before: [____________];
3.1.3 [____________] on or before: [____________].

3.2 The Licensee confirms that the Licensor's Logo shall be incorporated in the Product Package in the following specific manner:

packaging: [____________];
labels: [____________];
publicity, advertising and promotional literature: [____________];
radio commercials: [____________];
television commercials: [____________];
any other material: [____________].

3.3 The Licensee agrees that it shall be solely responsible for all costs and expenses incurred in respect of reproducing and incorporating the Licensor's Logo in the Product Package.

3.4 The Licensee agrees that the Licensor shall be entitled to approve all material of the Licensee's Product and the Product Package prior to production, manufacture and distribution and the Licensee acknowledges that such approval must be in writing.

3.5 The Licensee undertakes to supply at its sole cost such samples of the Licensee's Product and the Product Package in the exact form and material in which the Licensee proposes to manufacture, distribute, sell and market the Licensee's Product and the Product Package.

3.6 The Licensee agrees that it is solely responsible for all costs incurred in respect of the development, production, manufacture, distribution, marketing and any other commercial exploitation of the Licensee's Product and the Product Package.

3.7 The Licensee undertakes that the Licensee's Product and the Product Package, together with all other products or services owned or controlled by the Licensee, which the public would reasonably associate with the Licensee shall be safe and fit for their intended use and comply with all statutes, regulations, directives and codes in force.

3.8 The Licensee confirms that a comprehensive public and product liability insurance policy is and will be in force covering any claims, actions or damages which may arise as a direct or indirect result of the use by the public of the Licensee's Product and the Product Package, together with all other products or services owned or controlled by the Licensee, which the public would reasonably associate with the Licensee and the Licensee agrees to provide the Licensor with a copy of all relevant insurance policies upon request.

3.9 The Licensee confirms that it has and will retain good title and authority to enter into this Agreement and is not bound by any previous agreement which adversely affects this Agreement.

3.10 The Licensee undertakes that the Licensee's Product and the Product Package will not be offensive or obscene in nature or derogatory of any third party and will not expose the Licensor to any civil or criminal proceedings during the Licence Period.

3.11 The Licensee will ensure that the use of the Licensor's Logo will not infringe any sponsorship or advertising rules which may apply.

3.12 The Licensee undertakes that the Licensee's Product and the Product Package will not contain any material which infringes the intellectual property rights including copyright, design rights or any other rights of any third party in the Territory during the Licence Period.

3.13 The Licensee acknowledges and agrees to ensure that all third parties to be contracted by the Licensee in respect of the Licensee's Product and the Product Package will agree that all intellectual property rights including copyright and any other rights concerning the Licensor's Logo, together with any goodwill are and shall remain the sole property of the Licensor.

3.14 The Licensee agrees that it shall not deviate from the style book of the trademark supplied by the Licensor and that the Licensee shall use the trademark in the exact form, size, manner, colour and position specified.

3.15 The Licensee shall ensure that the Licensee's Logo is given suitable prominence in respect of any material and that no other third party's trademark or logo is more dominant.

3.16 The Licensee agrees that the Licensor's Logo shall not be used for any other purpose other than the promotion and endorsement of the Licensee's Product.

3.17 The Licensee agrees not to enter into any agreement to endorse, promote, advertise or use the logos, trademarks or other intellectual property rights of the following third parties during the Licence Period: [____________], whether in conjunction with the Licensee's Product or some other product or service of the Licensee.

3.18 The Licensee accepts that nothing in this Agreement shall prevent or restrict the Licensor at any time from granting or licensing rights in the Licensor's Logo to any other third party.

3.19 The Licensee accepts and shall ensure that there is no alteration or change of the Licensor's Logo in any of the Licensee's Product without the prior written approval in each case by the Licensor.

3.20 The Licensee shall provide the Licensor with a minimum number of [__________] free copies in each and every medium and/or format in which the Licensee uses the Licensor's Logo whether commercially released to the public or not.

4. OBLIGATIONS OF THE LICENSOR

4.1 The Licensor confirms that it is a bona fide registered company under [English Law] with the following registration number: [____________].

4.2 The Licensor confirms that it is the sole owner of or controls all intellectual property rights including copyright, trademark and service mark rights and any other rights in the Licensor's Logo throughout the Territory.

4.3 The Licensor confirms that it has full title and authority to enter into this Agreement and is not bound by any previous agreement which adversely affects this Agreement.

4.4 The Licensor confirms that the Licensor's Logo does not contain any obscene, offensive or defamatory material and will not expose the Licensee to any civil or criminal proceedings during the Licence Period.

4.5 The Licensor confirms that the Licensor's Logo does not contain any material which infringes the intellectual property rights including trademarks, service marks, copyright or any other rights of any third party throughout the Territory during the Licence Period.

4.6 The Licensor agrees to provide written approval or reject any of the material relating to the Licensee's Product and the Product Package provided by the Licensee within [____________] of delivery in each case.

4.7 The Licensor agrees not to reject any of the material relating to the Licensee's Product and the Product Package except on reasonable grounds and in good faith.

4.8 The Licensor agrees to supply at its sole cost such copies, in its possession or control, of the material of the Licensor's Logo on loan to the Licensee for reproduction purposes for the purposes of this Agreement: [list].

4.9 The Licensor acknowledges that the Licensee shall be entitled to retain all sums received from the exploitation of the Licensee's Product and the Product Package and that the Licensor shall not receive any sums.

4.10 The Licensor agrees that the Licensee shall be entitled to sell off on a non-exclusive basis, the Licensee's Product and the Product Package incorporating the Licensor's Logo previously manufactured under this agreement within the License Period for the purpose of commercial sale for a period of [____________] from the date of expiry or termination, provided that the Licensee adheres to the terms of this Agreement.

4.11 The Licensor shall be responsible for the clearance of all rights and the payment thereof in respect of the Licensee's use of the Licensor's Logo in the Licensee's Product.

5. CONFIDENTIALITY

The Licensor and the Licensee shall not disclose to any third party any confidential business or future plans of the other party at any time acquired during the existence of this Agreement and no reference is to be made to the terms of this Agreement by either party in any advertising, publicity or promotional material without the prior written consent of the other party.

6. AMENDMENTS

This Agreement supersedes all previous agreements, representations or promises and sets out all the terms agreed between the parties. Any amendment or alteration to this Agreement must be in writing and signed by an authorised signatory of each party.

7. NO PARTNERSHIP

This Agreement shall not be deemed to create any partnership, agency or employment relationship between the parties. Neither party shall be entitled to act on behalf of the other, or comment or pledge any matter on their behalf.

8. NOTICES

Any notice served under this Agreement shall be in writing. For the purposes of this Agreement, all notices shall be sent to the following addresses:

The Licensor: [Fax] [e-mail] [address] [name] [title];
The Licensee: [Fax] [e-mail] [address] [name] [title].

9. VALLUE ADDED TAX

All sums payable under this Agreement are exclusive of any value added tax that may be payable by either party.

10. THIRD PARTY TRANSFERS

10.1 The Licensee shall assign, transfer, charge or make over this Agreement or any of its rights or obligations without the prior written consent of the Licensor.

10.2 The Licensor may at any time transfer, assign, charge or make over the benefit of or obligations under this Agreement to any third party.

11. SELL-OFF PERIOD

After the expiry or the termination or the completion of the sell of period then the Licensor shall be entitled to instruct the Licensee to return or destroy all master material, licensed material of the Licensee's Product and the Product Package bearing the Licensor's Logo in the possession or under the control of the Licensee.

12. LIABILITY

12.1 The Licensee shall be fully liable to the Licensor for all acts or omissions with respect to any third party engaged or appointed by the Licensee in respect of the Licensor's Logo and the Licensee's Product.

12.2 The lists and materials of the Licensor's Logo delivered to the Licensee shall be complete and accurate. The Licensee shall not be liable to the Licensor provided that the Licensor's Logo has been used in the manner and detail authorised and approved by the Licensor.

12.3 The Licensee is responsible for any loss or damage to the Licensor's material for the Licensors Logo between the time that it is delivered on loan until it is returned at the Licensee's cost to the Licensor.

12.4 Neither party shall be liable to the other for any indirect or consequential loss or damages that may arise from this Agreement whether loss of profits, loss of publicity or failure to enhance reputation.

12.5 Any failure to renew or extend this Agreement once it is expired shall not constitute grounds for any claim or payment.

13. INDEMNITY

13.1 The Licensee agrees to indemnify the Licensor and any assignee against all actions, claims, costs, demands and expenses which may be suffered or arise out of the breach or alleged breach of any of the terms of this Agreement by the Licensee including death or personal injury resulting from the Licensee's Product.

13.2 The Licensor agrees to indemnify the Licensee in respect of all actions, claims, costs, demands and expenses which may be suffered or arise out of the breach or alleged breach of any of the terms of this Agreement by the Licensor relating to the Licensor's Logo.

14. LEGAL PROCEEDINGS

In the event that there is any claim, action, dispute, writ or summons arising out of the Licensor's rights to the Licensor's Logo, the use of the Licensor's Logo by the Licensee, or the Licensee's Product at any time during the Licence Period or sell-off period. Then written notice shall be given to the other party within [____________] who shall provide all such assistance as may be required to settle or defend the matter. Each party shall pay its own legal costs but may seek to later recoup them on an indemnity basis. Each party shall be entitled to settle, defend or act as they think fit in the circumstances.

15. TERMINATION

15.1 Either party may terminate this Agreement at any time after [____________] by notice in writing provided that no refund of the Licence Fee shall be made and the balance of the Licence Fee shall be paid if termination is by the Licensee.

15.2 This Agreement may be terminated at any time by either party to the other defaulting party where a breach of a form of this Agreement shall have occurred or the other party is bankrupt, ceased trading, been wound up or reached an agreement with creditors or is otherwise unable to pay its debts as they fall due.

16. GOVERNING LAW

The Law of [____________] shall be the jurisdiction for the construction, interpretation and litigation in respect of this Agreement.

[THE LICENSOR]: [____________]
[NAME/TITLE/DATE]

[THE LICENSOR]: [____________]
[NAME/TITLE/DATE]

DOCUMENTS ATTACHED TO THIS AGREEMENT:

SCHEDULE 1—THE LICENSOR'S LOGO
SCHEDULE 2—THE LICENSEE'S PRODUCT

OUTLINE—PROMOTIONAL USE OF COMPANY'S LOGO

This is a non-exclusive licence agreement for the promotional use of a Company's Logo. The party whose logo is being used is referred to as the Licensor and the party using the logo as the Licensee. An example of this type of Agreement is where a Licensee wants its product associated with an "environmentally friendly" organisation through the incorporation of the Licensor's Logo on the packaging or promotional literature concerning the Licensee's Product. The public would be likely to perceive such an arrangement as an endorsement of the Licensee's Product by the Licensor. This Agreement therefore protects the Licensor by ensuring that specific undertakings are given by the Licensee concerning the Licensee's Product.

The Licensee is paying the Licensor a Licence Fee for the non-exclusive use of the Licensor's Logo in respect of a specified territory for a fixed period in relation to a specified product. There is no sales related payment. The Licensee is agreeing that the Licensor's Logo will be incorporated in a specific manner in relation to its product, including packaging, labels, publicity, advertising and promotional literature, television and radio commercials. The Licensee is responsible for all costs incurred for the use of the Licensor's Logo.

The Licensee is to provide samples to the Licensor for written approval prior to the production, manufacture and distribution of all material which incorporates the Licensor's Logo. The Licensee is responsible for the insurance of its products and all associated material and is agreeing to provide a copy of all such policies to the Licensor.

It is the Licensee's responsibility to ensure that the use of the Licensor's Logo does not infringe any sponsorship or advertising rules.

The Agreement could be amended to entitle the Licensor to receive a sales related royalty for each item or some other additional payment over and above the Licence Fee. A full understanding and statement of the type of material for the Licensor's Logo is important. The more detailed the type of use by the Licensee of the Logo then the more specific the Agreement can be as to the mode of approval. The Licensee is not to acquire any rights in the Licensor's Logo except those set out. The Licensor is not responsible for the safety of the Licensee's Product, but confirmation of the safety tests carried out are important in the negotiation process.

TELEVISION ADVERTISEMENT AGREEMENT

AN AGREEMENT made this [____________] day of [____________]

BETWEEN:

(1) [____________]
of [____________] (to be known as the Television Company in this Agreement)

AND

(2) [____________]
of [____________] (to be known as the Agent in this Agreement).

IT IS AGREED as follows:

1. DEFINITIONS

The words below are agreed to mean as follows:

1.1 "The Product" shall be the subject matter of the Advertising Copy which is briefly described as follows: [____________].

1.2 "The Advertising Copy" shall be the film and any associated sound recording of the Product, which is intended for broadcast or transmission purposes as set out below:

Title: [____________];
Reference code: [____________];
Format: [____________];
and shall be [____________] seconds in duration.

1.3 "The Advertising Package" shall be the following material of the Advertising Copy:

1.3.1 technical material of first class quality comprising: [____________];
1.3.2 typed transcript of the Script; and
1.3.3 music cue sheet listing each musical work with the name of the composer, author and publisher, including the duration of each musical work and the description of use in each case.

1.4 "The Delivery Date" shall be the following date by which the Agent agrees to deliver the Advertising Package to the Television Company: [____________].

1.5 "The Advertiser" shall mean the individual, partnership or company on whose behalf the Agent is acting in respect of this Agreement.

1.6 "Working Day" shall mean Monday to Friday inclusive but shall not include any bank or public holidays.

1.7 "The Script" shall mean the typed copy of the final script of the Advertising Copy.

1.8 "The Transmission Fee" shall be the following amount due to be paid by the Agent to the Television Company in consideration for the transmission or broadcast of the Advertising Copy: [____________].

1.9 "The Transmission Times and Dates" shall be the following times and dates at which the Advertising Copy shall be transmitted or broadcast by the Television Company: [____________].

1.10 "The Agent's Commission" shall be [figure] per cent [_____]% of the Transmission Fee.

1.11 "The Territory" shall be the following countries: [____________].

2. NON-EXCLUSIVE LICENCE

2.1 In consideration of the Transmission Fee less the Agent's Commission, the Television Company agrees to transmit or broadcast the Advertising Copy on the Transmission Times and Dates throughout the Territory.

2.2 The Agent accordingly grants to the Television Company a non-exclusive licence to transmit or broadcast the Advertising Copy on the Transmission times and Dates throughout the Territory.

3. COPYRIGHT

The Television Company acknowledges that all copyright and any other rights in the Advertising Copy and the Advertising Package are and shall remain the sole and exclusive property of the Advertiser and that the Television Company shall not acquire any rights or interests in the Advertising Copy or the Advertising Package.

4. OBLIGATIONS OF THE AGENT

4.1 The Agent agrees to pay to the Television Company the Transmission Fee after deducting the Agent's Commission on or before: [____________].

4.2 The Agent agrees to provide the Television Company with the Advertising Package at its sole cost and expense on or before the Delivery Date.

4.3 The Agent confirms that the Advertising Copy has been or will prior to delivery to the Television Company be cleared for transmission or broadcast by the Television Company within the Territory by : [____________] and conforms with the Code of [____________] or any other similar advertising rules issued by [____________].

4.4 The Agent confirms that the Advertising Copy complies with all rules and guidelines regulations issued by any committee or body to oversee advertising which apply to the Television Company or television franchise holders in general at that time, including notes of guidance and copy clearance bulletins or other similar guidelines, policies or directives in force prior to or at the time of transmission or broadcast of the Advertising Copy.

4.5 The Agent confirms that the Advertising Copy complies with all statutes, regulations, rules, directives and codes in force.

4.6 The Agent confirms that all copyright and any other rights (musical or otherwise) in the Advertising Copy are owned or controlled by the Agent and the Advertiser.

4.7 The Agent undertakes that all copyright and any other rights (musical or otherwise), including consents have or will be cleared and paid for in respect of the transmission or broadcast by the Television Company of the Advertising Copy, including any sums due for the performing rights in any music and the mechanical reproduction of the Advertising Copy. That the Television Company is not and will not be liable for any such payments, except for such sums due in respect of the performing rights in any music for the broadcast or transmission by the Television Company.

4.8 The Agent confirms that the director of the Advertising Copy has waived his moral rights.

4.9 The Agent confirms that the Advertising Copy does not contain any material which infringes the copyright or any other rights of any third party in the Territory.

4.10 The Agent confirms that the Advertising Copy does not contain any obscene, offensive or defamatory material and will not expose the Television Company to any civil or criminal proceedings.

4.11 The Agent confirms that it has and will retain good title and authority to enter into and perform this Agreement and is not bound by any other agreement which adversely affects this Agreement. The Agent confirms in particular that there is an agreement between the Agent and the Advertiser which fully authorises the Agent to act on the Advertiser's behalf in respect of this Agreement.

4.12 The Agent undertakes at any time not to disclose to any third party any confidential information concerning the business or future plans of the Television Company acquired during the course of this Agreement.

4.13 The Agent confirms that no information concerning the transmission or broadcast details of the Advertising Copy shall be released to the public or trade press without the prior written consent of the Television Company.

4.14 In the event that the Advertising Copy is not of a suitable technical or broadcast quality and the Agent cannot deliver an acceptable replacement on or before the Delivery Date. Then the Television Company shall not be obliged to transmit or broadcast the Advertising Copy and shall be entitled to retain the Transmission Fee, less the Agent's Commission.

4.15 The Agent confirms that all costs and expenses incurred in respect of the Advertising Copy have been paid for and that the Agent has no reason to believe that any action, claim, demand or legal action against the Television Company will ensue as a result of the transmission or broadcast of the Advertising Copy.

5. OBLIGATIONS OF THE TELEVISION COMPANY

5.1 In consideration of the Transmission Fee less the Agent's Commission the Television Company agrees to transmit or broadcast the Advertising Copy throughout the Territory on the Transmission Times and Dates.

5.2 The Television Company agrees not to transmit or broadcast, either directly before or after the transmission or broadcast of the Advertising Copy, any other commercial advertising products which directly compete with the Product in the field of: [____________].

5.3 The Television Company agrees either to accept or provide written reasons for its rejection of the Advertising Package within [____________] of its receipt. The Television Company agrees to reject the Advertising Copy only on reasonable grounds and in good faith.

5.4 The Television Company undertakes to use all its endeavours to abide by its obligations to transmit or broadcast the Advertising Copy at the Transmission Times and Dates and in the event that such times and dates are to be altered The Television Company shall inform the Agent at the earliest opportunity.

5.5 The Television Company agrees that if for any reason the Advertising Copy is not transmitted or broadcast at the Transmission Times and Dates. Then the Television Company shall offer the Agent a comparable alternative time and/or date for the transmission or broadcast of the Advertising Copy and agrees that the Agent shall not be obliged to accept such alterations.

5.6 In the event that the Advertising Copy is not transmitted or broadcast on the Transmission Times and Dates and the Agent does not accept any alternative proposals. Then the Agent shall be entitled to repayment of all or part of the sums paid by the Agent, taking into account any transmissions or broadcasts already made.

5.7 The Television Company agrees that the Advertising Package shall remain the property of the Advertiser and that at the end or within [____________] of the completion of this Agreement the Advertisement Package shall be returned to the Agent at the [____________] expense.

5.8 The Television Company agrees that it shall not be entitled to authorise any third party to edit, adapt or alter the Advertising Copy without the prior written consent of the Agent.

5.9 The Television Company agrees that the Advertising Package shall be covered by a comprehensive insurance policy of the Television Company while it is in the possession or under the control of the Television Company.

6. MISCELLANEOUS

MUTUAL INDEMNITY

6.1 The Television Company and the Agent mutually undertake to indemnify the other against all liabilities, claims, demands, actions, costs, damages or loss arising out of any breach by either party of any of the terms of this Agreement.

6.2 In the event of any claim, dispute, action, writ or summons in connection with clause 6.1, the Television Company and the Agent agree to provide full details to the other party at the earliest opportunity and shall not settle any such matter without first consulting the other party.

CONFIDENTIALITY

6.3 The Television Company and the Agent shall not disclose to any third party any confidential business or future plans of the other party at any time acquired during the existence of this Agreement and no reference is to be made to the terms of this Agreement by either party in any advertising, publicity or promotional material without the prior written consent of the other party.

AMENDMENTS AND ALTERATIONS

6.4 This Agreement supersedes all previous agreements, representations or promises and sets out all the terms agreed between the parties. Any amendment or alteration to this Agreement must be in writing and signed by an authorised signatory of each party.

CANCELLATION

6.5 In the event that the Agent or the Advertiser gives notice to the Television Company to cancel the broadcast or transmission of the Advertising Copy on the Transmission Times and Dates. Then the Television Company shall be entitled to the following percentages of the Transmission Fee, after the deduction of the Agent's Commission:

6.5.1 where the Television Company receives notice of such cancellation [____] working days or more prior to the Delivery Date: [____________] %

6.5.2 where the Television Company receives notice of such cancellation less than [___] working days prior to the Delivery Date:[____________]%

NO PARTNERSHIP

6.6 This Agreement shall not be deemed to create any partnership or employment relationship between the parties.

NOTICES

6.7 Without prejudice to the right to serve notices by any other means any notice served under this Agreement shall be as follows:

6.7.1 First class, pre-paid post which shall be deemed to be received 48 hours thereafter (excluding Saturdays, Sundays and public holidays) if sent to the following addresses:

the Television Company: [____________];
the Agent: [____________].

6.7.2 By a telex or facsimile machine which shall be deemed to be received within 24 hours, provided that the notice is sent to the other party using the following codes:

the Television Company's telex number: [____________];
the Television Company's facsimile number: [____________];
the Agent's telex number: [____________];
the Agent's facsimile number: [____________].

VALUE ADDED TAX

6.8 All sums payable under this Agreement are exclusive of any value added tax that may be payable by either party.

THIRD PARTY TRANSFERS

6.9 Neither party shall assign, charge or make over this Agreement or any of its rights or obligations without the prior written consent of the other party.

FORCE MAJEURE

6.10 In the event that this Agreement cannot be performed or its obligations fulfilled for any reason beyond the reasonable control of the Television Company or the Agent, including such events as war, industrial action, floods, or Acts of God or unforeseen technical failure, then such non-performance or failure to fulfil its obligations shall be deemed not to be a breach of this Agreement. In the event that this Agreement cannot be performed or its obligations fulfilled for any reason beyond the reasonable control of the defaulting party for a continuous period of [____________]. Then the other party may, at its discretion, terminate this Agreement by notice in writing at the end of that period. Provided that both parties agree to negotiate, in good faith, an equitable settlement in respect of work already performed to the date of termination.

TERMINATION AND EXPIRY OF THE AGREEMENT

6.11 In addition to any other rights and remedies at law, this Agreement may be terminated by giving written notice to the other party who has breached this Agreement or defaulted in the following circumstances:

6.11.1 where the Agent has failed to account or make payments as required under this agreement;

6.11.2 where the Agent or the Television Company has committed a serious breach of its obligations under this Agreement, unless such party rectifies the position, as far as reasonably possible, within [____________];

6.11.3 where the Agent, the Advertiser or the Television Company goes into voluntary or involuntary liquidation;

6.11.4 where the Agent, the Advertiser or the Television Company is declared insolvent,either in bankruptcy proceedings or other legal proceedings;

6.11.5 where an agreement with creditors has been reached by the Television Company, the Agent or the Advertiser due to its failure or inability to pay its debts as they fall due; or

6.11.6 where a receiver is appointed over the whole or part of the Agent's, the Advertiser's or the Television Company's business.

GOVERNING LAW

6.12 This Agreement shall be subject to the Laws of [England].

Signed by: [____________]
FOR AND ON BEHALF OF THE TELEVISION COMPANY

Date: [____________]

Signed by: [____________]
FOR AND ON BEHALF OF THE AGENT

Date: [____________]

OUTLINE—TELEVISION ADVERTISEMENT AGREEMENT

This is an agreement between a Television Company and an Agent for the broadcast or transmission of an Advertisement on television. This Agreement does not purport to exactly reflect standard practice. The Agent is providing the Advertising Package of the technical material required for broadcast or transmission purposes. The Television Company is receiving a Transmission Fee after the deduction of the Agent's Commission.

In the event that the Advertisement is not transmitted or broadcast at the agreed times and dates, then the Agent has the right to reject any alternative proposals by the Television Company, although a comparable transmission or broadcast arrangement may be offered by the Television Company. The Agent is agreeing to be responsible for the copyright clearances and payments in respect of the broadcast of the Advertisement in the Territory, including any sums in respect of the mechanical reproduction of the Advertisement and the performing rights in any music. The Television Company will be responsible for any performing rights payment due for the transmission or broadcast of the advertisement. This type of agreement is very different from a sponsorship of a programme where the product or name is shown before the film begins and when it ends.

PRODUCTION OF AN ADVERTISEMENT FOR TELEVISION

BETWEEN:

(1) [_____________]
of [_____________] (to be known as the Production Company in this Agreement)

AND

(2) [_____________]
of [_____________] (to be known as the Commissioning Company in this Agreement).

IT IS AGREED as follows:

1. DEFINITIONS

The words below are agreed to mean as follows:

1.1 "The Advertisement" shall be the following film and any associated sound recording based on the Treatment entitled: [_____________], which shall be [_____________] seconds in duration.

1.2 "The Treatment" shall be the synopsis of the Advertisement for the Product. A copy of the Treatment is attached to and forms part of this Agreement in Schedule A.

1.3 "The Product" shall be the subject-matter of the Advertisement which is described as follows: [_____________].
A two-dimensional copy of the Product is attached to and forms part of this Agreement in Schedule B.

1.4 "The Production Fee" shall be the sum of [figure/currency].

1.5 "The Key Personnel" shall be as follows: [_____________].

1.6 "The Budget" shall be the costs of making the Advertisement, whether direct or indirect, inclusive of all locations, facilities and other items necessary for the development, pre-production, production, post-production and delivery of the Advertisement. A copy of the Budget is attached to and forms part of this Agreement in Schedule C.

1.7 "The Production Schedule" shall be the agreed dates, times and locations of making the Advertisement, including pre-production, production, post-production and delivery of the Advertisement. A copy of the Production Schedule is attached to and forms part of this Agreement in Schedule D.

1.8 "The Payment Schedule" shall be the details of the payment of the Budget by the Commissioning Company. A copy of the Payment Schedule is attached to and forms part of this Agreement in Schedule E.

1.9 "The Advertisement Package" shall be the following material of the Advertisement:

1.9.1 technical material of first class broadcast quality comprising of a fully edited pristine [format];
1.9.2 not less than [______ format] VHS copies of the Advertisement;
1.9.3 a complete list of the technical and master material and any copies in any format and in any gauge, including but not limited to rushes, out-takes, video tapes, sound recordings, music and effects tracks, title and subtitle tracks and viewing copies in the possession or under the control of the Production Company;
1.9.4 a complete list of the laboratories and any other locations at which any material relating to the Advertisement is held, together with access letters giving the Commissioning Company irrevocable authority to obtain the material and copies for use at its sole discretion.
1.9.5 typed transcript of final script.
1.9.6 music cue sheet listing each musical work with the name of the composer, author and publisher, including the duration of each musical work and the description of use in each case; and
1.9.7 a detailed written statement with supporting documents setting out all intellectual property rights including copyright, trademarks, service marks, logos, designs, slogans, text, artwork, title, recordings, scripts, music, photographs, artworks, products, artistes, graphics, and computer generated material, and all other consents, moral rights and contractual obligations obtained and paid for and/or due in respect of the Advertisement.

1.10 "The Territory" shall be all countries, areas, ships, aeroplanes, oilrigs and any other locations throughout the world and the universe.

2. ENGAGEMENT OF SERVICES

2.1 In consideration of the payment of the Production Fee and the Budget, the Production Company agrees to provide its non-exclusive services to produce and deliver the Advertisement based on the Treatment to the Commissioning Company.

2.2 The Commissioning Company agrees to engage the exclusive services of the Production Company to produce and deliver The Advertisement based on the Treatment.

3. FULL ASSIGNMENT OF RIGHTS

In consideration of the Production Fee and the Approved Budget, the Production Company assigns to the Commissioning Company all present and future copyright and any other rights in all media, whether in existence now or created in the future in the Advertisement and any parts and in the Advertisement Package and any developments throughout the Territory for the full period of copyright and any extensions and renewals including but not limited to:

3.1 all forms of television, digital, satellite, cable, terrestrial;

3.2 all forms of radio;

3.3 all forms of video and videogram, cassette, disc, laser;

3.4 all forms of publishing, hardbacks, paperbacks, newspapers, magazines;

3.5 all theatre, films, advertisements, educational, social, cultural and religious use;

3.6 all forms of merchandising whether based on characters, logos or images, toys, stationery, clothes;

3.7 all forms of electronic reproduction, dissemination and distribution, internet, electronic devices and gadgets, interactive games, multi-media, interactivity, in sound, vision, text, or graphics, CD-ROMs;

3.8 all other forms of any nature.

4. MORAL RIGHTS

The Production Company agrees to ensure, as far as reasonably possible, that the Director of the Advertisement will unconditionally waive all moral rights in the Advertisement.

5. OBLIGATIONS OF THE PRODUCTION COMPANY

5.1 The Production Company undertakes that it shall produce the Advertisement using the Key Personnel, in accordance with the Treatment, the Budget and the Production Schedule.

5.2 The Production Company confirms that the Advertisement shall be produced in colour, in the English language and in the following format: [____________].

5.3 The Production Company shall deliver the scripts and storyboard of the Advertisement to the Commissioning Company for approval on or before the following dates:

the draft scripts: [____________];
the final script: [____________];
the storyboard: [____________].

5.4 The Production Company agrees that the prior approval of the Commissioning Company shall be required in respect of the Advertisement in respect of:

5.4.1 [the artistes/voice-overs/music/stills/footage/other];
5.4.2 any other material:

5.5 The Production Company agrees that the final editorial decisions in respect of the Advertisement shall be at the sole discretion of the Commissioning Company.

5.6 The Production Company confirms that a representative of the Commissioning Company shall be entitled to attend the filming and editing of the Advertisement at any stage prior to its completion.

5.7 The Production Company shall deliver the Advertisement Package to the Commissioning Company on or before: [date].

5.8 The Production Company confirms that it is the sole owner of or controls all present and future copyright and any other rights in the Advertisement which are assigned under this Agreement, except for the Product and any other material provided by the Commissioning Company.

5.9 The Production Company confirms that it has and will retain good title and authority to enter into this Agreement and is not bound by any previous agreement which adversely affects this Agreement.

5.10 The Production Company undertakes, as far as reasonably possible, that all production personnel, artistes and musicians involved in the production of the Advertisement shall be members of recognised craft or trade organisations.

5.11 The Production Company undertakes that the Advertisement will not contain any obscene, offensive or defamatory material and will not expose the Commissioning Company to any civil or criminal proceedings throughout the Territory, except for the Product and any other material provided by the Commissioning Company.

5.12 The Production Company confirms that it will ensure that the Advertisement will conform to all statutes, rules, directives, guidelines and advertising codes of conduct in relation to exercise and exploitation by the Commissioning Company of the Digital, Cable and Satellite Television rights in [______________].

5.13 In the event of the Budget being exceeded by up to [______________]. The Production Company agrees to inform the Commissioning Company in advance and to provide the Commissioning Company with a statement of costs incurred to date and details of the additional costs.

5.14 In the event of the Budget being exceeded by more than [______________]. The Production Company agrees that the prior written approval of the Commissioning Company shall be required in order to authorise any further expenditure and that any further payment shall be at the Commissioning Company's sole discretion.

5.15 The Production Company undertakes that the Advertisement will not contain any material which infringes the intellectual property rights including the copyright or any other rights of any third party in the Territory except for the Product and any other material provided by the Commissioning Company.

5.16 The Production Company shall set out a clear statement of all material to be cleared and acquired for the Advertisement and the cost of clearance for all forms of digital, satellite and cable television on [______________]. The Production Company shall use the Budget to clear and pay for such rights. Where possible the Production Company shall acquire all media rights but where this would result in the Budget being exceeded, they should merely advise the Commissioning Company of this fact and not acquire additional rights. The Production Company shall only be responsible for clearance and payment for material set out in the Budget.

6. OBLIGATIONS OF THE COMMISSIONING COMPANY

6.1 In consideration of the production of the Advertisement, the Commissioning Company shall pay to the Production Company the Budget in accordance with the Payment Schedule.

6.2 In consideration of rights assigned under this Agreement, the Commissioning Company shall pay to the Production Company the Production Fee as follows:

6.2.1 [____________] upon signature of this Agreement;
6.2.2 [____________] on or before [____________];
6.2.3 [____________] upon acceptance of the Advertisement Package.

6.3 In the event of the Budget being exceeded by up to [____________], the Commissioning Company agrees to pay such additional costs, provided that the Production Company informs the Commissioning Company in advance and provides upon request to the Commissioning Company a statement of costs incurred to date and details of the additional costs.

6.4 In the event of the Approved Budget being exceeded by more than [__________], the Commissioning Company agrees to pay such additional costs, provided that it has given prior written approval of the expenditure to the Production Company.

6.5 The Commissioning Company agrees either to accept or provide written reasons for their rejection of the scripts, storyboard and the Advertisement Package within [____________] of delivery in each case.

6.6 The Commissioning Company confirms that it shall be responsible at its sole cost for all copyright and other clearance payments not set out in the Budget, including any sums due in respect of the distribution and exploitation of the Advertisement in any media throughout the Territory, including any sums due in respect of the performing rights in any music and the mechanical reproduction of the Advertisement.

6.7 The Commissioning Company agrees to provide the Production Company with such information, documentation, historical background and any other material concerning the Commissioning Company and its products as may be reasonably required by the Production Company for the purpose of fulfilling its obligations under this Agreement.

6.8 The Commissioning Company confirms that it is the sole owner of or controls all intellectual property rights including copyright and any other rights in the Commissioning Company and the Product in all media throughout the Territory, including any trademark, logo, title, artwork, slogan, packaging and any developments or variations provided by the Commissioning Company under this Agreement.

6.9 The Commissioning Company confirms that it has full title and authority to enter into this Agreement and is not bound by any previous agreement which adversely affects this Agreement.

6.10 The Commissioning Company confirms that the Product does not contain any obscene, offensive or defamatory material and will not expose the Production Company to any civil or criminal proceedings.

6.11 The Commissioning Company confirms that the Commissioning Company and the Product, including any trademark, logo, title, artwork, slogan, packaging and any developments or variations provided by The Commissioning Company under this Agreement, do not contain any material which infringes the intellectual property rights including copyright and trademarks or any other rights of any third party in the Territory.

6.12 The Commissioning Company agrees to supply at its sole cost copies of such artwork and other material relating to the Commissioning Company and the Product in its possession or control including any goods, packaging, trademark or logo which may be required by the Production Company for the purposes of this Agreement.

6.13 The Commissioning Company undertakes that the Product, together with all other products or services owned or controlled by the Commissioning Company, which the public would reasonably associate with the Product shall be safe and fit for their intended use and shall comply with all statutes, regulations, directives and codes in force on: [date].

6.14 The Commissioning Company confirms that a comprehensive public and product liability insurance policy is and will be in force covering any claims, actions or damages which may arise as a direct or indirect result of the use by the public of the Product, together with all other products or services owned or controlled by the Commissioning Company which the public would reasonably associate with the Product.

7. MISCELLANEOUS

MUTUAL INDEMNITY

7.1 The Production Company and the Commissioning Company mutually undertake to indemnify the other against all liabilities, claims, demands, actions, costs, damages or loss arising out of any breach by either party of any of the terms of this Agreement.

7.2 In the event of any claim, dispute, action, writ or summons in connection with clause 7.1, the Production Company and the Commissioning Company agree to provide full details to the other party at the earliest opportunity and shall not settle any such matter without first consulting the other party.

CONFIDENTIALITY

7.3 The Production Company and the Commissioning Company shall not disclose to any third party any confidential business or future plans of the other party at any time acquired during the existence of this Agreement and no reference is to be made to the terms of this Agreement by either party in any advertising, publicity or promotional material without the prior written consent of the other party.

AMENDMENTS AND ALTERATIONS

7.4 This Agreement supersedes all previous agreements, representations or promises and sets out all the terms agreed between the parties. Any amendment or alteration to this Agreement must be in writing and signed by an authorised signatory of each party.

RELATIONSHIP

7.5 This Agreement shall not be deemed to create any partnership or employment relationship between the parties. Neither party shall pledge, commit or authorise any sums on behalf of the other under this Agreement unless set out in the Budget and agreed in advance.

NOTICES

7.6 Any notice served under this Agreement shall be in writing. For the purposes of this Agreement, all notices shall be sent to the following addresses:

the Production Company: [Address] [Title];
the Commissioning Company: [Address] [Title].

VALUE ADDED TAX

7.7 All sums payable under this Agreement are exclusive of any value added tax that may be payable by either party.

THIRD PARTY TRANSFERS

7.8 The Production Company shall not assign, transfer, charge or make over this Agreement or any of its rights or obligations without the prior written consent of the other Commissioning Company.

7.9 The Commissioning Company may assign, charge, transfer or make over the benefits and obligations and rights under this Agreement to any third party at any time provided that the obligations to the Production Company will continue to be fulfilled.

FORCE MAJEURE

7.10 In the event that this Agreement cannot be performed or its obligations fulfilled for any reason beyond the reasonable control of the Production Company or the Commissioning Company, including such events as war, industrial action, floods or Acts of God. Then such non-performance or failure to fulfil its obligations shall be deemed not to be a breach of this Agreement. In the event that this Agreement cannot be performed or its obligations fulfilled for any reason beyond the reasonable control of the defaulting party for a continuous period of [____________] then the other party may, at its discretion, terminate this Agreement by notice in writing at the end of that period subject to settlement for payment for work completed to date, and delivery of all material.

TERMINATION AND EXPIRY OF THE AGREEMENT

7.11 In addition to any other rights and remedies at law, this Agreement may be terminated by a party giving written notice to the other party who has breached this Agreement or has defaulted in the following circumstances:

- 7.11.1 where the Production Company or the Commissioning Company has failed to account or make payments as required under this Agreement;
- 7.11.2 where the Production Company or the Commissioning Company has committed a serious breach of its obligations under this Agreement;
- 7.11.3 where the Production Company or the Commissioning Company goes into voluntary or involuntary liquidation;
- 7.11.4 where the Production Company or the Commissioning Company is declared insolvent, either in bankruptcy proceedings or other legal proceedings;
- 7.11.5 where an agreement with creditors has been reached by the Production Company or the Commissioning Company due to its failure or inability to pay its debts as they fall due; or
- 7.11.6 where a receiver is appointed over the whole or part of the Production Company's or the Commissioning Company's business.

GOVERNING LAW

7.12 This Agreement shall be subject to the Laws of [England].

Signed by: [______________]
FOR AND ON BEHALF OF THE PRODUCTION COMPANY

Signed by: [______________]
FOR AND ON BEHALF OF THE COMMISSIONING COMPANY

DATE of this Agreement: [______________]

OUTLINE—PRODUCTION OF AN ADVERTISEMENT FOR TELEVISION

In this Agreement, a company is commissioning a commercial Advertisement for television from a Production Company. The Production Company is agreeing to produce an Advertisement for a specified product based on a treatment. The Commissioning Company is agreeing to pay to the Production Company a Production Fee as well as the costs of producing the Advertisement, referred to as the Budget. The Commissioning Company has complete editorial control of the Advertisement and has the right to approve all artistes, scripts and music. The Production Company is assigning all rights in all media in the Advertisement to the Commissioning Company. The Production Company has agreed to deliver both technical and other material of the Advertisement to the Commissioning Company by a specified date.

There are no provisions for the Production Company to receive a credit in respect of the Advertisement and there is agreement that the Director will unconditionally waive all moral rights in the Advertisement. It is important to realise that the Budget only allows for clearance and payment of all forms of digital, cable and satellite television in a normal country. Clearance and payment of all media rights assigned will be an additional cost.

GENERAL ADVERTISING/PROMOTION AGREEMENT

AN AGREEMENT made this [____________] day of [____________]

BETWEEN:

(1) [____________]
of [____________] (to be known as the Promoter in this Agreement)

AND

(2) [____________]
of [____________] (to be known as the Company in this Agreement).

IT IS AGREED as follows:

1. DEFINITIONS

The words below are agreed to mean as follows:

1.1 "The Promotion Period" shall commence on [the date of this Agreement] and shall continue until [____________].

1.2 "The Company's Products" shall mean the products and services of the Company, which are briefly described as follows: [____________].
A two-dimensional copy of the Company's Products is attached to and forms part of this Agreement in Schedule 1 setting out all intellectual property rights including copyright, trademarks, service marks, logos, designs, slogans, text, artwork, title, recordings, scripts, music, photographs, artwork, products, artistes, graphic, computer generated material, all consents, releases, moral rights, contractual obligations obtained, paid for or due.

1.3 "The Territory" shall be the following countries: [____________].

1.4 "The Promotion Fee" shall be the total sum of [figure/currency].

1.5 "The Promotion Expenses" shall be all costs reasonably and properly expended by the Promoter in furtherance of this Agreement which are not recouped from any third party:

1.5.1 survey and marketing reports;
1.5.2 the creation supply and placing of advertisements in local and national press, including any photographs;

1.5.3 the development, production, post-production and distribution of a promotional video;

1.5.4 the development, production, post-production and distribution of an advertisement for radio;

1.5.5 the commissioning of any artwork for publicity, advertising and promotional material;

1.5.6 delivery, storage, shipping, customs duties, freight, handling charges and insurance;

1.5.7 artistes, stills, recordings, copyright, music, moral rights and other consents, clearances or other material or rights which are acquired;

1.5.8 any other costs specifically agreed between the Promoter and the Company as follows: [____________].

1.6 "The Promotion Budget" shall mean the combined costs and expenses of the Promotion Fee and the Promotion Expenses, which shall not exceed: [figure/currency].

1.7 "The Non-Theatric Rights" shall mean the right to exhibit any film to non-paying audiences in all businesses and commercial industries and organisations of an educational, cultural, religious, charitable and social nature, including but not limited to schools, churches, evening institutions, museums, hospitals, prisons, summer camps, drama groups, film societies, professional associations, public libraries, colleges and universities, hotels and private clubs.

2. APPOINTMENT OF EXCLUSIVE PROMOTER

2.1 The Company agrees to appoint the Promoter as the sole and exclusive advertising and promotion agent for the purpose of promoting and advertising the Company throughout the Territory for the duration of the Promotion Period in accordance with the terms of this Agreement.

2.2 In consideration of the payment of the Promotion Fee and the Promotion Expenses, the Promoter agrees to provide its non-exclusive services to the Company to act as agent to promote and advertise [the Company and] the Company's Products throughout the Territory for the duration of the Promotion Period in accordance with the terms of this Agreement.

3. COPYRIGHT

3.1 The Promoter confirms and acknowledges that all intellectual property righs including trademarks, copyright and any other rights in the Company's Products, together with any goodwill, are and shall remain the sole and exclusive property of the Company and that the Promoter shall not acquire any rights or interests in the Company's Products, including any developments or variations at any time.

3.2 The Promoter assigns to the Company all present and future intellectual property rights including copyright and any other rights in the product of its services in respect of the Company and the Company's Products within its possession or control throughout the universe for the full period of the copyright and any extensions or renewals in perpetuity.

3.3 The Promoter undertakes to ensure, as far as reasonably possible, that all third parties engaged to produce any material in furtherance of this Agreement shall agree to assign the product of their services in all media throughout the world for the full period of the copyright and any extensions and renewals to the Company so that they retain no intellectual property rights whatsoever.

3.4 The Promoter agrees to execute any document or do anything required by the Company to confirm that all intellectual property rights including copyright and any other rights in the product of its services under this Agreement belong to the Company.

3.5 The Company confirms and acknowledges that all copyright, trademark, service mark, logo and any other rights in the Promoter's trademark, design and logo, together with any goodwill are and shall remain the sole and exclusive property of the Promoter and that the Company shall not acquire any rights or interests in the Promoter's trademark, design or logo, including any developments or variations.

4. OBLIGATIONS OF THE PROMOTER

4.1 The Promoter acknowledges and confirms that the principal aims of this Agreement are to:

4.1.1 promote and increase the sales of the Company's Products;
4.1.2 raise public awareness of the Company's existence throughout the Territory;
4.1.3 inform the general public of the Company's positive track record within its industry;
4.1.4 improve the consumer image of the Company throughout the Territory;
4.1.5 create a favourable image of the Company to the public in general and in particular for the purpose of recruiting potential future employees;
4.1.6 increase and improve the Company's goodwill and understanding amongst its present customers; and
4.1.7 any other specific aims: [____________].

4.2 The Promoter agrees to provide its services to the best of its skill and ability and shall perform all services under this Agreement diligently to ensure that [the Company and] the Company's Products are promoted and marketed in the most cost effective manner during the Promotion Period within the Promotion Budget.

4.3 The Promoter undertakes that all promotions and advertising under this Agreement in respect of [the Company and] the Company's Products will not be offensive or obscene in nature or derogatory of any third party. The Promoter will ensure that all material produced under this Agreement will not infringe any sponsorship or advertising rules, statutes or directives currently in existence.

4.4 The Promoter shall, as far as possible, keep the Company fully informed on a regular basis as regards any negotiations with any third party in respect of the Promoter's obligations under this Agreement.

4.5 The Promoter confirms that it has full power and authority to enter into and perform this Agreement and is not bound by any other agreement which adversely affects this Agreement.

4.6 The Promoter confirms that this Agreement will not cause any conflict of interest with any of its existing clients and undertakes not to enter into any agreement with any third party during the Promotion Period which would result in conflict within this Agreement. In particular the Promoter shall not work for the following parties: [____________].

4.7 The Promoter undertakes not to use any commercially sensitive information provided by the Company to the Promoter during the Promotion Period to the commercial detriment of the Company at any time.

4.8 The Promoter shall not be entitled at any time to exploit commercially any mailing lists provided by the Company to the Promoter during the course of this Agreement without the prior written consent of the Company.

4.9 In the event of the Promotion Budget being exceeded by up to [____________], the Promoter agrees to inform the Company in advance and to provide the Company with a statement of costs incurred to date and details of the additional costs.

4.10 In the event of the Promotion Budget being exceeded by more than [__________], the Promoter agrees that the prior written approval of the Company shall be required in order to authorise any further expenditure and that any further payment shall be at the Company's sole discretion.

4.11 The Promoter undertakes that it and its sub-agents and sub-licensees and distributors shall keep full and accurate books of account, records and contracts, software and other material showing all allocation of and expenditure of the Promotion Budget.

4.12 The Promoter agrees that the Company shall be entitled to arrange for an audit to inspect and make copies of the Promoter's books of account, records, contracts, software and any other relevant material at any time at the Company's cost in order to verify the payments made from the Promotion Budget.

4.13 The Promoter agrees to provide in advance to the Company for its prior approval, all copies and samples of all material of any nature to be produced or distributed under this Agreement including advertising, publicity, promotional and packaging material concerning the Company and the Company's Products.

4.14 The Promoter agrees to provide the following copyright notice, trademark, service mark, logo and credit to the Company in any publicity, promotional, advertising and packaging material and [____________] concerning the Company and the Company's Product: [____________].

4.15 The Promoter acknowledges that the Company shall be entitled, upon request, to be provided with a copy of any contract, record, document, software or other material in the possession or under the control of the Promoter relating to the Company or the Company's Products.

4.16 The Promoter agrees to provide the Company with the following details and materials in respect of the production of any promotional video for the Company's prior approval:

4.16.1 background details concerning the proposed production and post-production company including the producer, director, writer, cameraman, presenter and senior editor;
4.16.2 any synopsis, treatment and scripts;
4.16.3 any production schedule, including all relevant filming times, dates and locations;
4.16.4 technical details of the material on which the film is to be shot;
4.16.5 a full breakdown of the production budget, whether direct or indirect, which is inclusive of all locations, facilities, computer-generated graphics and any other items necessary for the development, pre-production, production and post-production and delivery of the promotional video, including any contingency allowance, completion guarantee, insurance and the producer's fee,
4.16.6 a full breakdown of copyright clearances and any other consents and payments due required for the use by the Company of the Non-Theatric Rights in any promotional video, including those concerning artistes, performers and musicians and music, together with details of all payments that will be required to any royalty collecting society in respect of the mechanical reproduction or performing rights.

5. OBLIGATIONS OF THE COMPANY

5.1 The Company agrees to pay to the Promoter the Promotion Fee as follows:

5.1.1 [____________] upon signature of this Agreement,
5.1.2 [____________] on or before: [____________];
5.1.3 [____________] on or before: [____________].

5.2 In the event of the Promotion Budget being exceeded by up to [____________] the Company agrees to pay such additional costs provided that the Promoter informs the Company in advance and provides upon request to the Company a statement of costs incurred to date and details of the additional costs.

5.3 In the event of the Promotion Budget being exceeded by more than [__________], the Company agrees to pay such additional costs provided that it has given prior written approval of the expenditure to the Promoter.

5.4 The Company agrees to pay to the Promoter the Promotion Expenses on a quarterly basis in each year of the Promotion Period, subject to suitable receipts or other records being provided by the Promoter upon request by the Company.

5.5 The Company agrees to provide the Promoter with such information, documentation, historical background and any other material concerning the Company and the Company's Products on loan at the Company's cost and risk as may be reasonably required by the Promoter for the purpose of fulfilling its obligations under this Agreement.

5.6 The Company confirms that it is the sole owner of or controls all intellectual property rights including copyright and any other rights in the Company and the

Company's Products throughout the world in accordance with the statement set out in Schedule 1 for the Company's Product during the Promotion Period.

5.7 The Company confirms that it has full title and authority to enter into this Agreement and is not bound by any previous agreement which adversely affects this Agreement.

5.8 The Company confirms that [the Company and] the Company's Products do not contain any obscene, offensive or defamatory material and will not expose the Promoter to any civil or criminal proceedings during the Promotion Period.

5.9 The Company confirms that the Company and the Company's Products do not contain any material which infringes the copyright, trademarks or any other rights of any third party in the Territory.

5.10 The Company agrees to supply at its sole cost and expense on loan at the Company's risk, copies of such artwork and samples of material relating to the Company and the Company's Products in its possession or control, including any trademark, logo or other credit which may be required by the Promoter for the purposes of this Agreement.

5.11 The Company confirms that a product liability insurance policy is and will be in force throughout the Territory covering any claims, actions or damages which may arise as a direct or indirect result of the use by the public of the Company's Products, together with all other products or services owned or controlled by the Company which the public would reasonably associate with the Company. The Company confirms that the insurance company is [____________], policy number [____________], a copy of which is available upon request.

5.12 The Company undertakes not to use any commercially sensitive information provided by the Promoter to the Company during the Promotion Period to the commercial detriment of the Promoter at any time.

6. MISCELLANEOUS

MUTUAL INDEMNITY

6.1 The Company and the Promoter mutually undertake to indemnify the other against all liabilities, claims, demands, actions, costs, damages or loss arising out of any breach by either party of any of the terms of this Agreement.

6.2 In the event of any claim, dispute, action, writ or summons in connection with clause 6.1, the Company and the Promoter agree to provide full details to the other party at the earliest opportunity and shall not settle any such matter without first consulting the other party.

CONFIDENTIALITY

6.3 The Company and the Promoter shall not disclose to any third party any confidential business or future plans of the other party at any time acquired during the existence of this Agreement and no reference is to be made to the terms of this Agreement by either party in any advertising, publicity or promotional material, without the prior written consent of the other party.

AMENDMENTS AND ALTERATIONS

6.4 This Agreement supersedes all previous agreements, representations or promises and sets out all the terms agreed between the parties. Any amendment or alteration to this Agreement must be in writing and signed by an authorised signatory of each party.

NO PARTNERSHIP

6.5 This Agreement shall not be deemed to create any partnership, employment, or agency relationship between the parties. Neither party shall be entitled to pledge, comment or authorise any matter which is not set out under the terms of this Agreement.

NOTICES

6.6 Without prejudice to the right to serve notices by any other means, any notice served under this Agreement shall be served as follows:

6.6.1 First class prepaid post which shall be deemed to be received [____________] thereafter (excluding Saturdays, Sundays and public holidays) if sent to the following addresses:

the Company: [____________];
the Promoter: [____________].

6.6.2 By a telex or facsimile machine or e-mail, which shall be deemed to be received within[____________], provided that the notice is sent to the other party using the following codes:

the Company's codes: [____________];
the Promoter's codes: [____________].

VALUE ADDED TAX

6.7 All sums payable under this Agreement are exclusive of any value added tax that may be payable by either party.

THIRD PARTY TRANSFERS

6.8 The Promoter shall not assign, transfer, charge or make over this Agreement or any of its rights or obligations without the prior written consent of the Company. The Company may transfer, charge or make over any part of this Agreement to any third party provided that the Promoter is paid the Promotion Fee.

FORCE MAJEURE

6.9 In the event that this Agreement cannot be performed or its obligations fulfilled for any reason beyond the reasonable control of the Company or the Promoter, including such events as war, industrial action, floods or Acts of God. Then such non-performance or failure to fulfil its obligations shall be deemed not to be a breach of this Agreement. In the event that this Agreement cannot be performed or its obligations fulfilled for any reason beyond its reasonable control for a continuous period of [____________]. Then either party may, at its discretion, terminate this Agreement by notice in writing at the end of that period.

TERMINATION AND EXPIRY OF THE AGREEMENT

6.10 In addition to any other rights and remedies at law, this Agreement may be terminated by giving written notice to the other party who has breached this Agreement or defaulted in the following circumstances:

- 6.10.1 where the Company or the Promoter has failed to account or make payments as required under this Agreement;
- 6.10.2 where the Company or the Promoter has committed a serious breach of its obligations under this Agreement;
- 6.10.3 where the Company or the Promoter goes into voluntary or involuntary liquidation;
- 6.10.4 where the Company or the Promoter is declared insolvent, either in bankruptcy proceedings or other legal proceedings;
- 6.10.5 where an agreement with creditors has been reached by the Company or the Promoter due to its failure or inability to pay its debts as they fall due; or
- 6.10.6 where a receiver is appointed over the whole or part of the Company's or the Promoter's business.

GOVERNING LAW

6.11 This Agreement shall be subject to the Laws of [England].

Attached to and forming part of this Agreement is Schedule 1: The Company's Product.

Signed by: [____________] Date: [____________]
FOR AND ON BEHALF OF THE COMPANY

Signed by: [____________] Date: [____________]
FOR AND ON BEHALF OF THE PROMOTER

OUTLINE—GENERAL ADVERTISEMENT/PROMOTION AGREEMENT

This is a general advertising/promotion agreement where a Company is engaging the exclusive services of a Promoter to act as an Agent to promote and market the Company's Products. The Agreement can be amended to increase the significance of the cross-promotion of the Company, but this is not the main strategy.

There is no renewal or option to renew even if the project is successful.

There is no direct editorial control clause but the Company is to approve copies and samples of all material before it is produced or distributed.

It is important that the Budget for this Agreement is not unlimited and so a ceiling limit is fixed by adding the Promoters Fee to the Promotion Expenses, resulting in the Promotion Budget.

There could be more detail added as to the nature of the strategy for the Company's Products, and the consideration of other issues that the Company wishes to promote, *i.e.* environmentally-friendly products, or the age and category of the target group.

The Company is paying an agreed Promotion Fee to the Promoter. In addition, there are Promotion Expenses to be paid by the Company. These two sums are referred to as the Promotion Budget. The Promotion Budget can be exceeded by up to a fixed amount or percentage where the Promoter fully informs the Company of all costs incurred. The Company may refuse liability for any sums in excess of that amount over the original Promotion Budget.

The Promotion Expenses cover survey and marketing reports, press and radio advertisements and a promotional video. A television advertisement is not within the terms of this Agreement.

The transfer of all rights in all media in this Agreement is important. There is an assignment clause from the Promoter and a document should be drawn up which all third parties sign. This will allow the Company at a later stage to exploit all material in all media, subject to any additional clearance payments that may be needed for items such as music. The copyright ownership of all material created by or on behalf of the Promoter in furtherance of the Agreement is assigned to the Company.

The Company confirms that there exists product liability insurance cover, which the Company may inspect.

A two-dimensional copy of the Company's Products should be attached to the Agreement.

SPONSORSHIP AGREEMENT WITH A SPORTS ASSOCIATION FOR A TELEVISION CHAMPIONSHIP EVENT

AN AGREEMENT made this [____________] day of [____________]

BETWEEN:

(1) [____________]
of [____________] (to be known as the Sponsor in this Agreement)

AND

(2) [____________]
of [____________] (to be known as the Association in this Agreement).

IT IS AGREED as follows:

1. DEFINITIONS

The words below are agreed to mean as follows:

1.1 "The Event" shall be the following competition arranged and organised by the Association entitled [____________], which is to take place between the dates [____________] inclusive.

A summary of the format and structure of the Event is described in the attached Event Schedule which forms part of this Agreement in Appendix A.

1.2 "The Venue" shall be the following premises at which the Event is to take place: [Name of Venue] at [Address].

1.3 "The Proprietor" is the following owner of the Venue: [Name]; whose registered office is at [Address].

1.4 "The Promotional Logo" shall be the design, logo, service mark and/or trademark together with any accompanying words, slogan or text of the Association to be used for all promotion, advertising and marketing of the Event. A two-dimensional representation of the Promotional Logo is attached to and forms part of this Agreement in Appendix B.

1.5 "The Sponsor's Logo" shall be the design, logo, service mark and/or trademark, together with any accompanying words, slogan or text of the Sponsor to be used for all promotion, advertising and marketing of the Event. A two-dimensional representation of the Sponsor's Logo is attached to and forms part of this Agreement in Appendix C.

1.6 "The Promoter" shall be the following company: [____________], whose registered office is at [____________].

1.7 "The Licence Period" shall commence on [the date of this Agreement] and shall continue until: [date].

1.8 "The Sponsorship Fee" shall be the sum of [figure/currency].

1.9 "The Recordings" shall mean the right to exercise and make the film and/or film soundtrack of the Event and/or part, meaning a recording on any medium from which a moving image may by any means be produced and/or the sound recording of the Event and/or any part regardless of the medium of which the sound recording is made or the method by which the sounds are produced or reproduced whether in existence now or created in the future.

1.10 "The Recording Rights" shall mean the right to exercise and make the Recordings of the Event and/or part(s) and to reproduce, supply, distribute all such material arising from the Recordings and authorise others to do so.

1.11 "The Production Company" shall mean the following company which has been appointed by the Association to make the Recordings: [Name] of [Address].

1.12 "The Television Company" shall mean the following company which has been licensed by the Association to broadcast, transmit or supply the Recordings: [Name] of [Address].

1.13 "All Media Rights" shall mean the right to export the Recordings and any part(s) and any development or adaptations whether in existence now or created in the future including but not limited to:

1.13.1 all forms of exploitation through the medium of television and radio, satellite, cable, digital and terrestrial;
1.13.2 all forms of telecommunication systems;
1.13.3 all forms of mechanical reproduction including videogram, cassette, laser, disc, DVD;
1.13.4 all forms of theatric and non-theatric audiences;
1.13.5 all forms of publishing;
1.13.6 all forms of electronic reproduction and dissemination, computers, software, CD-ROM internet, multi-media and otherwise;
1.3.7 all forms of merchandising and any other medium of any nature.

1.14 "The Title Rights" shall mean the exclusive right to have the Event referred to for all commercial and promotional purposes, including the broadcast, transmission or supply of the Recordings by any form of cable, satellite, digital, terrestrial as follows: [____________].

2. LICENCE OF RIGHTS

2.1 In consideration of the Sponsorship Fee, the Association grants to the Sponsor the following rights in respect of the Event for the duration of the Licence Period throughout [the world] set out in clauses [2.2 to 2.7] below.

2.2 The Title Rights.

2.3 The right to have the Sponsor's Logo displayed in the following circumstances:

2.3.1 on any promotional literature including flysheets, advertisements in local or national press, posters, programmes, tickets, stationery and any publicity material under the control of the Association;

2.3.2 the exclusive right to have displayed the Sponsor's Logo on each competitor's clothing during the course of the Event in the following manner: [____________];

2.3.3 the exclusive right to have displayed the Sponsor's Logo on the clothing of all stewards, staff and personnel employed by the Association on public duty at the Event in the following manner: [____________]; and

2.3.4 the non-exclusive right to have displayed the Sponsor's Logo on display banners, score-boards, electronic display systems, perimeter fencing and advertising boards within the Venue itself in accordance with the Display Schedule which is attached to and forms part of this Agreement in Appendix D.

2.4 The exclusive right of an appointed representative of the Sponsor to present the championship trophy to the winner of the Event, including the use of the following words during the course of the presentation: [____________].

2.5 The exclusive right to have engraved on all trophies awarded during the course of the Event the following words: [____________].

2.6 Any other specific rights: [____________].

2.7 The right to veto the advertising of any third party to be displayed at the Venue during the course of the Event in any form if, in the reasonable opinion of the Sponsor, such advertising is of a product which directly conflicts or competes with the following products of the Sponsor: [____________].

3. TELEVISION COVERAGE

3.1 The Association confirms that it has reached an unequivocal and binding agreement in writing with the Production Company to produce the Recordings and the Association undertakes to permit the Sponsor (or an appointed representative) to inspect such agreement at the request of the Sponsor but not to take any copies or view financial details.

3.2 The Association confirms that it has reached an unequivocal and binding agreement in writing with the Television Company for the broadcast, transmission or supply of the Recordings in [the following countries]. The Association undertakes to permit the Sponsor (or an appointed representative) to inspect such agreement at the request of the Sponsor but not to take copies or view financial details.

3.3 The Sponsor acknowledges that the Association has no editorial control in respect of times, dates, duration and content of the broadcast, transmission or supply of the Recordings by the Television Company. Nor will the Sponsor seek to receive any compensation, refund or damages from any alteration or disruption or delay in the scheduling of the Recordings by the Television Company.

3.4 The Association agrees that in the event that the Production Company does not produce or deliver the Recordings of the Event for any reason, [figure] per cent of the Sponsorship Fee will become immediately repayable to the Sponsor by the Association.

3.5 The Association agrees that in the event that the Television Company does not broadcast, transmit or supply the Recordings for any reason [figure] per cent of the Sponsorship Fee will become immediately repayable to the Sponsor by the Association.

3.6 The Sponsor acknowledges that no sums shall become repayable by the Association, provided that the Television Company has broadcast, transmitted or supplied not less than [____________] minutes of the Recordings on or before [date].

3.7 The Association agrees that the Sponsor shall not be liable for any costs incurred in respect of the Recordings or the Recording Rights.

4. COPYRIGHT

4.1 The Sponsor and the Association agree to the following:

4.1.1 All Media Rights and intellectual property rights including copyright and any other rights shall be the sole and exclusive property of the Association for the full period of copyright and any extensions or renewals. The Association shall be entitled to retain all sums received at any time from the exploitation of any of these rights in any form of the Recordings.

4.1.2 The Sponsor confirms that it is the sole owner of or controls all copyright, trademarks and any other rights in the Sponsor's Logo and that the use of the Sponsor's Logo by the Association and the Television Company under this Agreement will not expose the Association or the Television Company to any criminal or civil proceedings during the Licence Period.

4.1.3 The Association confirms that it is the sole owner of or controls all copyright, trademarks and any other rights in the Promotional Logo and that the use of the Promotional Logo under this Agreement will not expose the Sponsor to any criminal or civil proceedings during the Licence Period.

4.1.4 All intellectual property rights including copyright and any other rights in the Sponsor's Logo, together with any goodwill, shall be the sole and exclusive property of the Sponsor and the Association shall not acquire any rights or interests in the Sponsor's Logo, including any developments or variations.

4.1.5 All intellectual property rights including copyright and any other rights in the Promotional Logo, together with any goodwill, shall be the sole and exclusive property of the Association and the Sponsor shall not acquire any rights or interests in the Promotional Logo, including any developments or variations.

5. OBLIGATIONS OF THE SPONSOR

5.1 In consideration of the rights granted under this Agreement, the Sponsor agrees to pay to the Association the Sponsorship Fee as follows:

5.1.1 [____________] upon signature of this Agreement;
5.1.2 [____________] on or before [____________];
5.1.3 [____________] within [____________] of the completion of the Event.

5.2 In addition to the Sponsorship Fee, the Sponsor agrees that it shall be responsible for the payment of all prize money to be paid to the successful competitors at the presentation ceremony in accordance with the Prize Money Schedule which is attached to and forms part of this Agreement in Appendix E. The Sponsor confirms that the total prize money, including any plate competition, amounts to not less than: [figure/currency].

5.3 In addition to the Sponsorship Fee and the prize money, the Sponsor agrees to provide and be responsible for the cost of the following trophies for the Event, which shall then be the property of the Association:

the winner: [____________];
the runner-up: [____________];
the losing semi-finalists: [____________];
the losing quarter-finalists: [____________];
the winner of the plate competition: [____________];
the runner-up of the plate competition: [____________];
all other competitors: [____________].

A Trophy Schedule is attached to and forms part of this Agreement, which describes the size, material and form of each of the trophies in Appendix F.

5.4 The Sponsor agrees to deliver all trophies to the Association not later than: [date].

5.6 The Sponsor confirms that a comprehensive insurance policy shall be arranged, at its sole cost, for the following:

5.6.1 loss, theft or damage to all of the trophies prior to and during the Event; and
5.6.2 the following specific matters: [____________].

5.7 The Sponsor agrees to provide to the Association, at its sole cost and expense, the following items of clothing bearing the Sponsor's Logo and the Promotional Logo: [____________]; of [____________] quantity.

5.8 The Sponsor acknowledges that the Association shall be entitled to approve in advance a pre-production sample of each of the proposed items of clothing to be supplied by the Sponsor under clause 5.7.

5.9 The Sponsor agrees to provide, at its sole cost and expense, all material of the Sponsor's Logo in a suitable form for its reproduction as required by the Association at the request of the Promoter.

5.10 The Sponsor undertakes to provide the following minimum number of free samples and giveaways of the sponsor's product during the course of the Event for the competitors, guests of the Association within the official hospitality suite, the press and all official stewards/referees/supervisors: [____________].

5.11 The Sponsor undertakes to provide, at its sole cost and expense, display banners, score-boards, software for any electronic display systems and perimeter advertising boards which solely bear or relate to the Sponsor's Logo.

5.12 The Sponsor confirms that it has and will retain full authority to enter into this Agreement and is not bound by any agreement with any third party which adversely affects this Agreement.

5.13 The Sponsor acknowledges that the Association, subject to clauses 2.3 and 2.7, is entitled to license or authorise third parties to advertise or promote their products or services during the course of and in relation to the Event, including the placement of advertisement and display boards at the Venue.

5.14 The Sponsor confirms that the Association shall be entitled to retain all sums received from the exploitation of the Event in any form, including ticket and programme sales, merchandising and advertising of the Event.

5.15 The Sponsor agrees that it shall not be entitled to authorise any third parties to assist it in the funding of the Event without the prior written consent of the Association. Nor shall the Sponsor authorise, pledge or commit the Authority to any third party.

5.16 The Sponsor shall be responsible for any costs arising from the hospitality suite and other facilities provided by the Association.

5.17 The Sponsor any not use the name of the Association, or any trademark, logo, diagram, or otherwise of the Event, Promoter or any other third party including competitors in any manner not specifically authorised under this Agreement. In particular it shall not promote or advertise any of its goods or services by any such unauthorised use.

6. OBLIGATIONS OF THE ASSOCIATION

6.1 The Association confirms that it is responsible for organisation and staging of the Event at the Venue in accordance with the Event Schedule.

6.2 The Association confirms that, whenever possible, it will ensure that the Sponsor's Logo will be present in accordance with this Agreement and that the Promoter undertakes to use its best endeavours to ensure that the title of the Event and the Sponsor's Logo are incorporated into all promotional and publicity material, particularly: [____________].

6.3 The Association confirms that it has full authority to enter into this Agreement and is not bound by any agreement with any third party which adversely affects this Agreement.

6.4 The Association confirms that the Sponsor shall not be responsible for any direct or indirect costs relating to the Event, other than those specifically set out in this Agreement.

6.5 The Association confirms that it has entered into an agreement with the Promoter for the purposes of the promotion, advertising and marketing of the Event.

6.6 The Association confirms that it shall be responsible for arranging and organising the following particular matters in respect of the Event:

6.6.1 the attendance of and payment for all referees, stewards, staff and any other personnel employed by the Association on duty throughout the Event; and

6.6.2 the printing and supply of flysheets, posters, programmes, tickets, stationery, publicity material and advertisements in local and national press and [____________].

6.7 The Association undertakes that all promotions and advertising will not be offensive or obscene in nature or derogatory of any third party. The Association will ensure that the use of the Promotional Logo and the Sponsor's Logo will not infringe any sponsorship or advertising rules currently in existence.

6.8 The Association confirms that printed programmes shall be made available to the general public which will bear the Promotional Logo and the Sponsor's Logo and a statement from the Sponsors of not less than [____________] words, and will refer to the Event throughout in the manner agreed in clause 2.

6.9 The Association confirms that not less than [____________] competitors have confirmed their participation in the Event.

6.10 The Association undertakes that the Event will be conducted in accordance with the rules and constitution of the Association, a copy of which is attached to and forms part of this Agreement in Appendix G.

6.11 The Association confirms that the Sponsor shall be provided with the following amenities:

6.11.1 a hospitality suite capable of accommodating not less than: [____________] official guests of the Sponsor, which shall be situated at: [____________].
6.11.2 an administrative headquarters for the Sponsor, which shall be situated at: [____________], which shall have available the following facilities: [____________].
6.11.3 the Association agrees to provide the Sponsor with not less than [____________] complimentary VIP tickets, together with appropriate car parking facilities for the Event.

6.12 The Association confirms that all competitors of the Event are or will be bona fide members of the Association and that all competitors have agreed [in writing] to co-operate with the Association in all applicable usage of the Sponsor's Logo.

6.13 The Association confirms that it has entered into a bona fide written agreement for the use of the Venue with the Proprietor and has made all administrative and financial arrangements necessary for the smooth running of the Event, including the hiring of the Venue and any prior arrangements required with the Proprietor, the local authority and the police.

6.14 Irrespective of any insurance cover provided by the Sponsor, the Association confirms that it will take out a comprehensive insurance policy for the Event, including adequate public liability insurance for injury or death of any competitors or spectators. The Association agrees to provide a copy of such insurance policy for inspection to the Sponsor upon request.

6.15 The Association accepts that, notwithstanding the obligations of the Association and the Promoter to promote and advertise the Event within the terms of this Agreement. The Sponsor shall be entitled to advertise, publicise, promote and otherwise commercially exploit its own products, goodwill and reputation as a result of the Sponsor's involvement in the Event for the duration of the Licence Period.

7. MISCELLANEOUS

MUTUAL INDEMNITY

7.1 The Sponsor and the Association mutually undertake to indemnify the other against all liabilities, claims, demands, actions, costs, damages or loss arising out of any breach by either party of any of the terms of this Agreement. In the event of any claim, dispute, action, writ or summons the Sponsor and the Association agree to provide full details to the other party at the earliest opportunity and shall not settle any such matter without first consulting the other party. Each party shall bear its own legal costs but may later seek to reclaim them on an indemnity basis.

7.2 It is agreed that the maximum liability for any reason of each of the parties under this Agreement shall be fixed at:

[figure/currency] in total for the Association
[figure/currency] in total for the Sponsor
[figure/currency] in total for the Promoter.

This limit shall include all costs, expenses, compensation, damages, losses or otherwise.

CONFIDENTIALITY

7.3 The Sponsor and the Association shall not disclose to any third party any confidential business or future plans of the other party at any time acquired during the existence of this Agreement. No reference is to be made to the terms of this Agreement by either party in any advertising, publicity or promotional material without the prior written consent of the other party.

AMENDMENTS

7.4 This Agreement supersedes all previous agreements, representations or promises and sets out all the terms agreed between the parties. Any amendment or alteration to this Agreement must be in writing and signed by an authorised signatory of each party.

RELATIONSHIP

7.5 This Agreement shall not be deemed to create any partnership, agency or employment relationship between the parties.

NOTICES

7.6 For the purposes of this Agreement, all notices shall be sent to the following addresses in writing by courier or recorded delivery postal service:

the Association: [____________];
the Sponsor: [____________].

VALUE ADDED TAX

7.7 All sums payable under this Agreement are exclusive of any value added tax that may be payable by either party.

THIRD PARTY TRANSFERS

7.8 Neither party shall assign, transfer, charge or make over this Agreement or any of its rights or obligations without the prior written consent of the other party.

FORCE MAJEURE

7.9 In the event that this Agreement cannot be performed or its obligations fulfilled for any reason beyond the reasonable control of the Sponsor or the Association, including such events as war, industrial action, floods or Acts of God. Then in the event that this Agreement cannot be performed or its obligations fulfilled for any reason beyond the reasonable control of the defaulting party for a continuous period of [____________]. Then the Agreement will automatically terminate at the end of that period of force majeure. At that time the parties shall enter into mediation to reach an amicable settlement of the outstanding issues relating to this Agreement.

TERMINATION AND EXPIRY OF THE AGREEMENT

7.10 In addition to any other rights and remedies at law, this Agreement may be terminated by giving written notice to the party who has breached this Agreement or has defaulted in the following circumstances:

7.10.1 where the Sponsor has failed to account or make payments as required under this Agreement;
7.10.2 where the Sponsor or the Association has committed a serious breach of its obligations under this Agreement, unless the party committing the breach rectifies the position, as far as reasonably possible, within [____________];
7.10.3 where the Sponsor or the Association goes into voluntary or involuntary liquidation;
7.10.4 where the Sponsor or the Association is declared insolvent, either in bankruptcy proceedings or other legal proceedings;
7.10.5 where an agreement with creditors has been reached by the Sponsor or the Association due to its failure or inability to pay its debts as they fall due; or

7.10.6 where a receiver is appointed over the whole or part of the Sponsor's or the Association's business.

GOVERNING LAW

7.11 This Agreement shall be subject to the Laws of [England].

ATTACH THE FOLLOWING DOCUMENTS:

APPENDIX:
A—EVENTS SCHEDULE
B—PROMOTIONAL LOGO
C—SPONSOR'S LOGO
D—DISPLAY SCHEDULE
E—PRIZE MONEY SCHEDULE
F—TROPHY SCHEDULE
G—CONSTITUTION AND RULES OF ASSOCIATION

FOR AND ON BEHALF OF THE SPONSOR: [____________]

FOR AND ON BEHALF OF THE ASSOCIATION: [____________]

OUTLINE—SPONSORSHIP AGREEMENT WITH A SPORTS ASSOCIATION FOR A TELEVISED CHAMPIONSHIP EVENT

This Agreement is between a Sports Association and a Sponsor for the purpose of funding televised championship Event. It is fundamental to this contract that the Event is to be recorded and then broadcast or transmitted on television. The Association has reached a binding agreement with a Production Company and Television Company to that effect. The Television Company could also be the Production Company. The rules concerning the funding of programmes by sponsors and sports bodies should be reviewed.

The Association is responsible for organising and arranging the Event, which is being promoted by a named Promoter appointed by the Association. In addition to the Sponsorship Fee, the Sponsor is responsible for the prize money and trophies. The Sponsor is entitled to have its logo displayed on most items associated with the Event, such as official clothing, display boards, promotional literature, tickets and programmes. The Sponsor is also acquiring the exclusive title rights to the championship. The sponsor has the right to a specific number of VIP tickets and other hospitality facilities. The Association is entitled to retain all income from the Event, including the exploitation of the recordings of the Event together with the gate and programme money and third party advertising.

It is significant to note that the Sponsor itself is not acquiring any media or television rights directly as such from the Association. There is only a reassurance that there has been a television agreement which the Sponsor can inspect with the financial details removed. It is important that no rights are acquired by either party on each other's trademarks or logos, or any goodwill. There are provisions for a refund of part of the Sponsorship Fee if only a proportion of the Recordings are shown on television. The definition of the Recordings covers film and film soundtrack and sound recordings in any medium.

AGREEMENT BETWEEN ORGANISERS AND PROMOTERS OF AN EVENT

AN AGREEMENT made this [____________] day of [____________]

BETWEEN:

(1) [____________]
of [____________] (to be known as the Promoter in this Agreement)

AND

(2) [____________]
of [____________] (to be known as the Organisers in this Agreement).

IT IS AGREED as follows:

1. DEFINITIONS

The words below are agreed to mean as follows:

1.1 "The Event" shall be the following series of performances, recitals, readings and events collectively entitled [____________]; which is to take place between the following dates [____________] inclusive.
A summary of the format, content and structure of the Event is described in the Event Schedule which is attached to and forms part of this Agreement in Schedule 1.

1.2 "The Venue" shall be the premises where the Event is to take place which are situated at [Name][Address].

1.3 "The Proprietor" is the owner of the Venue as follows: [____________], whose registered address is at [____________].

1.4 "The Organisers' Logo" shall be the artwork, design, logo, service mark and trademark including any associated words, slogan or text of the Organisers to be used for the promotion, advertising and marketing of the Event. A two-dimensional copy of the Organisers' Logo is attached to and forms part of this Agreement in Schedule 2.

1.5 "The Sponsor" shall mean the following company which is contributing to the funding of the Event: [Name] of [Address].

1.6 "The Sponsor's Logo" shall be the artwork, design, logo, service mark and trademark including any associated words, slogan or text of the Sponsor to be used for the promotion, advertising and marketing of the Event. A two-dimensional copy of the Sponsor's Logo is attached to and forms part of this Agreement in Schedule 3.

1.7 "The Promoter's Logo" shall be the artwork, design, logo, service mark and trademark including any associated words, slogan or text of the Promoter to be used for the promotion, advertising and marketing of the Event. A two-dimensional copy of the Promoter's Logo is attached to and forms part of this Agreement in Schedule 4.

1.8 "The Promotion Period" shall commence on [date] and shall continue until: [date].

1.9 "The Territory" shall be the United Kingdom of Great Britain, Northern Ireland, the Republic of Ireland, the Channel Islands, the Isle of Man and the following countries: [____________].

1.10 "The Promotion Fee" shall be the total sum of [figure/currency].

1.11 "The Promotion Expenses" shall be the following costs reasonably and properly expended by the Promoter in furtherance of this Agreement, which are not recouped from any third party:

1.11.1 the placing of advertisements in local and national press, and in particular, in the following newspapers and periodicals: [____________];
1.11.2 the commissioning of artwork printing and the distribution of promotional, publicity and advertising material;
1.11.3 the cost of setting, printing and distributing the admission tickets and the official programme; and
1.11.4 any other costs specifically agreed between the Promoter and the Organisers as follows: [____________].

1.12 "The Promotion Budget" shall mean the combined costs and expenses of the Promotion Fee and the Promotion Expenses, which shall not exceed the following sum: [figure/currency].

1.13 "The Recording Rights" shall mean the right to make any film and/or film soundtrack of the Event or part(s) meaning a recording on any medium from which a moving image may by any means be produced and/or the sound recording of the Event and/or part(s) regardless of the medium on which the sound recording is made or the method by which the sounds are produced or reproduced whether in existence now or created in the future. Together with the right to exercise and make the recordings of the Event and/or part(s) and to reproduce, supply, distribute and authorise others to do so in respect of all such material.

1.14 "The Title Rights" shall mean the exclusive right to have the Event for all commercial and promotional purposes, including the broadcast, transmission or supply of the Event on all forms of television referred to as [____________].

2. APPOINTMENT OF EXCLUSIVE PROMOTER

2.1 The Organisers agree to appoint the Promoter as the sole and exclusive promoter of the Event throughout the Territory for the duration of the Promotion Period.

2.2 In consideration of the payment of the Promotion Fee and the Promotion Expenses, the Promoter agrees to provide its exclusive services to promote, market and advertise the Event throughout the Territory for the duration of the Promotion Period in accordance with the terms of this Agreement.

3. SPONSOR'S RIGHTS

3.1 The Promoter acknowledges that the Organisers have granted to the Sponsor the following rights in respect of the Event for the duration of the Promotion Period throughout the Territory:

3.1.1 the Title Rights
3.1.2 the right to have the Sponsor's Logo displayed on any promotional literature, including flysheets, advertisements in local or national press, posters, the official programme, admission tickets, stationery and publicity material;
3.1.3 the exclusive right to have displayed the Sponsor's Logo on the clothing of all stewards, staff and personnel employed by the Organisers on public duty at the Event in the following manner: [____________];
3.1.4 The non-exclusive right to have displayed the Sponsor's Logo on display banners, score-boards, electronic display systems, perimeter fencing and advertising boards within the Venue itself in accordance with the Display Schedule, which is attached to and forms part of this Agreement in Schedule 5; and
3.1.5 any other specific rights: [____________].

3.2 The Promoter acknowledges that the Organisers have granted to the Sponsor the right to veto the advertising of any third party to be displayed at the Venue during the course of the Event in any form if, in the reasonable opinion of the Sponsor, such advertising is of a product which directly conflicts or competes with the following products of the Sponsor: [____________].

4. COPYRIGHT

4.1 The Organisers and the Promoter agree to the following:

4.1.1 All intellectual property rights including copyright and any other rights in the Event and the Recording Rights are and shall remain the sole and exclusive property of the Organisers throughout the world. The Organisers shall be entitled to retain all sums received from the exercise of the Recording Rights in any media throughout the world.
4.1.2 The Organisers confirm that it is the sole owner of or controls all intellectual property rights including copyright and any other rights in the Organisers' Logo and that the use of the Organisers' Logo under this Agreement will not expose the Promoter to any criminal or civil proceedings and that the Promoter shall not acquire any rights or interests in the Organisers' Logo, including any developments or variations.
4.1.3 The Promoter confirms that it is the sole owner of or controls all intellectual property rights including copyright and any other rights in the Promoter's

Logo and that the use of the Promoter's Logo under this Agreement will not expose the Organisers to any criminal or civil proceedings and that the Organisers shall not acquire any rights or interests in the Promoter's Logo, including any developments or variations.

4.1.4 All intellectual property rights including copyright and any other rights in the Sponsor's Logo, together with any goodwill, shall be the sole and exclusive property of the Sponsor and the Organisers and the Promoter shall not acquire any rights or interests in the Sponsor's Logo, including any developments or variations.

5. OBLIGATIONS OF THE PROMOTER

5.1 The Promoter shall provide its services under this Agreement to the best of its skill and ability and agrees to use its reasonable endeavours to perform the following duties in respect of the Event:

5.1.1 to organise the commissioning and printing of all admission tickets, the official programme, posters and flysheets in the following quantities: [____________];

5.1.2 to distribute and have displayed in an efficient and proper manner all printed posters and flysheets;

5.1.3 to promote and advertise the Event on local and national radio and press;

5.1.4 to arrange for the production and supply of the following merchandising material: [____________];

5.1.5 to obtain free news television coverage of the Event wherever possible; and

5.1.6 any other specific duties: [____________].

5.2 The Promoter shall perform all services under this Agreement diligently to ensure that the Event is promoted, marketed and advertised cost effectively throughout the Territory for the duration of the Promotion Period.

5.3 The Promoter undertakes that all promotions, advertising and marketing of the Organisers, the Sponsor and the Event pursuant to this Agreement will not be offensive or obscene in nature or derogatory of any third party. The Promoter will ensure that all material produced under this Agreement will not infringe any sponsorship or advertising rules, statutes or directives currently in existence and in particular of the following bodies: [____________].

5.4 The Promoter shall, as far as possible, keep the Organisers fully informed on a regular basis as regards any negotiations with any third party in respect of the Promoter's obligations under this Agreement.

5.5 The Promoter confirms that it has full power and authority to enter into and perform this Agreement and is not bound by any other agreement which adversely affects this Agreement.

5.6 The Promoter confirms that it will not disclose to any third party any confidential information concerning the Organisers or their future plans acquired during the Promotion Period without the consent of the Organisers.

5.7 In the event of the Promotion Budget being exceeded by up to [____________], the Promoter agrees to inform the Organisers in advance and to provide the Organisers with a statement of costs incurred to date and details of the additional costs.

5.8 In the event of the Promotion Budget being exceeded by more than [__________], the Promoter agrees that the prior written approval of the Organisers shall be required in order to authorise any further expenditure and that any further payment shall be at the Organisers' sole discretion.

5.9 The Promoter undertakes that it and its sub-agents, sub-licensees and distributors shall keep full and accurate books of account, records, contracts, software and other material showing all allocation receipts and expenditure of the Promotion Budget.

5.10 The Promoter agrees that the Organisers shall be entitled to arrange for an audit at anytime either during or up to the expiry of one year from the end of the Promotion Period in order to inspect and make copies of the Promoter's books of account, records, contracts, software and any other relevant material in order to verify the Promotion Budget.

5.11 The Promoter agrees to provide in advance to the Organisers for their prior approval, copies and samples of all proposed advertising, publicity, promotional, merchandising and packaging material, the official programme and admission tickets prior to the production and distribution of any such material.

5.12 The Promoter agrees to ensure that all proposed advertising, publicity, promotional, merchandising and packaging material, including the official programme and admission tickets, shall bear the Organisers' Logo, the Sponsor's Logo and the Promoter's Logo in such positions and dimensions as the Organisers may direct.

5.13 The Promoter agrees to ensure that all proposed advertising, publicity, promotional and packaging material, including the official programme and admission tickets shall incorporate the agreed title of the Event.

5.14 The Promoter acknowledges that the Organisers shall be entitled to retain all sums and benefits received from the commercial exploitation of the Event, including admission charges, sales from the official programme and any advertising, sponsorship or merchandising material and that the Promoter shall not be entitled to any part of such sums.

5.15 The Promoter agrees to provide the following copyright notice to the Organisers in any publicity, promotional, advertising, merchandising and packaging material concerning the Organisers and the Event: [____________].

5.16 The Promoter agrees to ensure that all third parties to be contracted by the Promoter under this Agreement will agree that all intellectual property rights including copyright and any other rights concerning the Organisers' Logo and the Sponsor's Logo shall remain the sole and exclusive property of the Organisers and the Sponsor respectively and that the Promoter and all such third parties shall not acquire any rights in any trademark, logo, title, artwork, words, slogan or text and any developments or variations.

5.17 The Promoter acknowledges that the Organisers shall be entitled, upon request, to be provided with a copy of any contract, record, document, software or other material in possession or under the control of the Promoter relating to the Event at the Promoter's cost.

5.18 The Promoter acknowledges that the Organisers, in accordance with and subject to the terms of this Agreement, are entitled to license or authorise third parties to advertise during the course of the Event, including the placement of advertising boards at the Venue.

6. OBLIGATIONS OF THE ORGANISERS

6.1 The Organisers agree to pay to the Promoter the Promotion Fee, as follows:

6.1.1 [____________] upon signature of this Agreement;
6.1.2 [____________] on or before: [____________];
6.1.3 [____________]on or before [____________].

6.2 In addition to the Promotion Fee, the Organisers agree to pay to the Promoter the Promotion Expenses within [____________] of [the last day of each month] following the receipt of a detailed invoice, together with supporting documents.

6.3 In the event of the Promotion Budget being exceeded by up to [____________], the Organisers agree to pay such additional costs, provided that the Promoter informs the Organisers in advance and provides, upon request, to the Organisers a statement of costs incurred to date and details of the additional costs.

6.4 In the event of the Promotion Budget being exceeded by more than [__________], the Organisers agree to pay such additional costs, given that they have provided prior written approval of the expenditure to the Promoter.

6.5 The Organisers agree to provide the Promoter with such information, documentation, historical background and any other material concerning the Organisers, the Event and the Sponsor as may be reasonably required by the Promoter for the purpose of fulfilling its obligations under this Agreement at the Organiser's cost and risk on loan.

6.6 The Organisers confirm that they have full title and authority to enter into this Agreement and are not bound by any previous agreement which adversely affects this Agreement.

6.7 The Organisers confirm that the Event and the Organisers' Logo do not contain any obscene, offensive or defamatory material and will not expose the Promoter to any civil or criminal proceedings during the Promotion Period.

6.8 The Organisers confirm that the Event and the Organisers' Logo do not contain any material which infringes the copyright or any other rights of any third party throughout the Territory during the Promotion Period.

6.9 The Organisers agree to supply, at their sole cost and expense, copies of such artwork and other material of the Organisers, the Event, the Organisers' Logo and the Sponsor's Logo which may be in the possession or under the control of the Organisers required by the Promoter for the purposes of this Agreement. Such material shall be supplied to the Promoter at the Organiser's cost and risk on loan.

6.10 The Organisers agree to provide the following amenities and facilities for the Promoter during the Event:

6.10.1 an administrative headquarters which shall be situated at [____________] and which shall have available the following facilities: [____________]; and

6.10.2 the Organisers agree to provide the Promoter with not less than [____________] complimentary VIP tickets, together with appropriate car parking facilities for the Event.

6.11 The Organisers confirm that they have entered into a bona fide written agreement for the use of the Venue with the Proprietor and have made all administrative and financial arrangements necessary for the smooth running of the Event, including the hiring of the Venue and any prior arrangements required with the Proprietor, the local authority, the local community and the police.

6.12 The Organisers confirm that it will take out at its sole cost and expense, a comprehensive insurance policy for the Event, including adequate public liability insurance.

6.13 The Organisers confirm that it shall be solely responsible for all sums incurred in respect of the Event and that the Promoter shall not be responsible for any sums, except for any unauthorised expenditure and costs incurred by the Promoter which are not within the Promotion Expenses and which are not agreed in advance with the Organisers.

7. MISCELLANEOUS

MUTUAL INDEMNITY

7.1 The Organisers and the Promoter mutually undertake to indemnify the other against all liabilities, claims, demands, actions, costs, damages or loss arising out of any breach by either party of any of the terms of this Agreement.

CANCELLATION OF THE EVENT

7.2 The Organisers and the Promoter agree that where the Promoter is given notice of the cancellation of the Event by the Organisers on or before [date]; then the Promoter shall only be entitled to be paid [figure] together with all sums incurred in respect of the Promotion Expenses.

7.3 Where the Event is cancelled after [date], the Organisers and the Promoter agree that the Promoter shall be entitled to be paid the Promoter's Fee in total, in addition to all sums incurred in respect of the Promotion Expenses.

7.4 Clauses 7.2 and 7.3 shall not apply where the Event is cancelled due to force majeure.

CONFIDENTIALITY

7.5 The Organisers and the Promoter shall not disclose to any third party any confidential business or future plans of the other party at any time acquired during the existence of this Agreement except where the information is in the public domain or for which the Organiser has provided its consent. No reference is to be made to the terms of this Agreement by either party in any advertising, publicity or promotional material without the prior written consent of the other party.

AMENDMENTS

7.6 This Agreement sets out all the terms agreed between the parties and any amendment or alteration must be in writing.

RELATIONSHIP

7.7 This Agreement shall not be deemed to create any partnership, agency or employment relationship between the parties.

NOTICES

7.8 For the purposes of this Agreement, all notices shall be sent to the following parties:

The Organisers: [____________];
The Promoter: [____________].

VALUE ADDED TAX

7.9 All sums payable under this Agreement are exclusive of any value added tax that may be payable by either party.

THIRD PARTY TRANSFERS

7.10 The Promoter shall not assign, transfer, charge or make over this Agreement, or any of its rights or obligations, without the prior written consent of the Organisers.

FORCE MAJEURE

7.11 In the event that this Agreement cannot be performed or its obligations fulfilled for any reason beyond the reasonable control of the Promoter or the Organisers, including such events as war, industrial action, floods or Acts of God. Then such non-performance or failure to fulfil its obligations shall be deemed not to be a breach of this Agreement. In the event that this Agreement cannot be performed or its obligations fulfilled for any reason beyond the reasonable control of the defaulting party for a continuous period of [____________], then the other party may, at its discretion, terminate this Agreement by notice in writing at at any time once they are aware that the Agreement cannot be fulfilled for that period.

TERMINATION

7.12 In addition to any other rights and remedies at law, this Agreement may be terminated by giving written notice to the other party who has breached this Agreement or has defaulted in the following circumstances:

7.12.1 where the Organisers or the Promoter has failed to account or make payments as required under this Agreement,

7.12.2 where the Organisers or the Promoter has committed a serious breach of its obligations under this Agreement;

7.12.3 where the Organisers or the Promoter goes into voluntary or involuntary liquidation;

7.12.4 where the Organisers or the Promoter is declared insolvent, either in bankruptcy proceedings or other legal proceedings;

7.12.5 where an agreement with creditors has been reached by the Organisers or the Promoter due to its failure or inability to pay its debts as they fall due; or

7.12.6 where a receiver is appointed over the whole or part of the Organisers or the Promoter's business.

GOVERNING LAW

7.13 This Agreement shall be construed and interpreted by the Courts of [__________] in the jurisdiction of the Laws of [__________].

DOCUMENTS ATTACHED:

SCHEDULE 1—Event Schedule
SCHEDULE 2—Organiser's Logo
SCHEDULE 3—Sponsor's Logo
SCHEDULE 4—Promoter's Logo
SCHEDULE 5—Display Schedule.

FOR AND ON BEHALF OF THE PROMOTER: [____________]
Name/Title/Date

FOR AND ON BEHALF OF THE ORGANISERS: [____________]
Name/Title/Date

OUTLINE—AGREEMENT BETWEEN ORGANISERS AND PROMOTERS OF AN EVENT

This is an agreement between the Organisers and the Promoter of an Event. The situation envisaged is one where the Organisers have arranged the Venue, the artiste/performers/musicians, etc., and sponsorship, and are engaging the services of a company to promote, market and advertise the Event.

The Event is being sponsored, although the Sponsor is not party to this Agreement. In consideration of the Sponsor's contribution to the funding of the Event, the Sponsor is granted certain rights, and include the title rights to the Event and the right to have the Sponsor's Logo displayed in defined circumstances. There may be more than one Sponsor in which case the Agreement should be amended accordingly. Although television coverage is not envisaged under this Agreement, if the Event is recorded the copyright and all income from the commercial exploitation of the recordings are retained by the Organisers. The Organisers also retain all the proceeds from the commercial exploitation of the Event, including the gate money, programme sales and advertising.

In return for the services of the Promoter a Promotion Fee is being paid by the Organisers. In addition, the Organisers are liable to reimburse the Promoter for the Promotional Expenses. The combined costs of the Promotion Fee and the Promotional Expenses are referred to as the Promotion Budget. There are provisions for the Budget being exceeded.

The Promoter is also responsible for organising and printing the admission tickets, the official programme, posters and flysheets, all of which shall bear the Organiser's, the Sponsor's and the Promoter's logos. The final decision in respect of the relative position and size of the logos remains with the Organisers. The Organisers are also agreeing to provide the Promoter with non-monetary benefits such as car parking facilities, free tickets, in-house amenities and an administrative headquarters.

There is an agreed fixed sum of payment in the event that the Organisers decide to cancel the Event before a particular date. After that time the Promoters will be paid all the Promoter's Fee whether or not the Event takes place, together with such Promoters Expenses as they have occurred.

SPONSORSHIP OF MUSIC/ARTS FESTIVAL

BETWEEN:

(1) [____________]
of [____________] (to be known as the Sponsor in this Agreement)

AND

(2) [____________]
of [____________] (to be known as the Organisers in this Agreement).

IT IS AGREED as follows:

1. DEFINITIONS

The words below are agreed to mean as follows:

1.1 "The Festival" shall be the following series of events collectively entitled [____________], which is to take place between the following dates [____________], inclusive.

A Festival Schedule which includes a full description of the content of the Festival is attached to and forms part of this Agreement in Appendix A.

1.2 "The Venue" shall be the premises where the Festival is to take place, which are situated at [Name][Address].

1.3 "The Proprietor" is the following owner of the Venue: [Name][Company].

1.4 "The Organisers' Logo" shall be the artwork, design, logo, service mark and trademark, together with any accompanying words, slogan or text of the Organisers, to be used for all promotion, advertising and marketing of the Festival. A copy of the Organisers' Logo is attached to and forms part of this Agreement in Appendix B.

1.5 "The Sponsor's Logo" shall be the artwork, design, logo, service mark and trademark, together with any accompanying words, slogan or text of the Sponsor to be used for all promotion, advertising and marketing of the Festival. A copy of the Sponsor's Logo is attached to and forms part of this Agreement in Appendix C.

1.6 "The Sponsor's Product" shall mean the following articles/services [____________].

1.7 "The Promoter" shall be the following company: [____________].

1.8 "The Promoter's Logo" shall be the artwork, design, logo and trademark, together with any accompanying words, slogan or text of the Promoter, to be used for all promotion, advertising and marketing of the Festival. A copy of The Promoter's Logo is attached to and forms part of this Agreement in Schedule D.

1.9 "The Sponsorship Fee" shall be the sum of [figure/currency].

2. NON-EXCLUSIVE LICENCE OF SPONSORSHIP RIGHTS

2.1 In consideration of the payment of the Sponsorship Fee, the Organisers grant to the Sponsor the following rights in respect of the Festival set out in clauses 2.2 to 2.4 below.

2.2 The non-exclusive right to have the Sponsor's Logo reasonably, prominently and clearly displayed in the following circumstances:

2.2.1 on any promotional literature, including flysheets, advertisements in local or national press, posters, programmes, admission tickets, stationery, publicity material and merchandising of material under the control of the Organisers;
2.2.2 the exclusive right to have displayed the Sponsor's Logo in the main public reception foyer in the following manner: [____________];
2.2.3 the non-exclusive right to have displayed the Sponsor's Logo on the clothing of all stewards, staff and any other personnel employed by the Organisers on public duty in the following manner: [____________];
2.2.4 the non-exclusive right to have displayed the Sponsor's Logo on display banners, electronic display systems, perimeter fencing and advertising boards within the Venue itself, in accordance with the Display Schedule which is attached to and forms part of this Agreement in Appendix E; and
2.2.5 any other specific promotional rights: [____________].

2.3 The right to veto the advertising of any third party to be displayed during the course of the Festival in any form if, in the reasonable opinion of the Sponsor, such advertising is of a product which directly or indirectly conflicts or competes with the following products of the Sponsor: [____________].

2.4 The right to exhibit, sell and promote the Sponsor's Product during the course of the Festival at the following sites at the Venue: [____________].
A copy of the Layout of the Venue showing the relative dimensions and positions of all commercial sites including the Sponsor's is attached to and forms part of this Agreement in Appendix F.

3. COPYRIGHT

3.1 The Sponsor and the Organisers agree to the following:

3.1.1 All intellectual property rights including trademarks, copyright and any other rights in the Sponsor's Logo shall be the sole and exclusive property of the Sponsor, together with any goodwill, and the Organisers shall not acquire any rights in the Sponsor's Logo, including any developments or variations.

3.1.2 All intellectual property rights including trademarks, copyright and any other rights in the Organiser's Logo shall be the sole and exclusive property of the Organisers, together with any goodwill, and the Sponsor shall not acquire any rights in the Organisers' Logo, including any developments or variations.

3.1.3 All intellectual property rights including trademarks, copyright and any other rights in the Promoter's Logo shall be the sole and exclusive property of the Promoter, together with any goodwill, and the Sponsor and the Organisers shall not acquire any rights in the Promoter's Logo, including any developments or variations.

3.1.4 All material produced for the Festival, excluding the Sponsor's Logo and the Promoter's Logo, shall remain or be assigned to become the sole and exclusive property of the Organisers.

4. OBLIGATIONS OF THE SPONSOR

4.1 In consideration of the rights granted under this Agreement, the Sponsor agrees to pay to the Organisers the Sponsorship Fee as follows:

4.1.1 [____________] upon signature of this Agreement;
4.1.2 [____________] upon commencement of the Festival; and
4.1.3 [____________] upon completion of the Festival.

4.2 The Sponsor agrees to provide to the Organisers, at the Sponsor's sole cost and expense, all suitable material including artwork of the Sponsor's Logo in order for it to be reproduced under the control of the Organisers by the following date: [____________].

4.3 The Sponsor agrees to arrange for and bear the cost of all banners, bill-boards, computer software for any electronic display system and any other promotional material relating solely to the Sponsor. The Sponsor undertakes that all such material shall be in place and safely secured in good time before the commencement of the Festival and to adhere to all directions and safety guidelines issued by the Organisers.

4.4 The Sponsor confirms that it is the sole owner of or controls all intellectual property rights, trademarks, copyright and any other rights in the Sponsor's Logo and that the use by the Organisers of the Sponsor's Logo under this Agreement will not expose the Organisers or the Promoter to any criminal or civil proceedings during the term of this Agreement.

4.5 The Sponsor confirms that it has and will retain full authority to enter into this Agreement and is not bound by any previous agreement with any third party which adversely affects this Agreement.

4.6 The Sponsor acknowledges that the Organisers, in accordance with and subject to the terms of this Agreement, are entitled to license or authorise third parties to advertise and sponsor the Festival.

4.7 The Sponsor confirms that the Organisers shall be entitled to retain all sums received from the exploitation of the Festival, including ticket and programme sales and any income from any third parties for advertising, merchandising, film, soundtrack or sound recordings.

4.8 The Sponsor confirms that it shall arrange a comprehensive insurance policy, at its sole cost, for the following:

4.8.1 public liability at the Venue during the course of the Festival, in respect of the Sponsor's Product and any other materials or goods owned or controlled by the Sponsor, which, in respect of any individual claim is not less than [____________];

4.8.2 loss, theft or damage to any of the Sponsor's Product or other materials or goods owned or controlled by the Sponsor; and

4.8.3 to cover any loss, damage or claim arising directly or indirectly by the use by the public of the specific product or services being promoted by the Sponsor, together with all other goods or services associated with the Sponsor's Logo.

4.9 The Sponsor undertakes to provide free samples, giveaways and promotional material of the Sponsor's Product in sufficient quantities to all guests of the Organisers within the official hospitality suite, the press and all official stewards/referees/supervisors, at its sole cost.

4.10 The Sponsor undertakes that the specific products or services being promoted under this Agreement, together with all other products or services owned or controlled by the Sponsor, which the public would reasonably associate with the Sponsor's Logo, shall be safe and fit for their intended use and comply with all statutes, regulations, directives and codes in force.

5. OBLIGATIONS OF THE ORGANISERS

5.1 The Organisers undertake to organise the Festival at the Venue using the Promoter at their sole cost and expense in accordance with the terms of this Agreement.

5.2 The Organisers confirm that it has full authority to enter into this Agreement and is not bound by any agreement with any third party which adversely affects this Agreement.

5.3 The Organisers confirm that it shall be responsible for arranging and organising the following matters:

5.3.1 The attendance of and payment for all performers, artistes, musicians, stewards, staff and personnel on public duty employed by the Organisers throughout the Festival;

5.3.2 the printing and supply of flysheets, posters, programmes, admission tickets, stationery, publicity material and advertisements in local and national press which shall bear the Sponsor's Logo, the Promoter's Logo and the Organiser's Logo; and

5.3.3 the supply of the following clothing to be worn by all stewards, staff, and personnel on public duty which shall bear the Sponsor's Logo and the Organiser's Logo: [____________].

5.4 The Organisers undertake that all promotions and advertising for the Festival will not be offensive, obscene or derogatory in nature or defamatory of any third party. The Organisers will ensure that the use of the Promoter's Logo, the Organisers' Logo and the Sponsor's Logo will not infringe any sponsorship or advertising rules, statutes, directives and codes in force in relation to the Festival.

5.5 The Organisers confirm that an official printed programme shall be made available to the general public during the Festival at a price within the sole discretion of the Organisers. The Organisers undertake that the official programme shall bear the Sponsor's Logo on the front cover, a statement from the Sponsor of not less than [____________] words on page [____________] and a full page advertisement of the Sponsor's Product on [the inside of the back cover].

5.6 The Organisers confirm that the following performers, artistes and musicians have agreed to participate in the Festival: [____________].

5.7 The Organisers confirm that, whenever possible, they will ensure that the Sponsor's Logo will be present in accordance with this Agreement and that the Promoter has undertaken to the Organisers to use its best endeavours to ensure that the Sponsor's Logo is incorporated into all promotional, advertising and publicity material.

5.8 The Organisers confirm that the Sponsor shall be provided with the following amenities:

5.8.1 a hospitality suite capable of accommodating not less than [____________] official guests of the Sponsor, which shall be situated at: [____________].

5.8.2 the Organisers agree to provide the Sponsor with not less than [____________] complimentary VIP tickets, together with appropriate car parking facilities for the Festival.

5.9 The Organisers confirm that the detail of the Sponsor's Logo shall be at the sole discretion of the Sponsor, subject to prior consultation with the Organisers.

5.10 The Organisers confirm that it has entered into a bona fide, written agreement for the use of the Venue with the Proprietor and have made all administrative and financial arrangements necessary for the smooth running of the Festival, including the hiring of the Venue and any prior arrangements required with the Proprietor, the local authority, the local community and the police.

5.11 Irrespective of any insurance cover provided by the Sponsor, the Organisers confirm that it will take out a comprehensive insurance policy for the Festival, including adequate public liability insurance for injury or death of any participants, performers or spectators.

5.12 The Organisers accept that, notwithstanding the obligations of the Organisers to promote the Festival within the terms of this Agreement, the Sponsor shall be entitled to advertise, publicise, promote and otherwise commercially exploit its own products, goodwill and reputation through the Sponsor's association with the Festival.

6. MISCELLANEOUS

MUTUAL INDEMNITY

6.1 The Sponsor and the Organisers mutually undertake to indemnify the other against all liabilities, claims, demands, actions, costs, damages or loss arising out of any breach by either party of any of the terms of this Agreement.

6.2 In the event of any claim, dispute, action, writ or summons in connection with clause 6.1, the Sponsor and the Organisers agree to provide full details to the other party at the earliest opportunity and shall not settle any such matter without first consulting the other party.

CONFIDENTIALITY

6.3 The Sponsor and the Organisers shall not disclose to any third party any confidential business or future plans of the other party at any time acquired during the existence of this Agreement and no reference is to be made to the terms of this Agreement by either party in any advertising, publicity or promotional material without the prior written consent of the other party.

AMENDMENTS AND ALTERATIONS

6.4 This Agreement supersedes all previous agreements, representations or promises and sets out all the terms agreed between the parties. Any amendment or alteration to this Agreement must be in writing and signed by an authorised signatory of each party.

NO PARTNERSHIP OR EMPLOYMENT

6.5 This Agreement shall not be deemed to create any partnership or employment relationship between the parties.

NOTICES

6.6 Without prejudice to the right to serve notices by any other means any notice served under this Agreement shall be in writing. Any notice which has been sent by first class, pre-paid post shall be deemed to be received 48 hours thereafter (excluding Saturdays, Sundays and public holidays). For the purposes of this Agreement, all notices shall be sent to the following addresses:

The Organisers: [____________];
The Sponsor: [____________].

VALUE ADDED TAX

6.7 All sums payable under this Agreement are exclusive of any value added tax that may be payable by either party.

THIRD PARTY TRANSFERS

6.8 Neither party shall assign, transfer, charge or make over this Agreement, or any of its rights or obligations, without the prior written consent of the other party.

FORCE MAJEURE

6.9 In the event that this Agreement cannot be performed or its obligations fulfilled for any reason beyond the reasonable control of the Sponsor or the Organisers, including events such as war, industrial action, floods or Acts of God. Then either party may terminate or suspend this Agreement by notice in writing.

TERMINATION

6.10 In addition to any other rights and remedies at law, this Agreement may be terminated by a party giving written notice to the other party which has breached this Agreement or has defaulted on any of the following grounds:

6.10.1 where the Sponsor has failed to account or make payments as required under this Agreement;

6.10.2 where the Sponsor or the Organisers has committed a serious breach of its obligations under this Agreement, unless such party rectifies the position, as far as reasonably possible, within [____________];

6.10.3 where the Sponsor or the Organisers goes into voluntary or involuntary liquidation;

6.10.4 where the Sponsor or the Organisers is declared insolvent, either in bankruptcy proceedings or other legal proceedings;

6.10.5 where an agreement with creditors has been reached by the Sponsor or the Organisers due to its failure or inability to pay its debts as they fall due; or

6.10.6 where a receiver is appointed over the whole or part of the Sponsor's or the Organisers' business.

GOVERNING LAW

6.11 This Agreement shall be subject to the Laws of [England].

APPENDICES: A—FESTIVAL SCHEDULE
B—ORGANISER'S LOGO
C—SPONSOR'S LOGO
D—PROMOTER'S LOGO
E—DISPLAY SCHEDULE
F—LAYOUT OF VENUE

[______________]
THE SPONSOR

[______________]
THE ORGANISER

DATE OF THIS AGREEMENT: [______________]

OUTLINE—SPONSORSHIP OF MUSIC/ARTS FESTIVAL

This is a non-exclusive Agreement between the Organisers of a music/arts Festival and a Sponsor. The Organisers would be permitted to have other sponsors, provided that their products or services do not directly or indirectly compete with the product of the Sponsor in this Agreement. A named Promoter has already been appointed by the Organisers and, as this Agreement stands, the logos of the Organisers, the Sponsor and the Promoter would all appear on the publicity and promotional material.

The Agreement is on the implicit basis that no radio or television coverage is envisaged. In return for the Sponsorship Fee, the Organisers are permitting the Sponsor, on a non-exclusive basis, to have its products exhibited and sold during the course of the Festival. In respect of the official programme, the Sponsor is entitled to have its logo on the front cover, a full-page advertisement on the inside of the back cover and a statement on an agreed page of an agreed length. In addition, the Sponsor will have its logo on all tickets, flysheets, posters and other promotional material. The only exclusive right the Sponsor has under this Agreement is to have its own display banners within the main reception area.

END USE SOFTWARE LICENCE

IMPORTANT—PLEASE READ THIS DOCUMENT CAREFULLY BEFORE BREAKING THE SEAL TO RELEASE THE DISC FROM THE WALLET. BY REMOVING AND USING THE DISC YOU THE PURCHASER ARE AGREEING TO BE BOUND BY THE TERMS SET OUT IN THIS DOCUMENT.

The disc and all the data included thereon is supplied to you the purchaser by the publisher, based entirely on the book. If you do not wish to be bound by the terms and conditions of use of the disc and data please do not remove the seal from the wallet. The following terms shall apply to the use of the book, disc and data whilst it is in the possession or control of the purchaser:

1. The Purchaser is granted a non-exclusive licence by the Publisher to use the disc and data for the purpose for which it is intended in conjunction with the book in the normal course of business, namely negotiating, drafting and concluding contracts. This right is personal to the Purchaser and shall also permit the Purchaser to copy the files from the floppy disc to their hard disc and also to make one security copy of the floppy disc itself. The Purchaser shall not have the right to make any additional copies and/or to permit, authorise, sub-licence, assign, transfer and/or otherwise exploit the book and/or disc and/or data in any form, whether for commercial purposes or otherwise. It is accepted by the Publishers that lawyers and others in practice and/or the media industry may use the book and/or disc and/or data to provide legal advice and services to individuals and companies. However, there is no right to copy the disc, data and/or book for supply by the purchaser to such persons by photocopying or electronically supplying large sections of the book. Please advise your clients or company to purchase the book and disc.
2. The right granted is limited and personal to the Purchaser and does not permit the Purchaser to exploit the book and/or disc and/or data in any media of any nature at any time or to permit others to do so. The Purchaser shall not acquire any rights and/or interest in the book, disc and/or data at any time which may be exploited by the Purchaser, and all rights not specified are reserved by the Publisher and not permitted or authorised under this Licence Agreement.
3. The Publisher and the Authors do not accept any responsibility for the use of the disc and/or data by the Purchaser at any time and shall not be liable for any direct and/or indirect damages, loss, injury or otherwise that may arise in respect of the Purchaser and/or any business in which the Purchaser may be involved and/or to which the Purchaser may supply advice or material for any reason. The Purchaser shall use the disc and/or data entirely at the Purchaser's sole risk and expense and agrees that the Purchaser shall be liable for all its own costs and expenses or otherwise that may arise from any such use.

4. The Publisher confirms that all rights necessary for the specified use by the Purchaser of the disc and/or data have been obtained from the Authors. The Publisher has endeavoured to ensure that as far as possible the data is based on the book. The Publisher and the Authors do not accept any responsibility and/or liability for any errors, omissions, viruses, defects and/or any other matters of any nature in the disc and/or data which may be a legal, technical or material fault or problem or otherwise. The Purchaser must use the disc and/or data entirely at its sole risk and cost and accept that the contract clauses are for reference and guidance only and are intended to be adapted and varied accordingly by each Purchaser to suit their particular circumstances. In the event that there is a technical defect in the disc itself, the Publisher agrees to replace the disc within [____________] days of purchase provided that the disc and/or data has been treated with all due care and not mistreated in some manner or damaged by some other means at a later date after purchase. If the disc and/or data is incompatible with the Purchaser's hardware and there is no alternative product available then there is no liability on the part of the Publisher to provide any other disc and/or data or any refund or reimbursement of any nature at any time.

5. In the event of any claim, demand, actions or otherwise by the Purchaser and/or any business for any reason arising from the use of the disc and/or data. Then the Publisher shall only be liable in total to repay the full purchase price of the book to the Purchaser. The Purchaser agrees that it is the Purchaser's responsibility to arrange and bear the cost of insurance cover for the benefit of the Purchaser, any business and/or third party for the use of the disc and/or data by the Purchaser and that the Publisher and the Authors shall not bear any responsibility and/or liability for the use of the disc and/or data by the Purchaser, any business, third party or otherwise which is supplied directly or indirectly by the Purchaser at any time.

6. The copyright owners of the data contained on the disc are the Authors of the book. The Authors assert all their moral rights in respect of the book, disc and data to be identified accordingly and provided with a clear and prominent credit as the Authors and the copyright owners as: [____________]. Similarly, the Publisher should be identified where appropriate as: [____________].

7. In the event that the Authors and/or the Publisher became aware and/or have reasonably grounds to believe that the Purchaser, business and/or third party is using the disc and/or data in a manner which was not set out in this document and which is prejudicial and/or detrimental to the interests of the Publisher and/or Authors and/or is in the breach of any intellectual property rights including copyright of such parties. The Publisher and/or the Authors shall be entitled without notice to the Purchaser to terminate the licence provided under this document without prejudice to any other rights and remedies of the Publisher and/or Authors. The Purchaser shall be obliged upon written notice to surrender all copies of the discs and/or data to the Publisher and/or Authors.

8. The Purchaser agrees that it shall not use and/or authorise the use of the disc and/or data in any manner or nature which is inconsistent with the intended purpose of the licence given in this document. Nor shall the Purchaser deface, erase, remove and/or alter any party of the copyright notice, trademarks, Author and Publisher details displayed on any part of the disc, cover and/or data.

9. This licence shall be governed by the Laws of [England], whether this disc and/or data is supplied and/or used in [the United Kingdom] and/or in any part of the universe.

OUTLINE—END USE SOFTWARE LICENCE

This is an end-use software licence intended to impose conditions of use of software which may, for example, accompany a book. It is important to distinguish between the detailed terms and their legal enforceability, which is a separate matter to be addressed by the seller of the product. As with all such terms and conditions where negotiation is not feasible, the end-user must have the terms clearly brought to their attention before they make the purchase. The essential restriction is that the end-user may not use the software, except for private and non-commercial use or for such other purposes as are specifically authorised. For example, with precedent contracts, the intention is for the end-user to use them in the course of their professional dealings with their clients, or for legal or permissions advisers to use them in the cause of their exploitation or rights. The licence makes it clear that large sections of the book are not to be copied and supplied. The purchaser is requested to advise third parties to use the book. Although the purchaser is permitted to make a copy of the disc for back-up purposes, they are not to make multiple copies for distribution purposes.

There is no named location for physical use of the software, since this is intended for a book sold with a disc in a normal trade shop. Where this end-use licence is location-specific and it is to be used as part of a computer software operator—for example for a sales force—then a different type of licence would be required.

INTERVIEW AGREEMENT WITH NEWSPAPER/MAGAZINE

BETWEEN:

(1) [____________]
of [____________] (to be known as the Publisher in this Agreement)

AND

(2) [____________]
of [____________] (to be known as the Person in this Agreement).

IT IS AGREED as follows:

1. DEFINITIONS

The words below are agreed to mean as follows:

1.1 "The Article(s)" shall mean the written record of the interview(s) between the Interviewer and the Person to be published by the Publisher in the Periodical.

1.2 "The Fee" shall be the following sum to be paid by the Publisher to the Person: [figure/currency].

1.3 "The Interviewer" shall be the following individual acting on behalf of the Publisher: [____________].

1.4 "The Periodical" shall be the following newspaper, owned or controlled by the Publisher, in which the Article(s) are to be published, entitled: [____________].

1.5 "The Artwork" shall mean any photographs, drawings, sketches, pictures, diagrams, maps or any other illustrations which are supplied by the Person intended to be included as part of the Article.

1.6 "The Photographs" shall mean all recordings of light or other radiation on any medium on which an image is reproduced or from which an image may by any means be produced and which is not part of a film commissioned by the Person or the Publisher or taken by them directly and shall include any negatives or prints howsoever stored or reproduced.

1.7 "The Publication Date(s)" shall be the following date(s) on which the Article is to be published by the Publisher in the Periodical: [____________].

1.8 "The Recordings" shall mean all sound recordings made of the Person for the purpose of the Article(s), namely a recording of sound from which sounds may be reproduced or a recording of the whole or part of literary, dramatic, or musical work from which sounds reproducing the work may be produced. This shall apply regardless of the medium in which the recording is made or the methods by which the sounds are reproduced or produced.

1.9 "The Territory" shall mean all countries, bases and locations throughout the world and universe.

2. EXCLUSIVE INTERVIEW

2.1 In consideration of the Fee the Person agrees to provide the following co-operation, information and material:

2.1.1 to answer verbal questions;
2.1.2 to answer written questions;
2.1.3 to be photographed both at home at [address] and on locations specified by the Interviewer at the Publisher's cost;
2.1.4 to provide on loan such Artwork as may be available to assist the Interviewer, to be reproduced at the Publisher's cost;
2.1.5 to answer and assist in any questions and facts required by the Publisher's legal advisers;
2.1.6 to provide a sworn statement on oath in support of any information documents and Artwork at the Publisher's cost.

2.2 The Person agrees that from [date] until [date] he/she shall not give any interview, inform, advise, disclose or release any details or other material to the media (including newspapers, periodicals, television and radio) or grant permission for or consent to the reproduction of any article, film, photograph or recording by any third party throughout the Territory.

2.3 The Publisher acknowledges that after the expiry of the last day of the Publication Date(s), the Person shall be entitled to divulge the same or similar information provided under this Agreement to any third party.

3. COPYRIGHT

3.1 In consideration of the Fee, the Person acknowledges that the Publisher owns all present and future intellectual property rights including copyright and all other rights in the Article(s) and the Recordings and the Photographs in all media, whether in existence now or created in the future throughout the Territory for the full period of copyright and any extensions and renewals in perpetuity.

3.2 The Interviewer and the Publisher agree that they shall not be entitled to exploit in any media the Article(s) and the Recordings, the Photographs and the Artwork for any purpose other than for publication in the Periodical on the Publication Date(s), without the prior written consent of the Person.

3.3 The Interviewer and the Publisher agree that in the event that the Article(s), the Recordings and/or the Photographs and/or the Artwork are exploited in any other media or form other than that set out in this Agreement. Then the Person shall be entitled to receive such additional payments as may be agreed between the Person and the Publisher.

3.4 The Person grants to the Publisher the non-exclusive licence to publish the Artwork in conjunction with the Article(s) in the Periodical on the Publication Date(s) throughout the Territory.

3.5 The Person confirms that he owns or controls all intellectual property rights including copyright and any other rights in the Artwork and that the supply by the Person and publication of the Artwork in the Periodical throughout the Territory will not infringe the copyright or any other rights of any third party and will not expose the Publisher to any civil or criminal proceedings.

3.6 The Publisher and the Interviewer agree that the Artwork, documents or other material supplied by the Person to the Publisher shall be on loan and that the copyright and all other rights in respect of the Artwork and any documents or other material provided by the Person pursuant to this Agreement are and shall remain the sole property of the Person.

4. RIGHT OF CONSULTATION

4.1 The Interviewer and the Publisher agree that the Person shall be entitled to be consulted regarding the accuracy and detail of the Article(s) prior to publication in the form in which it is intended to be published in the Periodical.

4.2 In the event that the Person is not satisfied that the Article is accurate and that the detail is correct, and the Publisher and/or Interviewer are not willing or able to change the Article(s). Then they agree that the Article(s) shall not be published by them, and the Publisher and the Interviewer agree that the Person may terminate the Agreement and repay all sums previously paid by the Publisher to the Person.

4.3 The Publisher agrees that the Person shall be entitled to be paid all the Fee, provided that he has not objected to the accuracy or detail of the Article, regardless of whether the Publisher publishes the Article or not.

5. OBLIGATIONS OF THE PUBLISHER

5.1 In consideration of the rights granted in respect of the Interview, the Artwork and the Photographs. The Publisher shall pay to the Person the Fee as follows:

5.1.1 [____________] upon signature of this Agreement;
5.1.2 [____________] on or before [____________].

5.2 The Publisher agrees that the subject-matter of the Article(s) shall principally cover the following issues: [____________].

5.3 The Publisher confirms that the Person shall have the right to decline to answer questions pertaining to matters outside the perimeters of clause [5.2].

5.4 The Publisher confirms that all interviews which form the basis of the Article(s) shall be conducted by the Interviewer.

5.5 The Publisher agrees to pay or reimburse the Person in respect of all costs and expenses reasonably and properly incurred in providing his services under this Agreement, including travel, accommodation, mobile phone, hairdressing and wardrobe for photographs, subject to satisfactory receipts or records being produced upon request up to a maximum limit of [figure/currency].

5.6 The Publisher confirms that it shall be solely responsible for and bear the cost of all intellectual property rights including copyright, trademarks, service marks, logos, designs, slogans, text, artwork, title, graphics, computer generated material, all other consents, moral rights, contractual obligations due and/or arising to any third party on in respect of the Article(s) and/or any promotion and/or advertisement in respect thereof.

5.7 The Publisher confirms that it has full authority to enter into and perform this Agreement and that it is not bound by any previous agreement which adversely affects this Agreement.

5.8 The Publisher confirms that the exploitation of the Article(s), the Artwork, the Photographs in any form will be at the sole cost and expense of the Publisher and that the Person shall not be liable for any such payments.

5.9 The Publisher agrees that the exploitation of the Article(s), the Artwork and the Photographs in any form will not contain any obscene, offensive, derogatory, demeaning or defamatory material and will not expose the Person to any criminal or civil proceedings.

5.10 The Publisher agrees to keep the Person informed of changes in respect of the Publication Date(s).

5.11 The Publisher agrees to provide the Person, free of charge, with not less than [___] copies of each edition of the Periodical and promotion and advertisement in which the Article(s), the Artwork and the Photographs are published.

5.12 The Publisher agrees to provide the Person, free of charge, with a copy of all the Recordings and Photographs made by or on behalf of the Publisher.

6. OBLIGATIONS OF THE INTERVIEWEE

6.1 The Person agrees to be available to be interviewed by the Interviewer at the following times, dates and locations: [____________].

6.2 The Person confirms that the subject-matter of the Article shall principally cover the following issues: [____________].

6.3 The Person agrees, that to the best of his knowledge and belief, the facts and information which he shall provide to the Interviewer shall be true and accurate.

6.4 The Person confirms that he has full authority to enter into and perform this Agreement and that he is not bound by any previous agreement which adversely affects this Agreement.

6.5 The Person undertakes that all the product of his services under this Agreement shall be original and will not infringe the copyright or any other right of any third party.

6.6 The Person undertakes that all the product of his services under this Agreement will not contain any obscene, offensive, derogatory, demeaning or defamatory material and will not expose the Publisher to any civil or criminal proceedings.

6.7 The Person agrees that he shall be responsible for all his own national insurance, personal tax and value added tax which may become due as a consequence of this Agreement.

6.8 The Person confirms that he holds a passport of [____________] and is resident in [____________].

6.9 The Person confirms that the Artwork was not taken pursuant to a private commissioning arrangement with any third party and that the publication of the Artwork will not infringe the rights of any third party.

7. MISCELLANEOUS

INDEMNITY

7.1 The Publisher and the Person mutually undertake to indemnify the other against all liabilities, claims, demands, actions, costs, damages or loss arising out of any breach by either party of any of the terms of this Agreement. The Publisher and the Person agree to provide full details to the other party at the earliest opportunity and shall not settle any such matter without first consulting the other party.

7.2 In the event that legal proceedings are commenced by any third party against the Person or the Publisher in respect of the Recordings, the Artwork, the Photographs or the Article(s). Then the Person shall immediately advise the Publisher. The Publisher may at its discretion agree to act on behalf of the Person and bear all legal and other costs and to release the Person from any indemnity or contribution. In the event that the legal proceedings are against the Publisher and that it is necessary for the Publisher to join the person as a third party. Then the Publisher shall pay all legal and other costs of the Person.

CONFIDENTIALITY

7.3 The Publisher and the Person shall not disclose to any third party any confidential business or future plans of the other party at any time acquired during the existence of this Agreement. No reference is to be made to the terms of this Agreement by either party in any advertising, publicity or promotional material, without the prior written consent of the other party.

AMENDMENTS

7.4 This Agreement supersedes all previous agreements, representations or promises and sets out all the terms agreed between the parties. Any amendment or alteration to this Agreement must be in writing and signed by an authorised signatory of each party.

RELATIONSHIP

7.5 This Agreement shall not be deemed to create any partnership, agency or employment relationship between the parties.

NOTICES

7.6 For the purposes of this Agreement, all notices shall be in writing and sent to the following addresses by courier or hand delivered:

The Publisher: [____________];
The Person: [____________].

VALUE ADDED TAX

7.7 All sums payable under this Agreement are exclusive of any value added tax that may be payable by either party.

FORCE MAJEURE

7.8 In the event that, due to unforeseen or unusual circumstances, it is necessary to change the interview arrangements or the Photographs or the Publication Dates or some other reason of force majeure which prevents the fulfilment of this Agreement. Then it shall be suspended for such period, and the relevant date(s) adjusted accordingly to a later period up to a maximum of [date]. After that time either party may at its discretion terminate this Agreement.

LOSS

7.9 In the event that the Artwork provided by the Person on loan is not returned due to loss, or is returned only partially complete or damaged, then the Person shall be entitled to compensation of: [figure].

7.10 The Publisher agrees that the Person shall not be liable for any damages or loss of profit to the Publisher in respect of interruptions, delays, inaccuracies, errors, omissions, or failure to publish.

TERMINATION

7.11 Either party may terminate this Agreement before: [date]. After that time either party shall have the right to terminate this Agreement by notice in writing in the event that the other is unable to fulfil its obligations or commits a material breach or whose conduct or activities are considered seriously detrimental, derogatory of or offensive to the other party.

THIRD PARTY TRANSFERS

7.12 This Agreement cannot be assigned by either party except by: [____________] to [____________].

JURISDICTIONS

7.13 This document shall be with the jurisdiction of [country] and governed by the Laws of [____________].

Signed by: [____________] [Date]
FOR AND ON BEHALF OF THE PUBLISHER

Signed by: [____________] [Date]
FOR AND ON BEHALF OF THE PERSON

OUTLINE—INTERVIEW AGREEMENT WITH NEWSPAPER/MAGAZINE

This Agreement is between a newspaper publisher and an individual. It is anticipated that the Interview is conducted on a question-and-answer basis which is tape-recorded and subsequently edited for publication. The Agreement is exclusive in the sense that the Person is agreeing that, for a specified period, he will not give any interview or other information or material to the media.

In consideration of payment of a Fee the Person is granting the sole and exclusive right to the Publisher to publish the Articles in the Periodical throughout the Territory. Under this Agreement the Fee would have to be paid irrespective of publication. The copyright in the tape-recordings and the Article itself would belong to the Newspaper, although under this Agreement that would not pre-empt the Person from divulging the same information to a third party (whether for publication or not) after the agreed period of silence on the subject. The copyright in any artwork such as Photographs, Drawings, etc. supplied by the Person on loan are retained by him. The Publisher is only acquiring a non-exclusive licence to reproduce the Artwork on the publication dates. It should be noted that there is a right of privacy in respect of certain photographs commissioned for private and domestic purposes which should be considered.

The Person has also agreed to be photographed for the Articles. The Publisher is paying for the cost of hairdressing and wardrobe, and copyright in the Photographs will belong to the Publisher. Some expenses are being paid for mobile phone, travel and accommodation. In the event of legal proceedings, then the Publisher may take the case over and pay the Person's legal costs. There are provisions for suspension and for adjustment of the dates under force majeure.

COMMISSIONING OF COLLECTION OF THREE-DIMENSIONAL WORKS

AN AGREEMENT made this [____________] day of [____________]

BETWEEN:

(1) [____________]
of [____________] (to be known as the Licensor in this Agreement)

AND

(2) [____________]
of [____________] (to be known as the Licensee in this Agreement).

IT IS AGREED as follows:

1. DEFINITIONS

The words below are agreed to mean as follows:

1.1 "The Designs" shall be the original concept and two-dimensional designs for a range of items described as follows: [____________].
Full details of the Designs are attached to and form part of this Agreement in Schedule A.

1.2 "The Prototypes" shall be the three-dimensional reproductions of the Designs which are the final products upon which the manufacture of the Licensed Articles are based.

1.3 "The Licensed Articles" shall be the three-dimensional reproductions of the Prototypes to be manufactured and distributed by the Licensee.

1.4 "The Prototype Fee" shall be a sum to be agreed between the Licensor and the Licensee for the expenses and costs incurred in producing the Prototypes, including but not limited to the cost of all raw materials used in the creation of the Prototypes.

1.5 "The Complete Set" shall mean the full range of the Licensed Articles based on the Designs and the Prototypes.

1.6 "The Non-Returnable Advance" shall be the sum of: [figure/currency].

1.7 "The Territory" shall be the following countries: [____________].

1.8 "The Licence Period" shall commence on [date] and shall continue for a period of [____________].

1.9 "The Licensor's Royalties" shall be the following percentage of the retail selling price or any other sums at any time received by or credited to the Licensee in respect of the exploitation of the Licensed Articles:

1.9.1 in relation to sales of the Complete Set:

[____________] for the first [____________] thousand;
[____________] for the following [____________];
[____________] for the following [____________]; and
[____________] thereafter [____________].

1.9.2 in relation to individual sales of the Licensed Articles (disregarding any sales of the Complete Set):

[____________] for the first [____________] thousand;
[____________] for the following [____________];
[____________] for the following [____________]; and
[____________] thereafter [____________].

1.10 "The Licensor's Consultancy Fees" shall be at a rate of: [____________], excluding any stationery, telephone, travelling or accommodation expenses.

2. EXCLUSIVE LICENCE

2.1 In consideration of the payment of the Non-Returnable Advance and the Licensor's Royalties, the Licensor grants to the Licensee the sole and exclusive right to produce, manufacture, distribute, supply and sell the Licensed Articles in the form of the Complete Set and part(s) based on the Prototypes throughout the Territory for the duration of the Licence Period.

2.2 The Licensee undertakes that at the end of the Licence Period it shall execute any document or do anything required by the Licensor to confirm that all rights including copyright, design rights and artwork in any variations or developments of the Licensed Articles are the sole property of the Licensor.

2.3 The Licensor undertakes that he will not license or permit any third party to produce, manufacture, distribute or supply the Designs, the Prototypes or the Licensed Articles or any development or variation, in the Territory during the Licence Period.

3. COPYRIGHT

The Licensee acknowledges and agrees that all present and future copyright and design rights in the Designs, the Licensed Articles, the Prototypes and the Complete Set are and will remain the sole property of the Licensor and that this Agreement does not in any way purport to transfer any copyright or design rights to the Licensee.

4. OBLIGATIONS OF THE LICENSEE

4.1 In consideration of the rights granted under this Agreement, the Licensee shall pay to the Licensor the Non-Returnable Advance as follows:

4.1.1 [____________] upon signature of this Agreement;
4.1.2 [____________] upon approval by the Licensee of the Designs;
4.1.3 [____________] upon approval by the Licensee of the Prototypes; and
4.1.4 [____________] upon first release of the Licensed Articles for sale to the public but in any event not later than [____________].

4.2 The Licensee acknowledges that the Non-Returnable Advance is to be off-set against the Licensor's Royalties but is not returnable nor contingent upon any sales figures in relation to the Licensed Articles.

4.3 The Licensee agrees to pay to the Licensor the Prototype Fee within [__________] upon delivery of the Prototypes by the Licensor to the Licensee.

4.4 The Licensee confirms that it has full title and authority to enter into this Agreement and is not bound by any previous agreement which adversely affects this Agreement.

4.5 The Licensee confirms that where the Licensor is requested by the Licensee to attend the Licensee's premises or make travel arrangements for any purpose at the request of the Licensee. Then the Licensee will be obliged to pay the Licensor's Consultancy Fees in accordance with this Agreement.

4.6 The Licensee confirms that, in addition to any sums payable as the Licensor's Consultancy Fees or the Licensor's Royalties, the Licensee shall pay to the Licensor all such stationery, telephone, travel and accommodation expenses as are incurred by the Licensor at the request of the Licensee. The Licensee confirms that the travel arrangements by the Licensor may, at the Licensor's discretion, include travel within the United Kingdom and abroad by way of business class aeroplane travel and first class rail travel. The Licensee also confirms that any hotel accommodation for the Licensor whether within the United Kingdom or abroad shall be four star.

4.7 The Licensee undertakes that the minimum retail selling price for the Complete Set shall not be less than: [figure/currency] in [country].

4.8 The Licensee undertakes that it shall pay the Licensor's Royalties to the Licensor on [dates] in each year.

4.9 The Licensee and its sub-agents and sub-licensees and any other third parties engaged or appointed pursuant to this Agreement shall keep professional and accurate books of account, records and contracts and prices showing all dealings of the Licensed Articles and prices showing all dealings of the Licensed Articles and the Complete Set and any part(s), including the total number of units of the Licensed Articles manufactured, distributed, supplied and sold, whether by wholesale or retail, or distributed without charge for promotional purposes and all units lost, damaged or stolen and the calculation of the Licensor's Royalties in respect of the Licensed Articles and the Complete Set.

4.10 On [dates] in each year, the Licensee shall provide a detailed report to the Licensor showing all dealings of the Licensed Articles and the Complete Set, including the total number of units of the Licensed Articles manufactured, distributed, supplied and sold, whether by wholesale or retail, all prices and details of units distributed without charge for promotional purposes and all units lost, damaged or stolen and the calculation of the Licensor's Royalties in respect of the Licensed Articles and the Complete Set.

4.11 The Licensee agrees that the Licensor shall be entitled to arrange for an [annual] audit to inspect and make copies of the Licensee's books of account, records, contracts, computer software and any other relevant material in order to verify the sums due to the Licensor. In the event that in any audit an error is found to the detriment of the Licensor in respect of the amount to be paid by the Licensee which is in excess of [____________]. Then the Licensee shall be responsible for the payment of all reasonable costs incurred in such audit.

4.12 The Licensee agrees to provide the following copyright notice and credit to the Licensor in respect of the Licensed Articles and the Complete Set and in all publicity, advertising promotional and packaging material in respect of the marketing and distribution of the Licensed Articles and the Complete Set: [____________].

4.13 In addition to any credits to be given by the Licensee to the Licensor in accordance with this Agreement, the Licensee agrees that each of the Licensed Articles will bear the following hallmark punch in a shape and size to be agreed between the Licensor and the Licensee: [____________].

4.14 The Licensee agrees that the Licensor shall be entitled to approve the Licensed Articles prior to their manufacture, supply and distribution and the Licensee undertakes to supply at its sole cost, samples of the Licensed Articles in the exact form and material in which the Licensee proposes to manufacture, distribute, supply and sell the Licensed Articles. The Licensee acknowledges that such approval must be in writing.

4.15 The Licensee agrees that the Licensor shall be entitled to approve the appointment of any sub-agent, sub-licensee or any other third party in respect of the manufacture, distribution, supply or other exploitation of the Licensed Articles under this Agreement.

4.16 The Licensee undertakes that not less than [____________] of the Complete Sets of the Licensed Articles shall be manufactured within [____________] of the delivery of the Prototypes by the Licensor to the Licensee.

4.17 The Licensee acknowledges that it is solely responsible for all costs incurred in the commercial exploitation of the Licensed Articles and the Complete Set, including the production, manufacturing, distribution, supply, selling, advertising and promotion.

4.18 The Licensee confirms that the Prototypes will not be rejected by the Licensee except on reasonable grounds and in good faith. In the event that the Licensee does reject the Prototypes such rejection will be made in writing within [____________] of delivery of the Prototypes by the Licensor to the Licensee.

4.19 The Licensee confirms that in the event that the Prototypes are not accepted by the Licensee, all sums paid or due to be paid to the Licensor under this Agreement, including the Prototype Fee and the Licensor's Consultancy Fees, shall be paid by the Licensee to the Licensor.

4.20 The Licensee undertakes that all the Licensed Articles shall be safe for their intended use and shall comply with all statutes, regulations, directives and codes in force and that prior to distribution, supply and sale to the public comprehensive product liability insurance cover shall be arranged of not less than [____________] per claim.

4.21 The Licensee agrees to provide the Licensor with not less than [____________] Complete Sets of the Licensed Articles in the form in which they are distributed to the general public without charge.

4.22 The Licensee agrees to provide the Licensor with copies of all artwork, packaging, promotional and advertising work in relation to the supply, sale and distribution of the Licensed Articles and the Complete Set.

5. OBLIGATIONS OF THE LICENSOR

5.1 The Licensor confirms that he is the original creator and sole owner of or controls all copyright and any other rights in the Designs, the Licensed Articles, the Prototypes and the Complete Set.

5.2 The Licensor confirms that he has full title and authority to enter into this Agreement and is not bound by any previous agreement which adversely affects this Agreement.

5.3 The Licensor confirms that the Designs, the Licensed Articles and the Prototypes do not involve the use of any material which infringes the copyright or any other rights of any third party in the Territory in respect of the rights granted under this Agreement.

5.4 The Licensor shall deliver the Designs for the Complete Set on or before: [date].

5.5 The Licensor shall deliver the Prototypes for the Complete Set on or before [date].

5.6 The Licensor undertakes that the Designs and the Prototypes shall be of suitable technical and artistic quality for the Licensor to reproduce and manufacture the Licensed Articles.

5.7 The Licensor agrees to take into account the requirements of the Licensee in respect of the Designs and the Prototypes.

5.8 The Licensor agrees that the Prototypes shall be made of the following materials: [____________].

5.9 The Licensor agrees to provide receipts or other records in respect of all raw materials, expenses or other costs to be paid by the Licensee.

5.10 The Licensor agrees to attend such meetings, exhibitions and promotional events as may reasonably be required by the Licensee, subject to sufficient prior notice.

5.11 Subject to prior written approval, the Licensor agrees that the Licensee shall be entitled to use the Licensor's name, biography, photograph and image in any commercial exploitation of the Licensed Articles both on the packaging and in any advertising and promotional material.

5.12 The Licensor agrees that he shall be responsible for all his own national insurance, personal tax and value added tax which shall be due in consequence of this Agreement.

5.13 The Licensor agrees to provide written approval or reject the Licensed Articles or any samples created by the Licensee as soon as reasonably possible.

6. MISCELLANEOUS

MUTUAL INDEMNITY

6.1 The Licensor and the Licensee mutually undertake to indemnify the other against all liabilities, claims, demands, actions, costs, damages or loss arising out of any breach by either party of any of the terms of this Agreement.

6.2 In the event of any claim, dispute, action, writ or summons in connection with clause 6.1, the Licensor and the Licensee agree to provide full details to the other party at the earliest opportunity and shall not settle any such matter without first consulting the other party.

CONFIDENTIALITY

6.3 The Licensor and the Licensee shall not disclose to any third party any confidential business or future plans of the other party at any time acquired during the existence of this Agreement. No reference is to be made to the terms of this Agreement by either party in any advertising, publicity or promotional material without the prior written consent of the other party.

AMENDMENTS AND ALTERATIONS

6.4 This Agreement supersedes all previous agreements, representations or promises and sets out all the terms agreed between the parties. Any amendment or alteration to this Agreement must be in writing and signed by an authorised signatory of each party.

NO PARTNERSHIP OR EMPLOYMENT

6.5 This Agreement shall not be deemed to create any partnership or employment relationship between the parties.

NOTICES

6.6 For the purposes of this Agreement, the following addresses shall apply in respect of notices under this Agreement:

The Licensor: [____________];
The Licensee: [____________].

VALUE ADDED TAX

6.7 All sums payable under this Agreement are exclusive of any value added tax that may be payable by either party.

THIRD PARTY TRANSFERS

6.8 Neither party shall assign, transfer, charge or make over this Agreement or any of its rights or obligations without the prior consent of the other party.

FORCE MAJEURE

6.9 In the event that this Agreement cannot be performed or its obligations fulfilled for any reason beyond the reasonable control of the Licensor or the Licensee, including such events as war, industrial action, floods or Acts of God. Then such non-performance or failure to fulfil its obligations shall be deemed not to be a breach of this Agreement. In the event that this Agreement cannot be performed or its obligations fulfilled for any reason beyond the reasonable control of the defaulting party for a continuous period of [____________]. Then the other party may, at its discretion, terminate this Agreement by notice in writing at the end of that period.

TERMINATION

6.10 In addition to any other rights and remedies at law, this Agreement may be terminated by giving written notice to the other party who has breached this Agreement or defaulted in the following circumstances:

6.10.1 where the Licensee has failed to account or make payments as required under this Agreement;
6.10.2 where the Licensor or the Licensee has committed a serious breach of its obligations under this Agreement, unless such party rectifies the position, as far as reasonably possible, within [____________];
6.10.3 where the Licensee goes into voluntary or involuntary liquidation;
6.10.4 where the Licensee is declared insolvent, either in bankruptcy proceedings or other legal proceedings;
6.10.5 where an agreement with creditors has been reached by the Licensee due to its failure or inability to pay its debts as they fall due; or
6.10.6 where a receiver is appointed over the whole or part of the Licensee's business.

SELL-OFF PERIOD

6.11 The Licensee shall be entitled to sell off, on a non-exclusive basis, licensed material and stocks previously manufactured under this Agreement for the purpose of commercial sale for a period of [____________] from the date of expiry or termination, provided that the Licensee adheres to the terms of this Agreement.

6.12 After the expiry or the termination or the completion of the sell-off period, then the Licensor shall be entitled to instruct the Licensee to deliver or destroy all master material, licensed material, any copies of the master or licensed material and stocks previously manufactured under this Agreement in the possession of or under the control of the Licensee relating to the rights granted under this Agreement.

GOVERNING LAW

6.13 This Agreement shall be subject to the Laws of [England].

SCHEDULE A: THE DESIGNS

Signed by: [____________]
FOR AND ON BEHALF OF THE LICENSOR

Signed by: [____________]
FOR AND ON BEHALF OF THE LICENSEE

DATE OF THIS AGREEMENT: [____________]

OUTLINE—COMMISSIONING OF COLLECTION OF THREE-DIMENSIONAL WORKS

This is an Agreement for the manufacture and distribution of a series of three-dimensional works based on original Designs and Prototypes. The original creator is referred to as the Licensor and the manufacturer and distributor as the Licensee. It is assumed that the parties have already agreed on the Designs.

An exclusive Licence is being granted to the Licensee by the Licensor to manufacture and sell Licensed Articles based on the Prototype. The Prototype is to be provided by the Licensor. The Licensee is paying to the Licensor a Non-Returnable Advance, which is to be off-set against the Licensor's Royalties. The Licensor is to receive an escalating percentage of the retail selling price of the Licensed Articles which could be in thousands or a much smaller amount.

The copyright and design rights in the Designs, Prototype and Licensed Articles remain the property of the Licensor. The Licensee is also paying a Consultancy Fee to the Licensor in the event that he is requested to attend meetings and other events by the Licensee. The Consultancy Fee is in addition to the stationery, mobile phone, travel and accommodation expenses incurred by the Licensor.

Although the Licensor is not asserting any moral rights which might theoretically exist, the Licensee is agreeing to provide the Licensor with a copyright notice and credit in respect of the Licensed Articles and all publicity and promotional material relating to the Licensed Articles.

The Licensor is entitled to approve the Licensed Articles themselves prior to manufacture as well as approve any third party appointed for the purpose of manufacturing the Licensed Articles. A copy of the Designs should be attached to and form part of this Agreement.

COMMISSIONING FROM FASHION DESIGNER

BETWEEN:

(1) [______________]
of [______________] (to be known as the Designer in this Agreement)

AND

(2) [______________]
of [______________] (to be known as the Purchaser in this Agreement).

IT IS AGREED as follows:

1. DEFINITIONS

The words below are agreed to mean as follows:

1.1 "The Designs" shall be the original concept and two-dimensional designs, sketches, drawings and patterns for an individual piece of clothing described as follows: [______________].

1.2 "The Garment" shall be the three-dimensional reproduction of the Designs to be created and supplied by the Designer which shall principally be of the following material: [______________]; and in the following colour(s): [______________].

1.3 "The Designer's Fee" shall be the sum of: [figure/currency].

1.4 "The Delivery Date" shall be the date by which the Garment is to be delivered by the Designer to the Purchaser.

2. PURCHASE OF THE GARMENT

2.1 In consideration of the Designer's Fee, the Designer agrees to create, produce and deliver the Garment based on the Designs to the Purchaser by the Delivery Date.

2.2 The Purchaser confirms and agrees that this Agreement relates solely to the sale and purchase of the Garment by the Purchaser for personal use and that the Designs and the Garment are not to be commercially exploited by the Purchaser in any form.

2.3 The Purchaser acknowledges that the Designer shall be entitled to sell, license or exploit the Designs and any reproduction of the Designs or the Garment in any form at any time throughout the world.

3. COPYRIGHT AND ANCILLARY RIGHTS

3.1 The Purchaser acknowledges, confirms and agrees that all present and future copyright, design rights and any other rights in the Designs and the Garment are and will remain the sole property of the Designer and that this Agreement does not in any way purport to transfer any copyright, design rights or any other rights to the Purchaser.

3.2 The Purchaser undertakes that it will not license or permit any third party to copy, reproduce, manufacture or distribute the Garment or the Designs including any development or variation, at any time throughout the world.

4. OBLIGATIONS OF THE PURCHASER

4.1 In consideration of the creation, production and supply of the Garment, the Purchaser shall pay to the Designer the Designer's Fee as follows:

4.1.1 [____________] upon signature of this Agreement; and
4.1.2 [____________] upon acceptance of the Garment by the Purchaser.

4.2 The Purchaser agrees to attend the premises of the Designer on not less than [____________] occasions for fittings for [the toile and the Garment].

4.3 The Purchaser agrees to accept or reject the Garment within [____________] of delivery.

4.4 The Purchaser confirms that in the event that the Garment is rejected then all sums previously paid to the Designer shall be retained by the Designer unless:

4.4.1 the Garment is substantially different from the Designs; or
4.4.2 the Garment is not made in the principal fabric requested; or
4.4.3 the Garment is of such poor technical quality and standard that it is unfit for its intended purpose; or
4.4.4 the Garment does not conform to the dimensions specified in the Designs which were confirmed at the last fitting; or
4.4.5 the Garment is of a different colour scheme from that which was originally agreed; or
4.4.6 [other].

5. OBLIGATIONS OF THE DESIGNER

5.1 The Designer agrees to create and deliver the Garment based on the Designs to the Purchaser by the Delivery Date.

5.2 The Designer confirms that he/she is the original creator and sole owner of or controls all copyright, design rights and any other rights in the Designs and the Garment.

5.3 The Designer confirms that he/she has full title and authority to enter into this Agreement and is not bound by any previous agreement which adversely affects this Agreement.

5.4 The Designer confirms that the Garment shall be of suitable quality to be used for its intended purpose.

5.5 The Designer agrees to bear the costs of the creation of the Designs and all labour and material used for the purpose of creating and supplying the Garment, including all fabric.

Signed by: [______________]
FOR AND ON BEHALF OF THE DESIGNER

Date: [______________]

Signed by: [______________]
FOR AND ON BEHALF OF THE PURCHASER

Date: [______________]

ATTACHMENTS: [Fabric, Photograph, Drawing].

OUTLINE—COMMISSIONING FROM FASHION DESIGNER

The purpose of this Agreement is to protect the copyright and design rights of a Designer in respect of an original creation. In the fashion industry most commissions and work are done without any reliance on documents and contracts, which results in ambiguity and the lack of solid evidence as to the intention of the parties. The Purchaser in this Agreement is not acquiring any rights to reproduce and exploit the Garment; such rights are retained by the Designer.

COMMISSIONING OF FILM TITLE AND CREDITS

AN AGREEMENT made this [____________] day of [____________]

BETWEEN:

(1) [____________]
of [____________] (to be known as the Assignor in this Agreement)

AND

(2) [____________]
of [____________] (to be known as the Production Company in this Agreement).

IT IS AGREED as follows:

1. DEFINITIONS

The words below are agreed to mean as follows:

1.1 "The Film" shall be the following film in which the Commissioned Work is to be incorporated, which is entitled [____________].

1.2 "The Commissioned Work" shall be the title sequences and end-credits to be prepared, produced and delivered by the Assignor to the Production Company, which is briefly described as follows: [____________]; which shall have an on-screen running period of [____________] seconds [____________] for the opening title sequence and [____________] seconds [____________] for the end-credits.

1.3 "The Delivery Date" shall be the following date by which the Commissioned Work, is to be delivered by the Assignor to the Production Company: [date].

1.4 "The Budget" shall be the maximum total payment to be made by the Production Company to the Assignor in respect of the Commissioned Work which shall not exceed [____________] and shall include:

1.4.1 the cost of all preparatory artwork and designs,
1.4.2 the cost of all raw materials expended in the course of making the Commissioned Work, including any film stock or videotape and the hiring of locations;
1.4.3 the cost of developing, printing and transferring any film stock from one format to another;
1.4.4 the cost of reproducing any videotape from one format to another;

1.4.5 the cost of any rostrum camera work;
1.4.6 any stationery, telephone, travelling and accommodation costs;
1.4.7 the cost of producing any computer-generated graphics;
1.4.8 the costs of insurance and delivery of the Commissioned Work;
1.4.9 all necessary copyright, consents, moral rights and other clearance payments;
1.4.10 labour costs of the Assignor; and
1.4.11 any other agreed costs: [____________].

1.5 "The Territory" shall be all countries, bases and locations throughout the world.

2. FULL ASSIGNMENT OF RIGHTS

In consideration of payment of the Budget, the Assignor assigns to the Production Company all present and future copyright and any other rights in the Commissioned Work and parts in all media, whether in existence now or created in the future throughout the Territory for the full period of copyright, including any extensions or renewals.

3. OBLIGATIONS OF THE ASSIGNOR

3.1 The Assignor undertakes that it shall produce the Commissioned Work in accordance with the Budget.

3.2 The Assignor confirms that the end product of the Commissioned Work shall be in the following format: [____________].

3.3 The Assignor confirms that it shall deliver the Commissioned Work to the Production Company on or before the Delivery Date.

3.4 In the event that the Budget is to be exceeded, the Assignor agrees that the prior written approval of the Production Company shall be required in order to authorise any further expenditure and that any further payment shall be at the Production Company's sole discretion.

3.5 The Assignor agrees that it is only authorised by the Production Company to take instructions in respect of the Commissioned Work from the following person(s): [____________].

3.6 The Assignor confirms that it is the sole owner of or controls all copyright and any other rights in the Commissioned Work, which are assigned under this Agreement.

3.7 The Assignor confirms that it has and will retain good title and authority to enter into this Agreement and is not bound by any previous agreement which adversely affects this Agreement.

3.8 In respect of the Commissioned Work, the Assignor undertakes that all copyright and any other rights, including consents and moral rights, shall be cleared and paid for in respect of the rights assigned under this Agreement for use by the Production Company.

3.9 The Assignor undertakes that the Commissioned Work will not contain any obscene, offensive or defamatory material and will not expose the Production Company to any civil or criminal proceedings.

3.10 The Assignor confirms that the Commissioned Work will not infringe the intellectual property rights including copyright, moral rights or any other rights of any third party throughout the Territory.

3.11 The Assignor agrees to take into account all specific requests made by the Production Company and that the contents of the Commissioned Work shall be at the sole discretion of the Production Company.

3.12 The Assignor agrees that the Commissioned Work will be of first class technical quality and will comply with the standards and requirements of: [____________].

3.13 The Assignor shall provide a full report to the Production Company of the costs incurred in respect of the Commissioned Work, upon request.

3.14 The Assignor shall keep full and accurate records and accounts of all costs incurred in respect of the Commissioned Work and agrees that the Production Company shall be entitled to inspect all such records and material upon request.

3.15 In the event that the costs incurred by the Assignor in respect of the Commissioned Work are less than the Budget then the Assignor agrees that the Production Company shall only be obliged to pay the lesser sum.

4. OBLIGATIONS OF THE PRODUCTION COMPANY

4.1 In consideration of the services provided by the Assignor and the acceptance of the Commissioned Work under this Agreement, the Production Company shall pay to the Assignor the costs incurred in respect of the Budget as follows:

4.1.1 [____________] upon signature of this agreement;
4.1.2 [____________] on or before [____________]
4.1.3 [____________] subject to acceptance by the Production Company of the Commissioned Work; and
4.1.4 [____________] on or before [____________],

subject to receipt by the Production Company of a report of all costs incurred in respect of the Commissioned Work.

4.2 In the event that the Budget is exceeded, the Production Company agrees to pay such additional costs provided that it has given prior written approval of the expenditure of the Assignor.

4.3 The Production Company agrees either to accept or provide written reasons for its rejection of the Commissioned Work within [____________] of delivery. The Production Company agrees to reject any material only on reasonable grounds and in good faith.

4.4 The Production Company confirms that it has and will retain good title and authority to enter into this Agreement and is not bound by any previous agreement which adversely affects this Agreement.

4.5 The Production Company confirms that it shall be solely responsible for the production of the Film and that the Assignor shall not be responsible for any such costs.

4.6 The Production Company agrees to provide the Assignor with the following end credit in the Film: [____________]

5. MISCELLANEOUS

TIME OF THE ESSENCE

5.1 Both parties agree that all times and dates referred to in this Agreement shall be of the essence.

MUTUAL INDEMNITY

5.2 The Assignor and the Production Company mutually undertake to indemnify the other against all liabilities, claims, demands, actions, costs, damages or loss arising out of any breach by either party of any of the terms of this Agreement.

5.3 In the event of any claim, dispute, action, writ or summons in connection with clause 5.2, the Assignor and the Production Company agree to provide full details to the other party at the earliest opportunity and shall not settle any such matter without first consulting the other party.

CONFIDENTIALITY

5.4 The Assignor and the Production Company shall not disclose to any third party any confidential business or future plans of the other party at any time acquired during the existence of this Agreement. No reference is to be made to the terms of this Agreement by either party in any advertising, publicity or promotional material without the prior written consent of the other party.

AMENDMENTS AND ALTERATIONS

5.5 This Agreement supersedes all previous agreements, representations or promises and sets out all the terms agreed between the parties. Any amendment or alteration to this Agreement must be in writing and signed by an authorised signatory of each party.

RELATIONSHIP

5.6 This Agreement shall not be deemed to create any partnership, agency or employment relationship between the parties.

NOTICES

5.7 All notices shall be in writing and may be sent by any means: fax, e-mail, post or otherwise.

VALUE ADDED TAX

5.8 All sums payable under this Agreement are exclusive of any value added tax that may be payable by either party.

FORCE MAJEURE

5.9 In the event that this Agreement cannot be performed or its obligations fulfilled for any reason beyond the reasonable control of the Assignor or the Production Company, including such events as war, industrial action, floods or Acts of God. Then either party may terminate this Agreement by notice in writing subject to agreement on the work, if any, completed to date.

TERMINATION OF THE AGREEMENT

5.10 In addition to any other rights and remedies at law, this Agreement may be terminated by giving written notice to the other party who has breached this or defaulted, on the grounds that the Production Company or the Assignor has failed to account or make payments as required under this Agreement or where the Assignor or the Production Company has committed a serious breach of its obligations under this Agreement and has not rectified the position within [____________].

THIRD PARTY TRANSFERS

5.11 The Assignor shall not be entitled to assign, transfer, charge or make over this Agreement or any of its rights or obligations without the prior written consent of the Production Company.

GOVERNING LAW

5.13 This Agreement shall be subject to the Laws of [England].

[____________]	[____________]	[DATE]
THE ASSIGNOR	**THE PRODUCTION COMPANY**	

OUTLINE—COMMISSIONING OF FILM TITLE AND CREDITS

This is an Agreement for the commissioning of title sequences and end-credits for a programme. The parties are referred to as the Assignor who are producing the Work and the Production Company who are commissioning it. The parties are agreeing to a maximum Budget for the Work which will not be exceeded without the prior written consent of the Production Company. This Budget includes the preliminary artwork, all raw materials used in making the title sequences and end-credits, labour costs, any computer-generated graphics and insurance.

The Assignor is transferring all rights to the Production Company and no further payment need be made to the Assignor in the event that the Work is commercially exploited by the Production Company.

The person who is authorised to give instructions to the Assignor on behalf of the Production Company is named in this Agreement and the Production Company would not be responsible for any costs incurred by the Assignor as a result of acting on instructions from any other individual unless prior written confirmation has been received.

There are no assertions of moral rights by the Assignor although the Production Company is agreeing to provide an on-screen credit to the Assignor.

EXCLUSIVE AGREEMENT FOR REPRODUCTION OF ORIGINAL DESIGNS

AN AGREEMENT made this [____________] day of [____________]

BETWEEN:

(1) [____________]
of [____________] (to be known as the Designer in this Agreement)

AND

(2) [____________]
of [____________] (to be known as the Licensee in this Agreement).

IT IS AGREED as follows:

1. DEFINITIONS

The words below are agreed to mean as follows:

1.1 "The Designs" shall be the original concept and two-dimensional designs for a range of [____________] and other products to be created and provided by the Designer. The Designs shall include all such designs which are set out in the attached Schedule A and form part of this Agreement, together with such other designs as are created by the Designer in accordance with the terms of this Agreement.

1.2 "The Licensed Articles" shall be the three-dimensional reproductions and adaptations of the Designs to be manufactured by the Licensee.

1.3 "The Trading Name" in respect of the commercial exploitation of all the Licensed Articles shall be under the title [____________].

1.4 "The Territory" shall be the following countries: [____________].

1.5 "The Licence Period" shall commence on [date] and shall continue for a period of [____________].

1.6 "The Gross Receipts" shall be the total proceeds from the commercial exploitation and sale of the Licensed Articles throughout the Territory at any time received by or credited to the Designer or any sub-agents or sub-distributors after the deduction of any value added tax or sales tax, customs duties, and exchange costs paid by the Designer.

1.7 "The Nett Receipts" shall be the Gross Receipts less:

1.7.1 the cost of all raw materials incurred by the Licensee during the course of making the Licensed Articles;

1.7.2 the reasonable costs incurred in the engaging of specialist services in the making of the Licensed Articles, including but not limited to: [____________];

1.7.3 all additional insurance costs incurred by the Licensee with respect to any comprehensive insurance policy to be taken out in accordance with the terms of this Agreement;

1.7.4 all reasonable additional security costs incurred by the Licensee in relation to the Business Premises, the Designs, the Licensed Articles and raw materials used or obtained for the purpose of producing the Licensed Articles; and

1.7.5 any other costs: [____________].

1.8 "The Licensee's Royalties" shall be [figure] per cent [______]% of the Nett Receipts.

1.9 "The Designer's Royalties" shall be [figure] per cent [______]% of the Nett Receipts.

1.10 "The Business Premises" shall mean: [____________].

2. EXCLUSIVE LICENCE

2.1 In consideration of the Designer's Royalties, the Designer grants to the Licensee the sole and exclusive right to produce and manufacture the Licensed Articles based on the Designs in accordance with the terms of this Agreement throughout the Territory for the duration of the Licence Period.

2.2 In consideration of the Licensee's Royalties, the Licensee agrees to produce and manufacture at the Business Premises the Licensed Articles in accordance with the terms of this Agreement for the duration of the Licence Period.

2.3 The Designer undertakes that he will not license or permit any third party to produce, make, manufacture or copy the Designs or the Licensed Articles or any development or variation of the Designs or the Licensed Articles throughout the Territory during the Licence Period and until the expiry of a period of one year from the end of the Licence Period.

3. COPYRIGHT

3.1 The Licensee acknowledges that all present and future copyright and design rights in the Designs are and will remain the sole property of the Designer and that this Agreement does not in any way purport to transfer any copyright or design rights to the Licensee in respect of the Designs.

3.2 The Designer agrees that all present and future copyright, design rights and any other property rights in the Licensed Articles manufactured during the Licence Period will be held jointly by the Licensee and the Designer. The Designer further agrees that where such joint copyright ownership has the effect of a transfer or assignment of copyright to the Licensee by the Designer then such transfer and assignment is acknowledged and agreed by the Designer.

4. OBLIGATIONS OF THE DESIGNER

4.1 The Designer agrees to create and deliver to the Licensee all the Designs as agreed between the Designer and the Licensee, whether such requests for the Designs are made in writing or otherwise by the Licensee during the term of this Agreement.

4.2 The Designer acknowledges the copyright ownership as stated under this Agreement in relation to the Designs and the Licensed Articles.

4.3 The Designer confirms that he is the original creator and sole owner of or controls all copyright and any other rights in the Designs provided to the Licensee under this Agreement.

4.4 The Designer confirms that he has full title and authority to enter into this Agreement and is not bound by any previous agreement which adversely affects this Agreement.

4.5 The Designer confirms that the creation and delivery of the Designs does not involve the use of any material which infringes the copyright or any other rights of any third party in the Territory in respect of the rights granted under this Agreement and will not expose the Licensee to any civil or criminal proceedings.

4.6 The Designer agrees that he shall be registered for value added tax in respect of the supply of any goods or services under this Agreement.

4.7 The Designer agrees that he shall be responsible for all his own national insurance, personal tax and value added tax which shall be due in consequence of this Agreement.

4.8 The Designer agrees to be responsible for all packaging, publicity, advertising, promotions, supply, distribution and sales of the Licensed Articles and confirms that such costs shall be at his sole cost and expense and that such costs are not to be offset in any manner in the calculation of the Nett Receipts.

4.9 The Designer agrees to be responsible for the collection and safeguarding of the Gross Receipts and to pay the Licensee's Royalties within [____________] of receipt of all such money to the Licensee.

4.10 The Designer agrees to open a bank account at [____________] for the specific purpose of depositing and dealing with all monies received from the commercial exploitation, supply, distribution and sale of the Licensed Articles and the payment of any third party remunerations.

4.11 The Designer agrees that the signatures of both the Designer and the Licensee shall be required for the payment of any money out of the bank account specified under clause 4.10.

4.12 The Designer agrees that the Licensee shall be entitled to order all materials necessary for the production and manufacture of the Licensed Articles through the Designer's credit facilities known as [____________] and the Designer confirms that such arrangements are in addition to the bank account specified in clause 4.11.

4.13 The Designer undertakes that it and its sub-agents, sub-licensees and distributors shall keep full and accurate books of account, records and contracts and prices showing all dealings of the Licensed Articles, including the total number of units of the Licensed Articles manufactured, supplied, distributed and sold, whether by wholesale or retail, distributed without charge for promotional purposes and all units lost, damaged or stolen and the calculation of the Designer's Royalties and the Licensee's Royalties in respect of the Licensed Articles.

4.14 The Designer agrees that the Licensee shall be entitled to arrange for an audit to inspect and make copies of the Designer's books of account, records, contracts and any other relevant material in order to verify the sums due to the Licensee. In the event that in any audit there is a discrepancy of [____________] or more to the detriment of the Licensee, then the Designer shall be responsible for all the costs of each such audit.

4.15 The Designer agrees to consult with the Licensee with respect to all publicity, advertising, promotional and packaging material of the Licensed Articles and, in any event, the Designer agrees that the address of the Licensee will not be used in respect of the marketing and distribution of the Licensed Articles.

4.16 In addition to any credits to be given by the Designer to the Licensee in accordance with this Agreement, the Designer agrees that each of the Licensed Articles will bear the following hallmark punch (the sponsor's mark): [____________].

4.17 The exact shape and size of such sponsor's mark shall be agreed between the Designer and the Licensee before the production of any of the Licensed Articles under this Agreement.

4.18 The Designer confirms that the Licensee shall have the right to reject any of the Designs on the grounds that, in the opinion of the Licensee, the Design is too vague or is generally of insufficient quality to be developed or manufactured as a Licensed Article.

4.19 The Designer agrees to provide the Licensee with copies of all artwork, packaging, publicity, promotional and advertising material in relation to the sale and distribution of the Licensed Articles upon request by the Licensee.

4.20 The Designer agrees to consult with the Licensee with respect to the prices at which the Licensed Articles are to be sold whether by retail, wholesale or at a discounted price.

5. OBLIGATIONS OF THE LICENSEE

5.1 The Licensee agrees to produce and manufacture the Licensed Articles based on the Designs created by the Designer in accordance with the terms of this Agreement.

5.2 The Licensee confirms that all manufacturing of the Licensed Articles under this agreement shall be at the Business Premises except where, in the opinion of the Licensee, specialist services in the development, production and manufacturing of the Licensed Articles are required.

5.3 The Licensee agrees to ensure that the Business Premises are comprehensively insured with respect to the Designs and the Licensed Articles.

5.4 The Licensee agrees to ensure that the Business Premises are comprehensively insured with respect to any raw materials used or obtained for the purpose of producing and manufacturing the Licensed Articles, where such raw materials are kept at the Business Premises.

5.5 The Licensee agrees to ensure that the Business Premises are suitably secure for all insurance purposes.

5.6 The Licensee acknowledges the copyright ownership as stated under this Agreement in relation to the Designs and the Licensed Articles.

5.7 The Licensee confirms that he has full title and authority to enter into this Agreement and is not bound by any previous agreement which adversely affects this Agreement.

5.8 The Licensee agrees that he shall be registered for value added tax in respect of the supply of any goods or services under this Agreement.

5.9 The Licensee agrees that he shall be responsible for all his own national insurance, personal tax and value added tax which shall be due in consequence of this Agreement.

5.10 The Licensee agrees that the Designer shall open a bank account at [____________] for the specific purpose of depositing and dealing with all money received from the commercial exploitation and sale of the Licensed Articles and the payment of any third party remuneration.

5.11 The Licensee agrees that the signatures of both the Designer and the Licensee shall be required for the payment of any money out of the bank account specified under clause 5.10.

5.12 In addition to all records to be kept by the Designer under this Agreement, the Licensee shall keep full and accurate books and records relating to all of the Licensed Articles produced and manufactured under this Agreement.

5.13 The Licensee agrees that the Designer shall be entitled to inspect the Business Premises during working hours subject to reasonable prior notice being given.

5.14 In the event at the Licensee rejects any of the Designs the Licensee confirms that such rejection will only be made in accordance with the terms of this Agreement and that the Licensee will notify the Designer of such a decision at the earliest opportunity.

6. MISCELLANEOUS

MUTUAL INDEMNITY

6.1 The Designer and the Licensee mutually undertake to indemnify the other against all liabilities, claims, demands, actions, costs, damages or loss arising out of any breach by either party of any of the terms of this Agreement.

6.2 In the event of any claim, dispute, action, writ or summons in connection with clause 6.1, the Designer and the Licensee agree to provide full details to the other party at the earliest opportunity and shall not settle any such matter without first consulting the other party.

CONFIDENTIALITY

6.3 The Designer and the Licensee shall not disclose to any third party any confidential business or future plans of the other party at any time acquired during the existence of this Agreement. No reference is to be made to the terms of this Agreement by either party in any advertising, publicity or promotional material without the prior written consent of the other party.

AMENDMENTS AND ALTERATIONS

6.4 This Agreement supersedes all previous agreements, representations or promises and sets out all the terms agreed between the parties. Any amendment or alteration to this Agreement must be in writing and signed by an authorised signatory of each party.

NO PARTNERSHIP OR EMPLOYMENT

6.5 This Agreement shall not be deemed to create any partnership or employment relationship between the parties.

NOTICES

6.6 Any notices served under this Agreement are to be at the following addresses:

6.6.1 in respect of the Designer: [____________].
6.6.2 in respect of the Licensee: [____________].

VALUE ADDED TAX

6.7 All sums payable under this Agreement are exclusive of any value added tax that may be payable by either party.

THIRD PARTY TRANSFERS

6.8 Neither party shall assign, transfer, charge or make over this Agreement, or any of its rights or obligations, without the prior written consent of the other party.

FORCE MAJEURE

6.9 In the event that this Agreement cannot be performed or its obligations fulfilled for any reason beyond the reasonable control of the Designer or the Licensee, including such events as war, industrial action, floods or Acts of God. Then such non-performance or failure to fulfil its obligations shall be deemed not to be a breach of this Agreement. In the event that this Agreement cannot be performed or its obligations fulfilled for any reason beyond the reasonable control of the defaulting party for a continuous period of [____________], then the other party may, at its discretion, terminate this Agreement by notice in writing at the end of that period.

TERMINATION AND EXPIRY OF THE AGREEMENT

6.10 In addition to any other rights and remedies at law, this Agreement may be terminated by giving written notice to the other party who has breached this Agreement or has defaulted on the following grounds:

- 6.10.1 where the Designer has failed to account or make payments as required under this Agreement;
- 6.10.2 where the Designer or the Licensee has committed a serious breach of its obligations under this Agreement;
- 6.10.3 where the Designer or the Licensee goes into voluntary or involuntary liquidation;
- 6.10.4 where the Designer or the Licensee is declared insolvent, either in bankruptcy proceedings or other legal proceedings;
- 6.10.5 where an agreement with creditors has been reached by the Designer or the Licensee due to its failure or inability to pay its debts as they fall due; or
- 6.10.6 where a receiver is appointed over the whole or part of the Designer's or the Licensee's business.

SELL-OFF PERIOD

6.11 The Designer shall be entitled to sell off, on a non-exclusive basis, licensed material and stocks previously manufactured under this Agreement for the purpose of commercial sale for a period of [____________] from the date of expiry or termination, provided that the Designer adheres to the terms of this Agreement.

6.12 After the expiry or completion of the sell-off period, the Licensee shall be entitled to instruct the Designer to deliver up or destroy all the Licensed Articles previously manufactured under this Agreement in the possession of or under the control of the Designer.

6.13 After [____________] following the expiry of the Licence Period, the Designer shall be entitled to have the Designs reproduced by a third party.

GOVERNING LAW

6.14 This Agreement shall be interpreted and governed by the Laws of [____________].

Attach Schedule A to the Designs.

THE DESIGNER: [____________] [Date]

THE LICENSEE: [____________] [Date]

OUTLINE—EXCLUSIVE AGREEMENT FOR REPRODUCTION OF ORIGINAL DESIGNS

This an exclusive Agreement between a Designer and a Licensee in respect of a series of Articles based on original Designs. The sort of situation that this would cover is where one party is creating designs and artwork, which could be anything from clothes to candlesticks, and the other is using some creative input to "translate" those designs into actual, marketable objects. This Agreement is not concerned with registered designs.

The Designer, who is the original creator of the series of two-dimensional Designs, is licensing their manufacture by the Licensee. It is important to distinguish between the two-dimensional Designs and the three-dimensional Licensed Articles, which are being produced from the Designs. Once the Articles have been produced, the original creator then markets and distributes the Licensed Articles. As this is a joint commercial venture, the trading name under which the Licensed Articles are distributed should be agreed in advance.

The financial arrangements between the parties is on the basis that the creator of the Designs receives all the income from the commercial exploitation of the Licensed Articles and then pays to the Licensee a royalty payment from the Nett Receipts. The Nett Receipts are defined as the Gross Receipts (which means all the proceeds from the sale of the Licensed Articles) less the specifically defined costs incurred by the Licensee during the course of making the Licensed Articles.

The copyright position is that all rights in the Designs remain vested with the original creator. The copyright in the Licensed Articles is held jointly between the parties. At the end of the Licence Period, the creator of the Designs would be entitled to have a third party make three-dimensional Articles based on the Designs. However, the commercial exploitation of the Licensed Articles actually made under this Agreement would be a matter to be agreed between the Designer and the Licensee. The business premises where the Licensed Articles are to be made should be stated in order to comply with the security and insurance aspects of the Agreement.

Where trademarks or service marks are relevant, ownership and title should be clearly set out.

COMMISSIONING OF SERIES OF PHOTOGRAPHS WITH FULL ASSIGNMENT

BETWEEN:

(1) [______________]
of [______________] (to be known as the Photographer in this Agreement)

AND

(2) [______________]
of [______________] (to be known as the Assignee in this Agreement).

IT IS AGREED as follows:

1. DEFINITIONS

The words below are agreed to mean as follows:

1.1 "The Commissioned Work" shall be the following series of photographs, based on the Summary to be created, produced, developed, printed and delivered by the Photographer to the Assignee.

1.2 "The Summary" means the subject-matter of the series of photographs to be produced by the Photographer, including specified locations, persons, themes, colours, items and words which are described as follows: [______________].

1.3 "The Delivery Package" shall mean the following material of the Commissioned Work:

1.3.1 number of developed prints, [______________] which shall be of the dimensions [______________] in colour/black and white;

1.3.2 all technical and master material and any copies in any format, including but not limited to negatives and prints in the possession or under the control of the Photographer; and

1.3.4 any other specified material: [______________].

1.4 "The Delivery Date" shall be the following date by which the Delivery Package is to be delivered by the Photographer to the Assignee: [______________].

1.5 "The Photographer's Fee" shall be the sum of [figure/currency].

1.6 "The Authorised Expenses" shall be the agreed costs of producing and supplying the Commissioned Work, which shall include:

1.6.1 film stock of not less than [____________] exposures, which shall be of the following technical description: [____________].
1.6.2 the development and printing costs of the film;
1.6.3 the travelling and accommodation costs incurred in making the Commissioned Work up to a limit of [____________]; and
1.6.4 the costs of insurance and delivery of the Delivery Package.

1.7 "The Territory" shall be all countries, bases and locations throughout the world.

2. FULL ASSIGNMENT

In consideration of the Photographer's Fee and the Authorised Expenses, the Photographer assigns to the Assignee all present and future copyright and all other rights in the Commissioned Work and any parts in all media, whether in existence now or created in the future, including but not limited to television, film, video merchandising, publishing and internet rights throughout the Territory for the full period of copyright and any extensions and renewals.

3. MORAL RIGHTS

The Assignee acknowledges that the Photographer asserts his moral rights generally in respect of the Commissioned Work and in particular to be reasonably, clearly and prominently identified as follows: [____________].

4. OBLIGATIONS OF THE PHOTOGRAPHER

4.1 The Photographer undertakes that he shall produce the Commissioned Work in accordance with the Summary and deliver the Delivery Package by the Delivery Date.

4.2 The Photographer confirms that he is the sole owner of or controls all copyright and any other rights in the Commissioned Work which are assigned under this Agreement.

4.3 The Photographer confirms that he has and will retain good title and authority to enter into this Agreement and is not bound by any previous agreement which adversely affects this Agreement.

4.4 The Photographer confirms that the Commissioned Work shall be the original work of the Photographer and will not infringe the copyright or any rights of any third party in respect of the rights assigned under this Agreement.

4.5 In respect of the Commissioned Work, the Photographer undertakes that all copyright and any other rights, including all consents, shall be cleared and paid for in respect of the rights assigned under this Agreement for use by the Assignee.

4.6 The Photographer undertakes that the Commissioned Work will not contain any obscene, offensive or defamatory material and will not expose the Assignee to any civil or criminal proceedings.

4.7 The Photographer confirms that the Commissioned Work shall not contain anything of an advertising or promotional nature, unless specifically requested by the Assignee.

4.8 The Photographer agrees that he shall be responsible for all his own national insurance, personal insurance for himself and his equipment, personal tax and value added tax, which may become due as a consequence of this Agreement.

4.9 The Photographer confirms that he is a British subject or national of a member state of the E.E.C.

4.10 The Photographer agrees to keep full and accurate records of the Authorised Expenses incurred for the purpose of fulfilling his obligations under this Agreement and shall provide satisfactory receipts or other records to the Assignee upon request.

4.11 The Photographer acknowledges that the Assignee has a right to privacy in respect of the Commissioned Work.

4.12 The Photographer acknowledges that the Assignee shall be entitled to commercially exploit the Commissioned Work in all media at any time and that the Photographer shall not be entitled to any further payment.

5. OBLIGATIONS OF THE ASSIGNEE

5.1 In consideration of the rights assigned under this Agreement, the Assignee shall pay to the Photographer the Photographer's Fee as follows:

5.1.1 [____________] upon signature of this Agreement;
5.1.2 [____________] on or before: [____________]; and
5.1.3 [____________] subject to acceptance of the Delivery Package.

5.2 In addition to the Photographer's Fee, the Assignee agrees to reimburse the Photographer in respect of the Authorised Expenses within [____________] of the presentation of an invoice or other record of expenditure.

5.3 The Assignee agrees either to accept or provide written reasons for the rejection of the Delivery Package within [____________] of delivery and the Assignee confirms that it will not reject any material except on reasonable grounds and in good faith.

5.4 The Assignee confirms that it has and will retain good title and authority to enter into this Agreement and is not bound by any previous agreement which adversely affects this Agreement.

5.5 The Assignee confirms that it shall be solely responsible for all sums due in respect of the distribution, marketing and exploitation of the Commissioned Work in any media throughout the Territory.

5.6 The Assignee undertakes not to use, reproduce or misrepresent the Commissioned Work in any way which is likely to bring the Photographer into disrepute.

5.7 The Assignee agrees to provide the Photographer with the following credit in any publicity, promotional, advertising and packaging material in respect of the marketing, distribution and exploitation of the Commissioned Work: [____________].

6. MISCELLANEOUS

TIME OF THE ESSENCE

6.1 Both parties agree that all times and dates referred to in this Agreement shall be of the essence. In the event that the Photographer fails to deliver the Delivery Package by the Delivery Date, then the Assignee shall have the right to terminate this Agreement by notice in writing and shall be entitled to be repaid all sums previously paid to the Photographer in respect of the Photographer's Fee.

MUTUAL INDEMNITY

6.2 The Photographer and the Assignee mutually undertake to indemnify the other against all liabilities, claims, demands, actions, costs, damages or loss arising out of any breach by either party of any of the terms of this Agreement.

6.3 In the event of any claim, dispute, action, writ or summons in connection with clause 6.2, the Photographer and the Assignee agree to provide full details to the other party at the earliest opportunity and shall not settle any such matter without first consulting the other party.

CONFIDENTIALITY

6.4 The Photographer and the Assignee shall not disclose to any third party any confidential business or future plans of the other party at any time acquired during the existence of this Agreement. No reference is to be made to the terms of this Agreement by either party in any advertising, publicity or promotional material without the prior written consent of the other party.

AMENDMENTS

6.5 This Agreement supersedes all previous agreements, representations or promises and sets out all the terms agreed between the parties. Any amendment or alteration to this Agreement must be in writing and signed by an authorised signatory of each party.

NO PARTNERSHIP

6.6 This Agreement shall not be deemed to create any partnership, agency or employment relationship between the parties.

NOTICES

6.7 All notices shall be in writing and by the following method: [____________].

VALUE ADDED TAX

6.8 All sums payable under this Agreement are exclusive of any value added tax that may be payable by either party.

FORCE MAJEURE

6.9 In the event that this Agreement cannot be performed or its obligations fulfilled for any reason beyond the reasonable control of the Photographer or the Assignee, including such events as war, industrial action, floods or Acts of God. Then such non-performance or failure to fulfil its obligations shall be deemed not to be a breach of this Agreement. In the event that this Agreement cannot be performed or its obligations fulfilled for any reason beyond the reasonable control of the defaulting party for a continuous period of [____________]. Then either party may, at its discretion, terminate this Agreement by notice in writing at the end of that period.

TERMINATION OF THE AGREEMENT

6.10 In addition to any other rights and remedies at law, this Agreement may be terminated by giving written notice to the other party who has breached this Agreement or defaulted on the grounds that the Assignee has failed to account or make payments as required under this Agreement or where the Photographer or the Assignee has committed a serious breach of its obligations under this Agreement and has not rectified the position within [____________].

GOVERNING LAW

6.11 Both parties agree that this Agreement shall as far as possible be first resolved by mediation through: [____________], and legal proceedings shall be instituted in: [____________] as a final resort.

THE PHOTOGRAPHER: [____________]

THE ASSIGNEE: [____________]

DATE: [____________]

OUTLINE—COMMISSIONING OF SERIES OF PHOTOGRAPHS WITH FULL ASSIGNMENT

This is an Agreement for the commissioning of a series of photographs. The parties are referred to as the Photographer and the Assignee. The Photographer is being paid a Photographer's Fee, which is payable in instalments. In addition to this fee, the Photographer is being paid certain authorised expenses, including film stock, printing and development costs, travel and accommodation.

It is important to specify in as much detail as possible the subject matter and content of the series of photographs, including themes, colours, locations, etc.

The Photographer is assigning all copyright in the commissioned work to the Assignee, which would entitle the Assignee to exploit commercially the photographs in the manner of their choosing. For example, it would be possible to have any one of the photographs reproduced on a poster or a book cover without any further payment to the Photographer. The commissioned work is to be delivered on or before a specified delivery date. In the event that the Photographer fails to deliver by the agreed date, the Assignee would have the right to terminate the Agreement and to be repaid all sums which had previously been made to the Photographer, apart from the authorised expenses.

The Photographer is agreeing to deliver not only the developed prints but all technical material in his possession or control relating to the commissioned work, including the original negatives.

Although this is an assignment agreement, the Photographer is asserting his moral rights in the commissioned work. This means that the Photographer must be identified as such in any commercial exploitation of the work.

The parties have agreed to try mediation before instituting legal proceedings in the event there is a dispute.

NON-EXCLUSIVE LICENCE FOR USE OF STILLS IN PROGRAMME

BETWEEN:

(1) [______________]
of [______________] (to be known as the Licensor in this Agreement)

AND

(2) [______________]
of [______________] (to be known as the Licensee in this Agreement).

IT IS AGREED as follows:

1. "The Stills" shall be the following photographs:

   reference code: [______________]
   title and description: [______________]
   source material: [______________]

2. "The Programme" shall be the following film in which the Stills are to be included:

   title: [______________];
   brief description: [______________];
   duration: [______________]; and
   producer: [______________].

3. "The Licence Fee" shall be the sum of [______________].

4. "The Research Fee" shall be the sum of [______________] per [______________].

5. "The Licence Period" shall commence on the date of this Agreement and shall continue until: [______________].

6. "The Territory/Licensed Area" shall mean: [______________].

7. "The Stills Material" shall be the following material to be reproduced and supplied by the Licensor to the Licensee at the Licensee's cost and risk:

   description: [______________];
   delivery date: [______________];
   delivery address: [______________].

8. In consideration of the Licence Fee the Licensor grants to the Licensee an EXCLUSIVE/ NON-EXCLUSIVE licence for the stills to be used in the Programme for the duration of the Licence Period in the TERRITORY/LICENSED AREA in the following media:

Film: [__________]		
Radio: [__________]:	Station:	[__________]
	Frequency:	[__________]
Television: Digital/Cable/Satellite/Terrestrial	Channel:	[__________]
	Transmissions:	[__________]
Video:	Format:	[__________]
	Distributor:	[__________]
Non-Theatric:	Format:	[__________]
	Distributor:	[__________]
Theatric:		[__________]
All Media:		[__________]
Internet [service]:	Website:	[__________]
	Software:	[__________]
Telecommunication System:		[__________]
Merchandising:		[__________]
Publishing:		[__________]
Right to sub-license rights:		[__________]
Right to reproduce computer generated image:		[__________].

9. **The Licensor** undertakes as follows:

9.1 to provide the Stills Material to the Licensee;
9.2 that it is the sole owner of or controls all copyright and any other rights in the Stills;
9.3 that it has and will retain good title and authority to enter into this Agreement;
9.4 that all copyright and any other rights have been obtained and that the Licensee is not liable for any payments other than those specified under this Agreement; and
9.5 that it shall indemnify the Licensee against all liabilities, claims, actions, costs, damages or loss arising out of any breach of this Agreement by the Licensor.

10. **The Licensee** undertakes as follows:

10.1 to pay the Licence Fee and the Research Fee to the Licensor within [__________] of receiving an appropriate invoice;
10.2 to report to the Licensor on the use of the Stills in the Programme as soon as reasonably possible following the final edit of the Programme;
10.3 to provide the Licensor with the following on-screen credit: [__________];
10.4 not to use, reproduce or misrepresent the Stills in any way which is likely to bring the Licensor into disrepute or which is defamatory of any person or offensive in manner;
10.5 to provide the Licensor with a viewing copy of the final version of the Programme upon request; and
10.6 not to transfer any of the rights granted under this Agreement to any third party.

11. **The Licensor and the Licensee** agree as follows:

   11.1 any amendment or alteration to this Agreement must be in writing and signed by an authorised signatory of both parties;

   11.2 this Agreement shall be subject to the Laws of [England]; and

   11.3 neither party shall be liable to the other for any loss or damage arising from its failure to perform any of its obligations in this Agreement for any cause whatsoever beyond its control.

Signed by: [____________]
FOR AND BEHALF OF THE LICENSOR

Date: [____________]

Signed by: [____________]
FOR AND BEHALF OF THE LICENSEE

Date: [____________]

OUTLINE—NON-EXCLUSIVE LICENCE FOR USE OF STILLS IN PROGRAMME

The contract could cover press cuttings by means of substitution. Often stills can be loaned and filmed with a rostrum camera under the supervision of the director, thereby avoiding unnecessary reproduction costs. The Licensor is the copyright owner of the material and the Licensee is the company acquiring the use of the stills.

Often these types of agreements are done by a short form or are not recorded at all, which leads to clearance problems years later. As much detail as possible should be given of the intended use, and it is preferable to clear the rights for future exploitation at an early stage; or to acquire an option fee which would be payable if exercised.

NON-EXCLUSIVE LICENCE FOR USE OF FOOTAGE IN PROGRAMME

BETWEEN:

(1) [______________]
of [______________] (to be known as the Licensor in this Agreement)

AND

(2) [______________]
of [______________] (to be known as the Licensee in this Agreement).

IT IS AGREED as follows:

1. "The Film" shall be the film and any associated sound recording entitled: [______________].

2. "The Footage" shall be the following parts from the Film:

   Reference code: [______________];
   Maximum duration: [______________];
   Format: [______________].

3. "The Programme" shall be the following film and any associated sound recording in which the Footage is to be included:

   Title: [______________];
   Brief description: [______________];
   Duration: [______________];
   Producer: [______________].

4. "The Licence Fee" shall be the sum of: [figure/currency].

5. "The Research Fee" shall be the sum of: [figure/currency] per [hour/day].

6. "The Licence Period" shall commence on [the date of this Agreement] and shall continue until: [date].

7. "The Territory Licensed Area" shall mean: [______________].

8. "The Footage Material" shall be the following material to be reproduced and supplied by the Licensor to the Licensee at the Licensee's cost and risk:

format: [______________];
delivery date: [______________];
delivery address: [______________],
and shall also include a music cue sheet.

9. In consideration of the Licence Fee the Licensor grants to the Licensee a non-exclusive licence for the Footage to be used in the Programme, including any associated promotional or advertising material, throughout the Territory for the duration of the Licence Period as follows:

Television rights: Digital: [______________]
Channel: [______________]
Cable: [______________]
Terrestrial: [______________]
Satellite: [______________]
Transmissions: [______________]
Options: [______________]
Video: [Format]; [Distributor]
Internet: [Website]
[Service]
[Software]
Telecommunication System: [______________]
All Media Rights: [______________]
Theatric & Non-Theatric: [______________]
Film: [______________]
Music: [______________]
Radio: [______________]; [station/frequency]
Merchandising: [item]
Publishing: [______________]
Sub-licence rights: [______________]
Computer generated images: [______________].

10. **The Licensor** undertakes as follows:

10.1 to provide the Footage Material to the Licensee;
10.2 that it is the sole owner of or controls all copyright and any other rights in the Footage;
10.3 that it has and will retain good title and authority to enter into this Agreement.
10.4 that all copyright, music and any other rights have been obtained and that the Licensee is not liable for any payments other than those specified under this Agreement;
10.5 the Footage does not contain any defamatory material and will not expose the Licensee to any civil or criminal proceedings; and
10.6 that it shall indemnify the Licensee against all liabilities, claims, actions, costs, damages or loss arising out of any breach of this Agreement by the Licensor.

11. **The Licensee** undertakes as follows:

11.1 to pay the Licence Fee and the Research Fee to the Licensor within [____________] of receiving an appropriate invoice;
11.2 to report to the Licensor on the exact duration of the Footage, which is included in the Programme as soon as reasonably possible following the final edit of the Programme;
11.3 to provide the Licensor with the following on-screen credit: [____________];
11.4 to be responsible for any payment in respect of the performing rights in any music in respect of the exercise of the rights granted under this Agreement;
11.5 not to edit or use the Footage in any way which is likely to bring the Licensor into disrepute or which is defamatory of any person or offensive in manner;
11.6 to provide the Licensor with a viewing copy of the final version of the Programme upon request; and
11.7 not to transfer any of the rights granted under this Agreement to any third party.

12. **The Licensor and the Licensee** agree as follows:

12.1 any amendment or alteration to this Agreement must be in writing and signed by an authorised signatory of both parties;
12.2 this Agreement shall be subject to the Laws of [England]; and
12.3 neither party shall be liable to the other for any loss or damage arising from its failure to perform any of its obligations in this Agreement for any cause whatsoever beyond its control.

THE LICENSOR: [____________]

THE LICENSEE: [____________]

DATE: [____________]

OUTLINE— NON-EXCLUSIVE LICENCE FOR USE OF FOOTAGE IN PROGRANMME

This is an Agreement for the non-exclusive right to use Footage, whether film or video tape of any gauge or format) in a Programme intended primarily for television or video. The Agreement has to be adapted and deleted as required. The Licence Fee may be a negotiated figure of an agreed rate relating to the duration of the material. The Licensee would usually have to pay a Researcher's Fee and any reproduction, delivery and freight costs incurred. The Licensor is the copyright owner of the material and the Licensee is the company acquiring the use of the Footage.

NON-EXCLUSIVE LICENCE FOR USE OF FOOTAGE IN CORPORATE VIDEO

AGREEMENT dated: [____________]

BETWEEN:

(1) [____________]
of [____________] (to be known as the Licensor in this Agreement)

AND

(2) [____________]
of [____________] (to be known as the Licensee in this Agreement).

IT IS AGREED as follows:

1. "The Film" shall be the film and any associated sound recording entitled: [____________].

2. "The Footage" shall be the following parts from the Film:

   Reference code: [____________];
   Maximum duration: [____________];
   Format: [____________].

3. "The Corporate Video" shall be the following film and any associated sound recording in which the Footage is to be included:

   Title: [____________];
   Duration: [____________];
   Brief Description: [____________];
   Commissioning Company: [____________].

4. "The Licence Fee" shall be the sum of: [figure/currency].

5. "The Research Fee" shall be at a rate of: [figure/currency].

6. "The Licence Period" shall commence on the date of this Agreement and shall continue until: [date].

7. "The Territory" shall mean all countries, bases and locations throughout the world, including ships, oil-rigs and aeroplanes.

8. "The Corporate Video Rights" shall mean the right to exhibit the Footage in the

Corporate Video to non-paying audiences in all businesses and commercial industries, corporate organisations, trade and promotional exhibitions and organisations of an educational, cultural, religious, charitable and social nature, including but not limited to schools, churches, evening institutions, museums, hospitals, prisons, summer camps, drama groups, film societies, professional associations, public libraries, colleges and universities, hotels and private clubs.

9. "The Footage Material" shall be the following material to be reproduced and supplied by the Licensor to the Licensee at the Licensee's cost and risk:

Format: [____________];
Delivery date: [____________];
Delivery address: [____________].

and shall also include a music cue sheet, if appropriate.

10. In consideration of the Licence Fee, the Licensor grants to the Licensee a non-exclusive licence to exercise the Corporate Video Rights and to authorise the Commissioning Company to do so throughout the Territory for the duration of the Licence Period.

11. The Licensor agrees and understands that the benefit of the Corporate Video Rights in clause 10, shall be transferred to and exercised by the Commissioning Company and not the Licensee but such transfer shall not release the Licensee from any of its obligations under this Agreement.

12. **The Licensor** undertakes as follows:

12.1 to provide the Footage Material to the Licensee as set out in clause 9;
12.2 that it is the sole owner of or controls all copyright and any other rights in the Footage;
12.3 that it has and will retain good title and authority to enter into this Agreement;
12.4 that all copyright and any other rights (whether musical or otherwise), including consents required under the Copyright, Designs and Patents Act 1988 have been obtained and that the Licensee is not liable for any payments other than those specified under this Agreement;
12.5 the Footage does not contain any obscene or defamatory material and will not expose the Licensee to any civil or criminal proceedings; and
12.6 that it shall indemnify the Licensee against all liabilities, claims, actions, costs, damages or loss arising out of any breach of this Agreement by the Licensor.

13. **The Licensee** undertakes as follows:

13.1 to pay the Licence Fee and the Research Fee to the Licensor within [14 days] of receiving an appropriate invoice;
13.2 to report to the Licensor on the exact duration of the Footage which is included in the Corporate Video as soon as reasonably possible, following the final edit of the Corporate Video;
13.3 to provide the Licensor with the following on-screen credit: [____________];
13.4 to be responsible for any payment in respect of the performing rights in any music as are controlled by the Performing Right Society (or any society affiliated to it) in respect of the exercise of the rights granted under this Agreement;

13.5 not to edit or use the Footage in any way which is likely to bring the Licensor into disrepute or which is defamatory of any person or offensive in manner;

13.6 to provide the Licensor with a viewing copy of the final version of the Corporate Video upon request; and

13.7 to ensure that the Commissioning Company undertakes to the Licensee to be bound by the terms of this Agreement in the event that it is to acquire the benefit of the rights granted under this Agreement.

14. **The Licensor and the Licensee** agree as follows:

14.1 any amendment or alteration to this Agreement must be in writing and signed by an authorised signatory of both parties;

14.2 this Agreement shall be subject to the laws of England; and

14.3 neither party shall be liable to the other for any loss or damage arising from its failure to perform any of its obligations in this Agreement for any cause whatsoever beyond its control.

Signed by: [____________]
FOR AND ON BEHALF OF THE LICENSOR

Date: [____________]

Signed by: [____________]
FOR AND ON BEHALF OF THE LICENSEE

Date: [____________]

OUTLINE—NON-EXCLUSIVE LICENCE FOR USE OF FOOTAGE IN CORPORATE VIDEO

This Agreement is specifically concerned with clearing Footage for corporate videos for use worldwide to all non-paying audiences. This Agreement does not give the right to use the Footage over the internet or on television. The Licensor is the copyright owner of the material and the Licensee is the Production Company and not the Commissioning Company. The rights granted under this Agreement would be transferred by the Licensee to the Commissioning Company under a contract between the Licensee and the Commissioning Company (*e.g.* Contract 13 in this book). To safeguard the Licensee's position the Commissioning Company should sign a copy of this Agreement agreeing to be bound by its terms.

ORDER FOR GOODS/SERVICES

AN AGREEMENT made this [____________] day of [____________]

BETWEEN:

(1) [____________]
of [____________] (to be known as the Purchaser in this Agreement)

AND

(2) [____________]
of [____________] (to be known as the Supplier in this Agreement).

IT IS AGREED as follows:

1. The Supplier shall provide the following goods/services to the Purchaser: [____________].

2. The Supplier agrees that the goods/services in clause 1 shall be exclusively available to the Purchaser for the following period:

   start date: [____________];
   end date: [____________].

3. In consideration of the goods/services, the Purchaser agrees to pay the Supplier the following fee/rates: [____________];
   payment shall be made in full subject to satisfactory goods/services, within 21 days of receipt of an invoice.

4. Details of the goods/services:
   Delivery date: [____________];
   Delivery address: [____________].
   Delivery shall be at the Supplier's risk and expense including packaging, shipping, carriage and insurance.

5. The Supplier agrees that the goods/services shall conform with the quality and description stated and shall be of merchantable quality and fit for their intended uses and free from all defects.

6. The Supplier's failure to deliver the goods/services on the dates specified shall entitle the Purchaser to cancel this order without liability to the Supplier as time is of the essence in this Agreement. Then the Supplier shall be held liable for any direct or indirect loss and additional costs incurred.

7. All specifications, drawings and any other material or information provided to the Supplier by the Purchaser shall remain the property of the Purchaser.

8. The Purchaser agrees that the risk shall pass immediately upon satisfactory delivery to the Purchaser but property shall remain with the Supplier until all sums due to the Supplier have been paid by the Purchaser.

9. The Supplier shall not assign, transfer, or sub-contract any part of this Agreement without the prior written consent of the Purchaser.

10. This Agreement shall be subject to the Laws of England.

Signed by: [____________]
FOR AND ON BEHALF OF THE PURCHASER

Date: [____________]

Signed by: [____________]
FOR AND ON BEHALF OF THE SUPPLIER

Date: [____________]

OUTLINE—ORDER FOR GOODS/SERVICES

This Agreement is a general order for goods/services. The details set out in the Agreement should be as specific as possible.

LABORATORY ACCESS LETTER

Dear Sir/Madam,

You are holding on deposit, in our name, certain master material of the film:

title: [____________];
reference code: [____________]; and
format: [____________].

We have entered into an agreement with the following party, [____________] of [____________].

You are authorised and instructed by us to accept and honour any orders for laboratory services from the above party with respect to the above film. This authorisation is effective from the date of this letter until further notice.

All laboratory services ordered by the above party will be at their sole cost and liability and on such terms as you and that party shall agree. In the event of any default of payment by the party no lien or charge will ensue in respect of any part of the master material. You agree that the master material of the film shall not be removed from your laboratory for any reason without our prior written consent.

It is not your responsibility to enquire whether any orders for laboratory services from the above party complies with the terms of their agreement with us.

Any alteration or amendment to the above terms must be in writing and signed by us.

Please sign and return the attached copy of this letter confirming your acceptance of the above terms.

Yours faithfully,

OUTLINE—LABORATORY ACCESS LETTER

This is a laboratory access letter. When the authority is to be withdrawn another letter must be sent to the laboratory to that effect.

LOCATION ACCESS LETTER

Dear Sir/Madam,

We are writing to confirm the arrangements made and the terms of your agreement to grant us filming facilities for material which we intend to use in our film entitled: [____________].

Duration: [____________];
Subject Matter: [____________].

We are pleased to confirm the following:

1. That you agree that we may film at the following location, [____________], on the following dates and times: [____________].
2. In consideration of your agreement to the filming facilities we agree to pay you the following fee, exclusive of any value added tax: [figure/currency].
   Such fee is to be paid on or before: [date].
3. The above fee is in full and final settlement and no further sums shall be due to you in respect of our use of the material in any form.
4. That you confirm that you are fully entitled to grant us the filming facilities and that no further consents are necessary.
5. There is no obligation on our part to use the material that we film on location in the film.
6. There is no obligation on our part to provide you with any on-screen credit in the film.
7. That we shall be responsible for arranging suitable insurance cover for our crew and in particular for public liability insurance.
8. We shall ensure that the location is left in good order after use and we agree that we shall be responsible for any loss or damage directly arising from our use of the location.
9. We agree that the material filmed on location will not be used by us in a manner which will bring you into disrepute or is defamatory to you.

We would be grateful if you would confirm your acceptance of these terms by signing and returning the enclosed copy of this letter.

Yours faithfully,

OUTLINE—LOCATION ACCESS LETTER

This is a location access letter. It is important to inspect the site shortly before filming to confirm its condition. A public liability insurance policy must be arranged. It may be advisable to take photographs as evidence of condition of the site.

MUSIC CUE SHEET

Production Company: [______________];
Production Title: [______________];
Title of music: [______________];
Performer: [______________];
Composer/arranger: [______________];
Publisher: [______________];
Record label: [______________];
Record number: [______________];
Duration of music used: [______________];

Description of use (delete as appropriate): background/featured/vocal/instrumental

OUTLINE—MUSIC CUE SHEET

This is a specimen music cue sheet for one piece of music. The point of this document is to spell out what information is required for each individual piece of music, which is to be included in the programme. Where there is more than one more item all the details should be listed chronologically. Details contained in this document are a summary of those required by PRS, MCPS and PPL.

CHECKLIST OF CLAUSE HEADINGS

Absence
Acceptance
Accounting Provisions
Act of God
Advances
Advertising
Affiliates
Agency
Amendments
Antiquities
Appointment
Approval
Arbitration
Artwork
Assignment
Assignment Fee
Assignment Period
Associated Company
Associated Person
Audit
Author
Authorisation
Bailment
Ballot
Bank Holidays
Bank Rate
Bankruptcy
Best Endeavours
Bill of Exchange
Bill of Lading
Bona Fide
Bonus
British Islands
Broadcasting
Broadcasts
Budget
Business Day
Buy-out
Cable
Cancellation
Capacity
Carriage Costs
Collaboration
Collection Agencies
Collective Works
Commission
Company
Completion Guarantee
Compliance
Computer Generated
Confidentiality
Consents
Consideration
Construction
Consultation
Continuous Employment
Control
Copyright Clearance
Copyright Ownership
Copyright Notice
Costs
Credits
Cover Versions
Damages
Death
Debenture
Declaration
Deed
Defamation
Default
Delay
Delivery
Deposit
Derivatives
Designs
Director
Disaster Recovery
Discharge
Disclaimer
Discount
Disputes
Distribution Expenses
Distribution Rights
Dividend
Dramatic Work
Due Diligence
Duration of Rights
Editorial Control
Electronic
Embargo
Endorsement
Entire Contract
Entry
Equal Opportunities
Equitable Relief
Error
Escrow
Essence
Estate
Europe
European Union Directive
Exclusivity
Executor
Expenses
Extension of the Agreement
Facility Access

Failure to Deliver
Fair Dealing
Fees
Films
Film Clips
First Refusal
Fixed Price
Fixed Term
Fixtures
F.O.B.
Force Majeure
Foreign
Format
Forum
Freight
Franchising
Frustration
Full Age
Goodwill
Governing Law
Grant of Licence
Gross Receipts
Group Accounts
Guarantee
Grievance Procedure
Hallmark
Hammer Price
Handsel
Headings
Health
Hire Purchase
Holding Company
Holidays
Hotel
Illegality
Implied Terms
Income
Indemnity
Index
Insolvency
Inspection of Accounts and Records
Insurance
Interest
Internet
Interpretation
Invalidity
Inventions
Jurisdiction
Know-how
Laboratory Access
Language
Legal Proceedings
Levies
Liability
Licence Area
Licence Fee
Licence Period
Loan Out
Location Access
Logo
Loss
Marketing
Material
Master
Mediation
Medical Report
Merchandising
Moral Rights
Multiple Occupation
Music Cue Sheets
Music Performance
Musical Work
Nett Receipts
New Editions
Notices
Novation
Nuisance
Obscenity
Omission
Option
Order
Originality
Outer Space
Ownership
Parties to Agreement
Partnership
Patent
Payment
Performance Bond
Performers
Performances
Permits
Personal
Personal Injury
Photographs
Phonogram
Pirated Goods
Power of Attorney
Preamble
Premises
Price
Privacy
Probationary Period
Product
Product Liability
Production Costs
Profit Share
Programmes
Promotional Excerpts
Promotional Material
Proofs
Property
Proxies
Publication

Publicity
Qualification
Quality Control
Quantity
Quorum
Quotations
Rates of Exchange
Recordings
Rejection
Remainders
Rental Surcharge
Residential Subscriber
Restraint of Trade
Rights
Risk
Royalties
Royalty Statement
Safety
Sales Commission
Sales Tax
Scripts
Secrecy
Sell-off Period
Series
Set Off
Severance
Shipment
Sick Leave
Signature
Specified Perils
Sound Recordings
Statements
Statutory Provisions
Stills
Sub-licence
Subsidiary
Surplus Stock
Suspension
Synopsis
Taxes
Television
Term of Agreement
Termination
Territory
Theatric
Third Party Transfer
Time of the Essence
Title
Trademarks
Translations
Treatment
Undue Delay
Unenforceable
Unfit
Union
Unlawful
Unsafe
Value Added Tax
Variation
Venue
Video
Videogram
Visas
Voluntary Departure
Voting
Waiver
War Damage
Warranties
Wayleave
Work
Xerography
X-Rated
Xylography
Year
Zero Rates

Instruction for use of the companion disc

Introduction

These notes are provided for guidance only. They should be read and interpreted in the context of your own computer system and operational procedures. It is assumed that you have a basic knowledge of Windows. However, if there is any problem please contact our help line on 020 7393 7266 who will be happy to help.

Disc Format and Contents

The disc which accompanies this book is suitable for MS-DOS or Windows 95 computers that can read high-density (1.44 MB) 3.5 inch discs. You will need approximately 4 MB of free hard disc space to store the data files.

This disc contains data files covering the precedents section of the book. It does not contain software, or other text or commentary.

The data files are in Windows 95 (v.6.0) and may be imported into later versions of Word for Windows. Again if you have any problems please contact our help desk on the number above who will be happy to help.

Installation

We strongly recommend that you make a backup copy of the distribution disc. The following instructions make the assumption that you will copy the data files to a single directory on your hard disc (*e.g.* C:\Fos&Laing), and that your disc drive is called A:\.

In Windows 95:
1. Insert the disc into the A drive of your computer
2. From Start button chose Run
3. Type A:\setup.exe as appropriate and click on the OK button (where A corresponds to your disc drive. If, for example, your disc drive letter is E, you should type E:\setup.exe)
4. Follow the on-screen instructions as prompted:
   - Press OK to the prompt "Fosbrook & Laing's The Media Contracts Handbook"
   - The WinZip Self-Extractor dialogue box will appear, type the name of the folder that you would like to save your files into and press Unzip
   - Press OK to the prompt "84 file(s) unzipped successfully"
   - The WinZip Self-Extractor dialogue box will reappear, press Close
   - The files are now stored in the C drive of your computer.

Using the precedents with Microsoft Word for Windows 6

N.B. For other versions of Word, and other Windows word processors in general, the instructions will be similar, but if you are not sure refer to the documentation that came with your word processor.

To open a document from The Media Contracts Handbook in Word, select **"File, Open"** from the menu. Highlight The Media Contracts Handbook directory in the "Directories" list box. Change **"Files of Type"** to **"All files"**. Select the desired document from the **"File Name"** list box and press **OK**.

The precedents have been supplied as read-only files. At this point it would be advisable to save the document before making any other changes.

Select **"File, Save As"** from the menu. In the **"Directories"** list box, highlight your working directory such as **"work"**. In the **"File Name"** list box, type a suitable document name such as **"newdoc"**. Press **OK**. Any other amendments can now be dealt with.

disc and data to be identified accordingly and provided with a clear and prominent credit as the Authors and the copyright owners as: Deborah Fasbrook and Adrian C. Laing. Similarly, the Publisher should be identified where appropriate as: Sweet & Maxwell Limited.

7. In the event that the Authors and/or the Publisher became aware and/or have reasonably grounds to believe that the Purchaser, business and/or third party is using the disc and/or data in a manner which was not set out in this document and which is prejudicial and/or detrimental to the interests of the Publisher and/or Authors and/or is in the breach of any intellectual property rights including copyright of such parties. The Publisher and/or the Authors shall be entitled without notice to the Purchaser to terminate the licence provided under this document without prejudice to any other rights and remedies of the Publisher and/or Authors. The Purchaser shall be obliged upon written notice to surrender all copies of the discs and/or data to the Publisher and/or Authors.

8. The Purchaser agrees that it shall not use and/or authorise the use of the disc and/or data in any manner or nature which is inconsistent with the intended purpose of the licence given in this document. Nor shall the Purchaser deface, erase, remove and/or alter any party of the copyright notice, trademarks, Author and Publisher details displayed on any part of the disc, cover and/or data.

9. This licence shall be governed by the Laws of [England], whether this disc and/or data is supplied and/or used in [the United Kingdom] and/or in any part of the universe.

Licence Agreement

IMPORTANT — PLEASE READ THIS DOCUMENT CAREFULLY BEFORE BREAKING THE SEAL TO RELEASE THE DISC FROM THE WALLET. BY REMOVING AND USING THE DISC YOU THE PURCHASER ARE AGREEING TO BE BOUND BY THE TERMS SET OUT IN THIS DOCUMENT.

The disc and all the data included thereon is supplied to you the purchaser by the publisher, based entirely on the book. If you do not wish to be bound by the terms and conditions of use of the disc and data please do not remove the seal from the wallet. The following terms shall apply to the use of the book, disc and data whilst it is in the possession or control of the purchaser:

1. The Purchaser is granted a non-exclusive licence by the Publisher to use the disc and data for the purpose for which it is intended in conjunction with the book in the normal course of business, namely negotiating, drafting and concluding contracts. This right is personal to the Purchaser and shall also permit the Purchaser to copy the files from the floppy disc to their hard disc and also to make one security copy of the floppy disc itself. The Purchaser shall not have the right to make any additional copies and/or to permit, authorise, sub-licence, assign, transfer and/or otherwise exploit the book and/or disc and/or data in any form, whether for commercial purposes or otherwise. It is accepted by the Publishers that lawyers and others in practice and/or the media industry may use the book and/or disc and/or data to provide legal advice and services to individuals and companies. However, there is no right to copy the disc, data and/or book for supply by the purchaser to such persons by photocopying or electronically supplying large sections of the book. Please advise your clients or company to purchase the book and disc.

2. The right granted is limited and personal to the Purchaser and does not permit the Purchaser to exploit the book and/or disc and/or data in any media of any nature at any time or to permit others to do so. The Purchaser shall not acquire any rights and/or interest in the book, disc and/or data at any time which may be exploited by the Purchaser, and all rights not specified are reserved by the Publisher and not permitted or authorised under this Licence Agreement.

3. The Publisher and the Authors do not accept any responsibility for the use of the disc and/or data by the Purchaser at any time and shall not be liable for any direct and/or indirect damages, loss, injury or otherwise that may arise in respect of the Purchaser and/or any business in which the Purchaser may be involved and/or to which the Purchaser may supply advice or material for any reason. The Purchaser shall use the disc and/or data entirely at the Purchaser's sole risk and expense and agrees that the Purchaser shall be liable for all its own costs and expenses or otherwise that may arise from any such use.

4. Publisher confirms that all rights necessary for the specified use by the Purchaser of the disc and/or data have been obtained from the Authors. The Publisher has endeavoured to ensure that as far as possible the data is based on the book. The Publisher and the Authors do not accept any responsibility and/or liability for any errors, omissions, viruses, defects and/or any other matters of any nature in the disc and/or data which may be a legal, technical or material fault or problem or otherwise. The Purchaser must use the disc and/or data entirely at its sole risk and cost and accept that the contract clauses are for reference and guidance only and are intended to be adapted and varied accordingly by each Purchaser to suit their particular circumstances. In the event that there is a technical defect in the disc itself, the Publisher agrees to replace the disc within 90 days of purchase provided that the disc and/or data has been treated with all due care and not mistreated in some manner or damaged by some other means at a later date after purchase. If the disc and/or data is incompatible with the Purchaser's hardware and there is no alternative product available then there is no liability on the part of the Publisher to provide any other disc and/or data or any refund or reimbursement of any nature at any time.

5. In the event of any claim, demand, actions or otherwise by the Purchaser and/or any business for any reason arising from the use of the disc and/or data. Then the Publisher shall only be liable in total to repay the full purchase price of the book to the Purchaser. The Purchaser agrees that it is the Purchaser's responsibility to arrange and bear the cost of insurance cover for the benefit of the Purchaser, any business and/or third party for the use of the disc and/or data by the Purchaser and that the Publisher and the Authors shall not bear any responsibility and/or liability for the use of the disc and/or data by the Purchaser, any business, third party or otherwise which is supplied directly or indirectly by the Purchaser at any time.

6. The copyright owners of the data contained on the disc are the Authors of the book. The Authors assert all their moral rights in respect of the book,